Engaging the
Doctrine
of Creation

Engaging the Doctrine of Creation

Cosmos, Creatures, and the Wise and Good Creator

Matthew Levering

Baker Academic

a division of Baker Publishing Group
Grand Rapids, Michigan

Published by Baker Academic
a division of Baker Publishing Group
P.O. Box 6287, Grand Rapids, MI 49516-6287
www.bakeracademic.com

Printed in the United States of America

Library of Congress Cataloging-in-Publication Data
Names: Levering, Matthew, 1971– author.
Title: Engaging the doctrine of creation : cosmos, creatures, and the wise and good creator / Matthew Levering.
Description: Grand Rapids : Baker Academic, 2017. | Includes bibliographical references and index.
Identifiers: LCCN 2016036526 | ISBN 9780801030994 (cloth)
Subjects: LCSH: Creation—History of doctrines. | Creationism—History of doctrines. | Catholic Church—Doctrines.
Classification: LCC BT695 .L478 2017 | DDC 231.7/65—dc23
LC record available at https://lccn.loc.gov/2016036526

17 18 19 20 21 22 23   7 6 5 4 3 2 1

In keeping with biblical principles of creation stewardship, Baker Publishing Group advocates the responsible use of our natural resources. As a member of the Green Press Initiative, our company uses recycled paper when possible. The text paper of this book is composed in part of post-consumer waste.

To Bishop Robert Barron

Contents

Acknowledgments

Among the many people I need to thank, first is David Augustine, now a doctoral student in systematic theology at Catholic University of America. David was my research assistant for the past three years here at Mundelein Seminary, and he became a dear friend. Among other things, he did the bibliography for this book and helped make major stylistic changes in the conclusions that made them much more readable.

Portions of this book were delivered at conferences, and earlier versions of chapters 5 and 7 have appeared in print (as have a small portion of chapter 3 and a section of chapter 6). A few paragraphs about Augustine and the New Atheists in the book's introduction will appear in a festschrift for Fr. Matthew Lamb, edited by Thomas Harmon and Roger Nutt. At a conference in which his former doctoral students honored Fr. Lamb, I delivered a keynote lecture on the divine ideas that formed the basis for chapter 1. Susan Waldstein gave me helpful insights during and after the conference. Chapter 2 began as a lecture at a conference on divine simplicity that I organized with George Kalantzis at Wheaton College. At the conference, papers by Brian Daley, SJ, Michel Barnes, David Luy, Marcus Plested, Keith Johnson, Paul Gavrilyuk, and Tom McCall challenged and instructed me, and their influence is found throughout chapter 2 even when my position ends up differing from theirs. Robert Wilken's keynote lecture at a conference organized by Christopher Thompson and David Meconi, SJ, inspired the section on Basil in chapter 3—as did the presence of Paul Blowers at that conference. In chapter 3, the section on the analogy of being began as an invited response to Michał Paluch, OP, at a conference hosted by the Dominican School of Philosophy and Theology in Berkeley, California, and organized by Bryan Kromholtz, OP; see my "Response to Michał Paluch's 'Analogical Synthesis: An Impossible Project?,'" *Nova et Vetera* 14 (2016): 609–17.

Chapter 5 began as a keynote lecture at the Thompson-Meconi conference on creation. It was improved by critical comments given me by Marie George during and after the conference (though I think that she would still disagree with my position). A version of chapter 5 has been published as "'Be Fruitful and Multiply, and Fill the Earth': Was and Is This a Good Idea?," in *On Earth as It Is in Heaven: Cultivating a Contemporary Theology of Creation*, edited by David Vincent Meconi, SJ (Grand Rapids: Eerdmans, 2016), 80–122. The discussion of Jonathan Edwards and Thomas Aquinas that appears in the last section of chapter 6 took shape through the kind invitation of Kyle Strobel, who introduced me to Edwards: a version of this section appeared as "Jonathan Edwards and Thomas Aquinas on Original Sin," in *The Ecumenical Edwards: Jonathan Edwards and the Theologians*, ed. Kyle C. Strobel (Burlington, VT: Ashgate, 2015), 133–48. Chapter 7 derives from a lecture given at Biola University under the friendly auspices of Oliver Crisp and Fred Sanders. It benefited from Ben Myers's paper at the same conference and from his gentle criticisms; and I also owe thanks to Eleonore Stump, Michael Horton, and Bruce McCormack for their contributions to the conference. A version of chapter 7 has been published as "Creation and Atonement," in *Locating Atonement: Explorations in Constructive Dogmatics*, edited by Oliver D. Crisp and Fred Sanders (Grand Rapids: Zondervan, 2015), 43–70.

At Baker Academic, my friend and editor Dave Nelson made possible this third volume in the "Engaging the Doctrine of" series, read through the whole manuscript in its penultimate form, and gave crucial counsel for improvement. John Betz, Gregory Doolan, and David Bentley Hart read the sections of the manuscript that addressed their work, and their insights and corrections have much improved the book. Danny Houck, a doctoral student at Southern Methodist University, offered me crucial corrections for chapter 6 on original sin, and I am also in debt to Fr. Paul Stein for helpful comments on that difficult chapter. Jörgen Vijgen read chapters 1 and 6, as well as the introduction, and gave me valuable insights and corrections. Mark Spencer of the University of St. Thomas transformed the first two chapters by his brilliant and penetrating comments and criticisms; I dread to think what these chapters would have been without his help. Alexander Pierce alerted me to the significance of Ian McFarland's work and provided other helpful tips. David Moser, now a doctoral student at Southern Methodist University, read the entire manuscript twice with an eye both to theological content and to stylistic clarity. He enhanced this book in so many ways by his extraordinary diligence and care. Lastly, during the copyediting process, David Cramer of Baker Academic (aided by proofreaders) made very helpful and welcome corrections, exhibiting a high level of theological acumen.

I am also deeply grateful to Mundelein Seminary and its excellent faculty and staff, including its rector and spiritual leader, Fr. John Kartje, and its academic dean, Fr. Thomas Baima, along with his administrative assistant Mary Bertram. I owe special thanks to James and Mary Perry, who generously endowed the chair of theology that I hold. The person who made the book truly possible—by her amazing work, her generosity and lightness of spirit, and her focus on important things rather than on things that are passing away—was my wife, Joy. "Like the sun rising in the heights of the Lord, so is the beauty of a good wife" (Sir. 26:16). Lord Jesus, bless Joy Levering for your name's sake with eternal life, and bless our children.

This book is dedicated to a great Christian leader, a theologian with a knack for seeing the whole of the Christian faith, a spiritual master who has given his life entirely to the Lord and whose ability to serve others is therefore extraordinary: Bishop Robert Barron. Let it be said of him, "Blessed is the man who makes the LORD his trust" (Ps. 40:4).

Introduction

Since the universe is a physical mechanism, and God plays no empirically evident role in it, does one need to postulate a "creator"? In what Roger Lundin has called "the *tacit creed* of contemporary intellectual life,"[1] Genesis 1–3 has long since been replaced with our new knowledge of the evolutionary development of hominids, the extinction of innumerable species, the millions of years when dinosaurs roamed the earth, and our discovery of the shocking vastness of time and space. When viewed from this perspective, does not the claim that humans are "in the image of God" (Gen. 1:27) merely exhibit yet again the familiar human need for self-aggrandizement? And if so, would it not be better to simply discard it as one more relic of—and, indeed, the anthropological counterpart to—an earth-centered cosmology that has long since been disproven? Moreover, given global population levels and the ecological crisis presently confronting us, is not God's command to humans to "be fruitful and multiply, and fill the earth" (Gen. 1:28) a recipe for disaster?

On a somewhat different front, granted what we know about human origins, is it really very likely that a handful of hunter-gatherer hominids in the grasslands of Africa could have committed an "original sin" that distorted the human race as a whole? Isn't "this" just how we are? (Indeed, an "original sin" becomes even more difficult to imagine given that the first humans would presumably have inherited the genetic selfishness that is found, by nature, in all animals, rational or otherwise.) Beyond even this, why would it be reasonable to think, given the vast expanse of the universe with its trillions of stars, that the supposed creator of all would become human on earth (bearing in mind that our cosmically insignificant race lives on a tiny speck of dust in

---

1. Lundin, *Beginning with the Word*, 3.

a remote corner of the galaxy) in Jesus of Nazareth and, moreover, that he would proceed to die on a cross—for our "sins," no less—and ascend to heaven, leaving us still in a big mess, a mess that is only getting bigger, and to which, incidentally, Christians have contributed much? For that matter, why death on a cross, of all gruesome things?

In sum, what I am getting at with this litany of questions is simply this: Given our modern worldview, is it not the more reasonable course to regard the authors of Genesis 1–3—as too the later authors of Scripture (including the New Testament)—as products of their "axial age" worldview, a worldview which has little to say to educated people today?[2] Why (and here my imaginary interlocutor throws his hands up in the air with a sigh of exasperation) should we still allow these ancient texts to have authority over our lives?

As an exercise in faith seeking understanding, the present book engages the Christian doctrine of creation with such concerns in mind. As for the plan of this book, I first emphasize that no theology of creation can succeed without distinguishing the wise and good creator from every kind of creaturely mode of being. If the creator is conceived in a way that logically identifies the creator as merely yet another (however powerful) creature, then there can in fact be no creator, no transcendent source of all finite modes of being. Thus, I begin the book with two chapters on the distinction of the creator from every kind of creaturely reality, emphasizing God's ideas and his simplicity as the underpinnings of creation *ex nihilo*, understood as the fruit of God's infinite goodness. With regard to God's free act of creation, David Burrell rightly observes that "the relation between Creator and creatures . . . is unlike any causal relation we know since God's causation in creating produces [in God] no change or motion or succession in time."[3]

---

2. See Bellah, *Religion in Human Evolution*; and Bellah and Joas, *Axial Age and Its Consequences*. Karl Jaspers originally developed the idea of the "axial age" (from the eighth to the third century BC); see his *Origin and Goal of History*. Judaism, Platonism, Buddhism, and Confucianism emerged during this period, in contrast to the earlier emphasis on multiple gods. For Jaspers (as for Bellah), "the spiritual foundations of humanity were laid simultaneously and independently in China, India, Persia, Judea, and Greece. And these are the foundations upon which humanity still subsists today" (*Way to Wisdom*, 98).

3. Burrell, "*Creatio ex Nihilo* Recovered," 18. As Robert Barron remarks, "Because God brought the whole of the finite universe into existence, God cannot be an ingredient within the universe; he must be other in a way that transcends any and all modes of otherness discoverable within creation" (*Exploring Catholic Theology*, 21). Barron goes on to examine Aquinas's discussion of the act of creation. In his *De potentia Dei*, as Barron says, Aquinas argues that only God can create finite beings, because of "the intensity of God's actuality. . . . God, who is totality actualized in his being, can affect things not simply through motion or change but through bringing forth the totality of their being, through creating them *ex nihilo*" (23).

My third chapter then examines the unfathomably vast profusion of organic and nonorganic creatures over time and space. How could this vast profusion reflect a truly wise creator, rather than being evidence of the absurd flux of things? I argue that the answer is cosmic theophany, although I recognize that the often brutal processes of material decay and destruction are, for now, deeply embedded in this theophanic creation.[4] My fourth chapter turns to the human being, who is unique among animals. What does it mean for the wise and good God to create human beings "in the image of God"? I suggest that the answer involves human rationality—knowing and loving—but not in a way that is separated from the wise and good stewardship of the creation that God calls humans to undertake.

My fifth chapter inquires into the wisdom and goodness of God's command to humans to "be fruitful and multiply, and fill the earth." I argue that this command, which may seem rather imprudent, does indeed embody the wisdom of the creator God, whose creative and redemptive love goes to extraordinary lengths in order to expand the creaturely communion of love, in which God shares his "beatitude" with us.[5] My sixth chapter explores whether Christians should believe in the historicity of the biblically attested fall, given the scientific issues involved as well as the fact that Genesis 3's portrait of this fall is highly symbolic. In my view, the connection between a fully free original sin and human death as we now experience it must be insisted upon, or else the wisdom and goodness of God's creative work would be undermined. My final chapter addresses the relationship of creation and atonement, by which the deepest consequences of human sin are reversed through the death of the incarnate Word. As will be clear, I agree with Jonathan Wilson's insistence upon "holding creation and redemption together," since Christ restores the created order of relational justice and thereby restores the human image in relation to the divine exemplar.[6]

---

4. Without such processes of decay and destruction, there would be no way for organic life to be sustained or for new life to emerge. As Arthur Peacocke puts it, "new forms of matter arise only through the dissolution of the old: new life only through the death of the old" (*Theology for a Scientific Age*, 63). See also Kenneth Miller, *Finding Darwin's God*, 245–46.

5. Thomas Aquinas, *Summa theologiae* (hereafter *ST*) I, q. 26, a. 3.

6. Jonathan Wilson, *God's Good World*, ix. Wilson does not mean to imply that sin (from which we are redeemed) was built into the created order. In a speculative fashion, he argues that "God created precisely the cosmos that God intended to create, a cosmos that would by God's work become the new creation by virtue of God's love for the cosmos and the cosmic response to God's love. In this view, if we had not turned from the telos of creation [by the fall], God would have brought about the new creation by the incarnation of God the Son and the perfection of creation in God's life. But the death of the Son of God would have been unnecessary" (119).

In an essay on Christian soteriology, John Webster makes a simple point that guides my book's engagement with the doctrine of creation: "The matter of the Christian gospel is the eternal God who has life in himself, and temporal creatures who have life in him. The gospel, that is, concerns the history of fellowship—covenant—between God and creatures."[7] It is this gospel, in the light of Genesis 1–3, that I examine through reflection upon "the eternal God who has life in himself" (chapters 1 and 2); "temporal creatures who have life in him" (chapters 3–5); and the "history of fellowship—covenant—between God and creatures," marred by original sin and restored by the cross of Christ (chapters 6 and 7).

Along the way, I seek to respond to the commonplace questions noted above about why a creator would produce such an unfathomably vast cosmos, why there is such a strange array of creatures, what makes humans distinctive and why the presence of humans is good, why anyone would believe in original sin, why the creator became incarnate and died on the cross, and so forth. I also aim to show appreciation for modern science without falling into what David Bradshaw insightfully describes as the erroneous view that "science provides the deepest possible insight into nature."[8]

Christ, the Trinity, and the Trinitarian Traces in Creation

The evident gaps in my book's engagement with the doctrine of creation require some explanation. Despite their integral links with the doctrine of creation, I do not explore divine providence and governance in this book, although how I would ground these topics will be evident from my first two chapters on the creator.[9] Nor do I devote a separate chapter to the angels.[10] Similarly, although I explore the divine ideas specifically in light of creation *ex nihilo*, I do not treat creation *ex nihilo* in a distinct chapter. This is not because of any lack of interest in or commitment to the doctrine, but rather because many other recent books on creation have concentrated with excellent results upon creation *ex nihilo*.[11] I hope that my chapter on the divine ideas will serve to elucidate what the doctrine of creation *ex nihilo* affirms, namely that, in John Webster's words, "in his work of creation, God inaugurates an order of

7. Webster, "It Was the Will of the Lord to Bruise Him," 15.
8. Bradshaw, *"Logoi of Beings in Greek Patristic Thought,"* 21.
9. See also Levering, "Eternity, History, and Divine Providence."
10. On the angels, see Bonino, *Angels and Demons.*
11. For recent books devoted to expositing creation *ex nihilo*, see, e.g., McFarland, *From Nothing*; Burrell, *Freedom and Creation in Three Traditions*; Burrell et al., *Creation and the God of Abraham*; and Soskice, *Creation 'ex Nihilo' and Modern Theology.*

being other than himself, and this work is presupposed in all subsequent assertions about that order of being."[12] Most importantly perhaps, I do not take
up the new creation, the eschatological goal of creation (see Rom. 8:22–23).
Although the ordering of creation to Christ (and thus to new creation) will
be evident in this book, I prefer to treat it in a book of its own. Some readers
may consider that I give insufficient place to Jesus Christ and to the distinct
persons of the Trinity, because my book lacks chapters on Christ the creator
and on the Holy Spirit's creative work. Colin Gunton argues that "it was
christology which enabled the emergence of the doctrine of creation, and
particularly creation out of nothing," and "it was christology which enabled
theology to conceive of a relation of God to the world, of eternity to time,
in which the two are *both* contingently *and* internally rather than necessarily
or externally related."[13] Gunton is surely right about the latter point, and he
is also right that "it is christology which enables theology to hold together
creation and redemption," although pneumatology is also central.[14] In this
book, I consistently have in view the Father, Son, and Holy Spirit, who, as
one God, *are* the wisdom, love, and power by which they (the divine persons)
create all things. When I address the vast profusion of creatures and the human
"image of God," I interpret these realities in light of Christ and the Spirit,
even when this is not explicit. As Webster says, "It is in the works of grace, in
which the end of God's act of creation is secured, that the natures of God's
creatures and of his own benevolence are most fully displayed."[15]

12. Webster, "Love Is Also a Lover of Life," 156.

13. Gunton, "Introduction," 4. For extensive elaboration of the latter point, see Anatolios,
Retrieving Nicaea. See also Gunton, *Triune Creator*; Gunton, *Christ and Creation*. In the
latter book, Gunton argues that "it is in the doctrine of the Holy Spirit that are to be found
many of the clues to a more adequate study of Christ and creation" (11; cf. Gunton, "End of
Causality?," 79–81). For a soteriological study that, like the present study of creation, focuses
on divine simplicity rather than on "trinitarian narratives" (37)—and does so with reference
to Gunton (and Aquinas)—see Holmes, "Simple Salvation?"

14. Gunton, "Introduction," 4. For an emphasis on the Jewish (as distinct from Christian)
contribution to the doctrine of creation *ex nihilo*, see Janet Soskice, "Creation and the Glory of
Creatures." Discussing Philo and his influence, Soskice observes: "I do not think that we should
complain that the wholesome streams of Judaism and Christianity are here contaminated by
Hellenistic philosophy. This is a discredited exercise and Robert Wilken is surely right in saying
that we should speak now not about the hellenization of Christianity but the Christianization
of Hellenism. And nowhere more so than in the distinctively Jewish and Christian teaching on
creation *ex nihilo* and the reflection on Being and participation attendant on it" (184). Soskice
holds that "the doctrine of creation *ex nihilo* is a biblically-inspired piece of metaphysics—not
a teaching of hellenistic philosophy pure and simple, but something that arises from what
Greek-speaking Jews found in their scriptures" (181).

15. Webster, "Love Is Also a Lover of Life," 157. Webster explains, with a perspicacity to which
I am much indebted: "Christian beliefs about the character of the creator and of his creative act
are shaped by what can be learned from considering providence and reconciliation, in which the

It behooves me here to say something more about what Jesus Christ has to do with creation. According to the New Testament, as Sean McDonough points out, "the Messiah, as the image of God, creates the world he rules."[16] McDonough echoes Karl Barth's insistence that the Father, Son, and Holy Spirit do not create as though the incarnation were an afterthought. Eternally, the Son is begotten by the Father, and the Father spirates the Holy Spirit through the Son. But the eternal Son is also the one who is sent in time as Jesus Christ, the divine image and the true human image. The incarnation of the Son reveals to the whole world that the entirety of creation was made by and for Jesus Christ.[17]

The first chapter of the Gospel of John distinguishes the Word as creator from the Word as incarnate at a particular historical moment, but John 1 carefully does not separate the creative Word from the incarnate Word. Of the Word as creator, John says, "In the beginning was the Word, and the Word was with God, and the Word was God. He was in the beginning with God; all things were made through him, and without him was not anything made that was made" (John 1:1–3). But since the creative Word is none other than the incarnate Word, when the incarnate Word entered the world he created, "He came to his own home" (John 1:11). Similarly, Ephesians 1 states that believers were chosen in Christ "before the foundation of the world" and that God's purpose for creation has eternally been "to unite all things in him [Christ], things in heaven and things on earth" (Eph. 1:4, 10). The act of creation is unthinkable without Jesus Christ, even if the hypostatic union, by contrast to the act of creation, came to be at a particular moment in time. Paul teaches

---

work of creation has its *terminus ad quem* (a point given its most extensive modern exposition in Barth's ordering of creation to covenant). Equally, however, beliefs about providence and reconciliation only make full sense when we attend to their *terminus a quo*, that is, when we bear in mind that the protagonists in the economy are the creator and his creatures, and that all being and occurrence that is not God is to its very depths *ex nihilo*" (157). Thus Webster recognizes that it can be appropriate to "prescind from discussing the trinitarian dimensions of creation as the work of the three persons of the godhead in order to concentrate upon creation as the operation of the undivided divine essence, about which a number of lines need to be followed" (160). For the full range of Webster's theology of creation, see also his "Trinity and Creation."

16. McDonough, *Christ as Creator*, 260.

17. Barth states, "If by the Son or the Word of God we understand concretely Jesus, the Christ, and therefore very God and very man, as He existed in the counsel of God from all eternity and before creation, we can see how far it was not only appropriate and worthy but necessary that God should be the Creator" (*Church Dogmatics* [hereafter *CD*] III/1, 51). Much depends here upon what Barth means by stating that Christ "existed in the counsel of God from all eternity." For the ongoing debate between George Hunsinger and Bruce L. McCormack on this point, see Hunsinger, *Reading Barth with Charity*; McCormack, *Orthodox and Modern*; McCormack, "Processions and Missions." See also Levering, "Christ, the Trinity, and Predestination."

that "for us there is one God, the Father, from whom are all things and for whom we exist, and one Lord, Jesus Christ, through whom are all things and through whom we exist" (1 Cor. 8:6). Thus, Christians confess both that "Christ is lord of creation" and that "Christ is part of creation."[18] It follows that, as R. R. Reno says, "Knowing the Lord Jesus is crucial to knowing the beginning in which and out of which all things come to be," and Jesus is preeminent and determinative among all the things that come to be.[19]

Given the significance of the creative Word, the trinitarian dimension of creation requires attention. With regard to Genesis 1:26–27, Bill Arnold observes that "early Christian interpreters often assumed trinitarian concepts were behind the plurals in vv. 26–27."[20] When Irenaeus read Genesis 1 (in the Greek Septuagint) in the second century AD, for example, the creative activity of God's "spirit" and speech led him, as Peter Bouteneff notes, "to make explicit the role of Father, Son, and Holy Spirit in the establishment of the world through the famous image of the Son and Spirit as God's two hands."[21] It may seem that my focus in chapters 1 and 2 on distinguishing the creator from creatures undervalues what could be learned by emphasizing that the creator is the Father, Son, and Holy Spirit—or, for that matter, what could be learned by emphasizing, with Denis Edwards, that it is the Holy Spirit as the "Breath of God who breathes fire into the equations and continues to breathe life into the exuberant, diverse, interrelated community of living things."[22]

In response, I note first that the divine persons, as one God, are distinguished only by their mutual relations, not by relations to creatures.[23] Because the act of creation does not in any way differentiate the persons from each other (if it could do so, then it would thereby produce new divine persons), the Father, Son, and Holy Spirit create by their common power or actuality. Michel Barnes remarks that according to Gregory of Nyssa, "God's primary δύναμις . . . is the capacity to produce or create, and it is this capacity that is the distinguishing characteristic of the divine nature."[24] The Trinity does

18. Gunton, *Christ and Creation*, 34.
19. Reno, *Genesis*, 36.
20. Arnold, *Genesis*, 44.
21. Bouteneff, *Beginnings*, 77.
22. Denis Edwards, *Breath of Life*, 33.
23. Here it is worth recalling Denys Turner's rejection of the view that "the mystery of the divine oneness is somehow less intense than that of the divine Trinity, as if the oneness of God were easier to get into your head than the Trinity. It is not. Christian Trinitarianism does not rock a unitarian boat that would otherwise be plain sailing" (*Thomas Aquinas*, 130).
24. Barnes, *Power of God*, 233–34. According to Barnes, "The unity between the divine δύναμις and divine φύσις is such that Gregory is led to speak of the transcendent δύναμις more than the transcendent φύσις, with the result that the title 'divine δύναμις' replaces 'divine φύσις' in Gregory's writings" (224). Thus Gregory thinks of "God's existence in terms of His

not divide the infinite divine power, because each of the persons (and all the persons) is none other than the divine power: God's "power is not what he has but what he is."[25] Of course, neither this divine creative power nor the act of creation can be conceived by finite minds, although we can know analogously that God is infinite act and infinite power.[26]

Second, however, the trinitarian dimension of creation is hardly insignificant: the creator is truly the Trinity, not merely the one God (as if God's essence subsisted on its own). The inseparable operation of the persons *ad extra* involves the glorious mystery of the trinitarian order, in which the Father works through the Son and in the Spirit. Given the creative Trinity, furthermore, every creature manifests a trace or vestige of the Trinity. In this regard, Lewis Ayres emphasizes that the fact that "the persons create together or operate inseparably" does not mean that creation lacks trinitarian traces or *vestigia*.[27] Augustine rightly "sees a reflection in each aspect of creation of the manner in which the Father creates through Word and in Spirit."[28]

Indeed, the creative Trinity is the reason why creaturely difference is good, rather than constituting a falling away from divine unity and simplicity. Gilles Emery remarks that for Thomas Aquinas, "The distinction of the persons is

---

causal capacity" (240). Admittedly, in his controversy with Eunomius, Gregory suggests that (in Barnes's words) "it is the Father who generates the Son, and it is the Son who creates the cosmos" (259). Barnes makes clear that Gregory nonetheless accepts "the distinction between *in se* and *ad extra* activities, or the understanding that all divine activities are actions by all divine persons in common," not least since "whoever has the power to create has a divine nature" (259, 262; cf. 290).

25. Webster, "Love Is Also a Lover of Life," 161.

26. Ibid., 162: "The act of creation is ineffable, having no analogues in our experience of causation or agency." Colin Gunton complains that in Aquinas, God's "act of willing is rather monistically conceived. The Trinity plays little or no constitutive part in his treatment of the divine realisation of creation" ("End of Causality?," 67). But to say that the persons act through their shared power is not to devalue the persons or to render creation a nontrinitarian act. Gunton raises a few other concerns about Aquinas's position, which are well answered (without mentioning Gunton) in Webster's "Love Is Also a Lover of Life." In Gunton's view, Aquinas lacks "a central place for the doctrine of creation out of nothing" and indeed finds this doctrine to be "scarcely of interest" ("End of Causality?," 70–71), but as Burrell, Webster, and many others have shown, the very opposite is the case. For a defense of creation *ex nihilo* that, in my view, conceives God too much along the lines of a creaturely agent and would benefit from reflection upon the divine ideas, see Robson, *Ontology and Providence in Creation*.

27. Ayres, *Augustine and the Trinity*, 277–78; cf. 279–80.

28. Ibid., 278. Roger Lundin bemoans the fact that "while the search for a *vestigia trinitatis* may have been plausible in the enchanted cosmos inhabited by St. Augustine and St. Bonaventure, such a search would be fruitless in the disenchanted universe of late modernity. For we live, not in the cosmos of Dante Alighieri, but the universe of Franz Kafka" (*Beginning with the Word*, 72). Lundin provides a helpful summary of Karl Barth's theological critique of the *vestigia trinitatis*, which in Barth's view amount to an attempt to ascend to God (who for Barth can only be known through his free self-revelation) through human language and the cosmos.

. . . the cause of that other distinction which is the production of creatures (creation implies a distinction between God and that which proceeds outside of God), and is also the source of the distinctions between creatures (their multiplication)."[29] Aquinas grounds the existence and goodness of creaturely difference in the "difference" characteristic of the trinitarian persons, namely, the Father's speaking of his Word and the spiration of the Holy Spirit as the love of the Father and Son: "God the Father made the creature through his Word, which is his Son; and through his Love, which is the Holy Spirit."[30] It is this trinitarian difference, a mystery of wondrous communion, that is the true ground of all finite difference.

There are other ways of thinking about the goodness of finite difference. D. C. Schindler, for example, argues that difference belongs even to the divine existence/essence. On this view, God's pure *esse* as such can be distinguished from God's pure *esse* as subsisting. Schindler concludes that "all of the things we associate with difference, even in their apparently negative aspects, can become surprising reflections of God himself."[31] I think that divine subsis-

29. Emery, "Trinity and Creation," 67. This essay sets forth the main lines of Emery's *La Trinité créatrice*.

30. *ST* I, q. 45, a. 6 and ad 1. Gunton holds that the Father's creative action through the Son is "an instance and paradigm of a form of *mediated* action that requires no *intermediaries*" ("End of Causality?," 78). Similarly he states that "the Son of God in free personal relation to the world, indeed identification with part of that world, is the basis for an understanding of God the Father's relation with his creation" (77–78). He continues in the same vein: "The Spirit is the one who mediates the action of God the Father in such a way that the life of the Son, while deriving from the Father and dependent upon him, is given space to remain authentically human" (79). The notion of the Son mediating the Father's act of creation is troubling, since they create by their shared actuality/power, although certainly the Son receives this actuality/power from the Father. "Mediation" is not the right term here.

31. Schindler, "What's the Difference?," 614. Schindler goes on to argue that "the Son participates, so to speak, in the Father's being, not at all as a defective copy, but as Perfect Image" (615). This way of putting it seems to differentiate the persons from the divine being (whereas in fact the persons are the divine being, and not by a participatory relationship, no matter how perfect). For Hans Urs von Balthasar, even the difference that is death has an analogous mode in the Trinity: thus in summing up his perspective, Balthasar remarks that "earlier we spoke of death as a mode of (eternal) life, of suffering as a mode of joy, of separation as a mode of union. Now we have seen dereliction as a mode of eternal communion between Father and Son in the Spirit, and in conclusion we begin to see how the 'economic' modes of relations between the Divine Persons are latent in the 'immanent' modes, without adding a foreign element to them as such" (*Theo-Drama*, 5:268). See also Balthasar's well-known (but, in my view, mistaken) contention that in the Trinity,

> there must be *areas of infinite freedom* that are *already there* and do not allow everything to be compressed into an airless unity and identity. The Father's act of surrender calls for its own area of freedom; the Son's act, whereby he receives himself from and acknowledges his indebtedness to the Father, requires its own area; and the act whereby the Spirit proceeds, illuminating the most intimate love of Father and Son, testifying to it and fanning it into flame, demands its area of freedom. . . . Something like infinite

tence is implied by and included in *ipsum esse*, and so I do not follow the
path taken by Schindler.

With regard to the goodness of finite difference, Christopher Malloy suggests an alternative way forward (drawn from Aquinas) that conceives of "the
universe as a hierarchically heterogeneous whole composed of irreducibly
diverse parts."[32] We must view each thing in relation to the whole. Aquinas argues that God "brought things into being in order that his goodness
might be communicated to creatures, and be represented by them"; and this
required many different creatures, so that "what was wanting to one in the
representation of the divine goodness might be supplied by another."[33] In this
light, it is fitting that creaturely difference includes imperfection on the part
of individual creatures, because the universe of creatures has its own proper
(relational) perfection.[34] Here we can see why creation's fulfillment comes in
the new creation that is the supremely interrelated mystical body of Christ,
composed of many members.[35]

By viewing the goodness of creaturely difference in terms of the *relationships* of each thing in the universe to other things and to the whole (so that
the relational whole is what best reflects God's own goodness), we can gain a
deeper appreciation for the vestiges or traces in creation of the creative Trinity.
Thus, Peter Leithart proposes that all creatures imitate the Trinity because
creatures display a "perichoretic" pattern, a pattern of mutual indwelling. As
Leithart observes, "Within the Trinity, each person both wholly envelops yet is
wholly enveloped by the others. Each person is both the dwelling place of and
is indwelled by each of the others."[36] Likewise, each created thing is what it is
by and through a profound relational presence to other things. Leithart shows
that the structure of such things as bodiliness, human identity, marriage, time,

---

"duration" and infinite "space" must be attributed to the acts of reciprocal love so
that the life of *communio*, of fellowship, can develop. . . . True, all temporal notions
of "before" and "after" must be kept at a distance; but absolute freedom must provide
the acting area in which it is to develop—and develop in terms of love and blessedness.
(*Theo-Drama*, 2:257)

32. Malloy, "Participation and Theology," 633. Malloy rightly sees his approach here as
"furthering the core of Schindler's thesis" even while taking it in a different direction (634).

33. *ST* I, q. 47, a. 1. Aquinas adds that "goodness, which in God is simple and uniform, in
creatures is manifold and divided; and hence the whole universe together participates in the
divine goodness more perfectly, and represents it better than any single creature whatever"
(ibid.). See also Pope Francis's *Laudato Si'*, §86, which cites Aquinas in praise of the multiplicity
and diversity of creatures.

34. See Blanchette, *Perfection of the Universe according to Aquinas*.

35. See also Guy Mansini, OSB, who makes the point that "the actual complications of reality
go far beyond that of the distinction and multiplicity of creatures" and include such things as the
incarnation of the Word ("Tight Neo-Platonist Henology and Slack Christian Ontology," 600).

36. Leithart, *Traces of the Trinity*, 134.

language, and sound/music exhibits a "pattern of mutual interpenetration" or "Love."[37] This pattern is the distinctive mark of the power and presence of the triune creator. In the interpenetration of creatures we can perceive, in faith, "the traces, fingerprints, and footprints of the God who is Trinity."[38]

Drawing upon Irenaeus, Robert Barron makes a similar point. He observes that "time is not simply one thing after another but rather a web, a nexus of meaning, one moment calling out to, indicating, or echoing another; and space is not simply an empty grid occupied by a variety of objects but rather a weave of interdependence and mutual implication."[39] Since God is one and three, Barron adds, we should expect salvation history to be a unity, and yet to exhibit multiplicity as well. We should expect the unity of the saints to be like a symphony, in which real multiplicity (rather than monotone) comes together to make one harmony. Like Leithart, Barron concludes that "all reality is . . . marked by a kind of being-with or being-for."[40]

With regard to the trinitarian traces or vestiges, Aquinas considers that each creature "represents" the Holy Spirit (love) via relationality, the Son (Word) via form, and the Father (paternity) via substantial subsistence.[41] More generally, Aquinas proposes that since "every effect in some degree represents its cause," creatures cannot help but represent the Trinity.[42] In rational creatures, this representation has the dignity of an image, because the rational processions of the soul, through their production of a word and love, are the image of the divine processions of the Son and Spirit. But in all creatures (and in human bodiliness), there is a "trace of the Trinity, inasmuch as in every creature are found some things which are necessarily reduced to the divine Persons as to their cause."[43]

Aquinas does not draw a connection here to mutual indwelling, though he does connect the trinitarian trace with the relationality inherent in each

37. Ibid., 132.
38. Ibid., 145.
39. Barron, *Exploring Catholic Theology*, 55. See also Barron's reflections on Charles Williams's theory of "coinherence," as set forth in Williams's *Region of the Summer Stars* and *Image of the City, and Other Essays*.
40. Barron, *Exploring Catholic Theology*, 226; cf. 38. Barron notes appreciatively that "Aquinas says that creation is *quaedam relatio ad creatorem cum novitate essendi*, a kind of relation to the Creator with freshness of being" (35). In this sense, "The creature does not have a relationship with God; instead it *is* a relationship with God" (ibid.). Jonathan Wilson, too, finds that "all creation lives by giving and receiving," but he emphasizes the present fallen condition of creation (and looks forward to the new creation that is already breaking in through Jesus Christ): "Right now, this supposed giving and receiving appears more like taking and keeping: animal predation, human conflict, perpetual violence" (*God's Good World*, 114).
41. *ST* I, q. 45, a. 7.
42. Ibid.
43. Ibid.

creature. In his view, the modes of indwelling possible for creatures are not radical enough to be an image or trace of the perfect mutual indwelling of the Father, Son, and Spirit.[44] With respect to the Father and Son, he observes that the creaturely mode that most nearly approximates their mutual indwelling is "that whereby something exists in its originating principle" (as for instance a son in a father).[45] The problem is that the indwelling here does not involve a perfect sharing of essence: "The unity of essence between the principle and that which proceeds therefrom is wanting in things created."[46] Even if the essence could be perfectly shared between a created principle and that which proceeds from it, a full-fledged *threefold* pattern would be needed for an image or trace of the persons' mutual indwelling. That said, Leithart's and Barron's insights into the relational fabric of creation are, indisputably, strong evidence of the creative Trinity.

Much that needs to be said theologically about the creator and his creation can be said, of course, without explicit reference to Christology and trinitarian theology. Katherine Sonderegger aptly points out that in theological investigation, "not all is Christology," in the sense that not all is grounded in or "derived from His incarnate life."[47] The same observation holds, *mutatis mutandis*, for trinitarian theology. As Sonderegger puts it: "God is supremely, gloriously One; surpassingly, uniquely One. Nothing is more fundamental to the Reality than this utter Unicity. . . . For *monotheism* is not a shame word!"[48] She goes on to caution, "So pronounced is the christological turn in modern theology that a doctrine of God shaped and set forth in other forms must appear to many readers as hardly biblical at all—nonbiblical in truth."[49] She is right to resist this limiting path. Although everything in the doctrine of creation relates to Christology and trinitarian theology, not everything in the doctrine of creation need be explicitly grounded in Christology and trinitarian theology, not least because Christ is, in his divine nature, the one, simple creator God.

44. For discussion of Aquinas's theology of the mutual indwelling or *perichoresis* of the persons of the Trinity, see Emery, *Trinitarian Theology of Saint Thomas Aquinas*, 298–311. For further background, see Durand, *La périchorèse des personnes divines*.

45. *ST* I, q. 42, a. 5, ad 1.

46. Ibid. In the *respondeo* of this article, Aquinas states that "there are three points of consideration as regards the Father and the Son; the essence, the relation, and the origin; and according to each the Son and the Father are in each other."

47. Sonderegger, *Systematic Theology*, 1:xvii.

48. Ibid., xiv. Sonderegger rightly adds that "the Mystery of the Trinity must in itself be a form of Oneness: here too the ineffable Unicity of God must govern, conform, and set forth the Triune Reality of God" (xv).

49. Ibid., xvii.

Creation and Modern Science

Books on creation are often expected to treat modern science extensively. Colin Gunton bemoans the resulting situation: "It is not too much of an exaggeration to say that in the modern world the doctrine of creation has in many places given way to discussions of the relation between science and religion."[50] Surely, as Gunton goes on to insist, the theological doctrine of creation must be much more than a dialogue with modern science. Given that the doctrine of creation inevitably interacts with science at various points, however, numerous excellent studies of creation-related themes—by Cynthia Crysdale and Neil Ormerod, Michael Hanby, Brendan Purcell, Conor Cunningham, Thomas Torrance, Stephen Barr, Hans Schwarz, and Lenn Goodman, among others—have focused a good deal of their energies on critiquing scientific materialism.[51]

As would be expected, modern scientific materialism is particularly obtuse when it comes to creation. In his *A Universe from Nothing*, for example, the physicist Lawrence Krauss argues that "all signs suggest a universe that could and plausibly did arise from a deeper nothing—involving the absence of space itself."[52] In modern physics, Krauss alleges, "the very distinction between something and nothing has begun to disappear."[53] He explains further that "quantum gravity not only appears to allow universes to be created from nothing—meaning, in this case, I emphasize, the absence of space and time—it may require them. 'Nothing'—in this case no space, no time, no anything!—*is* unstable."[54] Krauss also thinks that there may be "a multiverse, either in the form of a landscape of universes existing in a host of extra dimensions, or in the form of a possibly infinitely replicating set of universes in a three-dimensional space as in the case of eternal inflation."[55] Such a multiverse,

50. Gunton, "Introduction," 1.

51. See Crysdale and Ormerod, *Creator God, Evolving World*; Hanby, *No God, No Science?*; Purcell, *From Big Bang to Big Mystery*; Conor Cunningham, *Darwin's Pious Idea*; Torrance, *Divine and Contingent Order*. See also Stephen Barr, *Modern Physics and Ancient Faith*; Hans Schwarz, *Creation*; Goodman, *Creation and Evolution*; Haarsma and Haarsma, *Origins*; and Keith Miller, *Perspectives on an Evolving Creation*.

52. Krauss, *Universe from Nothing*, 183. Krauss imagines that believers in God must posit a nothingness in which "something" already is: "if one requires that the notion of true nothingness requires not even the *potential* for existence, then surely God cannot work his wonders, because if he does cause existence from nonexistence, there must have been the potential for existence" (174).

53. Ibid., 182–83.

54. Ibid., 170. For background to quantum theory, see especially Polkinghorne, *Quantum Theory*.

55. Krauss, *Universe from Nothing*, 176. See also the cognate discussion contained in James Lidsey, *Bigger Bang*, chap. 12. Lidsey remarks that "quantum fluctuations in the vacuum—that is, empty space—result in the spontaneous creation of particles and antiparticles. The idea is

he says, would do away with the need for identifying a "prescribed 'cause' for our universe," since it would relativize "the question of what determined the laws of nature that allowed our universe to form and evolve."[56] On these foundations, Krauss imagines himself to be in a position to deny that there is an all-powerful creative "external agency existing separate from space, time, and indeed from physical reality itself."[57]

More forcefully but on the basis of the same misunderstandings, Stephen Hawking and Leonard Mlodinow assert in their *The Grand Design* that "philosophy is dead"—a claim that the widespread embrace of their own philosophical arguments suggests may be all too true.[58] In light of quantum physics, Hawking and Mlodinow posit that "a great many universes were created out of nothing. Their creation does not require the intervention of some supernatural being or god. Rather, these multiple universes arise naturally from physical law."[59] As in Krauss, this physical law turns out to be the quantum law of gravity: "Because there is a law like gravity, the universe can and will create itself from nothing. . . . Spontaneous creation is the reason there is something rather than nothing, why the universe exists, why we exist. It is not necessary to invoke God to light the blue touch paper and set the universe going."[60] This

---

that a similar quantum fluctuation could also result in the creation of an entire universe. The argument goes as follows: initially, there was nothing, but then a quantum fluctuation occurred and caused a tiny, fledgling universe to emerge from the emptiness. This universe subsequently inflated and grew into the complicated structure that we observe today" (113). Lidsey adds that for the universe to emerge in this way, the law of the conservation of energy requires that "the total amount of energy present in the universe must be zero," which he thinks may be the case because "electromagnetic force is much stronger than the force of gravity, and so it would dominate the dynamics of the universe if the universe contained an excess of positive or negative electric charge" (115).

56. Krauss, *Universe from Nothing*, 176. For his part, Lidsey observes: "The idea that a quantum fluctuation can lead to the creation of the entire universe from nothing is very appealing, but a number of issues remain unresolved. It is far from clear how the quantum fluctuation arose in the first place" (*Bigger Bang*, 115). Here Lidsey would seem to be moving closer to questioning his own account of "nothing"; but he still fails to indicate any appreciation for the metaphysical issues involved.

57. Krauss, *Universe from Nothing*, 171.

58. Hawking and Mlodinow, *Grand Design*, 5.

59. Ibid., 8–9.

60. Ibid., 180. Earlier they observe that quantum theory's explanation of the space-time continuum "removes the age-old objection to the universe having a beginning, but also means that the beginning of the universe was governed by the laws of science and doesn't need to be set in motion by some god" (135). David Bentley Hart pointedly notes that contemporary scientists, when writing about God, fail even to rise to the level of atheism, since to be an atheist "one must genuinely succeed in not believing in *God*, with all the logical consequences such disbelief entails. . . . Beliefs regarding God concern the source and ground and end of all reality, the unity and existence of every particular thing and of the totality of all things, the ground of the possibility of anything at all. . . . The question of God, by contrast [to questions about

portrait of God intervening to "set the universe going" is utterly antithetical to the real doctrine of creation, and the quantum law of gravity is obviously not nothing. Nonexistence—which alone is truly "nothing"—is not merely the absence of matter (or of other stuff), but rather is the radical absence of existence of any kind whatsoever.

Indeed, the emergence of all finite things from an original, non-spatiotemporal finite reality is not a new idea, although the specific appeal to the quantum law of gravity is new. Indebted to Stoic philosophers, Gregory of Nyssa and Augustine already conceived of something broadly similar, at least with respect to an original formlessness logically prior to the spatiotemporal emergence of the stuff of the cosmos.[61] Thus Augustine envisions an original formless creation of "heaven and earth," which he calls "the very beginning of creation in its inchoate state," prior in origin (though not in time) to its reception of form.[62] Like Gregory, Augustine proposes a theory of *rationes seminales* by which all things are included in this original creation.[63] This original formless creation not only is broadly similar to the hypothetical scenario described by Krauss and Hawking/Mlodinow, but also makes clear that the scientists' hypothetical scenario does not in fact answer the problem identified by the doctrine of creation, which has to do with the *existence* of anything.[64]

---

gods], is one that can and must be pursued in terms of the absolute and the contingent, the necessary and the fortuitous, potency and act, possibility and impossibility, being and nonbeing, transcendence and immanence" (*Experience of God*, 32–34). Hawking and Mlodinow's work, argues Hart, has value when they stick with their expertise, physics; and in this regard they helpfully summarize the insights of the twentieth century into the first moments of the universe: "In the early universe—when the universe was small enough to be governed by both general relativity and quantum theory—there were effectively four dimensions of space and none of time. That means that when we speak of the 'beginning' of the universe, we are skirting the subtle issue that as we look backward toward the very early universe, time as we know it does not exist! We must accept that our usual ideas of space and time do not apply to the very early universe" (*Grand Design*, 134). Hawking and Mlodinow define a "law of nature" as "a rule that is based upon an observed regularity and provides predictions that go beyond the immediate situations upon which it is based" (ibid., 27).

61. See Blowers, *Drama of the Divine Economy*, 146–59. For background in Philo, see 54–61.

62. Augustine, *Literal Meaning of Genesis* 1.6.12, p. 25. See also 1.14.28, p. 35; 1.15.29–30, pp. 36–37; 5.5.16, p. 155.

63. For Gregory of Nyssa, as Blowers says, "the Creator is a grand Sower whose founding (καταβολή) of the world is an instantaneous 'throwing down' of the seeds of created things that funds the orderly and sequential production (κατασκευή)" (*Drama of the Divine Economy*, 146). See also D. Hart, *Experience of God*, 26. On the connections between Augustine's interpretation of Gen. 1–2 (including his doctrine of *rationes seminales*) and modern evolutionary theory, see Levering, "Augustine on Creation."

64. Quite rightly, therefore, Hart observes that

Hawking's dismissal of God as an otiose explanatory hypothesis . . . is a splendid example of a false conclusion drawn from a confused question. He clearly thinks that talk of God's creation of the universe concerns some event that occurred at some particular

In his writings on creation, Augustine shows that the creator God does not (and indeed could not) merely "set the universe going" as an external instigator. Rather, God, who is a mystery of unity and communion, of supreme wisdom and love, creates the universe from nothing by the sheer gift of finite existence, a gift that establishes and sustains the very core of every finite thing. As infinite eternal presence, God is intimately present to all time and space bestowing the gift of existence. God's gift of existence does much more than "set the universe going." Real creation, unlike the emergence of all things from the quantum law of gravity or from a formless non-spatiotemporal state, involves the inexpressibly powerful gift of being. Focused solely upon empirical realities, Krauss and Hawking/Mlodinow have not understood what actual creation from nothing requires. As Augustine is aware, only the transcendent God can give existence, as distinct from producing emergent realities or propagating new things. For giving and sustaining the *being* of things, a transcendent creator, infinite being (and not merely the infinite sum of all finite being), is necessary.

Another popular misunderstanding of the doctrine of creation comes from the evolutionary biologist Richard Dawkins, who has argued that "a God capable of continuously monitoring and controlling the individual status of every particle in the universe *cannot* be simple."[65] Dawkins thinks that the divine ideas—construed as God's "monitoring and controlling" of each and every thing—imply that God must possess a composite consciousness. He imagines that the theist must presume that "other corners of God's giant consciousness are simultaneously preoccupied with the doings and emotions and prayers of every single human being—and whatever intelligent aliens there

---

point in the past, prosecuted by some being who appears to occupy the shadowy juncture between a larger quantum landscape and the specific conditions of our current cosmic order; by 'God,' that is to say, he means only a demiurge, coming after the law of gravity but before the present universe, whose job was to nail together all the boards and firmly mortar all the bricks of our current cosmic edifice. So Hawking naturally concludes that such a being would be unnecessary if there were some prior set of laws—just out there, so to speak, happily floating along on the wave-functions of the quantum vacuum—that would permit the spontaneous generation of any and all universes. It never crosses his mind that the question of creation might concern the very possibility of existence as such, not only of this universe but of all the laws and physical conditions that produced it, or that the concept of God might concern a reality not temporally prior to this or that world, but logically and necessarily prior to all worlds, all physical laws, all quantum events, and even all possibilities of laws and events. From the perspective of classical metaphysics, Hawking misses the whole point of talk of creation: God would be just as necessary even if all that existed were a collection of physical laws and quantum states, from which no ordered universe had ever arisen; for neither those laws nor those states could exist of themselves. (*Experience of God*, 40–41)

65. Dawkins, *God Delusion*, 149. See D. Hart, *Atheist Delusions*, 4.

might be on other planets in this and 100 billion other galaxies."[66] In addition, Dawkins holds that any real communication from God to humans could be detected by science, and "a God who is capable of sending intelligible signals to millions of people simultaneously, and of receiving messages from all of them simultaneously, cannot be, whatever else he might be, simple."[67] Dawkins concludes, "God may not have a brain made of neurons, or a CPU made of silicon, but if he has the powers attributed to him he must have something far more elaborately and non-randomly constructed than the largest brain or the largest computer we know."[68] It is notable that the multiplicity of the divine ideas (if this phrase can be used in connection with the thoughts of Dawkins's hypothetical demiurge) fuels Dawkins's rejection of what he imagines to be the notion of divine simplicity. But Dawkins wildly misconstrues what philosophers and theologians have meant by the "ideas" and "simplicity" of the creator God.[69] My first two chapters correct such misunderstandings of the divine ideas and divine simplicity.

Dawkins also considers that Christianity is an instance of a deplorable "sado-masochism," since Christians believe that "God incarnated himself as a man, Jesus, in order that he should be tortured and executed in *atonement* for the hereditary sin of Adam."[70] Dawkins holds that this doctrine is "repellent"

66. Dawkins, *God Delusion*, 149.

67. Ibid., 154.

68. Ibid. Cf. the warning of Burrell against "presuming a computer-like inventory on the part of God, as though things were objects for God as they are for us. The next step would be to imagine possible trajectories, as though providence were a cosmic form of game-theory" (*Knowing the Unknowable God*, 93).

69. David Hume understands more clearly what philosophers and theologians mean by divine simplicity, but he claims (in the voice of "Cleanthes") that a nondiscursive, unchanging mind is a contradiction in terms:

> I can readily allow, said Cleanthes, that those who maintain the perfect simplicity of the supreme Being, to the extent in which you have explained it, are complete *mystics*, and chargeable with all the consequences which I have drawn from their opinion. They are, in a word, atheists, without knowing it. For though it be allowed, that the Deity possesses attributes, of which we have no comprehension; yet ought we never to ascribe to him any attributes, which are absolutely incompatible with that intelligent nature, essential to him. A mind, whose acts and sentiments and ideas are not distinct and successive; one, that is wholly simple, and totally immutable; is a mind which has no thought, has no reason, no will, no sentiment, no love, no hatred; or in a word, is no mind at all. It is an abuse of terms to give it that appellation; and we may as well speak of limited extension without figure, or of number without composition. (*Dialogues concerning Natural Religion*, in *Principal Writings on Religion*, 61)

The first two chapters of my book address the divine creative mind in its simplicity; suffice it to say here that the infinite fullness of mind, surely, need not be "no mind at all," even if it is not a finite mind.

70. Dawkins, *God Delusion*, 252.

and "barking mad" because it amounts to the notion that "in order to impress himself, Jesus had himself tortured and executed, in vicarious punishment for a *symbolic* sin committed by a *non-existent* individual [Adam]."[71] My final two chapters aim to correct false impressions such as these, in hopes that a clearer understanding of the doctrine of creation will also contribute to a clearer understanding of the doctrine of redemption. Given the level of misunderstanding among eminent scientists today, it should be evident that "discussions of the relation between science and religion" need a theologically and philosophically robust engagement with the doctrine of creation.[72]

Laudato Si', Contemporary Theologies of Creation, and Genesis 1–3

In his recent encyclical *Laudato Si'*, motivated by pressing ecological concerns, Pope Francis urges that "rather than a problem to be solved, the world is a joyful mystery to be contemplated with gladness and praise."[73] Indeed, for Pope Francis (as for my chapter 3), the world's various species "give glory to God by their very existence" and "convey their message to us" through their unique modes of embodying the gift of creaturely existence.[74] He observes that

71. Ibid., 253. In response to "the universal criticism of a cruel God who sacrifices his own innocent Son," Henk J. M. Schoot remarks in an essay on Thomas Aquinas's theology of the cross: "Christ's mission was voluntary, and undertaken on the basis of a charity which was divinely bestowed upon him. In fact, it seems never to cross Aquinas' mind to suppose an opposition between the man Christ and God his Father. His understanding of the ontological constitution of Christ would not allow for it, but one can easily suppose that, without such a background conception, some sort of opposition might be developed. This is exactly the point where a non-Chalcedonian christology is likely to fail, since it is much too vulnerable to the criticism of a cruel God, which was already voiced in Aquinas' days. But Christ was never detached from his divinity, not even when he suffered and died" ("Divine Transcendence and the Mystery of Salvation according to Thomas Aquinas," 279–81). See also the responses to Dawkins (and others) contained in John Hughes, *Unknown God*.

72. Gunton, "Introduction," 1. For an exemplary study in this regard, focused on modern science and divine causality, see Dodds, *Unlocking Divine Action*.

73. Pope Francis, *Laudato Si'*, §12.

74. Ibid., §33. See also Antonio López's appreciation for "both finite being and oneself as gift at whose respective centers is the divine mystery" (*Gift and the Unity of Being*, 27). Yet, as Jerry D. Korsmeyer points out, "Over ninety-nine percent of all species that ever lived are now extinct. . . . The universe contains finite creatures in competition, where one's gain is another's loss. It contains chance blunders of matter and energy that produce natural disasters, and violence of immense magnitude. Countless individuals and species have suffered and perished" (*Evolution and Eden*, 85). Korsmeyer continues, "Consider over a hundred million years of dinosaurs, half of which savagely hunted and ate the others. To what end? Was God pleased in some way with this spectacle? What about insects that have evolved to be parasites living within and destroying other life?" (ibid.). For Korsmeyer, the strange fruits of evolution show that creation "is not the result of an exact plan," since if it were an exact plan "existing from all eternity to produce

the creation accounts in Genesis 1–2 make clear that "human life is grounded in three fundamental and closely intertwined relationships: with God, with our neighbour and with the earth itself."[75] Due to "our presuming to take the place of God and refusing to acknowledge our creaturely limitations" (Gen. 3), however, the "three vital relationships have been broken, both outwardly and within us."[76] Pope Francis connects this brokenness with neglect of the truth of the doctrine of creation: "A spirituality which forgets God as all-powerful and Creator is not acceptable. . . . The best way to restore men and women to their rightful place, putting an end to their claim to absolute dominion over the earth, is to speak once more of the figure of a Father who creates and who alone owns the world."[77]

In making this argument, Pope Francis does not forget that the creator is the Trinity. As he states, "The world was created by the three Persons acting as a single divine principle, but each one of them performed this common work in accordance with his own personal property. . . . For Christians, believing in one God who is trinitarian communion suggests that the Trinity has left its mark on all creation."[78] Just as relationality describes the divine persons, so likewise "the world, created according to the divine model, is a web of relationships," with the result that "everything is interconnected."[79]

---

the human race," there would not be so much waste, destruction, and savage brutality, caused both by natural processes and by human sinners (ibid.). Frances Young sees the cycle of bodily deterioration–death–generation of new life from a different angle, with which I agree (though human death, which we experience as alienation, is a different matter, as I discuss in chap. 6): "Life depends on the consumption of other life, the stuff of life constantly being recycled, a process which can either be viewed as death-dealing or as constitutive of the surging diversity of living growth. Death is part of life, a prerequisite for the constant recycling that produces abundance. Should we be focussing on 'waste' or fecundity?" (Young, *God's Presence*, 67–68). See also Francis of Assisi, "Canticle of Brother Sun," 39; Nick Lane, *Life Ascending*; Schönborn, *Chance or Purpose?*, 89–103; Creegan, "Salvation of Creatures."

75. Pope Francis, *Laudato Si'*, §66.

76. Ibid.; see also the *Catechism of the Catholic Church*, §§399–400. Metropolitan Kallistos Ware similarly observes that "[man] repudiated the Godward relationship that is his true essence. Instead of acting as mediator and unifying center, he produced division: division within himself, division between himself and other men, division between himself and the world of nature. Entrusted by God with the gift of freedom, he systematically denied freedom to his fellows" (*Orthodox Way*, 58–59). For a contemporary historical-critical analysis of Gen. 2–3, see Blenkinsopp, *Creation, Un-Creation, Re-Creation*. Blenkinsopp emphasizes the original author's interest in "the question of how evil infiltrated into and undermined the good creation" (9). However, Blenkinsopp pays almost no attention to the nature of God as depicted in Gen. 1–11 or as an extratextual reality, and his knowledge of diverse historical contexts leads him to separate quite sharply, in a historicist manner, the Genesis narrative from later appropriations of it, whether by Paul (or other New Testament authors) or by the Church over the centuries.

77. Pope Francis, *Laudato Si'*, §75.

78. Ibid., §§238–39.

79. Ibid., §240.

Pope Francis also recognizes the christological dimension of creation, especially with regard to the divine Son, the creator, taking on flesh and uniting all things in himself. From this perspective, "the creatures of this world no longer appear to us under a merely natural guise because the risen One is mysteriously holding them to himself and directing them towards fullness as their end."[80]

Numerous theologians today promote environmental reform, and to this extent Pope Francis's *Laudato Si'* reflects widely shared concerns. But with regard to the full dimensions of the doctrine of creation (dimensions that are present in *Laudato Si'*), Jonathan Wilson rightly observes that "compared to other doctrines, the doctrine of creation has been neglected; the result is an atrophied doctrine."[81] The atrophy of this doctrine is all too apparent when one looks at the shelves of popular bookstores or when one examines the science textbooks typically used in colleges and universities. As Rudi te Velde observes, "With the rise of natural science and the prevalent naturalistic worldview, 'creation' has become more and more an anomaly, a mythical and anthropocentric remainder which can survive only in the weakened and non-cognitive sense of a metaphor."[82] Joseph Ratzinger likewise comments with concern that today "the creation account is noticeably and nearly completely absent from catechesis, preaching, and even theology."[83] Michael Welker, who has devoted much of his career to writing about the doctrine of creation, is similarly motivated by the growing disbelief in a creator and creation. He remarks sadly that in Europe, "more and more people are turning away

80. Ibid., §100; translation slightly altered.
81. Wilson, *God's Good World*, viii.
82. Te Velde, "Metaphysics and the Question of Creation," 73. As te Velde points out, the problem in contemporary culture's reception of the doctrine of creation is often related to the doctrine of God:

> It is not only that, from the conceptual horizon of natural science, the workings of a "supernatural agent" cannot be recognized as a genuine and acceptable scientific explanation; but what is more, such a "supernatural agent" must necessarily appear as an additional explanatory factor that concurs with other "natural" factors. In traditional language: it is as if one calls upon the "first cause" within the domain of the "second causes" of nature in order to explain particular features of natural processes and facts. "God" versus "natural evolution" is only an alternative when the immanent sphere of nature counts as the ultimate horizon of human self-understanding; but if this is so, "God" is reduced to "playing a part in the game" as nothing more than an additional factor within the one natural playing-field. (74)

See also Denis Edwards, *Breath of Life*, 9: "When a new worldview emerges that springs from a broadly held scientific consensus, theology must engage with it in order to be faithful to its own task."
83. Ratzinger, *'In the Beginning . . .'*, ix. Ratzinger directs attention to the significance of the Sabbath, to the creation of human beings in the image of God (in light of evolutionary theory), and to sin as an effort to free ourselves from creaturely limitations.

from belief in a personal figure who exists over and above this world, who has brought forth both himself and all reality, and who controls and defines 'everything' without distinction."[84]

Reinhard Hütter suggests that it may be Christian theologians themselves who are unwittingly making the doctrine of creation irrelevant.[85] Writing twenty-five years ago, Hütter perceptively cautions against "a reactive bandwagon theology: after environmentalists, scientists, politicians, philosophers etc., have pointed out and have very convincingly made the case for the ecological crisis, theologians would finally—always being the last—also join the choir in order to offer a *theology for* or *of* the meanwhile obvious ecological crisis."[86] Such theological baptizing of discourse drawn from other domains only persuades the broader culture that theological discourse, *as such*, is not necessary for knowledge of reality. Hütter's solution, which I find to be correct, involves developing a distinctive theology of creation focused on the *creator*.

Much like Hütter, Pope Francis cautions against making "the method and aims of science and technology an epistemological paradigm."[87] His focus is on ecological sustainability and on the need to respect nature's integrity and givenness. But he makes clear that a *sole* reliance on the scientific method as the arbiter of truth leads to an inability to discover the invisible and immaterial creator, as well as to an inability to recognize the deepest aspects of the

84. Welker, *Creation and Reality*, 1. The chapters of Welker's book therefore seek to reclaim the fundamental biblical concepts associated with creation. He explores such topics as how to read Gen. 1 and 2, "natural" knowledge of God in contrast to revealed knowledge of God, the meaning of "the heavens and the earth" (Gen. 1:1), angels and God's presence in creation, the image of God and "dominion" (Gen. 1:26–27), and the consequences of original sin.

85. Hütter, "*Creatio ex Nihilo*," 1.

86. Ibid. Hütter adds: "The very term *creation* is a *theological* term, and intelligible only as part and parcel of an encompassing theology, i.e., strictly put, the very term *theology of creation* is—if not a pleonasm—at least a tautology. *Creation* is only intelligible as *doctrine*, as part and parcel of the proclamation of the Gospel (*doctrina evangelii*), the redemptive story of God with Israel and with/in the life, death and resurrection of Jesus of Nazareth. The functional location (*Sitz im Leben*) of the doctrine is the theological, doxological, and ethical life of that community which was and constantly is created by the One whom this community confesses to be the Creator of Heaven and Earth" (3). More strongly than he would now put it, Hütter goes on to argue that "the statements of a theology of creation are an unfolding of a particular story and its reality claims. Yet these claims are eschatological by their very nature, i.e., they can neither be verified nor falsified, only testified" (3–4). For a recent reformulation of his position, from a Catholic perspective, see Hütter, *Dust Bound for Heaven*, esp. chaps. 2 and 10.

87. Pope Francis, *Laudato Si'*, §107. Hütter observes: "A theology of creation being deeply informed by the doctrine of creation *ex nihilo* will question philosophical implications of scientific reflection upon nature, i.e., will be a critical partner in the scientific endeavour, in raising the questions about the very possibility of *nature* being understood as *creatio*; and by pointing out the epistemological and ethical limitations of science as a human endeavour" ("*Creatio ex Nihilo*," 10).

human person.[88] When the scientific method becomes the "epistemological paradigm," notions of "sin" and "salvation," let alone of a "creator," can seem quaint, barely intelligible, and even perhaps a bit fanatical. Among the central tasks of the present book, therefore, is arguing for the reasonableness of belief in a creator and a creation as found in Genesis 1–3.

The Plan of the Work

In his well-known book on Thomas Aquinas, G. K. Chesterton presents him as "St. Thomas of the Creator" whose special task was to remind his contemporaries "of the creed of Creation."[89] Echoing this insight, Josef Pieper observes that Aquinas has "a fundamental idea by which almost all the basic concepts of his vision of the world are determined: the idea of creation, or more precisely, the notion that nothing exists which is not *creatura*, except the Creator Himself; and in addition, that this createdness determines entirely and all-pervasively the inner structure of the creature."[90] It is evident, then, that a book on creation can profitably draw upon Aquinas. My chapters aim to allow Aquinas's thought—and, equally important, that of his sources—to bear fruit in contemporary theology, often in light of a quite different set of problems than Aquinas (or his sources) faced.[91]

To some theologians, it has seemed that Aquinas's metaphysical profundity comes at the cost of separating the doctrine of creation from the history

88. As te Velde states, "The problem of the meaning of 'creation' in the modern world attests to the fact that current philosophical discourse remains silent about the metaphysical background of our experience of the world. The existence of the world, including the existence of human beings who know about the world as a whole, is taken for granted without asking further whether human beings can reach an adequate self-understanding within the horizon of the natural world. Much of contemporary thought, so it seems, prefers the brute facticity of existence as the ultimate truth of the world" ("Metaphysics and the Question of Creation," 74).

89. Chesterton, *Saint Thomas Aquinas*, 111, 119.

90. Pieper, *Silence of St. Thomas*, 47. For detailed exposition of this point, see Persson, *Sacra Doctrina*, 93–224. Persson notes that "the biblical idea of creation implies a radical reorientation in metaphysics, but this does not mean that metaphysics thereby ceases to be metaphysics. The primary modes of thought come from Greek philosophy, and though new formulations may in fact really be new when compared with earlier thought, they do not abrogate existing categories but rather bring existing lines of thought to completion" (141; cf. 280–82 for further reflection). With regard to creation, Persson observes that "God for Thomas is not a static and remote first principle without knowledge of the world, but is actively 'present' in all that happens in creation. Nothing exists or takes place that is not in its innermost being continually dependent on God for all that it receives. . . . The God whom we encounter in his [Thomas's] *sacra doctrina* is the Creator of whom the Bible speaks and who deals with his creation in grace and love" (271).

91. See Webster, "Theologies of Retrieval."

of salvation.[92] In the *Summa theologiae*, however, metaphysically informed reflection upon the Triune God's act of creation *ex nihilo* forms the basis for reflection upon the unfolding of creation in history. Thus David Burrell remarks with Aquinas's theology in view, "We are directed to this rich metaphysical mode of reflection by the scriptures themselves. . . . So we should no longer be surprised to find scripture demanding philosophical clarifications to display its own coherence."[93] Given his way of bringing together scriptural and metaphysical inquiries, Aquinas helps us to appreciate the creator God who is active in Genesis 1–3, which includes not only creation and fall but also commandments, punishment, and (proto-)redemption. Given the wisdom, goodness, and power of the creator God, creation and the history of redemption (and thus eschatology as well) are inextricably linked.

The first two chapters examine how it is possible that the wise and good creator God can know finite things and create finite things out of sheer infinite goodness, without losing his simplicity and freedom. Is it possible to conceive of the act of creation without conceiving of the creator God in such a way as to make him merely a powerful being among beings? In these two chapters, I explore and evaluate Aquinas's views of the divine ideas and divine simplicity in relation to the doctrine of creation. I undertake this task in light of trenchant criticisms offered by Vladimir Lossky and David Bradshaw, respectively. Their Eastern Orthodox commitment to the essence-energies distinction (especially in Lossky's version) strikes me as the best alternative way of accounting for the wisdom and simplicity of the creator God, but I argue that Aquinas's

92. For this concern, see Scheffczyk, *Creation and Providence*, 153. For Persson, by comparison, "in Thomas's *sacra doctrina* revelation does not simply provide the matter of theology and in this sense determine its content, but is a determinative principle as well in metaphysical conceptualisation" (*Sacra Doctrina*, 273). Yet Persson grants that at points in Aquinas, due to the dominance of the causal framework and because Aquinas's metaphysical outlook is not that of (for example) the author(s) of Gen. 1–3, there "is a certain ambivalent tension between *ratio* and *revelatio* of which, as far as we can judge, Thomas himself was not aware" (284). As an instance of this tension, Persson gives "the difficulty which Thomas finds in expressing adequately certain passages of the New Testament in terms of his preconceived definition of goodness and perfection," notably in 2 Cor. 5:21's statement that God "made him [Christ] to be sin" (287; cf. 290–91). I agree with Aquinas rather than Persson on 2 Cor. 5. But I can agree with Persson's observation that "the formal scriptural principle does not of itself guarantee a truly biblical theology" (288)—with the caveat that historical-critical reconstructions are not the only measure of a "truly biblical theology." After describing O. C. Quick's view of "the essential contrast between Greek and Hebrew thought," Persson rightly insists that "we cannot get to the heart of Thomas's thought simply by identifying his approach with one or other of these alternatives [Greek or Hebrew]. It is characteristic of Thomas that these are not alternatives but are in fact a conceptual unity" (291).

93. Burrell, "*Creatio ex Nihilo* Recovered," 19. This is the central argument of my *Scripture and Metaphysics*.

perspective offers a better way forward. With regard to God's eternal ideas of all the things he can create, it is necessary not to endow them with creaturely existence "prior" to their creation. As Henri de Lubac observes, "There are no eternal essences endowed with some kind of 'essential existence' until, by the creative act, they pass into 'actual existence'. In God there is only God."[94]

The middle three chapters then investigate the creation of "temporal creatures who have life in him."[95] In chapter 3, I seek to account theologically and philosophically for the extraordinary profusion of creatures in our unfathomably large universe, including the vast array of species of living organisms. How should theologians understand the seeming tension between contemporary scientific portraits of vast spatiotemporal expanses teeming with wildly strange creatures such as black holes and dinosaurs, on the one hand, and Genesis's description of a world of stars, plants, birds, and animals with which we are familiar, on the other? Why would a wise God have created dinosaurs to reign for hundreds of millions of years, something that seems rather absurd for the God of Genesis? In addressing such concerns, I draw upon Basil the Great's teaching about the six days of creation, and I argue that Aquinas's account of the analogy of being is helpful for awakening us to the theophanic significance of the diversity of creatures. Through this cosmic theophany, we can appreciate afresh the ancient Greek meaning of the word "cosmos," which, according to the Orthodox theologian John Anthony McGuckin, meant both "Beauty" and "World."[96]

I turn in chapter 4 to the creation of human beings "in the image of God" (Gen. 1:27). Contemporary biblical scholars and theologians find the patristic-medieval connection of the "image of God" with human rationality (wisdom and love) to be inadequate. This is so not only because some biblical scholars and theologians deny the existence of the spiritual soul, but also because students of the ancient Near Eastern literary context of Genesis have shown that the biblical author(s) likely understood the image of God in terms of human sharing in God's royal rule. Drawing upon the work of Richard Middleton, my chapter questions the modern dichotomy between the image of God as human rationality and the image of God as royal rule. In the wisdom and supreme love of Jesus Christ, we see the fullness of the royal priesthood that God wills to bestow upon humans; and we see the true image of the wise and good exemplar, God. In the words of the

94. De Lubac, *Mystery of the Supernatural*, 303–4.

95. Webster, "It Was the Will of the Lord to Bruise Him," 15.

96. McGuckin, "Beauty of the World and Its Significance in St. Gregory the Theologian," 36. See also the discussion of the beauty of creation in Vannier, *"Creatio," "conversio," "formatio" chez S. Augustin*, 124–31.

Second Vatican Council's Pastoral Constitution on the Church in the Modern World, *Gaudium et spes*, "Adam, the first man, was a type of him who was to come, Christ the Lord. Christ the new Adam, in the very revelation of the mystery of the Father and of his love, fully reveals man to himself and brings to light his most high calling."[97]

In light of the full meaning of the image of God, chapter 5 examines the first command that God gives to his image: "Be fruitful and multiply, and fill the earth" (Gen. 1:28). Although this chapter's main theme is whether the spread of human beings and their ongoing population growth are a suitable expression of divine wisdom and goodness, I also implicitly address whether the remainder of Genesis 1:28—"and subdue it [the earth]; and have dominion over the fish of the sea and over the birds of the air and over every living thing that moves upon the earth"—is an appropriate command. Should humans have "dominion" over nonrational creatures, and if so, how should this be squared with the ongoing growth of the human population, which is crowding out and endangering other species? If God is truly wise, why does he encourage the multiplication of fallen humans, as he does again after the flood (Gen. 8:17), well aware of how destructive humans are?

I next inquire into the origin of human destructiveness. Chapter 6 asks whether human sin comes about due to a free rebellion at the outset of human history or due to the first humans' genetically selfish dispositions. Genesis 2–3 portrays two first humans who freely disobeyed God, with profound consequences for their own condition and the condition of their descendants. Modern science has challenged this portrait on multiple fronts, as has contemporary historical-critical biblical exegesis, which has shown that Genesis 1–3 depicts a cosmic temple and has in view the sinfulness of the people of Israel. How should theologians address the tensions between the scientific evidence and the highly symbolic account of original sin in Genesis 3? In response, I survey various options for addressing the problems that have been raised regarding the doctrine of original sin. Arguing that God's wisdom and goodness in creation means that God originally made humans good and fully free, I contend that there was indeed a historical fall whose consequence is human death as we now experience it—namely, human death as alienation and as the cutting off of communion. Put another way, as John Henry Newman remarks, "*If* there be a God, *since* there is a God, the human race is implicated in some terrible aboriginal calamity. It is out of joint with the purposes of its Creator."[98]

97. *Gaudium et spes*, §22, p. 922.
98. Newman, *Apologia pro Vita Sua*, 320–21.

God's wise and loving response to sin, a response that eternally belonged to the simple Triune God's plan, is Jesus Christ, the incarnate Son who reveals the Father and (with the Father) sends the Holy Spirit in plenitude. Jesus fulfills the covenantal promises of God to Israel, such as Zechariah 13:1's prophecy of the triumphant day of the Lord: "On that day there shall be a fountain opened for the house of David and the inhabitants of Jerusalem to cleanse them from sin and uncleanness." Jesus instructs his disciples in the Gospel of Mark that he has come "to give his life as a ransom for many" (Mark 10:45). Paul teaches that "Christ died for us" and "we are now justified by his blood," since "we were reconciled to God by the death of his Son" (Rom. 5:8–10). But what does this language mean? In chapter 7, I propose that God's act of creation establishes an intricate order of relational bonds of justice. In order to interpret the cross rightly, then, we need to see the incarnate Word's suffering for our sins in light of the order of justice that pertains intrinsically to creation. In his wisdom and goodness, God chose the path of the cross not least because he willed to give humans—as his images—the dignity of restoring justice from within our human condition. Along these lines, N. T. Wright observes that "one of the greatest books in the New Testament (Romans) is about God's restorative justice."[99] At stake in this chapter is not only the wisdom of the divine ideas regarding creatures (including Christ, the incarnate Word), but also—in the words of Metropolitan Jonah Paffhausen—the human eschatological vocation "to offer the creation back to God in thanksgiving, as its priest, exercising dominion and care for all creatures in synergy with Divine love."[100]

99. N. T. Wright, *After You Believe*, 231. Wright's focus here is on the participation of believers in God's work of restorative justice, through "the corporate virtues of justice-work" (ibid.). As Wright says, "the notion of reflecting God's image once more into the world—the image of the generous, loving creator, filling his world with beauty, order, freedom, and glory—must go wider than community-creation on the one hand and evangelism on the other. The 'royal' vocation of Jesus's followers must give rise to the hard-won virtues of seeking, generating, and sustaining justice and beauty in a world where both have been at a discount for too long" (ibid.).

100. Metropolitan Jonah Paffhausen, "Natural Contemplation in St. Maximus the Confessor and St. Isaac the Syrian," 57. For a similar emphasis on the human being as "priest of the cosmos" (61), see in the same volume Louth, "Man and the Cosmos in St. Maximus the Confessor." Discussing how this priesthood makes sense even in an unfathomably vast universe, Louth draws also upon Blaise Pascal and explains, "Thought—*logos*: this it is that secures humankind its position in the universe, not any physical position at the center of the cosmos. In fact, the Fathers recognize this, for although they did see man as the culmination of creation, living on the earth at the center of the cosmos, it is his participation in *logos* that marks out his true dignity. . . . Maximus sees the universe given meaning by the *logoi* through which creatures participate in God. Science sees the universe as governed by laws to which we humans can give mathematical expression. But for all the impersonal objectivity of mathematics, it is only humans that can know it and understand it" (70).

———∞———

A final note before proceeding. In some of the chapters that follow, especially the first two, I refer to the divine "essence." Certainly there is no independent "divine essence," standing as an (impossible) fourth in the divine Trinity or in any way separable from the divine persons. I agree with Gilles Emery's observation that "in our language about God, we signify the essence as if we were referring to a form: we *signify* 'that through which' God is God, even though, in the divine reality itself, the divine essence is nothing other than the person (there is in God none of that composition of form and supposit which characterizes corporeal creatures)."[101] As Emery points out, our manner of accounting for the distinction of the persons likewise cannot satisfy on its own, since a divine person is not something "other than" the utterly simple divine essence.[102] Thus, God is not just one in his essence, but rather it is better to say that "God is one in three persons of one unique essence."[103] Given these parameters of trinitarian monotheism, we are justified in continuing to speak of the divine essence, as the patristic theologians did, and indeed as the New Testament does by applying the name "God" both to the Father and, at times, to Christ. The truth of the Trinity requires "the two aspects of the mystery of God (unity of essence and personal distinction) which the theologian constantly brings together, without conflating the divine reality with the language through which we refer to it."[104]

The difficulty of speaking at all about God's "essence," nonetheless, confirms the audacity of attempting to reason about the Triune God's work of creation, let alone about the vast wonders of creation and redemption—and the monstrous sadness of the fall—that Genesis 1–3 proclaims. Thus, not only as a preparation for undertaking this study, but also at every moment of the enterprise, let us remember our creatureliness and, with Sirach, give praise to the creator:

> By the words of the Lord his works are done. The sun looks down on everything with its light, and the work of the Lord is full of his glory. The Lord has not enabled his holy ones to recount all his marvelous works, which the Lord the Almighty has established that the universe may stand firm in his glory. . . . For the Most High knows all that may be known, and he looks into the signs of the age. He declares what has been and what is to be, and he reveals the tracks of

101. Emery, *Trinitarian Theology of Saint Thomas Aquinas*, 146–47.
102. Ibid., 147.
103. Emery, "Le 'monothéisme trinitaire,'" 167. For a different view, suggesting that Christians would do well to avoid using the term "God," see A. N. Williams, "Does 'God' Exist?"
104. Emery, *Trinitarian Theology of Saint Thomas Aquinas*, 150.

hidden things. No thought escapes him, and not one word is hidden from him. He has ordained the splendors of his wisdom, and he is from everlasting and to everlasting. Nothing can be added or taken away, and he needs no one to be his counselor. How greatly to be desired are all his works, and how sparkling they are to see! (Sir. 42:15–22)[105]

---

105. For background to the book of Sirach, see especially Perdue, *Wisdom and Creation*, 243–90. As Perdue says, "The world for Ben Sira is an object of great beauty whose operations and glory lead to wonderment and praise. Its marvelous nature is but a small indication of God's own greatness and glory" (290). Sirach 42:15–22 takes up the biblical motif of the "glory" (*kābôd*) of the Lord, in order "to speak of the revelation of the works of creation that point to the power, majesty, and benevolence of God. Thus God's glory, like the rays of the sun, is present in all of his works, and they in turn reveal his greatness" (279–80). See also John J. Collins, "Ben Sira in His Hellenistic Context," chap. 2 in *Jewish Wisdom in the Hellenistic Age*. Collins points out that "the core of Sirach's teaching is still traditional Near Eastern wisdom material. Much of it can be read as an elaboration of the teaching of Proverbs. Sirach had some acquaintance with Greek literature and philosophy, but he never refers to a Greek book, or indeed to any nonbiblical book, by name" (39).

ONE

Divine Ideas

And God said, "Let there be light"; and there was light.

Genesis 1:3

Few theologians today discuss the "divine ideas."[1] Yet Psalm 139 underscores that God knows everything about each human being even before he or she comes to be. The psalmist says of God, "Thy eyes beheld my unformed substance; in thy book were written, every one of them, the days that were formed for me, when as yet there was none of them" (Ps. 139:16). The psalmist presents God's "thoughts" as innumerable: "How precious to me are thy thoughts, O God! How vast is the sum of them! If I would count them, they are more than the sand" (Ps. 139:17–18).[2] Similarly, Job 28:24 teaches that God alone has wisdom, "for he looks to the ends of the earth, and sees everything under the heavens." Consider, too, Jeremiah 1:5, where God commissions Jeremiah as a prophet by telling him that this mission has been given to Jeremiah before he was even conceived in the womb: "Before I formed you in the womb I knew you, and before you were born I consecrated you; I appointed you a prophet to the nations." In the Gospel of Matthew, Jesus testifies to the extent of God's knowledge of creatures: "Are not two sparrows sold for a penny? And not one of them will fall to the ground without your Father's will. But

1. A valuable recent exception, which engages the ongoing Thomistic debate regarding the status of possibles, is the Catholic theologian Paul J. DeHart's "What Is Not, Was Not, and Will Never Be." Thomistic philosophers have continued regularly to engage the topic of the divine ideas. For a recent contribution on this topic by a Thomistic philosopher, see Doolan, "Aquinas on the Divine Ideas and the Really Real."
2. Cited in Boland, *Ideas in God according to Saint Thomas Aquinas*, 3.

even the hairs of your head are all numbered" (Matt. 10:29–30).[3] According to Scripture, then, God knows each and every particular thing in history, and God knows each thing even if it has not yet taken place in history. Indeed, God could not create things *ex nihilo* if he did not intimately know all that he could create.[4] This knowledge, since God is simple, must be profoundly

3. Thomas Aquinas distinguishes God's knowledge of things that exist at some time, from God's knowledge of pure possibles:

> Now a certain difference is to be noted in the consideration of those things that are not actual. For though some of them may not be in act now, still they were, or they will be; and God is said to know all these with the knowledge of vision: for since God's act of understanding, which is His being, is measured by eternity; and since eternity is without succession, comprehending all time, the present glance of God extends over all time, and to all things which exist in any time, as to objects present to Him. But there are other things in God's power, or the creature's, which nevertheless are not, nor will be, nor were; and as regards these He is said to have the knowledge, not of vision, but of simple intelligence. This is so called because the things we see around us have distinct being outside the seer. (*Summa theologiae* [hereafter *ST*] I, q. 14, a. 9)

This "knowledge of vision" still has to do with the divine ideas, rather than being somehow more "immediate" (as though the divine ideas were somehow wanting). In his ideas, God knows the modes in which things exist (or, in the case of possibles, do not exist). Thus Aquinas states: "God not only knows that things are in Himself; but by the fact that they are in Him, He knows them in their own nature and all the more perfectly, the more perfectly each one is in Him" (*ST* I, q. 14, a. 6, ad 1). Brian J. Shanley helpfully comments about the kinds of divine knowledge:

> The visual metaphor [knowledge of vision] cannot be taken to imply any perceptual passivity in the divine intellect; God does not know by being on the receiving end of a causal chain. . . . The distinctions between various kinds of divine knowledge, imposed by us according to different intelligible perspectives and different objects, do not imply any real distinction in God. There is no mental process whereby God first speculatively considers the various possibilities (*scientia simplicis intelligentiae*), then practically decides to execute one plan (*scientia approbationis*), and finally contemplates the finished product (*scientia visionis*); Molinists typically misread Aquinas in this way. This and other errors stem from an anthropomorphic failure to make the requisite distinctions between the human artist and the divine artist. God's practical knowledge of contingent singulars does not involve the kinds of logical, temporal, and operational stages involved in human production. ("Eternal Knowledge of the Temporal in Aquinas," 217–18)

4. As Augustine says, God "was not ignorant of what he was going to create" (*Trinity* 15.4.22, p. 414). Augustine, of course, excludes temporality from God; there is no "prior" to the act of creation. Thus Augustine affirms "the true eternity of the Creator": "his nature will never vary at different times, and his will is not external to his nature. It follows that he does not will one thing at one time, and another thing at another time. Once and for all and simultaneously, he wills everything that he wills. . . . My God, the eternal God, did not experience a new act of will when he made the creation, and his knowledge admits no transient element" (*Confessions* 12.15.18, pp. 254–55). As Augustine points out earlier in the *Confessions*,

> They say "What was God doing before he made heaven and earth?," or "Why did he ever conceive the thought of making something when he had never made anything before?" Grant them, Lord, to consider carefully what they are saying and to make the discovery that where there is no time, one cannot use the word "never.". . . A person singing or listening to a song he knows well suffers a distension or stretching in feeling and in sense-perception from the expectation of future sounds and the memory of past sound. With

personal. God's act of creation, of course, is an expression of sheer love, since "God is love" (1 John 4:16).

When reflecting upon the question of why God created, Thomas Aquinas answers that there is no other reason than the generous goodness of God. He states that "as God by one act understands all things in his essence, so by one act he wills all things in his goodness."[5] All things come forth from God's wisdom and will, without thereby being made of divine being, as Aquinas observes with regard to creation *ex nihilo*: "If the emanation of the whole universal being [creation] be considered, it is impossible that any being should be presupposed before this emanation. For nothing is the same as no being."[6]

In recent discussions of the doctrine of creation, many of which focus upon creation *ex nihilo*, God's will and goodness are highlighted. By comparision, God's wisdom and the divine ideas are generally either neglected or (with respect to the doctrine of the divine ideas) critiqued. In this chapter, then, I focus upon the divine ideas, always in light of the infinite divine love and goodness. The key reason for insisting upon the significance of the divine ideas in the act of creation *ex nihilo* has been expressed by John Hughes, who remarks that "the divine ideas, understood according to a Trinitarian logic, enabled Christian theologians to articulate creation *ex nihilo* in terms that avoided both necessary emanation and arbitrary choice."[7]

---

you [God] it is otherwise. You are unchangeably eternal, that is the truly eternal Creator of minds. Just as you knew heaven and earth in the beginning without that bringing any variation into your knowing, so you made heaven and earth in the beginning without that meaning a tension between past and future in your activity. (11.30.40–41, pp. 244–45)

5. *ST* I, q. 19, a. 5. See also *ST* I, q. 19, a. 2; *ST* III, q. 1, a. 1.

6. *ST* I, q. 45, a. 1. Note that creation *ex nihilo* is a different question from whether creation had a beginning. According to Aquinas, God *could* have willed for the world, created *ex nihilo*, to have always existed: "If the [creative, *ex nihilo*] action is instantaneous and not successive, it is not necessary for the maker to be prior to the thing made in duration. . . . Hence they say that it does not follow necessarily if God is the active cause of the world, that He should be prior to the world in duration; because creation, by which He produced the world, is not a successive change" (*ST* I, q. 46, a. 2, ad 1; cf. *ST* I, q. 45, a. 2). For further discussion of this point, see Mark F. Johnson's "Did St. Thomas Attribute a Doctrine of Creation to Aristotle?"

7. John Hughes, "*Creatio ex Nihilo* and the Divine Ideas in Aquinas," 137. See in the same volume the excellent essay by David B. Burrell, CSC, "*Creatio ex Nihilo* Recovered." As Burrell puts it, the doctrine of *creatio ex nihilo* "enables us to approach gingerly and modestly the daunting task of speaking of the universe as gift" (21). By contrast, the superb collection edited by Burrell, Cogliati, Soskice, and Stoeger, *Creation and the God of Abraham*, is devoted entirely to creation *ex nihilo* yet contains almost no mention of the divine ideas. An exception in this volume is a brief discussion of the divine ideas in Oliver, "Trinity, Motion and Creation *ex Nihilo*," 138–39. David Fergusson rightly observes that the Church fathers connected the doctrine of creation *ex nihilo* with "the manner in which the created order was expressive of

The doctrine of the divine ideas is not easily defended today. In the mid-twentieth century, Marie-Dominique Chenu deemed the doctrine of the divine ideas to be "the real spiritual and scientific home of theology," because of the way the doctrine both distinguishes and unites creatures and God, and because of its apprehension of creatures in light of their teleological perfection.[8] But eminent contemporaries of Chenu such as Étienne Gilson, A. D. Sertillanges, and Robert Henle considered the doctrine of divine ideas to be a misleading holdover from Augustinian (Neoplatonic) theology that Aquinas should have discarded.[9] More recently, the two pages of entries on the topic of "God" in the index of the *Catechism of the Catholic Church* contain no mention of "divine ideas" or "ideas," showing the general neglect into which this doctrine has fallen.

The key problem is that unlike the doctrine of creation *ex nihilo*, the doctrine of the divine ideas can seem to threaten the freedom of God's act of creation, by postulating that God merely makes actual an eternal pattern. In a particularly influential way, the Orthodox theologian Vladimir Lossky has argued that the Latin West's doctrine of divine ideas turns creation into an

---

the divine being," and (although Fergusson does not say so) this is a link to the divine ideas. See Fergusson, "Interpreting the Story of Creation," 157.

8. Chenu, *Toward Understanding Saint Thomas*, 312. He explains, "It simultaneously combines a rational explanation of things, which is drawn precisely from their natures, with a religious explanation since these natures in themselves and in their destiny are the realization of a divine idea" (ibid.). This passage is cited from the French edition in Boland, *Ideas in God according to Saint Thomas Aquinas*, 214. In a book originally published in 1945, Sergius Bulgakov notes that the doctrine of the divine ideas is a "normative one in contemporary Catholic theology" (*Bride of the Lamb*, 28), which no longer seems to be the case today.

9. See Gilson, *Christian Philosophy: An Introduction*, 103–8; Henle, *Saint Thomas and Platonism*, 359; Thomas Aquinas, *Somme théologique*, trans. Sertillanges, 2:403–5. For Gilson's earlier, quite positive account of the divine ideas, see his *Christian Philosophy of St. Thomas Aquinas*, 125–27. Gregory Doolan sums up the position of Gilson's *Christian Philosophy: An Introduction*: "Gilson does not even consider Thomas's doctrine of divine ideas to be philosophical at all; rather, he concludes, it represents a theological effort to reconcile an otherwise Augustinian doctrine with 'the strictest philosophical truth.' To speak of a multiplicity of ideas, he insists, is to employ a Platonic language foreign to the Aristotelianism of Thomas's theology. If we must use the language of ideas, Gilson thinks we should say instead that there is only one idea and that that idea is nothing other than God himself" (*Aquinas on the Divine Ideas as Exemplar Causes*, 112). The view that according to Aquinas there is only one idea, the divine essence, is advocated by Ross, "Aquinas' Exemplarism; Aquinas' Voluntarism." See the persuasive objections to Ross raised by Armand Maurer, CSB, and Lawrence Dewan, OP, as well as Ross's reply: Maurer, "James Ross on the Divine Ideas: A Reply"; Dewan, "St. Thomas, James Ross, and Exemplarism: A Reply"; Ross, "Response to Maurer and Dewan." Vivian Boland notes that in *De veritate* 3.2 Aquinas remarks that Avicenna and al-Ghazali did in fact hold that God has only one idea of all creatures, although they held this view in a Neoplatonic way. For this point, and for clear evidence that Aquinas consistently affirms many divine ideas, see Boland, *Ideas in God according to Saint Thomas Aquinas*, 206–13.

ontological fall, undermines the significance of history, and impinges upon God's freedom in the act of creation. Lossky proposes that formulating the divine ideas in terms of the divine energies solves the problems that, in his view, arise from Augustine's and Thomas Aquinas's equation of the divine ideas with the unchanging divine essence.[10]

In what follows, therefore, I first examine the relative disrepair into which the doctrine of the divine ideas has fallen in recent theologies of creation *ex nihilo*. With this background in place, I set forth Lossky's concerns about Aquinas's doctrine of divine ideas and explore the solution that Lossky offers through the distinction between the divine essence and energies. In light of Lossky's critique, I investigate Aquinas's doctrine of the divine ideas, with particular attention to his understanding of eternity and time. At issue is whether his doctrine of divine ideas has the Platonic problems that Lossky identifies, and thereby fails to do justice to the scriptural witness to the free creator of history—in which case it would make sense to defend creation *ex nihilo* by leaving behind the category of "divine ideas" or, better, by adopting Lossky's view of them. At stake in this chapter is how we can best affirm, with Vivian Boland, that "each single thing is, in some way, a trace of God" and that "the being and therefore the truth of this world and its history cannot be understood without reference to the wise love of God which originates and sustains it."[11]

Creation *ex Nihilo* and the Divine Ideas

In his influential *Creatio ex Nihilo: The Doctrine of 'Creation out of Nothing' in Early Christian Thought*, Gerhard May argues that the doctrine of creation *ex nihilo* is entirely absent from Scripture. For May, one cannot exegetically say that creation is "from nothing" even if the biblical text teaches clearly that "the world came into existence through the sovereign creative act of

---

10. With regard to the divine energies, Sergius Bulgakov's account of their relationship to the divine ideas deserves mention (not least because Lossky's view of the divine ideas is developed in opposition to Bulgakov, though not in opposition to Bulgakov's critique of Aquinas). Bulgakov finds the Palamite distinction between the essence and energies to be "essentially an unfinished sophiology" (*Bride of the Lamb*, 18). Bulgakov states that "Palamas considers the energies primarily in the aspect of *grace*, the supracreaturely 'light of Tabor' in the creaturely world. But these energies have, first of all, a world-creating and world-sustaining power which is a property of Sophia, the Wisdom of God, in both of her forms: the Divine Sophia, the eternal proto-ground of the world, and the creaturely Sophia, the divine force of the life of creation" (18–19). Bulgakov therefore understands himself to be undertaking "the sophiological interpretation and application of Palamism" (19).

11. Boland, *Ideas in God according to Saint Thomas Aquinas*, 331.

God, and that it previously was not there."[12] Rather, according to May, the biblical text must *explicitly* deny that God formed the world "out of eternal matter," or else the presence of an affirmation of creation *ex nihilo* cannot be assumed.[13] In his study, May directs attention to four main biblical passages that theologians have long used to defend the biblical foundations of the doctrine of creation *ex nihilo*. The first is Genesis 1:1–2: "In the beginning God created the heavens and the earth. The earth was without form and void, and darkness was upon the face of the deep; and the Spirit of God was moving over the face of the waters." Genesis 1:1 and 1:2 can be connected in different ways, due to ambiguities in the Hebrew. For the doctrine of creation *ex nihilo*, much depends on precisely how the second verse relates to the first. In his commentary on Genesis, Bill Arnold evaluates the evidence and finds that, much as May suggests, "Genesis 1 neither precludes nor defends the possibility" of creation *ex nihilo*.[14] Like Claus Westermann, however, Arnold considers that the concept of creation *ex nihilo* "is not false to the intent of Genesis 1. Indeed, had we an opportunity to pose the question to the author of this text, we may assume with Westermann . . . that he would 'certainly have decided in favor of *creatio ex nihilo*.'"[15]

12. May, *Creatio ex Nihilo*, 7.

13. Ibid. For perspectives indebted heavily to May, see, e.g., Young, *God's Presence*, 52–56; McFarland, *From Nothing*, 1–15. Like May, McFarland pays particular attention to the debate over gnostic Christianity: both Basilides (a gnostic) and Irenaeus appeal to the doctrine of creation *ex nihilo*. As McFarland notes, "Basilides' account of the world's origin seems to be grounded in a vision of divine transcendence in which creation from nothing provides a metaphysical basis for insulating God from direct contact with the created order. Since for Basilides the world that God creates 'from nothing' is a 'nonexistent' seed of pure potentiality, even the very moment of creation only approximates a genuine encounter between Creator and creature, and there is no possibility whatever for divine engagement with the world after this seed has been brought into being" (8).

14. Arnold, *Genesis*, 36.

15. Ibid., citing Westermann, *Genesis 1–11*, 108–9. He also cites Floss, "Schöpfung als Geschehen?," 311–18. In their evaluation of the evidence, Paul Copan and William Craig show that "a solid case can be made for *creatio ex nihilo* in the OT—that it is indeed demanded by the text, even if 'out of nothing' is implicit rather than directly stated" (*Creation out of Nothing*, 29). John H. Walton affirms that "God is fully responsible for material origins, and that, in fact, material origins do involve at some point creation out of nothing" (*Lost World of Genesis One*, 44). But he argues that Gen. 1 is not concerned with material origins. Instead, in Walton's view, Gen. 1 has to do with what Aristotle and patristic and medieval theologians think of as formal and final causes: Gen. 1 is about transforming chaos into a functionally ordered system, so that to bring something into existence is to give it form and purpose. Walton proposes that Gen. 1 is "an account of functional origins in relation to people in the image of God viewing the cosmos as a temple" (132). For a critique of Walton's perspective, arguing that Gen. 1 teaches that "the universe was indeed made ex nihilo by the word of God" and that it is certainly a mistake to suppose that Gen. 1 "altogether fails to address questions that have cosmological content," see Lennox, *Seven Days That Divide the World*, 134, 140. For ancient Jewish readings

The second regularly cited biblical passage is 2 Maccabees 7:28, which belongs to the Catholic and Orthodox canons of Scripture. In 2 Maccabees 7, we read of a mother of seven sons, six of whom have already been executed by Antiochus because of their refusal to renounce the Torah. Urging her last surviving son not to give in to Antiochus's requirement that he commit idolatry, she reminds him that God gives existence. If we suffer and die now for God, God will give us "everflowing life under God's covenant" (2 Macc. 7:36). In the relevant passage, she tells her son, "I beseech you, my child, to look at the heaven and the earth and see everything that is in them, and recognize that God did not make them out of things that existed [or: God made them out of things that did not exist]" (2 Macc. 7:28).[16] In May's view, shared by Jonathan Goldstein and other exegetes, this verse does not rule out an eternal substrate of unformed matter, since, given the philosophical background to 2 Maccabees, unformed matter can be thought of as not existing.

The third biblical passage comes from Romans. In the context of a discussion of Abraham's faith, in light of faith in the resurrection of the dead, Paul states that Abraham trusted in the promise of the God who "calls into existence the things that do not exist" (Rom. 4:17). May considers this verse

---

of Gen. 1 as bearing upon creation *ex nihilo*, see Kister, "*Tohu wa-Bohu*, Primordial Elements and *Creatio ex Nihilo*."

16. In his commentary in the Anchor Bible series, Jonathan A. Goldstein translates 2 Macc. 7:28 as follows: "I ask you, my child, to look upon the heaven and the earth and to contemplate all therein. I ask you to understand that it was not after they existed that God fashioned them, and in the same manner the human race comes to be" (*2 Maccabees*, 291). This rather convoluted translation seems aimed at ensuring that creation *ex nihilo* is not taken to be the meaning of the verse. Drawing upon the original German edition of May's book, Goldstein comments on verses 22–29:

> Christian writers, from Origen . . . on, took our passage (in particular v. 28) as the first unequivocal statement in scripture of the doctrine of creation *ex nihilo*, that God created the universe from absolutely nothing, not from some preexistent raw matter. In fact, there is no unequivocal statement of the doctrine either in the Hebrew Bible or in the New Testament, and statements can be found even in rabbinic literature supporting the view of creation from preexistent matter. . . . The crucial phrase in v. 28 is *ouk ex ontôn*, which I have translated "not after they existed." It might also be rendered "not from things which existed." *L* [a "Lucianic" manuscript] has *ex ouk ontôn*, which might be translated "from things which did not exist" or "from what did not exist." (307)

Goldstein notes that the reference may be to formless matter, which in a Platonic metaphysical sense has no existence; but Goldstein also grants that it is possible (though in his view not likely) that the author of 2 Maccabees "may have thought that the reading *ouk ex ontôn* was an unequivocal statement of creation *ex nihilo*," since it is possible that the author was "well enough versed in philosophy to have insisted upon creation ex nihilo as justification for the belief in resurrection" (308).

to have the same limitations as 2 Maccabees 7:28. By contrast, Luke Timothy
Johnson, among others, argues that Paul is claiming that God is "the source
and sustainer of *being* itself."[17]

The fourth and final commonly cited biblical verse is Hebrews 11:3: "By
faith we understand that the world was created by the word of God, so that
what is seen was made out of things which do not appear." May holds that
this verse should be read in light of Hebrews 11:1's insistence that faith is
"the conviction of things not seen." Rather than teaching creation *ex nihilo*,
Hebrews 11:3 probably has (in Harold Attridge's words) the Platonic implication that "the 'unseen' realities from which the visible world was created are
the constituents of the 'true,' 'heavenly' realm that is paradigmatic for the
world of sense."[18] This Platonic background might still allow for creation *ex
nihilo*, if these unseen realities are simply the divine ideas.

In his study of the Dead Sea Scrolls on creation *ex nihilo*, Markus Bockmuehl allows that creation *ex nihilo* "has no explicit terminological basis in
Scripture."[19] *Pace* May, however, Bockmuehl finds that "the meaning and
the substance of the doctrine, though not the terminology, is firmly rooted
in scripture and pre-Christian Jewish literature."[20] In the Qumran document
known as the Community Rule (first century BC), for example, we read,

17. L. Johnson, *Reading Romans*, 74.

18. Attridge, *Hebrews*, 316.

19. Bockmuehl, "*Creatio ex Nihilo* in Palestinian Judaism and Early Christianity," 269.

20. Ibid., 270. See also the overly positive assessment in O'Neill, "How Early Is the Doctrine
of Creatio ex Nihilo?"; and Winston, "Creation *ex Nihilo* Revisited." Regarding 2 Macc. 7:28,
Rom. 4:17, and Heb. 11:3, Ian McFarland (like May) argues:

> Although these three passages all seem to provide support for a biblical doctrine of
> creation out of nothing, closer examination suggests that such appearances are mislead-
> ing. Like most of the references to God's creative work in the Old Testament, these later
> texts speak of creation only in passing, as part of a broader appeal to divine power and
> trustworthiness. None of them can be read as part of an explicit theology of creation.
> Beyond these contextual considerations, moreover, is the question of just what creation
> "from things that do not exist/are not visible" means in these passages. . . . Absent the
> kind of explicit contrast that Theophilus draws with the Platonist scheme of creation
> from preexisting matter, however, such language cannot be taken as evidence of belief
> in creation from nothing. (*From Nothing*, 4–5)

I disagree that these biblical texts are not "part of an explicit theology of creation"; they
belong to Scripture's constant teaching that the creator is not solely the giver of form. I do not
think that we must wait for them to rule out preexistent matter explicitly, since they indicate
sufficiently that God is the creator of everything (including, if need be, preexistent matter) that
is not God. Indeed, I think McFarland may fundamentally agree with me, since in interpreting
John 1:1, he states: "No more than any other New Testament text does John contain the later
doctrinal language of creation from nothing, but thanks to this final clause, the upshot of the
Gospel's opening verse is that the sole precondition and only context for creation is God" (23).
If the "sole precondition" for creation is God, then I do not see how it could also be the case
that preexisting matter is a precondition.

"From the God of Knowledge comes all that is and shall be. Before ever they existed He established their whole design, and, when, as ordained for them, they came into being, it is in accord with His glorious design that they accomplish their task without change."[21] The Community Rule's emphasis that God is the creative source of all that has being accords well with Luke Timothy Johnson's view that Romans 4:17 teaches that God is "the source and sustainer of *being* itself."

Indebted to Arnold, Johnson, and Bockmuehl, I find that the cumulative weight of the four commonly cited biblical texts—when read in light of John 1:1–3 and other texts such as Psalms 33:6, 90:2, and 148:5, and when read in late Second Temple context[22]—requires that we hold that the God of Christian Scripture is the creator of all things rather than merely the giver of form to unformed matter, as if the latter could subsist in any way without a creator.[23] Even in Genesis 1:2, there is no suggestion that the primordial "deep" or "waters" should "be regarded as a second, pre-existent principle of Creation apart from God."[24] I therefore hold that like the Community Rule of Qumran, Christian Scripture should be read as affirming in a global sense that "from the God of Knowledge comes all that is and shall be." Even

21. This passage is cited in Bockmuehl, "*Creatio ex Nihilo* in Palestinian Judaism and Early Christianity," 261–62; Bockmuehl notes that he has drawn this translation of the Dead Sea Scrolls 1 QS 3.15–16 from Martínez and Tigchelaar, *Dead Sea Scrolls Study Edition*.

22. See also Philo of Alexandria (c. 20 BC–c. AD 50), *On the Creation* [*De opificio mundi*], 3–24. Although the significance of Philo's understanding of unformed matter is debated, I consider that Philo holds that all things were created from nothing in the deepest sense of dependence/causality: God is "the creator and father of all" (2.7, p. 3). Philo also suggests that God first created an exemplar realm of forms or divine ideas, from which God then created all the things of the cosmos. Ultimately, Philo leaves ambiguous the question of whether the divine ideas subsist in God or in a distinct realm of their own. For discussion, see Sterling, "*Creatio Temporalis, Aeterna, vel Continua?*"

23. Admittedly, there are also primordial-battle texts, such as Job 26:12–13; Pss. 74:12–14 and 89:10–11; Isa. 51:9; and others. Jon D. Levenson employs texts such as these to argue against creation *ex nihilo* (among other things) in his *Creation and the Persistence of Evil*. In the same way, biblical texts that suggest that YHWH is embodied or is one among many gods can be used—though not in my view persuasively—against God's transcendence and simple unity. For further discussion, see Levering, *Scripture and Metaphysics*, chap. 3; and Levering, *Engaging the Doctrine of Revelation*, chap. 8.

24. Scheffczyk, *Creation and Providence*, 6. Scheffczyk states: "Though the inconsistency observable in the Priestly document between primordial Creation and the chaos that is something intermediary between nothingness and created being does not seem to be resolved in conceptual terms, since we are not plainly told what relation subsists between the Creator and this chaos, still the chaos must not be regarded as a second, pre-existent principle of Creation apart from God. Rather, the notion of the chaotic is introduced here to give expression to a primordial human experience, to objectify our awareness of how Creation is jeopardized by the unformed, to emphasize by way of contrast how the Creator orders and sustains all things" (6–7).

everlasting unformed matter could only be such because it comes forth from the God who is the creative source of everything that is not God.

Many valuable recent theological and philosophical studies explore and defend creation *ex nihilo* and the free will of God, but neglect or critique "the God of Knowledge" as well as what Philo of Alexandria calls "the archetypal model, the idea of ideas, the Reason of God."[25] Let me review six instances of this trend before briefly surveying certain highlights of the patristic and medieval development of the doctrine of divine ideas.

David Fergusson's excellent short volume *Creation* includes a historical and constructive discussion of creation *ex nihilo*, but says nothing about the divine ideas. The closest that Fergusson comes to speaking about the divine ideas is in his appreciative description of Augustine's view that "the spiritual, moral, and aesthetic relation of the world to God is maintained by the manner in which the world derivatively possesses the form of the divine likeness. Created beings can participate, albeit in a manner appropriate to their created status, in the form, order, and weight of the divine life."[26] Here the divine ideas are at the very surface of the text, but Fergusson does not mention them. Instead, when he discusses Aquinas's theology of creation and providence, he highlights areas in which Aquinas "offers a more dramatic and less determinist account of the God-world relationship in which the divine initiative and creaturely response achieve a degree of mutuality."[27] The focus is the divine will in its relationship to human wills. It may be that the doctrine of the divine ideas is not present because it seems to offer a *less* dramatic and more determinist account of the God-world relationship.

Hans Schwarz's *Creation* stands even farther from the doctrine of the divine ideas. Schwarz surveys scientific developments in some detail before undertaking a critical retrieval of the doctrine of creation in light of nineteenth-century

---

25. Philo of Alexandria, *On the Creation* 6.25, p. 5. Mistakenly, Paul Copan and William Lane Craig suggest that Thomas Aquinas "basically disregarded the doctrine of a temporal creation out of nothing (not to mention the place of the Word of God—Christ—and the Spirit of God in creation)" (*Creation out of Nothing*, 10). In support of this claim, which is true only insofar as Aquinas distinguishes the question of creation *ex nihilo* from the question of whether there was a temporal beginning of the created order, they quote Gunton, "Doctrine of Creation," 150–51: "Although Aquinas affirms the doctrine of creation out of nothing, he makes little of it." For plentiful evidence to the contrary, see, e.g., Burrell, *Freedom and Creation in Three Traditions*; Burrell et al., *Creation and the God of Abraham*. See also Emery, *La Trinité créatrice*. For contemporary critics of the doctrine of *creatio ex nihilo*, see the essays in Oord, *Theologies of Creation*, many of which argue that creation consists in some form of divine matter. For a standard presentation of "panentheism," rejecting creation *ex nihilo* but affirming dependence on God, see Barbour, *Issues in Science and Religion*.

26. Fergusson, *Creation*, 24.

27. Ibid., 55.

responses to Charles Darwin and of notable twentieth-century Protestant theologies of creation. He treats creation *ex nihilo* in his concluding chapter, "Developing a Christian Understanding of Creation." Emphasizing the absolute freedom of God's will in creating, he argues that creation *ex nihilo* means that "God acts without preconditions" and that "there is nothing prior to the creation which limits God's sovereignty over against the world."[28] He goes on to defend God's providence and God's conservation of things in being, in relation to the evolutionary process. In conversation with recent science of the entropy of the universe, as well as with dire ecological predictions, he examines the biblical vision of the completion or goal of creation. Perhaps because his book begins with Johannes Kepler (1571–1630) and is particularly invested in the dialogue with modern science, rather than with Hellenistic and earlier Christian views, Schwarz's book contains no mention of the divine ideas.

Ian McFarland's *From Nothing* focuses, as its title indicates, on creation *ex nihilo*. McFarland extensively addresses aspects of the doctrine of creation that pertain to God's will, but aspects that pertain to God's intellect are relatively neglected. Much to his credit, however, McFarland has a doctrine of the divine ideas, although he does not use the term "ideas." Taking pains to rule out "divine arbitrariness," he provides a lengthy citation of Anselm's *Monologion* where Anselm states that "there is no way anyone could make something rationally unless something like a pattern (or to put it more suitably, a form or likeness or rule) of the thing to be made was in the reason of the maker."[29] In this context, McFarland both affirms that "the work of creation . . . is an expression of who God is, and therefore a work of reason," and also argues insightfully that "the invocation of the Word in John 1 is significant just because it points to difference within the divine life in a way that blocks the temptation to reduce God to sheer will."[30]

Very briefly, but significantly, McFarland also engages Maximus the Confessor's "image of creatures as distinct *logoi* spoken through (and as partial reflections of) the one divine *Logos*."[31] He uses Maximus's understanding of the *logoi* both to affirm a divine "order that is intrinsic to God's own life and immediately expressive of that life" so that creatures are ontologically grounded "in the inexhaustible richness of God's own life," and to distinguish between creation and preservation: "If a creature is the effect of a divinely uttered *logos*, one may posit that it subsists so long as that *logos* continues

28. Hans Schwarz, *Creation*, 173.
29. Ibid., 89; citing Anselm, *Monologion* 9, p. 22.
30. McFarland, *From Nothing*, 90.
31. Ibid., 140; cf. 90.

to be spoken."[32] Although he does not develop the doctrine of divine ideas beyond these two brief references, McFarland at least indicates its value for the doctrine of creation *ex nihilo*.

In Michael Hanby's brilliant engagement with evolutionary biology, *No God, No Science?*, there are a few brief references to the divine ideas. Hanby firmly places creation *ex nihilo* at the center of his work. He seeks "to retrieve the Christian doctrine of creation *ex nihilo* from the distortions imposed upon it by the totalizing claims of positivist science and especially by that most theological of sciences, evolutionary biology."[33] Specifically, he argues that the doctrine of creation *ex nihilo*, developed in light of the incarnation, enables "created being in its entirety" to "acquire the structure of a gift."[34] Critically evaluating the influence of William Paley in Darwinian biology's view of the living organism, Hanby lays his finger on the crimped philosophy that, despite its evident inadequacy in contemporary science, still dominates science today: "At the heart of this ontology is a reduction of being from act to facticity and a theological extrinsicism which reduces God to a finite object, nature to artifice, and creation to manufacture."[35] Hanby insists upon the "ontological primacy of form" in a manner that draws near to the divine ideas, and indeed in the context of trinitarian love he refers to Thomas Aquinas's view that "God knows the world by knowing himself and all the ways his being can be participated."[36] He makes a brief reference to the divine ideas when describing the medieval debate over the status of *natura*, a debate that involved the question of whether to place "comparatively greater emphasis on the exemplary form in the divine mind or the substantial form inhering in the thing itself."[37] These passing references to the divine ideas, however, are not developed further by Hanby, although he does pay significant attention to the Greek philosophers who laid the foundations for the doctrine of divine ideas.[38]

32. Ibid., 90, 140.

33. Hanby, *No God, No Science?*, 1; cf. 224–25.

34. Ibid., 86.

35. Ibid., 3; cf. 301. Hanby goes on to discuss positively "the so-called 'modern synthesis' of Darwinian evolution and Mendelian genetics and the return from exile of a developmental biology displaced by the evolutionary paradigm and intent on restoring the organism to the center of evolution" (4). As he notes, "This is a salutary development with metaphysical implications unrealized by its protagonists. . . . Even so, developmental biology has yet to escape fully from the mechanistic ontology it shares with Darwinism, and so it ultimately fails to fulfill this ambition" (ibid.).

36. Ibid., 337, 344; on the ontological primacy of form (strongly affirmed by Aristotle), cf. 60, 385.

37. Ibid., 88.

38. As Hanby observes with regard to the Greek philosophers, "The difficulty . . . is to conceive of the world's difference from God without conceiving of divine being as created

When Colin Gunton mentions the divine ideas in his *The Triune Creator*, he strongly criticizes the doctrine. Gunton lays particular blame upon Philo and Origen in this regard: "By interposing the platonic idea of a (semi-eternal) plan in the divine mind, Philo begins a process . . . of displacing biblical by platonic notions of mediation. By positing a world prior to and higher than the material universe Origen downgrades the part played in God's work by the one who became incarnate."[39] In Gunton's view, one can have either the Platonic divine ideas and a deity who does not act freely and historically, or the free creative and redemptive work of the Son and Holy Spirit as portrayed in Scripture. Gunton states, "When creation is mediated by the two hands of God, there is no need of intermediates like the platonic forms or their Aristotelian equivalents."[40] Gunton favors creation *ex nihilo*, therefore, not least because it supports "the autonomy of God's action."[41] He praises Athanasius for helping to make clear "the crucial distinction between the being and the will of God," so that "God's triune being is eternal, but not his willing of creation, which therefore becomes an act of free willing."[42] According to Gunton, it is by grounding God's free willing of creation in his Son, and thus in Jesus Christ, that we perceive how free God is vis-à-vis creation and how good creation is. Gunton briefly mentions Augustine's belief that "there are *eternal* forms of things . . . within rather than without the mind of the

being writ large, or what amounts to the same thing, collapsing created being into divine being such that God becomes the being of the world" (77). Hanby refers to Schindler, "What's the Difference?" It is noteworthy that Schindler takes up the divine ideas in his own essay, though not in a central way. He warns against "the problematic notion of creation as the free addition of existence (through an act of the divine will) to essences that, as so many logical 'possibles,' already exist 'separately,' as it were, in the mind of God" ("What's the Difference?," 608). This concern is shared in Burrell, "Creation and 'Actualism,'" 84–86; cf. Burrell, *Knowing the Unknowable God*, 89–91, 97–99. Burrell draws upon Ross, "God, Creator of Kinds and Possibilities." I disagree with Burrell's view that "it is only in the measure that God is creator that there is need at all for ideas" ("Creation and 'Actualism,'" 84). Ross's concerns are ably supported by DeHart, "What Is Not, Was Not, and Never Will Be." DeHart argues that "Aquinas can be read as envisioning a divine knowledge of non-existents quite distinct from his knowledge of creatures, a kind of knowing that points us away from a 'photo-exemplarist' array of discrete ideas of possibles eternally in God's mind, complete with all potential details of concrete state and interrelations (thus replicating the sort of knowledge God admittedly has of actual creatures)" (1012). Aquinas does distinguish in some places between "ideas" (of creatures) and "types" (of nonexistent things), and, as DeHart rightly emphasizes, he avoids conceiving of God as a discursive reasoner (as inevitably follows when one envisions God comparing sets of possible worlds). For a perspective opposite from Ross's, see Pruss, *Actuality, Possibility, and Worlds.*

39. Gunton, *Triune Creator*, 62.
40. Ibid.
41. Ibid., 65.
42. Ibid., 67.

creator," but he complains that this belief left Augustine "only half way to the doctrine of creation out of nothing."[43]

Lastly, Katherine Sonderegger, in her impressive *The Doctrine of God*, recognizes that "the riddle of the Divine Knowledge of particulars, of possibles, and of evils, mirrors—indeed is ingredient in—the riddle of time and Eternity."[44] In light of the teachings of John Calvin, she nicely summarizes the central questions: "Just in what way are we to understand God's comprehension of all that is and can be in the transcendent sphere of God's own eternal Being? Is it that Almighty God knows all things and events in His own Eternity in such a way that all creaturely reality and possibility exists and has always existed before all worlds in the very Being of God?"[45] If so, it would seem that divine determinism and the greater reality of things as they have always existed in God (as distinct from their existence in time) would follow necessarily.

Emphasizing "the dear Lord's humble Presence in all existents," Sonderegger makes a sharp division between reflecting upon "God's *mode of knowing* contingent events" and reflecting upon divine "Presence."[46] This emphasis on presence enables her to argue that "we must be able to affirm that God is Knowledge itself, perfect Intelligibility and Insight, such that He in His very Being is not simply a storehouse of every particular and all universals, but is rather the very life, the very heart and reins, the very taste of each living thing, in its own manner and way, its own indelible mark as this very one."[47] But she steers clear of the doctrine of divine ideas because it comes too close to Platonism, to the view that "the realities of creaturely life find their specific and larger life in God Himself" and that the cosmos is "the Mind of God, reified."[48]

Sonderegger also rejects the view that in knowing himself (his infinite essence, power, and goodness), God knows all things as finite participations in him, because she thinks that some things (such as evil and things which are not) stand beyond God. Grounding herself upon Scripture, she states, "There is . . . a 'reaching forth,' an extension and examination that moves outside the Reality that is the One God's Goodness and Life. . . . The Wisdom of God

---

43. Ibid., 78. For further criticism of Augustine (and Origen) as an instance of "Platonism Triumphant," see Gunton, "Between Allegory and Myth," 49–50, 55–58. Gunton emphasizes, mistakenly in my view, that "it is the marginalising of christology which so marks Augustine's teaching" (61).

44. Sonderegger, *Systematic Theology*, 1:347.

45. Ibid.

46. Ibid., 350.

47. Ibid., 360.

48. Ibid., 366.

is not closed up in its own Goodness, does not stay within its own Truth and Light, but may and is able to look into the abyss, to grasp it and to occupy it."[49] But her language here strikes me as risking both dualism and an anthropomorphic account of God's knowing of creatures. She goes on to reject still more firmly the notion that "every creaturely reality has an archetype and image and causal principle in the Being of God," and she notes that this problematic position "dogs the doctrine of Omniscience, and most especially, the doctrine of Divine Ideas, the particular *bête noir* of Colin Gunton."[50]

Although I disagree with Gunton's and Sonderegger's view that the divine ideas negate God's freedom in creating and reify all created things as divine existents—a view that, as we will see, also characterizes the seminal work of Vladimir Lossky—Gunton helpfully reminds contemporary theologians that Origen in the East and Augustine in the West greatly valued the contribution of the doctrine of the divine ideas to the theology of creation. Likewise, Sergius Bulgakov observes that "among a number of fathers (St. Gregory the Divine, St. John of Damascus, St. Maximus the Confessor, Pseudo-Dionysius, and St. Augustine), we encounter the doctrine of the prototypes, paradigms, or ideas of creaturely being in God."[51] For example, describing "the Cause which produced the sun and which produced everything else," Dionysius the Areopagite observes that "the exemplars of everything preexist as a transcendent unity within It. . . . We give the name of 'exemplar' to those principles which preexist as a unity in God and which produce the essences of things.

49. Ibid., 378–79.
50. Ibid., 386. See also her later remark:

> We are not asserting here that God's Communication of His own spiritual Perfection to creatures *entails* that the creaturely goods and faithful acts of the earthbound must find a likeness and representation in Almighty God. The Relation of Creator to creature that faith affirms in each creaturely act of knowledge does not imply that each limited truth, each rational concept, each earthly fact must be found "in God." The doctrine of divine ideas cannot be handled in this fashion! That God is the Uncreated Light mingled in our small lights does not carry in its wake the notion that the Lord is a spiritual inventory of all material objects and truths, nor that God in His own Reality is an elevated collection of all real things. This is Spinozism in theology, a danger we must carefully note and ward off. (450–51)

I think much depends upon what we mean when we say that things are found "in God," since of course God is not a database.
51. Bulgakov, *Bride of the Lamb*, 16. In Bulgakov's view, the fathers err by putting this "ideal proto-ground of the world, or of the entelechies of the world" in "a place *next* to christology" (ibid.). The fathers therefore do not resolve "the question of how one should properly understand the relation of these prototypes of the world to Logos, and then to the Divine Sophia and the creaturely Sophia. In particular, do these ideas have a divine and eternal character? Do they refer to divine being? Or are they created ad hoc, so to speak, as the ideal foundation of the world, as 'heaven' in relation to 'earth'?" (16–17). Bulgakov suggests that these questions require a deeper and more self-conscious sophiology, reflective of his own philosophical approach.

Theology calls them predefining, divine and good acts of will."[52] For his part, John of Damascus states about creation *ex nihilo*, "By thinking He creates, and, with the Word fulfilling and the Spirit perfecting, the object of His thought subsists."[53]

The fathers' strong connection between creation *ex nihilo* and the divine ideas appears, as we have already noted, in Aquinas. Affirming creation *ex nihilo*, Aquinas states that "all beings apart from God are not their own being, but are beings by participation. Therefore it must be that all things which are diversified by the diverse participations of being, so as to be more or less perfect, are caused by one First Being."[54] Likewise, while criticizing Plato's notion that the universal "forms" of all particular things have *independent* subsistence in an eternal realm of forms, Aquinas emphasizes that the creator God certainly has "ideas" of everything that can be created.[55] With regard

52. Pseudo-Dionysius, *Divine Names* 5.8, p. 102. Gregory Doolan notes, "Dionysius calls the ideas paradigms (Gr. παραδείγματα, Lat. *exemplaria*), rational accounts (Gr. λόγοι, Lat. *rationes*), predefinitions (Gr. προορισμοί, Lat. *praediffinitiones*), and willings (Gr. θελήματα, Lat. *voluntates*). Unlike Augustine, he offers a philosophical solution to the problem of the multiplicity of ideas by explicitly identifying them with the divine essence, itself the paradigm by which all things are created (*Divine Names*, 5.8–9 [*Dionysiaca*, 1.22.357–64])" (*Aquinas on the Divine Ideas as Exemplar Causes*, 108n61). For an extensive discussion of Dionysius on the divine ideas, in light of the viewpoint of Proclus, see Boland, *Ideas in God according to Saint Thomas Aquinas*, 93–142; cf. 297–312 for Aquinas's debts to the *Divine Names*. Boland remarks, "Saint Thomas sees no difficulty in combining Augustine's notion of a plurality of *rationes*, of horse, man, and so on, with Dionysius' notion of a plurality of 'considerations' or 'regards' (*respectus*) based on the degree to which creatures participate in being, life and intelligence" (202; cf. 146, 321, 324). See also the discussion of the divine ideas according to Dionysius, Augustine, and Aquinas in Riordan, *Divine Light*, 122–26. Riordan notes that for Dionysius "each creature is a growing participation in its exemplar or paradigm (παράδειγμα: *paradeigma*). Each exemplar-paradigm as it is in *God* actually is *God*" (123).

53. John of Damascus, *Orthodox Faith* 2.2, p. 205.

54. *ST* I, q. 44, a. 1. Allowing for the natural reproduction of species, Aquinas somewhat later observes that the act of creation is fundamentally "the emanation of all being from the universal cause," namely, God producing "being absolutely, not as this or that being" (*ST* I, q. 45, aa. 1 and 5). Vivian Boland, OP, observes that for Aquinas (as for Pseudo-Dionysius) "God's bestowal of *esse* means he is responsible for everything there is in things" and "God's knowledge therefore extends to the very least traces of existing things" (*Ideas in God according to Saint Thomas Aquinas*, 331).

55. For discussion of Aquinas's critique of Plato, see Doolan, *Aquinas on the Divine Ideas as Exemplar Causes*, 44–48; Doolan, "Aquinas on the Divine Ideas and the Really Real." For the Platonic understanding of "ideas" and the placement of these ideas within the divine intelligence (in significantly different ways) by such thinkers as Antiochus of Ascalon, Cicero, Seneca, Philo, Hippolytus, Origen, and Augustine, see Boland, *Ideas in God according to Saint Thomas Aquinas*, chap. 1. Sergius Bulgakov argues that Aquinas's doctrine of the divine ideas brings "Platonism . . . into the very heart of Christian philosophy" (*Bride of the Lamb*, 24), although Bulgakov also recognizes an Aristotelian influence: "Aquinas's doctrine of ideas that have their foundation in God and act in the world must be understood sophiologically as a doctrine of the Divine Sophia and the creaturely Sophia in their identity and difference,

to the intimacy of God's knowledge of individual things, he quotes Hebrews 4:12–13: "For the word of God is living and active, sharper than any two-edged sword, piercing to the division of soul and spirit, of joints and marrow, and discerning the thoughts and intentions of the heart. And before him no creature is hidden, but all are open and laid bare to the eyes of him with whom we have to do."[56] As further support for the absolute priority of God's ideas of things, Aquinas also cites Augustine's remark from *De Trinitate*: "It is true of all his [God's] creatures, both spiritual and corporeal, that he does not know them because they are, but that they are because he knows them. He was not ignorant of what he was going to create. So he created because he knew, he did not know because he had created."[57]

---

but . . . this doctrine is also an unfinished and underclarified combination of Platonism and Aristotelianism with Christian dogmatics" (25–26). For a sympathetic response to Bulgakov's concerns, see John Hughes, "*Creatio ex Nihilo* and the Divine Ideas in Aquinas." Hughes notes that Aquinas's acceptance of "the existence of a surplus of unrealised divine ideas, from which God arbitrarily chooses some to actualise, [does] in the end seem to leave a certain ambivalence towards the very goodness of creation, despite all Aquinas's supposed affirmation of the world" (135). Yet Hughes also fully recognizes that "for Aquinas, the divine ideas are clearly not some hangover from Platonic demiurgic or emanationist schemes of creation, but rather, understood according to the logic of the Trinity, are crucial to understanding creation as truly free and personal rather than proceeding from natural necessity, but also as in accordance with the intrinsic order of divine goodness and wisdom rather than simply formless, random, and arbitrary" (136–37).

56. Cited in *ST* I, q. 14, a. 6, *sed contra*. This is quite far from Aristotle's insistence in his *Metaphysics* that even if God could know individual things, God could only know things outside himself if they impressed themselves upon his thinking, which would negate his pure actuality. Since God knows creatures in themselves, rather than knowing only himself without knowing creatures, we are also no longer limited by the restrictions that Aristotle imposes in concluding that divine "Mind thinks itself, if it is that which is best; and its thinking is a thinking of thinking [ἡ νόησις νοήσεως νόησις]" (*Metaphysics* 12.9.4, p. 165); cf. John L. Farthing's observation that "Aristotle's God . . . is conscious only of Himself; such a God will not interrupt the contemplation of His own perfection and condescend to know that which is less perfect, *i.e.*, less real; to do so would be demeaning to the dignity of the divine intellect" ("Problem of Divine Exemplarity in St. Thomas," 183). Boland argues, however, that Aristotle is the ultimate source for the later tradition of placing the divine ideas in the divine mind and indeed for claiming that the divine ideas are the divine mind. See Boland, *Ideas in God according to Saint Thomas Aquinas*, 321–22; cf. 329.

57. Augustine, *Trinity* 15.4.22, p. 414; cited in *ST* I, q. 14, a. 8, *sed contra*. The "because" here does not mean that God has to create what he knows. For discussion of Augustine on the divine ideas (Augustine's preferred term is *rationes*), as well as Aquinas's appropriation of Augustine, see Boland, *Ideas in God according to Saint Thomas Aquinas*, 36–47, 274–84; Farthing, "Problem of Divine Exemplarity in St. Thomas," 191–93. Boland notes that Augustine's "*De Diversis Quaestionibus LXXXIII*.46 was the chief patristic source for the doctrine of the divine ideas in the Middle Ages. Under its influence Saint Anselm gives an account of the divine ideas in *Monologion X*. Peter Lombard links it with the divine attribute of knowledge at distinctions 35–37 of the first book of his *Libri Sententiarum*. Commentators on the *Sentences* then speak of the ideas when dealing with divine knowledge" (*Ideas in God according to Saint Thomas*

Vladimir Lossky on the Divine Ideas

In the view of Vladimir Lossky, however, Aquinas's account of the divine ideas not only does not succeed, but in fact profoundly undermines the divine act of creation. In chapter 5 of his masterwork, *The Mystical Theology of the Eastern Church*, Lossky addresses the topic of "Created Being." He begins by reflecting on the mystery of creation from nothing. As he points out, we cannot conceive of absolute nothingness, just as we cannot conceive of absolute being: "The nothingness of creatures is as mysterious and unimaginable as the divine Nothingness of apophatic theology."[58] What could it mean, furthermore, for God to create something that is not God? Given that God is infinite being, how could there *be* something that is not God? What ontological place could it occupy? Lossky notes that God himself must establish, mysteriously, such a place. He remarks, "We might say that by creation *ex nihilo* God 'makes room' for something which is wholly outside of Himself; that, indeed, He sets up the 'outside' or nothingness alongside of His plenitude."[59] God creates something "infinitely removed from Him," in the sense of ontological difference.[60]

When God creates, he does so freely. Lossky rules out any notion of necessary emanation due to the self-diffusive goodness of the Godhead. By contrast, the generation of the divine Word is an eternal work of God's nature rather than of the free will of the Father. Divine generation is eternal; divine generation has no beginning in God. Drawing on John of Damascus, Lossky argues that divine creation differs from the generation of the Word in that creation is the work of God's free will and has a beginning. Creatures are not co-eternal with God. Since creatures are not co-eternal, John of Damascus suggests that the act of creation, too, is not co-eternal. Lossky concludes, "We are, therefore, dealing with a work which has had a beginning; and a beginning presupposes a change, the passage from not-being into being."[61] The work of creation itself, God's work, involves a change and a beginning.

Lossky focuses in particular on the fact that God created with utter freedom and that "God could equally well not have created."[62] Against all Neoplatonic emanationism or emphasis on the self-diffusiveness of the good, he underscores that there is nothing in God that requires the existence of creatures. Creatures

---

Aquinas, 47). In this passage of *De Trinitate*, Augustine refers to Sir. 23:20: "Before the universe was created, it was known to him; so it was also after it was finished" (*Trinity* 15.4.22, p. 414).

58. Lossky, *Mystical Theology of the Eastern Church*, 92.
59. Ibid.
60. Ibid.
61. Ibid., 93.
62. Ibid.

were not necessary in any way. It is this that enables us to see both how close to nothingness creatures are, and how wonderfully free was God's choice to create. God's freedom, his will or desire, is the sole reason for our existence. Lossky points out that this does not mean that God may decide to annihilate creation at any instant of time. Rather, once God wills in favor of creatures, God wills immutably in favor of creatures. Thus creation "will never cease to be; death and destruction will not involve a return to non-being, for 'the word of the Lord endureth for ever.'"[63]

Lossky next argues that as a free act of God's will, the act of creation differs from "the shining forth of the divine energies" because it is not "a natural outpouring."[64] The divine energies, as Lossky earlier explains, "signify an exterior manifestation of the Trinity which cannot be interiorized, introduced, as it were, within the divine being, as its natural determination."[65] Some further definition of the energies will be helpful here. According to Lossky, the energies are "subsequent to the essence and are its natural manifestations, but are external to the very being of the Trinity"; and such energies as "Wisdom, Life, Power, Justice, Love, Being" manifest the divine essence while remaining "external to the very being of the Trinity."[66] The energies are natural manifestations, whereas the act of creation is not natural but free.

From John of Damascus's *The Orthodox Faith*, Lossky obtains the view that God, before creating, formulated all things in his mind, so that according

---

63. Ibid., 94; the internal quote is from 1 Pet. 1:25.
64. Ibid.
65. Ibid., 80.
66. Ibid., 80–81. Lossky adds:

> God, who is inaccessible in His essence, is present in His energies "as in a mirror," remaining invisible in that which He is. . . . Wholly unknowable in His essence, God wholly reveals Himself in His energies, which yet in no way divide His nature into two parts—knowable and unknowable—but signify two different modes of the divine existence, in the essence and outside the essence. This doctrine makes it possible to understand how the Trinity can remain incommunicable in essence and at the same time come and dwell within us, according to the promise of Christ (John xiv, 23). The presence is not a causal one, such as the divine omnipresence in creation; no more is it a presence according to the very essence—which is by definition incommunicable; it is a mode according to which the Trinity dwells in us by means of that in itself which is communicable—that is to say, by the energies which are common to the three hypostases, or, in other words, by grace—for it is by this name that we know the deifying energies which the Holy Spirit communicates to us. . . . In receiving the gift—the deifying energies—one receives at the same time the indwelling of the Holy Trinity—inseparable from its natural energies and present in them in a different manner but none the less truly from that in which it is present in nature. (86–87)

Lossky goes on to provide a further level of explanation: "The distinction between the essence and the energies is due to the antinomy between the unknowable and the knowable, the incommunicable and the communicable, with which both religious thought and the experience of divine things are ultimately faced" (87–88).

to God's eternal mind and will, each thing would receive its existence at the time assigned to it. Lossky places particular emphasis on John of Damascus's phrase κατὰ τὴν θελητικὴν ἀυτου ἄχρονον ἔννοιαν (according to his timeless will and thought), from which Lossky derives the phrase θελητικὴ ἔννοια (thought-will or volitional thought). For Lossky, this phrase sums up "the Eastern doctrine of the divine ideas."[67] In his view, the Eastern emphasis on will or volition ensures that God's ideas of created things are firmly connected with God's free will.

Lossky contrasts this Eastern view with the traditional Western theology of the divine ideas. In Augustine and most especially in Aquinas, he thinks, a crucial (Platonic) distortion of the divine ideas takes hold and profoundly undermines the theology of creation. Namely, the divine ideas come to be seen as "the eternal reasons of creatures contained within the very being of God, determinations of the essence to which created things refer as to their exemplary cause."[68] According to this Augustinian-Thomistic view, as presented by Lossky, creatures preexist in the unchanging knowledge of God, and since this knowledge is identical to the divine essence, creatures preexist in the divine essence. The divine ideas are God's eternal knowledge of the ways in which the divine essence (or existence) could be determined or communicated in a finite mode.

In Lossky's opinion, this understanding of the divine ideas is deeply distortive both because it removes free intentionality from God's ideas of creatures and because it implies that God's ideas of creatures are infinitely more real than are the changing, fleeting creatures of time and space. When the divine ideas become a realm of innumerable Platonic forms in God's very essence, indeed forms that are no different from God's very essence, these ideas of creatures have far more stability and dignity than any mere creature could ever have. The result, as Lossky puts it, is that the actual created universe appears "under the pale and attenuated aspect of a poor replica of the Godhead."[69] Surely it is greater to be a creature in the divine ideas, thus a component of the very divine essence, than to be a fleeting, suffering, pitiful creature here in the world of time and space. The place where our reality would be richest and fullest is in the eternal, unchanging divine ideas; and if so, then the value of history is profoundly compromised.

---

67. Ibid., 94. See John of Damascus, *Orthodox Faith* 1.9, pp. 189–90.

68. Lossky, *Mystical Theology of the Eastern Church*, 94. For discussion of John Duns Scotus's view of the divine ideas, which is quite different from Aquinas's and which argues both that the divine ideas are formally distinct from the divine essence and that they are produced in God's mind through what Scotus calls *ens cognitum* or *ens diminutum*, see Gilson, *Jean Duns Scot*, 279–306, 567–70; Shanley, "Eternal Knowledge of the Temporal in Aquinas," 221–22.

69. Lossky, *Mystical Theology of the Eastern Church*, 94.

Lossky argues that the undermining of history entailed by this doctrine of divine ideas both questions the goodness of God's actual creation and negates the radicality of creation *ex nihilo*. If all things exist eternally in the divine essence, as divine ideas, then creation from nothing is in fact creation from preexisting ideas, and is in fact a declension (in terms of being) rather than a gain. By contrast, Lossky points out, the Orthodox view of the divine ideas enables creation to appear truly "as an entirely new being, as creation fresh from the hands of the God of Genesis 'who saw that it was good', a created universe willed by God and the joy of His Wisdom, 'a harmonious ordinance', 'a marvelously composed hymn to the power of the Almighty', as St. Gregory of Nyssa says."[70] The Orthodox doctrine of creation achieves this, Lossky emphasizes, because it locates the divine ideas in the divine θελητικὴ ἔννοια, or volitional thought. The key point is that the divine ideas of creatures should not be associated with the divine essence, but rather with volitionally *free* divine thought.

It follows that the divine ideas are closely related to the divine energies, even though the divine ideas are not themselves divine energies.[71] Lossky explains that since for the Orthodox the divine ideas "are more dynamic, intentional in character" than they are for the West, it makes sense that they pertain to "the divine energies: for the ideas are to be identified with the will or wills (θελήματα) which determine the different modes according to which created beings participate in the creative energies."[72] These divine "wills"—or divine ideas—specify the particular creaturely "modes" of sharing in the creative divine energies. Put another way, the divine ideas freely establish the synergistic union of the "creative energies" and "created beings." Creatures exist as participations in the creative energies; and the divine volitional thoughts that freely produce such participations in the creative energies are the divine ideas.

Lossky underscores that this way of understanding the divine ideas allows for free creation, rather than a creation constricted by the patterns eternally known by the unchanging divine essence. He observes that "if the divine ideas are not the essence of God itself, if they are thus as it were separated from the essence by the will, then it follows that not only the act of creation but also the very thoughts of God Himself can no longer be considered as a necessary determination of His nature."[73] Since the divine volitional thoughts vis-à-vis creatures pertain to the divine energies, they are freed from the necessity of

70. Ibid., citing Gregory of Nyssa, *In inscriptiones psalmorum*, Patrologia Graeca 44:441 B.
71. For discussion of Lossky's perspective in this regard, see Papanikolaou, "Creation as Communion in Contemporary Orthodox Theology," 112–14, 117–18.
72. Lossky, *Mystical Theology of the Eastern Church*, 95.
73. Ibid.

the divine essence. The divine ideas thereby are truly intentional, free, and dynamic. Crucially, the divine ideas are not an eternal formal pattern in God that then, by God's will, gets transmitted or replicated into space-time realities.

In Lossky's view, if the Augustinian-Thomistic view of the divine ideas goes to one erroneous extreme, then Sergius Bulgakov and Russian sophio-logical theology go to the other erroneous extreme. According to Lossky, the Augustinian-Thomistic view of the divine ideas as God's essential, eternal knowledge of all the ways in which God's being could be participated in results in the disparagement of creation, which is "deprived of its original character as the unconditioned [free] work of the creative Wisdom."[74] Divine creation merely channels the "static" and "unmoving" data of the eternal divine ideas into a lesser, historical mode of being.[75] But Lossky thinks that Bulgakov makes the opposite error by inserting change and development into the divine essence, so that the divine essence—which is utterly unknowable—"itself becomes dynamic."[76] If anything, this is a worse distortion, tampering as it does with the ineffable Godhead; but it arises from the same mistake made by the Augustinian-Thomistic view, namely, the mistake of locating creation

74. Ibid., 96. For analysis of what creaturely ontological "participation" in God means for Aquinas (in terms of the relation of finite, created actuality to infinite, creative pure act), see especially te Velde, *Participation and Substantiality in Thomas Aquinas*; Wippel, *Metaphysical Thought of Thomas Aquinas*, 94–131.

75. Lossky, *Mystical Theology of the Eastern Church*, 96.

76. Ibid. Consider Bulgakov's sophiological statement that

positing alongside His divine world the becoming world, or the creaturely Sophia along-side the Divine Sophia, God realizes kenosis in His own life, whereby Sophia becomes in "nothing" or is created out of "nothing." Of course, Sophia as a nonhypostatic but natural mode of divine being cannot determine herself to kenosis. She can be determined to it only by God's hypostatic creative act. By virtue of this hypostatic act she is diminished to becoming, and this kenosis then becomes the state of her being, her own, although passively received, kenosis. . . . The positing of the Divine Sophia as the principle of the creaturely Sophia already constitutes a pre-creation of the world, of its *first*, preliminary and original, creation, so to speak. This *heavenly creation* (if one is permitted to use this expression) is defined in Scripture through the expression: "in the Beginning God created." (*Bride of the Lamb*, 61, 64)

See also Bulgakov's view that the divine ideas must be conceived "as divine life, the self-revelation of God in Divine Sophia, or as the divine world, which exists in God for God himself" (30). Far from considering that we can know that "God realizes kenosis in his own life," Lossky emphasizes the absoluteness of the apophatic path, which ultimately must seek union rather than knowledge: "Apophaticism is not necessarily a theology of ecstasy. It is, above all, an attitude of mind which refuses to form concepts about God. Such an attitude utterly excludes all abstract and purely intellectual theology which would adapt the mysteries of the wisdom of God to human ways of thought. It is an existential attitude which involves the whole man: there is no theology apart from experience; it is necessary to change, to become a new man. To know God one must draw near to him" (*Mystical Theology of the Eastern Church*, 38–39).

in the divine essence. A third, metaphysically absurd error is mentioned by Lossky: that of John Scotus Eriugena, who conceived of the divine ideas as the first *created* essences in order to avoid locating them in the divine essence. Eriugena serves as the Western exception who proves the rule with regard to the topic of the divine ideas: his Augustinianism made him "unable to identify the ideas with God's creative acts of will."[77]

For Lossky, therefore, the divine ideas may be "ideas," but their volitional or free (rather than eternal or static) dimension takes center stage. They are "acts of will," "the will of the craftsman," and they are freely creative in every sense.[78] Since they do not pertain to the essence, they are neither eternal patterns in the essence, nor revelations that the essence is in fact itself changing and dynamic. Lossky explains that the divine ideas, as thought-wills, "are the foundation of everything which is established by the divine will in the simple outpourings or energies."[79] The divine ideas relate God and creatures by foreordaining "the different modes of participation in the energies, the unequal statures of the various categories of beings."[80]

Do creatures then have freedom, or is everything determined by the free foreordinations of the divine ideas? Referencing Dionysius the Areopagite, Lossky holds that in the union with God to which all creatures are called, both created wills and the divine ideas play a part. He states that "all creatures are called to perfect union with God which is accomplished in the 'synergy', the

---

77. Lossky, *Mystical Theology of the Eastern Church*, 96. For discussion of Eriugena's position, see Boland, *Ideas in God according to Saint Thomas Aquinas*, 143–46. I agree with Lossky that Eriugena's position is unacceptable.

78. Lossky, *Mystical Theology of the Eastern Church*, 96–97. Bulgakov, by contrast, rejects any distinction between what is "necessary" and what is "free" in God's volition:

> This distinction brings into divinity the element of accident and arbitrariness, that occasionalism which is not appropriate to God's magnificence and absoluteness. To the idea of different and manifold *possibilities* in God, actualized and unactualized, we must oppose the idea of the uniqueness of the ways of God, a *uniqueness* that excludes all other, unactualized possibilities. . . . God posits His own natural being in absolute freedom, which is united with the absoluteness of this being's content as the only possible and, in this sense, necessary content. But one can say the same thing about God's creative act, which finds an absolutely sufficient ground in His essence and, in this sense, is just as necessary a self-determination of God as His being, though *in another way*. The notion, freely accepted by Aquinas and others, that God, by virtue of this "freedom" of His, could have refrained from creating the world must be rejected as not appropriate to His essence. If God created the world, this means that he *could not have refrained from creating it*. . . . Having in Himself the power of creation, God cannot fail to be the Creator. (*Bride of the Lamb*, 31; cf. 32)

Although God eternally willed to create, and although this volition was certainly not arbitrary, how does Bulgakov know that God could not have refrained?

79. Lossky, *Mystical Theology of the Eastern Church*, 97.

80. Ibid.

co-operation of the created wills with the idea-willings of God."[81] Creation is thereby linked closely with deification; it is a matter of the cooperative response of creatures to the divine ideas. As Lossky says, "Created beings have still to grow in love in order to accomplish fully the thought-will of God."[82] The divine ideas of creatures are volitions that are in the process of being synergistically accomplished through a free "agreement of wills" between humans and God.[83]

Drawing upon Maximus the Confessor, Lossky also notes that the created world, as it is (i.e., in its undeified state), reveals God to us through God's "creative 'thought-wills.'"[84] In Genesis (and Psalms), we find the divine ideas or "logoi [words]" of created things. These "logoi" lead upward, first to more general "logoi" (as the divine ideas of individuals are contained in the ideas of species) and ultimately to the Word, the Logos. Reflection on the divine ideas of created things therefore should lead us to their divine creative principle and goal. On this basis, Lossky asks whether the divine Word is the original divine idea or "thought-will." Economically speaking, he answers in the affirmative. The Word "is the manifestation of the divine will, for it is by Him that the Father has created all things in the Holy Spirit."[85] Furthermore, the ordering of all things to the Word (by whom all things were created) displays the ordering of creation to deification. Again, the divine ideas' association with creation is never solely with creation as it now is, but also as it will be when perfected—a process that in fact goes on forever due to "ever-increasing participation in the divine energies."[86] In this way, too, the divine ideas or "thought-wills" are utterly dynamic. Lossky observes, therefore, that "the divine ideas cannot really be made to correspond with the 'essences' of things" that philosophy postulates.[87] This is so because the divine ideas or "thought-

81. Ibid.
82. Ibid.
83. Ibid.
84. Ibid., 99.
85. Ibid., 98–99.
86. Ibid., 101.
87. Ibid. For discussion of Aristotle's critique of Plato's theory of separated forms, in light of Aristotle's understanding of substance/nature, god, and intelligence (among other topics), see Boland, *Ideas in God according to Saint Thomas Aquinas*, 148–73; for Aquinas's appropriation of Aristotle, cf. 284–96. Boland also provides a fascinating discussion of the Aristotelian tradition in the patristic and early medieval periods, and he notes "the importance of Aristotle's understanding of intelligence for the Plotinian doctrine of *nous*. . . . Plotinus' doctrine of *nous* is therefore a synthesis of platonism and aristotelianism. Placing the platonic ideas in the pure Aristotelian *nous* seems to meet the requirements of both philosophies" (60, 63). As Boland sums up Aquinas's position, "While Aristotle's rejection of Plato's theory of ideas is correct it leaves untouched the Christian theological understanding of creative divine

wills" include the deification of things, as should be expected given that the divine ideas are rooted in the Word "who brings all things, in the Holy Spirit, towards union with God."[88]

Already in their earthly lives, the saints can know the things of this world in this resplendent way, not only as created but also as deified. In contemplating God, the saints receive "the knowledge of the whole world of being in its first reasons which are the 'thought-wills' of God, contained in His simple energies."[89] Lossky gives the example of St. Benedict seeing the whole universe gathered in a beam of divine light, surely a magnificent vision.

Aquinas and the Divine Ideas: The Knowledge of the Eternal God

I hope that I have spent enough time with Lossky's views to show how powerful his approach is to the divine ideas. By placing the divine ideas on the side of the divine energies and by identifying them as volitional "thought-wills" rather than mere ideas, he strives to avoid an eternal data bank of the forms of creatures, which God then transmits into space-time reality—surely a lesser realm than that of the eternal forms. Lossky seeks to rescue God's full freedom in creating, to ensure that the divine ideas of creatures are not considered to be part of God's unchanging essence, and to allow for the synergistic and deifying "co-operation of the created wills with the idea-willings of God."[90] Plato haunts Lossky's reflection on the divine ideas. The question, then, is whether Aquinas's doctrine of divine ideas—which draws deeply not only upon Augustine but also upon Dionysius the Areopagite—possesses resources that Lossky overlooks.[91] Does Aquinas's doctrine of the divine ideas reduce

---

ideas which are responsible for the entire being of things and not only, as Plato would have it, for the essence of things" (296).

88. Lossky, *Mystical Theology of the Eastern Church*, 101.

89. Ibid., 99.

90. Ibid., 97.

91. For the contributions of Albert the Great to Aquinas's thinking on the divine ideas, see Boland, *Ideas in God according to Saint Thomas Aquinas*, 187–91. Boland concludes that medieval Aristotelian

> religious thinkers, Islamic and Christian, were aware of serious limitations in Aristotle's views, particularly in regard to God's knowledge of created things and his providential care for them. In that context the notion of ideas in the mind of God continued to be of importance, the philosophical facilities for this being found either in pagan neoplatonist attempts to reconcile Plato and Aristotle or in Christian neoplatonist corrections introduced by, for example, Dionysius. . . . It is not therefore correct to say that Saint Thomas dealt with the divine ideas only because Augustine did. All that he was taught and all that he read agreed that this was an essential part of the doctrine of God as creator. (192)

the living God's creative work to the production of a mere copy of a deterministic divine template?

The Divine Ideas and God's Eternity

In addressing this concern, let me begin by reflecting upon divine eternity with the help of the Catholic theologian Matthew Lamb. As Lamb observes, Plato's strong contrast between the eternal and the temporal is developed by Plotinus. For Plotinus, according to Lamb, "the divine eternal being is that which 'always exists' beyond all extension and duration. The eternal and the temporal are opposites, and the task of the true philosopher or mystic is to leave behind all the temporal for the super-intuition of the eternal."[92] Building upon divine revelation and upon his own profound conversion(s), Augustine overcomes this opposition between eternal and temporal by entering into his conscious self-presence and discovering there divine presence, which has no before or after. Describing the conclusion that Augustine draws from this discovery, Lamb states, "Augustine presents God as *totum esse praesens*, the fullness of Being as Presence freely creating, sustaining, and redeeming the universe and all of human history in the Triune Presence. All extensions and durations, all past, present, and future events, are present in the immutable and eternal understanding, knowing, and loving who are Father, Word, and Spirit."[93] Rather than being opposed to time, therefore, divine eternity—divine

92. Lamb, *Eternity, Time, and the Life of Wisdom*, 39. See also David Bentley Hart, "Hidden and the Manifest," 203. Much like Lamb, Hart notes that the solution was the "recognition of God's 'transcendent immediacy' in all things," which enabled the realization that "if God is himself the immediate actuality of the creature's emergence from nothingness, then it is precisely through becoming what it is—rather than through shedding the finite *idiomata* that distinguish it from God—that the creature truly reflects the goodness and transcendent power of God. The supreme principle does not stand over against us (if secretly within each of us) across the distance of a hierarchy of lesser metaphysical principles, but is present within the very act of each moment of the particular" (205).

93. Lamb, *Eternity, Time, and the Life of Wisdom*, 41–42. For Augustine's account of God as *totum esse praesens*, see, e.g, *Confessions* 11.11.13, pp. 228–29: "In the eternal, nothing is transient, but the whole is present. But no time is wholly present. . . . All past and future are created and set on their course by that which is always present." See also the reflections of Plotinus upon divine eternity:

Then we reconstruct; we sum all into a collected unity once more, a sole Life in the Supreme; we concentrate Diversity and all the endless production of act: thus we know Identity, a concept or, rather, a Life never varying, not becoming what previously it was not, the thing immutably itself, broken by no interval, and knowing this, we know Eternity. We know it as a Life changelessly motionless and ever holding the Universal content in actual presence; not this now and now that other, but always all; not existing now in one mode and now in another, but a consummation without part or interval. All its content is in immediate concentration as at one point; nothing in it ever knows development:

praesens or presencing—creates time. Time is related to eternity as finite (created) presence to infinite presencing.

With this insight in the background, we can turn to Aquinas. He takes his definition of divine eternity from Boethius: "Eternity is the simultaneously-whole and perfect possession of interminable life."[94] Discussing this definition, Aquinas notes that we can only conceive of divine eternity via time. Time, of course, includes a "before" and "after"; indeed, time is "the measure of before and after in movement."[95] The notion of eternity abstracts "before/after" and "succession" from time, leaving us solely with "the *now* of time."[96] Since the temporal "now"—the present moment—is obviously not eternity, the Boethian definition describes the "now" as "perfect" and replaces time's fleetingness with "simultaneously-whole [*tota simul*]." The word "interminable" likewise negates time's fleetingness, without positing any defect in eternity itself.

Aquinas goes on to ask whether eternity is something different from God, as time is different from the things that exist in time. Or is eternity God's "simultaneously-whole and perfect *possession* of interminable life," so that God's life is something different from his eternal possession of it? Responding that "eternity is nothing else but God himself," Aquinas argues that God's life, his infinite actuality, cannot be different from his "simultaneously-whole and perfect possession" of his life.[97] Only God, therefore, can be "eternal" in a proper sense, since all creatures have some kind of a beginning and are not pure actuality. Since eternity, unlike time, "is simultaneously whole," God's intelligent and loving presence is simultaneously whole and perfect rather than having duration or change.[98]

How does this understanding of eternity relate to the doctrine of the divine ideas? The divine ideas belong to God's simultaneously whole presencing

---

all remains identical within itself, knowing nothing of change, for ever in a Now, since nothing of it has passed away or will come into being, but what it is now, that it is ever. . . . That which neither has been nor will be, but simply possesses being; that which enjoys stable existence as neither in process of change nor having ever changed—that is Eternity. Thus we come to the definition: the Life—instantaneously entire, complete, at no point broken into period or part—which belongs to the Authentic Existent by its very existence, this is the thing we were probing for—this is Eternity. (*Enneads* 3.7.3, p. 216) Plotinus goes on to say that "a close definition of Eternity would be that it is a life limitless in the full sense of being all the life there is and a life which, knowing nothing of past or future to shatter its completeness, possesses itself intact for ever" (3.7.5, p. 219).

94. *ST* I, q. 10, a. 1, obj. 1. The Latin is *aeternitas est interminabilis vitae tota simul et perfecta possessio.*

95. *ST* I, q. 10, a. 1.

96. Ibid., ad 5. For clarification, emphasizing that this *now* is not a "divine time," see Maritain, *Existence and the Existent*, 113–14.

97. *ST* I, q. 10, a. 2, ad 3.

98. *ST* I, q. 10, a. 4.

(*totum esse praesens*) by which he is perfectly, intelligently, and creatively present to all things, and so the divine ideas should not be conceived of as a mere impersonal data bank upon which God draws. But if they should be conceived in a more personal way, what precisely might this involve? Here Gregory Doolan's discussion of Aquinas's theology of the divine ideas offers helpful precision. The divine ideas are not "that by which" God understands all things; rather they are God's understanding "that which" he understands.[99] As God's knowledge of that which he understands, the divine ideas are first and foremost God's knowledge of himself. In my view, this centrality of God's understanding of himself for Aquinas's account of the divine ideas of finite things emphasizes how intimate and personal the divine ideas are. When we think of the divine ideas, we cannot think of something separated from God's infinite self-presencing. Doolan adds that "although the ideas are many because of their relationships to created things, these relationships are not caused by things but rather by the divine intellect comparing itself with them."[100] This emphasis on the activity and priority of the divine intellect may be a starting point for addressing Lossky's concerns about divine freedom in creating, because the personal activity of intelligence is proper to freedom (once divine eternity is understood as an active rather than static realm).

If the divine ideas are God's understanding that which he understands, however, it might seem that there is really only one divine idea: God himself. Étienne Gilson and James Ross hold that this is in fact Aquinas's position. In this regard, Doolan distinguishes between a logical and an ontological multiplicity. The divine ideas involve the former kind of multiplicity: their logical multiplicity is founded on the ontological reality of the truth of the divine essence. At first, it might seem a problem that each distinct divine idea

99. Doolan, *Aquinas on the Divine Ideas as Exemplar Causes*, 102. See *ST* I, q. 15, a. 2, ad 2: By wisdom and art we signify that by which God understands; but an idea, that which God understands. For God by one understands many things, and that not only according to what they are in themselves, but also according as they are understood, and this is to understand the several types of things. In the same way, an architect is said to understand a house, when he understands the form of the house in matter. But if he understands the form of a house, as devised by himself, from the fact that he understands that he understands it, he thereby understands the type or idea of the house. Now not only does God understand many things by his essence, but he also understands that he understands many things by his essence. And this means that he understands the several types of things; or that many ideas are in his intellect as understood by him.

100. Doolan, *Aquinas on the Divine Ideas as Exemplar Causes*, 102. Cf. Boland, *Ideas in God according to Saint Thomas Aquinas*, 213. Bulgakov erroneously supposes that this means that Aquinas's doctrine of ideas is "constrained by instrumentalism, owing to which the very being of ideas (or at least their distinction) in God is connected with the existence of the world of things, and not vice versa" (*Bride of the Lamb*, 26).

"[falls] short of the infinite perfection of the divine essence," insofar as the idea is of a creature.[101] How can God be perfect if God has an eternal idea of Satan? The answer is that the logical rather than ontological status of God's ideas of finite things, including fallen angels and sinful actions, ensures that the divine ideas do not undermine God's perfection; indeed, multiple divine ideas, even ideas of defective modes of angelic freedom, are required precisely by the infinite perfection of God's knowledge. As Aquinas states, "So far, therefore, as God knows his essence as capable of such imitation by any creature, he knows it as the particular type and idea of that creature."[102] This knowledge is no mere backdrop to creation, nor is it solely self-referential; it is God's infinite presence ever at the root of all things, even those things that contain a defect that God permits rather than actively causes. Again, the divine ideas are not a static data bank that limits God's creative freedom; they are rather the expression of the simultaneously whole intelligence of the freely personal God whose eternal presencing (not only his will but also his intelligence) is more interior to creation than creation is to itself.[103]

In differentiating divine eternity from the "aeviternity" experienced by angels as immaterial rational creatures, Aquinas states that "since eternity is the measure of a permanent being, in so far as anything recedes from permanence of being, it recedes from eternity."[104] This "permanence of being" or *esse permanentis* sounds very much like the static domain that Lossky fears will overwhelm God's creative freedom. But by "permanent being," Aquinas means pure actuality, which has no composition and no potentiality and therefore possesses "the plenitude of perfection of all being."[105] Even so, this plenitude does sharpen the question of whether God can do anything freely vis-à-vis creatures, since God knows all possible things and

101. Doolan, *Aquinas on the Divine Ideas as Exemplar Causes*, 109. Boland states that "Saint Thomas explains the ideas as God knowing his own essence, the extent to which creatures imitate that essence and the measure in which creatures fall short of the divine essence in their imitation of it. Where is this measure and how does the falling short come about? Saint Thomas says that the hold on being of any creature is tenuous and infinitely inferior to the way in which God exists, that it is in fact nearer to non-being than to being" (*Ideas in God according to Saint Thomas Aquinas*, 271).

102. *ST* I q. 15, a. 2. For discussion see Dolezal, *God without Parts*, 172–77. Dolezal draws upon Wippel, *Thomas Aquinas on the Divine Ideas*, and Doolan, *Aquinas on the Divine Ideas as Exemplar Causes*.

103. See Augustine, *Confessions* 3.6.11, p. 43, where Augustine confesses to God: "You were more inward to me than my most inward part [i.e., Augustine's soul]." See also 10.27.38, p. 201: "Late have I loved you, beauty so old and so new: late have I loved you. And see, you were within me and I was in the external world and sought you there, and in my unlovely state I plunged into those lovely created things which you made. You were with me, and I was not with you."

104. *ST* I, q. 10, a. 5.

105. *ST* I, q. 9, a. 1.

cannot be more actual in any way. Aquinas accepts that God is not mutable in the ways that creatures are: God's "will must be entirely unchangeable."[106] Here again, however, the key is to discern the difference between eternity and time. If God were "entirely unchangeable" *in time*, God would be like a very solid stone. Such a God could not engage his people in any way. But God is "entirely unchangeable" precisely as eternal, which means as simultaneously and wholly possessing the fullness of life and the fullness of active presencing. There is no historical moment that is closed to God's infinitely personal presencing, not least because divine eternity (God himself) creates time; therefore God is fully free to be the electing and covenantal God. Without change to himself, God causes creatures (including free creatures) to participate in and be present to God in diverse ways, in accord with his wise and good plan "to unite all things in him [Christ]" (Eph. 1:10). Michael Hanby rightly concludes, "That there can be no 'intrinsic' constraint upon the freedom of divine generosity follows from the fact that God's superabundant fullness can admit no lack."[107]

As I will discuss further in the next chapter, Aquinas affirms that the eternal divine will determines itself freely vis-à-vis creatures, since the Triune God wills only his own Godhead in a necessary way. Eternally, God freely wills to create finite things and to be present in certain intimate ways to his creatures, but this willing does not change God (or depend upon a potency in God, other than his infinite power) since his will is his infinite actuality. As Aquinas states, "Although God's willing a thing is not by absolute necessity, yet it is necessary by supposition, on account of the unchangeableness of the divine will."[108]

Here again we would make a grave mistake if we imagined this "unchangeableness" on a temporal continuum. God's will is not unchangeable in the sense that God is not free later to change it or that beforehand he was free to do otherwise: the very supposition of a "later" or a "beforehand" in God indicates that one has misunderstood God's will from the outset. Rather, his will is unchangeable because he possesses himself wholly and simultaneously, without duration; his possession of himself is infinitely actualized, personal, intelligent, and free. Thus his infinite intelligent presence is characteristic of his volition vis-à-vis creatures, not least because, as Hanby points out (summarizing Aquinas), "the 'act' of creation can realize no unfulfilled potentiality in God. As *actus purus* already, God therefore needs to 'do' nothing further

---

106. *ST* I, q. 19, a. 7 and ad 4.

107. Hanby, *No God, No Science?*, 311. See also Dolezal, *God without Parts*, 86–88; Dodds, *Unchanging God of Love*, 159.

108. *ST* I, q. 19, a. 7, ad 4.

than *be* in order to cause the world."[109] Hanby adds helpfully, "Since God is already *actus purus*, and since what is received in the gift of creation is a share in the fullness of being as *act*, all of the 'action,' as it were, appears on the side of the world. Or rather, it appears *as* the world."[110]

The Divine Ideas and God's Knowledge

In the *Summa theologiae*, Aquinas divides God's ideas into "practical" and "speculative" knowledge, in accord with the fact that God does not will that every way that he can be participated in should come to be. Aquinas says that "so far as the idea is the principle of the making of things, it may be called an *exemplar*, and belongs to practical knowledge. But so far as it is a principle of knowledge, it is properly called a *type* [*ratio*], and may belong to speculative knowledge also."[111] With regard to the former, he observes that God's eternal understanding does not change when a contingent thing comes to be. Against the view that God could not know both that a thing will come to be and that it has come to be, Aquinas explains that "although contingent

109. Hanby, *No God, No Science?*, 322. Hanby adds with approval that "Aquinas will say that creation in the active sense is simply God himself with a certain rational relation to the world while creation in the passive sense is simply the world with a certain real relation to God" (323). The result is that "the doctrine of creation does not therefore seek to explain *how* the world came to be in any scientific sense of the world 'how.' Rather, it tells us what the world *is*" (324). Thus, God is the "cause" of creation in a highly analogous sense; God does not "move" or change in creating. Bulgakov misleads when he states that for Aquinas God's creative act "is wholly subsumed under the category of causality: God is the universal proto-cause"; here Bulgakov's criticisms are intensified by his reduction of causality to "mechanical and impersonal" action (*Bride of the Lamb*, 27, 37). Aquinas agrees with Bulgakov that *how* God creates is completely beyond our understanding (although for Bulgakov, it will be utterly unknowable even in eternal life). For an effort to completely separate God's omnipotence and action *ad extra* from the category of causality (understood as efficient causality), see also Sonderegger, *Systematic Theology*, 1:78–79, 177–85, 258–59, 316–25, and elsewhere. Sonderegger is concerned with determinism and especially with the problem of divine arbitrariness and predestination. Rather than causality, she speaks of God's "Personal Relation" (259, 268) to us, God's drawing us to himself by attraction, and "God's spiritual Nature" (316–18). I think that the concept of divine creation requires divine causality, analogously understood—and understood not solely in terms of efficient causality.

110. Hanby, *No God, No Science?*, 323.

111. *ST* I, q. 15, a. 3. Drawing upon the *De veritate*, Boland provides helpful background: "Saint Thomas always maintained that the idea belongs to both practical and speculative knowledge in God. Common usage and authoritative texts from Augustine, Aristotle and Dionysius might be taken to mean that the ideas belong exclusively to practical knowledge. . . . God's knowledge is 'actual practical knowledge' of what he has decided is to be and 'virtual practical knowledge' of what could be but never actually is. God's knowledge is 'speculative', knowing things not just as producible by himself but from every conceivable point of view and there are things (e.g., evil) which God knows of which his knowledge is not the cause" (*Ideas in God according to Saint Thomas Aquinas*, 252).

things become actual successively, nevertheless God knows contingent things not successively, as they are in their own being, as we do; but simultaneously."[112] God is not like a temporal knower who knows one thing at one time and knows it in a different way later. All things are present to him "as they are in their presentiality," because God is intelligently and freely present, in his eternity, to all the ways that they are temporally present; God eternally knows and wills everything that he knows and wills, though the effects of what he wills are in time.[113] Thus, for Aquinas, God's knowledge "must be altogether invariable."[114] Although this might sound like God's ideas limit him, in fact it is just another way of emphasizing that God's ideas of all things belong to his infinitely personal and free presencing. Aquinas comments, "God sees all things in one (thing), which is himself. Therefore God sees all things together, and not successively. . . . God sees his effects in himself as their cause."[115]

112. *ST* I, q. 15, a. 3. For discussion see Burrell, *Knowing the Unknowable God*, 100–103.

113. *ST* I, q. 15, a. 3. Harm Goris helpfully observes that "we can say that God knows from eternity what will happen tomorrow, but not that he creates from eternity tomorrow's events" ("Divine Foreknowledge, Providence, Predestination, and Human Freedom," 101). Goris also points out that "Anthony Kenny is famous for the logical reduction to absurdity of Boethius' solution. 'Present to' or 'simultaneous with,' he points out, is a transitive notion: if A is present to B, and B is present to C, then A is also present to C. Consequently, if all of time is present to God, then every temporal event must also be present to every other temporal event. In short, the whole of temporal extension would collapse into one singularity" (106). Eleonore Stump and Norman Kretzmann respond to this by emphasizing, as Goris says, that "in Boethius' solution one of the *relata* is not temporal but eternal" (ibid.). In Goris's view, "in order to prevent the misunderstanding that leads to Kenny's absurdity, one might better rephrase Boethius' statement that all events in time are 'equally present to God' as 'all events are (tenselessly) equally real to God'" (107). But in my view, the word "present" is worth retaining so as to underscore the dimension of personal intimacy. See Kenny, *Aquinas*; Stump and Kretzmann, "Eternity." In their essay, Stump and Kretzmann argue that Aquinas's way of conceiving eternity sounds too static and should be replaced by conceiving eternity as "atemporal duration," but this neither makes sense to me nor seems necessary. As Brian Shanley comments, "The presence of all of time to God is not a temporal presence but rather a causal presence; there is no relationship of simultaneity possible between the eternal God and anything temporal. All this makes it easy to see how facile is Anthony Kenny's contention that Aquinas is committed to the absurd claim that every moment of time is simultaneous with every other moment because every moment is present to divine eternity. . . . To start with time and eternity as two distinct realms or reference frames (à la Stump and Kretzmann) which must then somehow be brought together and coordinated is to misconstrue the issue from the start," by failing to apprehend the being of time as a created participation in eternity ("Eternal Knowledge of the Temporal in Aquinas," 222–23).

114. *ST* I, q. 14, a. 15.

115. *ST* I, q. 14, a. 7. In Bulgakov's view, this is a "purely pantheistic, Aristotelian definition of the relation between God and the world" (*Bride of the Lamb*, 21). Mistaking Aquinas for a univocal thinker, Bulgakov considers that for Aquinas "the existences of God and the world are essentially and indivisibly coordinated and merged" (20). In fact, Bulgakov's sophiology flirts closely with pantheism: "The entire positive force of the creaturely world's being is divine, is Sophia in her creaturely mode, for, in itself, 'nothing' has no force of being. . . . The uniqueness of the creaturely Sophia, or the world, consists in the fact that *uncreated* forces and energies,

Can this position avoid implying, however, that God knows himself and his eternal ideas of things but does not really know actual finite things in themselves? When Aquinas addresses the question of whether God knows individual things, he notes in an objection that "in God things are in the highest degree abstracted from materiality."[116] Since God has no contact with a material creature via material senses, how can God really know a material creature as it is? In an earlier objection, Aquinas had pointed out that "the created essence is as distant from the divine essence, as the divine essence is distant from the created essence. . . . Thus as God knows only by his essence, it follows that he does not know what the creature is in its essence, so as to know *what it is*."[117] On these grounds, it would seem that the divine ideas unavoidably lock God in himself, as would be the case if his infinite intelligence could not really know creatures as they are in themselves.

According to Aquinas, as we would expect, the contrary is the case: God knows "all contingent things not only as they are in their causes, but also as each one of them is actually in itself."[118] Since God knows everything to which his power extends, and God's power extends not only to forms but also to matter, God must know not only universals but also all individual things in themselves. In this context Aquinas reiterates that God "knows things other than himself by his essence, as being the likeness of things, or as their active principle."[119] If God did not know all other modes of being and other natures in themselves, he could not truly know himself. This is so, Aquinas explains, because "the nature proper to each thing consists in some degree of participation in the divine perfection. Now God could not be said to know himself perfectly unless he knew all the ways in which his own perfection can be shared by others. Neither could he know the very nature of being perfectly, unless he knew all modes of being."[120] God knows all things, then, in their deepest

---

submerged in nothing, receive a creaturely, relative, limited, multiple being, and the universe comes into being. The world as the creaturely Sophia is uncreated-created" (62–63). Bulgakov goes on to try to distinguish God and the world, but his sophiology tends to overwhelm his distinctions. Thus he argues, "Creation in the precise sense of the word is, first of all, the imparting of the image of the Divine Sophia to the creaturely Sophia, 'a prologue in heaven,' 'co-being' in Sophia. And this co-being refers wholly to God's eternity" (63).

116. *ST* I, q. 14, a. 11, obj. 2.

117. *ST* I, q. 14, a. 6, obj. 2.

118. *ST* I, q. 14, a. 13.

119. *ST* I, q. 14, a. 11.

120. *ST* I, q. 14, a. 6. Aquinas recognizes, as Boland comments, that ancient "philosophers had difficulties about God's knowledge because they did not accept that God works immediately in everything, that his creative power extends to everything including matter and that everything participates in the divine essence which is the principle and likeness of all that is in things whether material or formal" (*Ideas in God according to Saint Thomas Aquinas*, 198).

reality (their being), and he knows them precisely by knowing himself, because they participate in him by a likeness that he causes by his active presencing. As Aquinas observes, "God not only knows that things are in himself; but by the fact that they are in him, he knows them in their own nature and all the more perfectly, the more perfectly each one is in him."[121] Putting this point in terms of God's act of creation, Brian Shanley states that "God's eternal knowledge grasps each temporal effect in its own actual, temporal, determinate *esse* . . . because that *esse* is the terminus of God's creative activity."[122]

Granted that God has ideas of all the ways in which his being can be participated in, however, what kind of being do the divine ideas have? Aquinas makes two points in this regard: things in God have "intelligible being" rather than their "natural being"; and "an idea in God is identical with his essence," even though the logical content of the idea is less perfect than God's infinite being.[123] Surely, however, this returns us to two problems identified by Lossky. First, the divine ideas would seem to be "a necessary determination of his nature" or essence, thereby seemingly constricting the freedom of God's creative work.[124] Second, creatures would seem to be created not from nothing, but from a pattern in the divine mind, a pattern whose being is infinitely greater than that of the copy, thereby making the creation something of a disappointment.

Regarding Lossky's first concern, Aquinas has good reasons for thinking that his view does not restrict the divine freedom. As indicated above, in his infinite intelligent presence, God knows the infinite variety of finite modes that his essence can be participated in. Aquinas remarks, "Whatever therefore can be made, or thought, or said by the creature, as also whatever he himself can do, all are known to God, although they are not actual."[125] For

---

121. *ST* I, q. 14, a. 6.
122. Shanley, "Eternal Knowledge of the Temporal in Aquinas," 218–19.
123. *ST* I, q. 15, a. 1 and ad 3.
124. Lossky, *Mystical Theology of the Eastern Church*, 95.
125. *ST* I, q. 14, a. 9. Against the view that Aquinas's doctrine of the divine ideas is deterministic, see also Boland, *Ideas in God according to Saint Thomas Aquinas*, 327. Boland is here responding to Henri Bergson, whose position would also likely have been known to Lossky. See also Bulgakov's complaint that Aquinas's distinction between God's knowledge of things that have existed or will exist and of things that never exist, "is a highly obscure and arbitrary distinction, which admits in God an abstract, unreal thinking of bare possibilities, contrary to the fact that God's thoughts are also his deeds. This is pure anthropomorphism" (*Bride of the Lamb*, 22). But why should we claim that "God's thoughts are also his deeds"? Bulgakov's concern is ultimately rooted in his sophiology, which requires that divine and creaturely Sophia be one and the same. He bemoans the fact that for Aquinas, God could have created otherwise, so that this world is "only one of many possible types of worlds, so to speak. This supposition . . . introduces an element of irrational accident and arbitrariness in the relation of the Creator to creation. In any case, we get a quantitative noncorrespondence of ideas and things. The

Lossky, as we saw, the divine ideas unduly constrain God's creative work if these ideas are the divine essence and if they are not primarily volitional. But given Aquinas's understanding of eternity as God's intelligent and free self-presencing, the divine ideas should not be located "prior" to creation, as though God considered the panorama of his options (the divine ideas) and then implemented some of them volitionally in creation. Rather, there is only the triune creator God, who in his eternal intelligent presencing freely wills certain things to be, without changing his infinitely actual will. To understand Aquinas's theology of the divine ideas rightly, therefore, God's "plan for the fulness of time" (Eph. 1:10) cannot be a mere Leibnizian choosing among constraining sets of possible worlds. Again, the divine ideas belong to God's eternal intelligent self-presencing, in his infinite goodness, as he eternally wills himself and certain modes of participating in himself "on account of the love of his own goodness."[126]

Nor, with respect to Lossky's second concern, does Aquinas consider that the creation is a poor copy, ontologically speaking, of the divine ideas. Of course, there is nothing finite to which God's infinite intelligence is not utterly and actively present: "God knows even the thoughts and affections of hearts, which will be multiplied to infinity as rational creatures go on forever."[127] But ontologically speaking, creatures have their own (finite and participating) being. Aquinas observes that creatures "are not called beings through [per] the divine being, but through their own being."[128] In creating, God gives being

---

domain of ideas is larger than the domain of things; Divine Sophia does not coincide in content with creaturely Sophia" (26).

126. *ST* I, q. 32, a. 1, ad 3. James Dolezal points out that the same question addressed in this paragraph also comes up with regard to the act of creation vis-à-vis divine simplicity. If God's will is the same as God's unchanging being, how could any aspect of God's will truly be free? See Dolezal, *God without Parts*, chap. 7; on this topic see also chap. 2 of the present book. Norman Kretzmann mistakenly tries to solve this problem by arguing that to create is natural to God (rather than free), because it is natural to goodness to be self-diffusive. Kretzmann limits God's freedom to the choice of which particular things to create. See "General Problem of Creation"; "Particular Problem of Creation." John F. Wippel responds to Kretzmann's position in "Norman Kretzmann on Aquinas's Attribution of Will and Freedom to Create to God." As Dolezal notes, Wippel critiques Kretzmann for not differentiating between efficient and final causality: "When we ascribe free will to God we mean that he is free in respect to efficient causation, not that he is free in regard to final causation. If he wills anything at all, he *must* will himself as the end. If God efficiently wills (freely) to create he *must* diffuse his goodness into that creation. Kretzmann simply fails to perceive the crucial distinction between efficient and final causality in Thomas's texts" (Dolezal, *God without Parts*, 194n18).

127. *ST* I, q. 14, a. 12.

128. *ST* I, q. 6, a. 4, *sed contra*. Thus Aquinas's solution to Lossky's second concern is similar to his argument for a genuine secondary causality of things which is not in competition with God as first cause. See *ST* I, q. 19, aa. 8–9; *ST* I, q. 105, aa. 4–5.

to things that do not otherwise have any being whatsoever.[129] Although God eternally knows all things as they are, the ideas of things in God are not the existing created things. Creatures by definition could never be the divine ideas, since the divine ideas are coextensive with the divine essence. Aquinas points out, therefore, that God "brought things into being in order that his goodness might be communicated to creatures, and be represented by them."[130] Had things eternally possessed their own being in the divine ideas, they would not need to be brought into being. The only way to exist *as a creature* is to be created, to possess a distinct finite act of being. As Gregory Doolan sums up Aquinas's position, the divine "ideas exist simply as known beings rather than as real ones."[131]

129. See *ST* I, q. 46, aa. 1–2. Bulgakov rightly remarks: "Although creatures exist by the power of God and their being is affirmed in God, they nevertheless form a different and special world, a world that is *new* in a certain sense" (*Bride of the Lamb*, 55). But Bulgakov mistakenly considers the divine ideas to be a mere plan of creation, rather than being God's intimate, infinitely intelligent presence to all things. Thus Bulgakov complains with regard to patristic and medieval doctrines of the divine ideas, "The difference between the two worlds [the divine ideas and the created realm] must be understood as being much more profound than only the relation between a plan and its realization" (ibid.). Bulgakov's solution is to hold that the divine ideas "are the very seeds of being, implanted in the 'meonal' half-being of becoming" (ibid.). The characterization of the divine ideas as "seeds of being" causes a variety of conceptual problems, not least Bulgakov's conclusion that "God lives not only in Himself by His own life, but also outside Himself, in the becoming world" (56). Given the boldness of this view, it is odd that Bulgakov would complain so much of "Aquinas's pantheistic biases that have their origin in Aristotelianism" (57). Bulgakov goes on to translate his position into sophiological terms: "Having its foundation in the Divine Sophia, the world is not created but eternal, by this eternity of its foundation. But the world is also created and belongs to temporal being, for, in it, as the creaturely Sophia, the Divine Sophia acquires the mode of her being—not only in the eternal life of God in God and for God in His triune hypostases, but also by herself, in her becoming. . . . The creaturely Sophia is, in this sense, the kenosis of the Divine Sophia" (60).

130. *ST* I, q. 47, a. 1. As Boland says, "The idea is an exemplar because it is a way known to God whereby creatures may participate in God's own goodness which is the final end of all things" (*Ideas in God according to Saint Thomas Aquinas*, 261).

131. Doolan, *Aquinas on the Divine Ideas as Exemplar Causes*, 110. Boland helpfully observes, "Because of his understanding of the communication and participation of *esse* Saint Thomas can regard material things as more truly themselves in their material existence than in their existence in God's mind whereas for Plato and Augustine things were simply more truly themselves in their superior mode of being" (*Ideas in God according to Saint Thomas Aquinas*, 245). Bulgakov criticizes Aquinas for endorsing "the existence of . . . never-actualized ideas" (*Bride of the Lamb*, 26), but I do not see why God cannot have infinite ideas or *rationes* ("types") of things that do not actually exist. Indeed, God must have such knowledge. See also Doolan, "Aquinas on the Divine Ideas and the Really Real," where he distinguishes between the "fact of existence" and the "act of existence" and argues that created things are the "really real" with respect to the former but not with respect to the latter. He repeats his view that for Aquinas, "as regards *this esse* (*esse hoc*)—such as a man or a horse—created things exist more truly in their own nature (*propria natura*) than in the divine mind. From

As created, therefore, finite things are not ontologically fallen away from the divine realm. Instead, to speak of divine ideas is simply to affirm that God does not learn from the created order what the truth or being of things is. God, in his eternal presence that involves no before or after, "has ideas of all things known by him," and God gives finite being to the existing things that he knows in his eternal ideas.[132] Indeed, absent a proper account of the divine ideas, it can easily seem—as Aristotle Papanikolaou cautions in another context—that "creation, once created, is completely devoid of God's presence."[133] As we have seen, the very opposite is the case.

The Divine Ideas and the Divine Word

Aquinas frequently links the divine ideas to the Word of God. Thus, in the *Summa theologiae*, he states that "the Word is expressive of creatures," and he adds in this regard that "the Word of God is only expressive of what is in God the Father, but is both expressive and operative of creatures; and therefore it is said (Ps. xxxii. 9): 'He spake, and they were made'; because in the Word is implied the operative idea [*ratio factiva*] of what God makes."[134] Are the divine ideas, then, in some way unique or proper to the divine Word in the Trinity?

Gregory Doolan argues that Aquinas associates the divine ideas with the Word only by way of "appropriation." Citing *Summa theologiae* I, q. 32, a. 1, ad 1, Doolan holds that while the divine ideas pertain to the divine essence,

---

this perspective, Thomas again presents creatures, and not the divine Ideas, as the really real" (1089–90). Doolan draws here upon Kevin White, "Act and Fact." See also Clarke, "Problem of the Reality and Multiplicity of Divine Ideas in Christian Neoplatonism," 123: "It is true that my *intelligibility*, the *intelligible content* of the divine idea of me, exists in a higher, more perfect way in God than in me; but this is still not my true being, my *esse*." Clarke underscores the difference between Aquinas's position here and that of Augustine (and of Plato and Plotinus).

132. *ST* I, q. 15, a. 3, *sed contra*.

133. Papanikolaou, "Creation as Communion in Contemporary Orthodox Theology," 119. Papanikolaou is contrasting John Zizioulas's creation theology with that of Lossky and Sergius Bulgakov. Papanikolaou argues that "there is not a clear sense in Zizioulas on how creation as God's creation is always relating and participating in God's life. . . . Perhaps Zizioulas can learn something from Lossky and Bulgakov, who with the concepts of divine energies [inclusive of the divine ideas] or Sophia avoid any rigid set of dualisms" (ibid.). For confirmation of Papanikoloau's concerns, see Zizioulas's statement, in the same volume, that "the role of the human being, as the priest of creation, is absolutely necessary for creation itself, because without this reference of creation to God the whole created universe will die [return to nonbeing]. . . . Therefore, the only way to protect the world from its finitude, which is inherent in its nature, is to bring it into relation with God" ("Proprietors or Priests of Creation?," 167–68).

134. *ST* I, q. 34, a. 3 and ad 3.

the divine ideas are appropriated to the person of the Word in order to make more manifest the personal property that distinguishes the Word. He explains that "the Son of God proceeds by way of intellect as the Word; thus those things that pertain to intellect can be appropriated to him by similitude. Now, since ideas pertain to intellect, they can be appropriated to the Son."[135] For Doolan, however, this appropriation should not be taken to mean that in fact the divine ideas are uniquely connected to the Word in the Trinity. The divine ideas, as pertaining to the divine essence (God's knowledge), are not lacking from any of the persons. Thus Doolan concludes that the doctrine of divine ideas is primarily a philosophical doctrine, rather than a theological doctrine inextricable from the mystery of the Trinity.

While I agree with Doolan that the doctrine of the divine ideas does not require knowledge of the Trinity, and in this sense is philosophical, it seems to me that the connection with the Word is nonetheless more significant than Doolan suggests. Certainly, appropriation is at work when creation's intelligibility is linked to the Word. But in his theology of the Triune God, Aquinas distinguishes between the act of "understanding" (which pertains to the divine essence and thus to all three persons equally) and the act of "speaking an interior word" (which pertains to the personal property of the generation of the Son). Thus Gilles Emery comments that one must "make a distinction between *knowledge* in God (which is an act of his nature, shared by the whole Trinity), and *speech* (which is a personal or 'notional' action of the Father)."[136] Insofar as God understands himself and all the ways his essence can be imitated, the divine ideas are in the divine essence. But insofar as understanding involves "speaking an interior word," God the Father expresses the entire Trinity and all actual and possible creatures precisely in his Word. As Aquinas says, "But because God by one act understands himself and all things, his one only Word is expressive not only of the Father, but of all creatures."[137] For this reason, the divine ideas are not solely connected with the Word by appropriation; they are expressed in the Word. Vivian Boland adds in this regard, "Because *idea* signifies primarily the *respectus ad creaturam* the ideas are many. Because *verbum* signifies primarily the relationship to the sayer, and signifies creatures only

135. Doolan, *Aquinas on the Divine Ideas as Exemplar Causes*, 119. See also Boland, *Ideas in God according to Saint Thomas Aquinas*, 325.

136. Emery, *Trinitarian Theology of Saint Thomas Aquinas*, 187.

137. *ST* I, q. 34, a. 3. Bulgakov mistakenly asserts that Aquinas's "doctrine of ideas is therefore *not* brought into a connection with the doctrine of the Holy Trinity, does not belong to the trinitarian doctrine, but refers, so to speak, to the pre-trinitarian or extra-trinitarian (more Aristotelian than Christian) doctrine of God as mind, *noesis*" (*Bride of the Lamb*, 24).

in a consequent sense, the Word is one. There are therefore many ideas but only one Word for all creatures."[138]

Is it possible to be more precise regarding the role that the divine Word plays in the act of creation? On the one hand, the Triune God's creative act, in which his free, simultaneously whole presencing brings into existence some of the ways in which God knows that his essence can be imitated, does not differentiate the divine Persons from each other. Aquinas explains that "to create belongs to God according to his being, that is, his essence, which is common to the three Persons."[139] On the other hand, it is also the case that "the divine Persons, according to the nature of their procession, have a causality respecting the creation of things."[140] Aquinas likens the creator to an intelligent and loving craftsman, an analogy that when properly understood helps to illumine the trinitarian character of the act of creation: "God the Father made the creature through his Word, which is his Son; and through his Love, which is the Holy Spirit. And so the processions of the Persons are the type of the productions of creatures."[141] When God the Father speaks his Word, all creatures are spoken in the Word, since the Word is expressive of all things (both divine and creaturely). Created in the Word, we are redeemed in the Word, in accordance with the eternal plan of God: "For we are his workmanship, created in Christ Jesus for good works, which God prepared beforehand, that we should walk in them" (Eph. 2:10). The doctrine of the divine ideas helps to make clear that—in Leo Scheffczyk's words—"Creation and redemption are one in Christ."[142]

138. Boland, *Ideas in God according to Saint Thomas Aquinas*, 247.
139. *ST* I, q. 45, a. 6.
140. Ibid.
141. Ibid. Aquinas adds that "the processions of the divine Persons are the cause of creation" (ad 1). He further explains, "As the divine nature, although common to the three Persons, still belongs to them in a kind of order, inasmuch as the Son receives the divine nature from the Father, and the Holy Spirit from both: so also likewise the power of creation, whilst common to the three Persons, belongs to them in a kind of order. For the Son receives it from the Father, and the Holy Spirit from both" (ad 2). For discussion, see especially Emery, "Trinity and Creation." Bulgakov criticizes Aquinas here for holding that "the participation of individual persons in this causality [the creative act] takes place only '*secundum rationem suae processionis*,'" which Bulgakov considers to reflect "the general impersonalism of Aquinas's theology, which deduces the being of the hypostases solely from the distinctions and relations in divinity" (*Bride of the Lamb*, 27). But the criticism that the trinitarian persons act in creation only "according to the nature of their processions"—as if the latter were insignificant—misunderstands Aquinas's theology of the Trinity. See Emery's "Essentialism or Personalism in the Treatise on God in St. Thomas Aquinas?"
142. Scheffczyk, *Creation and Providence*, 32. Scheffczyk is critical of Aquinas's theology of creation on the grounds, mistaken in my view, that Aquinas's theology of creation is not sufficiently linked with Christ and history. Scheffczyk holds that "a metaphysical approach to and exposition of the truth of Creation—especially in the Aristotelian categories—tends to

Conclusion

In a brief treatment of the divine ideas at the end of the first volume of his *Theo-Logic*—originally published as *Truth in the World* in 1947—Hans Urs von Balthasar compares the creaturely image to its "archetype" in God. The rational creature can and does fall away from this divine "archetype." But even so, "there is no idea of the creature that can truly or ultimately be separated from this latter [the transcendent archetype]."[143] In understanding each creature, God understands his own "total truth" as imitated by the creature, and thus God knows each creature in his divine idea of the creature.[144] Balthasar explains that God considers the creature "in the medium of his own substance, of whose possible imitability the divine idea is the archetype. For God, all truth lies within his own essence, while everything else is true only insofar as it stands in relation to his essence."[145] This perspective echoes the position that we have seen in Aquinas. Balthasar differs somewhat from Aquinas, however, in the way he addresses the teleological or developmental dynamic of the divine ideas, governed by the "archetype." In this regard, Balthasar observes that when "a gulf opens up between the archetype in God and its realization in the creature," God shows his love by keeping his gaze upon the archetype and enabling the creature to attain it.[146] Thus, God mercifully overlooks the distance between the creature and its archetype, and God locates the creature's inadequacy firmly "within his archetypal knowledge."[147] In his infinite love, God ensures that the determinative divine idea is the archetype, no matter how imperfect and inadequate the creature may be. Balthasar states, "Because the archetype in God, that is, the higher reality into which the creature is elevated and that counts as its definitive truth before God, is a progeny of love, the creature knows that it is *kept safe* in this archetype."[148] On this view, it is the "eternal archetype," God's knowledge of the creature as perfected, that is in fact the "creative idea present in God" of each and every creature.[149]

---

represent Creation as something self-contained, an isolated event in the past, to treat it as a mere object of rational analysis, to the neglect of its import for salvation" (151).

143. Balthasar, *Theo-Logic*, 1:266.
144. Ibid.
145. Ibid.
146. Ibid., 265.
147. Ibid., 266.
148. Ibid., 266–67.
149. Ibid., 267. Balthasar states, "If it [the creature] looks at itself, its being in the archetype can seem only like an absolute and unjustified overtaxing; the 'idea' seems to float above reality in an unreal realm of mere ideal laws and unrealizable demands. But if, as the original evidence leads it to do, it looks to God, then it knows that it is kept safe in the archetype as its true reality, and it places confident faith in this creative idea present in God" (ibid.).

Aquinas's view has both convergences and differences with Balthasar's. Aquinas holds that the creative divine ideas are not solely the "archetypes" of perfected creatures—since if they were then all rational creatures would necessarily be saved—but also are ideas of creatures in their imperfection, including in some cases their permanent imperfection. God knows each creature in all of its modes of being, whether imperfect or perfect, because in God's simultaneously whole eternity, "the present glance of God [*praesens intuitus Dei*] extends over all time, and to all things which exist in any time, as to objects present to him."[150] Indeed, strictly speaking, even when rational creatures come to enjoy permanently the beatific vision, there is no absolutely final mode of being of rational creatures, since "God knows even the thoughts and affections of hearts, which will be multiplied to infinity as rational creatures go on forever."[151] Rather than appealing to a perfect "eternal archetype that is its [each creature's] idea,"[152] Aquinas allows that the divine ideas for some creatures include permanent (rebellious) imperfection. God "knows evil, not by privation existing in himself, but by the opposite good"—that is, by the good that should be present in the creature but is not.[153] In all this, Aquinas does not turn the divine ideas into a realm of divine necessity, as though God's creative plan were merely a transposition of the ideas contained in his eternal essence, or as though God's essence were not a realm of infinite intelligent freedom. Rather, God knows all the ways that his essence can be participated in, and thus he knows more than he determines to create. His plan of creation is eternal, but that does not mean that it is not freely willed.[154]

Like Balthasar (and Lossky), Aquinas firmly insists that God's ideas of each creature are not a mere jumble; they are ordered wisely within the whole of God's wise and loving plan for his creation. God knows and efficaciously wills the full "perfection and beauty of the universe," its perfect participation in or imitation of the divine wisdom and love.[155] Every creature's condition in

---

150. *ST* I, q. 14, a. 9.

151. *ST* I, q. 14, a. 12.

152. Balthasar, *Theo-Logic*, 1:267.

153. *ST* I, q. 14, a. 10, ad 1.

154. I return to the issue of God's free eternal will in the next chapter. For the eternal divine plan and the freedom of rational creatures, see Lonergan, *Grace and Freedom*.

155. *ST* I, q. 19, a. 9, ad 2. See Blanchette, *Perfection of the Universe according to Aquinas*. See also McGuckin, "Beauty of the World and Its Significance in St. Gregory the Theologian," 35: "The experience of beauty in the world was thus to Noetic Intelligence an epiphany of the underlying energy of the Logos who had made the world, to this end alone—that noetic intelligences would see his epiphany within it and glorify the maker through a rational ethical life aimed at divine communion. . . . Evagrius of Pontus and Maximus Confessor, with their doctrines of the *logoi* (revelatory principles) hidden within the world order, are perhaps the most explicit continuators of this master theme from Origen."

the eschatological new creation will be in full accord with the infinite divine wisdom and love, even if the result need not be the fully perfected archetypes that Balthasar has in view. Aquinas and Balthasar can agree that God's ideas of creatures reflect and express infinite wisdom and love. As Matthew Lamb has remarked with regard to the vast multiplicity of human beings, "Only an Infinitely Wise and Loving Father could know and love through the Holy Spirit so many countless human persons into existence as members of the mystical body of his own Son, the Word Incarnate."[156] Thus, as Lamb states in light of the terrible sins that humans have committed, "One of the great joys of the beatific vision will be finally to understand the beauty and wisdom of each and every thing that has occurred."[157]

To sum up: within the broader doctrine of creation, the doctrine of the divine ideas underscores most importantly that God's infinitely actual intelligence makes possible the countless array of created presences. In his simultaneously whole self-presencing, God is intimately present to all the modes of created being, as intelligibly ordered by his wisdom and as expressive of his love. This is where, in my view, Aquinas's doctrine of the divine ideas is particularly helpful, since it profoundly illumines this simultaneously whole, infinite intelligence whose perfect presencing creates, sustains, and governs all things. Viewed in this way, the divine ideas, far from being an impediment to appreciating God's free creation *ex nihilo* of historical creatures, underscore the immediacy of the Triune God's knowing and willing of each finite participation in his infinite act.[158] Moreover, the wise presencing of God to his whole creation shows the profound fittingness of the inestimable incarnation of the Word, in whom all creatures (and all divine ideas) are expressed. After all, as Vivian Boland observes, it is in the incarnate Word "that the uncreated God and his created world meet most intimately."[159]

And yet here a problem seems to emerge: For if God, in his eternal wise presencing, knows all things with a perfect and active personal immediacy at the heart of each thing, does not then this view of God's creative wisdom become (in Rudi te Velde's words) "tainted with . . . determinism," since "the plan of

156. Lamb, *Eternity, Time, and the Life of Wisdom*, 68.
157. Ibid., 64.
158. Metropolitan Kallistos Ware observes that the intimacy of the Triune God to creatures is such that it is a mistake to "speak of the created universe as if it were an artifact of a Maker Who has, so to speak, produced it from without"—since an artifact, by contrast to a work of art, today often implies a distant, mechanistic maker ("Through Creation to the Creator," 93). As Metropolitan Kallistos goes on to say, "Creation is not something upon which God acts from the outside but something through which he expresses Himself from within" (ibid.).
159. Boland, *Ideas in God according to Saint Thomas Aquinas*, 332.

providence, as it exists in God's mind, must be certain and immutable"?[160] Have we not here once again simply arrived at "the God of the *ancien régime*, the sovereign deity of absolute power who is in charge of everything," and who, as such, leaves "no room for genuine human freedom"?[161] I submit that the situation is just the opposite. For, as te Velde goes on to show, God's immediate and intimate wise presencing grounds the *participatory* actions of creatures, in accord with their own natures, on the gracious path of deification. The immediacy of the divine presencing, therefore, *enables, rather than negates*, created freedom. Ultimately, it is the God of the divine ideas—the God who is intimately and perfectly and intelligently present from divine eternity in and to each created thing—who is precisely the "God of participation, of letting other things share, from His own abundance, in being and goodness. The gift of being [thus] entails the gift of causality."[162] Creatures are free because God, who is our ontological source rather than our ontological competitor, knows us as free creatures in his eternal presencing and thereby enables our freedom as a participation in his own.

Here I agree with the formulation of Conor Cunningham: "Only in being thought by God, only in being called by God into existence—and thus being—and so inhabiting the *recollection* of this call, will life be possible."[163] Living as God's creatures, let us rejoice in the infinite wisdom of God, *totum esse praesens*, who (in Aquinas's words) is "the most perfectly liberal giver," the giver who is the source of the wondrously diverse, christologically ordered modes of creaturely imitation of his essence.[164]

---

160. Te Velde, "Thomas Aquinas's Understanding of Prayer in the Light of the Doctrine of *Creatio ex Nihilo*," 50.

161. Ibid.

162. Ibid., 50–51. Cynthia Crysdale and Neil Ormerod make a similar point: "God knows us through and through because God's loving wisdom is cause of all that is; and God's wise loving freely chooses us and everything else in this cosmos. . . . As such, we are intimately close to God; not the closeness of physical proximity, but the closeness of knowing and loving, an intimacy that causes us to be" (*Creator God, Evolving World*, 127). Of course, we are created from nothing; there is no substrate out of which we were made. When God creates "absolute being," the being of all things, God does not make this being out of himself, even though created beings "are diversified by the diverse participations of being" and are "being by participation" (*ST* I, q. 45, a. 5; *ST* I, q. 44, a. 1 and ad 1). All beings participate in God, but not as parts of God. Te Velde further observes that the Triune God as apprehended by Aquinas "grants the secondary causes (nature, human will) their own power and operation, not by 'retreating' as it were from the 'autonomous' space of the human world, but by being actively present in all things and by positing them in their own being and operation" ("Thomas Aquinas's Understanding of Prayer in the Light of the Doctrine of *Creatio ex Nihilo*," 50).

163. Conor Cunningham, "Being Recalled," 59.

164. *ST* I, q. 44, a. 4, ad 1.

TWO

Divine Simplicity

In the beginning God created the heavens and the earth.

Genesis 1:1

Can the wise and good creator God, who freely wills creatures in willing himself, be *simple* in the sense of possessing no composition of any kind and being utterly undivided and indivisible in any way?[1] In the previous chapter, I

1. For the view that divine simplicity, if understood to mean that all of God's actions are the same as God's essence, would negate God's omniscience and freedom (and thus the doctrine of divine simplicity must be erroneous), see Christopher Hughes, *On a Complex Theory of a Simple God*, 106 and elsewhere. See also the similar criticisms lodged against the doctrine of divine simplicity by Thomas V. Morris in *Our Idea of God* and by Alvin Plantinga in *Does God Have a Nature?* James E. Dolezal, *God without Parts*, 14–24, provides a helpful survey of the positions of Hughes, Morris, and Plantinga, which together represent the dominant perspective in contemporary (Protestant) analytic philosophy. As Dolezal makes clear, there are some rather deep misunderstandings at work here. For example, given his analytic conception of "being" along the lines of an accidental form, it is not surprising that "Hughes finds the identity of God with his act of existence non-compelling because he conceives existence to be 'thin,' functioning as nothing more than an on-off toggle switch, as it were. How can God possess all those other properties that Christians ascribe to him if he is nothing but existence itself?" (*God without Parts*, 15; cf. 105–10.) Hughes's view is also found in Kenny, *Aquinas on Being*. For the opposite view, see Klima, "On Kenny on Aquinas on Being"; Dewan, "Saint Thomas, Alvin Plantinga, and the Divine Simplicity." Citing Dewan, Dolezal comments, "It should be observed that the univocal concept of being in which God and creatures are simply different beings within one great ontological order is at the heart of recent 'possible worlds' semantics. . . . Placing God and creatures together as so many facts within the actual world inevitably tends toward ontological univocism. Gone is the ancient concern to sharply differentiate between God and creatures at the level of existence" (*God without Parts*, 117). Dolezal later specifies that those who "speak of God as though he were a property-bearing substance" do so "because of their instinctive commitment to ontological univocism" (147).

inevitably touched upon this question at numerous points. It seems right that a study of creation should begin with the divine ideas, and with God's work of creation *ex nihilo* in ordering all things to his goodness. But it is necessary now to engage more directly the question of whether the creator God can truly be simple. I recognize that at first glance, this question seems to require a negative answer, given that God acts not only *ad intra* but also *ad extra* and therefore seems to possess a multiplicity of actions. Thomas Aquinas tries to resolve this problem by arguing that God's act is not multiple, but instead—without ceasing to be perfectly simple and one—is both an immanent action (an action remaining in God) and a transitive action (an action terminating outside God).[2] Aquinas states that God possesses "the kind of operation that passes [*transeuntis*] into something extrinsic insofar as we say that he creates, conserves, and governs all things."[3] This transitive operation is *also immanent*, "for since his action is his essence, it does not pass outside of him."[4] But if God eternally has an operation that "passes into something extrinsic," then it surely seems that God has more than one act rather than being simple act.

One traditional way of addressing this problem, as we saw in the previous chapter, is through the essence-energies distinction. Given the previous chapter's critique of Lossky's approach to the divine ideas, I should note that defenders of the essence-energies distinction need not (in my view) reject the interpretation of divine simplicity that I will be defending in the present chapter.[5] Indeed,

2. In an unpublished essay "Aquinas on Creation," which he graciously shared with me, Gregory T. Doolan notes that although Aquinas does not use these later scholastic terms (immanent and transitive), Aquinas does use variants of *immanens* and *transiens* to make the same point. Doolan critiques the view of Susan Selner-Wright, who holds that Aquinas sees creation *solely* as an immanent act: see Selner-Wright, "Aquinas on Acts of Creation and Procreation." Doolan grants that there are texts in which Aquinas denies creation's transitivity in order to deny that creation is in any way like a physical motion or a movement outward.

3. Thomas Aquinas, *De potentia*, q. 10, a. 1; the translation is Gregory Doolan's, as found in his "Aquinas on Creation." The translation of q. 10, a. 1, in Aquinas, *On the Power of God*, appears to be missing some text. See also Aquinas, *Summa contra gentiles*, book 2, chap. 1, p. 29: "There are, however, two sorts of operation, as Aristotle teaches in *Metaphysics* IX [IX.8, 1050a 25]: one that remains in the agent and is a perfection of it, as the act of sensing, understanding, and willing; another that passes over into an external thing, and is a perfection of the thing made as a result of that operation, the acts of heating, cutting, and building, for example. Now, both kinds of operation belong to God: the former, in that He understands, wills, rejoices, and loves; the latter, in that He brings things into being, preserves them, and governs them."

4. Aquinas, *De potentia*, q. 3, a. 15 (Doolan's translation).

5. See, e.g., A. N. Williams, *Ground of Union*; Lévy, *Le créé et l'incréé*; Perl, "St. Gregory Palamas and the Metaphysics of Creation." See also the crucially important essay by John A. Demetracopoulos, "Palamas Transformed." For Palamas's theological milieu, in light of the history of Orthodox reception of Aquinas, see Plested, *Orthodox Readings of Aquinas*; see also such studies as Demetracopoulos, "Thomas Aquinas' Impact on Late Byzantine Theology and Philosophy"; Demacopoulos and Papanikolaou, "Augustine and the Orthodox."

Gregory Palamas strongly affirms divine simplicity; and in his debate with Barlaam and Akindynos (who accuse him of "speaking of many uncreated realities, and of making God composite"), Palamas's way of describing God's simple essence and multiple attributes strikes me as in accord with the position that I myself will defend, insofar as he argues that with respect to God we must "conceive of things indivisible as distinct" and we must appreciate that "God is indivisibly divided and is united dividedly, and yet in spite of this suffers neither multiplicity nor compositeness."[6] Since God is pure actuality—if God were not so, then he would be merely a finite being among other beings, and could not be the source of all finite being—Palamas is right that the Triune God is "indivisible" and "suffers neither multiplicity nor compositeness."[7]

At the outset, I should emphasize that we can have no *positive conception* of the infinite divine simplicity, because our minds are finite and rely upon

6. Gregory Palamas, *Topics of Natural and Theological Science and on the Moral and Ascetic Life*, 385 (for context, see 346–417). Regarding the creative Trinity, Gilles Emery, OP, remarks that for Aquinas, as also for the fathers, "The three divine persons act inseparably, in virtue of their common divine nature, and the whole Trinity is the source of all their works. But each person acts within the distinct mode of his relationship to the other persons within this common action. . . . It really is the divine nature which is the source of creation in each person; and a nature which each person has after the mode of his relative property" (*Trinitarian Theology of Saint Thomas Aquinas*, 349, 354). Emery goes on to explain that for Aquinas,

> the person distinction is not a matter of the three persons' action, which is one and single, or their power and principles of action, which come from their common nature and so are common to the three persons. Nor is it related to the effects of the divine action: these effects issue from the three as persons executing one single action. . . . The action of Son and Holy Spirit is thus no different from the Father's, since, because they are immanent to one another, the persons indwell one another's actions; they have one single operation. But the acting persons are distinct, and their acting modes reflect their relative personal property. The mode of action exhibits nothing more or less than the personal character itself. (351–52)

For the view that the God who freely acts in creation and in history cannot be metaphysically simple in the sense in which I have defined it, see, e.g., Novak, *Election of Israel*, esp. 81–84, 201–28; Rosenzweig, *Star of Redemption*; Hasker, *Metaphysics and the Tri-Personal God*, 38–39, 55–61; Pannenberg, *Systematic Theology*, 2:8–9. For the test case of the incarnation, see the superb treatment by Thomas G. Weinandy, OFMCap, in *Does God Change?*

7. David Bentley Hart bemoans the fact that "in analytic circles existence is quite often discussed in terms not of what 'being' is, or even of what it means for a thing actually to exist, but merely of the grammar of predication" (123) under the influence of Gottlob Frege: see Hart, *Experience of God*, 122–33. Among popular textbooks that reject divine simplicity, not least on the grounds that divine simplicity would negate divine freedom, Dolezal cites Moreland and Craig, *Philosophical Foundations for a Christian Worldview*. Dolezal observes critically, "The outstanding common denominator in each of these serious and sophisticated arguments against the DDS [doctrine of divine simplicity] is the strong commitment to ontological univocism. Each critic speaks as if God and creatures were 'beings' in the exact same sense, reducing the Creator-creature distinction to a difference of degrees. . . . This is, in effect, to offer a Platonic vision of the world in which even God possesses being and attributes through participation in ideal forms or universals" (*God without Parts*, 29).

sensibles. The fact is that we have no way of speaking about God's attributes and actions without depicting God as divided in himself. But I hold that it is possible to demonstrate that pure act exists, and this demonstration entails that God is simple.[8] God's simplicity is also arguably a corollary of God's naming himself "I AM" (Exod. 3:14) to Moses at the burning bush—a name (in its use of the verb "to be" without any modifier) that points to God's pure actuality.[9] Jesus names himself "I am" repeatedly in the Gospel of John. In Mark 14:62, too, Jesus makes use of "I am" to express his own divine status, in a manner that, as in John 8–10, results in the charge of blasphemy.[10]

When Aquinas reflects philosophically upon divine simplicity, then, he has in view divine revelation as the normative source of Christian knowledge of God. For Aquinas, as for almost all the Greek and Latin fathers, simplicity is both philosophically demonstrable and biblically revealed as an attribute that distinguishes the creator God from any creature—what the biblical scholar Kavin Rowe calls Scripture's "theological affirmation of the break between God and the cosmos."[11]

8. For discussion see, e.g., Thomas Joseph White, OP, *Wisdom in the Face of Modernity*, as well as Levering, *Proofs of God*.

9. See *Summa theologiae* (hereafter *ST*) I, q. 2, a. 3, *sed contra*. Lossky states, however: "Speaking generally, we must remark that it is too often forgotten that the idea of the divine simplicity—at least in the way in which it is presented in the manuals of theology—originates in human philosophy rather than in the divine revelation" (*Mystical Theology of the Eastern Church*, 78). Lossky complains specifically about Guichardan, *Le problème de la simplicité divine en Orient et en Occident au XIVe et XVe siècles*. Warning against grounding the doctrine of simplicity in anything but the scriptural witness to God's absolute trustworthiness, freedom, and love, Karl Barth comments, "If we examine its treatment of the *simplicitas Dei*, we can only be amazed at the way in which orthodox dogmatics entered on and lost itself in logical and mathematical reflections" (*Church Dogmatics* [hereafter *CD*], II/1, 457). Barth urgently calls upon theologians to ground the doctrine of simplicity solely in Scripture: "Rightly it [orthodox dogmatics] saw that God must be described as the absolutely simple. But this absolutely simple can only be God Himself—and not 'God Himself' as interpreted by the idea of the absolutely simple, but God Himself in His self-interpretation" (ibid.). For a rich accounting of the biblical foundation of divine simplicity, see Duby, *Divine Simplicity*. Duby's work is also helpful for its succinct differentiation of Aquinas's position on divine simplicity from the respective positions of John Duns Scotus and William of Ockham, both of which Duby gently (but persuasively) critiques.

10. Discussing Jesus's claim "Before Abraham was, I am" (John 8:58), Raymond Brown remarks, "In this verse the distinction is obvious between *ginesthai*, which is used of mortals, and the divine use of *einai*, 'to be,' in the form 'I AM'"; see *Gospel according to John (i–xii)*, 360. Francis J. Moloney, SDB, supposes that "there are no metaphysical claims here," but this assumes that claiming to be the unique "I am," and thus to name oneself simply in terms of unrestricted being, is not a "metaphysical" claim. See Moloney, *Gospel of John*, 287. Brown notes that this distinction between God's unique being—unqualified "I am"—and creaturely being is found also in Ps. 90:2.

11. Rowe, *World Upside Down*, 50. In light of the name "I am," Gregory of Nyssa argues that God, who is "incorruptible and incorporeal," cannot be a bodily composite: "the Divine is by its very nature infinite, enclosed by no boundary"; see Gregory of Nyssa, *Life of Moses*, 112, 115. See also Sokolowski, *God of Faith and Reason*.

Yet does divine simplicity entail that the creative act of the Triune God, or even God's simplicity itself, must be *identical* with the essence of God, as Aquinas supposes?[12] In response, David Bradshaw finds that the essence-energies distinction offers a better way forward, one that firmly excludes Aquinas's position. For Bradshaw, divine simplicity—as (in his view) a divine energy—is consistent with the affirmation that the divine act of creation is *not* identical with God's divine essence.

In this chapter, I first survey Bradshaw's treatment of Palamas and Aquinas on creation and divine simplicity, including Bradshaw's trenchant criticisms of Aquinas's position. I then examine how Aquinas defends his account of the simplicity of the creator who ineffably wills creatures in his one act of willing himself. For Aquinas, the transitivity involved in the act of creation (namely, its productiveness of creatures) does not involve any change or differentiation in the divine act, but rather requires precisely God's simple actuality and power. The act of creation, Aquinas says, does "not signify any perfection accruing [*advenire*] to God, but rather that a perfection comes to the creature from the divine perfection."[13]

In sum, I hope to show that it is unnecessary to conceive of God's will, let alone his simplicity, as an energy not identical with his essence. I will argue that given the necessity of divine simplicity for God to be the infinite, unconditioned creator of all finite being, God's free creative will is best conceived along Aquinas's lines, keeping in mind that, as David Burrell has noted, "the manner of that [creative] action will ever escape us, for its very simplicity belies any *manner* at all."[14]

---

12. Regarding the relationship of divine simplicity to divine unity, Dolezal shows that the issue is whether God's unity can be construed as that of one god among many. God possesses a unique "unity of singularity" only if God also possesses "unity of simplicity" (*God without Parts*, 73). As Dolezal says,

> Inasmuch as oneness is as common as being we will only be able to express the uniqueness and supremacy of God's unity by identifying the uniqueness of his mode of existence. How is it, then, that God's singularity is distinguished from and superior to the singularity of all other beings? Thomas answers this question by observing that the form of God's nature, unlike things in a genus and a species, is entirely incommunicable on account of his simplicity. . . . It is the *indivisibility* of divine simplicity that ensures that God is supremely and absolutely one. Other sorts of unity that we discover in creation—such as collective, potential, and abstract (or ideal) unities—fail to set God's unity apart from that of creatures. (75–76)

See also Stephen Duby's excellent discussion of divine unity and simplicity in his *Divine Simplicity*. For the view that God's free will requires that God be an act-potency composite in some way, see also Richards, *Untamed God*; Cooper, *Panentheism, the Other God of the Philosophers*. Cooper, however, supposes that he can still affirm a version of divine simplicity. Richards's views—and others like them—are persuasively criticized by Duby.

13. Aquinas, *De potentia*, q. 10, a. 1, as translated by Doolan.

14. Burrell, "Aquinas's Appropriation of *Liber de causis* to Articulate the Creator as Cause-of-Being," 82.

Divine Simplicity and Free Creation: David Bradshaw on Palamas and Aquinas

David Bradshaw's *Aristotle East and West: Metaphysics and the Division of Christendom* proposes that Thomas Aquinas's account of the simple Triune God's act of creation constitutes the foundation of Enlightenment rationalism. Bradshaw's critique of Aquinas on creation is influenced by Lossky, but Bradshaw expands significantly upon Lossky's own critique of Western views of divine simplicity.[15] I should note that Bradshaw's reading of Palamas is controversial, and I present it here in detail not because it is necessarily the correct reading—a matter that can only be settled by experts in Palamas's theology—but because it enables Bradshaw to develop a constructive alternative to Aquinas's theology of creation.[16] According to Bradshaw, Palamas

15. With regard to the divine simplicity, in light of criticisms of Palamas put forward by Barlaam and Akindynos (the latter being well read in Aquinas's *ST*), Vladimir Lossky states,

> It is clear that the doctrine concerning the energies is not a mere abstract conception, a purely intellectual distinction. We are dealing with a strictly concrete reality of the religious order, though it is one that is not easily grasped. Hence the formulation of the doctrine as an antinomy: the energies express by their procession an ineffable distinction—they are not God in His essence—and yet, at the same time, being inseparable from His essence, they bear witness to the unity and the simplicity of the being of God. . . . So this defence of the divine simplicity [by Barlaam and Akindynos], starting from a philosophical concept of essence, leads finally to conclusions which are inadmissible for practical piety and contrary to the tradition of the Eastern Church. For St. Gregory Palamas—as for all eastern theology, which is fundamentally apophatic—it was impossible to base the divine simplicity upon the concept of simple essence. The pre-eminent simplicity of the Trinity is the basis of his theological thought: a simplicity unimpaired by the distinction between the nature and the persons on the one hand, and that between the persons themselves on the other. Like every doctrinal statement about God, this simplicity can only be expressed in terms of an antinomy: it does not exclude distinction, but can admit neither separation nor division on the divine being. (*Mystical Theology of the Eastern Church*, 76–78)

16. For a summary of the position that Bradshaw takes in his book, see Bradshaw, "Concept of Divine Energies." See also the cognate view of Sherrard, *Greek East and the Latin West*. For a critique of Bradshaw's perspective, see Kappes, Goff, and Giltner, "Palamas among the Scholastics." In the volume *Divine Essence and Divine Energies*, which is bookended by essays defending Bradshaw's position (including his own "In Defence of the Essence/Energy Distinction"), see especially Lévy, "Woes of Originality"; and Milbank, "Christianity and Platonism in East and West." As in his *Le créé et l'incréé*, Lévy suggests that Palamas's position need not be taken as contradictory to Aquinas's (and Lévy also aptly critiques the exaggerated polemic present in Bradshaw's book). Milbank, who rejects the essence-energies distinction, suggests (in a critical way) that Palamas's position fits broadly with that of John Duns Scotus, who defends divine simplicity but insists that the divine attributes are formally distinct. (Kappes, Goff, and Giltner agree with Milbank regarding the affinity of Palamas's position with Scotus's.) See also elsewhere Lévy, "Introduction to Divine Relativity"; Milbank, "Ecumenical Orthodoxy." In his essay in *Divine Essence and Divine Energies*, Nicholas Loudovikos defends Bradshaw's book (though not in all particulars), critiques Milbank's connection of Palamas with Scotus, and charges

holds that God's "energies" are the "things around God."[17] Palamas describes God's energies as God's "essential energies," and he makes clear that they are uncreated.[18] The energies include God's goodness and life, and they differ from the essence not in the way that creatures differ from God's essence, but only insofar as they do not compose the "supraessential essence."[19] The key is that every essence has powers. The powers are inseparable from the essence, and when the essence exists the powers likewise exist, but the essence is not strictly speaking the same as the powers. Citing Palamas's *Triads* 3.2.6, Bradshaw states, "No essence can be without its powers or 'natural energies,' so in the case of God these too are without beginning."[20] For Palamas the divine energies include (among others) foreknowledge, will, providence, self-contemplation, reality (ὀντότης), infinity, immortality, life, holiness, and virtue. The divine essence is the cause of the divine energies, and thus the essence can be said to "transcend" the energies, even though the energies are uncreated. Importantly, the uncreated energies make possible a certain kind of divine change. Bradshaw explains that "at least one (foreknowledge) will have an end, and some, such as God's creative act, have both a beginning and an end."[21]

Bradshaw goes on to clarify this point regarding God's creative act. Certainly God's creative *power* does not and cannot have a beginning or end. But insofar as God acts to create, and the creation has a beginning in time, God is not eternally creating his creation. Instead, for Palamas, the divine activity of creating obviously has a beginning and an end.[22] This does not mean that things can exist without divine preservation in being, but rather it means that once God has caused the universe to be, God no longer needs to bring it forth *ex nihilo*; the act of creation has ended. Bradshaw emphasizes that the doctrine of the energies allows for there to be this kind of change in

---

Aquinas with developing an "onto-theo-logic" (134) that Aquinas then tried (unsuccessfully) to correct; see Loudovikos, "Striving for Participation." Loudovikos imagines that Aquinas's view that there can "be no real relation in God to the creatures" (141) would require Aquinas to deny God's real creative presence and action. For further background regarding the early Orthodox reception of Palamas and Aquinas, see Kappes, "Latin Sources of the Palamite Theology of George-Gennadius Scholarius"; Lévy, "Lost in *Translatio*?"

17. Bradshaw, *Aristotle East and West*, 237.
18. Ibid.
19. Ibid.
20. Ibid.
21. Ibid., 238.
22. In my view, whether or not his reading of Palamas is correct, Bradshaw here confuses creation as it is in God and creation as it is in creatures. The latter has beginning and end, but not the former, on Aquinas's view; rather, God just has a relation of reason to things in time, because God creates without movement or change as pure actuality (if he were not pure actuality, he could not create).

God, without the divine essence changing—just as a creature's essence can be distinguished from the acts (and changes) of its powers. Thus, Palamas is able to account for a divine action that has ended and yet is an action of the unchanging Triune God.[23]

In criticizing Palamas's doctrine of divine energies, his contemporary Barlaam denies that anything comes between the divine essence and creatures, because God (and thus the divine essence) creates. Why does Palamas differ from Barlaam by positing the energies? Bradshaw remarks that one reason is the fear of pantheism: "Palamas objects that in this case creatures would have to exist by participating in the divine essence, so that the divine essence itself would be the reality of creatures."[24] If creaturely being were a participation in the divine essence, the divine essence would be the ontological substrate of creatures.[25] To solve this problem, Palamas turns to the divine ideas or *logoi*, which "are both one and many, and indeed as many as there are participants."[26] Rather than existing as self-subsistent beings, the divine *logoi* belong to the predestination, foreknowledge, and will of God; as Bradshaw observes, they are "particularly related to God's creative act."[27] Those who see God will see all the *logoi*, and thus will know all created things. For Palamas, the divine ideas or *logoi* are divine energies rather than (as for Maximus) distinctively connected to the divine Logos or Son.

Given this insistence upon multiple divine energies, can divine simplicity truly be sustained? According to Bradshaw, Palamas puts this question on its head by including simplicity itself among the divine energies. God is simple, but God is also above the One. If even simplicity is among the divine energies, then divine simplicity cannot be said to be compromised by the multiplicity of the divine energies. It is one of the "things around God," all of which are

23. Colin E. Gunton argues somewhat similarly that while "creation is an act of the eternal," nonetheless creation is not "an eternal act," since it has an endpoint: creation *ex nihilo* is a divine act that, as such, has been completed. See Gunton, *Triune Creator*, 90. Gunton criticizes Augustine's view of "creation as a timeless act" of the utterly timeless God, which Gunton thinks makes it difficult for Augustine "to take the order of time and space seriously as the good creation of God" (81, 83). For Gunton, the solution is to emphasize that the creative (and redemptive) divine work of the Son and Spirit takes place precisely in *history* and shows the goodness of space, time, and materiality.

24. Bradshaw, *Aristotle East and West*, 239.

25. Participation in the divine essence, of course, need not imply that the divine essence is the being or substrate of things; such an implication would have been anathema to the great patristic and medieval theologians who employed a metaphysics of participation. For a survey of recent studies of Aquinas's theory of participation (in relation to creation), see Rziha, *Perfecting Human Actions*, chap. 1. See also Wippel, *Metaphysical Thought of Thomas Aquinas*, chap. 4; te Velde, *Aquinas on God*, 139–42.

26. Bradshaw, *Aristotle East and West*, 239.

27. Ibid.

true and uncreated, but none of which is yet the divine essence. But if God truly is simple, how is it that divine simplicity itself can be numbered among the multiplicity of energies? Would this not place simplicity on the side of multiple things, and thus render the doctrine incoherent?

Bradshaw observes that Palamas responds to this concern in more than one way. First, Palamas compares God to the soul: just as the soul is one, though possessed of many powers, so also God is one, though possessed of many powers or energies. Likewise, Palamas notes that a circle's center is one, even though a circle has the power to produce the points of the circle's perimeter. Bradshaw points out, however, that these responses neglect the fact that the energies involve more than powers. The energies are fully actual rather than potential, and they are realities that are participated in by creatures. Aware of this weakness, Palamas provides two further ways of thinking about the relationship of the divine essence and the energies. He compares the essence to the sun, and the energies to the rays of the sun. Second, he compares the essence to the mind, and the energies to the mind's ideas. The sun cannot be separated from its rays, and likewise the mind cannot be separated from its knowledge. The sun's rays are not mere powers of the sun, and the mind's ideas are not mere powers of the mind. Rather, the rays are ontologically actual and real in their own right, and they make manifest the sun, just as the mind's ideas have intelligible actuality and make manifest the mind.[28] According to Bradshaw, for Palamas the energies do the same for the divine essence: they lead us to the essence and make it known. We do not share or participate directly in the sun or in the mind, because our light and warmth are not a literal share in the sun and we cannot share someone else's intellect. But we can share or participate in the ideas that someone else has, and by sharing in these ideas, we are connected with the other person's mind and come to know it, just as by sharing in the sun's rays, we are connected with the sun and come to know it. Again, these comparisons do not involve separations, as though one could find ideas without a mind or rays without a sun. The energies have no subsistence of their own, since they subsist in the essence. Yet, in Bradshaw's view, Palamas holds that they are nonetheless distinct from the essence, as real manifestations of the essence.

In his description of Palamas's position, Bradshaw also underscores that the energies do not change in the sense of having less than perfect actuality. Although the divine creative act does have a beginning and ending, the divine

---

28. For Aquinas's use of the analogy of the sun and its light in his theology of creation, see Lévy, "Introduction to Divine Relativity," 221–29.

creative act is perfectly actual. When God is creating, his (uncreated) act of creation is perfectly actual. For Palamas, Bradshaw states, something that lacks simplicity shows this by being acted upon; its ability to be acted upon, and thereby to suffer change, reveals its composite ontological status. The divine energies have no ability to suffer change in this way, given their perfect actuality. They can gain nothing from outside themselves. Since they are not susceptible to being acted upon or gaining something, they are not composite. Thus the distinction between essence and energies does not mean that God, either in his essence or his energies, is anything but perfectly simple. As Bradshaw remarks, God's many powers, actualized in God's multiple "energies," only underscore God's perfect actuality: "To possess a multitude of powers is not a sign of composition, but of simplicity."[29] The more powers something has, the simpler it is.

Bradshaw considers that Palamas presents a successful portrait of divine simplicity, one that makes sense of uncreated acts such as the act of creation. Responding to critics of Palamas such as Rowan Williams, Bradshaw denies that Palamas's position implies a dichotomy between God-in-himself and God as participated in by creatures. The energies are not our participation in God, nor are they separate from God. Rather, they are manifestations of God. Against Eric Perl's view that for Palamas (in Bradshaw's words) "the *energeiai* are ultimately just the single act of creation that is differentiated in relation to creatures," Bradshaw insists upon the real multiplicity of energies and upon the fact that not all the energies are eternal, let alone necessary.[30] The energies are united by the fact that they are all acts of divine self-manifestation, ways in which God manifests himself. Since God is not composite but instead is perfectly actual, his many self-manifestations cannot make him composite; rather, they manifest him as the fully actual, personal, and free God that he is, and at the same time they protect him from the rationalistic desire to mold him to fit our concepts. In creation, the energies ensure that God can freely act (and not act, leaving certain potencies unrealized), without thereby affecting the divine essence.

Bradshaw's appreciative view of Palamas's position contrasts with his evaluation of the doctrine of divine simplicity advanced by Augustine and Aquinas. According to Bradshaw, Aquinas cobbles together portions of Aristotle's doctrine of pure act, Augustine's view of divine simplicity, and Boethius's and Dionysius's distinctive Neoplatonisms. Bradshaw notes that for Aquinas,

29. Bradshaw, *Aristotle East and West*, 241.
30. Ibid., 273. For the views that Bradshaw contests, see Perl, "St. Gregory Palamas and the Metaphysics of Creation"; Rowan Williams, "Philosophical Structures of Palamism."

God's *esse* is identical with his essence, since God is pure act. Everything that is in God must be God, since God is sheer self-subsisting form and has no "accidental" qualities. As infinite actuality, God possesses all perfections of being. These divine perfections are not different from God's supremely simple being. As Bradshaw says, for Aquinas, "God's *esse* is His understanding and willing; each of these is simply a different way of describing the single self-contained activity that is God."[31] God's act of creation, then, arises within God's understanding and willing of himself. For Aquinas, Bradshaw observes, "in knowing and willing Himself, God also knows and wills His effects."[32] When God wills (loves) his essence, he wills freely that his goodness be shared, and thereby wills creatures in the same act of willing or loving his own essence. Since the divine goodness is perfect, God need not have willed to share his goodness, and furthermore he need not have willed to share his goodness in the particular ways that he does.

Yet is there not potency in the divine act of willing, if there is real freedom in the divine act of willing? And if so, would this not undermine Aquinas's effort to insist that God is nothing other than simple actuality? As Bradshaw remarks, in *Summa contra gentiles* (book 1, chapter 82), Aquinas addresses the question of whether God's free choice with respect to creatures means that God is in potency. Aquinas answers that God's openness to different possibilities with respect to creatures does not make God less perfect, just as an artisan who can use different tools to make his art is not less perfect than an artisan who can use only one tool. However, Bradshaw thinks that this answer avoids the real problem. The problem is whether free choice involves a potency, not whether free choice involves an imperfection. Furthermore, since God (for Aquinas) is utterly simple, God's being is the same as his will. The point is that if God chooses freely with respect to creatures, then any particular choice thereby determines not only God's will but also God's being. And if God's being (or will) were changed by his choice in creating, then God could not be pure act, lacking any potency for change.

Bradshaw considers that this tension plagues the remainder of the *Summa contra gentiles*. Aquinas insists upon holding both God's absolute simplicity as pure act and God's free choice with respect to creation/creatures. The two

---

31. Bradshaw, *Aristotle East and West*, 246. Bradshaw finds that this perspective differs sharply from that of Dionysius and John of Damascus, for whom the divine names "are said of the divine processions (Dionysius) or operations (Damascene)" (245). Aquinas supposed that Dionysius and John of Damascus hold that the divine names are *known from* God's processions or operations, whereas in truth—according to Bradshaw—the position of these fathers is that the divine names *refer* to God's processions or operations (energies).

32. Ibid., 246.

claims, Bradshaw holds, are fundamentally irreconcilable. Thus, Aquinas distinguishes immanent operations that remain in the agent from transitive operations that pass into an external thing. Since God's transitive acts vis-à-vis creation are divine acts, they must be nothing other than God. They do not divide God's simple actuality. God's transitive acts are the same as God's being, and therefore are fundamentally immanent acts. Quoting various texts from book 2 of the *Summa contra gentiles*, in which Aquinas is discussing creation, Bradshaw shows that for Aquinas all of the actions that we attribute to God, although we rightly distinguish these actions in our way of thinking, are in God perfectly undivided, one, and simple, since everything that is in God is the utterly simple, purely actual God.

If God is utterly simple, could God have willed to create something different from what he in fact created? Bradshaw notes that having affirmed God's free choice in *Summa contra gentiles* book 1, Aquinas again affirms God's free choice in book 2, so as to make clear that God could have done otherwise than he has with respect to creatures. God knows everything to which his power extends, and therefore God knows many things that he has not willed to create but that he could have created. Yet Aquinas also argues that for the perfection of the universe, it was fitting or even necessary (given the universe that God made) for God to create certain things. The universe could hardly have been complete or perfect, for example, if it had not contained representatives of all kinds of being, not only rocks and plants and animals and rational animals, but also angels. Because God is good, God would not have willed to create an imperfect universe; rather, God wills to share his goodness with creatures in a perfect way. For Bradshaw, this line of argument inevitably suggests that God's goodness makes it necessary for him to create particular things so as to ensure the perfection of the universe, so that God is not truly free in terms of what he creates.

Bradshaw also examines how Aquinas's doctrine of creaturely existence as a finite participation in the divine *esse* affects God's simplicity. If creaturely being has its own act, then how is it that creatures have their being by "participating" in God's *esse*? What kind of "participation" is this? It cannot be the standard Platonic view of participation in a form, since if that were so, God would function like "universal being" rather than retaining his ontological transcendence. Since God is simple, all divine activity is the simple divine essence; therefore, creaturely being cannot be a mode of the divine activity without compromising the simple divine essence. Here Bradshaw observes critically, "In effect Aquinas ignores (within this context) the active dimension of *esse*, treating *esse* instead as a kind of quality that is possessed by God and replicated in creatures."[33] A similar problem occurs with respect to grace. In Bradshaw's view, Aquinas's doctrine of divine simplicity does not allow for true divine-human synergy, because the divine activity is the divine essence and therefore it cannot synergistically operate with creaturely activity. Instead, God operates as efficient cause and bestows "created grace," which is not God. Since divine simplicity requires that God will all that he wills in one single, simple act (the divine essence), it makes sense that things are predestined by God rather than synergistically involving creatures.

Finally, deification runs into the same basic problem. In order to see God, the creature sees the divine essence by a created intellectual light, the *lumen gloriae*. God is thereby known by creatures, rather than being beyond knowledge—which Bradshaw finds to be opposed to the views of Eastern Orthodoxy as represented by Gregory of Nyssa, Dionysius the Areopagite, and Maximus the Confessor.[34] For Aquinas, God is known extrinsically, since the *lumen gloriae* is created. By contrast, in the East deification turns on synergistic participation in the divine energies, and thus also on unending movement or progress toward the uncreated essence.

As Bradshaw observes, in *De potentia* q. 3, a. 15, Aquinas includes among his objections the view that divine simplicity requires that God's nature and will (or essence and operation) be utterly the same, so that God must do everything by his nature or essence, which would seem to rule out free choice. In reply, Aquinas explains that the distinction between God's nature and will is in our understanding; it is not a real distinction in God, given God's absolute simplicity, but nonetheless the content of the various formalities we attribute to God really are in God.[35] From the side of our understanding, we attribute

---

33. Ibid., 252.

34. Aquinas, however, repeatedly emphasizes that "no created intellect can comprehend God wholly" (*ST* I, q. 12, a. 8), even through the *lumen gloriae*. As Aquinas states, "Since therefore the created light of glory received into any created intellect cannot be infinite, it is clearly impossible for any created intellect to know God in an infinite degree" (*ST* I, q. 12, a. 7).

35. For discussion, with attention also to John Duns Scotus's and William of Ockham's views, see Dolezal, *God without Parts*, 127–36. Dolezal specifies that "Aquinas explains the distinction between God's attributes as a virtual distinction (*distinctio virtualis*), which is a distinction of reason with an extramental foundation in its object (*distinctio rationis ratiocinatae quae habet fundamentum in re*). As close as this may appear to Ockham's later nominalism, it is a decidedly different position inasmuch as the foundation of each attribute is not a distinct concept underlying it, but is, rather, the divine essence itself" (133). Dolezal is right to emphasize that, for Aquinas, the distinction among the divine attributes is not solely rooted in our concepts, a point that often eludes critics of Aquinas's position (including, interestingly enough, the nineteenth-century Reformed theologian Charles Hodge). The key is that Aquinas's "complex God-talk, though marked by the creaturely mode of imitating or reflecting the divine nature, conveys a real knowledge of God's essence. But by no means does this entail a direct comprehension of that essence or its simple mode of subsistence" (141–42).

free will to God, because the divine will is not determined vis-à-vis creatures. In God, mysteriously (in a manner beyond our understanding), even his free will is his nature. Yet we are nonetheless right to attribute free will to God, since to say the opposite would be to say that God is determined vis-à-vis creatures, which cannot be true. Bradshaw, however, considers this logic to be fallacious. After all, if God's free will is distinct from God's nature only in our mode of knowing, then it would seem that in God, the divine will is natural, not free.

In the *Summa theologiae*, as Bradshaw points out, Aquinas adopts a different approach. In I, q. 19, a. 3, Aquinas argues that whatever God chooses to will can be considered necessary, in a conditional sense, because God has eternally chosen to will it. Yet God does not necessarily, in a strict sense, will creatures, because he *could* have willed his own goodness without willing creatures (and creatures add nothing to his infinite goodness). Thus God does not and could not will creatures with the same necessity that he wills himself, although in willing his own goodness he can will it to be shared in by creatures.

Bradshaw notes that Aquinas's line of argument here has been explored by Eleonore Stump and Norman Kretzmann in their article "Absolute Simplicity."[36] They accept Aquinas's distinction between absolute and conditional necessity, and they ask whether this distinction negates divine simplicity. Their view is that it maintains divine simplicity, because it distinguishes logically

36. For an important critique of this essay, see Dolezal, *God without Parts*, 154–55. Dolezal observes that Stump and Kretzmann's "view still locates God upon a single ontological continuum with creatures and his perfections are still conceived as property instances, perfect and indistinguishable though they may be. By making 'perfection' the distinguishing mark between God's attributes and the creature's exemplification of the same attributes, Stump and Kretzmann seem to regard the divine attributes as a special *kind* or *species* of participated properties" (154n74). Dolezal rightly concludes with regard to approaches such as Stump and Kretzmann's,

> For all their orthodox and Thomistic intuition, these recent defenses are still beset by the metaphysical infelicity of claiming that God is a property or a property instance. Inasmuch as it is the nature of a property *qua* property to exist by dependence upon a substance, it seems best to abandon the Property Account of the DDS altogether. Properties can only really exist in a substance that is in potency to them and receives them as so many determinations of actuality. Denying that God is composed of act and potency requires that DDS proponents fashion a non-property explanation of God's identity with his attributes. (155; cf. 143–53)

For the same point, namely, that God cannot possess "properties," see Oderberg, *Real Essentialism*, 156–62; Dewan, "Saint Thomas, Alvin Plantinga, and the Divine Simplicity," 143–44. For further helpful insights in this regard, see Leftow, "Divine Simplicity"; Oppy, "Devilish Complexities of Divine Simplicity"; Brower, "Making Sense of Divine Simplicity"; Bergmann and Brower, "Theistic Argument against Platonism (and in Support of Truthmakers and Divine Simplicity)"; and Pruss, "On Two Problems of Divine Simplicity." For the opposite view, see Immink, *Divine Simplicity*; Swinburne, *Christian God*.

rather than metaphysically between components of the divine will or action. But Bradshaw does not find this explanation persuasive. In his view, God's willing of himself and God's willing of creatures surely involve some kind of metaphysical distinction, because the former could exist without the latter. If so, then God's willing of himself and God's willing of creatures cannot be metaphysically identical. Bradshaw's point is that "a *single* act need not be a *simple* one."[37] He goes on to show that Stump and Kretzmann's understanding of God's nature and will depends upon the claim that (in their words) "within any initial-state set of possible worlds God's nature is fully and immutably determinate, and is so as a consequence of the single, timeless act of will."[38] Bradshaw rightly responds that "Aquinas nowhere relativizes the determinate content of God's nature to a subset of possible worlds."[39] The distinction between God's natural willing (of himself) and God's free willing (of creatures) has to be made on grounds other than the fact that God's nature is "fully and immutably determinate" in the context of an "initial-state set of possible worlds." The claim that God's nature is determinate given "an initial-state set of possible worlds" differs significantly from Aquinas's insistence that God's nature and will are absolutely the same, absolutely simple, and not determined in any way by anything that is not God.

Before ending his discussion, Bradshaw treats one last effort to save Aquinas's position on divine simplicity and divine free will in the act of creation: John Knasas's "Contra Spinoza: Aquinas on God's Free Will." Knasas points out that an act is defined by its object, and so God's act—in which the object is always God even if God freely chooses to create—is the same single act. Bradshaw argues in response that God's willing his own goodness, and God's willing to communicate his goodness, are truly distinct. Aquinas does not merely say that in creating, God wills his own goodness; rather, Aquinas adds that in creating, God wills to communicate his goodness. For Bradshaw, this indicates that the object of God's will is not as simple as Knasas supposes.

37. Bradshaw, *Aristotle East and West*, 261.

38. Stump and Kretzmann, "Absolute Simplicity," 369, cited in Bradshaw, *Aristotle East and West*, 261.

39. Bradshaw, *Aristotle East and West*, 261. Stump develops this position further in her *Aquinas*, 111–15. Dolezal responds to Stump in *God without Parts*, 197–201. Noting that Stump argues God need not be "the same in all possible worlds in which he exists" so long as he is the same within the same world (*Aquinas*, 115), Dolezal presses the point that Stump has not properly understood what it means for God to be pure act. As Dolezal says, "Surely Aquinas did not simply mean to say that God is pure act in whatever world he happens to create but that he could have been a different pure act if he had chosen to create a different possible world. Pure act simply will not allow one to introduce *differentia* into the divine essence and existence" (*God without Parts*, 199).

Let me sum up Bradshaw's critique of Aquinas's doctrine of divine simplicity, as well as the Palamite alternative that Bradshaw offers:

1. Aquinas's claim that God's being is the same as his understanding and willing—and that the difference between these is solely in our mode of understanding, given our inability to grasp pure act—makes it impossible to defend adequately God's free will in creating. If God had free will in creating, then (given Aquinas's account) God would have a potency and not be pure act. If God's nature and will were the same, then God's natural willing of himself would be completely indistinguishable from God's free willing of creatures.

2. Aquinas's doctrine of divine simplicity rules out the synergistic participation of creatures in the divine activity. Aquinas's understanding of grace and deification is extrinsic, deterministic, and rationalistic (in its conception of the beatific vision).

3. Palamas argues that divine simplicity, which he views as one of the divine energies, is not contradicted by the multiplicity of energies. Just as every created essence possesses powers, while still remaining one essence, so also the one divine essence has divine powers or energies. Indeed, possessing many powers or energies is a mark of simplicity, since that which is "simple" always *acts* (by its powers) rather than ever being acted upon. The plurality of divine powers or energies ensures God's full actuality. In this sense, God is pure, simple act.

4. Palamas holds that some divine energies have a beginning and/or an end. God's foreknowledge has an end, and God's creative act had a beginning and an end (as described in Gen. 1). The divine powers or energies are freely directed toward the work of creation and (synergistically) toward creatures. There is no need to worry about whether this compromises God's perfect eternity, unity, and transcendence.

Thomas Aquinas on Divine Simplicity and Free Creation

Is Bradshaw right that the doctrine of divine simplicity, as understood by Aquinas, produces a rationalistic, emanationist theology of creation? Or is divine simplicity as understood by Aquinas necessary for affirming that the free act of creation is in fact the action of the living God, the God who is pure act ("I am")?[40] In what follows, I focus upon the first point above, namely, the simple God's freedom in creating. I deny that simplicity can include a real plurality in God of divine powers and acts (point 3 above). In my view, God's creative act—as his pure act—has no beginning or end, although from the side of creatures there is a beginning and an end to the moment of creation (point 4 above). In creation, it is creatures, not God, who change. Due to limitations of space, I must leave the issue of synergy (point 2 above) largely for a future work, while pointing the reader to such notable studies as Bernard Lonergan's *Grace and Freedom* and Joseph Wawrykow's *God's Grace and Human Action*.[41]

East and West

Despite the title of Bradshaw's book, it would be a mistake to construe this discussion of what pertains to the creator God as a debate between a

40. William Lane Craig proposes that God is timeless and that time is created but also that as soon as the universe of time and space comes into being, "God, in virtue of His real relation to the world, enters at that moment into time" (*God, Time, and Eternity*, 280). For Craig, "given the correctness of a tensed theory of time [which affirms the reality of temporal becoming] God cannot, insofar as He co-exists with the world, be timeless" (282). This strikes me as a misunderstanding of God's eternal presence—a misunderstanding rooted in a fundamentally univocal understanding of God's existence. For a better view of God's relationship to tensed time, see Helm, "Response to Nicholas Wolterstorff," 216–17, as well as the extensive discussion in Goris, *Free Creatures of an Eternal God*. Goris concludes that "the real presence of temporal things to eternity does not depend on their tenseless mode of being, but on the eternal mode of being of God. . . . We cannot express or grasp this eternal mode of being present" (253–54). See also Craig, "Timelessness and Omnitemporality." For a thoroughgoing defense of God's temporality, see Wolterstorff, "Unqualified Divine Temporality." Wolterstorff argues that God's everlasting temporality means that he can change and that he has a history, both of which Wolterstorff considers to be required by Scripture's narrative portrayals of God. See also, in favor of God's temporality, Mullins, "Doing Hard Time"; Novak, *Election of Israel*. For cogent defense of God's utter timelessness, see Helm, "Eternal Creation"; McCann, *Creation and the Sovereignty of God*, chap. 3.

41. In his "Introduction to Divine Relativity," Lévy shows that

while formulating Augustine's view on the interaction between God and the world in Aristotelian terms, Thomas remains faithful to the founding metaphysical intuition of the *Confessions*. In the example of Thomas Aquinas, it becomes once again plain that the Western theological tradition has neither neglected nor minimized the importance of the synergism that lies at the core of its Eastern equivalent. The post-Aristotelian, strongly Platonized scheme which, in Augustine's works, regulated the interaction between God and the world is taken up by Thomas in an apparently Neoaristotelian, yet intimately Neoplatonic form. From a doctrinal point of view, there is no difference between the ways the West and the East envisage the causal continuity and the essential discontinuity between God and the world. (228; cf. 186–89)

Yet Lévy finds that Palamas's approach to creation is "theocentric" while Aquinas's approach is "anthropological" (229), a conclusion that I would contest. Lévy states, "From the Eastern perspective, the phenomena, the visible and material realities, appear as continuously 'energized' by the Uncreated" (ibid.). Aquinas's view of the divine ideas and of God's creative action and conservation of things surely also rules out any autonomy (as distinct from integrity) of creatures.

monolithic "East" and "West," or even necessarily between Palamas and Aquinas. David Hart, whose debts to Gregory of Nyssa and Maximus the Confessor are profound and who also knows Palamas's writings well, remarks, "I am not at all convinced that Palamas ever intended to suggest a *real* distinction between God's essence and energies; nor am I even confident that the energies should be seen as anything other than sanctifying grace by which the Holy Spirit makes the Trinity really present to creatures."[42] Emphasizing that "God is never less than wholly God,"[43] Hart defends divine simplicity—understood along lines congenial to Aquinas—as necessary for God to be God. Hart points out in this regard: "No claim . . . has traditionally been seen as more crucial to a logically coherent concept of God than the denial that God is in any way composed of separable parts, aspects, properties, or functions."[44] Even more strongly, in a manner that rules out the kinds of composition that Bradshaw advocates, Hart observes, "If God is to be understood as the unconditioned source of all things, rather than merely some very powerful but still ontologically dependent being, then any denial of divine simplicity is equivalent to a denial of God's reality. . . . He cannot be composed of and so dependent upon severable constituents, physical or metaphysical, as then he would himself be conditional."[45]

Indeed, in an essay that has Bradshaw's work explicitly in view, Hart contests the notion that the Greek and Latin fathers differ in any significant way about divine simplicity.[46] Denying that Gregory of Nyssa holds that "the divine names apply only to the divine energies and not to the divine essence," Hart points out that "if the divine energies are genuine *manifestations* of God, however limited, then whatever names apply to the energies also necessarily apply to the essence, even if only defectively, immeasurably remotely, incomprehensibly,

---

42. Hart, *Beauty of the Infinite*, 204n75. Along similar lines, see also the sources cited above in nn. 2 and 14 of this chap.

43. Ibid., 174.

44. Hart, *Experience of God*, 134.

45. Ibid.

46. Sadly, Nikolaos Loudovikos responds to Hart's critique of Bradshaw by invoking the authority of anti-Thomism: "Hart is a gifted theologian, with a passionate devotion to the theology of participation, expressed by authors such as Gregory of Nyssa and especially Aquinas. But Hart seems not to be bothered by the pantheisizing passivity, the intellectualism, and the necessary identification of God with his revelation of the world to which his Thomist persuasions have led him" ("Striving for Participation," 147). In light of such polemics, I hope that the present chapter (and chap. 1 on the divine ideas) will be received by my readers as an exercise in theological contemplation rather than as yet another contribution to an unfortunate internecine squabble. In challenging specific readings of Aquinas put forward by Lossky and Bradshaw, I do not mean to suggest that Orthodox theology is unorthodox.

and 'improperly.'"[47] Turning directly to Bradshaw's arguments, Hart argues that for the Greek fathers no less than for the Latin fathers, "the divine essence and divine attributes are identical. . . . As the Damascene says, it is solely *because* God's attributes are, properly speaking, convertible with one another in the simplicity of his essence that we cannot comprehend what they are in him."[48] Hart concludes by pairing Gregory of Nyssa and Augustine: "Augustine's view does not differ significantly from Gregory of Nyssa's, as expressed in the first chapter of the *Oratio catechetica*: that we must assert that the divine will must be the same as divine goodness and commensurate with divine omnipotence, for otherwise we would introduce complexity and mutability *into the divine simplicity*."[49]

47. Hart, "Hidden and the Manifest," 212n38. As Hart observes in this same footnote,

> For all of the Cappadocians, we come to know anything of God only through his operations (or energies, if one prefers the Greek word); but none of them ever suggests that what is revealed of God therein is true of the energies alone (the Cappadocians were not Nominalists). Gregory [of Nyssa], certainly, has no notion of the divine energies as concretely other than or really distinct from God in himself—indeed, he explicitly rejects such a notion (*Contra Eunomium* 1 [GNO 2:87])—and I doubt it would have occurred to him or any of his contemporaries to speak of what *belongs* only to God's "energies" or "operations," even if the words we use of God are, from our side, names of those operations. (ibid.)

Hart adds that John of Damascus holds to the same position, rather than separating the energies from the essence:

> John of Damascus . . . argues that, while the "names" or "attributes" proper to God himself apply to the divine essence, we must not imagine that they are true of God in a plural way, which we could then understand; in God, who is infinitely simple, all of these attributes are one and identical with one another, and if we think of them in a composite fashion then we think of them as something outside his nature or as mere energies (which they are *not*); at the same time, as discrete predications, the positive names we apply to God "describe" God's nature, but still cannot "explain" God's essence to us (*De fide Orthodoxa* 1.9). John goes on to say that those attributes proper to "the whole God" (as opposed to the trinitarian relations) are attributes *of the essence*—which, nonetheless, we never understand in itself, just as we never understand the essence of anything merely by knowing its attributes. (ibid.)

Since Hart is defending analogous naming of God here, see also Hart, "Destiny of Christian Metaphysics."

48. Hart, "Hidden and the Manifest," 213n40. Thus, Hart challenges the "fanciful idea that there has always been some great difference between eastern and western patristic traditions regarding the nature of divine simplicity" (ibid.).

49. Ibid. See also the summary of the contributions of Basil the Great and Gregory of Nyssa in Holmes, "Simple Salvation?," 40–42; as well as Ayres, *Nicaea and Its Legacy*, 133–221, 273–301, 344–63. Hart's argument for the congruence of Greek and Latin patristic views of divine simplicity is at least partly in accord with Andrew Radde-Gallwitz's thesis that Basil and Gregory transformed the doctrine of divine simplicity in light of God's incomprehensibility. According to Radde-Gallwitz, Basil and Gregory hold both that "a certain class of divine attributes should be viewed as propria of the divine nature" and that these "propria do not define the essence. God's propria of goodness, wisdom, power, justice, and truth do not tell us what it is to be God," since our complex mode of knowing cannot know the simple God

Even so, what about Bradshaw's concerns that the doctrine of divine simplicity as articulated by Aquinas negates divine free will in creating? Does God's simplicity require—as Bradshaw suggests—solely that all of God's actions be perfectly actual? Or does simplicity in fact require that all of God's actions be (in God) identical to each other and to God's essence? All parties can agree in denying that "the particular determinations of God's will in time [i.e., created realities] are aspects of the divine essence," but is Aquinas right to defend "Augustine's claim that God wills all things in a single eternal act"?[50] For Aquinas, unless God's act is the same as his essence, then composition has been introduced into God, and God could not truly be the creator, because as a composite he would be in need of a cause, and could not be the source of all finite being.[51] Does Aquinas's position, then, allow for God's freedom in creating?

Aquinas on Divine Simplicity and Composition

In order to understand the issue more clearly, let me examine in more detail Aquinas's denial that the simplicity of the creator God can be squared with

---

(*Basil of Caesarea, Gregory of Nyssa, and the Transformation of Divine Simplicity*, 225). Hart would fully agree, as would Augustine and Aquinas. Radde-Gallwitz critiques Bradshaw's interpretation of Gregory of Nyssa on a number of grounds, and he rejects Bradshaw's effort to "make the goodness an *energeia* that in no way characterizes or reflects the divine *ousia*" (223). As Radde-Gallwitz says in response to Bradshaw, "To speak of divine *energeiai* that in no way reflect the nature or life of God is to pursue a line of argument not open to Gregory, given his concern to root the divine goods necessarily in the divine nature" (224). However, Radde-Gallwitz also argues that "Gregory's distinction between essence and substance allowed him to draw the distinction between common properties, which name the substance, and the essence, which is utterly unknowable" (216), and that Gregory defends the real multiplicity of God's properties, since otherwise God (in his perfect simplicity) could not be perfect. Radde-Gallwitz therefore holds that Gregory affirms "the non-identical relation between the goods and the divine nature (and among the goods)," and thus "Gregory's understanding of simplicity differs from the standard Thomist understanding" (221). By contrast, I think that Gregory of Nyssa's viewpoint, when placed in the context of all that he is trying to say, can be squared with Aquinas's position along the lines that Hart proposes.

50. Hart, "Hidden and the Manifest," 213n40. Hart is not referring to Aquinas here.

51. Dolezal, indebted to many earlier commentators, reminds us that for Aquinas no real distinction between "existence" and "essence" in God is possible, because "there can be nothing prior to God in the way that *esse* and *essentia* are prior to the complete *ens* in any created thing. If there were such priority to God then he could not be the first cause of all things and would himself need some extrinsic agent back of him to account for his actuality" (*God without Parts*, 65). Dolezal remarks earlier that Aquinas "speaks of divine 'substance' in an analogical and accommodated sense. . . . God is like a substance inasmuch as he is a complete being *per se* and does not exist by inherence in some other subject. But he is not a substance in the sense of being classified within a logical or natural genus (substance being the most common genus) or standing under any accidents" (60–61). For the difference between this understanding of "essence" (and "existence") and that of analytic philosophers and theologians, see Oderberg, *Real Essentialism*; see also the various discussions of this point in Duby, *Divine Simplicity*.

any kind of composition. In his treatment of divine simplicity in *Summa theologiae* I, question 3, Aquinas begins by addressing the numerous biblical texts that depict God anthropomorphically. He does so in light of his argument in question 2 that God must be pure act, because otherwise God would depend upon another for actuality. As I noted above, this understanding of God as pure act is necessary to exclude the notion that God is a being among beings. God can be the source and cause of all finite being, the *creator*, only if God ontologically transcends all finite being.[52] If divine being were finite, God could not "produce [finite] being absolutely," since no finite "being can produce a being absolutely, except forasmuch as it causes *being* in *this*."[53]

But even if God is not composite in the sense of being bodily or temporal, could God be composite in another way? For example, could God live by his life or be God by his Godhead (or divinity), so that *God* would be metaphysically distinct from his *Godhead*? In this regard, Aquinas admits that we have no way to think about God other than by imagining him as some kind of composite.[54] We cannot think of "God" without enumerating various divine formalities, such as "life," "Godhead," and so forth. In our thinking, we have no choice but to distinguish multiple powers and attributes of God, because to conceive of God requires that we conceive of a number of different perfections

---

52. This point is missing from the late Stephen H. Webb's proposal that "matter is one of the perfections of the divine" and that "division [or participation in divine matter] cannot be alien to God's nature"("*Creatio a Materia ex Christi*," 77). See also Webb, *Jesus Christ, Eternal God*. For versions of "the idea of God as the body of the world," an idea that Webb finds "congenial to my own approach" (Webb, "*Creatio a Materia ex Christi*," 78n5), see, e.g., Keller, *Face of the Deep*; Keller, "Energy We Are"; and Crain, "God Embodied in, God Bodying forth the World." The latter two works are appreciatively cited by Webb. I reviewed Keller's *Face of the Deep* in *Theological Studies* 66 (2005): 905–7. For the view that the God of the (Hebrew) Bible is consistently embodied, see Sommer, *Bodies of God and the World of Ancient Israel*. For further background, see Mark S. Smith, *Early History of God*. See also the valuable biblical theology (Old and New Testaments) of God's unity set forth by Feldmeier and Spieckermann, *God of the Living*, 93–124.

53. *ST* I, q. 45, a. 5 and ad 1. As Harm Goris remarks,

> One should not understand by this that God gives a kind of generic being, while created causes subsequently determine and particularize it. For Aquinas, "to be" is not a univocal, generic notion, but "the actuality of each thing," "more intimate and deeper than anything else." As each cause operates at a different level, the divine one on the transcendental level of being itself, and the created one on the level of its categorical determinations, there is no competition between the two, nor is there mutual exclusion. . . . God's incomprehensible act of giving being as such, including its modal qualifications, allows us to say that the Creator sustains the causal action of creatures and gives being to their effects in accordance with the necessity or contingency of the secondary causes. ("Divine Foreknowledge, Providence, Predestination, and Human Freedom," 114–15)

54. Thus, Robert M. Burns assumes that God can only exist in the way that we conceive him to exist, and Burns therefore turns God into an irreducibly complex (if internally harmonious) set of internal factors or properties; see Burns, "Divine Simplicity in St. Thomas."

and activities. In God himself, however, there is no real difference between the divine essence and all that pertains to God. As Aquinas repeatedly observes, God not only is his own nature or essence, but also his nature or essence is infinite actuality, infinite "to be" or *actus essendi*. Otherwise God would be "not essential, but participated being."[55] Since his essence is existence, he has absolutely no composition whatsoever. His essence literally cannot enter into composition with anything else, because nothing can be added to it.

Yet, just as a hot flame could be red or white, could there not be powers or attributes of God that differ from God's essence while still having divine status? This is, of course, Bradshaw's contention, in accord with his interpretation of Palamas. Could God be analogously similar to a hot flame, whose whiteness or redness is like a power of God that is divine but that does not pertain to the divine essence? Here Aquinas answers no, on the grounds that "although every essence may have something superadded to it, this cannot apply to absolute being."[56] If the divine essence had anything similar to the hot flame's whiteness, which is in the flame but not essential to the flame, the divine essence would be a composite of a certain kind; and if so, then the divine essence could not be *the same as* existence. Absolute and primal being is infinite being; its essence, therefore, cannot enter into composition with anything because it possesses the infinite fullness of existence.[57]

The seventh and eighth articles of question 3 make this point directly. In article 7, Aquinas asks whether God is altogether simple. In the objections of article 7, he places the issue of composition at the forefront. The first objection notes that everything that God has created is a composite of some kind. Since this is so, and since all things imitate God's goodness and come from God—"for from him and through him and to him are all things" (Rom. 11:36)—it would seem that all things bear witness to the fact that God, too, is a composite.[58] Although Aquinas does not give the example of the soul and its powers, this

55. *ST* I, q. 3, a. 4.
56. *ST* I, q. 3, a. 6.
57. As Aquinas observes (ibid.) further on, "It must be said that every being in any way existing is from God. For whatever is found in anything by participation, must be caused in it by that to which it belongs essentially. . . . Now it has been shown above (q. 3, a. 4) when treating of the divine simplicity that God is the essentially self-subsisting Being; and also it was shown (q. 11, aa. 3, 4) that subsisting being must be one; as, if whiteness were self-subsisting, it would be one, since whiteness is multiplied by its recipients. Therefore all beings apart from God are not their own being, but are beings by participation. Therefore it must be that all things which are diversified by the diverse participations of being, so as to be more or less perfect, are caused by one First Being, who possesses being most perfectly" (I, q. 44, a. 1). Aquinas adds that "from the fact that a thing has being by participation, it follows that it is caused" (ad 1).
58. Aquinas cites Rom. 11:36 in the crucial *sed contra* of *ST* I, q. 44, a. 1, where he asks whether it is necessary that every being be created by God.

example would be apropos: the soul (as the image of God) exhibits the goodness of a certain kind of composition, and it might seem that the creator God, source of all goodness, must analogously possess composition. The second objection moves along broadly similar lines, but this time by beginning with creatures rather than with God. In creatures, we can see that complex, composite things are better than more "simple" things: "Thus, chemical compounds [*corpora mixta*] are better than simple elements, and animals than the parts that compose them."[59] Likewise, if God is utterly simple, then it seems as though God would be less good than if he were composite in certain ways. As Bradshaw suggests, a God whose actions are composite (while essentially simple because infinitely actual) might be more powerful in freely creating and deifying, than would a God who possessed no kind of composition.

Aquinas's responses to these objections build upon the earlier articles of question 3, in which he has shown that God cannot be a composite of body and soul, of matter and form, of nature and individual supposit, of essence and existence, of genus and specific difference, of subject and accident, of primal cause and secondary causes or effects, or of actuality and potency. The key aspect involves essence and existence: once composition is ruled out with respect to essence and existence, then whatever has divine existence is the divine essence, and cannot be different from the divine essence in any way.[60] There can be no metaphysical composition or differentiated unity between any attribute/action of God and any other attribute/action of God, or between any attribute of God and the divine essence.[61] Aquinas remarks that if there

59. *ST* I, q. 3, a. 7, obj. 2. Aquinas here anticipates the objection of Dawkins, if only Dawkins knew it!

60. Dolezal points out that "Thomas's greatest contribution to the advancement of the DDS [doctrine of divine simplicity] is found in his teaching that every created thing, even relatively simple things such as human souls and angelic spirits, are [*sic*] at the very least composed of existence and essence. No created essence is identical with its act of existence and is therefore relative and dependent in some sense. But God's essence is identical with his existence and therefore God is absolutely necessary and self-sufficient" (*God without Parts*, 7; cf. 31–66). Dolezal also draws attention to how John Duns Scotus defends divine simplicity (lacking any composition) on the grounds of God's infinity: each attribute of God must be infinite and therefore cannot be less than fully God (see 7–8; cf. 77–81). For further discussion of Scotus's contribution, see Cross, *Duns Scotus on God*, 99–114. Lest such defenses of divine simplicity be imagined to be solely the province of Catholic theology, Dolezal cites similar defenses of divine simplicity (and rejection of composition in God) offered by theologians from Dolezal's own Reformed tradition, including Bavinck, *Reformed Dogmatics*, 2:176. For the significant contributions of Protestant scholastics such as Girolamo Zanchi, Amandus Polanus, John Owen, Francis Turretin, Peter van Mastricht, Bartholomäus Keckermann, Johann Alsted, and Johannes Maccovius, see Duby, *Divine Simplicity*. See also Muller, *Post-Reformation Reformed Dogmatics*.

61. By contrast, the argument could be made that since the divine persons are entitatively identical to the divine essence while still being really distinct from one another (without negating divine simplicity), then a similar kind of distinction for other things in God is possible. On this

were any composition of any kind, then the "parts" (or differentiated attributes/actions) that composed the "divine" would be in a *relation of potency* to the whole; they would be actualized as components of the whole. Indeed, "in wholes made up of similar parts, although something which is predicated of the whole may be predicated of a part (as a part of air is air, and a part of water, water), nevertheless certain things are predicable of the whole which cannot be predicated of any of the parts."[62]

This part-whole relationship certainly seems to be present in Bradshaw's God, composed of the ineffable essence and the energies or powers that diversely manifest that essence. For example, although all the energies are divine, some are not eternal—even though the essence is not less than eternal, and even though eternity is a divine attribute. The real differentiation of the divine energies means that the energies, though divine, are less than the whole of the "divine." Likewise, insofar as the divine energies are the manifestations of the divine essence, the divine essence is greater than a particular divine energy (such as divine foreknowledge or the divine creative act, both of which Bradshaw thinks come to an end). Composition is present here, not least in the fact that the divine energies, in their multiplicity, have a certain "potency" to the wholeness of the divinity.

The key point for Aquinas is that "nothing composite can be predicated of any single one of its parts."[63] Just as a human arm is not a human, if there is a component of God that is not absolutely and completely God, then God is a composite. And if God is a composite, then in God "either one of the parts actuates another, or at least all the parts are potential to the whole."[64] In such a case, there would be divine parts or aspects that in fact are not fully God, and therefore would not truly merit the name "divine." Thus Bradshaw's view that divine simplicity means solely that all God's powers are fully in act and never acted upon overlooks the fundamental problem of composition. In God, there cannot be parts, lesser elements, or potency.[65]

---

view, the divine attributes could be identical to the divine essence, but not to each other. I think this view is mistaken, however. The divine persons do not divide or differentiate the essence in any way, since the persons are distinct only vis-à-vis each other, not vis-à-vis the essence. If the divine attributes, which pertain to the divine essence, were really identical to the essence but not really identical to each other (in God, not simply in our mode of thinking), then the difference between the divine attributes vis-à-vis each other would introduce differentiation—and metaphysical composition—into the divine essence.

62. *ST* I, q. 3, a. 7.
63. Ibid.
64. Ibid.
65. Ibid.

If we return to the two objections in article 7—God need not be absolutely simple because his creatures (which reflect his goodness) are not absolutely simple, and a complex thing is always better than a simpler thing—we find that the answers to these objections are straightforward. Namely, attempting to conceive of God's simplicity in a manner that allows for composition (such as the composition found in the soul and its powers) means that one ends up conceiving a mere creature rather than God. Aquinas notes that "it is of the essence of a [caused] thing to be in some sort composite; because at least its existence differs from its essence."[66] Thus, the fact that all things that God has created reflect God's goodness, and that all these things are composite, does not mean that God is composite. Similarly, responding to the objection that complex material creatures are greater than less complex ones, Aquinas points out that this is "because the perfection of created goodness cannot be found in one simple thing, but in many things."[67] To imitate God's perfection, creatures must be and do many things. But the mystery of God's perfection is that God is perfectly simple. God's infinite actuality is not the product of many powers, as it would necessarily be if we conceived it in finite terms. Rather, God's infinite actuality, as sheer infinite fullness, entails perfect simplicity, utter lack of any kind of composition.[68]

In article 8, the question is whether the simple God can, nonetheless, enter into composition with his creatures. Bradshaw argues for the value of the divine energies in this regard, on the grounds that even if the divine essence cannot enter into composition with creatures, nonetheless grace and deification require the synergistic composition made possible by the activity of the divine energies. For his part, Aquinas thinks of God along the lines of an unlimited "form," and as the "exemplar" or "formal" cause of the being of things.[69] It would seem, however, that a "form" is precisely set up to enter into composition, as in the composition of form and matter. Surely, too, the divine cannot merely be extrinsically related to creatures as an efficient cause. If God cannot enter into some kind of composition with creatures, then how can God really have anything to do with creatures? This is Bradshaw's question, as we saw.

66. Ibid., ad 1.
67. Ibid., ad 2.
68. Dolezal notes that "since subsistent existent is unlimited and non-contracted, the absolute infinity of God is ontologically explained by his absolute simplicity"; it is divine "simplicity that provides the ontological conditions for God's absolutely infinite mode of life and perfection and sets it apart from all relatively infinite creaturely forms" (*God without Parts*, 81).
69. *ST* I, q. 3, a. 8, ad 2.

Aquinas strenuously resists the view that God (or the divine) must somehow enter into composition with creatures, a view that has a long philosophical history. His central point is this: "That which enters into composition with anything does not act primarily and essentially, but rather the composite so acts."[70] If God did not act "primarily and essentially"—that is to say, if God were not essentially act—God's essence would not be existence. And if this were so, then God would be a composite of essence and existence. The only way for God to enter into composition with creatures would be for God not to be God. As Aquinas observes, "No part of a compound can be absolutely primal among beings."[71] To be "absolutely primal" requires being pure actuality. How then is God the exemplar or formal cause of all things? God is so because all creatures are in some way imitations or reflections of the creator, since their finite being and goodness are created and belong to them by participation.

But does this inability to enter into composition make God extrinsic to creatures, as Bradshaw fears? It depends, I think, upon how we understand "efficient causality." God's efficient causality is not mechanistic and distant, like that of a watchmaker to a watch. Even among creatures, Aquinas notes that "an agent must be joined to that wherein it acts immediately, and touch it by its power."[72] This is unfathomably much more the case with God's creative agency, although of course God does not "move" in creating.[73] Aquinas

70. *ST* I, q. 3, a. 8.
71. Ibid.
72. *ST* I, q. 8, a. 1.
73. See *ST* I, q. 45, a. 3, ad 1: "Creation signified actively means the divine action, which is God's essence, with a relation to the creature. But in God relation to the creature is not a real relation, but only a relation of reason; whereas the relation of the creature to God is a real relation, as was said above (q. 13, a. 7)." Aquinas adds that "creation imports a relation of the creature to the Creator, with a certain newness or beginning" (ad 3). Here Dolezal's clarification is helpful:

> It should be noted that the classical DDS does not deny that God possesses active potency [the power to bring about a change] in some sense. As Weigel informs us, "Active potency *is* attributed to God as the first efficient cause, but not in the same way in which creatures have it. Creatures change and become further actualized when they use their powers. God does not." This is because the creature is ontologically correlative to those things upon which its active power operates so that effecting new forms of reality in others entails the appearance of a new relation in the creaturely agent. But Thomas rejects such correlativity between God and those things to which his active potency extends in operation. (*God without Parts*, 39, citing Weigel, *Aquinas on Simplicity*, 93)

See also Duby, *Divine Simplicity*, for the point that a reference to creatures does not alter or add to the Triune God's infinite actuality. God's will to create must not, therefore, be conceived as a further actualization of God, let alone a limiting of God. For discussion of the meaning of God's lack of "real relation" to creatures, a topic that has often provoked deep

observes that "since God is very being by his own essence, created being must be his proper effect; as to ignite is the proper effect of fire. Now God causes this effect in things not only when they first begin to be, but as long as they are preserved in being."[74] God is like a "fire" of "to be"; his infinite "to be" creates finite beings and sustains their being at every instant of their existence. This efficient causality is not like a match that lights the candle and then is taken away, with the candle now burning on its own. Rather, it is far more intimate: it is like a fire that burns at the very heart of all finite being. Indeed, according to Aquinas, "as long as a thing has being, God must be present to it," and present in the deepest, "innermost" way, since there is nothing more interior to a thing than a thing's being.[75] Harm Goris comments insightfully in this regard that "'presence' and 'causation' are said analogously of the Eternal One and of the Creator, and signify modes of presence and of causation that elude our grasp."[76] As we saw in chapter 1, precisely because God is

---

misunderstanding, see Weinandy, *Does God Change?*, 88–96. As Weinandy states, "To create demands that God acts by no other act than the pure act that he is as *ipsum esse* for no other act is capable of such an effect. But if the act of creation demands that God act by no other act than by the act that he is as *ipsum esse* then obviously creation does not change or affect God. The whole effect is in the creature precisely because it is in being related to God as *ipsum esse* that he comes to be" (92).

74. *ST* I, q. 8, a. 1. Weinandy rightly emphasizes that "God as pure act must be immutable not only because he is pure act, but also, since creation demands a cause that is pure act, he must by necessity be immutable to be creator. If God changed or was affected by the act of creation, it would mean that he acted by some act other than pure act, which is impossible both because God is pure act and can have no other act, and because no act other than pure act can create" (*Does God Change?*, 92).

75. *ST* I, q. 8, a. 1.

76. Goris, "Divine Foreknowledge, Providence, Predestination, and Human Freedom," 115. See also his observation at 110: "The relative expression 'being present to' has an analogous meaning when God fills in the blank. We can understand that a temporal being is present to another temporal being or event, or that it is past or future to it. But we do not know exactly what it means when a temporal being is said to be present to the eternal God. For if we did, we would also understand what God's own mode of being, eternity, is." Goris rightly adds, "It does not follow that 'being present to God' is just idle and nugatory talk" (ibid.). Similarly, Étienne Gilson distinguishes Christian understanding of God's creative causality from Greek philosophical understanding:

> On the Greek side stands a god who is doubtless the cause of all being, including its intelligibility, efficiency and finality—all, save existence itself; on the Christian side a God Who causes the very existence of being. On the Greek side we have a universe eternally informed or eternally moved; on the Christian side a universe which begins to be by a creation. On the Greek side, stands a universe contingent in the order of intelligibility or in the order of becoming; on the Christian side a universe contingent in the order of existence. On the Greek side, there is the immanent finality of an order interior to beings; on the Christian side the transcendent finality of a Providence who creates the very being of order along with that of the things ordered. (*Spirit of Medieval Philosophy*, 81; cited in Dolezal, *God without Parts*, 113–14n68)

ontologically transcendent, his efficient causality is so intimate and interior, so unfathomably present and immediate, that "nothing is distant from Him, as if it could be without God in itself."[77]

Furthermore, in rational creatures God is present not only as cause of being (and as "formal cause" inasmuch as beings are true and good), but also as the "object" of the spiritual acts of rational creatures. By graced knowledge and love of God, rational creatures enjoy the Triune God's presence through a personal relationship, a friendship. Sanctifying grace unites us to the persons of the Trinity: we gain "the power of enjoying the divine person," since "the divine person himself is given" by grace.[78] Even though the rational creature is ontologically other than God, therefore, our friendship with God cannot be characterized as "extrinsic," since even on earth the saints experience such friendship as more intimate than even the most intimate human marriage. In the beatific union with God, its intimacy will be inexpressible.[79]

In short, it seems to me that Aquinas is correct that God is not composite in any way. A composite God could not be the infinitely powerful, infinitely "present," infinitely generous creator God. Nothing that is "divine" enters into or possesses any kind of composition, since if it did it would be finite and unable to be the source of all finite being. *Pace* Bradshaw, in order for God to be the free creator, God must be utterly simple not only insofar as all of God's actions are pure actuality, but also insofar as all that is divine is none other than the simple God.

A Free Act of Creation

Henceforth, I will presume that no kind of composition can in fact apply to God. Yet I still must address Bradshaw's fundamental concern that the view of divine simplicity advocated by Aquinas (among others) negates the freedom of God in creating. This concern is a particularly pressing one in much contemporary philosophical theology, as can be seen in Ryan Mullins's recent essay "Simply Impossible: A Case against Divine Simplicity," in which Mullins argues that "all that is needed to show that divine simplicity is false" is "the claim that God is free."[80] If God's will is the same thing as God's being, how can there really be a distinction between *free will* and *necessary will* in God?

---

77. *ST* I, q. 8, a. 1, ad 3. For elaboration of this point, see Weinandy, *Does God Suffer?*
78. *ST* I, q. 43, a. 3 and ad 1. For discussion, see Emery, *Trinitarian Theology of Saint Thomas Aquinas*, 392–95.
79. For reflection upon eternal life, see Gaine, *Will There Be Free Will in Heaven?* See also Levering, *Jesus and the Demise of Death*, chap. 7.
80. Mullins, "Simply Impossible," 199. An unpublished essay by Thomas McCall drew my attention to Mullins's work.

How could God's will be different than it is, since if it were different, God's being would be different? If God's will could not be different, then creation is not free, but rather is a natural emanation from the Godhead.

My answer to this conundrum begins with God's infinite actuality, which supereminently and in an incomprehensibly simple manner possesses all perfections. God's causality of creatures must therefore be conceived analogously. As James Dolezal observes, we must not imagine that God's will, like ours, has a beginning or inheres in God as an "accident determining him to be this or that way."[81] The fact that God's will is pure act, however, does not mean that his necessary willing of his goodness renders creation necessary. What is excluded, instead, is the notion that God's will moves from an original indeterminacy to a decision to create, as though God's actuality could change or as though there were a God "prior to" the creator. This emphasis on the fact that the divine will (as infinite actuality) does not change does not make creation necessary; it simply confirms that the creator God truly is God, rather than a finite cause or mere being among beings. The essential point is well expressed by David Hart: "God's will . . . encompasses the whole span of his power and being, and is therefore perfectly free; all that God wills belongs naturally (though not necessarily) to that one eternal act whereby he wills his own goodness."[82]

How does Aquinas defend this position in the *Summa theologiae*? He first notes that God's act—analogously rather than univocally understood vis-à-vis created act—has only God as its (infinite) end. This entails that there is only one simple divine act, rather than many divine acts. How then can God will to create things other than God? Surely if God wills to create things other than God, he has other goals, other objects, that differentiate his will and action(s)? Bradshaw raises this objection particularly in view of Aquinas's claim that God wills "to communicate by likeness" God's own good, insofar as this can be communicated.[83] If God wills to communicate his goodness (and thereby to create creatures), surely this is distinct from solely willing himself as good.

In reply, Aquinas explains in article 2 of question 19 that when God wills himself as good, God infinitely wills infinite goodness. Within that one act of will, God can will "himself as the end, and other things as ordained to that end; inasmuch as it befits the divine goodness that other things should be partakers therein."[84] This willing of himself and willing of creatures need not require two acts of will, because creatures are befitting to the one "end"

81. Dolezal, *God without Parts*, 202.
82. Hart, "Hidden and the Manifest," 213n40.
83. *ST* I, q. 19, a. 2.
84. Ibid.

of the divine goodness that God wills. In the same act of willing his own in-finite goodness, God can will creatures as ordered to that goodness, without any change in his will, since the end of the volitional act is his goodness.[85] Admittedly, one cannot conceive of an act in which willing to communicate good to another is the very same act as willing one's own goodness. Aquinas, however, suggests that we can at least conceive analogously of such a supreme act of generous willing: "If natural things, in so far as they are perfect, com-municate their good to others, much more does it appertain to the divine will to communicate by likeness its own good to others as much as possible."[86] Given the will's natural inclination to communicate its own goodness to oth-ers, God's infinitely perfect (and thus ineffably mysterious) act of will can surely contain the communication of goodness to creatures. Put another way, if it belongs "to the nature of the will to communicate as far as possible to others the good possessed," then it should not surprise us that the infinite divine will, in perfectly willing the divine goodness, communicates its good-ness to creatures—a communication in which the change is all on the side of the creatures, not on the side of the divine will.[87]

Yet this approach seems to endanger God's freedom in creating, which may seem to be a necessary act of his self-diffusive will. Turning in article 3 of question 19 to the issue of whether God wills creatures freely, therefore, Aquinas lists some powerful objections. First, it seems that God could not will creatures by his one divine act of will, which is absolutely the same as his nature, in a mode that could truly be called "free." Second, surely God's will is absolute "to be," but if it were possible for God to will things that he does not will, then God's will would be a site of possibility and contingency, not of pure actuality (which has no potency whatever). Third, since all agree that God knows everything necessarily, there seems to be no room for God's will to be different, especially since God wills himself necessarily.

In his *respondeo*, Aquinas offers an analogy from creatures for under-standing how God's free will can be included within his necessary will. Namely,

---

85. See also *ST* I, q. 45, a. 3, ad 3, where Aquinas notes that "creation imports a relation of the creature to the Creator" rather than vice versa (given that the change is on the side of the creature, not on the side of God).

86. *ST* I, q. 19, a. 2.

87. Ibid.; cf. I, q. 45, a. 3. Aquinas's analogy comes from the finite will's intrinsic desire, in willing its own goodness, to communicate its own goodness to others. A different analogy is offered by W. Matthews Grant, who suggests that just as agents cause their immanent acts without change to themselves substantially, so God causes creatures without change to himself substantially. See Grant, "Aquinas, Divine Simplicity, and Divine Freedom." This approach hinges upon what it means to change substantially, and therefore may introduce further difficulties without removing the mystery present in any conception of infinitely perfect volition.

one may will to go from Milan to Rome, and this volition may be marked by necessity; but in willing to go to Rome, one does not will necessarily "things without which the end is attainable, such as a horse for a journey which we can take on foot, for we can make the journey without one."[88] Even humans, then, often will an end necessarily and will things conducive to that end freely. Surely God can do the same, and can do so in an infinitely more perfect way so that (unlike humans) he need not undertake two volitional acts. The transcendence and infinite power of God's will, its infinite activity and fecundity, means that we have no certain grounds for denying that God can will himself—precisely as participated in by other things—in one single act of will, even though we have only weak finite analogues for this transcendent act.[89]

Aquinas adds that God exists absolutely and necessarily, whereas creatures do not. God is the cause for which one does not need to look for a cause, since God alone, as pure act, accounts for his own actuality. It follows that God could be God without creatures, and so his willing of creatures *cannot* have the absolute necessity that his willing of himself has. Creatures are contingent by nature, whereas God is necessary by nature. Yet if God's will is his nature, how is it that God's will vis-à-vis creatures could be in any way otherwise than it is? Although Aquinas clearly affirms that "God can do what He does not," his answer does not rely on God's will actually being different than it is.[90] God's free will, being eternal, does not change. As Aquinas says of God, "supposing that he wills a thing, then he is unable not to will it."[91] Indeed, there is no "moment" in God's eternity in which he does not will all that he wills; there is no God "prior" to God's will to create.[92] In this sense, God *can* be said to will *necessarily* everything that he wills. The potency or possibility stems not from God's will, but from the contingent nature of the finite things willed; they do not and cannot determine the divine will. Aquinas also emphasizes that since "the divine being is undetermined, and contains

88. *ST* I, q. 19, a. 3.
89. For clarification of the meaning of divine "transcendence" according to Aquinas, see Rocca, "'Creatio ex Nihilo' and the Being of Creatures."
90. *ST* I, q. 25, a. 5.
91. *ST* I, q. 19, a. 3.
92. Some might think that because God is free and omnipotent, there must be "moments" or "formalities" in God (or in the divine nature per se) that are open to other possible worlds, although God has eternally willed this world. But, as Dolezal comments, because God's will is absolutely eternal, "there has never been a temporal or logical 'moment' in the divine life in which God stood volitionally open to other possible worlds. The actual world is conditionally necessary and every other possible world is conditionally impossible by virtue of the fact that God has *eternally* willed this particular world" (*God without Parts*, 207). Had God freely willed a different world, that world would have been necessary because of the eternal immutability of the divine will.

in himself the full perfection of being, it cannot be that he acts by a necessity of his nature, unless he were to cause something undetermined and infinite in being."[93] Finite things *cannot* be created necessarily, that is to say, with the same necessity with which God wills himself.

For Aquinas, therefore, the necessary and free modes of God's one will can be distinguished but not separated, because God's free creative will is his one eternal will (pure act). We know that in willing himself necessarily, God—in the very same act of willing, since God's infinitely actual will does not change or alter in any way—wills finite things freely in accord with their contingent mode of being. But we cannot say more, due to the limits of our analogous knowledge of God. As Michael Dodds observes, "The operation of God's will infinitely exceeds the capacity of our thought and language."[94] Paradoxically, given Bradshaw's denunciation on his book's last page of the "rationalist ideology" of Western "scholasticism," Aquinas's position insists upon apophatic caution when speaking of the creator God's utterly simple will.[95] Despite the appropriate role of analogy, since the true God really is the free creator, nothing that God is or does should be conceived along the lines of creaturely composite being and action.

Thus, Aquinas deliberately explains less than Bradshaw's account of the divine energies tries to explain. In Bradshaw, we find that some of God's energies or actions, such as creation and foreknowledge, are divine but not eternal. Bradshaw thereby seeks to illumine for us precisely how God's will and knowledge of creatures do not and cannot partake of the same necessity as God's will and knowledge of himself—although Bradshaw also utterly veils the divine essence. By contrast, in Aquinas we find that all of God's acts (and attributes) are none other than the utterly simple divine essence, with certain distinctions

93. *ST* I, q. 19, a. 5. Aquinas adds that the divine existence, divine knowledge, and divine will are in themselves necessary, but the divine will differs from the divine knowledge in that the will is ordered to "things as they exist in themselves" (I, q. 19, a. 3, ad 6). This accounts for the difference between God's necessary knowledge of *all* finite things and God's free willing of *some* finite things.

94. Dodds, *Unchanging God of Love*, 180. Citing Dodds, Dolezal states at the end of his discussion, "It should readily be confessed that the exact function of free will in God who is himself pure act is beyond the scope of human knowledge. Just as we cannot comprehend God as *ipsum esse subsistens*, we cannot comprehend the identity between God as eternal, immutable, pure act and his will for the world as free and uncoerced. Though we discover strong reasons for confessing both simplicity and freedom in God, we cannot form an isomorphically adequate notion of *how* this is the case" (*God without Parts*, 210).

95. Bradshaw, *Aristotle East and West*, 277. With regard to apophatic caution, Paul Gavrilyuk comments: "The function of apophatic qualifications, such as 'God is impassible', is fairly modest: it spells out the truth that emotionally coloured characteristics should not be conceived entirely along the lines of their human analogies" (*Suffering of the Impassible God*, 62).

that are true about God, such as that God supereminently possesses intellect and will, and that God wills himself necessarily (as befits necessary being) and wills creatures freely (as befits contingent being). These distinctions are true, but they are hedged in by apophatic qualifications. Although we have analogies, only in eternal life will we see—though still not fully comprehend—how God's eternal necessary willing of himself, which is also his free willing of himself as participated in by finite beings (which do not relationally change God's infinite actuality in any way), is the one simple divine act.[96]

Conclusion

I agree with David Burrell's remark about the simplicity of the Triune God: "The affirmation of simpleness," he writes, "is offered as an attempt to formulate 'the distinction' [between God and creation]. There is, in short, no simpleness but God's simpleness."[97] Burrell is right to emphasize that we cannot formulate a concept of what it means to be simple, absolutely speaking. The reason for this is that we do not know what it is to be infinite actuality.[98] The beings with which we are directly acquainted are all composite beings. And, as Rudi te Velde points out, if God were composite in any way, then God would be merely "one [being] amidst others, particularized within the common space of being," whence follows te Velde's well-grounded assertion: "The way of *simplicitas* leads ultimately to the identity in God of essence and being."[99] Nevertheless, although we cannot understand what it means for God to be simple, we *can* still affirm *the fact* of divine simplicity, because (as Norris Clarke puts it) "God can have no real composition of really distinct

96. See also Dolezal, *God without Parts*, 134–37; Duby, *Divine Simplicity*.

97. Burrell, *Knowing the Unknowable God*, 46. As Oliva Blanchette observes, therefore: Metaphysics, more than anything else in philosophy, has to do with the question of transcendence, especially the kind of transcendence that is presupposed in properly religious belief. . . . Metaphysics may not begin with any idea of God in mind, but pushed to its ultimate limit, metaphysics ends up with such an idea, as of something that is totally transcendent to anything that can be given in our experience. As a rational discourse it is an ontology, a science of being as being, not a theology, much less an ontotheology. If the idea of God or of the first universal Cause enters into its discourse, it is not as part of what is taken to be its subject, namely, being, which is inclusive of all that we can know immediately in experience, or mediately by reasoning from effect to cause. God is not known as another thing we can know in the universe, nor can be numbered among the things or finite spirits we do find in the universe. Metaphysics knows God only as totally transcendent to the universe. ("Metaphysics as Preamble to Religious Belief," 145)

98. See Dolezal, *God without Parts*, chap. 4; Wippel, *Metaphysical Thought of Thomas Aquinas*.

99. Te Velde, *Aquinas on God*, 79.

component parts of any kind, because all such compositions require an efficient composing cause," and because God, in order to be God rather than merely yet another finite being, must be absolutely unlimited "*Ipsum Esse Subsistens* (Subsistent To-Be itself), which by that very fact contains within itself the fullness of all possible real perfection."[100] Only the God whose essence is existence—who is thus supremely "simple"—can be the creator and ultimate source of all finite beings.

Even so, this affirmation of the divine simplicity raises a question: Can a simple triune creator God really will himself necessarily *and* will creatures freely (as ordered to himself), while still having one single, fundamentally undifferentiated volitional act that is identical to his act of being? The central problem here, so it seems to me, is that in *our* mode of thinking an act that has both necessary and free aspects, even if it does not necessarily consist of two discrete acts of the will, is still a highly differentiated action that does not fit readily under the label of absolute simplicity.

As we have seen, however, the key to the solution lies in our affirming that God's causality differs radically from creaturely causality. In defending the simplicity of the free creator, therefore, we need solely to show that divine simplicity does not logically entail that God cannot create freely. Certainly, God's willing of himself as participated in by creatures cannot be necessary in the same way that his willing of himself is necessary, since creatures are contingent. This distinction, however, does not mean that God has more than one volitional act. If God wills freely to include contingent creatures in his willing of his own goodness, surely God's infinite actuality can do it without dividing his will, especially since creatures add solely a relation of reason to the creator who is pure act and who does not change in creating. As Maximus the Confessor remarks with appropriate apophatic caution, the creator God is "completely free and simple and existing by itself," and at the same time is beyond "being conceived" by finite minds.[101]

Moreover, the fact that the creator is triune does not alter the divine simplicity. Aquinas would fully agree with Maximus's observation that "neither is the Godhead divisible nor are Father, Son, and Holy Spirit imperfectly God. . . . For there is one and the same essence, power, and act of the Father and Son and Holy Spirit."[102] Since the distinction of the persons does not

---

100. Clarke, *One and the Many*, 231. See also Gaven Kerr, "Aquinas, Stump, and the Nature of a Simple God."

101. Maximus the Confessor, *Chapters on Knowledge* 2.2–3, in *Maximus the Confessor*, 148.

102. Maximus the Confessor, *Chapters on Knowledge* 2.1, in *Maximus the Confessor*, 148. See also in the same volume Maximus's *Church's Mystagogy*, chap. 21, where Maximus praises "the mysterious oneness of the divine simplicity" (203).

arise from distinct acts of the divine essence, the Trinity does not make the divine "essence, power, and act" to be complex rather than simple.[103] Without complexifying the divine essence, the communion of the Father, Son, and Holy Spirit makes clear that creation is not necessary to God: God creates through the Word rather than by a necessary emanation of knowledge, and God creates through the Holy Spirit (who is love in person) rather than needing creatures in order to love.[104]

In sum, if God were not simple, then God could not be infinite actuality, infinite power and fecundity. It is only because God is simple actuality that (as Aquinas says) "creation is the proper act of God alone."[105] Only a simple God could "produce being absolutely," which is what the act of creation involves.[106] And since there is no reason that God could not exist without creation, the "proper act of God" in willing the existence of creatures through his eternal intelligent self-presencing must be supremely free. It follows, I submit, that the Triune God can be freely creative not despite, but precisely because he is simple. Beyond this, nothing more can be said.

---

103. For a superb discussion of why the Trinity does not negate the divine simplicity, see Duby, *Divine Simplicity*.

104. See *ST* I, q. 32, a. 1, ad 3.

105. *ST* I, q. 45, a. 5. See te Velde, *Aquinas on God*, 125, 129–32, 139–42.

106. *ST* I, q. 45, a. 5. Thus Barry Miller is justified in criticizing Richard Swinburne's failure to discern "the rationale of the identity thesis, which has nothing to do with unity in the wider sense, and everything to do with the special unity which is identity. The point is that only a being that is identical with its existence (and hence with its other real properties) can be the *creator* of the universe" (*Most Unlikely God*, 94; cited in Dolezal, *God without Parts*, 143).

THREE

Creatures

And there was evening and there was morning, a sixth day. Thus the heavens and the earth were finished, and all the host of them.

Genesis 1:31–2:1

The Universe of Creatures

Why has the wise and good God created not only birds, fish, animals, and humans, but also profoundly strange things such as billions of dinosaurs and innumerable strange species that are now extinct?[1] It may seem that this

1. Peter Holland notes, "The first dinosaurs evolved around 230 million years ago and diversified into a multitude of species of different sizes, shapes, and habits, until their sudden and famed extinction 65 million years ago" (*Animal Kingdom*, 103). For many scientists, as Christoph Schönborn notes, "What we regard as 'species' are in fact merely 'snapshots' in the great stream of evolution. Everything is just transition and a stage being passed through, and each individual is merely a fluke" (*Chance or Purpose?*, 60). It seems to me, however, that there are "species," in the sense of specific kinds of living things that can be reasonably classed together and that share a particular end or mode of flourishing. On the origins of life on earth, see Charlesworth and Charlesworth, *Evolution*, 53. The Charlesworths describe evolution as "pitiless," but they nonetheless hold that "the vision of the history of life revealed in the fossil record, and in the incredible diversity of species alive today, gives a sense of wonder at the results of more than 3 billion years of evolution" (ibid.). See also Fortey, *Life*, chap. 2, for the theory that life emerged partly due to meteorites called carbonaceous chondrites. Fortey proposes that "the creation of life happened because Earth had a gaseous atmosphere, and water. During the violent genesis of the planet whatever primitive atmosphere that might have been present would have been stripped away, just as the heat at the surface would have prevented the first, mysterious alchemy leading to the appearance of life" (32). He goes on to admit that the origin of life remains fully "the province of speculation" (33). He explains: "This is nothing less than

109

extraordinary and ever-changing diversity of creatures does not accord with or befit either the wisdom of God's ideas or the perfection of God's simplicity. My concern here is not the destruction and death that characterize the physical universe, which Paul Griffiths evocatively describes as "a charnel house, saturated in blood violently shed; an ensemble of inanimate creatures decaying toward extinction; a theater of vice and cruelty."[2] Rather, the challenge that I take up in this chapter is even more fundamental: why a wise and good God willed to create dinosaurs to rule the earth for more than 150 million years and then disappear, to create the sun as merely one among many octillion stars, and to create countless species of which 99.99 percent are now extinct. Why would such unfathomable multitude and such strange diversity, seemingly purposeless, absurd, and wasteful, characterize God's plan of creation?[3] In contemporary secular culture, negative views of creatures appear frequently, as for instance in Philip Kitcher's remark that "we easily might take life as it

---

the transformation of matter itself: to forge the indifferent elements into vital systems that can regenerate themselves. The search for the secret of this transformation is still far from complete, and rendering its myriad steps comprehensible is like trying to summarize what is known of human anatomy on a postcard: the shape might be broadly correct but the detail is inevitably approximate"—to say the least (ibid).

2. Griffiths, *Decreation*, 4. John Henry Newman remarks along broadly similar lines, though with the course of human history in view: "What strikes the mind so forcibly and so painfully is, His absence (If I may so speak) from His own world. It is a silence that speaks. It is as if others had got possession of His work" (*Essay in Aid of a Grammar of Assent*, 396–97; see also Newman, *Apologia pro Vita Sua*, 319–20). With regard to the distortive impact of sin in our relationships with each other and with God, the Gospel of John also often speaks of "the world" in a deeply negative way. Griffiths suggests that the proper theological response to the destruction and suffering that characterize the material universe is to include these aspects among the results of the primal angelic fall, made worse by the temporal fall of humans. He explains that what we see around us is a "damaged cosmos. . . . Traces of the cosmos' surpassing beauty remain, some evident to human creatures and some not. But for the most part, the world appears to human creatures as it is: a charnel house, saturated in blood violently shed; an ensemble of inanimate creatures decaying toward extinction; a theater of vice and cruelty" (*Decreation*, 4). In my view, this description does not sufficiently allow for the value of the material corruption, since without such corruption new things could not come to be. Even so, I certainly do not rule out that some of the nonrational cruelty and devastation that we see may well be the result of the angelic fall. Furthermore, Griffiths's position is preferable to arguing, as Norman Wirzba sometimes seems to do, that the eschatological new creation will simply be God coming back to earth, as though the fundamental problem with earthly life here and now is not destruction and death but rather is the fact that we are not caring for the earth properly (see Wirzba, *From Nature to Creation*, 1–5). For the view that material corruption and death are natural, even though human death is a punishment, see Thomas Aquinas, *On Evil*, q. 5, a. 5, pp. 225–32. See also Randall S. Rosenberg, "Being-toward-a-Death-Transformed"; Lewis, *Problem of Pain*; Blanchette, *Perfection of the Universe according to Aquinas*.

3. Indeed, one might deem the vast multitude of creatures (over space and time) to be a deviation from any "ideas" that a wise God might have and a malevolent falling away from God's simplicity. See Brakke, *Gnostics*.

has been generated on our planet as the handiwork of a bungling, or a chillingly indifferent, god."[4]

How might one respond to the concern that the extraordinary profusion of creatures over the aeons and across the universe's countless trillions of miles is far too random and fleeting to have come from a wise and good creator God? Since Genesis 1 chronicles the six days of the creation of all things, we might expect to find in Genesis 1 an account of the goodness of the huge multitude of creatures that have populated the cosmos. But what modern science now knows about the extreme diversity and strangeness of creatures and about the inconceivable vastness of the universe differs sharply from the serene and tidy portrait delivered by Genesis.[5] Genesis 1 does not answer the questions that our contemporaries urgently ask, such as (in Kenneth Miller's words) "Why should so many nonhuman species have preceded us on this planet?" and "What was God's purpose in allowing evolution to produce the great dinosaurs of the Jurassic?"[6]

It is not surprising, then, that many contemporary critics and defenders of Genesis 1 engage the biblical text through the concerns of modern science. I follow this path in the first three sections of this chapter by setting forth the three main options for reading Genesis 1 in relation to science. First, I examine the modern scientific account of the universe, as set forth by such authors as Bill Bryson, Martin Redfern, Timothy Ferris, Paul Davies, and Michael Benton. This modern scientific perspective challenges and often explicitly denies the relevance of Genesis 1. The chapter's second section examines the work of the Jewish physicist Gerald Schroeder, who aims to demonstrate the fundamental *correspondence* of Genesis 1 with modern science. Schroeder's insights open up avenues of rejoinder to the modern despisers of Genesis 1, by insisting upon the scientific relevance of the biblical text.[7] Yet, like others

---

4. Kitcher, *Living with Darwin*, 126.

5. For theological reflection on the size of the universe, see Haarsma and Haarsma, *Origins*, 150–57.

6. Kenneth R. Miller, *Finding Darwin's God*, 244. Writing as a scientist and a Christian, Miller answers his own questions as follows: "There is no religious justification for demanding that the Creator hold to a certain schedule, follow a defined pathway, or do things exactly according to our expectations. To God, a thousand years are as a twinkling, and there is no reason to believe that our appearance on this planet was for Him anything other than right on time" (245). Surely, however, a better answer can be found than this nonanswer—although I should add that in many respects I find Miller's book to be very helpful.

7. For studies of Gen. 1 and modern science that take a broadly similar approach to that of Schroeder, see, e.g., Brown, *Seven Pillars of Creation*; Lennox, *Seven Days That Divide the World*; Parker, *The Genesis Enigma*. Lennox highlights the significance of God creating by speaking a word: "This revelation, that God by his Word imparts energy and information to create and structure the universe, is profoundly new [in its ancient Near Eastern context]. Yet

who adopt this approach, Schroeder tends to overstate the correspondences between the text of Genesis 1 and the findings of modern science, and he also measures the value of Genesis too much in terms of these correspondences.[8]

In the chapter's third section, therefore, I turn to the patristic period for a better way forward for the task of reading Genesis 1 in light of science. In a series of homilies on Genesis 1, Basil the Great searches *not for correspondences* that show that Genesis 1 measures up to the standards of science, but rather for scientific *testimony* to the extraordinary complexity, beauty, and diversity of the kinds of creatures that appear in the six days of Genesis 1. Basil shows that scientific attention to the minute particularities of the vast array of creatures enhances our appreciation of the outpouring of creatures depicted by the six days. In turn, as Basil makes clear, the six days serve to locate the fruits of scientific study in their proper framework: namely, the wisdom and goodness of God's creation and its status as a cosmic theophany.[9] In making this claim about Basil's mode of employing science vis-à-vis

---

. . . it converges with some of the deepest insights of a modern science that has come to realize the fundamental nature of information and its irreducibility to matter and energy" (*Seven Days*, 141). In his instructive and erudite book, Brown grants that "the cosmos as portrayed in Genesis 1 bears little resemblance to its physical character as observed by scientists today" (*Seven Pillars*, 49). He goes on to compare the original "darkness . . . upon the face of the deep" (Gen. 1:2) with the "dark matter" of modern physics; the original formlessness (Gen. 1:2) with modern science's "primordial, 'soupy' state of the universe at its inception" and also with contemporary chaos theory; and the "waters" (Gen. 1:2) with "the interstellar dust and gas responsible for stars and planets" (51, 53). Brown notes that both Gen. 1 and modern science appreciate the close relationship of space and time and recognize that "the universe bears a history, a history that begins in symmetry" and that involves "broken symmetries or 'nonpredictable variations'" (52–53, 55). A number of other similarities are identified by Brown, much as Schroeder does. For example, he proposes that the evolutionary development of life from simple forms to highly complex ones is mirrored in Gen. 1, which begins with vegetation and ends with humans.

8. For a helpful critique of such approaches (focusing on examples from the eighteenth century), see Watson, "Genesis before Darwin." Watson comments, "Harmonization merely produces a new, artificial narrative that fails to respect the integrity of the discrete narratives and forces them into unnatural union. Rather than blending the narratives together, they should have been allowed to go their separate ways" (35). While I largely agree with Watson, I survey Schroeder's work here because I think that Scripture and science should be distinguished without going "their separate ways." For example, it is worth showing that Gen. 1 is not unsophisticated, even if its scientific sophistication (by modern standards) can be exaggerated; and it is worth insisting that scriptural narratives (such as the story of Adam and Eve) may bear upon science and history even while not themselves being scientific-historical narratives. For an effort to distinguish Scripture and science without allowing them to "go their separate ways," see Schönborn, *Chance or Purpose?*

9. The goal is to appreciate (in the words of Metropolitan Kallistos Ware) "the distinctive and peculiar flavor of each created thing" so as to "discover in and through it the divine presence." See Ware, "Through Creation to the Creator," 94. Metropolitan Kallistos goes on to explain, "The first step, then, is to love the world for itself, in terms of its own consistency and integrity. The second step is to allow the world to become pellucid, so that it reveals to us the

Genesis 1, admittedly, I am not breaking new ground. Frances Young remarks, "For Basil . . . Genesis is a summary account of the sheer gift of finite existence, a doxological invitation rather than a full philosophical or scientific exposition of origins."[10] I agree with Young that Basil's "work is a salutary warning against the temptation to accommodate current scientific thinking to Genesis and *vice versa*."[11]

Although Basil's theophanic approach to the diversity of creatures and the wisdom of God's plan is highly valuable, Basil has no awareness that the earth was ruled for millions of years by dinosaurs—which hardly seems like a wise divine idea, if the earth's purpose is to foster interpersonal communion. This

---

indwelling Creator-Logos. . . . We need to recognize the solidity of the world before we discern its transparency; we need to rejoice in the abundant variety of creation before we ascertain how all things find their unity in God. Moreover, the second level, that of theophanic transparency, does not in any way cancel out the first level, that of particularity and distinctiveness" (94–95). See also Schönborn, *Chance or Purpose?*, 57: "The world offers an enormous variety of creatures—the stars, the variety on our own planet, the world of plants and animals. The basic message [of Genesis] about this variety is that it is good, it is what God intends, it corresponds to the Creator's will."

10. Young, *God's Presence*, 47. For further background, see Louth, "Six Days of Creation according to the Greek Fathers." Louth identifies Basil's *Hexaemeron* as "the finest account of . . . the six days, in the Greek tradition" (44). See Glacken, *Traces on the Rhodian Shore*, 190; McGuckin, "Beauty of the World and Its Significance in St. Gregory the Theologian," 40. Glacken captures Basil's theophanic view of the world: "The world is a work of art from which one learns to know God" (*Traces on the Rhodian Shore*, 191).

11. Young, *God's Presence*, 47. As Young goes on to say, "Interpreted by the Fathers, Genesis invites us neither to devise some artificial integration with current physics, nor to deny its findings or its fascination. Science, its data, its assured results and the philosophical enquiries generated by science—all have the same status *vis à vis* theology as the hypotheses, questions and knowledge about the natural world which Basil and Augustine both challenged and embraced" (51–52). Similarly, Louth comments: "For Basil, there was no opposition between scripture and science; he used contemporary science to fill in the bare outline of the cosmos found in Genesis. He can do this because he is quite clear that the scriptural account is not a scientific account" ("Six Days of Creation according to the Greek Fathers," 48). Louth goes on to observe that for Basil, "it is no criticism of Moses . . . that he did not clarify whether the earth is a sphere, a cylinder, a disc, or like a great basket, hollowed out in the middle, or that he did not give the measurement of the circumference of the earth. All these things, interesting though they might be, are irrelevant to Moses's purpose: to proclaim God as Creator, the cosmos as his good creation, and the place of the human in all of this" (48–49; cf. 53). Francis Watson shows that John Calvin, in commenting on Gen. 1, similarly avoids harmonizing or conflating Scripture and science; see Watson, "Genesis before Darwin," 25–28. Watson demonstrates that Calvin both recognizes that "the scientific account operates within a different frame of reference from the scriptural one" and that "the scientific account is not to be neglected, as though the theologian had no stake in it," not least because the scientific account "provokes a more insightful reading of the scriptural text that is not content merely to note and paraphrase its fact-like assertions, but seeks to uncover their significance and rationale" (27–28). Watson argues that it was not until the seventeenth century, with its geological discoveries (which at first seemed to tell in favor of the literal historicity of the flood narrative), that Scripture and science began to be conflated in a way that Darwinian science has helped Christians to move beyond.

point of weakness in Basil's approach leads me to augment it by arguing that there is an intrinsic reason for the goodness of the vast diversity of creatures over space and time. Namely, I hold that the "analogy of being," especially when understood in terms of proper proportionality (diverse *rationes* of act/potency), serves to confirm the theophanic character of each and every creature. Each instance of finite actuality points intrinsically, and in a unique and irreplaceable way, to the unfathomable glory of pure act.

In sum, I propose that rather than constituting evidence of cosmic absurdity, such things as dinosaurs, octillions of stars, and the vast number of species intrinsically constitute a cosmic theophany of the wise and good God.[12] The wonder of this cosmic theophany should generate an appreciation not only for the creator's ideas and goodness, but also, as Andrew Louth says, for "the connectedness of everything created, a connectedness rooted in the creative energies of God, in the one word, or logos, of God, in whom all the diverse

12. D. Stephen Long has warned against the view that "metaphysics (the analogy of being) *conditions* revelation," in the sense of setting the epistemological terms for our understanding of created nature and divine nature. In my view, however, this concern is assuaged when one appreciates that the analogy of being itself involves theophany: creatures, in themselves, are theophanic, as befits their status as God's creation. Long asks, "Is the *analogia entis* what allowed first-century Jews to recognize God in Christ? What happened to the revelation given to Moses?" (*Saving Karl Barth*, 167). Certainly, the analogy of being is not a revealed datum, nor does it replace revelation, let alone stand in for theological faith. But on the other hand, if being were not knowable, and knowable as analogous (e.g., the being of a rock is analogous to the being of a dog, and being rock or being dog is not equivalent to being), then God would hardly have been able to reveal himself in a manner that could have been comprehended. The created order need not be set in opposition to the order of revelation. Long asks, "Are creatures able to tell God the conditions by which God can become incarnate?" (ibid.). The answer is no, because the Triune God himself sets the conditions in creation. When Thomas Joseph White, OP, argues for the distinction between Christology and natural theology (and defends the possibility of the latter), Long asks: "In what sense could 'nature' be distinguished from Christ if *omnia in ipso constant* (in him all things consist)[?] In other words, has White assumed a realm of pure nature, untouched from Christology that is more than hypothetical? Does nature-distinguished-from-Christ do actual work in theology?" (94). White, however, is simply discussing whether all that we can know about God can be known solely in and through divine revelation (as summed up in Christ). White does not assume "a realm of pure nature," in the sense of a nature that is not created in grace or not fallen and redeemed or not sustained by God. Rather, White holds that the gift of creation, as distinct (but not separated or cut off) from the gift of grace, itself includes rational powers that allow for some knowledge of God. The work done by "nature-distinguished-from-Christ" (not nature *separated* from Christ the creator) is the subject matter of the doctrine of creation. Long repeatedly criticizes "Ressourcement Thomism," but I do not think Long understands White's arguments. Long is engaging White, "Classical Christology after Schleiermacher and Barth"; and White, *Wisdom in the Face of Modernity*. Long also has in view Hector, *Theology without Metaphysics*. See also the important questions raised, and clarifications offered, in Hütter, *Dust Bound for Heaven*, chaps. 5 and 6.

meanings, or logoi, of creation find unity and harmony."[13] The discoveries of modern science regarding the vast profusion of creatures over space and time, therefore, can only enhance our appreciation of the universe's accordance with and glorious manifestation of the creative wisdom of God.

Modern Scientific Views of the Universe: Leaving Genesis Behind?

As is well known, many details about the universe offered by leading authorities on modern science differ significantly from the portrait given in Genesis 1's description of the six days. Inevitably, these differences have caused doubts that Genesis 1 really has much to tell us about creation, poetically rich though Genesis 1 might be.[14] For example, Bill Bryson indicates the enormity of the universe by pointing out that there appear to be around 140 billion galaxies. In our galaxy, the "Milky Way," there are between 100 billion and 400 billion stars, and the Milky Way is only a moderately sized galaxy. These stars are by no means clumped closely together: the average distance between stars is about 20 trillion miles.[15] The nearest star to our sun is about 25 trillion miles away, our sun is 28,000 light years away from the center of the Milky Way (each light year being about six trillion miles), and the closest galaxy to the Milky Way is 170,000 light years away.[16] Referring to a photo Voyager 1 sent of our solar system from *only* 3.7 billion miles away, Martin Redfern

13. Louth, "Six Days of Creation according to the Greek Fathers," 53. To quote Symeon the New Theologian, we can add that it is the Word incarnate who makes "completely visible" to the eyes of faith the infinitely wise and loving Creator who is "invisible to all" (*Divine Eros*, 85).

14. This situation has helped to place Judaism and Christianity on the defensive in contemporary popular culture. Thus, in a book published shortly before his death (and prior to the explosion of New Atheist popular writings), the Jewish paleontologist and evolutionary biologist Stephen Jay Gould felt compelled to defend religion, despite himself leaning toward atheism. Summing up the approach of his *Rocks of Ages*, Gould observes: "Irenics sure beats the polemics of ill-conceived battle between science and religion—a thoroughly false model (chapter 2) that too often continues to envelop us for illogical reasons of history (chapter 3) and psychology (chapter 4). I do get discouraged when some of my colleagues tout their private atheism (their right, of course, and in many ways my own suspicion as well) as a panacea for human progress against an absurd caricature of 'religion,' erected as a straw man for rhetorical purposes" (209). Gould argues for "the Principle of NOMA, or Non-Overlapping Magisteria" (5), but his account of the "Magisterium" of religion is unfortunately limited to meaning and value, with factual matters being the domain of science: "Science tries to document the factual character of the natural world, and to develop theories that coordinate and explain these facts. Religion, on the other hand, operates in the equally important, but utterly different, realm of human purposes, meanings, and values—subjects that the factual domain of science might illuminate, but can never resolve" (4).

15. See Bryson, *Short History of Nearly Everything*, 27.

16. See Lidsey, *Bigger Bang*, 2–4.

observes, "The planets are scarcely visible. The Earth itself is smaller than one picture element in Voyager's camera, its faint light caught in what looks like a sunbeam. This is our whole world, seemingly just a speck of dust."[17] The age of the universe is estimated to be almost fourteen billion years—a far cry from the depiction of six "days."

Although Genesis and modern science seem to agree that the universe had a beginning, Ferris helps us to appreciate the extraordinary oddity of big bang theory, which holds that the universe's unfathomably vast space and its countless stars emerged from "a *singularity*—a state of infinite curvature of spacetime. In a singularity, all places and times are the same. Hence the big bang did not take place in a preexisting space; all space was embroiled *in* the big bang."[18] People often imagine that the big bang took place in a particular point of space, but in fact the big bang happened in *all* the space that we see today, since all space was originally concentrated in a singularity. Bryson describes the original instants in a manner indebted to the cosmic-inflation theory of the physicist Alan Guth: "A fraction of a moment after the dawn of creation, the universe underwent a sudden dramatic expansion. . . . The whole episode may have lasted no more than 10^{-30} seconds—that's one million million million million millionths of a second—but it changed the universe from something you could hold in your hand to something at least 10,000,000,000,000,000,000,000,000 times bigger."[19] Bryson also reports that gravity, followed very shortly after by electromagnetism and the strong and

17. Redfern, *Earth*, 5.

18. Ferris, *Whole Shebang*, 17.

19. Bryson, *Short History of Nearly Everything*, 14. Indeed, James Lidsey notes that "there are strong arguments to suggest that the universe underwent a period of very rapid expansion when it was no more than 10^{-35} seconds old. At that time the matter currently contained within the observable universe (around one hundred billion galaxies) would have been squashed into a region of space considerably smaller than that occupied by a typical atom. Furthermore, the temperature of the universe would have been exceptionally high, many times higher than the temperature at the centre of the sun" (*Bigger Bang*, 6). Lidsey also notes that according to Jim Hartle and Stephen Hawking, "The quantity that we measure today as time does have a beginning in some sense. When the universe was smaller than the Planck limit [distances of 10^{-35} meters], there was no such thing as time. When the size of the universe was roughly 10^{-35} metres, the intrinsic quantum fluctuations associated with space and time became negligible. At that point, space and time began to take on separate identities, and the concept of time became meaningful. The origin of time in this picture may therefore be identified as the point where this transformation occurred. In this sense, the universe is not infinitely old, and time has not existed forever even though there is no boundary or edge to the time dimension. If we were to follow the time dimension backwards, we would find that it combines with the other space dimensions to form a smooth, *closed* surface" (120–21). Lidsey considers it possible that universes are or could be birthed by the processes within black holes, so that our universe would be part of "a network of closed baby universes" (125) with the result that, perhaps, "the global universe may never die and may produce baby universes into the infinite future" (126).

weak nuclear forces, emerged around "one ten-millionth of a trillionth of a trillionth of a trillionth of a second" after the big bang.[20] After the emergence of gravity, an unfathomably large number of photons, protons, electrons, neutrons, and other elementary particles emerged—"between 10^{79} and 10^{89} of each."[21]

The production of this vast universe could not have proceeded were it not for the precise strength of gravity: "Had gravity been a trifle stronger, the universe itself might have collapsed like a badly erected tent, without precisely the right values to give it the right dimensions and density and component parts. Had it been weaker, however, nothing would have coalesced. The universe would have remained forever a dull, scattered void."[22] Similarly, as Paul Davies points out, if the weak nuclear force in the universe had been just a tiny bit stronger or a tiny bit weaker, then "the dissemination of carbon and other heavy elements needed for life" could not have occurred; and if neutrons had not been 0.1 percent heavier than protons, then there could not have been a sufficient amount of hydrogen in the universe to allow for stars or for abundant water.[23] Neither Davies nor Bryson is thereby arguing that a creator exists; this cosmic "fine-tuning" or "anthropic principle" shows rather how strange the universe is.[24]

It is also worth noting that, as Ferris remarks, the phrase "big bang" can conjure the wrong image insofar as we might imagine a violent explosion. In fact, "things did not fly out into space but remained where they were, while the surrounding space expanded."[25] Additionally, Ferris reminds us that the phrase "big bang" can be used with different referents: "Some cosmologists use the term 'big bang' to refer to the initial singularity, and 'early universe' for the 'hot,' high-energy physics fest that ensued. Others use the term 'big bang' more broadly, to refer as well to the hot universe as it evolved through the first seconds and minutes of time."[26]

Even if the big bang is in certain ways compatible with understandings of creation that are grounded in Scripture, one has to wonder why Genesis gives

---

20. Bryson, *Short History of Nearly Everything*, 14.

21. Ibid., 15.

22. Ibid.

23. Davies, *Goldilocks Enigma*, 141. As Philip Ball remarks, "Hydrogen is solar fuel, and the sun 'burns' it, not by combining it chemically with oxygen . . . but by fusing its nuclei to make helium. . . . About 600 billion kilograms of hydrogen are burnt to helium in the sun every second. . . . All it takes to trigger fusion in hydrogen are conditions extreme enough: a high enough density of hydrogen, and a temperature of about ten million degrees" (*Elements*, 106–7).

24. Davies, *Goldilocks Enigma*, xi; cf. 266–68. Davies states bluntly, "I do *not* believe *Homo sapiens* to be more than an accidental by-product of haphazard natural processes" (268). Bryson would surely agree.

25. Ferris, *Whole Shebang*, 17.

26. Ibid.

no hint of the vast aeons, unfathomable distances, unimaginably numerous stars, solar systems, and so forth. Why would God create not simply thousands or millions of stars but 100 octillion stars, and why did God not reveal at least some of this vastness to us in the inspired narrative of creation? At the level of living things, we face similar questions, regarding which Genesis again seems to give us little help. For example, why is it that, as David Norman remarks, "the (reptilian) dinosaurs rose to dominance in the Late Triassic (220 Ma [million years ago]) and the mammals only began to increase in size and diversity after the dinosaurs had become extinct at the end of the Cretaceous period (65 Ma)"?[27] Why were the very first mammals, 205 million years ago, mere shrew-like creatures? Why was there a species of "feathered dinosaur with highly developed and complex wings, *Archaeopteryx*"?[28] Why has the progression of living creatures on earth moved so slowly, beginning about 3,600 million years ago? Why is it that there seems to be so much cosmic waste, so that, as Bryson points out, "of the billions and billions of species of living thing that have existed since the dawn of time, most—99.99 percent—are no longer around"?[29] In this regard, Bryson is right to say that "it is a curious feature of our existence that we come from a planet that is very good at promoting life but even better at extinguishing it."[30] This extinction of species is not something discussed in Genesis.

Indeed, one can see how nihilistic views of human life arise from concentration upon the seemingly purposeless existence of so many now extinct species, including powerful ones such as dinosaurs, over the vast expanse of time. Bryson reflects this nihilism in his observation—which he seeks to temper by expressing his gladness to have come to be, even for such a short time, given the evolutionary odds against it—that "even a long human life adds up to only about 650,000 hours. And when that modest milestone flashes past, or at some other point thereabouts, for reasons unknown your atoms will shut you down, silently disassemble, and go off to be other things. And that's it for you."[31]

Furthermore, 650,000 hours (or even a fraction of that) is much more than most living beings enjoy. Ernst Mayr comments, "Every species consists of thousands, millions, or even billions of individuals. Many of them perish every day and are replaced by new ones."[32] There are 2,500 known species of mayfly,

27. Norman, *Dinosaurs*, 109–10.
28. Ibid., 130.
29. Bryson, *Short History of Nearly Everything*, 3.
30. Ibid.
31. Ibid., 2.
32. Mayr, *This Is Biology*, 151.

and yet mayflies live no more than one day, and some species of mayfly have a life span of only half an hour. A housefly lives only four weeks; a dragonfly only four months. A mouse lives only one to three years. Why do these things come to be, only to perish so quickly? Why, too, do living creatures develop in such a strange way, as we see in the Cambrian explosion of 530 million years ago, with its brachiopods, arthropods, echinoderms, archaeocyathids, and chordates? Why all these forms of algae, jellyfish, sponges, priapulids, and so forth? Why would God create the species Anomalocaris, which could grow to two meters in length, and was a many-segmented predator that, according to Michael Benton, "probably swam by flapping large flexible lobes along the side of its body, and snatched prey with its large curved, flexible armoured arms that bore barb-like spikes"?[33] Why would God will for sea squirts, "fleshy bags that are fixed to the seabed and feed by pumping water in and out of their central cavity," to come into existence as part of his wise creative plan?[34]

Going back further into time, why did God begin the history of life on earth with such creatures as eukaryotes and prokaryotes, for instance the Grypania of 1.85 billion years ago, which look like "spaghetti-like coils of tubes about 5 millimetres wide"?[35] In fact, earth originally had no oxygen, and the first living organisms appear to have been stromatolites, dating from about 3.4 billion years ago and "made from many thin layers that apparently build up over many years or hundreds of years to form irregular mushroom- or cabbage-shaped structures" consisting of cyanobacteria, which is something like a less complex version of algae.[36] For almost three billion years, then, there were no living creatures on land. Benton states that "the land began to become green in the Ordovician [period], some 450 million years ago."[37] It was not until around 320 million years ago that life "exploded" on land, in the warm Carboniferous period, when forests and flying insects emerged and flourished. In the Carboniferous period, probably due to the atmosphere containing 35 percent oxygen (by contrast to 21 percent today), "there were dragonflies like birds, cockroaches as large as your hand, 2-metre-long millipedes, and so on."[38]

Genesis does not tell us that things proceeded in this way; no reader of Genesis comes away with knowledge of the Carboniferous period with its

33. Benton, *History of Life*, 61.
34. Ibid., 62.
35. Ibid., 41.
36. Ibid., 29.
37. Ibid., 71.
38. Ibid., 93.

"dragonflies like birds" and so forth. Bryson makes this point with his typical emphasis on sheer chance: "We are so used to the notion of our own inevitability as life's dominant species that it is hard to grasp that we are here only because of timely extraterrestrial bangs and other random flukes. The one thing we have in common with all other living things is that for nearly four billion years our ancestors have managed to slip through a series of closing doors every time we needed them to."[39]

Even today, when 99.99 percent of species that once came into existence have become extinct, the profusion of species is enormous. Why would God will such an exotic profusion? The animal kingdom alone, which includes insects, birds, fish, reptiles, and mammals, contains more than one million known species (and there are thought to be many millions more). About one million of the known species are insects; vertebrates compose only 5 percent of animal species. Indeed, the authors of *The Encyclopedia of Animals* estimate that the real number of insect species today "could be more in the region of 30 million."[40] We can understand why penguins, dolphins, monkeys, dogs, butterflies, lions, seals, and other beautiful animals were created, but why so many insects, to say nothing of the amazing number of bacteria that live upon these animals?[41]

39. Bryson, *Short History of Nearly Everything*, 349. In his book on Charles Darwin, Jonathan Howard voices a similar conclusion, one that is now commonplace in popular science writing: "It is no longer easy to look to spiritual authority for a satisfying account of the ultimate issues of human existence: why are we here? why does the world act so uncaringly? What is the sense of the sublime? The Darwinian revolution has been a cruel one in that it has taken away many of the customary sources of consolation. To realize that the physical construction of human bodies and brains is the outcome of processes as comprehensible as those which form the ocean waves may give intellectual satisfaction but it does not necessarily compensate for the loss of divine providence. In the physical continuity between humans, other forms of life, and non-living matter, there is no hint of a crack in which humans can find any special dispensation for themselves" (*Darwin*, 105–6). But there is no reason, of course, that the existence of comprehensible natural processes should rule out divine providence—in fact the best theologians have always thought that providence went hand in hand with natural processes—and likewise the physical continuity between humans and other material creatures is just what theologians have always expected ("the LORD God formed man of dust from the ground" [Gen. 2:7]).

40. Goodwin and Handley, *Encyclopedia of Animals*, 15.

41. Furthermore, animal life is often extraordinarily cruel and brutal—an issue that I hope to address more fully in a future work. Richard Dawkins comments in this regard, "If Nature were kind, she would at least make the minor concession of anesthetizing caterpillars before they are eaten alive from within. But Nature is neither kind nor unkind" (*River out of Eden*, 132, cited in Murray's *Nature Red in Tooth and Claw*, 4–5). Dawkins describes animals being eaten alive, running from predators, whimpering in terror, being eaten from within by parasites, dying of starvation and disease. At the present moment, thousands of animals are undergoing these horrific trials, which are a necessary process of the ecosystem. For Dawkins, therefore, a closer look at the biosphere gives the lie to the portrait in Gen. 1 of an earth teeming with

Mention should also be made of the genetic makeup of living beings. Each human contains about three billion base pairs of DNA; and when humans are compared with each other, 99.999 percent of our DNA is the same. Tara Robinson points out, "Less than 2 percent of the human genome codes for actual physical traits—that is, all your body parts and the ways they function."[42] What does the other (more than) 98 percent of the DNA in a human being do? It undeniably has some role, but it still seems as though DNA—like the cosmos, from all that we can tell scientifically—proceeds upon a principle of rather wasteful profusion, rather than with regard for the significance of each and every thing. As with the other evidence from modern science that we noted in this section, Genesis 1 does not tell us about DNA, let alone about the 98 percent of DNA whose function is unclear.

In sum, the modern scientific portrait of origins seems to be profoundly untidy and far vaster and stranger than what we can obtain from reading Genesis 1. The billions of years of cosmic unfolding involve more than enough odd and seemingly random events and outcomes to challenge our confidence that we are witnessing the plan of a wise and good creator God.

Gerald Schroeder: Correlating Genesis 1 and Modern Science

Given the modern scientific challenge not only to the reliability of the details of Genesis 1's depiction of the six days of creation, but also to the truthfulness of the claim that creation is "very good" (Gen. 1:31), the question inevitably becomes why educated persons—or indeed anyone at all—should pay any

---

happy creatures coming forth from God's commanding word, governed by humans as the "image of God," and worthy of the approbation "very good." In his view, far from manifesting the superabundance of divine gifting (or love), the vast array of creatures manifests "pitiless indifference" summed up in the constant cycle of meaningless suffering (*River out of Eden*, 132). See also Gould, *Rocks of Ages*, 183, which sets forth Charles Darwin's famous example of the reproduction of ichneumonid wasps, which involves the mother injecting her eggs into the body of a host and then the hatched larvae eating the host's body "from the inside—but very carefully, leaving the heart and other vital organs for last." Denis Alexander responds to such examples by noting that "once multicellular carbon-based life forms began to exist, then a dynamic order in which life and death are integral parts became an inevitable consequence. No change or development into new life forms would be possible without the death of the old. Carbon-based organisms (which are the only types that exist on planet earth) can only live by feeding on carbon-based molecules derived from other plants and animals" (*Rebuilding the Matrix*, 352–53). Alexander also notes that the ability to experience pain is necessary for the survival of higher-level organisms, and he concludes: "The natural world provides a constant source of wonder and fascination, but it is an amoral world, devoid of those qualities of foresight, conscious deliberation and ethical choice that would justify assessing it as either cruel or cooperative" (356).

42. Robinson, *Genetics for Dummies*, 266.

further attention to Genesis 1. One way of answering this question is to argue that in fact, Genesis 1 anticipates modern science, so that the seeming divergences are not as significant as first appears.[43] This way of answering the question frames the contribution of Genesis 1 largely in terms of modern science, with the benefit of directing attention to the perceptiveness of Genesis 1 even when measured by modern science. In a scientific age, it may seem that the best way to defend Genesis 1 is to show that its portrait of origins corresponds at least broadly to the findings of modern science.

For an example of this approach, I have chosen Gerald Schroeder's *Genesis and the Big Bang*. As the title of his book suggests, Schroeder reads Genesis 1 largely through the lens of modern science, though with some assistance from the medieval Jewish philosopher Nahmanides. Against biblical literalists, including some teachers at his child's Orthodox Jewish school who consider the world to be around 6,000 years old, Schroeder accepts modern science's evidence for the age and development of the universe. But he also considers that "beyond providing cultural insights, the Bible is also a valid source of cosmological insight," when interpreted correctly.[44] He states his basic argument as follows: "The duration and events of the billions of years

43. Stephen Jay Gould comments on the turning-of-the-tables that is involved here:
   Much as modern syncretism [which Gould defines as "the claim that science and religion should fuse to one big, happy family, or rather one big pod of peas, where the facts of science reinforce and validate the precepts of religion"] riles me, I can at least take comfort in a wry feature of the contemporary version—at least from the parochial perspective of a professional scientist. Older and classical forms of syncretism always gave the nod to God—that is, religion set the outlines that everyone had to accept, and science then had to conform. Irenics in this older mode required that the principles and findings of science yield religious results known in advance to be true. Indeed, such conformity represented the primary test of science's power and validity. . . . But the spectacular growth and success of science has turned the tables for modern versions of syncretism. Now the conclusions of science must be accepted a priori, and religious interpretations must be finessed and adjusted to match unimpeachable results from the magisterium of natural knowledge! The Big Bang happened, and we must now find God at this tumultuous origin. (*Rocks of Ages*, 212–13)
   I hope to show that Basil the Great is not a syncretist of what Gould calls the "older and classical" kind, because Basil takes his natural science from Hellenistic (pagan) culture and does not imagine that Genesis answers the questions that are central to this natural science. Nor is Basil a simple proponent of the view that (in Gould's words) "God shows his hand (and mind) in the workings of nature" (212)—but Basil does consider that nature, when rightly perceived, makes its creator manifest. This view need not be syncretistic in Gould's negative sense, although it goes further than Gould is willing to allow.

44. Schroeder, *Genesis and the Big Bang*, 10. However, he also notes that "today's best mathematical estimates state that there simply was not enough time for random reactions to get life going as fast as the fossil record shows that it did. The reactions were either directed by some, as of yet unknown, physical force or a metaphysical guide, or life arrived here from elsewhere" (25).

that, according to cosmologists, have followed the Big Bang and those events of the first six days of Genesis are in fact one and the same. *They are identical realities that have been described in vastly different terms.*"[45] After all, since time is relative (given Einstein's theory of relativity), God's perception of the time between the big bang and the creation of humans could be six days, even if by our reference points today, taking into account the space-time curvature, almost fourteen billion years have passed. Schroeder concludes that the big bang and the rapid expansion of the universe, as well as the modern scientific conclusion that space and time did not exist prior to the big bang, correspond with Genesis 1:1's "In the beginning" as well as with the view of Nahmanides, who held that (in Schroeder's words) "at the briefest instant following creation all the matter of the universe was concentrated in a very small place, no larger than a grain of mustard."[46]

Schroeder goes on to argue that a vast universe is needed for the creation of life, insofar as the various elements must be formed, temperatures (energy) must fall, and light (photon energies) must separate from other particles. As he points out, "When photon energies fell below 1 electron volt, the photons were no longer sufficiently powerful to eject the atomic electrons. Electrons were at once drawn into stable orbits around the hydrogen and helium nuclei by the electromagnetic charges of these nuclei."[47] The result was the separation of light and darkness. Schroeder states, "Prior to that time, there had been a mix of photons and free electrons, or light and matter, in a turmoil of continual collisions. These photon-electron collisions had been so frequent that the photons (light itself) had been literally held within the mass of the universe."[48] The removal of the electrons produced what Genesis 1:4 describes; and the prior existence of light (photon energies) is depicted in Genesis 1:3.

What about Genesis 1:5's claim that, when God separated the light from the darkness, "God called the light Day, and the darkness he called Night. And there was evening and there was morning, one day"? This verse may seem to presuppose the 24-hour period that we experience due to the earth's revolving around the sun. Indebted to Nahmanides, however, Schroeder argues that in fact the Hebrew word for "evening," in its root, expresses disorder; whereas the Hebrew word for "morning" expresses order. On this basis, he explores the second law of thermodynamics, which is about entropy. The cosmos is cooling, as stars expend their nuclear energy and burn up. Eventually, the universe will enter into a state of "heat death" and disorder due to lack of energy.

45. Ibid., 26.
46. Ibid., 65.
47. Ibid., 88.
48. Ibid., 88–89.

Indeed, the universe would never have had order had it not been for gravity, electromagnetism, and the strong and weak nuclear forces. In Schroeder's view, by stating that "there was evening and there was morning," Genesis is describing the movement from chaos to order that comes about, if only for a time, through the emergence of gravity, electromagnetism, and the strong and weak nuclear forces. These forces form the stars, points of power, energy, and order within an otherwise chaotic and cooling universe.

Turning next to the emergence of living organisms, Schroeder shows that "the individual chemical and physical reactions involved in the maintenance of life are quite similar to those found in reactions among non-living substances."[49] Can life emerge from the chemical reactions of nonliving molecules? As Schroeder points out, such was assumed to be the case by both patristic-medieval and modern thinkers, since meat left out for a few days appeared to generate maggots (or at least microbes). In the late nineteenth and twentieth centuries, this was disproved, but it was also demonstrated that natural processes could produce the building blocks of life, specifically amino acids. The more complex the compound, however, the more likely its spontaneous dissolution would also be. How then do living organisms develop such incredibly complex compounds? Schroeder explains, "Life does it by working in the highly protected environment within its cells, by using catalysts that have the ability to select and concentrate the needed chemicals and to increase rates and extents of reactions, and by expending considerable energy to accomplish the tasks."[50] The chemical compounds are unstable (as appears quickly after death), but living organisms produce their own "highly protected environment," including cellular walls. The catalysts are enzymes, which living cells produce. As Schroeder points out, "A reaction that may take seconds within an enzyme-driven, temperature-controlled 98° F system of an animal might take years or longer in an uncatalyzed system."[51] He also cites the calculations of the physicist Harold Morowitz, who estimated that all the random chemical reactions needed to form the chemical compound of one single-celled bacterium would require, for their random success, fifteen billion years (the age of the universe). But in fact, a billion years after the earth's crust cooled 4.5 billion years ago, life was present. Sedimentary rocks dated to 3.3 billion years ago already contain fossils of several living organisms.

Another difficulty raised by the rapid emergence of life is that each living cell possesses a genetic code, built of "long helixlike molecules, deoxyribonucleic

49. Ibid., 106.
50. Ibid., 109.
51. Ibid., 110.

acid (known as DNA) and ribonucleic acid (RNA)"; and all living cells depend upon twenty amino acids.[52] While amino acids can be formed by natural processes, "the probability of duplicating, by chance, two identical protein chains, each with 100 amino acids, is 1 chance in 20^{100}, which equals the digit 1 followed by 130 zeros or 10^{130}. To give perspective to the extraordinary magnitude of this number, realize that there have been less than 10^{18} seconds in the 15 billion years since the Big Bang."[53] How did the long helixlike chains that are present in every living cell come to be, and come to be so quickly? Living organisms, from bacteria to humans, share certain specific complex protein chains, and it would seem that there is only one viable basic genetic code for living organisms. How, then, could life have originated by random chemical reactions?

Schroeder points out, too, that both the universe and earth are conditioned in a marvelous way for the emergence of living organisms. He reviews some of the numerous conditions that other scientists refer to as the "anthropic principle."[54] Regarding the earth, for example, he notes that the T-Tauri phase

52. Ibid., 113.

53. Ibid. Note that scientists today estimate the age of the universe to be almost fourteen billion years rather than fifteen billion. For the argument that God is the only plausible source of the origin of life in the universe, see Axe, *Undeniable*. I agree with David Bentley Hart's assessment that

> if one looks at the extraordinary complexity of nature and then interprets it as a sign of superhuman intelligence, one is doing something perfectly defensible. . . . Moreover, if one already believes in God, it makes perfect sense to see, say, the ever more extraordinary discoveries of molecular biology, or the problem of protein folding, or the incredible statistical improbabilities of a whole host of cosmological conditions (and so on) as bearing witness to something miraculous and profoundly rational in the order of nature, and to ascribe these wonders to God. But, however compelling the evidence may seem, one really ought not to reverse the order of discovery here and attempt to deduce or define God from the supposed evidence of design in nature. . . . Seen in the light of traditional theology the argument from irreducible complexity looks irredeemably defective, because it depends on the existence of causal discontinuities in the order of nature, "gaps" where natural causality proves inadequate. But all the classical theological arguments regarding the order of the world assume just the opposite: that God's creative power can be seen in the rational coherence of nature as a perfect whole; that the universe was not simply the factitious product of a supreme intellect but the unfolding of an omnipresent divine wisdom or logos. (*Experience of God*, 37–38)

54. On the "anthropic principle," see also Baker, *50 Universe Ideas You Really Need to Know*, 112–15; Robin Collins, "Scientific Argument for the Existence of God"; Rees, *Just Six Numbers*; Stephen M. Barr, *Modern Physics and Ancient Faith*, 118–57; McGrath, *Fine-Tuned Universe*, esp. 115–65. McGrath supports his discussion by reference to a wealth of scientific literature, and he suggests that the "anthropic principle" should be seen as similar to Augustine's *rationes seminales*. Like Robin Collins, McGrath argues that "theism offers the best 'empirical fit' of the various theories which set out to account for anthropic phenomena. Yet it must be emphasized that Christian theology has never seen itself as charged with the task of inventing an explanation for these observations; rather, they fit within, and resonate with, an *existing* way of

of the sun produced (assuming it to be like the T-Tauri phase observed in other stars) a strong solar wind that swept away into outer space the atmospheres of the planets. Had our sun's T-Tauri wind occurred before matter aggregated into planets, then earth would have been left without water. Likewise, if our sun's T-Tauri wind had occurred after the volcanic eruptions that marked the period of the young earth's melting, then our planet would have looked like Mars, devoid of most of earth's present water and atmosphere. The distance of earth from the sun is also exactly what it needs to be for the sustaining of life, and the amount of volcanic activity on earth also was just right. As Schroeder states, "The internal heating of the Earth produced an amount of volcanic activity that was enough to liberate the water needed for oceans, the gases needed for the atmosphere, the molten iron core needed for our protective magnetic field, while being insufficient to make volcanoes and earthquakes a continual occurrence."[55]

When the earth cooled and dried (cf. Gen. 1:9), so as to bring about the difference between ocean and land, the first life that appeared was microscopic. Schroeder observes that the biblical authors could not have been expected to start their story with such forms of life. Instead, they started the story with vegetation (Gen. 1:11). But how could vegetation appear on the third "day," while the sun, moon, and stars appear only on the fourth "day"? Schroeder suggests that at first, the cloud cover of earth would have prevented the luminaries in the sky from being seen. The atmosphere was then cleared by early plant life, through the process of photosynthesis. Thus Genesis 1 is describing the scene as it appeared from earth. Photosynthesis, in turn, released quantities of oxygen, gradually turning the earth's atmosphere from oxygen-free to oxygen-rich. This made animal life possible. On the fifth "day," after the clearing of the atmosphere so that the sun, moon, and stars could be seen,

thinking [namely, the doctrine of creation], which proves capable of satisfactorily incorporating such observations" (121). McGrath denies that the anthropic principle should be taken as a demonstrative proof of the creator God's existence, as it is by William Lane Craig and others; here he cites approvingly the cautions raised by the Catholic philosopher Ernan McMullin in "Natural Science and Belief in a Creator." See also Craig, "Existence of God and the Beginning of the Universe." Stephen Jay Gould provides valid criticisms of the demonstrative power of both the "weak" and the "strong" anthropic principle; see *Rocks of Ages*, 218–20. For efforts to undermine the anthropic principle itself, either by positing observational bias or by positing multiple universes (neither of which seems much of an argument to me), see Leslie, *Universes*; Vilenkin, *Many Worlds in One*; Bostrom, *Anthropic Bias*. Stephen Barr comments aptly, "It is a very curious circumstance that materialists, in an effort to avoid what Laplace called the unnecessary hypothesis of God, are frequently driven to hypothesize the existence of an infinity of unobservable entities. . . . It seems that to abolish one unobservable God, it takes an infinite number of unobservable substitutes" (*Modern Physics and Ancient Faith*, 156–57).

55. Schroeder, *Genesis and the Big Bang*, 126.

fish appeared in the waters; and on the sixth "day," land animals appeared. As Schroeder comments, "It was the availability of oxygen that allowed the development of life forms larger than bacteria and algae and also produced the uv-absorbing ozone layer allowing the population of dry land."[56] With respect to the various species, which in Genesis are presented as essentially all appearing at once, Schroeder underscores that the fossil record does not show gradual evolution (although there are gradual changes within a particular species), but rather shows a pattern of sudden, large-scale emergence of new species, called "punctuated evolution."[57] Regarding the fossil record of development in the genus *Homo*, leading to modern *Homo sapiens*, Schroeder remarks that Genesis, too, describes a pattern of development, notably through the decline of life span. He comments, "What we learn from this is that it is in accord with biblical tradition for changes to occur within a given species and that these changes can be the result of environmental influences."[58] He affirms with regard to hominids that "a form of animal life that was very much like human life predated Adam and Eve."[59]

For Schroeder, then, the basic portrait offered by Genesis 1 corresponds well to the modern scientific vision of the order of the creation of the universe and the emergence of life on earth, as well as with the fact that time and space have a beginning. The order of the "days" is, on Schroeder's view, the correct order, once one allows for microscopic creatures being left out. Even the wide variation within a genus or species, such as one finds in the genus *Homo*, can be understood biblically, since early humans are depicted as having a much longer life span and also as having the bodies of giants.

Is Schroeder's approach the right way to think about the vast diversity of creatures and the enormous extent of the cosmos? Is it correct, for example, to map the emergence of fish, birds, and dinosaurs to days five and six, as described in Genesis 1:20–25? Is the separation of photons from other particles the divinely intended meaning of Genesis 1:4, "God separated the light from the darkness"?

I think that Schroeder does indeed provide some helpful correspondences, showing that the biblical story of creation should by no means be rejected as mere foolishness by those who adhere to the modern scientific understanding of the big bang, the expansion of the cosmos, and so forth. Schroeder's insights remind us that the biblical story of creation is not ignorant or embarrassing, even if we hold that the purpose of Genesis 1 is not to provide a scientific portrait of events.

56. Ibid., 132–33.
57. Ibid., 135.
58. Ibid., 138.
59. Ibid., 149.

Even so, Schroeder seeks to correlate the scientific story of creation and creatures too closely with the six days. This kind of correspondence exaggerates the similarities between biblical theology of creation and creatures and modern scientific portraits. While there are similarities, they are not of the kind that can or should be correlated with exactitude. Genesis does not have the insights of modern cosmology or modern biology in view, even if Genesis's basic portrait of the early development of the universe and of the stages in the emergence of life on earth displays some correspondences with modern science. This is not to say that theology today should be "content to leave the physical and biological sciences go their own way."[60] Theology—and especially the theology of creation—must engage the findings of natural science. But it should do so in a way that accounts more carefully for the genre and purposes of Genesis.

A Way Forward? The *Hexaemeron* of Basil the Great

Unlike Schroeder, Basil thinks that Genesis 1 does not intend to offer a scientific rendering of the exact content of creation. Had Genesis wished to do this, then it would have explained to us such details as whether the earth is "spherical or cylindrical," whether it resembles "a disc and is equally rounded in all parts, or if it has the form of a winnowing basket and is hollow in the middle."[61] Such scientific matters, Basil observes, are hotly debated by cosmographers but ignored by Genesis. Far from focusing upon what is of most interest to natural scientists, says Basil, Moses "has not said that the earth is a hundred and eighty thousand furlongs in circumference; he has not measured into what extent of air its shadow projects itself whilst the sun revolves around it, nor stated how this shadow, casting itself upon the moon, produces eclipses."[62] Natural scientists of Basil's day would have liked to know these things, but Genesis deems them unimportant for its purposes. What then is important for Genesis? Genesis focuses upon the wisdom and goodness of the creation, and upon the multitudes of diverse creatures that give glory to the creator in all sorts of ways.

Basil focuses upon the same, and therefore he eschews allegorical readings of Genesis 1: "For me grass is grass; plant, fish, wild beast, domestic

---

60. Ashley and Deely, *How Science Enriches Theology*, 29. Ashley and Deely observe, "Nor is it only theology, but traditional philosophy too that has to come to terms with the cosmos as we have learned it to be—not an unchanging heavens centered on a stationary earth, but an evolutionary whole which does not even have a center that we can determine in our present awareness" (29n48). This task has been central to Deely's extensive philosophical work.

61. Basil, *Hexaemeron* 9.1, p. 101.

62. Ibid., 102.

animal, I take all in the literal sense."[63] To understand Genesis 1, we need to recognize the theophanic character of the universe's extraordinary range of creatures. It is this theophanic character that Basil tries to show by means of his detailed attention to the creatures of the universe, aided by the Hellenistic science of his day. He values natural science because, as he observes, "grand phenomena do not strike us the less when we have discovered something of their wonderful mechanism."[64] This section will therefore survey Basil's approach with the goal of showing in detail how he employs natural science in his preaching on Genesis 1. Since Basil does not discuss the corruption and death of creatures in this work, but instead focuses upon their existence and life, the question of why God created a vast diversity of creatures is our focus here.[65]

At the outset of the *Hexaemeron*, Basil states that God's creation of "the heavens and the earth" (Gen. 1:1) should lead us to praise "the beauty of visible things" and "the grandeur of bodies," and through them to praise

63. Ibid., 101.

64. Ibid., 1.10, p. 57. Clarence Glacken comments that Basil "added little if anything to the store of knowledge regarding the earth; [fourth-century Christians'] biology, their geography, their natural history came entirely from pagan sources. Basil's hexaemeron is a compendium of classical science and natural history organized around a Christian principle; it is, in fact, a rich storehouse of ancient science, now in the service of the Christian religion" (*Traces on the Rhodian Shore*, 194). While Ambrose borrowed a great deal from Basil's *Hexaemeron*, Glacken notes that "Ambrose's hexaemeron is less intellectual than is Basil's; there is much more allegory and spiritual interpretation in it" (196).

65. Although I think that the corruption, suffering, and death of living things are an inevitable part of a temporally unfolding material creation, some scientists and theologians consider any suffering and destruction to be fundamentally out of place in the very good universe depicted by Gen. 1—assuming that it truly is very good. Michael Murray surveys the various responses that Christian theologians and philosophers have given to observations such as Dawkins's and Gould's (see note 41 above) with regard to the suffering of nonhuman animals. According to Murray, some theologians and philosophers argue that without suffering there could not be good animal action, or that pain pertains to animals' ability to protect themselves from serious harm. Murray holds that the universe moves from chaos to order in such a way that a long history of evolutionary development, including the development of nonhuman animals, is required for the emergence of humans. This long history requires, first, "the accumulation of complex states (molecular, planetary, galactic, biological, etc.)"; and second, "a long pedigree of prehuman animals capable of experiencing pain and suffering, since these animals will be necessary precursors to descendants capable of ever more complex forms of mental life and moral value" (*Nature Red in Tooth and Claw*, 8). Murray grants that this solution cannot be shown to be clearly sufficient for outweighing the evil of the animal suffering that God permits. In my view, in reflecting upon the problem of brutality, suffering, and waste in creation, we cannot merely undertake a comparative weighing of temporal goods (as done by Murray, despite his salutary insistence upon the impossibility of philosophically demonstrating either that creation is good or that it is not). That said, I value Murray's clarity that an evolving material universe, insofar as it contains living organisms, must include bodily decay and death absent a miraculous stability, which in my view could characterize only the eschaton.

their creator.[66] At the same time, Basil reflects on such scientific problems as how the earth is held in space. He proposes some solutions, both scientific and theological: perhaps it "reposes on a bed of air" or "rests upon itself" or "rides on the waters."[67] As he notes, Genesis 1 does not try to give us the answer. Whatever might be the scientific case, says Basil, in a deeper sense the earth surely "is sustained by the Creator's power."[68]

Discussing God's first words, "Let there be light" (Gen. 1:3), Basil urges us to consider "the pleasure and delight" that comes to us from physically basking in light.[69] Turning to the "waters" and "firmament" (Gen. 1:6) of the second day, he emphasizes the importance of the earth's superabundant water, without which the earth would be utterly overwhelmed by heat. He also notes that although it is generally held that "the firmament owes its origin to water, we must not believe that it resembles frozen water or any other matter produced by the filtration of water; as, for example, rock crystal, which is said to owe its metamorphosis to excessive congelation."[70] He explores the gathering together of waters, which he presents as having taken place in "a single mass" or ocean; and he compares the water of the ocean to the water that is in lakes and rivers.[71] In all these ways, he takes the opportunity to speculate on scientific matters, beyond what Genesis tells him, not in order to prove Genesis right but in order to ponder on how each distinct creature is beneficial to the whole and manifests the creator God.

With respect to the third day, Basil reflects at length upon the "vegetation, plants yielding seed, and fruit trees bearing fruit in which is their seed" (Gen. 1:11). Here he continues his practice of supplementing Genesis with the science of his time in order to gain insight into the value that each creature, no matter how humble, possesses among the whole profusion of creatures.[72] He

66. Basil, *Hexaemeron* 1.11, p. 58. As Frances Young observes, "In his *Hexaemeron* Basil constantly uses anagogy to lift the vision from the wonders of creation to a sense of the Creator's presence. Genesis states that God saw that each creation was good, and this allows Basil to emphasize its beauty—not just the beauty in the eye of the beholder, for what God esteems beautiful is the capacity of a thing to fulfil its divinely intended purpose. . . . Each thing created indicates ineffable [divine] wisdom" (*God's Presence*, 72–73).

67. Basil, *Hexaemeron* 1.8–9, p. 57.

68. Ibid., 1.9, p. 57.

69. Ibid., 2.7, p. 64. Since at this stage the sun had not yet been created, however, he supposes that the light of the first day came forth directly from God's will—going beyond any scientific theory.

70. Ibid., 3.4, p. 67.

71. Ibid., 4.4, p. 73.

72. As Glacken points out, Basil counters the worship of the sun by arguing that the sun is not the cause of vegetation, in a manner that erroneously goes against the natural science of his day. For Basil, Glacken states, "it was necessary . . . to insist, following Genesis, that plants were growing before the sun was created" (*Traces on the Rhodian Shore*, 193). Basil remarks in this

urges his audience: "I want creation to penetrate you with so much admiration that everywhere, wherever you may be, the least plant may bring to you the clear remembrance of the Creator."[73] With this goal in view, he inquires carefully into why "the reed, couch-grass, mint, crocus, garlic, and the flowering rush and countless other species, produce no seed."[74] He examines the relationship of the germ, seed, sprout, leaves, stalk, and fruit. He argues that the roots draw nourishment from the soil, aided by warmth and moisture; and the stem pumps this nourishment to the other parts of the plant. He notes that some stalks have joints or supports that enable them to bear their fruit (such as wheat). He reflects upon the mixture of plants, which include both those good for food and those that are poisonous. All plants, he argues, serve some good purpose, even if we do not know what it is. Thus he points out that certain birds, specifically the starling and the quail, can eat hemlock and hellebore without being poisoned. In certain doses, too, otherwise poisonous plants serve as medicine: for example, opium dulls terrible pain, and even hemlock and hellebore can mitigate diseases. He differentiates between diseased wheat and varieties of healthy wheat. This scientific inquiry into plants, which goes on at much greater length than I have surveyed here, is not about demonstrating the scientific validity of Genesis 1, but rather seeks to serve Genesis 1's larger purpose of manifesting the goodness of the creator and the richness of the creation.

When he comes to the fourth day, Basil praises "the great and prodigious show of creation" insofar as it is manifested in the heavenly bodies.[75] He compares the stars to flowers dotted across the sky, and he compares the universe to a great city filled with marvels. In contemplating the universe, we realize that we are capable of raising our minds beyond earthly things and seeking the cause of all things. The beauty of the stars, like the beauty of earthly creatures, reminds us that a creator of so much temporal and visible beauty surely must have in store for us an unimaginably beautiful eternity in the contemplation of invisible things. Similarly, the vastness of

---

vein, "Some consider the sun as the source of all productiveness on the earth. It is, they say, the action of the sun's heat which attracts the vital force from the centre of the earth to the surface. The reason why the adornment of the earth was before the sun is the following; that those who worship the sun, as the source of life, may renounce their error. If they be well persuaded that the earth was adorned before the genesis of the sun, they will retract their unbounded admiration for it, because they see grass and plants vegetate before it rose" (*Hexaemeron* 5.1, p. 76). For Basil, as we have seen, God does not depend on the sun even for light, let alone for vegetative life, since God is the fundamental source of all things: see, e.g., *Hexaemeron* 2.8, p. 64.

73. Basil, *Hexaemeron* 5.2, p. 76.
74. Ibid., 5.1, p. 76.
75. Ibid., 6.1, p. 81.

the universe reminds us that we must remain humble before the infinitude of God. Basil compares the sun, which is "subject to corruption" but nonetheless of extraordinary beauty and greatness, to the Son of righteousness, although the latter infinitely surpasses the former.[76] The sun is so beautiful that God created it only on the fourth day so that people would refuse the temptation to worship it. He investigates how it is that the sun gives light: the sun's "body" cannot be separated from light (just as fire's brightness cannot be separated from its heat and flame), but yet the sun's body is not identical with light. Instead, he thinks, the sun's body serves as the vehicle of immaterial light.[77] He recognizes the vast size of the sun and moon, and the extraordinary rapidity of the rotations of the stars and planets. In a lengthy discussion, Basil rejects all forms of astrology: we do not depend upon the movement of the heavenly bodies for our free action.

When Basil arrives at the fifth day, with its fish, sea creatures, and birds, he indefatigably and joyfully discusses frogs, gnats, flies, seals, crocodiles, hippopotamus, dolphins, stingrays, fish, mussels, scallops, shrimp, oysters, conches, crabs, lobsters, cuttlefish, lampreys, eels, swordfish, dogfish, sharks, and whales. Regarding small fish, he observes, "What infinite variety in the different kinds! All have their own names, different food, different form, shape, and quality of flesh."[78] He investigates how fish reproduce (eggs dropped into the water), how fish feed, and how fish and sea creatures protect themselves. He notes the differences in their food: mud, seaweed, other sea plants, as well as big fish eating smaller fish. He describes the way in which the crab, with its claws, seeks cunningly to eat the oyster, which is protected by its two shells. He also depicts the squid that camouflages itself against a rock so as to consume unsuspecting fish.

Against the view that the ocean is merely a place of utterly chaotic scramble for life, he points out that the life of fish and sea creatures generally follows a very specific order or pattern. Each kind of fish or sea creature appears to flourish in a particular place or area of the ocean. At the same time, he recognizes the existence of migratory fish, which migrate for example between the North Sea and the Euxine Sea; in this regard he asks where this regular migratory instinct could come from. He also wonders about why ocean water is salty, about the plants that form rock-hard coral, about why an oyster contains something as beautiful as a pearl, about the beautiful byssus or fleece of the sea pinna, and about the extraordinary range of the color purple found in shells.

76. Ibid., 82.
77. Ibid., 6.2, p. 83.
78. Ibid., 7.2, p. 91.

With patient delight in the uniqueness of each creature, Basil next turns to birds, who float through the air like fish do through the sea. He distinguishes birds that have claws for catching prey, or that walk well, from birds who live on insects and whose feet are unstable (such as the swallow). Some birds are gregarious and communal; others are independent and carnivorous. Most birds are migratory. Many birds like to live around humans. The music of birds seems marvelously variable: "Some twitter and chatter, others are silent, some have a melodious and sonorous voice, some are wholly inharmonious and incapable of song; some imitate the voice of man."[79] Basil recognizes that "the creatures which fly differ infinitely in size, form and colour," and "in their life, their actions and their manners, they present a variety . . . beyond the power of description."[80] He explores eagles, bats, wasps, flying insects, doves, cranes, starlings, jackdaws, bees, roosters, peacocks, and partridges. Of all flying things, bees impress him the most, and he devotes a great deal of attention to them. He notes that they work together and dwell together, and they are ruled by one bee, who is of "superior size, beauty, and sweetness of character."[81] He is deeply impressed by the gathering of nectar from flowers, by the making of honey, and by the building of complex honeycombs, in comparison with which the discoveries of geometry and architecture seem negligible.

In his analysis of the sixth day, on which God created "cattle and creeping things and beasts of the earth according to their kinds" (Gen. 1:24), Basil ponders the fact—or so he thought it to be—that "nature always makes a horse succeed to a horse, a lion to a lion, an eagle to an eagle, and preserving each animal by these uninterrupted successions she transmits it to the end of all things."[82] He states that in some cases, however, animals emerge spontaneously from the earth; for example, in wet weather, insects come forth. In Egypt, he says, hot weather and lots of rain cause the spontaneous generation of mice from the earth. We now know such things to be untrue, but we can easily understand how this would have seemed credible to Basil. He then begins to investigate the variety of animals, both with regard to their distinctive characteristics and with regard to their level of intelligence. Regarding their distinctive characteristics, Basil observes, "The ox is steady, the ass is lazy, the horse has strong passions, the wolf cannot be tamed, the fox is deceitful, the stag timid, the ant industrious, the dog grateful and faithful in his friendships."[83] The lion exhibits a proud, tyrannical, and unsociable

79. Ibid., 7.3, p. 97.
80. Ibid., 96.
81. Ibid., 7.4, p. 97.
82. Ibid., 9.2, p. 102.
83. Ibid., 9.3, p. 102.

disposition. The panther has extraordinary power and quickness. The bear has a heavy, sluggish body and a sly and secret disposition.

According to Basil, animals can be quite intelligent. The bear knows how to heal its wounds by applying the plant mullein; a tortoise, after eating a venomous snake, will protect itself by eating marjoram. Sheep fatten themselves before winter to prepare for the time when there will be little food. During the summer, ants zealously store provisions, and they also dry grains in the sun and cut them in half so that they will not germinate. Oxen recognize when spring has come and prepare to leave their pen. Hedgehogs adjust the entrance of their hole based upon anticipating the direction of the wind. Basil does not suppose that these animals are rational in the way that humans are, but he argues that God gave them a kind of intelligence from which humans can learn much.

In addition to intelligence, animals show affection and intuition. Basil notes that the baby lamb recognizes its mother from among a thousand sheep, and likewise the mother recognizes her baby. Baby dogs defend themselves against teasing, and baby calves butt with their heads even though they as yet have no horns. Dogs can track hunted animals with extraordinary accuracy. Dogs, too, show more gratitude and fidelity than do most humans. Basil also examines the procreation patterns and survival mechanisms of animals. He observes that those animals that are easiest to capture and kill produce the most offspring, whereas carnivores and venomous animals have few offspring. God has given each animal what it needs to survive: carnivores have big teeth and short necks (bears, tigers, lions); camels have long necks; elephants have trunks and no knee joints so that they keep their balance while standing; ruminating animals, which have few teeth, have many stomachs; scorpions have an exquisite delivery system for their venom.

Here, after a very brief exposition on the creation of humans in the image of God, Basil's *Hexaemeron* comes to an end. Even from my much-abbreviated survey, it should be clear how much attentive delight Basil takes in the manifold kinds of creatures—whose natures are illumined by science—that together compose the universe. Science helps Basil appreciate how the distinctive mode of being of each kind of creature manifests the wisdom and goodness of the creator God. Instead of trying to correlate Genesis 1 with modern science, then, we should allow Genesis 1 to stimulate our appreciation for the wondrous diversity of creatures that reveals so wise and good a creator—and we should do so by extensively availing ourselves of what science tells us about these diverse creatures. We should read Genesis 1 *alongside* modern science so as to accentuate and deepen Genesis's own interest in the amazing diversity of creatures coming forth from so great a creator.

The Analogy of Being and the Intrinsic Goodness of Beings

Nonetheless, Basil's approach, with its emphasis upon cosmic theophany and its corresponding appreciation for scientific detail about the wonders of creation, may still seem removed from the question of why God would make so many things that are doomed to die or crumble away, flashing in and out of existence in such rapid succession. To recall the questions that I noted at the outset of this chapter, why would God populate the earth with dinosaurs for millions of years, and why has God allowed more than 99 percent of the species that have ever existed on earth to become extinct?[84] I think that further light can be thrown on these questions by the philosophical doctrine of the analogy of being, abstract and arcane (and even antitheological) though this doctrine is sometimes imagined to be.[85]

Specifically, the analogy of being can help us to appreciate more deeply how it is that the finite actuality of each created being and of the totality of finite beings in their wondrous diversity is a theophany of God as pure act. The vast number of living creatures that once existed and the vast cosmic explosions and implosions are not a sign of cosmic failure; rather, each creature that has ever lived, and each nonliving thing, makes its theophanic contribution to the whole. As Reinhard Hütter says, every creature has a likeness to God, both because all creatures are participating beings and because all creatures "are ordered to God in order to obtain divine goodness and hence attain to the divine likeness according to their measure."[86]

In an essay that helpfully introduces the technical debates about the analogy of being, Michał Paluch asks why Aquinas conceived of this analogy both in terms of attribution and in terms of proportionality.[87] Paluch argues that these two versions of the analogy of being have complementary strengths. The analogy of attribution attributes the perfections of a created "effect" in a supereminent way to the divine cause. Aquinas employs this version of analogy in his *Summa theologiae*, and it serves to highlight the likeness between creatures and God, namely, the likeness (despite the ever-greater unlikeness) of an effect to its cause. The analogy of proportionality, for its part, appears in Aquinas's *De veritate* and serves to highlight God's transcendence by setting forth a "proportion": God's being is to God as created being is to creatures.

During the past fifty years, however, the analogy of proportionality has fallen out of favor. Paluch observes that for scholars such as Bernard Montagnes,

84. See Goodwin and Handley, *Encyclopedia of Animals*, 26.
85. See Thomas Joseph White, OP, "Introduction."
86. Hütter, *Dust Bound for Heaven*, 203–4.
87. Paluch, "Analogical Synthesis."

"only the analogy of attribution that is described in terms of causality, or participation understood as communication of act, may be the proper means to articulate the foundational bond between God and creatures."[88] By contrast, advocates of the analogy of proportionality, such as Steven A. Long, point out that it (and it alone) "allows us to establish in the center of our metaphysical analysis the Aristotelian distinction between act and potency."[89] As Long emphasizes, in the encounter with the actual beings that we see around us—composites of actuality and potency, in diverse and intrinsically analogous ways—we perceive both that being is not nonbeing and that act, as such, has no limits. The result is the "priority of the analysis of being before the reflection on being created."[90] On this view, the intrinsic analogicity of being, even before any reflection on the relationship of effect to cause, awakens the mind to the theophanic character of beings (from insects to stars to dinosaurs).

Long's approach to analogy serves the purposes of the present chapter. Let me therefore try to explain his position a bit further. He holds that the analogy from effect to cause presupposes the real being of the effect, which we discern through our contact with actual beings.[91] If so, then the analogy

88. Ibid., 604–5. See Montagnes, *Doctrine of the Analogy of Being according to Thomas Aquinas*. For the French version, see Montagnes, *La doctrine de l'analogie de l'être d'après Saint Thomas d'Aquinas*. For further criticism of the analogy of proportionality, see Wippel, *Metaphysical Thought of Thomas Aquinas*, chap. 13, esp. 552–55. Discussing Aquinas's defense of the analogy of proportionality in his *De veritate*, Wippel states, "His overriding concern throughout much of this discussion seems to be to protect divine transcendence. His theory of analogy of proportionality is not equally successful, however, in protecting him against the kind of agnosticism on our part which he associates with a theory of purely equivocal predication of the divine names" (554).

89. Paluch, "Analogical Synthesis," 604.

90. Ibid.

91. See Steven A. Long, *Analogia Entis*, 3–4. In his review of Long's book in *The Thomist*, Serge-Thomas Bonino, OP, states that "the critique addressed to B. Montagnes misses its goal to the extent that it omits any discussion of his essential thesis: the change of model for thinking about transcendental analogy comes in Thomas's thought from a deepening in the manner of conceiving divine causality: Thomas no longer thinks of the creature's relation to God 'as a resemblance of the copy to the model (formal causality) but as the dependence of one being in relation to another that produces it (efficient causality)' (Montagnes, *La Doctrine*, 91)" (631). Bonino differentiates philosophical and theological perspectives on analogy: "Just as it is legitimate that the philosophical approach begins by unifying the multiplicity of beings at the level of *ens commune* by means of the analogy of proportionality, extended then possibly to God, so the theological approach first grasps the unity of beings in light of their divine source and thinks of creatures first in terms of their relation to God by means of the analogy of intrinsic attribution" (632). For an erudite argument that—*pace* Montagnes and others, including most recently John Wippel and Gregory Rocca—Aquinas did not change his view of analogy, see Hochschild, "Proportionality and Divine Naming." Hochschild shows the analogy of proportionality to be fully at work in texts such as *Summa theologiae* (hereafter *ST*) I, q. 14, a. 3, ad 2, and *ST* I-II, q. 3, a. 5, ad 1.

of being arises from encountering actual beings, "diverse *rationes* of act" such as rocks and frogs, that are like each other insofar as they are actual, but that differ from each other insofar as they are limited (by potency) in diverse ways.[92] Long's view presumes the principle of noncontradiction (i.e., being is not nonbeing) and the distinction between act and potency.

Critics of the analogy of proportionality argue that it fails to account for its terms (specifically God's "being"), since infinite being is incomprehensible. Long responds that although pure act certainly "exceeds our knowledge" and transcends "the whole order of proportionate being," we can know that infinite being at least must be without any limitation of potency.[93] Long also emphasizes that "while the *esse* of the creature is an effect of God, it is not itself a receptive principle but rather the act of being of the substance that grounds the relation of creature to God."[94] Thus, Long anchors the analogy of being in actual finite beings. The analogy of being derives directly from our encounter with finite beings (diverse *rationes* of act/potency). In actual finite beings, we discover the analogicity of being, which is "the analogical unity of the likeness of diverse *rationes* of act and potency."[95] This "analogicity" of being means that all beings point to pure act; all beings are theophanic.

Another admirer of the analogy of proportionality, Erich Przywara, argues (not least in debate with Karl Barth) that it is in Jesus Christ that we see most clearly what the Fourth Lateran Council termed the similarity and the ever greater dissimilarity of creatures to God.[96] Paluch alludes to Przy-

92. Long, *Analogia Entis*, 4; cf. 68.
93. Ibid., 91; cf. 66: "*Esse* is limited in relation to essence as potency. That is to say, act is not self-limiting, but is limited only in relation to potency—finally, limited in function of the hypothetical but immutable divine intention to create that which He creates, namely, some limited type of being whose existence is caused by God as proportionate to its nature (which last is to that existence as potency is to act)."
94. Ibid., 70.
95. Ibid.
96. John R. Betz states that "the ultimate sense of analogy, as Przywara employs it, is *not* that of any analogy of attribution (which would highlight creaturely similitude to God as the *cause* of creaturely perfections) . . . but that of an analogy of proportionality (*analogia proportionalitatis*), understood . . . as a proportion of one alterity to another" ("Beauty of the Metaphysical Imagination," 55). Earlier Betz observes, along lines quite close to Long's: "This, then, in the briefest of terms, is what Przywara means by the analogy of being: an analogy between an absolute identity of essence and existence in God and an utterly contingent and gratuitous relation of essence and existence in creatures" (54). In email conversation with me on Sept. 15, 2015, Betz—who understands these matters deeply—commented that "the *analogia attributionis* and *proportionalitatis* seem conceptually equiprimordial (one has priority in one sense, the other in another sense, so that it is hard to come down on one over the other except as a matter of emphasis—as Przywara does)." In the same conversation, Betz suggested that "the *analogia proportionalitatis* provides a better way of addressing Heideggerian concerns about causality and onto-theology, and better explains the sense of wonder at the gift of being, as well as

wara's position by noting that "the doctrine explaining how human words may help us to discover the created and human similarities to God without compromising His always greater dissimilarity must lead us to His last and definitive Word—Christ. It is in Christ whose humanity became the tool of divinity that the logic of analogy reaches its ultimate confirmation and completion."[97] Without disagreeing with this appreciation for the instrumentality of Christ's humanity and its significant implications for the doctrine of the analogy of being (and for the openness of creation to new creation), I observe that the analogy of being is less a historical or eschatological claim than it is a metaphysical claim, even though these domains do not, in the end, conflict. All finite beings theophanically disclose pure act as their glorious and incomprehensible source, even though after the fall our minds may fail to perceive this theophany without the aid of grace.[98]

As an example of all created things' theophanic analogicity, consider the praise that, according to Psalm 148, all the beings of this world offer to God. Angels and humans, of course, should praise God freely and intelligently, and Psalm 148 does not leave this out. But Psalm 148 also exhorts the sun, moon, stars, highest heavens, sea monsters, fire, hail, snow, wind, mountains, trees, beasts, insects, and birds to praise the Lord. How could these irrational things praise God? The answer seems to be by simply existing, as actual things, in their wondrous diversity. Their praise of the creator is joined to the praise offered by "all peoples, princes and all rulers of the earth" (Ps. 148:11).[99] This union of humans and irrational creatures in praise of the creator accords with the fact that, as Christoph Schönborn remarks, humans "are related to all other creatures."[100]

Consider also God's response to Job, a response that highlights particular beings, including the earth, the sea, the thunderbolt, the torrents of rain, the

---

highlighting, as it does for Przywara, the *maior dissimilitudo* in every *similitudo*. It also captures the diversity of the acts of being, or diverse *rationes* of act and potency, that constitute the plenitude of being." For helpful exposition of Przywara's *Analogia Entis*, see Betz's "Translator's Introduction" in Przywara, *Analogia Entis*, as well as three essays in Thomas Joseph White, *Analogy of Being*: Betz, "After Barth"; Oakes, "Cross and *Analogia Entis* in Erich Przywara"; and Schenk, "Analogy as the *Discrimen Naturae et Gratiae*." For Hans Urs von Balthasar's concern that Przywara's analogy of being remained (despite itself) insufficiently christological, see Casarella, "Hans Urs von Balthasar, Erich Przywara's *Analogia Entis*, and the Problem of a Catholic *Denkform*," 204–5. It seems clear to me that in comparison to his *Analogia Entis*, Przywara's reflections on the analogy of being became increasingly christological over time.

97. Paluch, "Analogical Synthesis," 592. For elaboration of this point from a Thomistic perspective, see Thomas Joseph White, "'Through Him All Things Were Made' (John 1:3)."

98. On the effects of the fall, see White, "'Through Him All Things Were Made' (John 1:3)," 276–77.

99. Psalm 148:14 indicates that God's glory is manifested above all in Israel.

100. Schönborn, *Chance or Purpose?*, 116–17. See Berkowitz, *Stardust Revolution*.

stars, and the dew and frost, as well as the calving of deer, the horse's strength, and the soaring of the hawk and the eagle. In his response to Job (see Job 38–41), God especially emphasizes the strength of the hippopotamus and the crocodile. By their strength, these creatures bear witness analogically to God's strength. The analogy of being here begins with actual beings: arguably, God reminds Job of all these creatures so as to lead Job to God from the wildness and power of actual things. God repeatedly makes clear that these creatures are God's, and that God alone made them. The movement of God's response to Job is not so much from effect to cause—though such a movement is certainly included—but rather is from the modes of actuality of these wild and powerful things, to the God who as pure act transcends all such things, the God who can name himself "I AM" (Exod. 3:14).

Prior to God's response to Job, Elihu instructs Job in a manner that follows the path of effect-to-cause.[101] Each effect is said directly to point to the creative cause, God. Elihu begins with God as the reason why nonrational things behave in an intelligible and predictable manner. As Elihu urges: "Hear this, O Job; stop and consider the wondrous works of God. Do you know how God lays his command upon them, and causes the lightning of his cloud to shine? . . . Can you, like him, spread out the skies, hard as a molten mirror?" (Job 37:14–15, 18). The stability of the effect shows forth the power of God as transcendent cause, and assures Israel that God will not fail in the history of salvation.[102]

If the analogy of being is grounded primarily upon the encounter with the world as an analogical unity of diverse *rationes* of act/potency, without minimizing the path of effect-to-cause reasoning, then John Betz is right to say that "the reason why Plato and Aristotle began with wonder is that the sensible world *is* a revelation. This is why one *can* begin with the senses, and why one can—and *should*—begin with the experience of wonder."[103] From this

---

101. See Levering, "Book of Job and God's Existence."

102. This link between creation and God's covenantal promises is noted by Frances Young, in summarizing Augustine on the topic of the resurrection: "Created existence itself is the most powerful testimony for belief in the physical resurrection of Christ, the coming resurrection to the new age of humankind and the immortality of the body. God's promises are to be relied upon, God being the originator of creation, with all its marvels and surprises, and creation's goodness being rooted in God" (*God's Presence*, 103).

103. Betz, "Beauty of the Metaphysical Imagination," 47. For appreciation of the analogy of proportionality, see also Martin Bieler, "*Analogia Entis* as an Expression of Love according to Ferdinand Ulrich," 335, citing Ulrich, *Homo Abyssus*, 231. Bieler also directs attention to Cornelius Fabro's arguments for the necessary connection between the analogy of attribution and the analogy of proportionality: see Fabro, *Participation et causalité selon S. Thomas d'Aquin*, 510–35. For Ulrich and Bieler, once God is revealed as Trinity (and therefore as possessed of distinct processions that ground the distinction between God and the world), this "helps philosophy to

perspective, it seems quite possible that in Genesis 1's hierarchical movement toward greater actuality, from water and dry land (Gen. 1:9) to vegetation to fish and birds to animals and finally to humans (Gen. 1:26–28), we find a similar, though unthematized, "experience of wonder" with regard to the distinct ways in which actual things are limited by potency, and with regard to the special actuality of humans, since humans can know, love, and rule. In its portrait of creatures, Genesis 2 likewise appreciates the diversity of beings; in a short space, Genesis 2 mentions the ground, mist, trees, rivers, gold, bdellium, onyx, birds, animals. None of these things has an actuality equal to that of man/Adam. Man/Adam names all the living creatures, but finds no equal among them. Only woman/Eve, made specially by God for man/Adam, is actual in the way that man/Adam is: rationally. This confirms that the analogy of being finds its highest point, among bodily creatures, in the human person, as we would expect from Genesis 1:27's description of humans as created in the image of God.

Among all humans, the one who fully and truly images the wisdom and love of God is Jesus of Nazareth, who comes to us in what Betz calls "the novelty of revelation" that "exceeds rational comprehension."[104] In his human nature, Jesus Christ is the greatest creature and the one mediator, the true priest-king of all creation. His supreme offering of praise, through his salvific cross, embodies the (graced) perfection of human intelligence and love. Other creatures join in this praise insofar as they have actuality. The analogy of being, then, is a philosophical doctrine, but one consonant in the deepest possible way—as Przywara, Paluch, Betz, and many others rightly emphasize—with the revelation of God's "purpose which he set forth in Christ as a plan for the fulness of time, to unite all things in him, things in heaven and things on earth" (Eph. 1:9–10). As Kenneth Oakes puts it, the analogy of being "reflects and radiates the glory of Jesus Christ, the incarnate God."[105]

---

maintain the unity of its vision of created being as *completum et simplex sed non subsistens* instead of yielding to the temptation—out of angst—to close the gap between the finite and the absolute in a move toward univocation, which must then be counterbalanced by equivocation" (Bieler, "*Analogia Entis* as an Expression of Love according to Ferdinand Ulrich," 336).

104. Betz, "Beauty of the Metaphysical Imagination," 47.

105. Oakes, "Cross and *Analogia Entis* in Erich Przywara," 170. As Betz says in response to Karl Barth's critique: "The *analogia entis*, as a particular metaphysics . . . is, at the end of the day, simply a consistent development and philosophical clarification of the Church's doctrine of creation" ("Beauty of the Metaphysical Imagination," 49). Indebted to Przywara, Betz emphasizes that "the *analogia entis* (i.e., an ontological and not merely linguistic doctrine of analogy) is implied by Aquinas's doctrine of divine simplicity and his corresponding doctrine of a real distinction in creatures between essence and existence" (51; Betz's reference to a "merely linguistic doctrine of analogy" has in view such thinkers as Herbert McCabe and Ralph McInerny). See also Burrell, "Analogy, Creation, and Theological Language," cited approvingly by Betz.

It does so, however, in a way that allows for the theophanic analogicity of *all* creatures, from bacteria to dinosaurs to stardust and beyond, as befits the unity of creation in Christ, the perfect Image of God.

Conclusion

Without mentioning the book of Genesis, *The Encyclopedia of Animals* dismisses the biblical creation narratives (along with other ancient creation narratives) as mere "just-so" stories by which prescientific peoples tried to understand the origins of life. *The Encyclopedia of Animals* remarks in this vein: "Questions of how and where life began have fascinated and confounded people for millennia, giving rise to creation myths and legends in all human cultures."[106] In this way, *The Encyclopedia of Animals* simply assumes the correlational model that we found in Schroeder, albeit without Schroeder's appreciation for the deep intelligence and insight of Genesis.

In my view, attempts to present Genesis as a scientific account of material origins—the "how and the where life began" of *The Encyclopedia of Animals*, for example—fail to understand Genesis. It is better to recognize, as David Cotter observes, that in the six days "there are eight creative acts by God, first to create the physical environment and then to fill it with life. God orders, names, and distinguishes, putting things where they belong, blessing, and filling the now ordered and blessed world with life."[107] Life began because God, in his wisdom, willed that it be so; he "spoke" and things came to be. It is not the "how" of this, let alone the "where," that concerns Genesis. Rather, Genesis underscores the goodness and wisdom of all things precisely as the creatures of the wise creator. Genesis 1 is a liturgical celebration of the creator's gifting, and thus it is also a celebration of the magnificent diversity and profusion of creatures that pour forth from the creator and that reflect and even image his glory.[108]

---

106. Goodwin and Handley, *Encyclopedia of Animals*, 22. For the vast difficulty of explaining the origins of life, see Dawkins, *Blind Watchmaker*, chap. 6. See also the highly simplified perspective of J. Scott Turner's *Tinkerer's Accomplice*, 13: "I mean that life is, at root, a physiological phenomenon, and *no* attribute of life, including its evolution, really makes sense unless we view it through a physiological lens."

107. Cotter, *Genesis*, 16.

108. Joseph Blenkinsopp argues that the six days are intended to show that "human beings are created and sustained for the worship of God, and the world is created as a cosmic temple in which that worship takes place, a theme for which parallels can be found in Mesopotamian myth" (*Creation, Un-Creation, Re-Creation*, 21). Similarly, William Brown holds that Gen. 1 presents God as a generous builder of a cosmic temple, in a manner that undermines other ancient Near Eastern creation stories by underscoring God's serene generosity and by granting integrity

Reading Genesis 1 in this way, we need not be surprised to find that God governed dinosaurs for millions of years, or that God governed fiery rocks and gases for billions of years. The vast interstellar spaces, with their explosions and implosions, their black holes and dark matter and yet-to-be-discovered mysteries, are not meaningless. The extinct species that make up such an overwhelming majority of all species that have ever lived are not purposeless. Nothing is cosmic waste or cosmic absurdity, even though material things decay and die, collide with each other, and consume each other as part of the ongoing unfolding of spatiotemporal being. It is not for nothing that, as David Norman remarks, "the buzz of excitement created when children glimpse their first dinosaur skeleton is almost palpable."[109] Rather than being useless, dinosaurs and galactic systems are *theophanic*: in their finite actuality, they point to the creator who is pure act. We need not be surprised that God created so many kinds of plants and such amazing "swarms of living creatures" (Gen. 1:20) in the oceans, lakes, and rivers; nor that many such species have died off and given way to other species. Everything points to God, participates in God, and glorifies the wondrous actuality that God is. The diversity and profusion of creatures, including at its summit the human person gifted with rational communion in knowledge and love (the "image of God"), is indeed, as God says, "very good" (Gen. 1:27, 31).[110]

For Basil, as we saw, the profusion of creatures—which constitutes the unfathomably vast unity that we call the universe—shows that "nothing has been done without motive, nothing by chance. All shows ineffable wisdom."[111] For David Norman, by contrast—and reflecting the worldview prevalent among empirical scientists today—the universe and the creatures within it are mere happenstance. Certainly, Norman recognizes the uniqueness of the human race: "We are the first species ever to exist on this planet that has been able to appreciate that the Earth

---

and freedom to creatures. As Brown emphasizes, God's creative act involves the cooperation of creatures, since in Gen. 1:21 the waters themselves are to a certain extent responsible for the swarming of the sea creatures that God has made. Genesis 1 mentions seeds (Gen. 1:11) and implies sexual reproduction (Gen. 1:28). See Brown, *Seven Pillars of Creation*, 37–49. See also Bernhard W. Anderson's comments that Gen. 1 "presupposes the Jerusalem cult," which "gave special prominence to Yahweh's cosmic and universal kingship," especially "in the temple festival when Yahweh, 'the King of Glory,' entered into Zion" (*Creation versus Chaos*, 113).

109. Norman, *Dinosaurs*, 3. Norman concludes his book on an eschatological note that reflects his worldview: "The deeper question is: can we learn from past experiences and use them to help us to preserve an inhabitable Earth for other species to inherit when we are finally gone?" (166).

110. See Stephen M. Barr, *Modern Physics and Ancient Faith*; Purcell, *From Big Bang to Big Mystery*. See also, for the significance of natural beings precisely as "creatures," McGrath, *Reenchantment of Nature*.

111. Basil, *Hexaemeron* 5.8, p. 80.

is not just 'here and now' but has a deep history."[112] It is therefore with a tinge of sadness that he concludes, "The one thing we can be sure of, after studying the waxing and waning of species throughout the immensity of the fossil record, is that the human species will not endure for ever."[113] In this light, he urges us to preserve the earth as a habitable place for the species that will follow us just as we followed the dinosaurs. To preserve the earth, we need to recognize our own transience: "From our origins as *Homo sapiens* approximately 500,000 years ago, our species might last a further 1 million years, or perhaps even 5 million years if we are extraordinarily successful (or lucky), but we will eventually go the way of the dinosaurs: that much at least is written on the rocks."[114]

In this chapter, I have suggested that there is much more than this "written on the rocks," given the beauty of the rocks themselves, and the history of theophany that they preserve. If the human future were simply to become (eventually) a fossilized race, then our future would indeed be "written on the rocks" in a grim and ultimately meaningless way, since the rocks themselves will not care what gets written on them, and since there will be no one left to read the "writing" on the rocks; indeed even the rocks themselves will erode and eventually the whole earth will burn up when the sun dies. But as Genesis teaches, neither the rocks, nor humans, have such a meaningless destiny, because their origin is in the God who "created the heavens and the earth" (Gen. 1:1). Norman has not read the rocks rightly, nor, for that matter, has he properly understood the meaning of humans. There is the wondrous mystery of the unfathomably vast and bewilderingly rich profusion of creatures, and there is the unfathomably complex human brain, and there is the even greater mystery of rational, interpersonal communion.

As Eric Perl puts it—interpreting Dionysius the Areopagite—"all things at all levels, the least speck of dust no less than the greatest of the seraphim,

112. Norman, *Dinosaurs*, 166.
113. Ibid.
114. Ibid. It seems to me that this perspective, despite Norman's ecological intentions, in fact leads humans to live as though nothing in the universe has real meaning. Norman values each species, but in the end, everything will be just rocks and dust. If so, the deep value of each species (and future species) for my own life seems quite amorphous. As we see today, an environmentalist culture can be, at the same time, a consumerist culture. Norman Wirzba describes a consumerist perspective as follows: "To live in the world primarily as a consumer means that the world will come to be understood as one vast store or warehouse of commodities available for purchase. What matters most is that the world be made available to us efficiently, conveniently, copiously, and above all, cheaply" (*From Nature to Creation*, 39–40). Admittedly, Wirzba himself does not give a sufficient account of how, if food and resources are not relatively cheap, impoverished people will have access to them (that is, without a huge and rapid decrease in global human population). He assumes too quickly that modern economic and agricultural practices flow from "the worship of ourselves" (48).

are theophanies, the immediate manifestation and presence of God."[115] The rocks, in their finite actuality, are telling a story not of death or randomness, but of a purpose unfolding, as befits a creation that is "very good" (Gen. 1:31). Likewise, rather than telling a scientific story of origins, Genesis is telling what the rocks in fact tell: the glory of the God who is the origin of all things. For, ultimately, the purpose of the entire creation, rocks included, is cosmic praise and rejoicing—led by humans made in the image of God, and led even now (in the inaugurated but not yet consummated new creation, which will be marked by perfect charity and glorified bodiliness) by Jesus Christ, who is "the image of the invisible God, the first-born of all creation" (Col. 1:15).

Christoph Schönborn observes that for Aquinas, "God desired a multifarious world. No one creature alone can reflect God. It needs the whole plenitude of creatures to reflect God's plenitude. The variety of creatures is the multiform expression of the goodness of God."[116] And, as Basil shows, it is just this theophanic character that is adumbrated in Genesis 1. This is why modern scientific portraits of the cosmos of creatures do not render Genesis 1 irrelevant. Rather, Genesis 1 still provides the template for how to understand the vast profusion of things in relation to God and to each other. The infinite wisdom and goodness of the creator God are apparent in each and every finite thing, none of which is absurd or fails to manifest God—if only we know how to look rightly.

115. Perl, "Hierarchy and Love in St. Dionysius the Areopagite," 27.
116. Schönborn, Chance or Purpose?, 59–60.

FOUR

Image of God

God created man in his own image, in the image of God he created him; male and female he created them.

Genesis 1:27

Whither the Image of God?

In my first two chapters, on the ideas and simplicity of the creator God, I focused upon God's wisdom and freedom in the act of creation, which is rooted in the divine goodness. Chapter 3 then addressed the outpouring of creatures as not an absurd profusion, let alone a declension from the transcendental unity and simplicity of God, but a creaturely theophany of the infinite wisdom and goodness of God. Given the focus of my first three chapters upon God's wisdom, goodness, and freedom, it should not surprise that the present chapter interprets the "image of God" (Gen. 1:27) as the human imaging of the divine wisdom (above all by knowing God) and the human imaging of the divine goodness and freedom (above all by loving God). On this view, the human image of God is found in the human capacities for interpersonal communion, intellect, and will, since God possesses such spiritual perfections supereminently and the image mirrors the exemplar.

This understanding of the image of God, however, has fallen out of favor among contemporary theologians and biblical exegetes. Among theologians, it has become common to locate the image solely in human freedom. Thus, in light of the distinctive human ability to alter ourselves, Hans Urs von Balthasar argues that "the 'image of God' in the creature consists . . . in its *autexousion*, in the created mirroring of uncreated freedom" through "self-determination."[1] According to Balthasar, such an "image" cannot be grasped abstractly, but instead, like the divine freedom, can only be known in freely willed action. Balthasar therefore describes the image as lacking "all objective visibility and ascertainability."[2] Its content cannot be deduced from human "nature," since "it is by looking toward infinite freedom that finite freedom sees how it can and should realize itself in its finitude, its natural state."[3] Like divine freedom, human freedom "is *more* than what can be included in a conceptually clear definition."[4] Balthasar emphasizes that "just as the original, God, cannot be defined, neither can the copy, the 'image', whose distinctiveness comes precisely from the fact that it represents, in worldly and created terms, this nondefinable divine reality."[5]

Kathryn Tanner similarly proposes that since God is incomprehensible, human nature in the image of God must also be incomprehensible. She emphasizes human possession of "plastic powers, self-formative capacities" that ensure that humans, unlike other animals, "turn out in wildly different ways."[6] On this basis, she considers that humans "imitate God's incomprehensibility" because our spiritual capacities are not "limited by a predetermined nature"

1. Balthasar, *Theo-Drama*, 2:397.
2. Ibid.
3. Ibid.
4. Ibid., 345. Balthasar adds, however, "It is not simply mistaken and pointless to attempt such definitions. . . . While we can never come to the end of our attempt at integration, there are valid building stones to be used in the process. In the perspective of theo-drama, integration is God's act, not man's" (345–46).
5. Ibid., 320.
6. Kathryn Tanner, "Creation and Salvation in the Image of an Incomprehensible God," 68. Tanner integrated this essay into her *Christ the Key*. Somewhat similarly, Robert W. Jenson holds with regard to "the human" that "one cannot successfully think *about* what one cannot quite think at all. Our anthropological endeavors are at once impelled and checked by an epistemic quirk or set of quirks: notions we need to use and do use when we talk about ourselves as human resist thought" (*On Thinking the Human*, ix). Jenson's book achieves a great deal, but he would benefit from a stronger doctrine of human nature—as for example when he argues that the consciousness (the being-conscious) of all humans "is enabled by the existence of the church. Were there no community in creation that was itself centered around the One in whom divine community and created community have a common nexus, there might well be intelligent animals of our species, but the mystery we are pondering [i.e., the unity of consciousness] would not occur" (30). Jenson aims to avoid an individualistic anthropology by arguing that consciousness can only exist if it is located in community, primarily the triune divine community; human consciousness enters this community in the Son, Jesus Christ. But his admission that even without the Church "there might well be intelligent animals of our species" shows that his approach is tacitly grounded upon notions of "intelligent animals" and "our species" that require elucidation.

and, indeed, are not "anything in particular to start with."[7] She seeks to square this account of a fundamentally plastic, and thus incomprehensible, human nature with early Christian understandings of the image of God. From this perspective, she argues that the way in which the Greek fathers typically construed the image, namely, in terms of free will or self-rule, "could now be taken in a new light, not as the promotion of some vaunted power in a positive sense, an imitation of divine omnipotence, but as an interest in the unusual plasticity of human lives absent any predetermined direction by nature."[8]

Tanner's position seems to open the door to sheer voluntarism, which imagines that humans have no "nature" other than free will, and thus one can do anything one wishes with oneself without violating the proper ordering of human nature.[9] She attempts to limit this danger, however, by insisting that free will has nothing to do with "some vaunted power in a positive sense," because its purpose is simply to cleave to the sovereign divine image rather than to have any power of its own. In this vein, she remarks that it is only in clinging to the divine image (the incarnate Son) by God's grace that humans "have the image of God."[10] It still seems, however, that her portrait of human

7. Tanner, "Creation and Salvation in the Image of an Incomprehensible God," 75.

8. Ibid., 68. In Tanner's view, "like God who is incomprehensible because unlimited, humans might have a nature that imitates God only by *not* having a clearly delimited nature. . . . Humans are a definite sort of creature distinct from others, and in that sense of course still have a particular nature; they are not God who alone is different from others by not being a kind of thing. But humans can still stand out by their failure to be clearly limited by a particular nature as other creatures are" (64). Tanner goes on to suggest that this nondelimited nature is plastic because of its unlimited desire for good, because of its spiritual dynamism. But when Tanner defines this lack of limit, she does so more broadly: "What is of interest about human nature is its *plasticity*, its openness to formation through outside influences and the unusually wide range of possible effects of such a process of formation in the human case" (65).

9. I should note, however, that in her *Christ the Key* Tanner moves, more fruitfully in my view, along the lines of the divine ideas: "What creatures get from God pre-exists in God in exemplary fashion, and therefore when they participate in God in virtue of their creation creatures also image God" (9).

10. Tanner, "Creation and Salvation in the Image of an Incomprehensible God," 69. See Barth, *Church Dogmatics* [hereafter CD] III/1, 197: "Man is not created to be the image of God but . . . he is created in correspondence with the image of God. His divine likeness is never his possession, but consists wholly in the intention and deed of his Creator, whose will concerning him is this correspondence." For Tanner, "The image of God in a proper sense is just God, the second person of the Trinity" ("Creation and Salvation," 68). Tanner adds that "humans do become the divine image—by attaching themselves to it. It is by being identified with what they are not that the divine image becomes their own. Humans become the image of God in the strongest sense (not imaging the image [i.e., the Son] but simply identified with it) when they are not trying to *be* it at all, not trying to image the divine image in a human way, but are *brought near* to it, so near as to become one with it" (68–69). Thus humans "have the image of God only by clinging to what they are not—that divine image itself—in love" (69). Since Tanner holds that the "image of God" is the Son, her argument generally runs along lines other than

freedom as "not being anything in particular to start with" does not square with the reality that "our self-formative capacities" are indeed something distinctive and characterizable, with inscribed ends, inclinations, and potencies that mark out our proper flourishing, and in which our determinate bodily constitution participates.[11]

Tanner grants that her own position goes beyond the Greek fathers' emphasis on the image as free will or self-rule. But her reference to their position raises the question of how the Church fathers interpreted the image, and in fact their disagreements over the meaning of the image of God were already intense and deserve consideration here. As the patristics scholar Frances Young points out, Diodore, John Chrysostom, and Theodoret of Cyrus reserve the image of God (properly speaking) to men, with women imaging the male image of God. Clement of Alexandria holds that women are equally the image of God in the rational soul, but that women's bodies mean that men, on earth, are more in the image because they are more inclined to rational contemplation. Clement and Origen assume that the image of God is the human soul or mind, and they distinguish between the divine "image" and "likeness" (Gen. 1:26) by arguing that the latter involves the perfection acquired by the soul at the consummation of all things. Epiphanius of Salamis rejects the view that the image of God is the soul, but he displays even less patience for arguments that the image of God is the body (as argued by the desert monk Abba Apphou) or that the image of God is found in virtue or in baptism. He refuses to settle upon any candidate for the image of God, preferring to preserve it as an incomprehensible mystery—somewhat like Balthasar and Tanner, although they favor free will as the locus of the image.[12]

---

reflecting upon how humans image the *whole* divine Trinity or the divine essence. Thus, she envisions that humans "formed in Christ's image will follow the incomprehensible pattern of the Word's own relations with the other members of the Trinity" (75)—the "image" here is solely an image of the Word rather than of the whole Trinity. Yet she also speaks about our "imaging of the divine" (ibid.), presumably our imaging of the divine essence, and she argues that those who are saved by Christ will imitate in their "humanity the inclusiveness of the absolute being and goodness of God," seemingly another reference to imaging the divine essence in Christ (ibid.).

11. See MacIntyre, *Dependent Rational Animals*; MacIntyre, "Prologue: *After Virtue* after a Quarter of a Century," in *After Virtue*, ix–xvi. In his "Prologue," MacIntyre shows why indeterminate or voluntarist accounts of human nature do not work, by tracing a central development in his own thought since the first edition of his book: "It is only because human beings have an end toward which they are directed by reason of their specific nature, that practices, traditions, and the like are able to function as they do" (xi). To suppose that the end of human nature (itself now reduced to free will) lies solely in cleaving to Christ, and that human nature is otherwise indeterminate, is a mistake.

12. In his prologue to the *secunda pars* of the *Summa theologiae* (hereafter *ST*) Aquinas, too, emphasizes human freedom of action in connection with the image of God: "Since, as Damascene states (*De fide orthod.* ii. 12), man is said to be made to God's image, in so far as

Another approach appears in Irenaeus and Origen—namely, the image of God in Genesis 1 is Jesus Christ. Irenaeus and Origen offer distinct ways of understanding the claim that the image of God is Jesus Christ. For Origen, it is in Christ as the Word, whereas for Irenaeus, it is in Christ as human (that is, as the incarnate Word, who configures humankind to himself). Young explains that "what Irenaeus envisages is creation according to the image and likeness of God in Christ, and failure to realize this fully until the incarnation."[13] The difference between Origen and Irenaeus on whether Christ is the image as the Word or as human has significance for understanding the Arian crisis: for Arian sympathizers such as Eusebius of Caesarea, Christ is the image as Word, and therefore is similar but not identical to God (the Father). For the pro-Nicene Marcellus of Ancyra, Christ is image *only* in his human flesh, thus emphasizing that the Word is equal to the Father. Young credits Athanasius and the Cappadocians with developing an integrated account of the image, in which "the body is potentially the temple of God and the human person is God's image on earth, while the whole is held together in a Christology which sees Christ as intrinsically God's Image, both as Son of God and also as the new Adam, humanity as it was meant to be."[14]

For the purposes of the present chapter, it is noteworthy that the christological path marked out by Irenaeus is taken up by John Kilner in his recent *Dignity and Destiny: Humanity in the Image of God*, although he seems unaware of the extensive patristic discussion of Christ as the image (in his humanity and/or divinity). For Kilner, "the image of God is Jesus Christ. People are first created and later renewed according to that image."[15] Specifically,

---

the image implies 'an intelligent being endowed with free-will and self-movement': now that we have treated of the exemplar, i.e., God . . . it remains for us to treat of His image, i.e., man, inasmuch as he too is the principle of his actions." But Aquinas carefully unites the will with the intellect, as well as with the bodily components of human nature.

13. Young, *God's Presence*, 160.

14. Ibid., 173–74.

15. Kilner, *Dignity and Destiny*, xi. See also Kelsey, *Eccentric Existence*, 2:938: "I urge that the principal anthropological significance of the notion of the *imago Dei* emerges, not from its role in Genesis 1:26–27, but from its role in christological contexts in the New Testament. The significance of the notion of 'image of God' for theological anthropology emerges, I argue, when the question asked of the phrase 'image of God' is 'Who is the "image"?' rather than 'What is the "image"?' and when the answer is, 'Jesus Christ.'" For the point that the image of God is Jesus Christ in his humanity, see also 1009–34, 1045–51. Nonetheless, in affirming (with respect to Rom. 8:29) that "God's self-commitment to draw creation to eschatological consummation is equiprimordial with God's decision to relate creatively to all that is not God" (954), Kelsey insists that the content of the latter should not be reduced to the content of the former. In this regard he criticizes the approach of Grenz, *Social God and Relational Self*, 231–32. What is crucial is whether Gen. 1 (and not solely Gen. 1 in light of New Testament texts) reveals significant

Kilner holds that the image of God is Jesus Christ in his humanity.[16] We are created in the image of God in the sense that God creates us to be united with Christ, and we are renewed in the image of God when we are closely united with Christ (and with God through Christ).

Kilner warns repeatedly against "understanding God's image in terms of something that can be deformed by sin or other causes, as can any human attribute."[17] He recounts the deplorable ways in which theologians have excluded races, or the female gender, from the image of God. He denies that the image is the human soul and its powers, and he also denies that the image is "humanity's present ability to rule over creation."[18] The latter view inevitably leads to domination of creation, whereas the former view privileges those who are seen as more intelligent. Kilner points out that the Old Testament does not make fully clear what the image of God is, but the Old Testament does call humans to connection with God and urges humans to reflect the glory of God.[19] Kilner concludes that it is only when God reveals the image of God in Christ that we know what the image of God is. He explains, "Christ *is* God's image, according to the New Testament, and there is enough explanatory material in the relevant passages to offer many insights into what it means for humanity to be created *in* God's image."[20]

For Kilner, if the Bible tells us that Christ is the true image of God, then we do not need to look any further, especially when other options are so clearly conditioned by later cultural preferences (e.g., Greek privileging of the soul, Renaissance privileging of rulership over nature, Reformation emphasis on God's imputation of righteousness, twentieth-century emphasis on I-Thou relationship). His key point is that "the Bible's authors do not define God's image by ways that people are especially like God, that is, in terms of present

---

anthropological content. I think that it does, and that this revealed anthropological content fits well with (and is both illumined and in certain ways transformed by) what Jesus Christ reveals.

16. See also Barth's view that "the man Jesus in His being for man repeats and reflects the inner being or essence of God and this confirms His being for God. . . . The humanity of Jesus is not merely the repetition and reflection of His divinity, or of God's controlling will; it is the repetition and reflection of God Himself, no more and no less. It is the image of God, the *imago Dei*" (CD III/2, 219). Barth defines "real man" as "the covenant-partner of God" (203), and only Jesus, "in His being for man," is thus fully "real man" (and fully the image of God, since God, too, is "for man"). Barth adds that, of course, Jesus's humanity "is the image of God" and therefore "is only indirectly and not directly identical with God" (219).

17. Kilner, *Dignity and Destiny*, 21; cf. 28, 49, 95–115, 136, 178–230, and elsewhere.

18. Ibid., 36; cf. 44, 46.

19. See ibid., 116–32. See also such works as Briggs, "Humans in the Image of God and Other Things Genesis Does Not Make Clear"; and James Barr, "The Image of God in Genesis—A Study in Terminology"—both of which are cited by Kilner.

20. Kilner, *Dignity and Destiny*, 43.

human attributes."[21] Instead, it is the New Testament that defines the image of God, and it does so by identifying Jesus Christ as the image. This is made explicit in Colossians 1:15 and 2 Corinthians 4:4, and it is also evident in Hebrews 1:3, Philippians 2:6–8, Romans 8:29, and elsewhere.[22]

Kilner's position, however, raises a serious difficulty: If Christ is the image, how are all *other* humans in the image? Kilner cautions against conflating "the image of God with the human being," given our sinful and changing condition: we are only in the image because God created us to be configured to Christ.[23] Explaining this position, Kilner states that "creation *in* God's image is God's expressed *intention* that people evidence the special connection they have with God through a meaningful reflection of God"; the sinless Christ does this perfectly, and in Christ all people are called to do it.[24] Indeed, since God created humans in light of the predestined humanity of Christ, "the Ultimate Adam [Christ] is really the first—the one who not only created *adam* but also was the God-intended standard for *adam*."[25] It follows that when we are fully in the image (in Jesus Christ), then our reason, righteousness, rulership, and relationships—the attributes that are most often associated with the image—will be fully renewed and will be as God always intended them to be.

A similar stance against conceiving of the image of God as the human capacities for knowing and loving is adopted by Ian McFarland, who argues

21. Ibid., 51.

22. For discussion of these passages in light of significant recent biblical commentaries, see also Kelsey, *Eccentric Existence*, 2:951–1007. Kelsey notes that "in 2 Corinthians 4:4b and Hebrews 1:3, Jesus Christ is said to be the 'image of God,' or its functional equivalent, precisely in his humanity. However . . . Colossians 1:15 is open to the interpretation that it is the preexistent Son, God's agent in the creating and unifying of the cosmos, who is the image of God" (1003). Kelsey adds that these texts do not address how Jesus's "being is related to God's being," but rather address "how Jesus' identity images God's ways of actively relating to that which is not God" (1004). This fits with understanding the image of God in terms of royal rule, but it also raises underlying ontological questions. Functional and ontological renderings of the image of God should not be placed in opposition to each other.

23. Kilner, *Dignity and Destiny*, 135. Claus Westermann argues that the image pertains solely to the process or act of the creation of humans, so that Genesis 1:26–28 "is not making a generally and universally valid statement about the nature of humankind; if it were, then the Old Testament would have much more to say about this image and likeness" (*Genesis 1–11*, 155; cited in Kelsey, *Eccentric Existence*, 2:935). But the Old Testament does have more to say about the image and likeness; the story of the "image" continues with the fall, with the violence and pride culminating in the flood, with the covenantal election of Abraham, with the giving of the Torah and the effort to build up a holy people for God, and so on.

24. Kilner, *Dignity and Destiny*, 79. Kilner observes with regard to Colossians and 2 Corinthians, "There are two New Testament books that comment on the image status of both Christ and people, and they consistently distinguish between Christ, who is God's image, and people who need transformative growth according to the standard of that image" (91).

25. Ibid., 81.

that "so little is the *imago dei* an inherent property of humanity as such that it is described biblically as a state into which we are gradually transformed as the same Spirit that raised Jesus from the dead raises us to life with Christ by binding our lives ever more closely to his (see, e.g., Rom. 8:29; 1 Cor. 15:49; 2 Cor. 3:18; Col. 3:10)."[26] For McFarland as for Kilner, Jesus is the sole image, and other humans are "in the image of God" solely insofar as they "have been incorporated as members of Christ's body."[27] Since this position seems to exclude non-Christians from being created in God's image, McFarland clarifies it by stating that creation in God's image can simply refer "to the fact that God has chosen to relate to human beings" through Christ, and thus in this manner all humans are created to be in God's image.[28] Like Kilner, McFarland supposes that this position grounds rule and relationship by compelling us, when we ask where Christ's image is, to look precisely at those whom we have ignored or excluded but whom God made in his image: thus "in biblical perspective it is *Christ* who interposes himself between myself and my neighbor—and does so precisely so that I may see my neighbor as and for the person she is."[29]

By way of drawing these contemporary conversations together, let me note that Kilner's and McFarland's reflections on Jesus Christ as the sole image fit in certain ways with Balthasar's and Tanner's approaches. Balthasar suggests that since the image only expresses itself in free action, we only recognize the image truly when we see the free action or *mission* of the Image/image, Jesus Christ—within whose mission *each human being receives a specific and irreplaceable mission.*[30] Balthasar focuses on Christ's obedience and our obedience in Christ.[31] Tanner holds that humans possess the image insofar as they strive to cleave to *the* image, Jesus Christ, and since this happens by grace, God is sovereignly working out the mystery of his merciful and inclusive will for all humans in Christ.[32]

26. McFarland, *Divine Image*, 165. McFarland draws constructively upon Maximus the Confessor.

27. Ibid.

28. Ibid.

29. Ibid., 164. Cf. McFarland's *Difference and Identity*.

30. For freedom as the image of God, see also Bonhoeffer, *Creation and Fall; Temptation*, 40–43.

31. See Balthasar, *Theo-Drama*, vol. 4, part 3. See also Barth, *CD* III/1, 265, where Barth defines created freedom as fundamentally "the freedom to obey," while at the same time asserting that "this freedom has nothing whatever to do with man's divine likeness or the foolhardy assumption of divine responsibilities."

32. Another recent student of the image of God, Anthony Hoekema, proposes that Christ is the image of God, and therefore "the heart of the image of God must be love"; see *Created in God's Image*, 22; cf. 73–75 on Christ's being wholly directed to God, wholly directed to his

Instructed by the patristic and contemporary treatments of the image of God, the present chapter asks *how* Christ is at the center, not whether Christ is at the center. For Athanasius, as Young helps us to see, Christ's centrality as the image of God is both as creator and as redeemer. Athanasius goes beyond recent interpreters of the image of God because he sees a link between the creative Word and rationality.[33] If the Son is the Word, and humans are the image of the Word, then why should not this human image be associated uniquely with reason/word? As Athanasius points out, this association belongs to the New Testament's canonical testimony to the Word (John 1) as image of God (Col. 1:15). I agree with Athanasius that if the human image of God is connected uniquely with the Word, then it is connected with reason and freedom, intellect and will.[34]

Informed by this broadly Athanasian perspective, I structure this chapter in three sections. I first examine the evolutionary emergence and constitutive marks of the first humans as presented by contemporary paleoanthropologists. For such scholars, consciousness is a strictly biological phenomenon, whereas I consider consciousness to be the fruit of rational ensoulment prepared for by

---

neighbor, and ruling over nature (with respect to these three relationships, the human image of God is fallen and in need of renewal). For emphasis on love as the key to the image of God, see also Berkouwer, *Man*, 100–104; and Weber, *Foundations of Dogmatics*, 1:574. Both Berkouwer and Weber are cited by Hoekema, although he differentiates his own position from both of theirs.

33. For related concerns regarding the "Christological historicization of human nature," see Thomas Joseph White, OP, "The 'Pure Nature' of Christology," (quotation from 298). For the humanity of Jesus as revelatory of human nature, see Barth, *CD* III/2, 226; cf. 231.

34. In criticizing Thomas Aquinas's account of the image of God, Anthony Hoekema states that

> Aquinas finds the image of God solely in man's *intellectual* nature. This view has its roots in Greek thought rather than in Scripture. Both Plato and Aristotle call man's intellect divine; it was the spark of divinity within man. When Thomas asserts that the image of God must be seen particularly in the intellect, since the intellect is the most Godlike aspect of man, he is echoing a typically Greek idea. We may admit that there is in human intellectual ability a reflection of God who is the supreme Knower, but to say that the image of God is found exclusively or even primarily in man's intellect is to render a judgment that is more Greek than Christian. The Bible says that God is love; nowhere does it say that God is intellect. (*Created in God's Image*, 39)

But the Bible does say that God (the Son) is Logos, Word; and the Bible makes clear that God knows all things. Moreover, Aquinas never limits the image to the "intellect"; intellectual or rational nature includes both intellect and will for Aquinas. Hoekema also suggests that focusing on human rationality downplays "man's relatedness to God and others" (ibid.), when in fact human relatedness arises precisely in and through our rational dynamisms. When Hoekema presents his own constructive viewpoint, however, his position comes much closer to Aquinas's. Hoekema argues that the image "must include both man's structure and man's functioning" (69). For Hoekema, the soul and its powers are the "structure," and the functions include such things as worship, love, and rule.

body and brain evolution.[35] I accept that the first humans were intellectually primitive hunter-gatherers. A first component of the image of God, therefore, is that it should not require any developed level of culture, because otherwise the first humans could not have been created in the image of God.

In my second section, I examine the standard way that historical-critical biblical scholars today interpret the original meaning of the image of God for the author(s) of Genesis 1. Here I focus upon Richard Middleton's *The Liberating Image*, which surveys recent biblical exegesis on the topic and thoroughly investigates Genesis's meaning in light of Mesopotamian parallels. Middleton finds that the image of God is democratized royal rule or dominion. As Frances Young points out, for both Genesis and the Church fathers, humans are "in a kingly position in relation to the rest of the created order."[36] I conclude that royal rule, in imitation of the wise creator God, must pertain to the image of God.

On the basis of these first two sections, my third section argues that the image of God is in the human soul.[37] For Young, the "image of God" is present only in community and solidarity: the image "points away from discrete, supposedly autonomous, individuals to the solidarity of incorporation into the humanity of Christ, who is truly 'the image of the invisible God.'"[38] In

35. I agree with C. S. Lewis's remark: "I do not doubt that if the Paradisal man could now appear among us, we should regard him as an utter savage, a creature to be exploited or, at best, patronised"—though "God came first in his love and in his thought, and that without painful effort" (*Problem of Pain*, 78–79). Lewis adds, "He may have been utterly incapable of expressing in conceptual form his Paradisal experience. All that is quite irrelevant. From our own childhood we remember that before our elders thought us capable of 'understanding' anything, we already had spiritual experiences as pure and as momentous as any we have undergone since, though not, of course, as rich in factual content" (79).

36. Young, *God's Presence*, 137. See also N. T. Wright's chapters "Priests and Rulers" and "Virtue in Action: The Royal Priesthood," in his *After You Believe*, 73–100 and 219–55.

37. As C. John Collins remarks, "Suppose that someone is convinced of the *representative* or *relational* view [of the image of God]: this person must nevertheless recognize that these views actually presuppose that there are some distinctive human capacities that make the relationships and ruling possible. Therefore, no matter which interpretation of the image of God we prefer, we must, if we are to be careful, acknowledge that it implies that there is something about human capacities that is different from those in any other animal" (*Did Adam and Eve Really Exist?*, 94–95). Collins identifies these capacities (the divine image) as most importantly intelligence and love. He goes on to argue that Steven Pinker and others have radically underestimated the uniqueness of human language.

38. Young, *God's Presence*, 181–82. Young also considers that "God's image is not something inherent, nor is it similar to 'human rights', but rather a gift of grace" (181). But if humans are "created . . . in the image of God" (Gen. 1:27), why would the image not be "something inherent," that is to say, something that belongs inherently to the kind of creature we are? And why, given that "a gift of grace" signifies something distinct from "a gift of creation" (though both are gifts, and though they are not cut off from each other), why would the statement that "in the image of God he created him" (Gen. 1:27) signify a gift of grace? Indeed, Young herself

my view, conceiving of the image of God as expressed communally should be paired with the insistence that *each* individual human is in the image of God.[39] It seems to me that the best way to locate the image of God in each human, while retaining the royal rule emphasized by biblical exegetes and while insisting upon the relationality of the image, is to defend the view that the image of God is in the soul's powers of knowing and loving, and thus is fully manifested in Jesus Christ.[40] Augustine, of course, stands out for his influential account of how the image of God is in the individual soul. Even so, for Augustine the embodied human soul is never autonomous; it is always in various kinds of relationship to the Triune God, to Christ and his body the Church, and to other people and communities.[41] Drawing upon Thomas Aquinas as a representative of the Augustinian position on the image of God, my third section attempts to draw together the primitive, royal, rational, and christological dimensions of the image of God as revealed by Scripture.[42]

Human Origins according to Modern Science: From Hominid to Human

Theological accounts of the creation of humans "in the image of God" (Gen. 1:27) should not ignore the research on human origins that has been undertaken over the past century and a half. Paleontologists and paleoanthropologists now tell us that large populations of nonhuman hominids existed in the past,

states that the image or "God-likeness" is "given in principle at creation," and she affirms that "the gift of the image involves freedom and potential to make moral choices," both of which pertain to the human being as created (ibid.).

39. Karl Barth is certainly right that "every supposed humanity which is not radically and from the very first fellow-humanity is inhumanity" (*CD* III/2, 228). See also Barth's earlier statement, focused entirely (by contrast to III/2) on the image of God as consisting in the male-female conjunction: *CD* III/1, 195; cf. his treatment on 196 of "the relationship between the summoning I in God's being and the summoned divine Thou."

40. It would be a mistake to adopt the strict opposition proposed by David Kelsey, who holds that "it is humankind as some sort of corporate whole that is created according to or after the image of God" (*Eccentric Existence*, 2:922). Hoekema similarly concludes that "the image of God in its totality can only be seen in humankind as a whole" (*Created in God's Image*, 99). Hoekema cites Herman Bavinck, who argues that "only the whole of humanity is the fully developed image of God" (Bavinck, *Reformed Dogmatics*, 2:577).

41. On christological configuration to the image of God, see Gioia, *Theological Epistemology of Augustine's "De Trinitate,"* 232–97; Ayres, "Christological Context of *De Trinitate* XIII." In Augustinian fashion, Joseph Ratzinger concludes that the image of God fundamentally "means that human persons are beings of word and of love, beings moving toward Another, oriented to giving themselves to the Other and only truly receiving themselves back in real self-giving" (*In the Beginning . . .*, 48).

42. For further discussion of the image of God according to Aquinas, see Torrell, *Saint Thomas Aquinas*, 2:80–100; Dauphinais, "Loving the Lord Your God"; O'Callaghan, "Imago Dei." See also Levering, *Jewish-Christian Dialogue and the Life of Wisdom*, chap. 3.

including *Australopithecus* (3–1.4 million years ago), *Homo habilis* (2.4–1.5 million years ago), *Homo erectus* (1.9 million years ago), and prerational *Homo sapiens* (400,000–approx. 150,000 years ago). Describing the current scientific consensus regarding the evolutionary emergence of humans, Michael Benton states, "It seems that all modern humans arose from a single African ancestor, and that the *H. erectus* stocks in Asia and Europe died out. *H. sapiens* spread to the Middle East and Europe by 90,000 years ago."[43] From 90,000 to 30,000 years ago, Neanderthals were dominant in Europe. Benton presents them as large-brained, stocky and powerful, and possessed of "an advanced culture that included communal hunting, the preparation and wearing of sewn animal clothes, and religious beliefs."[44] Their bodies were adapted to life in the ice ages. Benton classifies them among *Homo sapiens*, although he notes that some other scientists classify them separately.[45] He finds that they "disappeared as the ice withdrew to the north, and more modern humans advanced across Europe from the Middle East."[46] This advance eventually populated the whole habitable world: "This new wave of colonization coincided with the spread of

43. Benton, *History of Life*, 164. For a somewhat more complicated view, see Stringer, *Lone Survivors*, 250–64.

44. Benton, *History of Life*, 164. Klein and Edgar hold that Neanderthals lacked a complex culture, and that it was this lack of culture that led to their extinction. They note that "the Neanderthals manufactured a relatively small range of recognizable stone tool types, and they probably used a single type for multiple tasks like butchering, wood working, or hide processing. In contrast, their fully modern successors generally made a much wider variety of discrete types, and they probably designed each type for a relatively narrow purpose" (*Dawn of Human Culture*, 180). Klein and Edgar do not include religious beliefs among the abilities they attribute to Neanderthals, but they do view Neanderthals as sharing, in general, a common "humanity" with modern humans. They state, "Neanderthals and Cro-Magnons shared many advanced behavioral traits including a refined ability to flake stone, burial of the dead, at least on occasion, full control over fire (implied by the abundance of hearths in their sites), and a heavy dependence on meat probably obtained mainly through hunting. In addition, both Neanderthal and Cro-Magnon skeletal remains sometimes reveal debilitating disabilities that imply that the people cared for their old and their sick. There could be no more compelling indication of shared humanity" (189). For a more detailed and nuanced discussion, suggesting that "shared humanity" is an exaggeration, see Stringer, *Lone Survivors*, 142–70, 190–204. On 168–70 Stringer discusses the ongoing controversy among archaeologists regarding whether Neanderthals made and used symbolic objects. For the evolutionary development of the hominid brain, see 207–13.

45. Stringer, for instance, urges that even though Neanderthals and modern humans interbred, they should still be classed as different species. As he says, merging the two into one species would produce "a *Homo sapiens* characterized by, for example, a high and rounded skull, and a long and low skull; by no continuous brow ridge, and a strong continuous brow ridge; by a well-developed chin even in infants, and no chin; by no suprainiac fossa in adults, and a suprainiac fossa in adults; by an inner ear of modern shape, and an inner ear of Neanderthal shape; by a narrow pelvis with a short thick superior pubic ramus, and a wide pelvis with a long thin superior pubic ramus—and so on" (*Lone Survivors*, 266).

46. Benton, *History of Life*, 164.

Homo sapiens over the rest of the world, crossing Asia to Australasia before 40,000 years ago, and reaching the Americas 11,500 years ago, if not earlier."[47] According to Benton, Neanderthals possessed religious beliefs, but modern humans had larger brains and "brought more refined tools than those of the Neanderthals, art in the form of cave paintings and carvings, and religion."[48] Around 10,000 years ago, settlements and agriculture replaced the previously nomadic life of *Homo sapiens*.

The paleontologist Richard Fortey tells the story a bit differently. He reviews various hominid fossils, including *Australopithecus*, from which emerged the species *Homo*, and he notes that bipedal hominid footprints have been discovered from 3.6 million years ago, preserved in volcanic rock. He argues that *Homo habilis* (around 2.5 million years ago) "was probably the original toolmaker."[49] For around a million years, there was no change in the production of tools, indicating that such tools are not a sign of intelligence. *Homo erectus* (1.7 million years ago, according to Fortey) made slightly more sophisticated tools, as do chimpanzees. Fortey reports that according to recent scholars such as Chris Stringer, building upon genetic evidence, modern *Homo sapiens* emerged around 40,000 years ago in Africa and spread throughout the world.[50] Between 110,000 and 35,000 years ago, there were also Neanderthals, who made intricate tools, buried their dead, and placed flowers in the graves. While admitting that the fossil record is sparse, Fortey observes, "The origin of *H. sapiens* was from among a series of populations spanning a time interval between 700,000 and 125,000 years ago."[51] But with the spread of modern *Homo sapiens* around the world beginning about 40,000 years ago, we find "spectacular advances in the technology of stone tools; within the compass of a few thousand years more innovation had been achieved than in the previous million years by *H. erectus* and his 'archaic *sapiens*' successor—whatever they should be called."[52]

According to Fortey, genetic evidence indicates that all humans living today possess "genetic material derived from one woman" who lived in Africa,

47. Ibid.
48. Ibid. See also Cook, *Ice Age Art*, and the remarks on this text by Rowan Williams, *Edge of Words*, 25–26.
49. Fortey, *Life*, 300.
50. See Stringer, *African Exodus*; Wood, *Human Evolution*. See also Stringer and Andrews, *Complete World of Human Evolution*; Stringer, *Lone Survivors*, 256–68. In *Lone Survivors*, Stringer acknowledges an "added complexity and evidence of interbreeding with Neanderthals and Denisovans," but he concludes that "if the evidence for archaic assimilation [interbreeding between modern humans and archaic humans] remains modest and restricted to Africa and the dispersal phase of modern humans from Africa, constituting less than 10 percent of our genome, I think 'mostly Out of Africa' is the appropriate designation" (265).
51. Fortey, *Life*, 304.
52. Ibid., 305.

although this does not imply that we all descend directly from one human couple.[53] Modern *Homo sapiens* includes "Cro-Magnon man" (30,000–15,000 years ago), whom Fortey dubs "Man the Artist," since "Cro-Magnons drew exquisite icons of the animals they held sacred, or those they hunted. These outline drawings, in ochre, in charcoal, or in natural pigment, portray mammoths, antelopes, bison, oxen, horses. Man himself appears as an emblem, rather than a portrait, a spindly figure, a dark, attenuated sprite."[54] Fortey considers that *Homo sapiens* developed separately from Neanderthals, and he argues that Neanderthals showed sufficient signs of consciousness, with the result that *Homo sapiens* can no longer be said to be the sole species possessed of consciousness. In order for "consciousness" to be possible, he notes, there must be various developments in the hominid body, including prominent development of the frontal lobes of the brain, as well as the larynx and vocal cords, since thought and language should be expected to develop in tandem.[55]

53. Ibid., 306.
54. Ibid., 307. Stringer remarks that

there is not yet any strong evidence for figurative or clearly representational art anywhere before the European material dated at about 40,000 years. . . . However, the processing and use of red pigments in Africa does go back considerably farther, to beyond 250,000 years, at sites like Kapthurin and Olorgesailie in Kenya. The record is sporadic after this but emerges at Pinnacle Point in South Africa at about 160,000 years, and much more strongly at sites in North and South Africa from about 120,000 years. In particular, there is the rich material from Blombos Cave, South Africa, which includes about twenty engraved ocher fragments and slabs, dated to around 75,000 years ago and some which extend back to 100,000 years. These fragments seem to be generally accepted as symbolic in intent rather than accidental or utilitarian, but many of the earlier examples are only suggestive of symbolic meaning, rather than definitive. (*Lone Survivors*, 213–14)

Regarding the use of symbolism, Stringer goes on to conclude: "Personally I think the proliferation of shell beads and red ocher use along the length of Africa between 75,000 and 100,000 years ago must reflect an increasing intensity of symbolic exchanges both within and probably between early modern human groups. But perhaps the highest levels of symbolic meaning were still only nascent then" (215).

55. Similarly, Stringer argues that "simple languages must already have existed in early human species, given the complexity of behavior that is apparent at sites like Boxgrove and Schöningen in Europe and Kapthurin in Kenya, and so Neanderthals would have inherited and built on the language or languages acquired from their ancestors. But in my view it was only with the growing complexity of early modern societies in Africa that sophisticated languages of the kind we speak today would have developed, through the need to communicate increasingly intricate and subtle messages" (*Lone Survivors*, 217). Stringer argues that the development of complex language would have been stimulated by "humanly driven cultural or sexual selection, favoring the best communicators" (ibid.). It is worth noting that, as William Brown points out, "the human brain is of such complexity that quantifying it reaches astronomical proportions. One estimate is 10^{13} neurons, each equipped with several thousand synapses" (*Seven Pillars of Creation*, 64). On the development of thought and language, and the irreducibility of human consciousness to material elements, see Braine, *Language and Human Understanding*. Braine concludes his vastly complex work by stating:

After the spread of *Homo sapiens* around the globe during the ice age, the end of the ice age resulted in the rising of the oceans and the isolation of groups of *Homo sapiens*. Fortey states, "The cultural diversity of humankind arose during 10,000 years or so of tribal differentiation."[56] He pays attention here to religious rituals and to war. He explores the domestication of animals, the development of agriculture, the rise of settlements, and the making of pottery between 15,000 and 5,000 years ago.[57] As he concludes, "The popula-

---

> The judgments we make are not limited by any set of mechanically applicable rules capable of representation or embodiment in the workings of a physical organ, and are situated within the setting of the unitary framework of understanding, involving a general logic which cannot be formalized. . . . Our thinking is not embodied in speech; nor is it embodied in neural or imaginative sequences. Thus, when we say that a man had the sudden thought, "Heavens! The post has gone!", it is evident that the man has already thought the "has gone" when he thinks "Heavens!", since it is the post having gone which is the object of his surprise; hence it is evident that, although these words express the thought he has had, his having the thought did not consist in saying these words successively to himself; rather, he had the thought in an indivisible act. . . . Yet these activities are at the same time, of their very nature, expressed through speech and coordinated with the use of the imagination, both involving the brain and how its activity is organized, notably in the exercise of memory of vocabulary and accidence, while the acquisition of concepts depends in varied ways on sensory experience. (753)

56. Fortey, *Life*, 311.

57. On this period, see the fascinating reconstruction by Mithen, *After the Ice*. The extent of global climate change and development of civilization during this period is well summarized by Mithen:

> The peak of the last ice age occurred at around 20,000 BC and is known as the last glacial maximum, or LGM. Before this date, people were thin on the ground and struggling with a deteriorating climate. Subtle changes in the planet's orbit around the sun had caused massive ice sheets to expand across much of North America, northern Europe and Asia. The planet was inundated by drought; sea level had fallen to expose vast and often barren coastal plains. Human communities survived the harshest conditions by retreating to refugia where firewood and foodstuffs could be found. Soon after 20,000 BC global warming began. Initially this was rather slow and uneven—many small ups and downs of temperature and rainfall. By 15,000 BC the great ice sheets had begun to melt; by 12,000 BC the climate had started to fluctuate, with dramatic surges of warmth and rain followed by sudden returns to cold and drought. Soon after 10,000 BC there was an astonishing spurt of global warming that brought the ice age to its close and ushered in the Holocene world, that in which we live today. It was during these 10,000 years of global warming and its immediate aftermath that the course of human history changed. By 5000 BC many people throughout the world lived by farming. New types of animals and plants—domesticated species—had appeared; the farmers inhabited permanent villages and towns, and supported specialist craftsmen, priests and chiefs. Indeed, they were little different to us today: the Rubicon of history had been crossed—from a lifestyle of hunting and gathering to that of farming." (4)

Mithen notes that such radical climate change is not unusual in human evolutionary history: "Our ancestors and relatives—the *Homo erectus, H. heidelbergensis* and *H. neanderthalensis* of human evolution—had lived through equivalent periods of climate change as the planet see-sawed from ice age and back every 100,000 years. They had responded by doing much the

tion doubled, and redoubled. More people meant more inventiveness: the rush of invention tracked the population and has never ceased. Writing began in the most functional way—the tally of lentils or the baking of a dozen loaves recorded on a clay tablet."[58] In this way, the period of human history as we know it arrived.

To recap: Benton argues for an origin in Africa some 150,000 years ago of all hominids possessed of "consciousness," counting Neanderthals among those. Benton classifies Neanderthals as *Homo sapiens*, and credits Neanderthals with a rather high level of culture. For his part, Fortey draws a sharp distinction between Neanderthals and modern *Homo sapiens*—who emerged 40,000 to 50,000 years ago in Africa—even though he considers both to have "consciousness." Benton's view would place the first hominids possessed of consciousness in Africa around 150,000 years ago, at a very primitive level, while Fortey's view emphasizes the significance of modern *Homo sapiens*, but would also allow for at least one earlier species of nonhumans possessed of consciousness, namely Neanderthals, a species that no longer exists.

In light of these viewpoints regarding human evolution, it seems that a good deal depends upon what it means to credit Neanderthals—and premodern *Homo sapiens* in the period between 150,000 and 50,000 years ago—with "consciousness." Certainly, once the level of culture can be shown to have reached a certain point, free and rational consciousness must be present; but the question is when this point was actually reached. Fortey speaks of consciousness as "the final threshold . . . freeing the mind from the confines of mere cells, allowing imagination to probe situations not yet encountered: a sense of self—and reason."[59] David Bentley Hart offers a more elaborate account of consciousness, against reducing the emergence of consciousness solely to the evolution of brain functions (such as memory), important though the latter must have been.[60] Hart appreciates the mind's "seeming indivisibility, intentional orientation toward formal and final objects of thought,

---

same as they had always done: their populations expanded and contracted, they adapted to changed environments and adjusted the tools they made" (ibid.).

58. Fortey, *Life*, 314.

59. Ibid., 308.

60. For the reductionist view, see Rose, *Making of Memory*. Along broadly similar lines, Chris Stringer cites Stanley Ambrose's view that

> what was most important was the integration of working memory with prospective memory (dealing with near-future tasks) and constructive memory (mental time traveling), which are centered in the front and lower rear of the frontal lobes. Such links would have facilitated everything from the construction of composite artifacts to the development of the fullest levels of mind reading and social cooperation. In his view, archaic humans like the Neanderthals had developed the memory for short-term planning and the production of composite artifacts, but they lacked the full brain integration and hormonal

incommunicable privacy of perspective, capacity for abstract concepts, and all its other mysterious powers," including its immediacy, its "extraordinary openness to the physical world," its "reflective awareness of itself," and "the liberty of its conceptual and imaginative powers from the constraints of its material circumstances."[61]

The stunning breakthrough that occurred around 40,000 to 50,000 years ago—a breakthrough whose first African origins may perhaps have been even earlier, although Chris Stringer notes that "signs of 'modern' traits such as symbolism and complex technology are hardly apparent until after 45,000 years ago"[62]—exhibited the kind of consciousness that Hart describes. Modern *Homo sapiens* quickly moved far beyond the few advances of premodern *Homo sapiens* and Neanderthals, who buried their dead, produced composite tools and weapons with blades, used pigments, made pendants from seashells, and harnessed fire. Richard Klein and Blake Edgar have aptly described the breakthrough as a "dawn" that has resulted in a "series of ever more closely spaced 'revolutions,' starting with agriculture and running through urbanization, industry, computers, and genomics."[63] This dawn, which Klein and

---

    systems that promoted the levels of trust and reciprocity essential for the much larger social networks of modern humans. (*Lone Survivors*, 212)

    Memory has long been recognized—not least by Thomas Aquinas—to belong to the cognitive powers that humans share with other animals possessed of complex brains. Stringer adds that "several archaeologists and biologists" have attributed the new abilities of humans around 50,000 years ago to the brain-strengthening "fish oils obtained by early moderns when they began to seriously exploit marine resources" (213).

    61. David Bentley Hart, *Experience of God*, 155–56. For the argument that rational consciousness cannot be reduced to material or physical components, no matter how complex their interactions, see—in addition to Hart's book and Braine's *Language and Human Understanding*—such works as Braine, *Human Person*; Ross, *Thought and World*, chap. 6; Feser, *Last Superstition*, chaps. 5–6; Chalmers, *Character of Consciousness*; Koons and Bealer, *Waning of Materialism*.

    62. Stringer, *Lone Survivors*, 235; cf. 219, 224. Stringer argues that "large, stable populations may have a greater ability to survive and to develop and maintain innovations, and I think that is actually the key to what must have been happening in Africa about 60,000 years ago. Research suggests that the optimal conditions for rapid cultural changes are those where there are large groups of interacting social 'learners,' and this is the case not only in humans but in our closest living relatives, the great apes" (222). Although Stringer assumes that modern human intelligence exceeds that of premodern *Homo sapiens* (and Neanderthals) not qualitatively but only by degree—i.e., he assumes that there is no spiritual soul, but rather consciousness can be accounted for by the increasing complexity of the brain—he is aware of the uniqueness of modern humans, which he describes as "the ability of members of our species to interact with each other not just face-to-face at one time, as other animals do—and earlier human species did—but also at a distance in both time and space through indirect symbolic communication" (223).

    63. Klein and Edgar, *Dawn of Human Culture*, 270; for Klein and Edgar, this dawn was caused by "a fortuitous mutation that promoted the fully modern human brain" (ibid.). Stringer comments: "Unfortunately for Richard Klein's views of a significant cognitive event about 50,000

Edgar associate with the arrival of "the modern capacity for rapidly spoken phonemic language," inaugurated "the extraordinary modern human ability to innovate," that is to say, "the uniquely modern ability to adapt to a remarkable range of natural and social circumstances with little or no physiological change."[64]

Although Genesis 1–2 describes humans as "in the image of God [bəṣelem 'ĕlōhîm]" (Gen. 1:27) and as possessing earthly "dominion" (Gen. 1:28), Adam and Eve exhibit no complex ability other than language, which makes possible their communion with each other and with God.[65] In Genesis, complex toolmaking and other arts begin only with the descendants of Cain. Whenever

years ago, the heightening of the frontal and the expansion of the parietal lobes had apparently already occurred 100,000 years earlier, as shown by the shape of the early modern skulls from Omo Kibish and Herto" (*Lone Survivors*, 212–13). Indeed, Klein and Edgar grant that their "neural hypothesis . . . cannot be tested from fossils. The connection between behavioral and neural change earlier in human evolution is inferred from conspicuous increases in brain size, but humans virtually everywhere had achieved modern or near-modern brain size by 200,000 years ago. Any neural change that occurred 50,000 years ago would thus have been strictly organizational, and fossil skulls so far provide only speculative evidence for brain structure" (*Dawn of Human Culture*, 272). A "strictly organizational" change fits quite well with the emergence of humans who were endowed with rational souls.

64. Klein and Edgar, *Dawn of Human Culture*, 271. Robert Bellah places the development of language much earlier: "Sometime between 250,000 and 100,000 years ago, full grammatical language developed, making complex narratives possible" (*Religion in Human Evolution*, xviii). Bellah is drawing upon Donald, *Origins of the Modern Mind*; Donald, *A Mind So Rare*.

65. In *Seven Pillars of Creation*, 77, William P. Brown argues that humans are unique among all animals because of our ability to invent and share "symbolic language," including the language of prayer. For discussion of human language from a scientific perspective, emphasizing the uniqueness of humans, see the chapters "From Darwinism to Darwinitis" and "Bewitched by Language" in Tallis, *Aping Mankind*, 147–82 and 183–208. Stringer proposes that all languages may have their origins in one African language; see *Lone Survivors*, 218. The scientist-theologian John Polkinghorne, who advocates a "dual-aspect monism" (similar, I imagine, to Tallis's ultimate position, and differing from my own view), argues that we should be "no longer restricted to the notion of Darwinian survival necessity as providing the sole engine driving hominid development. In these noetic realms of rational skill, moral imperative and aesthetic delight—of encounter with the true, the good and the beautiful—other forces are at work to draw out and enhance distinctive human potentialities. Survival is replaced by something that one may call *satisfaction*, the deep contentment of understanding and the joyful delight that draws on enquirers and elicits the growth of their capacities. No doubt the neural ground for the possibility of psychosomatic beings like ourselves to be able to develop aptitudes in this way was afforded by the plasticity of the hominid brain. Much of the vast web of neural networking within our skulls is not genetically predetermined, but it grows epigenetically, in response to learning experiences" (*Exploring Reality*, 56–57; cf. 46–49 on the human "soul," conceived of in an Aristotelian but not Thomistic manner). A similar view of human evolution, emphasizing selection for "courtship tools," is proposed by Stringer, *Lone Survivors*, 226. See also McCabe, "Organism, Language and Grace." For an emphasis on the "connection between the prelinguistic and the linguistic" (51) even while allowing for the significant distinction between the two, see MacIntyre's *Dependent Rational Animals*.

the first truly free and rational hominids actually came into existence, therefore, all parties can agree that at the outset they were still deeply primitive, though possessed of the extraordinary power of free rational consciousness.

Richard Middleton on the Image of God in Genesis 1

What does it mean to be "in the image of God," and what is "dominion" supposed to look like?[66] In his comprehensive engagement with the past half-century of biblical scholarship on Genesis 1:26–28, Richard Middleton has argued that "the author of Genesis 1 (whenever he lived) was acquainted (in either oral or written form) with the Mesopotamian notion of the king as image of a god (as a particular crystallization of royal ideology) and that he intentionally challenged this notion with the claim that all humanity was made in God's image."[67] Indebted to Edward Curtis and others, Middleton carefully reviews the Near Eastern parallels to Genesis 1, including the Akkadian *Gilgamesh Epic*, the Egyptian *Instruction for Merikare*, the Egyptian *Instruction of Ani*, the Near Eastern practice of a king setting up an image of himself to "rule" over a land where the king could not be present, and the numerous Egyptian and (less frequent, but equally compelling) Mesopotamian instances of describing kings or queens as images of a god.[68] With regard to the Egyptian examples, he observes that "the notion of image is but one among many other ways of expressing the pharaoh's divine origin and kinship to the gods. The notion is distinctive, however, in that it picks up specifically on

66. Ellen F. Davis argues that the meaning of the "image of God," not least for christological reasons, "cannot be fully grasped within the first chapter of the Bible, even by the most thorough exegete. Rather, one must keep reading, and living in biblical faith, in order to know what our creation in the image of God yet might mean" (*Scripture, Culture, and Agriculture*, 56). This position seems right to me, although (as Davis surely would agree) a great deal can be gained from focusing on Gen. 1. For reflection upon what "dominion" should involve today, see, e.g., Verhey, *Nature and Altering It*.

67. Middleton, *Liberating Image*, 145. For discussion of Middleton's position, see Kelsey, *Eccentric Existence*, 2:930–33. Kelsey argues that Middleton conflates the question "What are we?" with the question "Who are we?"; and Kelsey also finds that Middleton reads Gen. 1:26–28 explicitly in relation to the Christian canonical narrative of redemption. I think that Middleton does both of these things, but not in a way that compromises his interpretation of Gen. 1:26–28. In Kelsey's view, creation in a democratized image "would be liberating good news for those whose identities had been defined as slaves of the gods," but the problem is that Gen. 1, on its own terms, "does not presuppose that there is anything 'there' from which humankind would need to be redeemed" (933). Middleton's position, however, requires simply that God create all humans in his royal image; it does not require the fall, although it helps to make sense of God's response to the fall.

68. See Curtis, "Man as the Image of God in Genesis in the Light of Ancient Near Eastern Parallels."

the central *function* of the king, namely, his cultic, intermediary function of uniting the earthly and divine realms."[69] The king is not only of divine origin, but has a function or office that makes him the god's image. Among the Mesopotamian instances that Middleton cites is a letter from a Babylonian astrologer to an Assyrian king (seventh century BC), in which the astrologer describes the king as the image of the god Marduk. Middleton holds that in the Mesopotamian cases, too, the king is the image of the god primarily because of the king's status as a cultic intermediary and earthly representative of the god.[70] The king, though not divine as in the Egyptian worldview, mediates the god's rule on earth as the god's viceroy.

According to Middleton, the great difference in Genesis 1 is that *all* humans are in the image of God. In Middleton's words, "Humanity in Genesis 1 is called to be the representative and intermediary of God's power and blessing on earth."[71] No longer is this representative and mediating role limited to the king (or to a priest).[72] Middleton considers that the most direct influence on Genesis 1 came from Mesopotamia, where the phrase "image/likeness of god" had become part of the theopolitical lexicon. Indeed, Genesis 1 and 2 share a wide variety of elements with Mesopotamian creation accounts such as the *Enuma Elish* and the *Atrahasis Epic*. For example, "the sequence, in Genesis 1:1–2:3, of the creation of humanity *followed by* divine rest is a distinctly Mesopotamian motif," by contrast to Egyptian creation narratives.[73] In Genesis 2, Eden is located in Mesopotamia. Abraham himself was born and raised in Mesopotamia. The status of the general run of human beings in Mesopotamian narratives was lowly, namely, that of slaves whose purpose is to do the grunt work that the gods would otherwise have to do. In both the *Atrahasis Epic* and another creation narrative called *Enki and Ninmah*, the gods originally have to produce their own food and dig out the canals needed for agriculture. They create humans to do this work for them. In Mesopotamian narratives, the service that humans render to the gods includes building and repairing the temple.

---

69. Middleton, *Liberating Image*, 110.

70. See ibid., 118.

71. Ibid., 121. See the similar conclusions of Arnold, *Genesis*, 44–45. See also the discussion of humans as mediators in Harrison, *God's Many-Splendored Image*, 124–37. Harrison's treatment of Maximus the Confessor on this topic is particularly illuminating. She notes that for Maximus, we regain our "original vocation" of mediation by sharing in "Christ's work of mediation" (132).

72. Some earlier commentators such as William P. Brown make the same point, and Middleton argues that major commentators (such as Claus Westermann) who rejected this notion of a democratized image were constrained by a particular reconstruction of the purposes of the Priestly author. See Brown, *Ethos of the Cosmos*, 44; Westermann, *Genesis 1–11*, 153. See also Brown, *Seven Pillars of Creation*, 66.

73. Middleton, *Liberating Image*, 132.

In the *Enuma Elish*, the god Marduk constructs the cosmos out of the dead body of the goddess Tiamat (the ocean), whom he has killed. Marduk then sets the gods to work in building Babylon, but they complain about the heavy labor. In response, Marduk creates humans out of the blood of a sacrificial victim, the evil god Qingu. Humans are created to do the work of the gods, who are credited with having finished the building of Babylon and its temples. In Babylon, the king and temple priests (servants of the cultic image of Marduk) held court; they were the privileged members of the society, and the other members of the society existed to serve them. Middleton sums up the especially privileged status of the king: "If the purpose of the mass of humanity is to serve the gods and if the king represents those gods as their son and image, then the gods are served precisely by serving the king."[74] He also notes that the fact that humanity was created from the blood of an evil god means that humanity has inherited his evil tendencies. By contrast, since Mesopotamian kings were thought to be in the god Marduk's image as his exalted functionaries, they were able to justify their own violent conquest and repression.

For Middleton, the entirety of Genesis 1–11 serves to provide an alternative to the Mesopotamian creation narratives and worldview. Indebted to Frank Moore Cross, he especially emphasizes Israel's critique of sacral kingship, inclusive of Israel's prophetic critique of the pretensions of its own kings. As Middleton remarks, the "dominion" granted to Adam and Eve in Genesis 1:28 does not include dominion over each other, or for that matter over any other humans that might come to be. In Middleton's reading, Genesis 1–2 stands in tension with notions of priestly hierarchy found elsewhere in Scripture, despite the long-standing historical-critical attribution of Genesis 1–2 to the hypothetical "Priestly" source. Middleton argues that God's teaching that humans are created "in the image of God" means that "all persons have equal access to God simply by being human. . . . Just as the *imago Dei* in Genesis 1 democratizes royal ideology, the text suggests that human beings as the image of God are *themselves* priests of the creator of heaven and earth."[75] Here, indebted to Walter Brueggemann, he connects Israel's aniconism with the fact that only humans—and *all* humans—can be said to be God's authorized images.[76] Noteworthy, too, is the fact that in Genesis 1 God does not suggest that he creates humans in order for them to be of service to God or to the heavenly court. God provides food for humans, rather than the other

---

74. Ibid., 173.
75. Ibid., 207.
76. Ibid. See Brueggemann, *Genesis*, 32. For background, see Mettinger, *No Graven Image?*

way around. The relegation of the heavenly bodies to creaturely status also accentuates human dignity and freedom, by contrast to the role played by astrology in Mesopotamia.

Middleton shows that the references in Genesis 5:1–3 and 9:6 to humans as in the likeness and image of God are also instructive. He states, "Not only does the human race in the genealogy of Genesis 5 take the place that the line of ancient kings occupies in the preflood section of the *Sumerian King List*, but Adam as the first person created in God's image is clearly equivalent to A-lulim, the first king."[77] Adam is not the only image of God. As Middleton observes, the fact that Adam himself has a son "in his own likeness, after his image" (Gen. 5:3) indicates that all humans, as descendants of Adam, are in God's image.[78] For its part, Genesis 9:6 belongs to God's instructions to Noah after the flood, at the outset of the new start for the human race. God decrees that those who kill humans will be killed by humans. Whether this commandment favors capital punishment, or simply depicts the likely destiny of violent humans, is not clear. But the dignity and value of each human life is clear. This is underscored by the final clause of the sentence, which appeals to the fact that humans are in the image of God: "Whoever sheds the blood of man, by man shall his blood be shed; for God made man in his own image" (Gen. 9:6).[79] Each human, not solely Adam, is in the image of God. The point that Middleton wishes to make is that "the *imago Dei* in Genesis constitutes a democratization of Mesopotamian royal ideology."[80]

Middleton then strives to differentiate Israel's God from the Mesopotamian god Marduk, who creates by an act of primordial violence against the powers of chaos. Admittedly, some biblical scholars, such as Jon Levenson, Hermann Gunkel, and James Crenshaw, have suggested that Israel's God similarly creates by conquering the primordial chaos. If so, then violent action to control

77. Middleton, *Liberating Image*, 213.

78. See also Hoekema, *Created in God's Image*, 15–16. Bill Arnold comments that Gen. 5:3 means that "the image of God is carried forward, so Seth will rule and have dominion over that which was his father's. Without this statement [i.e., Gen. 5:3], we might have taken Genesis 1:26–27 as *sui generis*, leaving open the possibility that a primeval human being in God's image might have been unique to that ancient period and having little to do with later humans. But since Seth was made in Adam's image, and Adam was made in God's, the image of God becomes an actuality for all humans" (*Genesis*, 86). At the same time, Arnold argues that all humans after Adam are also in the (fallen) image of Adam, and therefore are a combination of royal image of God and sinful image of Adam. By contrast, Kelsey argues (mistakenly in my view) that "*neither adam* ('humankind' in Gen. 1:26–27) nor any individual human being is ever said to be the image of God in Genesis" (*Eccentric Existence*, 2:956).

79. See also Hoekema, *Created in God's Image*, 16–17.

80. Middleton, *Liberating Image*, 214.

chaotic forces would be a significant part of what the image of God means, especially insofar as the image of God entails "dominion." Middleton identifies three texts in which the Old Testament depicts creation clearly as involving a primordial conflict. The first is Job 26:7–14, in which God's creative work is seen as overcoming chaos, symbolized by the waters and darkness. In Job 26:12, Job specifically mentions God's overcoming "Rahab": "By his power he stilled the sea; by his understanding he smote Rahab." The second text is Psalm 74:12–17. Here we find, in the same context as a description of God establishing the stars and the sun, God's primordial work of "break[ing] the heads of the dragons on the waters" and "crush[ing] the heads of Leviathan" (Ps. 74:13–14). The third text is Psalm 89:5–14, where again in the context of God's creative work there appears the image of the primordial destruction of "Rahab." Indebted to Jon Levenson's work, Middleton underscores the connection made in Psalm 89 between God's violent marking out of the world's boundaries and King David's work of boundary-marking for Israel. Middleton comments, "Psalm 89 thus illustrates very well the function of the creation-by-combat theme to legitimate the monarchy, via a motif remarkably like the *imago Dei*."[81]

Yet, in Middleton's view, these texts should not govern our understanding of God's creative work, not least because the result would be to legitimize violence and to produce a boundary mentality of us-versus-them.[82] As an example of this mentality, he shows how the Christian Reconstructionist theologian David Chilton, in his *Paradise Regained: A Christian Theology of Dominion*, develops an oppositional theology that explicitly calls for the destruction and death of the opponents of Christianity as understood by Chilton.[83] Nor are left-wing political interpretations of the image of God acceptable to Middleton. He denies that Genesis 1's presentation of the image of God intends to turn the tables politically upon Babylonian ideology, by replacing Babylon and its god and kings with Israel and its elect people. If this were the case, it would simply replace a violent Babylon with a violent Israel. In fact, the waters (or the deep) are not presented as God's *opponent* in Genesis 1. God is the *creator* of "the great sea monsters" (Gen. 1:21), by contrast to the combat texts' portraits of Rahab. Similarly, God creates by his word, without a struggle or conflict; God encounters "no resistance in creating the world."[84] God's dominion is marked by primordial peace, not

81. Ibid., 249. See also Levenson, *Creation and the Persistence of Evil*, 22–23.
82. Here Middleton draws upon the work of Pedro Trigo and Catherine Keller; see Trigo, *Creation and History*; Keller, *Face of the Deep*; Keller, *From a Broken Web*.
83. See Middleton, *Liberating Image*, 259–60; see also 35–36.
84. Ibid., 264.

by primordial violence.[85] Thus, God finds the whole of creation to be "very good" (Gen. 1:31). The goodness of creation amplifies the sense of a lack of combat or violence. As Middleton says, "God is pictured here not as warrior, but as craftsman or artisan."[86]

Genesis 1, then, is not an Israelite transposition of Mesopotamian creation narratives, but rather is a radical alternative, in the sense of showing the creator—and thus his human images—to be primordially peaceful. Thus when humans exercise dominion in the image of God, humans cannot do so in a violent manner, as though God's whole creation were not good or as though God were himself fundamentally a warrior-creator. God's power is not domineering or dominating, but rather is exercised in creation as pure gift, pure delight in the coming to be and flourishing of creatures. Human dominion, exercised in the image of God, must have the same characteristics.

Yet, having admitted the existence of at least three biblical texts that depict God as a warrior in his creative act, why should we privilege Genesis 1's portrait of God's creative work over against, say, the combat myth of Job 26? For Middleton, the canonical placement of Genesis 1 gives it a distinct authority in governing the reading of other, briefer creation narratives in Scripture. In addition, it seems to me that one could make a case that the texts in Job and the Psalms are mainly about God's power in a world marked by human sin and death. They are affirmations of God's power to accomplish his good will, rather than being attempts to depict how God created. In Job and the Psalms, the issue at stake is not how things were made, but rather whether God is truly powerful.[87]

---

85. Influenced by John Howard Yoder and Willard Swartley, Jonathan R. Wilson rightly emphasizes that "peace is the very shape of the life of creation. The God of creation and redemption is also the God of peace" (*God's Good World*, 121).

86. Middleton, *Liberating Image*, 266.

87. See, e.g., Janzen, *Job*, 234–35. Janzen goes on to discuss the image of God in the book of Job: "Job's dilemma is one that is intrinsic to the human status as divine image. This dilemma consists in the fact that the image or symbol in some sense participates in the reality which it symbolizes but is not that reality" (242). God's power is not totalitarian or domineering, but something in which God enables creatures to share. According to Janzen, therefore, God speaks "out of the whirlwind" in order to show himself as "a cosmic creator who delights in a world sufficiently ordered to make life possible and worthwhile, but sufficiently free to allow for the possibility of bilateral participation" (257). Janzen also points out that "Job's continuing affirmation, 'you [God] can do all things, and no purpose of yours can be thwarted,' is one version of the Yahwistic refrain which runs through the old and the New Testaments, 'all things are possible.' Here as elsewhere the refrain comes, not as a human assessment on the basis of a reading of worldly conditions, but as a human affirmation of the inexhaustible resources of the covenant God" (252). Similarly, David B. Burrell, CSC, comments on the experience of Job as a discovery that relating to God "is not so much a task as it is a surrender to the 'facts of the matter,' a letting-go of a posture of 'existential autonomy' (or separateness) to submit to

Middleton also cautions against what he shows to be the common scholarly practice of pitting Genesis 1 against Genesis 2, as though the creator God of Genesis 1 were remote, and the creator God of Genesis 2 were personal and caring.[88] Middleton points out that Genesis 1, rather than being in tension with Genesis 2, sets up (as a kind of "prelude") the "normative conditions" for the action that occurs in Genesis 2.[89] In Genesis 1, he emphasizes, God is not "an extrinsic, transcendent force or will unilaterally imposing order upon creation as an inert object."[90] God is not a remote tyrant. Middleton's thesis is that according to Genesis 1, "God's founding exercise of creative power . . . is an act of generosity, even of love," with the result that we should not "separate our vision of God's redemptive love from an understanding of God's creative power."[91] This seems to me to be quite right. God must be seen not as "a Newtonian lawgiver" but rather as "a strange attractor" who gives creatures a "noncoercive freedom" and a real participation in the ongoing flourishing of creation. This freedom and participation appear not only in the "dominion" that humans receive, but also in the sun and moon ruling "over the day and over the night" (Gen. 1:18), among other instances.[92] The creator God of Genesis 1 enables creatures to participate in their own governance. Middleton rightly observes that "attention to these rhetorical features points us to a God who does not hoard divine creative power, with some desperate need to control, but rather to a God who is generous with power, sharing it with creatures, that they might make their own contribution to the harmony and beauty of the world."[93] The God of Genesis 1, like the

---

the innate desire toward 'the Good' that spells our fulfillment. Relating to the Creator, then, is like a free fall, yet for intentional beings, the term *free* has a double connotation: not only unhindered, but deliberate as well. That is the dynamic that Augustine's *Confessions* articulate, and the one that the creator-God's responses to Job make evident" (*Deconstructing Theodicy*, 133). For the genre of royal psalms, see Estes, *Handbook on the Wisdom Books and Psalms*.

88. This contrast can be seen even in Arnold, *Genesis*, 56: "A distinction in theology is also noticeable [between Gen. 1 and 2]. Genesis 1 portrays the transcendent and sovereign Creator commanding order from chaos by a series of cuts and separations, structuring the world and its inhabitants according to types and categories. Now, 2:4–25 complements that portrait with one in which the immanent and intensely personal Yahweh Elohim, LORD God, shapes humanity from clay like a potter (2:7)."

89. Middleton, *Liberating Image*, 291.

90. Ibid., 276.

91. Ibid., 278, 297.

92. Ibid., 287–88.

93. Ibid., 289. Yet Middleton oversteps when he later adds, "Genesis 1:1–2:3 thus portrays God as taking the risk first of blessing human beings with fertility and entrusting them with power over the earth and the animals and then of stepping back, withdrawing, to allow humans to exercise this newly granted power, to see what develops" (294). This anthropomorphic understanding of divine causality, seemingly in competition with human power, requires positing a God who makes himself remote from the action of his creatures. Middleton associates his position with

God of the New Testament, is a giver of goodness and blessing, who invites us to participate in his life.

Middleton notes that the standard view among exegetes today is that Genesis 1:26–27 refers "to humanity's office and role as God's earthly delegates," insofar as humans image by their royal and priestly rule on earth the sovereign and creative work of God, who dwells in his cosmic temple.[94] Middleton calls this position the royal-functional view of the image of God, and he develops it, as we have seen, to make clear its distinctive democratization of the royal-functional "image of God" vis-à-vis the Egyptian and especially Mesopotamian understandings of the image as being solely the king (and, in some instances, the high priest). As we have seen, Middleton also argues for the identity of the creator God of Genesis 1–2 as the generous giver, whose power is gift and blessing rather than domination.

In making his case, Middleton complains that "the vast majority of interpreters right up to recent times have understood the meaning of the image in terms of a metaphysical analogy or similarity between the human soul and the being of God, in categories not likely to have occurred to the author of Genesis."[95] He blames this identification of the image of God with the spiritual soul (or "reason") on the influence of Platonic philosophy upon patristic and medieval theology. For Middleton, the tide began to turn only when Martin Luther argued that the image of God is a relational reality, namely, the original justice that was lost by Adam's sin. The relational model of the image was further developed by Karl Barth, along the lines of Martin Buber's I-Thou personalism and with an emphasis on our creation as male and female, but according to Middleton, Barth's relational model does not stand up exegetically.

Clark Pinnock's "open theism," but he seems (unfortunately) to have read little in philosophical theology, despite complaining about "the long history of misreading both divine and human power in Genesis 1" (297). He does cite Pasewark, *Theology of Power*, which credits Martin Luther with developing a notion of non-zero-sum power in his commentary on Genesis.

94. Middleton, *Liberating Image*, 60; see also 29, 87–90. N. T. Wright remarks in representative fashion: "The 'image' does not refer principally to some aspect of human nature or character which is especially like God. As many writers have shown, it points to the belief that, just as ancient rulers might place statues of themselves in far-flung cities to remind subject peoples who was ruling them, so God has placed his own image, human beings, into his world, so that the world can see who its ruler is" (*After You Believe*, 76). Similarly, Brueggemann comments, "It is now generally agreed that the image of God reflected in human persons is after the manner of a king who establishes statues of himself to assert his sovereign rule where the king himself cannot be present. . . . The image of God in the human person is a mandate of power and responsibility. But it is power exercised as God exercises power. The image images the creative use of power which invites, evokes, and permits. There is nothing here of coercive or tyrannical power, either for God or for humankind" (*Genesis*, 32).

95. Middleton, *Liberating Image*, 18.

However, significant problems are associated with Middleton's own view of the image of God, as Kilner helps us to see. Namely, if imaging God consists (as Middleton thinks) in advancing culture, sharing in governance, and mediating God's blessings to the world, then no matter how much one insists upon a democratized image, it remains the case that leaders have much more opportunity to advance culture, share in governance, and widely mediate blessings than do other humans. If so, then a community's leaders would still be more in the image of God than other humans can be. In addition, if humans are in the image of God when they are sharing in God's royal rule, then when they behave badly, do they lose the image? How can a brutal tyrant, ruling in the exact opposite way of God's way, be in the image of God, if by this we mean participating in "the special role of representing or imaging God's rule in the world"?[96] Furthermore, do severely mentally disabled humans possess the image? How do humans who have no capacity for significant mental function, due to a bodily defect, image God's rule in the world?

These questions should prompt further inquiry into what human capabilities the royal image depends upon. Middleton suggests that "the *imago Dei* designates the royal office or calling of human beings as God's representatives and agents in the world, granted authorized power to share in God's rule or administration of the earth's resources and creatures."[97] He goes on to specify that God's rule is one of generosity, love, and gift, not of domination. In a brief section on God as an artisan or craftsman of the cosmic temple, he also reflects upon the wisdom of God's rule. As he points out, Bezalel, the master builder of the tabernacle in Exodus 31, receives wisdom, understanding, and knowledge—"precisely the same triad by which God is said to have created the world in Proverbs 3:19–20."[98] Middleton recognizes that the depiction of Bezalel here should inform our understanding of the image of God: "Bezalel's Spirit-filled craftsmanship, which imitates God's primordial wise design and construction of the cosmos, is functionally equivalent to the *imago Dei*."[99] If this is so, then underlying what it takes to be in the image of God is wisdom; and in imitating God's *wise* rule, we are imitating the God "who calls the world into being as an act of generosity."[100] In imaging God's wise rule, we are imaging "an act of generosity, even of love."[101] Our imaging of God, therefore, requires wisdom and love.

96. Ibid., 26.
97. Ibid., 27.
98. Ibid., 87.
99. Ibid.
100. Ibid., 297.
101. Ibid., 278.

But what about the problem of losing this image (of wisdom and love) through evildoing? When humans sin, do they lose the image, as would seem to be the case since their sins certainly do not image the royal rule of the all-good God? Genesis 5:3 may seem to suggest that sinners lose the image, insofar as it is the good son of Adam (namely Seth) who alone is explicitly said to bear the image: "When Adam had lived a hundred and thirty years, he became the father of a son in his own likeness, after his image, and named him Seth." Is Adam's sinful son Cain, then, not in the image of God?

The answer can be found in Genesis 9:6: "Whoever sheds the blood of man, by man shall his blood be shed; for God made man in his own image." The implication is that even the blood of a sinner is the blood of someone made in God's image.[102] This resonates with God's promise to Cain, when after slaying his brother Cain feared for his life: "The LORD said to him, 'Not so! If any one slays Cain, vengeance shall be taken on him sevenfold'" (Gen. 4:15). Even Cain is in God's image, despite the fact that his murderous action was the very opposite of God's rule. But if this is so, then the image cannot simply be based upon acts of wise and generous "ruling" (as Middleton suggests) in imitation of the wise and generous creator God.[103] Cain does not act in a wise and loving way, yet he is still in God's image. It must be, then, that Cain is in God's image because Cain possesses the *ability* to act wisely and lovingly (cf. Gen. 4:7)—an ability that pertains to his human nature, and arguably, therefore, to his embodied soul and its rational powers.[104] Middleton

102. In this regard, see Anthony Hoekema's critical response to Klaas Schilder and G. C. Berkouwer, who argue that after the fall humans should not be said to be in the image of God: Hoekema, *Created in God's Image*, 17–18; cf. 61 for further engagement with Berkouwer on this point. Hoekema cites Schilder, *Heidelbergsche Catechismus*, 1:296–98, and Berkouwer, *Man*, 56–59. In arriving at his interpretation, Berkouwer draws upon Schilder's exegetical work. See also Hoekema's discussion of James 3:9 (With it [the tongue] we bless the Lord and Father, and with it we curse men, who are made in the likeness of God") in *Created in God's Image*, 19–20.

103. For this argument, though without identifying the image in the soul and its powers, see von Rad, *Wisdom in Israel*, 57.

104. Although Genesis 4 obviously does not contain a teaching on the soul, I think that the spiritual or immaterial nature of the embodied soul of human beings is indeed taught by Scripture; see Levering, *Jesus and the Demise of Death*, chap. 6, in critical dialogue with Green, *Body, Soul, and Human Life*. The patristic bishop-theologian Nemesius of Emesa rightly holds that the immateriality and immortality of the soul is a *biblical* doctrine, by contrast with the *philosophical* position of Aristotle and the Stoics. For discussion, see Young, *God's Presence*, 114. Young, however, thinks that Nancey Murphy's nonreductive physicalism is sufficient to uphold what the fathers wanted to uphold through their affirmation of a spiritual soul. Young concludes that "what we now need is a mean between the Enlightenment tendency to overestimate the superiority of human rationality and the tendency of naturalism to treat our whole being, personal and social, as explicable through biochemistry and evolutionary theory" (*God's Presence*, 130). In contrast to Young, I do not think that nonreductive physicalism works; in addition to the relevant section of *Jesus and the Demise of Death*, see my review of Murphy's

criticizes this position as the "substantialistic image."[105] Yet, far from being an isolated or autonomous substance, the soul is always relationally inclined toward God (and toward the true and the good in all creation). The image of God in the embodied human soul is certainly found in a substance, but the image is relational and interpersonal rather than "substantialistic" in a negative way.

With regard to the embodied spiritual soul as the locus of the human image of God, however, Hans Reinders has raised a strong concern: What about people who, due to a bodily disability, are not able to know and love? For Reinders, since the "capacity to act requires a body that is suitable to its actualization," and since "some human beings do not have a potential for the activity of reason and will residing in their bodies," the traditional Catholic view of the image of God as located in the soul and its powers leaves no place for the full humanity of the severely mentally disabled.[106] Fortunately,

---

Bodies and Souls, or Spirited Bodies? in *National Catholic Bioethics Quarterly* 7 (2007): 635–38. For an exemplar of pro-soul argumentation, Young relies upon Ward, *Defending the Soul*, but this book strikes me as quite weak, not least by contrast to the excellent essay by W. Norris Clarke, SJ, "Immediate Creation of the Human Soul by God and Some Contemporary Challenges." See also Josef Pieper's instructive observation that "Thomas [Aquinas] in no way thinks that the true overcoming of death lies in the natural indestructibility of the spiritual soul. But he does think that, if the human soul were not immortal by virtue of creation, there would be nothing and nobody to *receive* the divine gift of resurrection and eternal life" ("Immortality—a Non-Christian Idea?," 84–85; cf. Pieper's profound discussion of death and the human person on 76–81).

105. Middleton, *Liberating Image*, 19.

106. Reinders, *Receiving the Gift of Friendship*, 114–15. Reinders holds that "fulfilling the ultimate end of being human is God's gift," and therefore severely mentally disabled humans can still attain to the goal of the image of God, an attainment that is sheer gift in every case. For my part, I emphasize that severely mentally disabled persons are intrinsically in the image of God due to their fully rational soul, despite their severe bodily incapacity. God can transform the soul even if the powers are unable to be in act. Even when the acts of faith and charity are not possible, the habits of faith and charity can be present in the soul by sanctifying grace, as in infant baptism or the baptism of severely mentally disabled humans: for Aquinas's position in this regard, see *ST* III, q. 68, aa. 9 and 12. For further discussion, including a response to Reinders, see Romero, "Aquinas on the *Corporis Infirmitas*," esp. 109–16. Amos Yong notes that the sin of "ableism" consists in dehumanizing, marginalizing, or fearing humans who suffer from significant bodily disability, and to his great credit Reinders has been a leader in insisting upon the full humanity of persons who suffer from even the most severe bodily disabilities and who are therefore unable to share in intimacy and communion with others (many such persons, horrendously, are aborted in the womb). For Yong, however, combating "ableism" requires insisting that "there is nothing intrinsically wrong with the lives of people with disabilities, that it is not they who need to be cured, but we, the non-disabled, who need to be saved from our discriminatory attitudes and practices" (*Bible, Disability, and the Church*, 118). See also Miguel Romero's compilation of Aquinas's texts on bodily disability in Brock, *Disability in the Christian Tradition*, 125–51; as well as Tranzillo, *John Paul II on the Vulnerable*; and Brennan, *John Paul II*.

this concern is not well founded. Reinders fails to appreciate that for Aquinas (and the fathers), even if the powers of the soul are not in act or are unable in this life ever to be in act due to a bodily defect, the grace of the Holy Spirit can still transform the soul and elevate the person relationally to union with the persons of the Trinity. By being united to God through the infused habits of faith and charity, a severely mentally disabled human being can share in God's rule even in the present life. Indeed, since the capacity to share in God's rule characterizes the image of God, it is *only* if the image of God is in the embodied rational soul that humans who endure severe mental disability can be created in the image of God. The key is that the soul, even when it lacks the bodily capacity for knowing and loving, retains its ability to receive infused relational habits that enable the human person to share in God's sovereignty.[107]

Aquinas's Approach to the Image of God

Biblical Challenges for the (Merely) Human Image of God

When Aquinas approaches the image of God from a biblical perspective, he first examines two texts that seem to rule out the notion of an image of God in human nature.[108] The first such text is Isaiah 40:18: "To whom then will you liken God, or what likeness will you compare with him?" The context here is Isaiah's critique of idolatry among God's covenant people. There is no man-made icon or image that can truly be a likeness of God, because God is living and active. There is also the fact that, for Isaiah, God is utterly incomparable: "I am God, and there is no other" (Isa. 45:22).

Aquinas treats this incomparability earlier in the *Summa theologiae*. Citing Isaiah 40:18, he observes that "although it may be admitted that creatures are in some sort like God, it must nowise be admitted that God is like creatures."[109] This is because God and creatures are not on the same ontological level: God is infinite, creatures finite. Creatures may be like God analogously, and rational creatures can even be the image of God, but it remains the case that infinite act is incomparable to finite act. Citing Pseudo-Dionysius's *The Divine Names*, Aquinas explains that "'the same things can be like and unlike to God: like,

---

107. For further reflection on our embodied rationality, in light of experiences such as clinical depression and dramatic religious experience, see the essays in Jeeves, *From Cells to Souls— and Beyond*. Although the essays in this volume generally affirm a doctrine of "nonreductive physicalism," which I find inadequate, the volume has significant value.

108. See *ST* I, q. 3, a. 1, objs. 1 and 2.

109. *ST* I, q. 4, a. 3, ad 4.

according as they imitate Him, as far as He, who is not perfectly imitable, can be imitated; unlike according as they fall short of their cause,' not merely in intensity and remission . . . but because they are not in agreement, specifically or generically."[110] The key point is that God is in no way like a creature, because God is not a mere *mode* of being but rather the infinite source of the finite being of all creatures.

Once God's radical ontological difference from creatures is understood, then what it means to be God's "image" can be better appreciated. Aquinas states that will is an intellectual aptitude or appetite for the goodness known by the intellect. The fact that God analogously possesses will, which is his love for his infinite goodness (including this goodness as participated in by the finite creatures that he creates), is testified to repeatedly in Scripture, not least in Paul's praise for "what is the will of God, what is good and acceptable and perfect" (Rom. 12:2).[111] Although we cannot know what infinite divine will is, we can know that God supereminently possesses the perfection of willing the good. God, too, must have infinite wisdom or else he could not know himself or us. Again, Paul's testimony is apropos: Paul praises the incomparable "depth of the riches and wisdom and knowledge of God" (Rom. 11:33).[112]

Idols, by contrast, have neither understanding nor will. Isaiah emphasizes that not only can these images not move, but also they cannot answer the pleas of their devotees (see Isa. 46:7). Thus, Aquinas observes in response to Isaiah 40:18 that while humans cannot make an image of God, God can make an image of himself, as in fact God has done by creating humans. Given the kind of creatures that humans are, Aquinas considers it "manifest that in man there is some likeness to God, copied from God as from an exemplar."[113] But he adds that the divine exemplar infinitely exceeds the image. To share in God's rule—Middleton's royal image—requires that humans share in a finite way in the infinite divine perfections of intellect and will. It is logically necessary that human nature possess intellect and will in order for humans to image God's royal rule.

The other biblical text that Aquinas cites against the view that the image of God is in each human is Colossians 1:15. This is where the Son is described as "the image of the invisible God, the first-born of all creation; for in him

110. *ST* I, q. 4, a. 3, ad 1.
111. *ST* I, q. 19, a. 1, *sed contra*.
112. Aquinas cites this passage in showing that "in God there exists the most perfect knowledge"; see *ST* I, q. 14, a. 1.
113. *ST* I, q. 93, a. 1.

all things were created, in heaven and on earth."[114] If the "image" of God is the Son, then certainly the image of God is not in mere humans. This argument has similarities with Kilner's and McFarland's. Aquinas answers that the divine Son is the perfect image, whereas humans are only imperfectly the image of God. The perfect likeness of God can appear only in one of the same divine nature, whereas an imperfect likeness of God can appear in one of an alien (human) nature.[115] In Jesus Christ, these two natures are united in one person, so that we see the divine image through the human image—specifically, through the embodied wisdom and love of Jesus. Aquinas's approach here resonates with that of Athanasius's emphasis on the rationality of the Word.

In Genesis 1, God makes clear that humans alone, and not birds or any other animals, are made "in the image of God" (Gen. 1:27). But given the association of the image of God with "dominion" (Gen. 1:28), one might ask why other animals, too, might not share in God's royal rule in their own domains. After all, lions might be said to exercise dominion over other animals in the African savannah; or sharks over other fish in the ocean; or eagles over other birds in the air. Similarly, Aquinas points out that the whole cosmos might be called an image of God, since God calls his whole creation as a unity "very good" (Gen. 1:31). If the whole creation is very good, why is not the *whole* creation (inclusive of humans) the best "image" of God, who is infinitely good? This idea is found in Plato's *Timaeus*, although Aquinas does not cite it.[116] In response, Aquinas argues that to be God's "image," a creature must be rational. The God of Isaiah 40, we recall, is active, free, and intelligent. All true images of God must also be active, free, and intelligent, or at least possess the capacity to be so. As Aquinas explains, "The universe is more perfect in goodness than the intellectual creature as regards extension and diffusion; but intensively and collectively the likeness to the divine goodness is found rather in the intellectual creature, which has a capacity for the highest good."[117]

Among all intellectual creatures, Jesus Christ, in whom "human nature is raised to its highest perfection," is the truest and fullest human image of God.[118] Summarizing the position of Aquinas, Augustine Di Noia remarks, "The perfect image of God is the incarnate Word who is both the exemplar

114. See *ST* I, q. 93, a. 1, obj. 2. Aquinas's Latin translation of this verse reads not "all creation" but "all creatures" (*omnis creaturae*).
115. See *ST* I, q. 93, a. 1, ad 2.
116. See Plato, *Timaeus*, 31a, p. 1163.
117. *ST* I, q. 93, a. 2, ad 3.
118. *ST* III, q. 1, a. 6.

of the created of God in man and the pattern for its graced transformation."[119] Even though Christ comes as a "servant" (Phil. 2:7), in his earthly life he already rules humankind by wisdom and love—rules in the sense of bestowing good gifts upon others, since he comes to restore and perfect the image of God in us by his words and deeds.[120] Christ shows us perfect love, so that "man knows thereby how much God loves him, and is thereby stirred to love Him in return."[121] Likewise, Christ exhibits perfect wisdom, not least in the fact that "His will was ruled by the divine wisdom."[122] Christ also rules the created order, as he shows through miracles; thus "the more lowly He seemed by reason of His poverty, the greater might the power of His Godhead be shown to be."[123] Having ascended to the right hand of the Father, Christ now "reigns together with the Father, and has judiciary power from Him."[124] The rule of Christ is supreme: he "possesses over all other creatures royal and judiciary power" in his glorified humanity.[125] As the risen Christ says to his apostles in the Gospel of Matthew, "All authority in heaven and on earth has been given to me" (Matt. 28:18). This emphasis on rule fits with the emphasis of Middleton; in this respect, Aquinas fully agrees with the contemporary exegetical perspective.

Yet the Bible often seems to suggest that angels are greater sharers in God's royal sovereignty than are humans, and so Aquinas gives some attention to the question of whether the angels are in the image of God more than any human is. Consider Peter's experience in prison, just after Herod had executed James the brother of John. We read in Acts 12:6–7, "The very night when Herod was about to bring him out, Peter was sleeping between two soldiers, bound with two chains, and sentries before the door were guarding the prison; and behold, an angel of the Lord appeared, and a light shone in the cell; and he struck Peter on the side and woke him, saying, 'Get up quickly.'" The angel led Peter out, despite the soldiers and iron gate that normally would have barred entrance into the city. We find a similar presence of angels in the Gospels. To name just one example, in the Gospel of Matthew, Mary Magdalene and "the other Mary" go to Jesus's tomb on Sunday morning and encounter an angel who brings news of Jesus's resurrection (Matt. 28:1–7). Indeed, Middleton notes that the plural "our image, after our likeness" (Gen. 1:26) may indicate

---

119. Di Noia, "Imago Dei—Imago Christi," 268.
120. See *ST* III, q. 1, a. 2.
121. *ST* III, q. 46, a. 3.
122. *ST* III, q. 46, a. 9.
123. *ST* III, q. 40, a. 3.
124. *ST* III, q. 58, a. 2. In this regard Aquinas cites such texts as Mark 16:19 and Acts 7:55.
125. *ST* III, q. 58, a. 3.

"the presence of an (adumbrated) royal metaphor in the background of the text, in which God is pictured as ruling the cosmos from his heavenly throne room, attended by angelic courtiers and emissaries."[126] If this is so, as Middleton thinks it is, then the "image of God" may be a reference not only to the likeness of humans to God, but also to the likeness of humans to God's heavenly court of angels. Humans are to share in God's rule on earth and are to spread the message of the gospel, just as angels share in God's rule in heaven and act as messengers for God (cf. Heb. 1:14).

Middleton does not press this point, however; and other scholars such as Kilner argue that "there is no biblical warrant for maintaining that angels are in the image of God, as people are."[127] Kilner suggests that the Bible avoids identifying angels as in the image of God because the Bible does not conceive the image in terms of attributes (such as rationality). For Kilner, rather than now having any attributes that make us in the image of God, humans "are created to develop according to God's image in Christ."[128] However, surely the good angels, at least, are now configured to God's image in Christ? If they were not configured to Christ, how could they worship him, as Hebrews 1:6 says that they do? Likewise, if they were not configured to Christ, it hardly seems that they would have "ministered to him" (Mark 1:13) after his temptation in the desert. In addition, countless angels appear in the vision of the seer of the book of Revelation as proclaiming (in the very midst of the heavenly Church's worship), "Worthy is the Lamb who was slain, to receive power and wealth and wisdom and might and honor and glory and blessing!" (Rev. 5:12). Hebrews describes those who hope steadfastly in the gospel as having "come to Mount Zion and to the city of the living God, the heavenly Jerusalem, and to innumerable angels in festal gathering," who are joined with "the spirits of just men made perfect" and above all with "Jesus, the mediator of a new covenant" (Heb. 12:22–24). This is a clear portrait of the Church as composed of angels and humans in Christ. First Timothy 5:21 also shows that angels belong to the Church of Christ: "In the presence of God and of Christ Jesus and of the elect angels I [Paul] charge you to keep these rules." If angels were not in the image of God, they could hardly be members of Christ's Church alongside humans. In my view, therefore, Aquinas is biblically justified in asking whether angels are "more" in the image of God than are humans.

126. Middleton, *Liberating Image*, 59.
127. Kilner, *Dignity and Destiny*, 112.
128. Ibid.

In one way, Aquinas thinks that the answer must be yes, since the good angels have far greater wisdom than humans do on earth.[129] The angels' greater wisdom appears, for example, in the angel Gabriel, who according to the Gospel of Luke knows the full plan of salvation, including the mystery of how the incarnation will occur: "Do not be afraid, Mary, for you have found favor with God. And behold, you will conceive in your womb and bear a son, and you shall call his name Jesus" (Luke 1:30–31). Hebrews 2:2 presents angels as having delivered the Torah, "the message declared by angels"; therefore angels must be wise indeed. But in another sense, humans image God more than angels do, not least in imaging (via *bodily* generation) the procession of the Son from the Father. Aquinas concludes that angels are more in the image of God than are humans by nature, but by grace humans can be more in the image of God than are angels. The exemplar of this is Jesus Christ, whose charity in his passion was so great that he merited "to be exalted above the angels" (cf. Heb. 1:4 and 2:9) and who was already the head of the angels from the instant of his conception, since Christ in his humanity "is nearer God, and shares His gifts more fully, not only than man, but even than angels; and of His influence not only men but even angels partake."[130]

If the status of the angels vis-à-vis the image seems difficult to resolve, 1 Corinthians 11:7 poses even more serious problems for the theology of the

129. Against this view, Thomas Weinandy, OFMCap, argues that "there is very little, if any, biblical warrant for saying that angels are more in the image and likeness of God. Nowhere in the Bible is such a statement made" ("Of Men and Angels," 295). In addition to this scriptural point, Weinandy's key argument is that "angels are not, in the absolute sense, created in the image and likeness of God because, while they may most closely resemble his intellectual ability, they are unable to reproduce themselves," and thus are unable to image the intratrinitarian generation and spiration (297). Aquinas recognizes that by being able to reproduce themselves, humans are more in the image of God than are angels; but he still considers that angels are strictly speaking more in the image of God than are humans. For Weinandy, "Human beings are, in the absolute sense, created in the image and likeness of God precisely because they are fecund; they are life-giving" (ibid.). Weinandy comments, "Human beings' ability to procreate rationally and lovingly is not something then apart from who they substantially are as human beings and so not something apart from who they substantially are as images and likeness of God" (ibid.). I agree with this, but in my view, it does not derogate from the point that rationality (embodied in the case of humans, not embodied in the case of angels) is what enables humans, and not other animals, to be in the image of God. Indeed, Weinandy goes on to suggest that humans are not so much the image of God (either the divine essence or the divine persons), but rather are the image specifically of one person of the Trinity: God the Father (much as the Son is the image of the Father). This strikes me as a mistake, but one can see that it flows from locating the image in generative fecundity rather than in wisdom and love. For further discussion of the angels' status, see Bonino, *Angels and Demons*; Goris, "Angelic Knowledge in Aquinas and Bonaventure."

130. *ST* III, q. 59, a. 6; III, q. 8, a. 4. For discussion, see Levering, *Engaging the Doctrine of the Holy Spirit*, chap. 4.

image. What could Paul mean by saying that a man "is the image and glory of God; but woman is the glory of man"? Aquinas's translation, which differs from the Vulgate, states that "woman is the image of man"—making even more troubling an already troubling passage. The verse seems to imply rather clearly that women either are not in the image of God or are less so than men. Concerns arising from this implication motivate much of Kilner's exegetical insistence that only Jesus is the image of God.

Although Aquinas does not recognize all the dimensions of the equality of women that the Church now affirms, he firmly defends the full status of women as the image of God. Women and men both possess rational souls; therefore both are equally in the image of God. For Aquinas, God makes this equality clear in Genesis 1:27: "So God created man in his own image, in the image of God he created him; male and female he created them."[131] The last clause serves as a commentary upon what it means to say that "man ['ādām]" is in the image of God. Indeed, only this interpretation can fit with Paul's theology elsewhere, for example, his claim in 1 Corinthians 15:49 that "just as we have borne the image of the man of dust, we shall also bear the image of the man of heaven," and his teaching in Galatians 3:28: "There is neither male nor female; for you are all one in Christ Jesus."

In his epistle to the Romans, Paul raises another problem for the theology of the image of God. Speaking of "those who love him [God], who are called according to his purpose" (Rom. 8:28)—and thus evidently not speaking of all humans—Paul states (8:29) that "those whom he [God] foreknew he also predestined to be conformed to the image of his Son." If all humans are not conformed to the image of the Son, then will some humans eventually not be in the image of God? Aquinas responds by insisting that to lack "the conformity of the image" is not the same as to lack the image per se.[132] Since he grounds the image of God ontologically in human nature, Aquinas is able to affirm that the image cannot be lost by sin or by a physical defect that prevents full and free exercise of the rational powers. All humans, without exception (and thus even the damned), possess "a natural aptitude for understanding and loving God; and this aptitude consists in the very nature of the mind."[133]

131. See *ST* I, q. 93, a. 4, ad 1.
132. *ST* I, q. 93, a. 4, obj. 2.
133. *ST* I, q. 93, a. 4. In *God's Presence*, Young repeatedly speaks of her son Arthur, who suffers from "the microcephaly and brain damage consequential upon intra-uterine deprivation of oxygen" (68) and who requires the aid of caretakers for eating, defecating, and other everyday tasks, including "preparing his twisted and impaired body for bed" (107). In Young's view,

> Arthur's limited experience, limited above all in ability to process the world external to himself, is a crucial element in who he is, in his real personhood. An ultimate destiny in which he was suddenly 'perfected' (whatever that might mean) is inconceivable—for he

But the image as given, the natural image, is not yet the perfected image. Not only can the image of God be obscured by sin, by diminishing and obstructing "the natural inclination to virtue," but also the image of God can be elevated and perfected.[134]

Degrees of Possession of the Image of God (God the Trinity?): The Soul and Its Powers

For Kilner, the view that the image can be obscured or enhanced is disastrous. Kilner explains his concern: "In this view, sin can damage such attributes [rationality, rule, righteousness, relationship] and thus damage God's image. Accordingly, people vary in the extent to which they have these attributes—and are in God's image. For many, that means how much people warrant respect and protection varies from person to person."[135] But this is hardly Aquinas's position. Everyone who possesses a rational soul—that is to say, everyone who possesses human nature, *not* only saintly people or only wise people—deserves "respect and protection." In this regard, Aquinas's discussion of charity exemplifies his perspective. Asking whether sinners should be loved out of charity, he lists a number of objections, all favoring the view that "sinners should be hated rather than loved" (cf. Ps. 119:113).[136] In his response, Aquinas appeals to the image of God in the embodied soul. With regard to a sinner, we must keep in view that "according to his nature,

---

would no longer be Arthur but some other person. His limited embodied self is what exists, and what will be must be in continuity with that. There will also be discontinuities—the promise of resurrection is of transcendence of our mortal "flesh and blood" state. So there's hope for transformation of this life's limitations and vulnerabilities, of someone like Arthur receiving greater gifts while truly remaining himself. Perhaps the transformation to be hoped for is less intellectual or physical advance and more the kind of thing anticipated in the present when the fruits of the Spirit are realized in relationships. (107)

I question whether a "perfected" condition of Arthur's body, or his reception of full (indeed glorified) intellectual capacities for processing his experience, would be "inconceivable" as an "ultimate destiny." In the state of glory, everyone will receive such an extraordinary "intellectual and physical advance" that Arthur's own intellectual and physical advance will hardly seem out of scale. For the view that "the marks of impairment follow not only Jesus but all those who are resurrected in his train," see Yong, *Bible, Disability, and the Church*, 130. Yong envisions "the redemption rather than the elimination of disabilities" (132). Although he adds that he is "not insisting that people with disabilities will exist literally as such eschatologically" (135), a *bodily* disability cannot *not* exist unless it is eliminated. Helpfully, Yong goes on to say that he does not "want to romanticize or even divinize disability" (139–40). See also Hauerwas, *Suffering Presence*; Le Pichon, "Sign of Contradiction."

134. *ST* I-II, q. 85, a. 1.
135. Kilner, *Dignity and Destiny*, 1.
136. *ST* II-II, q. 25, a. 6, obj. 1.

which he has from God, he has a capacity for happiness, on the fellowship of which charity is based . . . wherefore we ought to love sinners, out of charity, in respect of their nature."[137] In accord with Jesus's command, we must love even our enemies (cf. Matt. 5:44), because they are in the image of God and are called to be everlastingly united to Christ's Church.

At the same time, the image of God is obscured in sinners. Aquinas states that when the wicked seek the good of their bodies in contempt for the good of their souls, "they do not love themselves aright," and indeed they distort themselves by "evil and horrible" actions and habits.[138] It remains the case, however, that sinners, who seem to have dehumanized themselves by losing the image of God through their misrule, are still in the image of God.[139] No matter what we do, we cannot dispossess ourselves of the image of God, which "consists in the very nature of the mind, which is common to all men"[140]—keeping in view that the nature of the human mind or soul (our rationality) is to be embodied and is not equatable to such things as IQ, which depend upon the bodily instrument through which the mind operates, namely, the brain.

Although we cannot lose the image of God in us, the image is not a static property. With respect to the diverse ways in which the image of God exists in us, Aquinas cites the medieval gloss on Psalm 4:6 where the gloss "distinguishes a three-fold image, of 'creation,' of 're-creation,' and of 'likeness.' The first is found in all men, the second only in the just, the third only in the blessed."[141] God's grace restores and renews the image of God in sinners. Thus

137. *ST* II-II, q. 25, a. 6.

138. *ST* II-II, q. 25, a. 7.

139. See also Aquinas's references to Augustine, *De Trinitate* 14.2.6: "The image of God abides ever in the soul; 'whether this image of God be so obsolete,' as it were, clouded, 'as almost to amount to nothing,' as in those who have not the use of reason; 'or obscured and disfigured,' as in sinners; or 'clear and beautiful,' as in the just" (*ST* I, q. 93, a. 8, ad 3). See Augustine, *Trinity*, 374. Aquinas emphasizes that all humans possess the image of God, even though he wishes to affirm that the image is exercised and perfected in acts of knowing and loving. In those who lack the use of reason, sanctifying grace can perfect the image of God by infusing the habits of faith and charity. See also Hoekema's account of Calvin's stringent view of the effects of the fall upon the image: "At times he speaks of the image of God as having been *destroyed* by sin, *obliterated* by the Fall, *wiped out* or *lost* by sin, *cancelled* by sin, 'as it were, *blotted out* . . . by Adam's sin,' or *utterly defaced* by sin. A closer look, however, reveals that there is a real sense in which, according to Calvin, fallen man is still in the image of God. The image of God, Calvin says, is not totally annihilated by the Fall but is frightfully deformed" (*Created in God's Image*, 43).

140. *ST* I, q. 93, a. 4.

141. *ST* I, q. 93, a. 4. On the "natural image," the "image of grace," and the "image of glory," see Cessario, *Introduction to Moral Theology*, 29–31. See also, for the importance of the natural image, Cessario, "Sonship, Sacrifice, and Satisfaction," 79–81. For further discussion, see Eschmann, "Ethics of the Image of God." The notion of a "natural image" raises the complex topic of "nature and grace." In the debate over whether Henri de Lubac's interpretation

Paul comments after listing a number of sinful actions and habits: "And such were some of you. But you were washed, you were sanctified, you were justified in the name of the Lord Jesus Christ and in the Spirit of our God" (1 Cor. 6:11). By grace, we are conformed to the image of Jesus Christ, so that the image of God is healed and elevated in us, even though we are still imperfect. The perfecting of the image of God will be accomplished in eternal life, in the state of glory, when the blessed will know and love God perfectly, insofar as this is possible for a creature.[142] Paul remarks in this regard, "Now I know in part; then I shall understand fully, even as I have been fully understood" (1 Cor. 13:12); and even more clearly, he affirms that we who are "beholding the glory of the Lord, are being changed into his likeness from one degree of glory to another" (2 Cor. 3:18).[143] As Augustine Di Noia emphasizes, "the dynamic character of the *imago Dei* is clear: Human beings must be active in

---

of Aquinas on this matter is correct, the question is often thought to be whether grace (the dynamism of trinitarian communion) is unrelated to created nature as such or is connatural to created nature as such. In both cases, created nature would hardly seem to need transformative grace for its fulfillment, even after the fall. Thus Stanley Hauerwas imagines that the debate is about "de Lubac's insistence that grace is not extrinsically related to nature but rather is a gift that makes possible a narrative of our lives otherwise unavailable" ("Seeing Peace," 123n15). No one in the actual debate, however, conceives of grace as "extrinsically related to nature" in the sense of "unrelated" or "unfulfilling"; the purpose of theories of obediential potency was precisely to combat such extrinsicism, while at the same time retaining conceptually (through theoretical construals of "pure nature" intended to identify certain aspects of our humanity that belong to created nature) precisely the view of grace as "a gift that makes possible a narrative of our lives otherwise unavailable." See also Stratford Caldecott's insistence that "there is no purely natural man whose 'due' is determined solely by his natural needs. For in fact our natural needs include the need for love, which is supernatural" (*Not as the World Gives*, 65). No one in the debate, with the possible exception of a few early Franciscans, supposes that a "purely natural man" ever existed on earth; yet there remains the question of whether supernatural love transforms and perfects a created, natural dynamism of the will that deserves the name "love" even in persons who lack supernatural charity. The complexity of the issues involved can be seen in the recent article by Thomas Joseph White, OP, "Imperfect Happiness and the Final End of Man," the final two paragraphs of which begin, respectively, with "Against Barth and with de Lubac" and "Against de Lubac and with Barth." See also Levering, "Note on John Milbank and Thomas Aquinas."

142. See *ST* I, q. 93, a. 4; I, q. 12, a. 7. Aquinas affirms both that we will know God "as he is" (1 John 3:2) and that "no created intellect can know God infinitely. For the created intellect knows the divine essence more or less perfectly in proportion as it receives a greater or lesser light of glory. Since therefore the created light of glory received into any created intellect cannot be infinite, it is clearly impossible for any created intellect to know God in an infinite degree" (*ST* I, q. 12, a. 7). For reflection on pertinent issues, see Levering, *Jesus and the Demise of Death*, chap. 7, as well as Gaine, *Will There Be Free Will in Heaven?* See also the discussion by Romanus Cessario, OP, of "image-perfection and image restoration" (177) in his *Godly Image*. See also Levering, *Paul in the "Summa theologiae,"* chap. 5.

143. See Hoekema, *Created in God's Image*, 23–24. Like Aquinas, Hoekema counsels that "we must always see man in the light of his destiny" (96).

the grace-enabled actualization of the image of God within them."[144] Insofar as the Spirit enables us to imitate God's wisdom and generous love in Christ Jesus, we become more perfectly in the divine image as our infused habits of faith and charity are enriched and strengthened. Jean-Pierre Torrell helpfully remarks that for Aquinas, "the man-image does not reflect the God-Trinity like a mirror, but in the way an actor imitates a real person, whom he represents by entering more and more deeply into the life of the character."[145]

Torrell's reference to reflecting "God-Trinity" prompts the question of whether the image of God in us is an image of the Trinity. Rooted in Genesis 1, Middleton defines the image of God as "the royal office or calling of human beings as God's representatives and agents in the world, granted authorized power to share in God's rule or administration of the earth's resources and creatures."[146] This "royal" image imitates God in his unity—as one would expect from Genesis—but not so clearly in his Trinity. Here Aquinas's deepening of the royal image in terms of the soul and its powers can help us once more.[147] Indebted to Augustine, Aquinas argues that our wisdom and love image the divine unity, while the inner processions by which we know and love are an image of the divine Trinity. With respect to the latter, Aquinas observes that "as the uncreated Trinity is distinguished by the procession of the Word from the Speaker, and of Love from both of these . . . ; so we may say that in rational creatures wherein we find a procession of the word in the intellect, and a procession of the love in the will, there exists an image of the uncreated Trinity."[148] He goes on to specify that the image of the Trinity exists in the soul concretely when we

144. Di Noia, "Imago Dei—Imago Christi," 276. Di Noia is combating the stereotype of the "static" Thomistic image of God. This unfortunate stereotype is found, for example, in Hoekema, *Created in God's Image*, 40: "Thomas's understanding of the image of God is an abstract, static conception, far removed from the dynamics of biblical language about man."

145. Torrell, *Spiritual Master*, 89. Torrell draws this analogy from Merriell, *To the Image of the Trinity*, 245. Aquinas's position is the same as that drawn by Anthony Hoekema on the basis of a careful study of a number of biblical texts: "(1) The image of God as such is an unlosable aspect of man, a part of his essence and existence, something that man cannot lose without ceasing to be man. (2) The image of God, however, must also be understood as that likeness to God which was perverted when man fell into sin, and is being restored and renewed in the process of sanctification" (*Created in God's Image*, 32).

146. Middleton, *Liberating Image*, 27.

147. The democratized "royal" image might allow for a certain kind of social image of the Trinity, but intratrinitarian agency would be privileged (the Father "rules" more clearly than does the Son). For an exemplar of the "social" image of the Trinity, arguing for the equal value of receptivity, see Grenz, *Social God and Relational Self*.

148. *ST* I, q. 93, a. 6; cf. I, q. 28, a. 3. See also Emery, *Trinitarian Theology of Saint Thomas Aquinas*; Merriell, "Trinitarian Anthropology."

are knowing and loving *God*.[149] We can do this by our created powers, but much more so by grace.[150]

Commenting on Aquinas's "trinitarian anthropology," Juvenal Merriell observes that while "man is able in some limited way to actualize the trinitarian potentiality of his being at the natural level," humans "are enabled through grace to know God and love God better than mere nature allows."[151] Indeed, Middleton's focus on rule (even wise and generous rule in imitation of God) seems more "substantialistic"—because more strictly related to the divine substance or unity—than Aquinas's view that the trinitarian "image of God is found in the soul according as the soul turns to God, or possesses a nature that enables it to turn to God."[152]

On the grounds that it prejudices the discussion of Genesis 1:26–27 in the direction of identifying the image with rationality, Middleton, Kilner, Anthony Hoekema, and others criticize the patristic-medieval question, "In what way are humans *like* God and *unlike* animals?"[153] But this question cannot be repressed with respect to Genesis 1–2, since God first creates animals and then creates humans "in our image, after our likeness" (Gen. 1:26) with the specific injunction that humans are to "have dominion over the fish of the sea, and over the birds of the air, and over the cattle, and over all the earth, and over every creeping thing that creeps upon the earth" (Gen. 1:26). This passage appears to differentiate deliberately between humans as the image of God, on the one hand, and all other animals and earthly creatures, on the other. Furthermore, in Genesis 2:18–23 God shows each of the animals to Adam, and since Adam cannot find a true partner among any of them, God

149. See *ST* I, q. 93, a. 8.

150. For Tanner, by contrast, our graced identity diverges from our natural identity. She argues that when we cleave to the incomprehensible divine image (the Son incarnate), we gain "a new identity in him apart from anything one is oneself" ("Creation and Salvation in the Image of an Incomprehensible God," 75). While recognizing that creatures are always utterly dependent upon God, Aquinas holds that the image of God truly is in us as a created gift, and that the graced and glorified image is not an entirely new human. If our new identity were literally "apart from anything one is oneself," then our new identity could not be said to be the transformation or salvation of our old identity; it could only be said to be an utterly new creation *ex nihilo*. Tanner nonetheless speaks of "our community of nature with the humanity of Christ" (74). Surely—as Aquinas's approach allows—this "community of nature" involves something that "one is oneself."

151. Merriell, "Trinitarian Anthropology," 138. See also Cessario, "Trinitarian Imprint on the Moral Life."

152. *ST* I, q. 93, a. 8. This turning to God is also a turning to Christ; see Hibbs, "*Imitatio Christi* and the Foundation of Aquinas's Ethics"; Bailleux, "À l'image du Fils premier-né,"; Di Noia, "Imago Dei—Imago Christi."

153. Middleton, *Liberating Image*, 18–19. See Kilner, *Dignity and Destiny*, 109–11; Hoekema, *Created in God's Image*, 23.

makes Eve. Once again, this differentiates quite plainly between humans and other animals. If the "image of God" arises in the context of the differentiation between humans and other animals, however, does this necessitate the identification of the mind or rational soul as the key differentiating factor between humans and other animals?

Regarding the distinctive element in human nature, Aquinas highlights Ephesians 4:23–24: "Be renewed in the spirit of your minds, and put on the new nature, created after the likeness of God in true righteousness and holiness."[154] This "new nature," as opposed to the corrupt and sinful "old nature" of Ephesians 4:22, is "created after the likeness of God" precisely because it involves a renewal "in the spirit of your minds" so as to be marked by "true righteousness and holiness." It is therefore our minds that are renewed so that we, in our new nature, can once more be "after the likeness of God." To this passage, Aquinas adds another very similar one from Colossians 3:10, where Paul extols those who "have put on the new nature, which is being renewed in knowledge after the image of its creator."[155] When we are renewed "in knowledge," this is the renewal of "the image" of God in us. These texts strengthen Aquinas in his view that the distinctive human image of God must be in the rational soul and its powers. Furthermore, when addressing the question of whether any creature can be like God, Aquinas's response combines the "image of God" in Genesis 1:27 with 1 John 3:2: "When he appears we shall be like him, for we shall see him as he is."[156] This "seeing" is an experiential "knowing"; and thus putting "on the new nature" and "being renewed in knowledge" have

---

154. See *ST* I, q. 93, a. 6.

155. Christopher R. Seitz comments on Col. 3:10, "We are being renewed in a knowledge—not of the tree of knowledge—that brings about renewal, as the garments of our old Adam are being replaced by the garments of Christ the new Adam. . . . 'Knowledge' here is the form of Christian provisioning that stands in contrast to the deathly knowledge in disobedience. It is knowledge of God, not self-knowledge of our loss of God" (*Colossians*, 159). Seitz is right to distinguish between the knowledge of good and evil gained by sin, on the one hand, and the knowledge of Col. 3:10, a "knowledge after the image of its creator," on the other. Aquinas's observation that to be in the image of the creator centrally includes knowledge—above all "knowledge of God"—is consonant with Seitz's interpretation. Another contemporary exegete, Marianne Meye Thompson, does not make much of the connection of knowledge with the image, but she argues that the key element of the passage, in light of Christ's status as "the image of the invisible God" (Col. 1:15), is that "Christ is the image of the renewed humanity; and, hence, the renewal of humanity according to the image of its Creator takes place in Christ, the 'firstborn' of all creation" (*Colossians and Philemon*, 78). This interpretation makes sense, but the question is why the renewal in those who are in Christ of the image of God is described as being "renewed in knowledge" (Col. 3:10). It would seem to favor the interpretation that the image of God in us has to do with knowing. For further emphasis that "Colossians 3:9–10 can plausibly be read to mean by 'image of its creator' the 'image of Christ,'" see Kelsey, *Eccentric Existence*, 2:947.

156. *ST* I, q. 4, a. 3, *sed contra*. Jean-Pierre Torrell highlights this pairing in his *Spiritual Master*, 80.

as their goal (in Torrell's words) contemplative "union with God, whom the soul enjoys like an object of love freely possessed."[157]

This does not mean, however, that our bodiliness, or for that matter the bodiliness of other creatures, lacks reference to God. On the contrary, as I discussed in the book's introduction, Aquinas (like the fathers) considers that there is a "likeness by way of a *trace*" in every creature, so that every creature is like a footprint of God, showing God's presence and action as the wise and loving creator.[158] Moreover, our bodiliness is specially adapted to the relational dimension of the image of God, as appears, for example, in the erect stature that enables us to establish face-to-face bonds of knowing and loving with fellow humans.[159] We are able to image the love of Christ and the Church—and thereby to be configured to Christ's image of selfless love—in marriage: "Husbands, love your wives, as Christ loved the church and gave himself up for her" (Eph. 5:25). Our bodies are none other than "the temple of the living God" (2 Cor. 6:16), and we must therefore "cleanse ourselves from every defilement of body and spirit" (2 Cor. 7:1). Building upon Augustine's *De Trinitate*, Aquinas adds some comments about whether the image of God is found in the relationship between man and woman, which may seem to be suggested by Genesis 1:27's statement "in the image of God he created him; male and female he created them." Here the Father would be the man, the Son the child, and the Spirit the woman. Aquinas deems this position to be "absurd," not least because "one man would be only the image of one Person."[160] The image of the Triune God cannot be an image of solely *one* divine person.

157. Torrell, *Spiritual Master*, 93. Rudolph Schnackenburg observes, "Those who sin lose their credibility as people who have 'seen' Christ or 'known' him. 'To see' is a Johannine term for the experience of faith leading to fellowship" (*Johannine Epistles*, 173).

158. *ST* I, q. 93, a. 6. For a contemporary development of this point, see Leithart, *Traces of the Trinity*, which I discuss in the conclusion to the present book.

159. Aquinas explains that "this is not to be understood as though the image of God were in man's body; but in the sense that the very shape of the human body represents the image of God in the soul by way of a trace" (*ST* I, q. 93, a. 6, ad 3).

160. *ST* I, q. 93, a. 6, ad 2. Pope John Paul II argues, however (like Karl Barth and others), that the account of the creation of man in Genesis 1 affirms from the beginning and directly that man was created in the image of God inasmuch as he is male and female. The account in Genesis 2, by contrast, does not speak of the "image of God," but reveals, in the manner proper to it, that the complete and definitive creation of "man" . . . expresses itself in giving life to the "*communio personarum*" that man and woman form. In this way, the Yahwist account agrees with the content of the first account. If, vice versa, we want to retrieve also from the account of the Yahwist text the concept of "image of God," we can deduce that *man became the image of God not only through his own humanity, but also through the communion of persons*, which man and woman form from the very beginning. The function of the image is that of mirroring the one who is the model, of reproducing its own prototype. Man becomes an image of God not so much in the moment of solitude as in the moment of communion. He is, in fact, "from the

A final exegetical point mattered a good deal to some of the fathers of the Church: Why did God say not only "image" but also "likeness" (Gen. 1:26)? Are they synonyms or two different things?[161] In this regard, Aquinas begins with Aristotle, who holds that likeness is caused by "oneness in quality" and therefore "is a kind of unity."[162] This unity, Aquinas observes, can either be a preamble or a perfection. He explains that "since *one* is a transcendental, it is both common to all, and adapted to each single thing."[163] As common to all, likeness identifies a preamble that exists in a wider array of things than does the image; as adapted to particular things, likeness signals a perfection of the specific image. John of Damascus thinks of "likeness" in Genesis 1:26 as meaning a perfection of the image, whereas Augustine thinks of it as meaning a preamble to the image. Aquinas agrees with both interpretations. Thus, in accord with John of Damascus, Aquinas affirms that "likeness" involves degrees of imaging God, insofar as likeness "signifies a certain perfection of image."[164] But in his commentary on 1 Corinthians 15:49, "Just as we have borne the image of the man of dust, we shall also bear the image of the man of heaven," Aquinas observes that "inasmuch as we are sinners, the likeness of Adam is in us"—thereby defining likeness in terms of a preamble rather than a perfection.[165]

Conclusion

Middleton's democratized royal image, focused on God's power as generosity and gifting rather than as domination, offers helpful insights into the content

---

beginning" not only an image in which the solitude of one Person, who rules the world, mirrors itself, but also and essentially the image of an inscrutable divine communion of Persons" (*Man and Woman He Created Them*, 163).

I find this view persuasive as a description of the innately relational character of the image of God, but I think that in fact the soul and its powers uphold this relational character better than does locating the image in the communion of man and woman (or of man, woman, and child). I agree that there is no individual human that is not relational (toward God and toward neighbor), but I want to retain the insistence, both on exegetical and on theological grounds, that each individual human is fully in the image of God. For a development of Pope John Paul II's position, see Scola, *Nuptial Mystery*. See also Hoekema, *Created in God's Image*, 97. Hoekema goes so far as to say that "man can only be fully human in fellowship and partnership with woman," although he adds that "every person . . . is in the image of God" (97–98).

161. For further discussion of this point, see Hoekema, *Created in God's Image*, 13, 30.

162. *ST* I, q. 93, a. 9.

163. Ibid.

164. Ibid.

165. Thomas Aquinas, *Commentary on the Letters of Saint Paul to the Corinthians*, chap. 15, lect. 7, §998, p. 376. For discussion of 1 Cor. 15:49 as bearing upon the theology of the image of God, see also Hoekema, *Created in God's Image*, 30.

of the image of God. Nonetheless, Kilner's concerns about locating the image of God in particular attributes tell against Middleton's position, insofar as Middleton rejects as "substantialistic" and unbiblical the identification of the image of God with the rational soul and its powers. The royal image, no matter how democratized, would seem to unavoidably favor leaders, who have the opportunity to do more good "royal" things for others than can less privileged members of the community—even if everyone has a vote. Rebels, too, are hardly royal in the good sense, and in fact could lose the image entirely by acting persistently against God's rule. The royal image would also not be present among people who, due to severe mental disability, cannot imitate God's rule in any way. These concerns are significant because, as Henri de Lubac says, in its fundamental meaning "the divine image does not differ from one individual to another: in all it is the same image."[166]

Throughout this chapter, I have argued that solutions to these concerns can be found by turning to what underlies our royal rule, namely, the knowing and loving that form the basis for our communion with God and neighbor. As we saw, the paleontologist Richard Fortey finds such knowing and loving in the most primitive first modern *Homo sapiens* (and, in his view, Neanderthals). Fortey observes that "we cannot question that the sense of 'I-ness' is one of the defining possessions of our species," and he argues that language and conscious thought developed together.[167] For Fortey, the evolutionary evidence suggests that consciousness was a solely material development, but he does not address the arguments for the immateriality of the soul—arguments that I find persuasive and have defended elsewhere.[168] Here, the point is that the placement of the image of God in the powers of knowing and loving—which are fulfilled not in a mere mastery of facts or in high IQ but in relationships, above all in the relationship with God—ensures that both the most primitive and the most advanced humans are in the image of God. This becomes crystal clear once it is realized that the human soul is not a bodily organ, even though it works through bodily organs. Even those who cannot exercise the powers of the soul due to a bodily defect possess in full the rational soul and its powers. Thus even severe mental disability—let alone being a primitive hunter-gatherer—cannot remove the image of God by which humans are related to the creator.

166. De Lubac, *Catholicism*, 29.
167. Fortey, *Life*, 308–9.
168. I argue for this position in chap. 6 of *Jesus and the Demise of Death*, but David Bentley Hart (without adopting a strictly Aristotelian understanding of the soul) and others have made the case far more extensively. The immateriality of the soul is a philosophical doctrine, but it is also part of the Catholic doctrinal inheritance.

At the same time, the position I am advocating fully accounts for the royal dimension that Middleton emphasizes. This is so because, as Middleton recognizes, to share in God's rule means to exercise wisdom and generous love, which is none other than to exercise the powers of the soul. Moreover, my position resolves a difficulty raised by Middleton's: although severely mentally disabled persons and children prior to the age of reason cannot share in God's rule in this way due to a bodily lack, they are still in the image of God and called to a supernatural participation in God's life because of their possession of the rational soul. Indeed, Genesis makes clear that God called the very first rational *Homo sapiens*, in all their primitiveness, to this very same goal of divine communion. As Nonna Verna Harrison comments, "The good news is that God, who has created the world out of nothing, has made all human persons—everyone, without exception—to be people of real value, for he has placed his own value, the divine image, in each of us."[169]

Admittedly, when Aquinas describes the paradisal condition of Adam and Eve, he imagines them to possess a breadth of knowledge that far exceeds what is plausible or necessary.[170] Fortunately, his overall account of what the image of God involves does not require the possession of extensive knowledge, and in fact fits quite well with the portraits of primitive humans that I surveyed at the outset of the chapter. Aquinas's account of the image of God as being in the (embodied) soul and its powers also accords with Genesis's depiction of the first humans as distinguished from the other animals solely by rationality and linguistic communication. Furthermore, his presentation of the image of God connects with contemporary biblical exegesis by exhibiting what it means for humans to exercise royal rule as God's representatives on earth. Above all, such royal rule must mean to be like God by the right embodied exercise of the powers that sustain our communion with God and each other and that enable us to be good stewards of the earth—namely, the powers of knowing and loving, since "the intellectual nature imitates God chiefly in this, that God understands and loves himself."[171] Of course, God "infinitely

169. Harrison, *God's Many-Splendored Image*, 44.

170. See *ST* I, q. 94, a. 3. Aquinas argues that Adam could only have named the animals if he knew their natures, and he thinks that this implies that Adam "was possessed of the knowledge of all other things" (I, q. 94, a. 3, *sed contra*). Among the things that Adam would not have known, in Aquinas's view, are "the thoughts of men, future contingent events, and some individual facts, as for instance the number of pebbles in a stream" (I, q. 94, a. 3). Because Adam had to teach his descendants, and since actuality precedes potentiality, Aquinas supposes that God infused Adam's mind with "whatever truths man is naturally able to know" and also the "supernatural truths" befitting Adam's state (ibid.).

171. *ST* I, q. 93, a. 4. Metropolitan John Zizioulas of Pergamon both defends and critiques the term "steward": it is a positive term "from the point of view of what it intends to exclude,

excels" the soul and its powers, so that whereas "the Image of God exists in his first-born Son" perfectly, the image of God "exists in man as in an alien nature, as the image of the king is in a silver coin."[172]

In sum, I contend that when we read Middleton and Aquinas together, thereby combining the fruits of modern exegesis and patristic-medieval exegesis, we gain a deeper appreciation of why God describes humans as "in our image, after our likeness" (Gen. 1:27). Created as rational, that is, with the capacity for wisdom and love, humans are called to communion with God, with each other, and in a certain sense with the whole creation. The intelligent capacity for royal-priestly communion with God, a free participation in God's wise governance and gifting, is what distinguishes the human race from all other animals.[173]

---

namely, that the human being is the lord and proprietor of creation"; but it is a negative term insofar as it "implies a *managerial* approach to nature" and insofar as it seems to neglect our responsibility to cultivate (rather than simply conserve) creation; see "Proprietors or Priests of Creation?," 163–64. In my view, "steward" need not carry these two negative connotations. Metropolitan John prefers the term "priest of creation." He helpfully distinguishes between "a development of nature that treats it as *raw material for production* and distribution, and . . . development that treats nature as an entity that must be developed *for its own sake*" (170). I think that the latter definition allows for a development of nature in service to humanity.

172. *ST* I, q. 93, a. 1 and ad 2. Aquinas draws this comparison of the "image" of a king in his son and on a coin from Augustine. Aquinas specifies that creatures imitate the divine, even though God is not "like a creature" (I, q. 4, a. 3, ad 4; cf. I, q. 13, aa. 6–7). By contrast, Tanner holds that "the divine simply cannot be imitated, strictly speaking, in what is not divine" ("Creation and Salvation in the Image of an Incomprehensible God," 72). As I noted in chap. 1 on the divine ideas, Aquinas insists that the divine can be imitated by the nondivine. Tanner, who knows Aquinas's thought well, may here be putting her point in an intentionally exaggerated form, in order to accentuate the complete difference between the nondivine image and the divine image. After all, she grants that "we image God in and through what we are as creatures," even though "we do not do so independently of God" (71). Similarly, she affirms that humans "are more in the image of God than animals, and more the image of God in certain respects than others" (ibid.). She shows her appreciation for Aquinas's teaching on analogy in her *God and Creation in Christian Theology*, 12, although she attempts to make analogy solely about our discourse (our "God-talk") rather than about God. On this problem, see Francesca Aran Murphy, *God Is Not a Story*.

173. See the title of chap. 7 of Middleton, *Liberating Image*, "Imaging God's Primal Generosity." Middleton comments, "Given the portrayal or rendering of God's power disclosed by a careful reading of Genesis 1, I suggest that the sort of power or rule that humans are to exercise is a generous, loving power. It is power used to nurture, enhance, and empower others, noncoercively, for *their* benefit, not for the self-aggrandizement of the one exercising power. In its canonical place in the book of Genesis, the creation story in 1:1–2:3 thus serves as a normative limit and judgment on the violence that pervades the primeval history, indeed the rest of the Bible and human history generally" (295).

Be Fruitful and Multiply

And God blessed them, and God said to them, "Be fruitful and multiply, and fill the earth and subdue it."

Genesis 1:28

After the big bang occurred fourteen billion years ago, 4.5 billion years ago the sun and solar system came to be, perhaps due to the explosion of a supernova. During its formative period, the earth first became so hot that its inner core became molten, after which the gradual cooling of the earth produced millions of years of torrential rain, forming the oceans.[1] The simplest forms of life emerged 3.5 billion years ago, a shockingly short time after the cooling of the earth. Multicellular animals evolved 550 million years ago or thereabouts. Nonrational hominids, from which human bodies evolved, broke away from primates about seven million years ago. The development of *Homo sapiens* almost came to a dead end between 90,000 and 135,000 years ago. Tropical Africa endured a severe drought, with the result that, as Edward O. Wilson states, "the size of the total *Homo sapiens* population on the African continent descended into the thousands, and for a long while the future conqueror species risked complete extinction."[2] Had the drought not lifted, the earth might forever have remained a place for nonrational animals and the profusion of plant life. It was only because the drought lifted that

1. See Bellah, *Religion in Human Evolution*, 52–53.
2. Edward O. Wilson, *Social Conquest of Earth*, 82. Although I have chosen to highlight Wilson's narrative here, Chris Stringer gives a more up-to-date and thorough rendition of climate change in Africa between 195,000 and 57,000 years ago; see *Lone Survivors*, 230–35.

human population expanded again and moved out of Africa, through "a corridor of continuous habitable terrain up the Nile to Sinai and beyond."[3]

Wilson reports that this "breakout from Africa" led to a "vast overall increase in population size," as well as to beneficial cognitive mutations and innovations.[4] The next step was cultural change, which began to occur rapidly around fifty thousand years ago and has not stopped since. Humans arrived in Europe "no later than 42,000 years before the present," entirely displacing the native Neanderthals within twelve thousand years.[5] In Wilson's view, the reason that there are no other hominids possessed of human intelligence is "the extreme improbability" of each of the "preadaptations" occurring at precisely the right time, so as to enable each of the necessary evolutionary adaptations.[6] As a species, says Wilson, humans "have made every one of the required lucky turns in the evolutionary maze."[7]

Have these "lucky turns" for the human species been lucky for the earth? The emergence of large communities of human beings soon began to have a significant impact upon the earth, especially beginning ten thousand years ago, when "the Neolithic revolution began to yield vastly larger amounts of food from cultivated crops and livestock, along with rapid growth in human populations."[8] This environmental impact of human communities has increased dramatically in the last few centuries, since for thousands of years there were less than ten million people on earth, and even in the year 1650 there were only 500 million. Thanks to much lower mortality rates and numerous technological/agricultural improvements, there are now almost seven and a half billion people on the planet. This vastly increased presence of human populations was predictable, Wilson notes, because "region by region, recent studies show, the populations have approached a limit set by the supply of food and water"—and human multiplication simply does not

---

3. E. Wilson, *Social Conquest of Earth*, 82.

4. Ibid., 88.

5. Ibid.; on the cultural explosion, including the development of agriculture, see 91–93. Later in the book Wilson observes,

> The beginnings of the creative arts as they are practiced today may stay forever hidden. Yet they were sufficiently established by genetic and cultural evolution for the 'creative explosion' that began approximately 35,000 years ago in Europe. From this time on until the Late Paleolithic period over 20,000 years later, cave art flourished. Thousands of figures, mostly of large game animals, have been found in more than two hundred caves distributed through southwestern France and northeastern Spain, on both sides of the Pyrenees. Along with cliffside drawings in other parts of the world, they present a stunning snapshot of life just before the dawn of civilization. (278–79)

6. Ibid. 45.

7. Ibid.

8. Ibid., 76.

stop until such limits are reached.[9] The impact of humans on the earth has thus become enormous.

For his part, Wilson argues that the rise and spread of humans mean that "Darwin's dice have rolled badly for Earth."[10] More optimistically, the Catholic thinker Brendan Purcell celebrates the human revolution: "The range of our feeling and imagination, of our understanding and our effective freedom, while still rooted in incarnate finitude, opens out to a transfinite horizon of beauty, truth and goodness."[11] But even Purcell is no romantic; he fills out his portrait of human beings with examples taken from the Nazi period, including among his examples not only the heroic death of Sophie Scholl, but also the evil actions of Albert Speer. Moreover, the genocidal Nazi reign has given way to an era in which humans now seem to be on the verge of destroying the earth's entire ecosystem, whether by nuclear conflagration, or by carbon emissions, or simply by overpopulation that crowds out and extinguishes other species.[12]

Is Wilson then right that, in the emergence and spread of the "image of God" (Gen. 1:27), "Darwin's dice have rolled badly for Earth"? Or does

9. Ibid.

10. Edward O. Wilson, "Is Humanity Suicidal?," cited in Derr, "Environmental Ethics and Christian Humanism," 96. Derr critiques the leading voices of the environmentalist movement for being overly negative and alarmist about the numbers of humans on earth. Derr applauds the drop in fertility rates brought about by the use of contraception; see his "Environmental Ethics and Christian Humanism," 74–76. Even so, Derr strongly opposes organized "birth control campaigns" (75), coerced birth control and abortion, and the tendency to blame the ecological crisis upon population. See also the insightful critique of the view that "if man cannot accept his circumscribed place on the earth, it would be best if he were to become extinct" (184), in Carey, "Sedimentation of Meaning in the Concepts of Nature and the Environment." Carey remarks: "This view of things is manifestly idolatrous: it elevates the visible world above both man and the invisible God in whose image he is made" (ibid.).

11. Purcell, *From Big Bang to Big Mystery*, 271.

12. Regarding religion, Wilson considers that humans began with "just-so" stories, around which have built up the elaborate "myths and gods of organized religions," myths and gods that "are stultifying and divisive" and that "encourage ignorance, distract people from recognizing problems of the real world, and often lead them in wrong directions into disastrous actions" (*Social Conquest of Earth*, 292). While religion is divisive and occult, science is empirical and open to everyone. For Wilson, therefore, "The conflict between scientific knowledge and the teachings of organized religions is irreconcilable. The chasm will continue to widen and cause no end of trouble as long as religious leaders go on making unsupportable claims about supernatural causes of reality" (295). For a profound defense of the arguments for God's existence and for the immateriality of rational consciousness, see David Bentley Hart, *Experience of God*. As Diogenes Allen points out, "Attempts to reduce human agency to a deterministic connection of events we observe, say to stimulus and response patterns, or to neurological connections in the body and brain, always *presuppose* the very agency they are supposedly describing in non-agency terms" ("Persons in Philosophical and Biblical Perspective," 172). See also Schönborn, *Chance or Purpose?*, 120–22; Clarke, "Immediate Creation of the Human Soul by God and Some Contemporary Challenges."

the growth of human population express the wisdom of God in creation? In the context of such questions, I reflect in this chapter upon God's command in Genesis 1:28 to "be fruitful and multiply, and fill the earth," a command that God repeats elsewhere in Genesis. What should we make of this command today? Randall Smith, Hava Tirosh-Samuelson, and others have rightly contested the view that Genesis 1 is negative toward the environment.[13] While I agree with their arguments, I think that the command to "be fruitful and multiply, and fill the earth" requires more attention, especially in light of the growing consensus articulated by the theologian Michael Northcott that "reductions in population in both North and South are highly desirable in the light of the environmental crisis."[14]

The first section of this chapter examines God's command to "be fruitful and multiply, and fill the earth." I emphasize the fact that God reaffirms this command even after fallen humans exhibited their destructive tendencies, including their destructive ecological tendencies. The value that God accords to his human images is such that God strongly promotes human multiplication even after it has led (in the Genesis narrative at least) to the near annihilation of life on earth. My second section then explores a quite different perspective on the multiplication of human images of God, namely, that found in the Christian environmentalist Bill McKibben's *Maybe One: A Case for Smaller Families*. McKibben argues that Americans need to limit family size to one child or else face imminent, catastrophic ecological disaster. His position accords with the biblical scholar Richard Bauckham's view that in Genesis 1:28–30, God shows humans "that the produce of the earth is not intended to feed them alone, but also all the living species of the earth. Humans are

13. See Randall Smith, "Creation and the Environment in the Hebrew Scriptures"; Tirosh-Samuelson, "Judaism and the Care for God's Creation." See also such works as Davis, *Scripture, Culture, and Agriculture*; and Shochet, *Animal Life in Jewish Tradition*. Critiques of Gen. 1 are generally focused upon God's command to "subdue" the earth and "have dominion over the fish of the sea and over the birds of the air and over every living thing that moves upon the earth" (Gen. 1:28).

14. Northcott, *Environment and Christian Ethics*, 28; cf. 300–301 for strategies to accomplish this reduction, indebted to Daly and Cobb, *For the Common Good*. Northcott observes, "The United Nations Population Fund estimates that world food production can sustainably (that is without soil erosion, desertification, ground-water depletion etc.) feed around 5.5 billion people with an adequate calorific intake if everyone was on a vegetarian diet. If, however, the population derives 25 per cent of calorie intake from meat products, as North Americans and West Europeans do, then the number which can be sustainably fed reduces to around 2.8 billion" (27). Does this number assume that soil erosion, desertification, and so forth are impossible to address in ways that do not reduce food production? For a theology of the Holy Spirit in light of climate change, emphasizing the work of the Spirit in "the restoration of creation and of human and creaturely relations" (58), see Northcott, "Holy Spirit"; cf. Wallace, "Green Face of God."

not to fill the earth and subdue it to the extent of leaving no room and no sustenance for the other creatures who share the earth with them."[15]

Having set forth this tension, my third section develops a theological framework for approaching the command to "be fruitful and multiply" in a manner that is not closed to concerns about population growth but that is mindful that "the Church stands for life: in each human life she sees the splendor of that 'Yes,' that 'Amen,' who is Christ Himself."[16] My fourth and final section, then, draws some conclusions in dialogue with contemporary theologians about whether the Church should now encourage couples to have small families or should continue to recognize the value of large families even in an ecologically strained world of almost seven and a half billion people. Pope Francis remarks, "Because all creatures are connected, each must be cherished with love and respect, for all of us as living creatures are dependent on one another."[17] Should this interconnectedness suppress "be fruitful and multiply" in the case of humans, in light of the need for humans to rule wisely over the earth? Or is a still-expanding human population justified by what Pope Francis identifies as the "unique dignity" of each human being?[18]

"Be Fruitful and Multiply, and Fill the Earth"

According to the first chapter of Genesis, after creating human beings male and female, "God blessed them, and God said to them, 'Be fruitful and multiply, and fill the earth'" (Gen. 1:28). In a brief note on this passage in his recent *Commentary on the Torah*, the Jewish exegete Richard Elliott Friedman states simply, "This commandment has now been fulfilled."[19] From an evangelical Christian perspective, Bill Arnold's commentary on Genesis treats Genesis 1:28 with similar brevity, remarking solely that God's blessing consists in his

15. Bauckham, *Living with Other Creatures*, 227. See also, for a related emphasis on the "sacred trust" that humans have received to be "preservers and conservers of all life," Hall, *Imaging God*, 200. In my view, the extinction of other species can sometimes be an acceptable cost of the expansion of human interpersonal communion: for example, I do not consider the massive loss of species that came about due to the populating of America by nonnative peoples to be a tragedy, since these humans could not have survived in large numbers without extensive clear-cutting of forests for agricultural use of the land. Likewise, I do not mourn the first arrival of humans in the Americas (which took place when "a single Siberian population reached the Bering land bridge no sooner than 30,000 years ago, and possibly as recently as 22,000 years"), despite what Edward O. Wilson identifies as "its catastrophic impact on the virgin fauna and flora" (*Social Conquest of Earth*, 83).

16. Pope John Paul II, *Familiaris consortio*, §30.

17. Pope Francis, *Laudato Si'*, §42.

18. Ibid., §43.

19. Friedman, *Commentary on the Torah*, 13. Alter, *Genesis*, does not comment on this verse.

favorable disposition toward humankind and his desire that they "fill up and inhabit that portion of the cosmos set apart especially for them."[20] Likewise, Walter Brueggemann connects the passage with other texts of "blessing" and observes that the point is that God's creative activity is intended to flow through "the generative power of life, fertility, and well-being that God has ordained within the normal flow and mystery of life."[21] Among the recent commentaries on Genesis that I have read, R. R. Reno has the most to say on Genesis 1:28. Reno focuses on the fact that procreation "gives us a future" and "realizes the capacity of creation to have time and history."[22] He points to Scripture's later connection of idolatry with immoral sexual practices, and he observes that the ultimate goal of fruitful procreation consists in a blessing that we cannot give to ourselves or to our children, namely, Christ's gift of eternal life. For Reno, human parenthood is a paradigmatic act of self-surrendering trust in the goodness of God.

Yet was God's command to humans to "be fruitful and multiply, and fill the earth" a good idea? Does the earth really need to be filled by humans, and even if so, what about the risk of overfilling it? It would seem that God's command, even if one granted that it is good for the earth to become full of humans, unwisely leaves out what happens when the earth is filled with humans. Since humans breed more humans, an earth filled with humans is at severe risk of becoming overfilled with humans. In his seemingly rather blithe command, God does not appear to take this risk into account.

Various responses might be given from the text or from the text's reconstructed historical context. Perhaps filling the earth is a good command, and a good idea, so long as humans remain without sin.[23] After all, in Genesis 1:28

20. Arnold, *Genesis*, 47.

21. Brueggemann, *Genesis*, 37. Brueggemann cites Westermann, *Blessing in the Bible and the Life of the Church*.

22. Reno, *Genesis*, 56.

23. John Hart, for instance, argues that "environmental crises do not result when human activity is natural. Crises result when humans deny their place in creation as its integrating consciousness reflecting on itself and as its complexity evolving beyond itself. When humans lose their sense of place—their setting and their role—they lose a sense of the sacred, they reject intrinsic value in abiotic nature and in species and individuals of the biotic community, they deny natural rights to nature, and they reject humanity's situation in creation as one of the uncounted numbers of all species who have complementary roles in the community of life, and are related to each other as the common offspring of cosmic becoming" (*Sacramental Commons*, 203). Hart defines a "natural" human action as one that "is integrated with human biological-personal-social-psychological-spiritual identity and aspirations; is consonant with the integration of humans within the biotic community and with abiotic nature; is compatible with Earth's evolutionary flow of time, energies, elements, and events; and represents or complements generally accepted social values and conduct. Humans are most natural when they are social beings who live in and with nature, and relate to nature while they work to ensure the commons

there is as yet no mention of human sin. Created in the royal image of God, humans are part of the whole creation that God has reason to deem "very good" (Gen. 1:31). After the first humans sin, therefore, does God rescind his command to be fruitful and multiply, and fill the earth?

The answer is no. Instead, after Adam and Eve's fall and their alienation from God and each other, God foretells that humankind's relationship to the earth will be marked by conflict and pain. He tells Adam, "Cursed is the ground because of you; in toil you shall eat of it all the days of your life; thorns and thistles it shall bring forth to you; and you shall eat the plants of the field" (Gen. 3:17–18). There is a sense here that Adam and the ecosystem will be opposed to each other, that the ecosystem has been "cursed" because of Adam and that its well-being (the well-being of the "plants of the field") is now set in opposition to Adam's ("thorns and thistles it shall bring forth to you").[24] Given this conflictual relationship, it seems that Adam's sin has permanently marred the ecosystem and that Adam's efforts to obtain food will cause the ecosystem pain. Yet, despite God's foretelling of this conflictual relationship between Adam and the ecosystem, God proceeds to help Adam and Eve have children—and thus to help Adam and Eve "be fruitful and multiply, and fill the earth." When Eve conceives a child, she rejoices, "I have gotten a man with the help of the LORD" (Gen. 4:1). The child she conceives is Cain.

The arrival of Cain, murderer of his brother Abel and the first builder of a city, seems a rather ominous start to "be fruitful and multiply." Was God right to "help" Eve have a child (Gen. 4:1) who would introduce violence and

---

good and the common good through an equitable distribution of commons goods as common goods" (202). The goal of human natural action is "to bear fruit not only for itself but for the extended biotic community and for Earth for generations to come" (ibid.). For this goal to succeed, the number of fallen humans in the world would likely need to be quite small.

24. For a somewhat contrasting (agrarian) vision, see Fred Bahnson and Norman Wirzba's argument that "ecological amnesia" has been produced by the separation of most modern people from food production. Bahnson and Wirzba state rather romantically that "whether as hunters and gatherers or, more likely, as peasants and farmers, people understood that in order to eat, they had to understand and respect the soil, climate, plants and animals. . . . Although it did not guarantee a fully satisfied or comfortable life, such work refined and reinforced the understanding that survival was deeply implicated in the lives of other creatures. It taught humans that the basis for health and well-being was thoroughly bound up with the health and well-being of the fields, waters and animals that warmed and fed them. In short, this was an understanding of humans as embodied beings in multiple, unfathomably complex relationships with nonhuman bodies" (*Making Peace with the Land*, 35). Bahnson and Wirzba suggest that the meaning of God's Sabbath blessing is that "no creature, no body whatsoever, should be neglected, despised or abused. Each body is God's love made visible, touchable, smellable, hearable and delectable" (40). I agree with this, although it needs to be emphasized that human (ensouled) bodies in a special way are "God's love made visible" and that human interpersonal communion, even if it displaces or in some way causes harm to other nonhuman bodies, is a supreme instance of "God's love made visible."

urban life to the very good world, with its wondrous plants, birds, fish, and animals as described in Genesis 1? Furthermore, Cain's descendant Tubal-cain became the first "forger of all instruments of bronze and iron" (Gen. 4:22). Thus the God who commanded that humans be fruitful and fill the earth, the same God who helped the fallen Adam and Eve have a child (Cain) and who thereby set in motion human multiplication and filling of the earth, is also responsible in a certain sense for the rise of the technology that has balefully harmed the earth's ecosystem—namely, "instruments of bronze and iron." That such instruments are made by the descendants of Cain is of course significant; due to the correlation of Cain with violence, we already have a sense that such instruments, which would have been unnecessary before the fall, are going to wreak a good deal of havoc. But my point is simply that God does not take back his commandment to multiply and fill the earth after the sin of Adam and Eve. In fact, according to Eve, God helps her have a child and thereby helps to set the whole thing rolling. Having failed to rescind the command to be fruitful and multiply, God sets up the situation in which human sinners build cities and forge iron and bronze tools that inevitably are going to threaten the ecosystem, in accord with God's foretelling that Adam and his descendants would be in a conflictual relationship with the ecosystem.

For those who might wish to see a victory of the ecosystem over the steadily multiplying human sinners, things improve somewhat in the next few chapters of Genesis. The line of Seth emerges as a counterpoint to the city-building, tool-forging Cainites. Seth has good descendants, including Enoch, who "walked with God" (Gen. 5:24). From this line, Noah is born. God also perceives that the multiplication of human beings, their filling of the earth, has produced baleful fruit. We read, "Now the earth was corrupt in God's sight, and the earth was filled with violence. And God saw the earth, and behold, it was corrupt; for all flesh had corrupted their way upon the earth" (Gen. 6:11–12). According to the narrative, God's solution is to flood the entire earth, thereby destroying almost all animals, plants, and birds, as well as all humans other than Noah and his family. But had God stuck to his original plan (as described in Gen. 6:7) to entirely wipe out all humans, the life-sustaining beauty of the earth would not today be threatened by nuclear holocaust or by the turning of the entire habitable earth into a polluted pavement.[25]

25. As Bahnson and Wirzba point out,
> The nightmare is not over. God promised to never again destroy the world, but we humans just might. The findings of ecologists and environmental historians show that people have yet to learn what is required to live harmoniously on and with the earth. God's soil and water are daily being poisoned and wasted. God's forests and glaciers are quickly disappearing. God's animals, particularly the agricultural animals that we have

Noah, however, is found to be righteous, and so God decides not to follow through on his earlier decision: "I will blot out man whom I have created from the face of the ground, man and beast and creeping things and birds of the air" (Gen. 6:7). Instead, God commands Noah to make an ark, so that Noah and his family can survive the catastrophic flood that God has decided to unleash. Noah becomes the means of survival for many animals and plants as well. God commands Noah, "Of every living thing of all flesh, you shall bring two of every sort into the ark, to keep them alive with you; they shall be male and female. Of the birds according to their kinds, and of the animals according to their kinds, of every creeping thing of the ground according to its kind, two of every sort shall come in to you, to keep them alive" (Gen. 6:19). Noah also brings into the ark a sample of every edible plant. In a second version of the story, Noah goes so far as to bring seven pairs of each clean animal, along with one pair of each unclean animal—the Mosaic law here being explicitly introduced into the flood accounts, thus reminding us not to read these accounts in a literalistic way.

Even though the flood accounts are not intended to be read as literal history, their presentations of God, humans, and nature retain deep significance.[26] According to Genesis, God goes ahead with the worldwide flood and blots out almost all the representatives of all land-based species.[27] Yet God does not learn what seems to be the obvious lesson of the multiplication of sinful human city-builders and tool-users.[28] On the contrary, once the floodwaters

---

domesticated, are systematically being abused. And perhaps worst of all, we are causing the "dome in the midst of the waters," that protective mantle we call the *atmosphere*, to rupture (Gen. 1:6). Polar ice is melting, hurricanes and droughts are becoming more frequent and severe, sea levels are rising, and the tropics have expanded by two degrees latitude. (*Making Peace with the Land*, 17)

Nuclear war also remains a real possibility, as more and more countries gain nuclear weapons. Although Bahnson and Wirzba do not raise the issue of population, and in fact suggest that their solutions will serve "the world's poor" (ibid.), it seems that the growth of the world's population to more than seven billion fallen humans is a factor in many of the ecological problems that Bahnson and Wirzba recount.

26. Thus Bill Arnold points out, "The cosmic phenomena described in [Gen.] 7:11–24 are not some banal punishment for the sin of that ancient generation, but they represent a reversal of creation, or 'uncreation' as it has been called. . . . Strikingly the sequence of annihilation, 'birds, domestic animals, wild animals, all swarming creatures that swarm on the earth, and all human beings' (7:21), follows closely that of creation itself in Genesis 1:1–2:3" (*Genesis*, 103).

27. Bahnson and Wirzba describe the flood in evocatively agrarian terms: "Human disobedience, arrogance and violence—to which the soil constantly bears witness—had so degraded and destroyed creation's order. What began as a garden of 'delight' (which is what *Eden* really means) quickly became a nightmare of drowning and death" (ibid.). They urge us to cultivate our own food as much as possible, by cultivating our own gardens (18).

28. In making this point, of course, I am aware that the flood stories, as redacted into a unity in Gen. 6–9, have other purposes than ecological ones, even if the stories can teach us something about God and ecology.

recede and Noah and his family together with all the animals return to the land, God gives to Noah and his family the *very same blessing* that God gave to Adam and Eve before the fall.[29] Rather than preserving the earth's ecosystems from the corruption that human sinners inevitably carry with them, "God blessed Noah and his sons, and said to them, 'Be fruitful and multiply, and fill the earth. The fear of you and the dread of you shall be upon every beast of the earth, and upon every bird of the air, upon everything that creeps on the ground and all the fish of the sea; into your hand they are delivered'" (Gen. 9:1–2).[30] This hardly sounds like a wise plan! Why deliver the ecosystem once more into the hands of humans? Why encourage humans, once again, to "fill the earth"?

Perhaps, at this stage of the story, we might imagine that Noah was righteous, and that paradise had been restored.[31] But such a reading would be

29. In this regard, H. Tristram Engelhardt Jr. is right to emphasize that "environmental ethics is set first within the condition of Adam after the Fall, when nature is no longer in harmony with man. . . . Even before the flood, man is to subdue the earth and to fill it with humans, such that man is implicitly blessed to change the environment through his presence. This commission is expanded after the flood" ("Ecology, Morality, and the Challenges of the Twenty-First Century," 280).

30. Rachel Muers observes that "the core biblical images of peaceable relationships between humanity and nonhuman creatures are eschatological as much as, or more than, protological" ("Creatures," 101). She notes that in the eschatological covenant renewal described in Hosea 2:18–23,

> God is represented as instituting a new covenant between humanity and nonhuman animals—particularly the animals that are *not* humanity's immediate "neighbours"—in order to restore both human security and the fertility of the land, in the context of a restored relationship between "the heavens" and "the earth" (2.21). In the context of Hosea, the cause of the disruption is human wrongdoing. . . . The promised covenant amounts, on one possible reading, to a *re*-creation that reaches back before the flood; hence it draws attention, in any particular context of reading, to present failures and problems of co-creaturely existence, and to the impossibility of a final peace. At the same time, it draws attention to the everyday lived needs of humanity and the other creatures for one another, and to the ongoing reshaping of creaturely life by their interactions (for example, in the reference to crops bred and grown for food, Hosea 2.22). (101–2)

Muers concludes that Hosea, and other such texts, underscore "the urgent need for interim and local forms of peace-making to enable creaturely life to continue" (102). See also the discussion of Hosea 2:18–23 in Davis, *Biblical Prophecy*, 84–89 (cf. 104–8); as well as Christopher J. H. Wright, *Old Testament Ethics for the People of God*, 184–86.

31. The idea that it might be possible to retrieve or renew a paradise on earth has parallels in contemporary ecological theology. Thus, in his *Political Theology of Climate Change*, Michael Northcott holds not simply that "for the early Christians, salvation was an ecological as well as a political and spiritual reality in which the earth and all its creatures, as well as human society, were being redeemed through the worship and the witness of the saints and under the kingly rule of Christ," but also that "the restoration of Paradise on earth was for more than a thousand years understood to be the work of the Christian Church" (199). I would note that the fathers of the Church understood the new creation (not a "restoration of Paradise") as the work of the Triune God, not of the Church, even though the Church certainly is the inaugurated kingdom

contrary to God's recognition, after Noah's disembarking from the ark and before God's words of blessing, that "the imagination of man's heart is evil from his youth" (Gen. 8:21). And in fact, after receiving God's covenant of blessing as symbolized by the rainbow, Noah started a farm, planted a vineyard, and got drunk. As Noah lay naked on the ground stone drunk, his son Ham "saw the nakedness of his father" (Gen. 9:22). After waking up, Noah retaliated by cursing Ham's son Canaan.

Hardly a chapter later, we find that the expansion of humans across the earth had begun—with predictably dire consequences. At this time the human population was still so small that "the whole earth had one language and few words" (Gen. 11:1). A group of migrating humans built a city and a tower whose purpose was to "make a name for [them]selves" (Gen. 11:4).[32] This was an act of pride, and the punishment that God delivered was to multiply human languages and to scatter the people "abroad over the face of all the earth" (Gen. 11:9). For the earth's ecosystem, it would seem, a worse solution could hardly be found. When humans had been small in numbers and contained in one city, their sinfully destructive capabilities could be contained; but when humans were spread "over the face of all the earth," they were liable

---

and the Triune God works through the Church to transform the world and to prepare for the gift of the new creation. Northcott suggests that medieval monks, in their desire to restore "Paradise on earth," were moved "to create gardens and herbariums and to develop crafts and workshop techniques and technologies which were labour saving while also increasing the fertility and productiveness of the earth" (ibid.). Northcott relies here upon a work whose scholarly value on this point seems to me to be minimal: Brock and Parker, *Saving Paradise.* Northcott advances a similar argument in his "Holy Spirit," 58–60; here Northcott cites Whitney, *Paradise Restored;* Ovitt, *Restoration of Perfection.* Indebted to Taubes, *Occidental Eschatology,* as well as to William Blake, Northcott reflects at length upon the eschatologies of Augustine and Joachim of Fiore, with the latter (along with Paul) as the revolutionary hero; see Northcott, *Political Theology of Climate Change,* 271–305. Northcott is sympathetic to distributivist "Transition" movements. For positions similar to Northcott's, see Stueckelberger, "Who Dies First? Who Is Sacrificed First?"; Zachariah, "Discerning the Times."

32. See also the concerns regarding "anthropocentrism" in Wirzba, *Paradise of God.* Wirzba connects "anthropocentrism" with the view that "we are the only species that really matters" and also with "the vast scope of our manipulation of the earth" (95). Rather than demonizing the human race, Wirzba states that "we are a species that, far from being an alien or cancerous presence, must learn to take up its proper place and role" (192). He is aware, too, that "traditional agrarian societies" can be criticized, just as our modern urban society can be (ibid.). From his agrarian perspective, he proposes the following solutions to the ecological crisis: become gardeners, support local economies, rethink energy use, unplug the media, design a generous household economy, and develop Sabbath rituals. He explains his viewpoint: "There are limits to what we can and should do, limits set by the integrity of the land. The way to show that we respect those limits is to make ourselves the students and servants of the land, for in being servants we relinquish our own will and desire for the sake of the creation's well-being. Anthropocentrism is replaced not by ecocentrism but by theocentrism, a vision that is focused on God's intention together with the sweep of God's creative work" (139).

to multiply, build new cities, and generally run amuck. And this is precisely what they do as the narrative continues.

Prior to blessing Noah and his family and fatefully commanding them once again to multiply and "fill the earth," God promised: "I will never again curse the ground because of man . . . neither will I ever again destroy every living creature as I have done" (Gen. 8:21). The destructive power of humans, however, remains fully present. During the time of Abraham, with whom God makes covenant so that by Abraham "all the families of the earth shall bless themselves" (Gen. 12:3), we find a new cause of devastation: war.[33] The rulers of the various cities make war on each other. We read, "In the days of Amraphel king of Shinar, Arioch king of Ellasar, Chedorlaomer king of Elam, and Tidal king of Goiim, these kings made war with Bera king of Sodom, Birsha king of Gomorrah, Shinab king of Admah, Shemeber king of Zeboiim, and the king of Bela (that is, Zoar)" (Gen. 14:1–2). As if this kind of destruction were not enough, the citizens of Sodom and Gomorrah turn out to be so sinful that God brings upon them utter destruction as the punishment for their sins. This does nothing good for the ecosystem, although as yet the destruction involves only a small portion of land. After the destruction of Sodom and Gomorrah, Abraham "looked down toward Sodom and Gomorrah and toward all the land of the valley, and beheld, and lo, smoke of the land went up like the smoke of a furnace" (Gen. 19:28).

According to Genesis, in the years before the wars and the destruction of Sodom and Gomorrah, Abraham became "very rich in cattle," and Lot "also had flocks and herds and tents, so that the land could not support both of them dwelling together" (Gen. 13:2, 5–6). Such proliferation of flocks and herds hardly benefits the ecosystem. Likewise, both before and after Sodom and Gomorrah, the human population continued to grow and to seek new land upon which to live. Indeed, the history of the people of Israel is a history of struggle for land upon which to survive, in competition with many other peoples who want to control the same land. In two ways, the Bible recounts the people's entrance into the land after their escape from generations of Egyptian slavery: first the entrance under Joshua, in which the people of Israel win decisive victories over the peoples of the land; then the stories of the book of Judges, which reveal a time of petty chieftains and constant warfare, culminating in a long territorial war with the Philistines. During the time of Saul and David, civil warfare is added to the struggles against the Philistines,

---

33. Matthew A. Shadle points out that although military leaders have always wreaked destruction upon the environment, modern warfare's technological advances mean that its "potential to harm the natural environment has increased exponentially" ("No Peace on Earth," 407).

and the briefly united twelve tribes divide again during the reign of David's grandson Rehoboam. The people of Israel in both the northern and southern kingdoms soon find themselves pinched between Egypt on the one side and various empires—Assyrian, Babylonian, Persian, Greek, and eventually Roman—on the other. If the endless territorial wars and frequent periods of famine are any indication, the land hardly suffices for its population.

Nonetheless, in the midst of the formative period of the people of Israel, we consistently find God blessing his favored ones by promising them many descendants and by encouraging them to have children. Thus God promises Abraham, "[I] will multiply you exceedingly" and "I will make you exceedingly fruitful; and I will make nations of you, and kings shall come forth from you" (Gen. 17:2, 6–7). Nor does God bless only his favored people in this way. God says of Ishmael, whom Abraham expelled from his home: "I will bless him and make him fruitful and multiply him exceedingly; he shall be the father of twelve princes" (Gen. 17:20). Again, in the very midst of the terrible strife caused by the rape of Jacob's daughter and the brutal attack upon the city of Shechem by Jacob's sons, God gives Jacob the new name Israel and proclaims: "I am God Almighty: be fruitful and multiply; a nation and a company of nations shall come from you, and kings shall spring from you" (Gen. 35:11). God intends not only for the Israelites to flourish and spread, but also for Abraham and Jacob (and Ishmael) to father many nations, many peoples. In fact, God tells Abraham, "I will multiply your descendants as the stars of heaven and as the sand which is on the seashore" (Gen. 22:17). Even granted that this statement is hyperbole, it remains the case that God has no worry whatsoever about overpopulation, notwithstanding the fact that the land of Canaan itself already seems overcrowded, with wars and brutal violence of all kinds.

Can this promotion of human multiplication really be a wise decision on God's part? Why does God repeatedly command humans, both before and after the fall, to "be fruitful and multiply, and fill the earth"? God is certainly aware that after the fall, ever-increasing human population inevitably leads (as it does in Genesis) to cities, wars, famines, and ecological disasters. God nonetheless presses forward with his command regarding human multiplication and with his promise that Abraham will have an enormous number of descendants—not only through Sarah but also through Hagar, to whom the "angel of the Lord" promises, "I will so greatly multiply your descendants that they cannot be numbered for multitude" (Gen. 16:10). In the Mosaic law, too, God forbids sexual intercourse during a woman's period and thereby focuses sexual intercourse upon the fertile time of the female cycle.

One could interpret these blessings, promises, and laws as simply the human authors' desire to aggrandize their own nation, or as simply the result of a mentality marked by the presence of a high mortality rate. But even if this reductive interpretation were partly true, it cannot explain (at least for those for whom the Torah is Scripture and mediates divine revelation) why the same God who knows full well what terrible troubles are caused by fallen humans, nonetheless encourages humans to spread around the entire earth. The God who promises Abraham, "I will make nations of you, and kings shall come forth from you" (Gen. 17:6), and who swears, "I will multiply your descendants as the stars of heaven and as the sand which is on the seashore" (Gen. 22:17)—despite the grave conflicts over water and land that are already emerging (cf. Gen. 21:25–34)—is no opponent of human urbanization. Aware of the troubles caused by powerful and populous cities and nations, God blesses and encourages rapid population growth and the formation of new nations.[34]

The question, then, is why God has so much interest in multiplying the population of fallen humans, even at the cost of other goods of creation. Surely a significant part of the answer, according to Genesis, is that God desires to make covenant with humans: humans are uniquely made for a relationship with God (cf. Gen. 9:12–17). Each human who comes into existence is an irreplaceable individual known to God, as can be seen not only in the line of the Abrahamic covenant, but also, for example, in the careful lists of Esau's sons Eliphaz, Reuel, Jeush, Jalam, and Korah and their children, and in the lists of Seir the Horite's sons Lotan, Shobal, Zibeon, Anah, Dishon, Ezer, and Dishan and their children (cf. Gen. 36). These are not God's chosen people, but they are named. Indeed, in Genesis childbearing consistently has in view "God Almighty who will bless [Joseph] with blessings of heaven above, blessings of the deep that couches beneath, blessings of the breasts and of the womb" (Gen. 49:25).

Bill McKibben's *Maybe One*

Bill McKibben is a leading contemporary environmentalist and an active Methodist Christian. In the acknowledgments of his 1989 book *The End of Nature*, he thanks "the men and women of the Johnsburg United Methodist Church and our pastor, Rev. Lucy B. Hathaway." Even more clearly, he dedicated his 1998 book *Maybe One* to his three godchildren and to "the many,

---

34. By contrast, for a Marxist reading of the first books of Scripture, arguing that the Yahwist author favors rural laborers (especially sheep and cattle herders) over city-state elites, see Coote and Ord, *Bible's First History*. For salutary appreciation of "human dominion over creation" as *service*, of our intrinsic "relatedness and interdependence," and of the need for showing "gratitude for the gift of life that we and the creation as a whole are," see Wirzba, *Paradise of God*, 137.

many children of the Johnsburg and Mill Creek United Methodist Church Sunday School."[35] In the latter book, he specifies that he regularly teaches Sunday school at Mill Creek United Methodist Church.

From his perspective as a Christian environmentalist, McKibben argues in *Maybe One* that couples should have no more than one child.[36] He makes clear that he does not intend to imply that couples who want to have more than one child are guilty of a sin, since he considers that children "are magnificent."[37] Nor is he proposing that government, as in China, should mandate a family-size limit.[38] Rather, he is simply trying to address what he considers to be

35. See McKibben, *End of Nature*, ix; McKibben, *Maybe One*.

36. Note also the recent work of the philosopher Sarah Conly, which echoes and elaborates upon McKibben's position: Conly, *One Child*. Not surprisingly, McKibben is joined by most environmental activists in his wish to sharply and quickly reduce human population. See, e.g., Kaufmann, *Shall the Religious Inherit the Earth?*, 263:

> The earth's growing population is combining with economic development to produce unsustainable levels of carbon emissions. In the present climate, a falling global population may be exactly what the doctor ordered—at least until we find the technological fix required to meet our energy needs while cooling the planet. . . . According to Andrew Watkinson of the Tyndall Centre for Climate Change Research, three-quarters of climate change is caused by population growth. This was recently recognised by the UN Population Fund in its 2009 report, *The State of World Population*. Coming just a month before the Copenhagen conference on climate change, the report broke fresh ground in challenging its decades-long reticence about broaching the population-environment link. . . . The UN report also hints that family planning could be the most effective green policy of all. UN projections suggest that world population will rise from 6.8 billion today to between 8 and 10.5 billion at mid-century. If fertility cuts reduce world population by a billion in 2050, this would achieve the same effect as the daunting task of constructing all new buildings to the highest energy-efficiency standards or replacing all coal-fired power plants with wind turbines.

For recent works of philosophy that raise wide-ranging doubts about the morality of bringing children into the world, see also Weinberg, *Risk of a Lifetime*; Hannan, Brennan, and Vernon, *Permissible Progeny?*

37. McKibben, *Maybe One*, 12. Raising the issue of sin, Elizabeth A. Johnson, CSJ, holds that "not all levels of human birth are morally correct" (*Ask the Beasts*, 245). By contrast, fifty years ago Vatican II's *Gaudium et spes* strongly approved of married couples "who after prudent reflection and common decision courageously undertake the proper upbringing of a large number of children" (§50, p. 954). It has become commonplace in many circles to view having a large family as unethical, as titles such as *One Child*, *Risk of a Lifetime*, and *Permissible Progeny?* make clear.

38. Other scholars advocate this option; see, e.g., Conly, *One Child*, 3, 103–40, and elsewhere, although Conly rejects "[literally] forced abortions and sterilizations," which she distinguishes (inaptly, in my view) from the same results when brought about by stringent legal and economic sanctions (132). In his characteristically colorful language, Dave Foreman remarks that "to say that women have the right to have as many children as they want is much the same as saying that men have the right to as many gas-guzzling, land-ripping SUVs as they want. Except it is worse. Either way, it says that it is okay for anyone to act on selfish whims that ransack wild things. As in so many things, we scramble rights with irresponsibility. Freedom becomes no better than a two-year-old's temper tantrum" ("Great Backtrack," 63).

humankind's biggest problem: our consumption habits and use of fossil fuels, especially in rich countries such as America, are literally causing the destruction of the planet. Once Americans realize this, Americans will be able to "develop new social norms" that address the problem, without needing to coerce people or make anyone feel guilty. McKibben grants that limiting families to one child would eventually "yield populations smaller than almost anyone would want."[39] But he strongly favors fewer people. If the United States can get its birthrate down to 1.5 and can simultaneously cut immigration, there could be only 230 million Americans in the year 2050, which would be millions less than we have now.[40] If the birthrate remains the same and immigration goes unchecked, there will be 400 million Americans by the year 2050, with a profoundly negative environmental effect. In McKibben's view, it is important to work to ensure that the hypothetical extra 170 million people are never conceived or born, in order that the good of the ecosystem not only of America but also of the world might be preserved and strengthened.

McKibben tells us that he and his wife thought for a long time that they might have no children, but they eventually decided to have one—after which they surgically ensured that they could not have another child. As he points out, the spread of birth control around the world may mean that the world's population will not go much beyond ten billion. But were birthrates not to continue to go down worldwide, the world's population would reach 296 billion by 2150, assuming hypothetically that so many humans could be fed. Indeed, if worldwide birthrates fell only to 2.5 children per woman, this would mean a world population of 28 billion by 2150. Of course, a significant factor here is life expectancy: in the United States, for example, if the mortality rate was the same as it was in 1900, the population would be half of what it presently is.

These numbers, McKibben observes, will get us off track if we fail to realize that the most pressing problem today is the human appetite for consumption—the amount of timber, pasture, precious metals, and oil that our lifestyle requires. If humans were willing and able to stay on small farms and used little or no electricity, oil, chemicals, or manufactured products, then population growth would be *less* of a problem than in fact it is. McKibben runs quickly through the list of population doomsayers: Thomas Malthus, William Vogt, Fairfield Osborn, William and Paul Paddock, Paul Ehrlich.[41] So far they have

39. McKibben, *Maybe One*, 13.

40. For an essay on immigration congenial to McKibben's position, see Cafaro and Staples, "Environmental Argument for Reducing Immigration into the United States."

41. In a book published in 1971, when he occupied a prominent position in left-wing politics (but was an opponent of Paul Ehrlich), Richard John Neuhaus offers a telling sketch of the 1970 Earth Day protest in New York City, in which a university scientist spoke of the earth having

all been wrong, but McKibben points out that there must be some population number that will prove to be unsustainable.[42] Against those who might wish to ignore the problem of population growth, McKibben cites evidence that the earth's environment is *already* buckling under the strain of providing for so many eaters and consumers.

McKibben argues that the earth is being crippled by the gases that our consumption habits pour daily into the atmosphere. During the industrial revolution, cities discovered that their air became unlivable if too much pollution was poured into it. But it now appears that the atmosphere itself, and not just the air of a few cities, is reaching an unlivable amount of pollution: nitrous oxide, carbon dioxide, methane. McKibben warns especially against human-caused climate change, which he argues will produce environmental catastrophes of various kinds, including a large rise in temperatures in the twenty-first century.[43] The only practicable solution is to try immediately to limit this damage by limiting our population growth.

only ten years left to (forcibly) reduce human population before mass starvation would become unavoidable. See Neuhaus, *In Defense of People*, 23. The stories that Neuhaus tells from the period remind us that the environmental activism of the 2010s was already fully present in the elite culture of 1971, though the scientific warnings then were based not on global warming but on resource scarcity. For further background to the period, see Veldman, *Fantasy, the Bomb, and the Greening of Britain*. For a vigorous defense of the fundamental accuracy of Ehrlich's warnings, see Weisman, *Countdown*, 399–406.

42. Alan Weisman suggests that the unsustainable population number is in fact seven billion (which we have now exceeded). He states that "there are other, simpler ways that nature will halt our unimpeded growth if we don't take the reins ourselves. The most basic is the world's oldest: cutting off our sustenance. The bottom line of the twenty-first century is that we will have less food—not more as we did, only briefly, during the Green Revolution. That is what an odds maker would bet on: We will not be able to grow, hunt, or harvest enough for the 7 billion we already are, let alone the 10.9 billion we're racing toward" (*Countdown*, 383; cf. 384–85; although on 424–27 he suggests that it might theoretically be possible to feed 8–10 billion people for a short time). Weisman credits global warming and the end of the "Green Revolution" for this approaching food scarcity. Just prior to this discussion, however, Weisman warns about fertility problems linked to "endocrine disruptors found not just in agro-chemistry, but in pharmaceuticals, household cleaners, detergents, plastics, and even cosmetics and sunscreens. . . . From animals to us, fertility is dropping not by choice, but by exposure to molecules that never existed before. The term we've invented to describe them, *gender-benders*, is precisely accurate, but unfortunately too snappy to be taken as seriously as it truly is. This is a tragedy—and it is also nature rejecting an unnatural act, making life inhospitable for the actors" (382). This would suggest that population is going to drop no matter what we might wish. In making the case for the urgent need to expand the use of contraception, Weisman suggests focusing on male contraception, and he also devotes an extensive section to promoting abortion, not least because the existence of billions of young males in poor countries is generating violence. From a similar population-control perspective, see also Bartlett, "Reflections on Sustainability and Population Growth."

43. For a recent summary of climate data and prediction of the grave consequences of global warming caused by man-made carbon emissions, see Northcott, *Political Theology of*

McKibben is aware that some population-control advocates blame the countries of the "Third World" and focus upon increasing the use of contraception in those countries. But McKibben focuses instead upon wealthy countries such as the United States because of their tremendously elevated carbon footprint. Each member of the richest tenth of Americans causes the emission of twenty-two times as much carbon dioxide as does each person in the poorer countries of the world. Some might suppose that this problem could be solved solely by Americans living more simply and with technology that is more energy efficient. But McKibben points out that reducing our number of children will likely be much easier than changing our consumption and energy-usage patterns in the radical ways that will also soon be necessary.[44] As he states, "If we can cut the birthrate, that's 50 or 100 million fewer cars and furnaces; 50 or 100 million fewer dinners to serve and thermostats to set each day; 50 or 100 million fewer giant balloons [of energy-use pollution] hovering above the landscape."[45] Speaking practically, McKibben points out that humans are not going to easily give up the cars, air travel, computers, technology, spacious houses, health care, television, heating, air-conditioning, and so forth that characterize the economically developed countries of the world. Given the imminence of the ecological threat, therefore, it is fortunate

---

Climate Change. Citing Betts, Collins, Hemming, et al., "When Could Global Warming Reach 4° C?," Northcott observes that the "current best scientific guess for the timing of a four degree temperature rise is 2070. The world has not been that warm for three million years, and never in the time of *Homo sapiens.* According to climate scientist Kevin Anderson, a four degree warmer world is 'incompatible with organised global community, is likely to be beyond "adaptation," is devastating to the majority of ecosystems, and has a high probability of not being stable (i.e., 4° C would be an interim temperature on the way to a much higher equilibrium level)'" (*Political Theology of Climate Change,* 164; the interior quotation is from Anderson, "Going beyond Dangerous Climate Change"). Civil debate about climate data is now nearly impossible, as was already apparent in the response to Lomborg, *Skeptical Environmentalist;* cf. Lomborg's *Cool It;* Scruton, *Green Philosophy.* Warning against "climate denialists," Northcott points out that "predictions of climate catastrophe . . . represent a *politics* because climate science indicates that, absent a *leveling* of unequal uses of fossil fuels between rich and poor and between developed and developing countries, the earth itself will enforce a leveling on the presently disequalising tendencies of fossil-fuelled industrial capitalism through climate catastrophe. Unmitigated climate change by the end of the century will flood the rich cities of the powerful and disrupt their global resource extraction and wealth accumulation systems, as well as turning the lands of the poor into deserts" (*Political Theology of Climate Change,* 16–17). I do not share Northcott's (or McKibben's) certitude about the extent of man-made global warming or about its sole possible solutions.

44. McKibben adds that this is so especially given the fact that consumption and energy use are on the rise in China, India, and other developing countries. Similarly, Weisman observes that since no one really has "a solution for overconsumption," the main plan for addressing the ecological crisis must in fact be "lowering the number of consumers" (*Countdown,* 418).

45. McKibben, *Maybe One,* 125.

that the evidence shows that people generally are glad to accept contraception and sterilization. He argues that since this crisis will reach its peak during the next fifty years, now is the time to have one or fewer children, if we care about the environment.

Describing his own vasectomy, McKibben admits that "it felt sad" and even "a little *shameful*," feelings that he attributes to his biologically built-in urge to reproduce.[46] In this context, he addresses God's injunctions in Genesis to "be fruitful and multiply, and fill the earth." He rejects as "canards" the commonplace attacks upon the Pope (or upon Hasidic Jews and Mormons), and he seeks to take seriously the religious critique of contraception.[47] He first explores Jewish understandings of the passages in Genesis. Indebted to the work of David Feldman, he notes that the most relevant religious duty in this regard is not procreation but marriage, which "is good in its own right"; since sexual intercourse aids marriage, it too "is considered a great good."[48] According to Jewish teaching, each married couple can obey the command-ment to be fruitful and multiply simply by having a boy and a girl, "but the Talmud urges that parents keep going, if only to make sure that their children are not sterile, or don't die before reproducing *themselves*."[49] The Jewish teaching seems straightforward enough: it involves the survival of the people of Israel. McKibben comments, "It celebrates sex but not self-indulgence, and it has helped assure growth from a tiny band and survival against odds more daunting than any other race has ever faced."[50]

Christianity, however, does not require the survival of a particular nation, and Jesus makes "scant comment on birth control or marriage or reproduction."[51] In his discussion of Christianity, McKibben is particularly indebted to John Noonan. According to Noonan, early Christians rejected what they considered to be the hedonism of Roman culture, and they adopted certain ascetic ideas current at the time. Given his expectation of the imminent end of the world, Paul favored celibacy and said little about procreation. The early Church fathers likewise favored celibacy and did not encourage procreation, and Tertullian even praised natural disasters for reducing population in overcrowded nations. Yet from the third century onward, the Church has condemned contraception. Why so, given that the Church has encouraged celibacy and has not made a big deal out of the command to "be fruitful and multiply"?

46. Ibid., 184.
47. Ibid., 185.
48. Ibid., 186.
49. Ibid., 186–87.
50. Ibid., 187.
51. Ibid.

McKibben argues that the historical reason for the Church's teaching against contraception is to be found not in God's commands in the book of Genesis, but in the Church's controversies against metaphysically dualistic splinter groups. On this view, Augustine's fight against the Manichaeans, who believed matter was evil and practiced birth control, was especially significant. Reacting against the extreme position of the Manichaeans, Augustine arrived at the other extreme. He forbade all contraception and held that sexual intercourse is only good when its purpose is procreation. Augustine's position won the day, although during the Renaissance the Church began to allow for the value of pleasure and companionship (and not just procreation) with regard to marriage and sex.[52] During the French Revolution, McKibben observes, a 20-percent reduction in the birthrate indicated changing social mores, and the late nineteenth century introduced widespread birth control movements, culminating in the Anglican Church's decision in 1930 to allow contraception. Even the Catholic Church now allows for the rhythm method, and most Catholics in the West ignore the Church's formal teaching against contraception.

McKibben grants that the Church's teaching, while rooted in an Augustinian extreme, nonetheless identifies a real danger: selfishness. Not having children can be an excuse for American couples to give way even more fully to consumerism and self-indulgence. Positively citing contemporary theologians such as Gilbert Meilaender and John Berkman, McKibben praises the New Deal–era Catholic priest and moral theologian John Ryan for arguing in favor of large families on the grounds that living a self-sacrificial life is good for the parents, as well as for the children. McKibben agrees that in order to lead Christian lives, we need to be trained in self-sacrifice. He accepts that parenting often instills self-sacrificial habits in people, and he also accepts that parenting large families can do this particularly well. But as he points out, "The problem, of course, is that now we live in an era—maybe only a brief one, maybe only for a few generations—when parenting a bunch of kids clashes with the good of the planet."[53] How then to become people who focus on others, who are willing to sacrifice rather than indulge? McKibben suggests that the statements of Pope John Paul II in preparation for the 1994 Cairo Conference on population rightly emphasize both the need to avoid selfishness and the need to make informed, responsible decisions

52. For a better view of medieval understandings of marriage, against such caricatures, see Parmisano, *Craft of Love*. See also Cahall, *Mystery of Marriage*, in which Cahall presents a balanced view of the history of Catholic teaching on marriage and shows how the doctrine of marriage has developed.

53. McKibben, *Maybe One*, 196.

about procreation. But in McKibben's view, given the current environmental situation and the fact that world population is going to balloon to ten billion (even if birthrates continue to go down), responsible decisions about procreation now mean having no more than one child.[54] Indeed, it would be selfish and irresponsible to sacrifice the earth's ecosystem by insisting on having many children. As it stands, we have already reached the point where "huge swaths of God's creation are being wiped out by the one species told to tend this particular garden."[55] Part of an unselfish, sacrificial life today involves using contraception so as to keep our number of children low.

Has McKibben thereby rejected or devalued God's command to be fruitful and multiply? On the contrary, he argues that humans have already succeeded in amply fulfilling this commandment of God. The entire earth has been marked and refashioned by human presence. On the negative side, we have corrupted the environment; but on the positive side, we have "spread wondrous

54. Weisman points out, in a hopeful moment, that if "the entire world adopted a one-child policy tomorrow," then "by the end of this century, we would be back to 1.6 billion, our population in 1900. . . . That would reduce our numbers by three-quarters, freeing billions of acres for other species, on whose existence a functioning ecosystem—including our place in it—depends" (*Countdown*, 415). He points out that women in developed countries freely and radically limit their fertility, without need for a government edict. In this context, he raises a line of thought quite similar to McKibben's, but with more governmental involvement:

"There is not a single problem on Earth that wouldn't be easier if there were fewer people," said a woman in Salt Lake City, and surprisingly, no one objected. That made me wonder: Was there something in the histories or holy books of the rest of the world's cultures and religions that might embrace the idea of, so to speak, refraining from embracing as much during the next two or three generations, limiting our progeny to bring us back into balance with the rest of nature—at which point, having reached an optimum number, we could resume averaging two children per family? . . . Might we benefit *right now* if everyone agreed to bring population down in the twenty-first century, much as the world's nations came together during the last century to sign a protocol to save our flickering ozone layer? (417)

55. McKibben, *Maybe One*, 197–98. On this point, from a population-control perspective, see the following essays in Cafaro and Crist, *Life on the Brink*: Kolankiewicz, "Overpopulation versus Biodiversity"; McKee, "Human Population Footprint on Global Biodiversity"; Staples and Cafaro, "For a Species Right to Exist." From this perspective, see also Foreman, *Man Swarm and the Killing of Wildlife*; E. O. Wilson, *Future of Life*; McKibben, *Deep Economy*. Citing McKibben's *Deep Economy*, Staples and Cafaro point out that "ever more people and ever more human economic activity are impossible to square with sustaining the resources and ecosystem services necessary for *people* to lead comfortable and enjoyable lives in the future. That is the clear, if largely unacknowledged, lesson of climate change and other examples of planetwide environmental degradation" ("For a Species Right to Exist," 297). Staples and Cafaro look forward to a much less populated world (they estimate 2–3 billion) "where people are less likely to suffer hunger, sickness, resource wars, and other ills stemming from the overuse and collapse of ecosystems. It would be a world where the human right to experience and celebrate wild nature is more widely ensured" (ibid.).

and diverse cultures, full of love and song."[56] Now that we have fulfilled this first commandment of God, says McKibben, we should focus our attention on fulfilling the other commandments, rather than on having large families. We can lead self-sacrificial lives by helping to ensure that people around the globe have food, clothing, and comfort. We can also lead self-sacrificial lives by ensuring that the earth remains environmentally able to sustain life. This means ensuring clean water and the survival of species, and it also means strengthening parenthood and freeing societies from violence. The energy that we would have spent raising large families, we can now spend on these crucial communal, environmental, and societal goals—goals that answer to God's other commandments. He concludes that the call to have only one child, and to use birth control to avoid large families, accords with the Pope's focus on self-sacrifice in a way that fits with "the signs of the times" regarding the need to care for the environment.[57]

Even so, what about people who rule out birth control (and abortion) as a further instance of the modern technological desire to control nature? McKibben cites the example of a group of "conservative" or radical Quakers who, like the Amish, have large families. In response to this subset of the environmentalist movement, he argues that precisely in order to preserve God's earth, we now need to plan, since "there are so many of us, and we have done

56. McKibben, *Maybe One*, 198. Weisman evocatively underscores the negative side of population growth, namely, the paving of many green spaces: "No matter where people are from, or whatever age or politics or faith, everyone remembers a place where they used to go to escape the clamor and congestion of their lives. A place not too far away, where they could hike, or picnic, or ride a dirt bike. Where they could watch birds—or if they like to hunt, kill birds. Where they could hug trees, or cut them for firewood, or just fall asleep beneath one. But now, that favorite place is gone, vanished beneath strip malls or industrial parks or condominia. Everyone remembers a world that was better. Less crowded. Lovelier. Where they felt freer" (*Countdown*, 420).

57. Weisman, too, reaches out in a certain way to Christian leaders. As he describes, he once met

with Reverend Richard Cizik, a former Washington Lobbyist for the National Association of Evangelicals. In 2008 he left them and founded the New Evangelical Partnership for the Common Good, a Christian organization with an environmental mission he calls "Creation Care." For the past three years, he told me, "I've been laying theological groundwork for interpreting how the mandate to be fruitful and multiply applies to today, in light of the current crisis of the planet." A thin, intense man with straight, receding blond hair, he'd just come out publicly in support of family-planning funding a few weeks earlier in a piece for the *Washington Post*'s faith blog. "Family planning is not only moral: it's what we should be doing. Be fruitful and multiply was superseded by a post-flood mandate to live peacefully with all of God's creatures." He was undaunted by the pushback from conservative evangelicals, he said, and encouraged by the response of a new generation of concerned young Christians. "*Thy will be done on Earth as it is in heaven*, Jesus says in the Lord's Prayer. If that's the case, then we should bring the values of heaven to Earth. In heaven things don't go extinct. Sustainability means you don't make things go extinct. Yet that's what we're doing, to entire species." (*Countdown*, 428)

such a poor job of planning for our numbers."[58] On this view, if today we refuse any technological intrusion in our reproductive lives, we will simply be facilitating the ongoing destruction of the earth by other uncontrolled human technologies.

Reading Genesis and McKibben: God's Blessings and Human Procreation

Thus far, I have advanced two contrasting views. First, I noted that the God of Israel, in commanding humans—even fallen humans—to "be fruitful and multiply, and fill the earth," does not include the prudential limitations that we might expect. God seems to be well aware of the damaging results (including ecologically damaging results) of increasing the population of fallen humans, and yet God continues to promote such increase. Furthermore, God does not qualify the commandment prudentially, by suggesting that once the world (or the land of Israel) is full, the commandment can be set aside. Second, I surveyed Bill McKibben's proposal that Americans should have no more than one child. For McKibben, promoting the widespread use of contraception and sterilization is now necessary, not only because of his view of the current ecological crisis, but also because otherwise world human population would quickly jump beyond ten billion.[59] Such a vast human population, if it did not result in mass starvation and devastating conflict over scarce resources, would certainly result in the extinction of numerous plant and animal species and would turn much of the earth into pavement and apartment buildings.[60]

---

58. McKibben, *Maybe One*, 203.

59. Ronald E. Osborn warns against an approaching "ecological holocaust in which manic human greed and unchecked exploitation of the earth threaten to destroy entire species and render God's creation a wasteland" (*Death before the Fall*, 172). It should be clear that I do not blame "manic human greed" for the problem; like McKibben, I think that the problem is also, and even primarily, caused by the existence of a huge number of humans on the planet, all trying to figure out ways to obtain food and to improve their material welfare and opportunities for cultivated leisure. Here I depart from the insistence of (for instance) Metropolitan Kallistos Ware, who urges that "the crisis is not first and foremost an ecological crisis. The fundamental difficulty lies not outside but inside ourselves, not in the ecosystem but in the human heart" ("Through Creation to the Creator," 102). Granted that we are sinners, and therefore that we need conversion in every way (including ecologically), it still seems to me that we treat our planet in the way that we do at least partly in order to allow for many billions of humans to live and to have a lifestyle that is not that of a mere drudge.

60. See also the alarm expressed by Eric Kaufmann about the fact that religious couples have more children than secular couples in his *Shall the Religious Inherit the Earth?*, though he distinguishes between liberal churches and more conservative or fundamentalist ones. Kaufmann remarks rather disturbingly: "Liberals are aware that tolerating illiberal groups is risky. . . . The problem arises when illiberal groups such as religious fundamentalists demographically increase to the point where they are able to threaten the freedom of others" (262). With fundamentalist

The purpose of this third section is to provide a broader context for evaluating the messages of Genesis and McKibben. In this regard, it is noteworthy that in Genesis 1:1–2:4, God explicitly blesses creatures three times. The first blessing has to do with the fish and the birds: "And God blessed them, saying, 'Be fruitful and multiply and fill the waters in the seas, and let birds multiply on the earth'" (Gen. 1:22). The second blessing has to do with humans: "And God blessed them, and God said to them, 'Be fruitful and multiply, and fill the earth and subdue it; and have dominion over the fish of the sea and over the birds of the air and over every living thing that moves upon the earth'" (Gen. 1:28).[61] Finally and most importantly, the third blessing involves the completion of all things: "So God blessed the seventh day and hallowed it, because on it God rested from all his work which he had done in creation" (Gen. 2:3).

Is there a relationship of these three blessings to each other? John Walton and others have suggested that "we should think of Genesis 1 in relation to a cosmic temple."[62] In Genesis 1:1–2:4, Walton observes, we find "a seven-day inauguration of the cosmic temple, setting up its functions for the benefit of humanity, with God dwelling in relationship with his creatures."[63] If this is so, then the three blessings do not solely express God's approval of procreation, but also express the goal of human existence, namely, to share in God's

---

Muslims and Christians in view, he goes on to state, "what [Alex] Renton and the UNFPA report deliberately fail to mention are the taboos of immigration and religious fertility. Without (largely religious) immigration and the impact of religious fertility, the American population would be closer to 300 million in 2050 instead of its projected 400–500 million. Western Europe's population would be falling instead of soaring. . . . Seculars and moderates can encourage the fastest-growing fundamentalists to integrate, pointing out that high fertility is a political act which, for the sake of harmony, should be moderated. All the same, we must be prepared for the possibility that religious demography cannot be killed with kindness" (264). The implication is that political coercion will be necessary, although Kaufmann—who describes himself as a libertarian who hopes for a world freed from religious superstition and who rejects such things as "free will and the Self" (267)—avoids drawing this conclusion.

61. Bill Arnold comments:

God's blessing of all living creatures [Gen. 1:22] here anticipates his blessing of humankind in v. 28, and with similar effect. In both cases the divine blessing is articulated as a command to "be fruitful and multiply," and fill those reaches of the universe intended for them. Indeed, the blessing to procreate distinguishes "living creatures," animals and humans alike, from sun, moon, stars and other parts of the universe. The capacity to reproduce is the fundamental definition of what it means to be a "living creature." The command "be fruitful and multiply" is a verbal play (*pĕrû ûrĕbû*), which may be intended to bring to mind the nominal hendiadys "formless void" of v. 2 (*tōhû wābōhû*). In this case, the living creatures of God's creation are hereby empowered to perpetuate God's life-giving creativity by bringing still more life into the world, by filling up and inhabiting that which was previously empty and uninhabitable. (*Genesis*, 43)

62. Walton, *Lost World of Genesis One*, 87.

63. Ibid., 163. See also Arnold, *Genesis*, 50–51; Bernhard W. Anderson, *Creation versus Chaos*.

Sabbath. The second blessing (of humans) is intimately related not only to the first blessing (of living creatures), but also most fundamentally to the third (of the Sabbath). Human life is at its fullness in giving temple praise to God, thereby lifting up all creation into worship of the creator. R. R. Reno rightly remarks, "The created order is organized so as to prepare for the ascending logic of fellowship with God."[64] Similarly, Abraham Joshua Heschel comments, "The Sabbath is not for the sake of the weekdays; the weekdays are for the sake of the Sabbath. It is not an interlude but the climax of living."[65]

If sharing in God's Sabbath is the purpose of human existence, what does this purpose mean for being fruitful and multiplying? Most importantly, the people that come to be in the process of human multiplication have an everlasting vocation. Thus, Paul remarks that we were created so as not only to be the "image of God" (Gen. 1:27) but also "to be conformed to the image of his Son, in order that he might be the first-born among many brethren" (Rom. 8:29). The resurrection of Jesus shows that people are called to fellowship with God not only here and now, but also for eternity. As Paul states, "Though our outer nature is wasting away, our inner nature is being renewed every day. For this slight momentary affliction is preparing for us an eternal weight of glory beyond all comparison, because we look not to the things that are seen but to the things that are unseen" (2 Cor. 4:16–18).

Do such appeals to life beyond the grave involve, for Paul, indifference about the earth's ecosystem? On the contrary, Paul appreciates the unity of all creation. He observes in Romans 8:21 that "the creation itself will be set free from its bondage to decay and obtain the glorious liberty of the children of God," and he is quite sure that we and the whole creation are united in our purposeful striving toward God. At the same time, however, the whole creation strives toward an interpersonal communion, a "royal priesthood, a holy nation, God's own people" (1 Pet. 2:9).[66] This is the purpose of creation, in the plan that God made "before the foundation of the world," "a plan for

64. Reno, *Genesis*, 56.
65. Heschel, *Sabbath*, 14.
66. The whole creation groans toward this interpersonal consummation, even if, as Scripture indicates, some rational creatures, angels and humans, permanently resist God's love and thus never come to belong to "God's own people." For Aquinas, as Oliva Blanchette says, "the universe is ultimately a community of intellectual beings, each intelligent and free, all capable of the highest good, moving toward completion through an activity in which this community expresses and perfects itself. Material things are ordered by nature to serve these intellectual creatures, to be used by them as they tend toward their own perfection, which is identically the perfection of the universe. This is the end or the perfection of material things themselves. They are more perfect when they serve in this way than when they are in any other state, even if it were to be according to their purely natural state" (*Perfection of the Universe according to Aquinas*, 300).

the fulness of time, to unite all things in him [Jesus Christ]" (Eph. 1:4, 10).[67] It is this purpose—the blessing of eternal sharing in the life of the Trinity (the Sabbath blessing)—that makes human life so extraordinarily meaningful and valuable.

Does this mean, then, that humans must have all the children that we can physically have, so as to give as many people as possible the opportunity of eternal life with God?[68] The commandment that Jesus gives us is not to have all the children that we can possibly have, but rather is: "Love one another as I have loved you" (John 15:12). Not all will be called to married life. The bearing of children is neither the "pearl of great price" (Matt. 13:46) nor the "new commandment" (John 13:34). Jesus tells a parable about a wedding banquet—an image of the eschatological consummation—and, among those invited to the banquet, one refuses to come on the grounds that he has "married a wife, and therefore . . . cannot come" (Luke 14:20). This excuse is not accepted as a good one by the Lord of the banquet. Furthermore, Jesus approves of renouncing marriage for the sake of bearing witness to the kingdom that he has inaugurated: "There are eunuchs who have made themselves eunuchs for the sake of the kingdom of heaven" (Matt. 19:12). Paul, too, argues that the ability to focus upon the Lord is hampered by marriage and children, good though the latter are. Paul states that "he who marries his betrothed does well; and he who refrains from marriage will do better" (1 Cor. 7:38).

Nonetheless, far from rejecting marriage or children, Jesus affirms both quite strongly. With regard to marriage, he explains to the Pharisees who seek to test him by questioning him on the lawfulness of divorce for any cause: "Have you not read that he who made them from the beginning made them male and female, and said, 'For this reason a man shall leave his father and

---

67. For reflection on this theme in relation to ecology, see Neuhaus, "Christ and Creation's Longing," 128–37. Neuhaus remarks,

> The creation has, in Christ, been incorporated into the very Godhead. . . . Citing, and affirming, the wisdom of the Athenians, St. Paul declares, "In him we live and move and have our being" (Acts 17:28). And what is true of us human beings is true of all that is, the macrocosmic and microcosmic, the galaxies beyond numbering and the subatomic particles beyond discernment. In creation and redemption, God's covenantal faithfulness holds all that is, was, and ever will be to himself. In the dynamic of creation, even the millions of species that have disappeared are not finally lost. This, I believe, is the sensibility that is consonant with Jesus' words about every hair being counted and every fallen sparrow taken into Divine account. It is in this context, a context decisively shaped by God's redemptive purposes in Christ, that we can join with St. Francis of Assisi in hymns of familial and filial piety toward nature. (135)

68. This view is held by the groups that Kathryn Joyce chronicles in her *Quiverfull*. See Hess and Hess, *Full Quiver*; Provan, *Bible and Birth Control*. For more recent works in this direction, see Houghton, *Family UNplanning*; Nancy Campbell, *Be Fruitful and Multiply*.

mother and be joined to his wife, and the two shall become one'? So they are no longer two but one" (Matt. 19:4–5). In the same context, Jesus underlines the importance of children. The disciples have sought to keep people from bringing their children to Jesus for his blessing. Jesus rebukes his disciples and commands, "Let the children come to me, and do not hinder them; for to such belongs the kingdom of heaven" (Matt. 19:14). Elsewhere Jesus tells his disciples that they must become like children in order to enter the kingdom of heaven. Calling a child to himself, he instructs his disciples, "Whoever receives one such child in my name receives me" (Matt. 18:5). When we welcome "children" (whether literal children, or disciples of Christ) in Christ's name, we welcome unique humans whom Christ has called to become adopted sons and daughters of God in the eternal kingdom.

How then should Christians balance these two aspects, Jesus's affirmation of the choice not to marry and have children on the one hand, and Jesus's affirmation of the importance of welcoming children on the other? Should we envision, as McKibben does, a world in which some become eunuchs for the kingdom of heaven, and others (married couples) become somewhat like eunuchs—via contraception, sterilization, and perhaps even direct abortion (McKibben leaves this point ambiguous)—for the planet's long-term sustainability? Here we can note that Jesus, in his discussion of "eunuchs" in Matthew 19:12, does not envision a situation in which married couples become somewhat like eunuchs. Arguably, the nature of marriage itself excludes, morally speaking, the possibility of deliberately sterilizing the act of marital intercourse.[69] It is not possible here for me to give a full account of the reasons why contraception distorts the meaning of sexual intercourse, but the fundamental point is that contraception turns the marital embrace inward upon lesser goods rather than allowing it to be what God created it to be, namely, the embodied enactment of the couple's spiritual gift of self in

69. For reflection on relevant scriptural texts, see Pope John Paul II, *Man and Woman He Created Them*. Although Jesus does not explicitly condemn contraception or abortion in urging the welcoming of children, both contraception and abortion were of course known in his world. Thus, in his pro-contraception study *Contraception*, John T. Noonan states: "The existence of contraceptive methods in the world from which the Christians came is established: by the Old Testament, by the Talmud, by Aristotle, by Pliny, by the physicians, and by imperial law. Coitus interruptus, potions, pessaries, spermicides, genital salves, postcoital exercises, the sterile period—a very wide range of possible techniques was known" (28–29). For his part, Weisman rejoices in the power of soap operas to popularize contraception in our time. As he notes, the 1970s Mexican soap opera "*Acompáñame* is widely credited for the 34 percent drop in Mexico's fertility rate during the decade the series aired. [Miguel] Sabido's method inspired the work of the Population Media Center in Burlington, Vermont, which today produces soap operas that promote family planning in twenty-two languages: electronic analogs of the family-planning street theater I witnessed in Pakistan" (*Countdown*, 432).

a manner that opens the couple to welcoming a new human life, rather than focusing their love solely on each other.[70] McKibben recognizes the connection of contraception with the danger of selfishness, but he underestimates the way in which the bodily constitution of marital intercourse matters spiritually.

Yet, in McKibben's view, as we saw, the loss of contraception—when combined with the better health care that has resulted in such gains in life expectancy—would produce a catastrophic ecological event as population quickly moved over ten billion. Even if the Church cannot promote contraception, should the Church urge believers in Christ not to "be fruitful and multiply," at least for a generation or two, so as to keep the earth going longer and to respect the place of other species? Given that Christians surely "have an obligation to take future generations into account" by caring for the earth, should the Church at least promote increased use of natural family planning (to avoid conception) and a new emphasis upon adopting unwanted children rather than begetting new children?[71]

In this regard, Thomas Aquinas offers some helpful principles. He remarks that God's command, "Be fruitful and multiply, and fill the earth," should be obeyed not blindly but with attention to "the good of the species."[72] Thus he finds that "the precept of procreation regards the whole multitude of men, which needs not only to multiply in body, but also to advance spiritually."[73] He does not hold that Christians should have as many children as possible in order to build up the kingdom of God. Instead he considers that "sufficient provision is made for the human multitude, if some betake themselves to carnal procreation, while others abstaining from this betake themselves to the contemplation of divine things, for the beauty and welfare of the whole human race."[74] He thinks of this as a division of labor for the common good, as in an army some are sentries and others fight. As important as bearing and raising children is, "virginity that is consecrated to God is preferable."[75] Although he certainly does not foresee the ecological crisis that McKibben argues is now taking hold, Aquinas's emphasis on the common good seems to tell in the direction of less marriage and many fewer children among Christians today.

Yet Aquinas also thinks of God's perfect goodness as self-diffusive, and the purpose of human life is to imitate God's goodness in Christ Jesus. Aquinas

---

70. For a fuller account, see Pruss, *One Body*; Kupczak, *Gift and Communion*. See also the Pontifical Council for Justice and Peace's *Compendium of the Social Doctrine of the Church*, §§217–21, 230–34, 237.

71. The quotation is from Derr, "Environmental Ethics and Christian Humanism," 88.

72. *Summa theologiae* (hereafter *ST*), II-II, q. 152, a. 2, obj. 1.

73. *ST* II-II, q. 152, a. 2, ad 1.

74. Ibid.

75. *ST* II-II, q. 152, a. 4, ad 3.

states that "what belongs to the essence of goodness befits God. But it be-longs to the essence of goodness to communicate itself to others."[76] God communicates himself to us supremely by becoming incarnate as one of us, in the womb of Mary. We, too, seek to share our goodness, the goodness of human life. Thus we have a natural inclination toward the procreation and raising of children, and, far from bemoaning human multiplication per se, we should love all humans as created to be members of Christ's mystical body. The Holy Spirit "communicates the goods of one member to another," and so we all benefit from each expansion of the circle of interpersonal com-munion.[77] Aquinas comments that "what we ought to love in our neighbor is that he may be in God," since this is the greatest good, and the good for which humans are made.[78]

Does Aquinas pay any attention to nonhuman creatures? Aquinas recog-nizes that "the multitude and distinction of things is from God" and is good.[79] As Aquinas puts it, "The divine wisdom is the cause of the distinction of things for the sake of the perfection of the universe," since "the universe would not be perfect if only one grade of goodness were found in things."[80] He remarks further that God "brought things into being in order that his goodness might be communicated to creatures, and be represented by them; and because his goodness could not be adequately represented by one creature alone, he pro-duced many and diverse creatures."[81] In chapter 3, we observed that Aquinas finds a "trace" of the Trinity in all creatures, and an "image" of the Trinity in rational creatures. The final perfection of all things, therefore, will be a glorious reflection of the divine goodness.[82] Yet in this final perfection, the

76. *ST* III, q. 1, a. 1.
77. *ST* III, q. 68, a. 9, ad 2.
78. *ST* II-II, q. 25, a. 1. For discussion, see Levering, *Betrayal of Charity*.
79. *ST* I, q. 47, a. 1.
80. *ST* I, q. 47, a. 2.
81. *ST* I, q. 47, a. 1. In her *Ask the Beasts*, Elizabeth A. Johnson comments that "if the diversity of creatures is meant to show forth the goodness of God which cannot be well represented by one creature alone, as Aquinas saw, then extinction of species is rapidly erasing testimony to divine goodness in the world now and for the foreseeable future" (255). Given that almost all species that have ever existed have long been extinct, and also given the vast numbers of species that exist today, I think that ample testimony to the divine goodness remains present. Yet it is evident that the extinction of a species, let alone many species, is not something that humans would wish to bring about. Edward O. Wilson predicts, "If global changes caused by HIPPO (Habitat destruction, Invasive species, Pollution, Overpopulation, and Overharvesting, in that order of importance) are not abated, half the species of plants and animals could be extinct or at least among the 'living dead'—about to become extinct—by the end of the century" (*Social Conquest of Earth*, 294).
82. See *ST* I, q. 44, a. 4. For an excellent discussion of Aquinas's view, see Blanchette, *Perfection of the Universe according to Aquinas*. See also chap. 7 of Levering, *Jesus and the Demise of Death*.

"kingdom of God" or the "new creation," humans will have a special place, although not the sole place. Aquinas states that "of all creatures the rational creature is chiefly ordained for the good of the universe," since the blessed attain to the highest possible participation in God's happiness.[83] The universe is created for the saints, not in the sense that the universe is a discardable shell, but in the sense that the new creation, the goal for which God makes all things, will have as its pinnacle the unfathomable intimacy of glorified humans and angels with God in Christ and the Holy Spirit.

Simply as created, humans participate in the ontological goodness of God: it is good to be. Wondrously, God also calls humans to share in his own happiness, to be God's friends and to know him as he knows us. This extraordinary union with God is the friendship to which we and any children that we have are called by God's grace (although humans can reject this grace). Already, simply as created, "parents love their children as being part of themselves."[84] In charity, however, we also love our children in light of God's supreme self-diffusion in the incarnation, as "heirs of God and fellow heirs with Christ" (Rom. 8:17). The begetting and raising of children involves the self-diffusion of goodness in a way that participates deeply in the divine gifting. For Christians, then, the begetting and raising of children displays not only a natural desire to share the good of human life, but also the charitable desire for extending and expanding the fellowship of humans and God in the mystical body of Christ. Since the Church is ignorant of the time of the second coming and the final judgment,[85] we cannot put off doing good today solely because the presence of fewer people might hypothetically allow the earth to sustain life for more generations than otherwise would have been the case.[86]

83. *ST* I, q. 23, a. 7.
84. *ST* II-II, q. 26, a. 9.
85. See *ST* III, q. 10, a. 2, ad 1.
86. By contrast, from a perspective that does not see each additional human life as an inherent good (due to overpopulation), see Edward O. Wilson, *Consilience*, 288:

> Population growth can justly be called the monster on the land. To the extent that it can be tamed, passage through the bottleneck [i.e., the current ecological crisis] will be easier. Let us suppose that the last of the old reproductive taboos fade, and family planning becomes universal. Suppose further that governments create population policies with the same earnestness they devote to economic and military policies. And that as a result the global population peaks below ten billion and starts to decline. With NPG (negative population growth) attained, there are grounds for hope. If not attained, humanity's best efforts will fail, and the bottleneck will close to form a solid wall.

Wilson recognizes that human scientific ingenuity can and will continue to devise surprisingly helpful fixes for the ecological and agricultural problems facing an overpopulated world, but he warns that "each advance is also a prosthesis, an artificial device dependent on advanced expertise and intense continuing management. Substituted for part of the Earth's natural environment, it adds its own, long-term risk"—and these risks multiply over time as more

The charitable married couple, then, will be loath not to share the gift of existence. Yet, for the sake of other important goods (including the common good of the ecosystems of the earth), a charitable married couple may prudently abstain from procreation.[87] Given the greatness of the potential good involved—a child of God—there must be an important good that motivates the couple's abstinence. The blessing of life is the greatest blessing that a married couple can share, and so having children is the charitable norm, and marriage entails the commitment to having children when it becomes prudently possible.

Conclusion

According to Catholic social teaching, although governments must not interfere in a married couple's decision making with respect to family size, nonetheless, "granted that rapid population growth may at times impede the development process, governments have rights and duties, within the limits of their own competence, to try to ameliorate the population problem."[88] In this regard, James McHugh takes heart from the United Nations' demographic estimate

---

and more prosthetic fixes are developed (289). Although Wilson consistently sees population reduction as the fundamental goal, he notes that for the time being "the common aim must be to expand resources and improve the quality of life for as many people as heedless population growth forces upon Earth, and do it with minimal prosthetic dependence. That, in essence, is the ethic of sustainable development" (ibid.). As he does elsewhere in his work, Wilson also urges that biodiversity be recognized as a paramount good. He notes that "biologists . . . generally agree that on the land at least, species are vanishing at a rate one hundred to a thousand times faster than before the arrival of *Homo sapiens*," with destruction of tropical rain forests being the main culprit today (293).

87. See Fisher, *Sinner's Guide to Natural Family Planning.*

88. McHugh, "Catholic Perspective on Population," 88. See Pope Paul VI, *Populorum progressio,* §37:

> It is true that too frequently an accelerated demographic increase adds its own difficulties to the problems of development: the size of the population increases more rapidly than available resources, and things are found to have reached apparently an impasse. From that moment the temptation is great to check the demographic increase by means of radical measures. It is certain that public authorities can intervene, within the limit of their competence, by favouring the availability of appropriate information and by adopting suitable measures, provided that these be in conformity with the moral law and that they respect the rightful freedom of married couples. Where the inalienable right to marriage and procreation is lacking, human dignity has ceased to exist. Finally, it is for the parents to decide, with full knowledge of the matter, on the number of their children, taking into account their responsibilities towards God, themselves, the children they have already brought into the world, and the community to which they belong. In all this they must follow the demands of their own conscience enlightened by God's law authentically interpreted, and sustained by confidence in Him.

that world population will likely not go much beyond ten billion—although admittedly this figure depends upon continued growth in the use of birth control.[89] For McHugh, reflecting the position of the Church's magisterial teaching on this topic, the real problem is not population but development. Namely, rich countries' consumption of resources results in environmental devastation in poor countries due to developmental imbalances.[90]

By contrast, John Schwarz has argued that the Catholic Church errs when it tries to sideline or ignore the role of population in the ecological crisis. Schwarz states: "Excessive population as well as excessive consumption and abuse of resources damages the environment."[91] Due to his concern for the way in which increasing population contributes to environmental damage, he rejects the Church's teaching against birth control.[92] He gives the example

89. For diverse sociological responses to the current striking decline in fertility in developed countries, see Wattenberg, *Fewer*; Krause, *Crisis of Births*; Greenhalgh, *Situating Fertility*.

90. See also Ryan, "Introduction," in Ryan and Whitmore, *Challenge of Global Stewardship*, 1–16. Ryan argues that the fact that something is deeply wrong with our current choices can be seen in what she calls the "deepening poverty for many of the world's people, depletion of natural resources, and persistent conflict around the world. We need not agree on the question of contraception to agree that 'something must be done'" (8).

91. John C. Schwarz, *Global Population from a Catholic Perspective*, 173. For this position, see also Sen, "Population." Contemporary Catholic theologians writing on ecology tend to avoid the issue of population, while circling around it nervously due to questions about the status of nonhuman species, land use, and so forth. See, e.g., Vogt, "Catholic Social Teaching and Creation"; Mescher, "Neighbor to Nature"; Finn, "Theology and Sustainable Economics," esp. 109. For an exception, see Elizabeth A. Johnson, *Ask the Beasts*, which confronts "the problematic impact of population growth on the world of other species" and affirms population control, although without explicitly coming out in favor of contraception: "While the question of *how* to control population growth does indeed divide interested parties at the global and national level, it is important to note that in recent decades the Roman Catholic Church has endorsed the basic idea that it is legitimate to limit human births" (244). Citing Pope John Paul II's General Audience of September 5, 1984, Johnson states, "If the good of future children, the material conditions of the times, and the interests of society are factors in weighing the ethical rightness of reproductive activity [as John Paul II's General Audience address suggests], the good of the ecological world which sustains human society is also profoundly relevant" (244–45). Johnson warns of the unsustainable environmental destruction (especially species extinction) caused by current human population levels and "rapacious habits" (253); see also 245–59. She concludes that "Christians personally and as church are called by the power of the Spirit to enter into solidarity with suffering creation and exercise responsibility for a new project of ecojustice. . . . The long-term goal is a socially just and environmentally sustainable society in which the needs of all people are met and diverse species can prosper, onward to an evolutionary future that will still surprise" (284–86). For an evangelical work that bemoans "the ecological realities caused by too many people, too many cars, the proliferation of invasive (non-native) species and the global effects of climate change," see Edward R. Brown, *Our Father's World*, 97.

92. Schwarz does not discuss global warming, no doubt because he was not yet aware of it at the time of writing. For recent Catholic and Protestant theological responses to global warming, see Richard W. Miller, "Global Climate Disruption and Social Justice." Miller argues that the world is facing an "unimaginable tragedy" and that "people need to start demonstrating en

of China's population of 1.2 billion; surely without birth control the population growth in China would destroy the ecosystem (both China's and the
world's) even more rapidly than the already over-high population is presently
doing. Approvingly, Schwarz cites John Haught's argument that a truly pro-
life ethic today "cannot turn away from the global population problem and
the additional pressures placed on the earth's systems by the sheer force of
human numbers."[93] This fits with an urgent warning issued in 2012 by over
one hundred science academies worldwide regarding not only overconsumption, but also population growth.[94]

Whereas Schwarz, Haught, McKibben, and most contemporary scientists
consider preventing the human population from growing much beyond its
current level to be a positive good, I maintain that the unique greatness of
each human existence and the value of expanding the human interpersonal
communion still make increasing human population to be justifiable today. I
am aware of the risks inherent in my position. As Alan Weisman comments on
global warming: "Only over time, scientists caution, can we know if mounting
weather events add up to a trend that means the climate has entered a phase
shift. But if we wait to act until all the numbers are in, we'll have waited too
long."[95] What is true of global warming is also true of scarcity of resources,
extinction of species, destruction of forests and green spaces, and other possible threats that follow upon increased population: if we wait too long, it
may be too late.

Why then do I propose further waiting with regard to efforts to restrict
population growth? I do so principally because each new human life that today
enters the world is a priceless addition to the interpersonal communion of life
and love that God is building up for the heavenly city, and, also, because I am

---

masse in the streets all across the globe, especially in the United States" (22, 25). Miller focuses
upon cutting carbon emissions rapidly via renewable energy sources. He does not speak about
trying to solve global warming by reducing population, but rather warns that global warming
itself will produce a huge loss of population: "While the planet's population is projected to
reach 9 billion by 2050, Hans Joachim Schellenhuber, one of the leading climate scientists in the
world, carefully argued at a major international climate conference that at a 5 degree Celsius (9
degrees Fahrenheit) increase from pre-industrial temperatures, which is where we are headed on
our current path, the planet could probably support only about 1 billion people" (18).

93. Haught, *Science and Religion*, 200, cited in Schwarz, *Global Population from a Catholic
Perspective*, 198. Ian Hore-Lacy makes the same point but with a greater recognition of human
ability to overcome apparent limits; see Hore-Lacy, *Responsible Dominion*, 41–42; cf. 84–100.
Against Steven Bouma-Prediger's *For the Beauty of the Earth*, which he suggests suffers from
romanticism, Hore-Lacy makes clear the need to understand "the world of agriculture, mining
and forestry" as part of care for the environment (45).

94. See Weisman, *Countdown*, 404.

95. Ibid., 422–23.

hoping that we will find other, less radical ways to adapt. I take heart from the seeming recklessness of the provident God who, despite the destruction caused by fallen humans and despite the overpopulation of the land of Israel and its environs, commands his people to be fruitful and multiply. Furthermore, I agree with the Orthodox philosopher H. Tristram Engelhardt, who calls upon the Church to recognize that "in environmental policy, as with all empirically driven policy choices, there are good grounds for caution with regard to apodictic statements," especially given the inevitable "uncertainty regarding predictions with respect to the environment" and "the special complexity of environmental studies and their attempts to predict the future."[96] Thus, at present, the generous welcoming of children seems to me to be the path that charitable married couples, with due prudence, should pursue.[97]

96. Engelhardt, "Ecology, Morality, and the Challenges of the Twenty-First Century," 276–77. Pope Francis's *Laudato Si'* occasionally would benefit from more attention to this complexity. For his part, Engelhardt seems to have a good sense of the prudentially evaluated "tradeoffs between costs and benefits flowing from different changes to the environment. For example, more productive fields have always meant fewer virgin forests and untilled plains" ("Ecology, Morality, and the Challenges of the Twenty-First Century," 281).

97. Norman Wirzba observes that in Gen. 2–3, "we can see that the rejection of limit is ultimately a rejection of God" ("Art of Creaturely Life," 17). Wirzba has in view not population limits but rather the ways in which humans construe their identity vis-à-vis natural limits. Since I agree with Wirzba about "the rejection of limit," I wish to make fully clear that in this chapter I am not rejecting any limits to human population on earth per se, even though I am arguing that the goodness of each additional human being is so great that, at the present time, our pursuit of potential ecological gains should not be undertaken at the cost of the responsible conception and birth of children. For further insight into Catholic views of responsible procreation, see also Caldecott, *Not as the World Gives*, 82; *Gaudium et spes*, §50, p. 953. For a much different vision, see Wilson, *Social Conquest of Earth*, 297.

Original Sin

And the LORD God commanded the man, saying, "You may freely eat of every tree of the garden; but of the tree of the knowledge of good and evil you shall not eat, for in the day that you eat of it you shall die."

Genesis 2:16–17

The biblical story of the first humans' first sin is well known. Commenting on Genesis 3:6, where the woman and man eat of the forbidden fruit of the tree of the knowledge of good and evil (cf. Gen. 2:16–17 and 3:2–3), Gordon Wenham remarks that "the essence of man's first sin was his disobedience to the only divine command he had received: not to eat of the tree of knowledge."[1] In tempting Eve to disobey God's command, the "serpent" (Gen. 3:1–4) assures Eve that God has oppressively misled her about the tree of the knowledge of good and evil, and that in fact when she eats from it her eyes will be opened and she "will be like God, knowing good and evil" (Gen. 3:5).[2] According to

1. Wenham, *Genesis 1–15*, 90.
2. Robert Alter supposes that Gen. 3:15 records a mere just-so story about the origin of antagonism between snakes and humans. See Alter, *Genesis*, 13: "Although the serpent is by no means 'satanic,' as in the lens of later Judeo-Christian traditions, the curse records a primal horror of humankind before this slithering, viscous-looking, and poisonous representative of the animal realm. It is the first moment in which a split between man and the rest of the animal kingdom is recorded." For a more nuanced interpretation, see Arnold, *Genesis*, 69. In *Creation, Un-Creation, Re-Creation*, Joseph Blenkinsopp notes that "the word *nāḥāš* ('snake') would inevitably have brought to mind the idea of magic, divination, the occult, expressed by the same lexeme (verbal stem *nḥš* and corresponding substantive . . .). The snake has earned this reputation since it lives underground, like the wise Enki lord of the underworld, and, like the snake in *Gilgamesh* (XI 279–89), it has discovered a way of perpetually rejuvenating itself" (73). For the view that the serpent in Gen. 3 does not truly tempt Adam and Eve, and that the serpent in fact tells the truth, see Charlesworth, *Good and Evil Serpent*. For a response to Charlesworth

Genesis 3, then, the first abuse of human freedom comes from the desire to "be like God" and to "know good and evil" as breakers of God's command, as though humans could be like God by countermanding God. Thus Adam and Eve, God's royal images whom God created to know and love God and neighbor, fall by rejecting their dependence upon the wise and good creator.

Yet did such a first human couple, sinless royal images of God, ever actually exist?[3] This question has become pressing due in part to modern science's discovery that the age of the human race is not six thousand years as Scripture implies, but forty thousand to fifty thousand years or more.[4] The question has also become pressing due to genetic studies that indicate that there was not an original pair of humans from whom, in direct descent, all other humans can trace their ancestry. Although these studies affirm the existence of a man and a woman from whom all humans alive today can trace their descent, this man and woman lived at quite different times from each other and do not appear to have been the first man or first woman. Scientists today argue that our genetic variability requires a much larger (though still relatively small) group of ancestors, perhaps ten thousand and at least a few thousand.[5]

---

from a strictly historical-critical perspective, see Day, *From Creation to Babel*, 36–40. Like most historical-critical interpreters, Day emphasizes that "the serpent was not Satan (the devil) in J's understanding. The concept of Satan developed later, and we find him first equated with the Eden serpent in the apocryphal book of Wisdom" (35). In my view, while the serpent may not have been conceived as "Satan" by the original author, neither is the serpent merely a sly talking beast; rather, the serpent is a powerful, fallen creature whose physical attributes are symbolic.

3. For discussion of the content of the doctrine of original sin, including the fact that the doctrine belongs within the broader framework of redemption, see Gary A. Anderson, "*Necessarium Adae Peccatum*." As Anderson notes, "For Christians, the affirmation that God's mercy defines the very ground of human existence is founded on the basis of Adam's sin and redemption" (44). Although I focus in this chapter primarily upon how and why we should defend the view that there was a freely committed original sin at the dawn of human history, this chapter should be paired with the chapter that follows (on redemption). See also Stanley Hauerwas's marvelous "Sinsick," including his appreciative discussion of Thomas Aquinas's understanding of original sin in relation to death. For the view that modern science has ruled out monogenesis at least in its "classical form," see McFarland, *In Adam's Fall*, 143–44.

4. Denis O. Lamoureux holds that "the archaeological record discloses that humans who behaved like us (creating art, sophisticated tools, and intentional burials) appeared roughly 50,000 years ago" ("No Historical Adam," 64). Lamoureux adds that Scripture "reveals that humans are the only creatures who bear the Image of God, and *only* humans are sinful. I suspect that the manifestation of these spiritual realities coincides with the appearance of behaviorally modern humans about 50,000 years ago" (ibid.). This seems plausible to me. For a helpful sketch of various options for accounting for human origins in light of the evolutionary development of hominids, see Hurd, "Hominids in the Garden?" See also Tattersall, *Fossil Trail*.

5. See Lamoureux, "No Historical Adam," 64. For scientific discussion, see most notably Ayala et al., "Molecular Genetics of Speciation and Human Origins." See also the scientific articles suggesting that genetic diversity can increase faster than Ayala et al. supposed, cited in C. John Collins, *Did Adam and Eve Really Exist?*, 119n28. Some scientists have proposed theories of

Another difficulty for the historicity of Adam and Eve is that Genesis 2–3 is not history in either ancient or modern understanding of that genre, and so Genesis 2–3 should not be expected to provide literal historical details about human origins. Edward Yarnold, in his 1971 study of original sin, is surely correct when he says that "the account of the Fall in the third chapter of Genesis is not literally accurate as history or science."[6] This lack of literal accuracy does not mean that there could not have been a pair of humans who, at the outset of the human race, committed a first sin that affected the whole of human nature. But Yarnold argues that in fact the doctrine of the fall is "not about man's origins but about his present condition and his future," so that "original sin" means simply "my entry into membership of a sinful society" and my doing so *without grace*."[7] When Yarnold takes up the question of whether "original sin" entails a primal fall, he concludes that "there is no need to postulate an original representative group in whose sin we all share."[8]

A different approach, more congenial to the one I adopt in this chapter, comes from Karl Barth. While granting that Genesis 3 is not literal history, Barth insists that "in these passages we have to do with a genuine consideration

human origins that are "polygenist" in the sense of involving lines of rational hominids emerging at various places and developing in parallel. But as Collins states, "The models that are more in favor among paleoanthropologists today focus more on unified origin" (121).

6. Yarnold, *Theology of Original Sin*, 74. See also Schoonenberg, *Man and Sin*; Dubarle, *Le péché originel dans l'Écriture*. For the debate during this time period, see de Villalmonte, *El pecado original*. In his *Evolution and the Doctrine of Original Sin*, S. G. M. Trooster, SJ, underscores that Gen. 2–3 "has no intention of presenting 'history' as we understand the term today," since Gen. 2–3 "arose from the author's prophetic vision of the condition of depravity and of salvation in which the people of his own times were living" (55). Trooster emphasizes that Gen. 2 is a protology pointing already to our eschatological end, and that in fact "this original state of blessedness is not realized anywhere" (71), which means that there was indeed no first sin. Instead, humans have always been sinners. Thus Trooster speaks of "man's refusal *from the very beginning of time* to embrace God's redemptive goodness and to realize it in himself and the world. It is precisely the scientifically demonstrated primitivity of the (chronologically) first human beings, including their mortality, that could be additional proof of the unfathomable and universal nature of this mystery of human refusal and negation" (ibid.)—a mystery that for Trooster has no beginning, since it was already present at the very beginning. For a similar view, see Hayes, *Gift of Being*, chap. 7.

7. Yarnold, *Theology of Original Sin*, 76, 79. It should be noted that in denying the historicity of Adam, Yarnold and his contemporaries were not breaking new ground; already in his Hulsean Lectures of 1901–2, for example, F. R. Tennant had denied a historical fall. See Tennant, *Origin and Propagation of Sin*. See also Savage, *Religion of Evolution*. Both Tennant and Savage are cited in Madueme, "Most Vulnerable Part of the Whole Christian Account."

8. Yarnold, *Theology of Original Sin*, 90. See also, e.g., Duffy, "Our Hearts of Darkness," 618; Korsmeyer, *Evolution and Eden*, 121; Mahoney, *Christianity in Evolution*, chap. 3; Haught, *God after Darwin*, 149; Wiley, *Original Sin*, 207; McFadyen, *Bound to Sin*, 248; LaCocque, *Trial of Innocence*, 41.

of real events, persons and things."[9] If so, then the event that we describe as "original sin" took place in time and involved real human beings who lived in a real place on earth. At the same time, for Barth Genesis 2–3 is rooted "in imagination," as befits "sagas" that "do not aim to present 'history' but 'pre-historical' history."[10] C. S. Lewis offers a somewhat similar proposal, but unlike Barth he tries to correlate his proposal broadly with the scientific evidence. In what he calls "a not unlikely tale," Lewis presents what he intends to be a plausible defense of the historical possibility of an original sin.[11] He describes the gradual evolution of the hominid body, and he suggests that advanced hominids may have existed for tens of thousands of years, and may indeed have been quite clever (bearing marks of intelligence) without yet being rational or human.[12] Finally, at some unidentifiable point in history, God created the

9. Barth, *Church Dogmatics* (hereafter *CD*) III/1, 252. For a position similar to Barth's, see Schönborn, "Die kirchliche Erbsündenlehre im Umriss." Earlier in his career, in his commentary on Romans, Barth argues that "the sin which entered the world through Adam is, like the righteousness manifested to the world in Christ, timeless and transcendental"; that "Adam has no existence on the plane of history and of psychological analysis"; and that "the entrance of sin into the world through Adam is in no strict sense an historical or psychological happening" (*Epistle to the Romans*, 171; cf. Barth, *Christ and Adam*). Some commentators have taken these statements to mean that Barth considers Rom. 5 to refer "to a non-historical fall" in the sense of a fallenness that has no source in an original human sin (Collins, *Did Adam and Eve Really Exist?*, 39). But in the same place, Barth insists that death "entered into the world as a result of the original and invisible sin by which the life, which is the relationship of men to God, was damaged" (*Epistle to the Romans*, 170). In a rather confusing way, Barth affirms of Adam that "neither he nor the Christ risen and appointed to the life of God, the Christ of whom he is the projection, can be 'historical' figures. Leaving out of account what may have occurred to the historical Adam, it is clear that the sin which Adam brought into the world precedes death, just as the righteousness which Christ brought follows it" (ibid., 171). Barth's view of original sin is in certain ways similar to that of Søren Kierkegaard; see Kierkegaard, *Concept of Anxiety*, 26 and elsewhere. As Henri Blocher points out, "Kierkegaard is commonly credited with a denial of the 'historic view' of Genesis 2–3, but we should not underestimate the subtlety of his position. . . . His reluctance to let go entirely of a primeval element, seen in a historical sequence, deserves notice" (*Original Sin*, 52–53). For the view that Barth makes the historicity of Adam irrelevant, see Trueman, "Original Sin and Modern Theology," 176–79. See also Conor Cunningham's claim, indebted to Barth's way of reading Romans, that "there is no Fall before Christ"—and thus no strictly historical Adam (*Darwin's Pious Idea*, 378).

10. Barth, *CD* III/1, 252–53. Later in the *CD*, Barth explains that God chose this genre (saga or prehistorical history) so as to ward off a fundamental misreading. Namely, if we were to attempt to read Gen. 2–3 "as history, relating it either favourably or unfavourably to scientific palaeontology, or to what we now know with some historical certainty concerning the oldest and most primitive forms of human life," we would miss the very point of Gen. 2–3: we can only know sin (and thus human history itself) insofar as we accept by faith "the prophetically attested Word and judgment of God" (IV/1, 508).

11. Lewis, *Problem of Pain*, 77.

12. See John M. Rist's contention that (since there is no evidence of a "Golden Age" before the fall) it may be that "our earliest ancestors, with no moral awareness and therefore no moral responsibility, simultaneously became, at least to an extent, conscious of moral responsibility

first rational hominids as the priests of creation. In Lewis's version, we need not know how many first humans God made or how long they remained in their original holy condition.[13] We know simply that eventually they rebelled against God—with the result that human nature itself became disordered, since "the total organism which had been taken up into his spiritual life was allowed to fall back into the merely natural condition from which, at his making, it had been raised."[14]

Pope Pius XII's 1950 encyclical *Humani generis* teaches that "the faithful cannot embrace that opinion which maintains that either after Adam there existed on this earth true men who did not take their origin through natural generation from him as from the first parent of all, or that Adam represents a certain number of first parents."[15] Responding to this teaching, however, Karl Rahner highlights Pius XII's next sentence, which I quote here: "Now it is in no way apparent how such an opinion can be reconciled with that which the sources of revealed truth and the documents of the Teaching Authority of the Church propose with regard to original sin, which proceeds from a sin actually committed by an individual Adam and which, through genera-tion, is passed on to all and is in everyone as his own."[16] In Rahner's view,

---

and of being immersed in a fatal (or at least potentially fatal) 'infection' of the human race" (*Augustine Deformed*, 382; cf. 384–88). Rist's thesis is that the human race grew in an evolutionary way, somewhat as each individual human grows into rational maturity. It seems to me that Rist errs by dissociating the fatal "infection" from a free moral act.

13. See also Robin Collins, "Evolution and Original Sin." Collins hypothesizes that there was an original group of hominids (or, possibly, two hominids) who "became aware of God and God's requirements," but who "were subject to various temptations arising both from the desires and instincts they inherited from their evolutionary past and from various new possibilities for self-centeredness, self-idolization, self-denigration, and the like" (469–70). According to Collins, the fall of these hominids, not through one sin but through "sinful acts," "created a form of spiritual and moral darkness along with an accompanying bondage to sin" (470).

14. Lewis, *Problem of Pain*, 82–83. N. T. Wright similarly argues that "perhaps what Genesis is telling us is that God chose one pair from the rest of early hominids for a special, strange, demanding vocation. This pair (call them Adam and Eve if you like) were to be the representatives of the whole human race" (*Surprised by Scripture*, 37). Reading Genesis through the lens of Israel's election, Wright thinks it biblically plausible that "Adam and Eve" were chosen from the early hominid population "to take the creator's purposes forward to a new dimension of life. But if they fail—if they abdicate their image-bearing vocation and follow the siren call of the elements of chaos still within creation—they will come to share the entropy that has so far been creation's lot," namely death (38). See also N. T. Wright, "Letter to the Romans," 524–26.

15. Pope Pius XII, *Humani generis*, §37.

16. Ibid. In this chapter I do not treat the section on original sin in Rahner's late work *Foundations of Christian Faith* (originally published in 1976). In this section Rahner develops an existential reading of "original sin" in light of God's gracious self-communication from the outset of the human race. He argues that the "co-determination of the situation of every person by the guilt of others is something universal, permanent, and therefore also original. There are no islands for the individual person whose nature does not already bear

this sentence implies that *Humani generis*'s condemnation of polygenism is conditional. *If* it could be made apparent how polygenism could be reconciled with what is taught about original sin by Scripture and the magisterium, then polygenism could be allowed. Suffice it here to say that Rahner's conclusion is that from among the first rational hominids, God chose a pair (or a group) as the representative head of humanity, and the sin of these representatives brought about the fall of all of humankind and the beginning of the human race as we know it.[17]

I think that Rahner's reading of *Humani generis* and of the doctrine of original sin is plausible. The first section of my chapter, therefore, sets forth Rahner's position in the light of a recent proposal offered by the Catholic philosopher Kenneth Kemp. Kemp aims to show that science (in this case, genetic studies) does not require Christian thinkers to give up on the possibility of monogenism, as Rahner supposed.[18] Despite their differences, Kemp

---

the stamp of the guilt of others, directly or indirectly, from close or from afar" (109). He then proposes that "such a universal, permanent and ineradicable co-determination of the situation of every individual's freedom by guilt, and then of course of every society's too, is conceivable only if this ineradicable co-determination of the situation of freedom by guilt is also *original*, that is, is already imbedded in the origin of this history to the extent that this origin of the single history of the human race is to be understood as established by man" (110). Given this preparation, he proposes that God's gracious absolute self-communication "is what is most radical and most deep in the existential situation of human freedom," and the original sin was a rejection of this grace, so that "the *loss* of such a sanctifying self-communication assumes the character of something which *should not be*" in the whole human race (113). One can see here a transposition of certain elements taken from Aquinas, but in my view—paradoxically given the goal of the transposition—Aquinas's language is clearer and less time bound.

17. For his part, John H. Walton suggests that at some point in history, "perhaps at the moment that geneticists refer to as the bottleneck when humanity nearly became extinct," God bestowed the "image of God" upon the entire human population ("Historical Adam," 114), though what Walton specifically has in mind here is unclear. Walton argues that since there was as yet no law, these humans were not punished for their sins by God, although they did experience death (which in my view certainly seems to be a punishment). He proposes that "sometime later, perhaps tens of thousands of years, individuals whom the Bible designates as Adam and Eve are chosen by God as representative priests in sacred space" (114–15), and Adam and Eve's sin brought moral responsibility and punishment upon all later humans. Similarly, Denis Alexander has proposed that around 10,000 years ago, God uniquely revealed himself to "Adam and Eve," whom God chose to spread the knowledge of God around the world; Adam thus became the "federal head" of all humans living at that time and after, although humans lived prior to Adam's time. In Alexander's view, too, death was natural to humans, but sin spread only after Adam's fall. See Alexander, *Creation or Evolution*. I am not persuaded by Walton's or Alexander's positions, because they stretch the imagination without seeming to account for anything of real significance. See also C. John Collins, "Historical Adam," 172; Kidner, *Genesis*, 26–31.

18. Somewhat similarly, but with a much different time frame, Catholic philosopher Dennis Bonnette proposes that the first rational hominids, the first to be endowed with a rational

and Rahner agree in holding that there could have been a real original sin, notwithstanding the scientific evidence that has challenged the doctrine.

My second section then functions as a *sed contra* to both Rahner and Kemp. For the biblical scholar Peter Enns, no approach that attempts to square Scripture and modern science can work as an interpretation of Genesis 3. Enns emphasizes that the first chapters of Genesis are about the story of Israel.[19] On this view, one can only rightly read Genesis 1–3 for what it teaches about Israel; one cannot read it for what it seemingly teaches about human origins, because the original author solely intended to be offering a cosmic backdrop to Israel's story.[20] Despite its exegetical acuity, however, Enns's interpretation of Genesis 3 is in my view too impatient with efforts to square Genesis 3 and modern science. I think that Enns does not pay sufficient attention to the connection that Genesis and Paul draw between Adam and Eve's sin and human death.[21] For Enns, sin is built into the human condition rather than

soul, "predate, or are contemporary with, *Homo erectus*," unless the first humans were in fact members of *Homo erectus* (*Origin of the Human Species*, 167).

19. Along these lines, Raymund Schwager, SJ, argues that just as the biblical author or authors projected back to primordial origins a specific covenantal sin on the part of Israel, Christians need to interpret the primordial history in light of Christ (*Banished from Eden*, 88; cf. Ligier, *Péché d'Adam et péché du monde*). Schwager, however, also offers a number of scenarios or "thought experiments" that strive to describe a plausible "original sin" (not a reflective decision, but an affective "shrinking back" from God's call) in light of evolutionary theory (*Banished from Eden*, 95; cf. 105–11).

20. Indebted to Gerhard von Rad, Leo Scheffczyk similarly observes in his 1970 history of the doctrine of creation that "even those accounts, which form the basis of the OT theology of Creation, do not treat of Creation for its own sake. The sacred authors write in the context not of belief in Creation as such but of a belief in salvation and election which reaches back to the very beginning and also includes the fact of Creation. . . . Creation is envisaged as essentially the beginning of Yahweh's saving works and at the same time constitutes the proto-history of God's mercies to his chosen people" (*Creation and Providence*, 5, 8). More recently, regarding Paul's assumption that there was a historical Adam (see Rom. 5; 8; 1 Cor. 15), Denis Lamoureux argues that to deliver the gospel of Jesus Christ, "the Holy Spirit accommodated and allowed Paul to use the biology-of-the-day as an incidental vessel" ("No Historical Adam," 62–63).

21. Given the connection between sin and human death as we now experience it, the *Catechism of the Catholic Church* describes the doctrine of original sin as "an essential truth of the faith," and states plainly that "the Church, which has the mind of Christ [cf. 1 Cor. 2:16], knows very well that we cannot tamper with the revelation of original sin without undermining the mystery of Christ" (§389). The *Catechism* notes that with the certainty of faith, "the Church has always taught that the overwhelming misery which oppresses men and their inclination toward evil and death cannot be understood apart from their connection with Adam's sin and the fact that he has transmitted to us a sin with which we are all born afflicted, a sin which is the 'death of the soul'" (§403; the interior citation is from the Council of Trent). The same point is made by the evangelical scholar Philip G. Ryken in his "We Cannot Understand the World or Our Faith without a Real, Historical Adam." See also the anathemas contained in the Council of Trent's "Decree on Original Sin" (June 17, 1546), in Norman Tanner, *Decrees of the Ecumenical Councils*, 2:665–67.

being chosen at the outset with full freedom, and human death as we now experience it is thus a creational given rather than a punishment. I think that this position inevitably undermines the goodness and justice of the creator, by implicating the creator in our sinfulness and by having no answer (other than our created condition) for why our alienation and death are so terrible.[22] Furthermore, the unity of all humans not only in Christ, but also in the first rational hominids ("Adam and Eve") as the original or representative bearers of human nature, cannot be lightly dismissed, given the importance of the unity of all those whom Christ redeems.

In this light, my third section explores a set of theological themes: death as a punishment for original sin, the relationship of original sin and original justice, and the unity of all humans in Adam and Eve. For this task, I have recourse to Jonathan Edwards and Thomas Aquinas. Edwards provides an instructive exposition of the biblical testimony to human death as a punishment and to Adam's free will in sinning. Aquinas defines original sin vis-à-vis original justice, reflects upon human unity in Adam as one body or one family, and addresses the question of why we still labor under the consequences of original sin even after Christ.[23] I argue that Edwards and Aquinas help us to see fully the theological significance of holding to the existence of an actual first sin committed by free, rational, and innocent humans.[24]

22. I distinguish human death, which involves an experience of alienation or of the cutting off of communion, from death per se, which was already present three billion years prior to the emergence of rational hominids. For an evolutionary account of the aging and death of organisms, see Charlesworth and Charlesworth, *Evolution*, 117–21.

23. See also Austriaco, "Theological Fittingness Argument for the Historicity of the Fall of *Homo Sapiens*." Austriaco argues that it would have been fitting for God to give "preteradaptive" gifts to the first humans, as evolved hominids possessed of rationality and ordained to eternal union with God. These "preteradaptive" gifts ensure that inherited evolutionary adaptations did not, in the case of the first humans, impede their virtuous exercise of reason and will. I agree with Austriaco but remain within the traditional category of original justice. On original justice, see two articles cited by Austriaco: DeLetter, SJ, "If Adam Had Not Sinned . . ."; Vollert, "Two Senses of Original Justice in Medieval Theology."

24. Ian A. McFarland critiques as "theologically problematic" and scientifically implausible the cause-effect framework of "Adam sinned (cause), and therefore all humanity is burdened with original sin (effect)" (*In Adam's Fall*, 153). He argues that the theological problem is both how one person's sin can "*constitute*" all other persons "as sinful," and the fact that the available answers to this question produce "a fundamental asymmetry between Adam and all other human beings, since it is only in the case of this one human being that a particular act of the will is able to cause damage to the human will in general" (ibid.). I grant that there is a certain "asymmetry" in that Adam and Eve received the grace of original justice, but in my view this grace befits them (given their unique place in human history), just as Christ's grace befits him (and Mary's grace befits her). The grace of original justice ensures that God made humans fully good. The loss of this grace does not produce an asymmetry of natural goods, even if there is an asymmetry with respect to full holiness. The latter kind of asymmetry does

On the basis of Edwards's and Aquinas's insights, I return to the approaches of Rahner and Kemp in the chapter's conclusion. *Pace* Enns, I argue that Rahner's and/or Kemp's ways of squaring Genesis and modern science are serviceable for upholding the doctrinal content that Edwards and Aquinas suggest must be upheld. This doctrinal content includes death as a punishment for original sin, Adam and Eve's full freedom prior to the fall (due to the grace of original justice), and Adam and Eve as the physical or royal-representative "first movers" of the human race whose sin justly affects the state of human nature in the whole human race.

Karl Rahner and Kenneth Kemp on Adam and Eve

In the wake of *Humani generis*, the question for Catholic scholars is whether we can deny that "after Adam there existed on this earth true men who did not take their origin through natural generation from him as from the first parent of all." Put simply, does *Humani generis* require that we deny that there have been any humans who did not descend physically from Adam and Eve? The question is whether Pius XII's way of phrasing his condemnation allows for some version of polygenism *if* it became clear how this version could be adequately reconciled to the doctrine of original sin as taught by Scripture and the Church. As noted above, Pius XII insists that all humans have descended directly from Adam and Eve (monogenism), on the grounds that Scripture and magisterial teaching require that original sin "proceeds from a sin actually committed by an individual Adam and which, through generation, is passed on to all and is in everyone as his own." Here Pius XII has in view Trent's *Decree on Original Sin* (June 17, 1546), which anathematizes anyone who holds that the "sin of Adam which, one by origin and passed on to all by propagation and not by imitation, inheres in everyone as something proper to each, is removed by human and natural powers, or by any remedy other

---

not strike me as theologically problematic, since it is simply part of the historical unfolding of the human race. McFarland produces the problematic asymmetry by rejecting the view that original sin's punishment is the loss of original justice, and by instead construing original sin as directly damaging the human will (so that Adam and Eve's wills would have power that other wills do not). For McFarland, "If original sin [in us] is not itself genuine sin (viz., active resistance to God that merits condemnation), then it is hard to see how the various actual sins that it generates can be counted as genuine either, since the congenital condition of debility under which they are committed would appear to constitute a mitigating circumstance of the highest order" (38–39). I note in response that original sin in us does produce a punishment absent God's grace (namely, exclusion from our ultimate end) and that we remain free to do good or evil, so that the debility under which we operate does not mean that our actual sins are not genuine.

than the merit of the one mediator, our lord Jesus Christ."[25] Trent's anathema is aimed at those who claim that something other than Christ's passion can remove original sin. But the anathema can obviously also be read as requiring that original sin be understood as "passed on to all by propagation," which would require monogenesis.

This is indeed a formidable set of magisterial texts for Catholics who wish to hypothesize polygenist scenarios without breaking with definitive dogmatic teaching. Nonetheless, Karl Rahner argues that neither Trent nor *Humani generis* is yet decisive regarding whether all other humans descended from one original couple. He holds that Trent's central teaching in the passage cited is that original sin cannot be "removed by human and natural powers, or by any remedy other than the merit of the one mediator," and Trent defines this central teaching *without* formally defining the corollary that original sin is "passed on to all by propagation and not by imitation." Likewise, as we have seen, Rahner finds it significant that *Humani generis*, in teaching that all humans descend physically from Adam, makes this proposition conditional upon the seeming impossibility of squaring any other view with the necessary content of the doctrine of original sin. On these grounds, Rahner holds that the question remains open about whether a polygenist approach to original sin "can be reconciled with that which the sources of revealed truth and the documents of the Teaching Authority of the Church propose with regard to original sin."[26]

As I mentioned above, I accept Rahner's claim that there may be forms of polygenism that the teaching of Trent and *Humani generis* does not definitively rule out. But what specific forms of polygenism does Rahner have in mind? In his *Hominisation: The Evolutionary Origin of Man as a Theological Problem*, published shortly after Vatican II, Rahner proposes that Genesis 2–3 should be conceived as a "historical aetiology, that is, as statements which man made from the standpoint of his later experience of the history of salvation and perdition in his relations with God."[27] For Rahner, the experience of salvation history is what teaches the author(s) of Genesis 2–3 that humankind is a unity. As an aetiology, Genesis 2–3 cannot be expected to provide factual information about how the unity of all humans came to be, but rather it simply testifies to this unity. On this view, the term "Adam" need not refer to one particular man as the source of the unity of all humans, but instead should be taken to mean "humanity in that form in which it existed at the beginning of its own

25. Council of Trent, *Decree on Original Sin*, §3, in Norman Tanner, *Decrees of the Ecumenical Councils*, 2:666.
26. Pope Pius XII, *Humani generis*, §37.
27. Rahner, *Hominisation*, 37–38.

history, and from which all subsequent humanity originated, from which we are all descended."[28]

Rahner then suggests that in the beginning of human history, a decision of human freedom negatively determined the situation of humanity. He thinks that the decision of one individual could have been determinative for an original group of humans if God willed that the "*humanitas originans*" would "mediate grace only if it had continued as a *whole* and wholly sinless through its decision."[29] As it happened, therefore, one free human decision—whether by a group or by an individual in the group—destroyed forever the original unity and sinlessness of humankind. Rahner adds that the beginning of human history, "humanity in the process of achieving itself," should be understood to coincide with the decision that constitutes original sin.[30]

In my view, it seems unlikely that God would have appointed a large group and allowed it to "mediate grace only if it had continued as a *whole* and wholly sinless through its decision." The larger the number of representative first humans, the more likely that someone will sin; and surely God did not wish to stack the deck in favor of human sin. However, in an earlier essay on the same topic, published not long after the promulgation of *Humani generis*, Rahner moves in a direction that seems more promising. As always, he first proposes that *Humani generis*'s condemnation "is not a positive declaration of the irreconcilability of polygenism and the Catholic doctrine of original sin, but a denial of the obviousness (not in fact to be had) of a possibility of reconciliation."[31] The question then is whether one can find a version of polygenism that does not fall into the pitfalls named by *Humani generis*: in other words, "whether the single sinful ancestor of all men, of whom the definition speaks, must *necessarily* be understood in the sense of monogenism alone."[32]

By way of answering this question, Rahner treats the 1909 decree of the Pontifical Biblical Commission, which argues that the corporal descent of all humans from one man is a historical truth that Genesis 2–3 inerrantly wills to teach. In Rahner's view, this position still theoretically leaves room for the development of an alternative concept of unity, unknown to the authors of the decree, that "does as much justice to the ultimate theological intention of the decree as monogenistic unity."[33] Remarking that many theologians find monogenism to be at least implicitly defined by Trent, Rahner argues that a

28. Rahner, "Sin of Adam," 252.
29. Ibid., 261.
30. Ibid., 262.
31. Rahner, "Theological Reflexions on Monogenism," 237.
32. Ibid., 238.
33. Ibid., 239.

council's formulation of a doctrine (in this case original sin) can include time-bound elements that turn out to be unnecessary for the truth of the doctrine. As an example, he notes that the idea that original sin was transmitted through carnal generation was taught by the Council of Carthage, but is not in fact a necessary element of the doctrine of original sin. He holds that the fathers of Trent, in insisting on an original sin that is spread by propagation (not imitation), were rejecting views that denied hereditary sin rather than attempting to define a doctrine of monogenism. Although the fathers of Trent had in view one specific man, Adam, whom they understood to have "handed down original sin to his posterity by means of the natural bond of generation,"[34] this view of Adam was arguably not what the council fathers were defining. Rahner adds that the plans for the First Vatican Council included a schema in which polygenism would have been defined to be heretical, but the discontinuation of the council meant that these plans did not come to fruition.

Rahner goes on to observe that from the perspective of historical-critical exegesis, it is not possible to show that the author of Genesis 2–3 intended to insist historically upon the literal origin of all humans from one man, Adam. Instead, the author of Genesis may have been making a theological claim about the unity of the human race and depicting this unity through an image. Rahner finds, too, that Wisdom 10:1 or Acts 17:24–26 cannot rightly be used to confirm a historical Adam as the father of all people. At the same time, Rahner readily grants that "what Genesis says is *positively open* to a revealed doctrine concerning monogenism arrived at elsewhere and by other means and guaranteed by the *magisterium*."[35] Regarding Pauline theology, he considers that "a genuine unity of origin of all men must be understood in St Paul in a really monogenistic way if it is to retain its meaning."[36] Even so, he does not think that monogenism, in the strict sense of physical descent of all humans from one man, is thereby necessarily required. To show this, he describes a hypothetical scenario in which "the first man created in the state of original justice is nominated by God as the trustee, in respect of the justice compulsorily intended by God for all men, for all the men who follow him, whether they descend from him physically or not."[37] Were this particular man

---

34. Ibid., 244.
35. Ibid., 257–58.
36. Ibid., 266.
37. Ibid., 270. Insofar as it relies upon a notion of a human being "nominated by God as the trustee," Rahner's position here has Jesuit antecedents. Liam G. Walsh, OP, notes that the seventeenth-century Jesuit Francisco de Lugo held that God decreed "Adam the moral, juridical head of humanity. Adam and Eve were established as the legal representatives of all humans. They are presented as having acted on behalf of all humans; it is because they sinned in that capacity that all humans are taken to have sinned" ("Thomas Aquinas, the Doctrine of Original

to sin, then the gift of original justice would be removed from humanity, and all humans would be subject to the consequences of original sin.

Rahner then addresses the question of whether Jesus Christ's assumption of human nature requires that human nature have monogenistic origins. Specifically, Rahner asks "whether Christ can only be Head and Mediator of humanity because and only because he is a member of a humanity monogenistically one from the origin."[38] On the basis of Pauline texts, Rahner argues that the human race, of which Christ became a member, must share one "history of guilt," which requires that the human race be one "physically real common stock."[39] Those who share in this "common stock" are in a situation of damnation and thus in need of Christ's redemption. Rahner emphasizes—and I very much agree—that the members of this common stock (humankind) could not all be in this same situation unless their situation were traceable to "a single real individual in the beginning and in his act."[40] Yet, in Rahner's view, this single real individual could have belonged to an original community, so long as it was truly the *original* human community in which humanity formed a unity of some kind. It follows that Adam need not be the physical progenitor of all other humans, since the other members of the original community need not have been his children. Rahner thereby differentiates his position from "monogenism in the strict sense," which requires that there was one original human pair from whom all other humans physically descend.[41] In sum, Rahner holds that the unity of all people in one fallen condition can be defended even if one concludes, in light of scientific evidence, that the biblical account of all humans originating from Adam is not accurate with regard to physical descent.

Rahner bases his reflections upon the view that science has likely ruled out "monogenism in the strict sense." By contrast, Kenneth Kemp has recently argued that science has in fact not ruled out monogenesis, and so theologians need not give up on an actual Adam and Eve from whom all other humans have descended physically. At first glance, this claim—which, if true, would

---

Sin, and the Dogma of the Immaculate Conception," 119). For a succinct presentation of the Reformed scholastic Francis Turretin's similar federalist view, see Rea, "Metaphysics of Original Sin," 326. See also Weir, *Origins of the Federal Theology in Sixteenth-Century Reformation Thought*; and McFarland's comparison of "realist" and "federalist" views of our inclusion "in Adam" (*In Adam's Fall*, 150–53). I agree with Rea when he holds that Jonathan Edwards's account is not "a federalist view, even though it is consistent with the claim that Adam is the federal head of the human race" ("Metaphysics of Original Sin," 331n25).

38. Rahner, "Theological Reflexions on Monogenism," 274.
39. Ibid., 276.
40. Ibid., 281.
41. Ibid., 286.

offer an important alternative to Rahner's position—seems to run counter to the scientific evidence that Kemp himself accepts. As Kemp observes, genetic studies indicate that "although man probably came into being at 'one place,' the size of that place is only probably a relatively small place (say, East Africa), and could be as large as (nearly) the entire Old World. The population size might be small, but only relatively so—probably at least a few thousand; surely not a single couple."[42] Scientists also hold that the human race did not emerge suddenly, but rather developed gradually in an evolutionary fashion.

It seems as though these scientific findings rule out any kind of monogenesis. But Kemp proposes that a solution might be found by distinguishing, with regard to *Homo sapiens*, "biological species" from "philosophical and theological species."[43] Biologically speaking, all those who interbreed are one species. Philosophically, however, the human species emerges only with the infusion of a rational soul; and theologically the human species is constituted by God's free offer of eternal life (grace). As Kemp says, therefore, scientists might be able to detect the presence of the biological human species well before the "philosophical and theological species" came on the scene. Kemp describes this biological human species simply as "hominids," and argues that they did not possess a rational soul with its concomitant power of free rational thought.

Kemp notes that from within this cognitively advanced but nonrational hominid population, God could have infused rational souls into an original pair of full-fledged humans, to whom God could also have given the gifts that compose "original justice." After their fall, these two humans would have bred with each other, and their children would have bred with nonrational hominids—which would explain the age-old question of where Cain's wife (Gen. 4:17) comes from, even while it also means that these acts of intercourse would have been less than fully personal.[44] When these events would have oc-

42. Kemp, "Science, Theology, and Monogenesis," 225.

43. Kemp credits this distinction (made, however, in different terms) to Andrew Alexander, CJ, "Human Origins and Genetics." For recent engagement with Kemp's position, see Bonnette, "Impenetrable Mystery of a Literal Adam and Eve." Bonnette is not sure "whether successful mating is actually possible between subhumans and humans." He grants its theoretic possibility, however, and goes on to suggest various ways in which God could have arranged matters so as to minimize the extent of interbreeding between humans and nonrational hominids.

44. By taking this approach, Kemp aims to address the difficulties indicated by David Wilcox (among others), who states: "The coalescence points for most lines of [genetic] evidence indicate 100,000 to 200,000 years ago. That would suggest a bottleneck—although perhaps extended—during this period. And, this is the time period that seems to show the appearance of modern morphology. But there is not a clear consensus. For instance, several recent studies with large Y chromosome data bases and new analytical techniques have reported a coalescence point of around 50,000 years ago, a far more recent root than previous studies. Other studies—of beta

curred depends upon when one supposes that true rationality emerged. Kemp thinks that the emergence of rationality must have happened at least by sixty thousand years ago, after which archaeologists date "a variety of artifacts that seem clearly to require rationality, of which Cro-Magnon art is only the most spectacular example."[45] In short, Kemp finds that strict monogenism—Adam and Eve as the physical source of all humans—remains quite possible.

Peter Enns: A *Sed Contra*

Peter Enns's recent *The Evolution of Adam: What the Bible Does and Doesn't Say about Human Origins* sifts contemporary science and historical-critical exegesis to offer a powerful and synthetic case, building upon the work of many other scholars, for the view that Genesis 2–3 should not be expected to deliver historical details about the first humans, including about a supposed first sin that infected the entire human race. Enns begins by remarking that "the Human Genome Project, completed in 2003, has shown beyond any reasonable scientific doubt that humans and primates share common ancestry."[46] If this is so, then what should we make of Genesis 2's account of God's creation of the first man "of dust from the ground" (Gen. 2:7) and of the first woman from one of Adam's ribs (Gen. 2:21–22)? It should be clear that Genesis teaches the special creation of Adam and Eve, not the infusion of spiritual souls into two hominid bodies. Enns's point is that those who seek to defend the historical accuracy of the *biblical* portrait of human origins must do so by rejecting the scientific evidence for shared human and primate ancestry. In Enns's view, defenders of Genesis 2–3's portrait of human origins cannot appeal to a biblical-scientific hybrid that is *neither* biblical *nor* scientific.

---

hemoglobin, PDHA1, a noncoding sequence in chromosome 22, and the HLA antigen presenting series—indicate the presence of much older polymorphisms, perhaps dating back as far as 1.5 million years ago" (Wilcox, "Finding Adam," 250–51). The studies of the Y chromosome databases cited by Wilcox include Underhill et al., "Y Chromosome Sequence Variation and the History of Human Populations"; Thomson et al., "Recent Common Ancestry of Human Y Chromosomes: Evidence from DNA Sequence Data." Wilcox adds:

> Whether Adam and Eve were created by providence through descent from a hominid lineage or are an original pair created without ancestors, they can have only 4 DRB1 alleles between them. If one human pair is the sole ancestor of all living people, all the human HLA alleles must be descended from those four "adamic" alleles. All the diversity must have been produced by modifying those four versions of the HLA-DRB1 gene since Adam and Eve were created. Yet a 5–10 million year coalescence would apparently make Adam a "monkey's uncle" (ancestral to at least chimps, gorillas, and humans). ("Finding Adam," 251–52)

See also Venema, "Genesis and the Genome."

45. Kemp, "Science, Theology, and Monogenesis," 235.
46. Enns, *Evolution of Adam*, ix.

Having established this point, Enns proceeds to ask whether biblical authority requires Christians to reject the scientific evidence and insist that Adam, created by God directly "from the dust of the ground," was the first human. In this regard, it may seem that Paul's arguments about Adam in Romans 5 and 1 Corinthians 15 are decisive: "After all, what purpose does the actual obedience of the second Adam (Christ) have if there was no first Adam who disobeyed? So, as the argument often goes, if there was no first Adam, then there was no fall. If there was no fall, there is no truly inescapably sinful condition and so no need for a Savior."[47] It seems, then, that the Adam created from the dust of the ground must be a historical figure, as Paul thinks him to be, and so Christians must reject the seemingly compelling scientific evidence to the contrary.

In light of this apparent scientific conflict with Scripture, Enns takes a closer look at Genesis 1–3. As he shows in detail, Genesis 1–3 engages in constructive and creative ways with perennial theological issues that were also taken up in roughly contemporaneous Near Eastern literature such as the *Enuma Elish* and the *Atrahasis Epic*.[48] Summing up the results of a wide body of historical-critical research on Genesis 1–3, Enns rightly states that "Israel's creation stories were not simply accounts of 'how it all began.' They were statements about the continuing presence of the God who acted back then. Israel's creation stories rooted their present experiences in the very origins

47. Ibid., xvi. For the view that the act of Adam and Eve was in fact a liberative one, enabling them to attain to true human consciousness, see Béresniak, *Le mythe du péché originel*. Béresniak identifies Augustine as the (Manichaean) creator of the myth of original sin, and he devotes attention to the harmful development of correlative myths regarding sorcery, witchcraft, and Lilith. For his part, Paul Ricoeur strongly rejects a historical fall that had a distortive effect upon the human race (as opposed to a symbolic meaning); see Ricoeur, *Histoire et vérité*; Ricoeur, "Original Sin." Ricoeur argues that "we *inaugurate* evil. It is through us that evil comes into the world. But we inaugurate evil only on the basis of an evil already there, of which our birth is the impenetrable symbol" ("Original Sin," 286). He adds, "We never have the right to speculate on either the evil that we inaugurate, or on the evil that we find, without reference to the history of salvation. Original sin is only an antitype. But type and antitype are not only parallel ('just as . . . so too'), but there is a movement from one to the other, a 'how much more,' an 'all the more': 'where sin abounded, grace did much more abound' (Rom. 5:20)" (ibid.).

48. Although Enns's particular focus leads him to emphasize the (nonscientific) similarities between Gen. 1–2 and other ancient Near Eastern creation accounts, I expect that he would agree with Bill T. Arnold's point regarding the theology of Gen. 1 that "we have overemphasized the similarities between Genesis 1 and the other ancient cosmogonies without fully appreciating the differences. The text soars above them in such a way as to deny *implicitly* any possibility of the theologies expressed in the Egyptian or Mesopotamian accounts" (Arnold, *Genesis*, 32). Arnold grants that "the Egyptian material offers several interesting parallels with Genesis 1, including the belief in a creator god who made the universe by verbal fiat" and that "the Mesopotamian materials are helpful for understanding the broader worldview" of Gen. 1 (33).

of the cosmos."[49] As Enns observes, biblical scholars have made a very strong case that when read in its historical context, the depiction of Adam (and Eve) in Genesis 2–3 should be seen as a depiction of a "proto-Israel" proceeding from creation by God, to law/commandments and land/garden, to disobedience and exile.[50] Enns adds that, in the story of Cain and Abel, "there are evidently other human beings assumed to exist outside of the garden, people whom Cain fears will retaliate for his murder of Abel and from whom he picks a wife and settles in the 'land of Nod' (Gen. 4:16)."[51] The best explanation for this is not that Adam and Eve had many other children who wished to retaliate against Cain and from whom Cain chose a wife, but rather that in the genre of Genesis 2–3, Adam is proto-Israel, an explanatory backdrop to Israel's own history. Adam is a literary device of a kind commonplace in ancient Near Eastern stories of origins, not an actual historical figure.[52]

In discussing the ways in which Genesis 1 corresponds to the *Enuma Elish* and Genesis 2–3 to the *Atrahasis Epic* (two Babylonian creation myths generally dated to around 1700 BC), Enns directs attention to the fact that the Hebrew word *'ādām*, which appears in both Genesis 1 and Genesis 2–3, refers to humanity as a whole in Genesis 1. He suggests that "the editor might be signaling that the individual man Adam in chapter 2 is a subset of the humanity *'ādām* in chapter 1."[53] Arguing that this fits with the depiction of Adam as proto-Israel, Enns reconstructs the original meaning as follows: "There is *'adam* in the universal sense outside of Eden, but inside Eden, God's garden, there is no *'adam* but one Adam—the one human with

49. Enns, *Evolution of Adam*, 62.

50. Ibid., 67.

51. Ibid., 67–68.

52. For an approach to Gen. 2–3 that differs from the standard view Enns offers but that shares its focus upon historical and (especially) cultural context, see Zevit, *What Really Happened in the Garden of Eden?* Zevit argues that in the late third century BC, 200 years after the book of Nehemiah rehearsed Israel's sins without mentioning Adam and Eve, certain Jewish commentators popularized reading Gen. 2–3 as "the fall," and this view then entered into late Second Temple interpretations such as those of 2 Baruch, 2 Esdras, and Paul. Zevit dates Gen. 2–3 (which he ascribes to the Yahwist source) to the ninth century BC and suggests that it is based upon oral tradition from around 1100 BC. Zevit summarizes his interpretation of Gen. 2–3: "In its own historical time it was not a story about sin—no word for sin, rebellion, disobedience, or the like occurs in it—although it does deal with the circumvention of a divine instruction. It was not a story about death or redemption. It was a story about the origins of humanity and human nature, about proper comportment, dignity, the acquisition of knowledge, and, ultimately, ethical self-awareness" (261). It seems to me that Zevit has neglected the disobedience to God's command and the importance that the problem of death has throughout Gen. 2–3. Zevit adds that "the image of Eden as untroubled and serene is medieval, fashioned from non-Israelite ideas about a place identified as paradise before the Fall" (102).

53. Enns, *Evolution of Adam*, 69.

whom he has a unique relationship, the progenitor of God's chosen people, Israel. The question is whether this Adam will be obedient to God and stay in Eden, or join the other *'adam* outside of the garden, in exile."[54] Since Enns concludes that the early narratives of Genesis have to do with Israel's own self-definition, he rejects as unbiblical the attempt to turn the Adam story into an account of the origin of all human beings. Noah's story in Genesis 9 might seem to complicate Enns's thesis, since it teaches that all people descend from his three sons; accordingly, this would be a universal story, and not merely one focused primarily on Israel. But Enns notes that the genealogies of Genesis 10–11 focus solely on the progenitors of Israel and exhibit "the same pattern of privileging the one among the many that began in the Adam story."[55] Thus the Noah story, too, turns out to be about proto-Israel, privileged among the nations.

Enns grants that Genesis 1 depicts the creation of the whole universe, not only of Israel. But Genesis 1 does so in a manner that shows that the created world is God's temple; and the tabernacle that God commands the Israelites to construct in Exodus is a minicreation, "an instantiation of God's true temple, the heavens and the earth."[56] As Enns explains, "There is no more holy place on earth than the sanctuary and no more holy time than the Sabbath. The sanctuary is the microcosm where Israel participates in Yahweh's cosmic victory."[57] The key point, again, is that we must learn to read Genesis according to its real biblical genre, which is focused upon Israel rather than upon scientific or historical questions of human origins.

Enns also makes a good deal out of the fact that Adam, after Genesis 5:3, barely appears in the Old Testament at all, and certainly not in connection with universal sinfulness. Further, as Enns points out, the curses listed in Genesis 3:14–19 do not include being born into a state of original sin.[58] In my view, however, Enns overlooks the punitive element implied by exile from Eden and thus from the intimacy with God enjoyed by Adam and Eve in Eden. I am not persuaded that "Adam's disobedience is not presented as having any causal

54. Ibid.
55. Ibid.
56. Ibid., 72.
57. Ibid., 73.
58. Bill Arnold argues that "the subsequent concept of 'original sin' articulated by the New Testament and codified in church dogma is altogether reasonable and compatible with this text (e.g., Rom. 5:12–21). But that is not to say that 'the fall' is explicitly taught here, nor any abstract concept of universal sin transmitted to successive generations infecting all humanity" (*Genesis*, 73). Nonetheless, Arnold holds that Gen. 3 "is primarily interested in why the individual human, *by nature of his or her humanity*, is forever afflicted by alienation, guilt, and the inevitability of death, and yet why humans still have this potential for life with God" (ibid.).

link to Cain's."[59] On the contrary, Cain's rebellious envy and violence flow from the disorder introduced by Adam and Eve's rebellion against God, and Cain's rebelliousness represents the fallen condition of humans after Adam and Eve's exile from "the garden of Eden" (Gen. 3:24). Adam and Eve's sin does not cause Cain to sin, since Cain has free will (cf. Gen. 4:6–7), but Cain's sin is nonetheless linked causally to the rebellion and exile experienced by Adam and Eve. Exile from Eden is a state of punishment and of alienation. This state of disordered alienation from God and from neighbor is what the doctrine of original sin aims to describe: not only Israel but in fact all peoples are in this state of exile, which began at the outset of the human race due to a free act of disobedience.[60] It is true that the Old Testament almost never returns to Adam's role, but I do not see why it must do so, since the state of exile/alienation is always clear enough despite the presence of holy people who "walked with God" (Gen. 5:24). Adam and Eve's rebellion paves the way for the situation that follows both in the entire world and in Israel: "The LORD saw that the wickedness of man was great in the earth, and that every imagination of the thoughts of his heart was only evil continually" (Gen. 6:5).

Enns next turns his attention to Paul. When Paul presents Adam as the first man and the ancestor of all humans and as the one whose disobedience caused universal sin and death, Enns finds that "Paul is not doing 'straight exegesis' of the Adam story. Rather, he subordinates that story to the present, higher reality of the risen Son of God, expressing himself within the hermeneutical conventions of the time."[61] Regarding Romans 5:12–21 specifically, Enns argues that Paul is thinking soteriology, not human origins. Furthermore, for Enns, Paul's exegesis should not "settle what Adam means in Genesis itself, and most certainly not the question of human origins as debated in the modern world."[62] Enns also denies that we can appeal to Paul to support a modern version of origins such as a "representative 'head' of humanity," whereby "the act of this 'Adam' has affected the entire human race not because all humans are necessarily descended from him but because God chose to hold all humans

59. Enns, *Evolution of Adam*, 86. Enns makes the same point a bit later: "What does not seem to be of interest in the Old Testament is tying Israel's disobedience—or that of humanity at large—to Adam's one act of disobedience" (87).

60. Paul J. Griffiths, who considers animal suffering and death and the destruction of inanimate things to be the result of the primal angelic fall, argues that Eden "is distinct from the cosmos because it is not the place of the angels, and because it is a paradisial enclave within a cosmos-become-world already devastated by the angelic fall" (*Decreation*, 4). For a contrary perspective, see Haught, "Evolution, Tragedy, and Cosmic Purpose."

61. Enns, *Evolution of Adam*, 81.

62. Ibid., 117.

accountable for this one act."[63] Paul himself, after all, never envisioned such an Adam, so to construct such an Adam is not a valid way of saving Paul's own meaning. Likewise, Kemp's way of presenting the first rational hominids also would not work, again because neither Paul nor Genesis is thinking of such a being: they have in view the "Adam" directly created from the dust by God, and reconstructions such as Kemp's lead us away from this Adam rather than closer to the biblical texts.[64]

In building his case against a historical original sin, Enns also distinguishes between Augustine's account of Genesis 2–3 as a devastating fall, and Irenaeus of Lyons's account of Genesis 2–3 as a pedagogical description of how not to pursue wisdom.[65] According to Irenaeus as interpreted by Enns, God wants us to become like God, but to do so we must become humble to God's instruction rather than grasping childishly and foolishly at what is beyond our powers. We must follow the path of wisdom, a path sketched, for example, in Proverbs 9. In light of Irenaeus's approach, Enns concludes that it is appropriate to read Genesis 2–3 "as a wisdom text—a narrative version

63. Ibid., 120. Enns does not mention Rahner.

64. Enns does not mention Kemp's article, but he is aware of "attempts to preserve an 'Adam' who is not the first human as Paul has it but is the first 'spiritual' hominid (or group of hominids) endowed with a soul and so forth" (123). Enns remarks in this regard that

> it is ironic that in trying to hold on to biblical teaching a scenario is proposed that the Bible does not recognize: gradual evolution over millions of years rather than the sudden and recent creation of humanity as the Bible has it. Now I will say it is *possible* that, tens of thousands of years ago, God took two hominid representatives (or a group of hominids) and with them began the human story where creatures could have a consciousness of God, learn to be moral, and so forth. But that is an alternate and wholly ad hoc account of the first humans, not the biblical one. One cannot pose such a scenario and say, "Here is your Adam and Eve; the Bible and science are thus reconciled." Whatever those creatures were, they were not what the biblical authors presumed to be true. They may have been the first beings somehow conscious of God, but we overstep our bounds if we claim that these creatures satisfy the requirements of being "Adam and Eve." (139)

In my view, certain elements of the Adam and Eve story can be preserved, above all the fact of real human responsibility for alienation and exile, without presenting one's hypothesis as an alternative Scripture. Enns also voices the concern that the rational hominid proposal equates Genesis's "image of God" with rationality or the spiritual soul, whereas in fact Genesis's "image of God" "refers to humanity's role as ruler over creation, as God's earthly representatives" (ibid.). Here I think that Enns makes an opposition where one is not necessary, since rationality is at the root of representative rule.

65. For an erudite summary of Augustine's position on original sin in light of the positions of earlier fathers (East and West), see Couenhoven, "St. Augustine's Doctrine of Original Sin." Couenhoven concludes: "The fundamental point is that [in the patristic era and today] one can believe in primal sin, a doctrine of solidarity with Adam (suitably understood), universal negative consequences of sin, and some sort of theory about how those consequences are transmitted, without being committed to a doctrine of inherited sin, and thus *without* being committed to Augustine's doctrine of original sin" (387). See also Couenhoven, *Stricken by Sin, Cured by Christ.*

of Israel's failure to follow Proverbs' path of wisdom."[66] Enns argues that such a reading of Genesis 2–3 accords with universal sinfulness but does not seek to explain it in terms of Adam and Eve's causality. Rather, Adam and Eve are exemplars of the childish condition that impedes us all. They show us both the consequences of failure to follow the path of wisdom, and the true lineaments of that path. I think, however, that Irenaeus would have been surprised to see his account of original sin dissociated from an actual sin of Adam and Eve, since Irenaeus attaches the just punishment of the whole human race precisely to Adam and Eve's culpable rebellion.[67]

Enns sums up his own view of universal sin by distinguishing between "original sin" and "sin of origin." An "original sin" would require a historical Adam, and would depend at least partly on Augustine's explication. By contrast, to speak of a "sin of origin" means to affirm "the absolute inevitability of sin that affects every human being from *their* beginnings, from birth."[68] To know why sin is inevitable for every human is beyond our powers, but we can know that all humans are sinners, inclined to sin from birth. The concept of "sin of origin" fits much better, in Enns's view, with the Old Testament portrait of human existence, both with regard to the overall fallenness of individual and collective history, and with regard to explicit testimonies to our sinfulness such

66. Enns, *Evolution of Adam*, 91.

67. Robert Sherman considers that "the Eastern Orthodox tradition," which he identifies with Irenaeus, thinks of "original sin as less a matter of willful rebellion and more a kind of youthful indiscretion that nevertheless had very unfortunate consequences" (*Covenant, Community, and the Spirit*, 20). For Irenaeus and Basil, while original sin may have been a "youthful indiscretion," it was also a "willful rebellion" truly deserving of punishment. Summarizing the position of Basil the Great, Dumitru Staniloae observes that "God could not create the human being evil, but he wanted man to strengthen himself in the good through his own cooperation as well" (*Experience of God*, 2:177). God wanted Adam and Eve to grow in freedom by loving God, but instead Adam and Eve took their freedom as an occasion for turning away from God and claiming autonomy, with the result that they enslaved themselves. Yet Basil identifies a positive outcome, since Adam was thereby "led to the knowledge of his own nakedness and hence to the knowledge of shame," and thus to repentance (ibid., 182). For his part, Irenaeus holds that at the outset, Adam was "a young child, not yet having a perfect deliberation" (*On the Apostolic Preaching*, §12, p. 47). Adam disobeyed God's commandment, and in so doing became a sinner. His disobedience came about in significant part because of his immaturity—"he was easily deceived"—and God had placed Adam in Eden because "it was necessary for him [Adam] to reach full-development by growing in this way," though (crucially) it was not necessary for him to sin (ibid.). God justly and sternly punished Adam and Eve for their sin by placing them "far from His face" (ibid., §16, p. 50). See also Irenaeus of Lyons, *Against Heresies*, book 3, chaps. 22–23; book 5, chap. 22. Regarding the interpretation of Gen. 3 offered by Irenaeus's gnostic opponents, Thomas Holsinger-Friesen comments in this regard: "Both Gospel of Truth and the Sethian *Apocryphon of John* assert that human beings accrue the benefit of knowledge of the Father by eating fruit from a tree" (*Irenaeus and Genesis*, 97).

68. Enns, *Evolution of Adam*, 124. He is relying upon George L. Murphy, "Roads to Paradise and Perdition."

as Psalm 51:1–5 and Job 14:1–4. Enns argues that we should be silent about why we are sinners ("original sin"), just "as Scripture is silent."[69]

In my view, however, Scripture is not silent about the "why" question. The depiction of Adam and Eve's sin, and especially the penalty of alienation and exile from Eden (with the corresponding curses), indicates a free origin of the human experience of exile or fallenness, even if Genesis's primary concern is Israel. Scripture begins with humans in a state of harmony with God and each other. This is not a state of harmony pure and simple—the "serpent" does indeed lurk[70]—but it is nonetheless a state of real harmony with God, with each other, and interiorly within themselves. Even if it is about proto-Israel, the Adam story presents the creation of humans (and not solely Israel) in this state of harmony, so that a state of exile was not simply inevitable for humanity/Israel but rather was the free choice of the first humans. At bottom, what is at stake exegetically is not only the situation of Israel but also the goodness of creation and the insistence that the present situation of both Israel and the nations is the fault neither of God nor of human finitude per se but of the first humans who freely turned away from the creator God.

Enns grants, of course, that "even without attributing their cause to Adam, sin and death are with us, and we cannot free ourselves from them."[71] The question then is whether God made us in such a way that to be human is

69. Enns, *Evolution of Adam*, 125.

70. For a sensitive reading of the dialogue between the serpent and the woman, see Levin, "Genesis 2–3," 95–98.

71. Enns, *Evolution of Adam*, 125. He adds: "They remain the foes vanquished by Christ's death and resurrection" (ibid.). As he observes, evolutionary theory holds that "death is not the unnatural state introduced by a disobedient couple in a primordial garden," but rather death "is the means that promotes the continued evolution of life on this planet and even ensures workable population numbers" (147). In his book *How We Die*, Sherwin B. Nuland puts it this way:

> Nature has a job to do. It does its job by the method that seems most suited to each individual whom its powers have created. It has made this one susceptible to heart disease and that one to stroke and yet another to cancer, some after a long time on this earth and some after a time much too brief, at least by our own reckoning. The animal economy has formed the circumstances by which each generation is to be succeeded by the next. Against the relentless forces and cycles of nature there can be no lasting victory. . . . Mankind, for all its unique gifts, is just as much a part of the ecosystem as is any other zoologic or botanical form, and nature does not distinguish. We die so that the world may continue to live. We have been given the miracle of life because trillions upon trillions of living things have prepared the way for us and then have died—in a sense, for us. We die, in turn, so that others may live. The tragedy of a single individual becomes, in the balance of natural things, the triumph of ongoing life. (262)

When viewed in terms of the ongoing unfolding of material creation, human death is natural and positive; but human death in its concrete individual (and communal) form, experienced as radical exile and loss of communion, is a punishment. See also Randall S. Rosenberg, "Being-toward-a-Death-Transformed."

inevitably to fall into sin and death. Did God create the human race in such a way that it was already broken? Enns's position requires, logically speaking, that it be so. The point of the doctrine of "original sin" is that it was not so. Behind Paul's assumptions about a historical Adam stands his concern to emphasize that alienation and exile were not part of the original creation of humanity, but instead came about through freely chosen sin, which disordered the original harmony once and for all. As Paul puts it in emphasizing the "reconciliation" that Jesus Christ brings "by his blood" (Rom. 5:9–11), "Sin came into the world through one man and death through sin" (Rom. 5:12). Reconciliation is needed because of an original disordering caused freely by the first humans. If instead sin and alienation were conceived as intrinsic to the human condition, there might need to be a healing, but one could hardly speak of a need for reconciliation, since the creator God would be responsible for humans' original disharmony. The "why" issue is crucial to Paul, and it must retain a central place today.

I agree with Enns that Genesis 2–3, Romans 5, and 1 Corinthians 15 were not intended to solve the historical and scientific problems that we now know about. But the Genesis narrative, while aiming fundamentally to render an account of proto-Israel, also instructs the reader about the origins of sin and human death. Specifically, Genesis 2–3 shows (just as Paul says, and as Genesis 1 helps to clarify) that these origins cannot be traced to God's creative activity, which instead reflects the goodness of God and the original goodness and harmony of God's creation. Indeed, as in the case of Israel's history, sin and death entered into universal human history not because of something intrinsic to how God made humans, but because of a free choice at the very outset of the human race. In this sense, Paul was right to read a historical Adam into Genesis 2–3, even though the Genesis text itself has other purposes. It follows that notwithstanding Enns's otherwise salutary cautions about interpreting the biblical text according to its own parameters, hypotheses such as those regarding the "representative man" (Rahner) or the two first rational hominids who interbred with nonrational hominids (Kemp) are helpful precisely for understanding the testimony of Scripture, even if Genesis and Paul were not addressing our contemporary scientific challenges and did not have these hypotheses in view.

Jonathan Edwards and Thomas Aquinas on Original Sin

Despite the differences between their solutions, Rahner, Kemp, and Enns all write from the conviction that the traditional Christian understanding of the doctrine of original sin needs adjustment in light of contemporary science and historical-critical exegesis. While agreeing that the traditional interpretation of Genesis 2–3 needs adjustment, I argue in this section of the chapter that central theological elements of the Augustinian interpretation of original sin remain necessary for Christian faith. These elements include the following three: human nature, which is a unity, was created entirely good rather than marked by sinful tendencies; the first sin was entirely free; and this first sin has a corruptive impact on all humans and brings about human death as we now experience it. Genesis 2–3's testimony to the sin of Adam and Eve should be interpreted in a manner that preserves these three elements, while also attending to the concerns and insights that we found in Rahner, Kemp, and Enns (and that are widely shared by other scholars as well). In this section, therefore, I set forth what I consider to be the enduring elements of the broadly Augustinian tradition, as represented by Jonathan Edwards and Thomas Aquinas.

Jonathan Edwards: Death as Punishment, and the Freedom of the Original Sin

In his *The Great Christian Doctrine of Original Sin Defended*, the last work that he wrote before his death (published posthumously), Jonathan Edwards strives to answer the objections to the doctrine of original sin contained in John Taylor's *The Scripture-Doctrine of Original Sin Proposed to a Free and Candid Examination* and *Key to the Apostolic Writings*, published with *A Paraphrase and Notes on the Epistle to the Romans*.[72] I will begin

---

72. It is worth noting that John Wesley, too, also responded in 1757 to Taylor's book; see Wesley, *Doctrine of Original Sin*. For the similarity of Edwards's and Wesley's responses, see Andrew C. Russell, "Polemical Solidarity." Admittedly, after reading an earlier work of Edwards's, Wesley complained that it relied too much upon philosophy, a criticism that Wesley would no doubt have equally lodged against Edwards's response to Taylor. See also Thomas H. McCall's excellent survey, "But a Heathen Still." McCall shows that "Wesley and the early Methodist theologians . . . generally held to a federalist account of original sin" (165; cf. 148–51 for Wesley's response to Taylor). For a succinct introduction to Edwards, *Great Christian Doctrine of Original Sin Defended* (and to critical reception of this work), see McClymond and McDermott, *Theology of Jonathan Edwards*, 346–56. For further background to Taylor, whose theology became especially influential in the unitarian movement, see Eddy, *Dr Taylor of Norwich*; Sell, *Philosophy, Dissent and Nonconformity*. See also Mark A. Noll's references to Taylor in *America's God*, 140, 273. Clyde A. Holbrook, himself rather dubious of the doctrine of original sin except insofar as it expresses the "enigmatic surd" at the heart of human morality, argues that Edwards "unwittingly anticipated twentieth-century criticisms of the doctrine which were virtual copies of Taylor's contentions"; in particular he names the criticisms of original sin advanced by H. D. Lewis and Albert C. Knudsen. See Holbrook, "Jonathan Edwards Addresses Some 'Modern Critics' of Original Sin," 212, 230. See also Quinn, "Disputing the Augustinian Legacy."

with Edwards's discussion of death, even though Edwards himself does not take up this point until his second chapter. For Edwards, death is a punishment, whereas for Taylor, death is a benefit that God gave the human race after Adam's sin. In Taylor's view, death benefits humanity after Adam's sin by helping us to avoid turning life on earth into our sole desire. As Edwards summarizes Taylor's view, suffering and death "increase the vanity of all earthly things, and tend to excite sober reflections, and to induce us to be moderate in gratifying the appetites of the body, and to mortify pride and ambition."[73] In our current state, Taylor thinks, death constitutes not a punishment but a real gift, without which we would be far worse off with respect to our relationship with God.

Edwards grants that there is indeed an angle from which one can look at death as a gift. Our mortality and our sufferings dampen our pride and restrain our disordered desires. Yet, as Edwards points out, Taylor's position that death is a gift cannot account for the death of young children, who can hardly be expected to use the thought of death to mortify their disordered desires and pride. According to Edwards, Taylor suggests that perhaps God intends the death of children to be a gift to the parents, by serving to dampen the parents' disordered desires and pride. Edwards answers forcefully: "But hath God any need of such methods to add to parents' afflictions? Are there not other ways for increasing their trouble, without destroying the lives of such multitudes of those who are perfectly innocent, and who, on the supposition [of Taylor], have in no respect any sin belonging to them?"[74] Even if there are ways of construing death to be a blessing for adults who have lived a relatively full life, the death of children reveals death to be a punishment.

But could it not be that the death of children is simply a result of human finitude and mortality, as with the death of all other animals? Has not God simply inscribed death within the universal condition of humans, due to our materiality rather than to an original sin? Edwards grants that "God has a sovereign right to set bounds to the lives of his own creatures, be they sinful or not," since life is a pure gift that God can take away without fault.[75] But Edwards pushes the point further, and shows that it is a mistake to describe death as simply the taking away of life. The question is "how far God has a right to bring extreme suffering and calamity on an innocent moral agent."[76] Death involves more than the peaceful removal of life; it is generally experienced

73. Jonathan Edwards, *Great Christian Doctrine of Original Sin Defended*, 174.
74. Ibid.
75. Ibid., 173.
76. Ibid.

as a devastating, horrific event. The death that humans experience is hardly coterminous with animal death. Edwards remarks that for humans, "capable of conceiving of immortality, made with an earnest desire after it, capable of foresight and reflection on approaching death, and having an extreme dread of it," death must be conceived in the most severe terms.[77] For those who insist solely upon God's sovereign power to give and take life, it may be possible to imagine that God could bring "so great a calamity on mankind when perfectly innocent."[78] But Scripture testifies that God, in his goodness, has not in fact done so.

According to Scripture, death, as we experience it, is a calamity that is properly describable only as a punishment for sin. Edwards points out that "Scripture every where speaks of all great afflictions and calamities, which God in his providence brings on mankind, as testimonies of his displeasure for sin, in the subjects of those calamities; excepting those sufferings which are to atone for the sins of others."[79] He draws attention to the numerous texts in Scripture where "calamities consisting or issuing in death" are attributed to God's punitive "wrath."[80] He observes, too, that Scripture repeatedly identifies death not only as a punishment, but as the most fearsome one. He cites a variety of biblical passages, such as 1 Samuel 5:11, Isaiah 17:11, Matthew 26:38, and Psalm 17:9, in which reference to death is employed to indicate a state of maximum threat to the human person. As he notes, Jesus's suffering for our sins constitutes the maximum suffering because he "became obedient unto death, even death on a cross" (Phil. 2:8). When God wishes to punish people for particularly wicked crimes, he inflicts the punishment of death: here Edwards instances the destruction produced by the flood, the obliteration of Sodom and Gomorrah, the death of Onan, the killing of the firstborn of Egypt, the killing of Nadab and Abihu, the swallowing up of the rebels led by Korah, the destruction of the Canaanites, the deaths of Ananias and Sapphira, and the destruction of Jerusalem in AD 70. In each of these cases, death appears explicitly as a punishment for sin. This connection between sin and death (as the punishment for sin) appears also in numerous warnings given by God with regard to ritual profanation.

Edwards provides a lengthy quotation from Psalm 90, which merits attention here for its complex analysis of God's role in human death. This psalm begins by observing that God, in some real sense, wills the death of humans: "Thou [God] turnest man back to the dust, and sayest, 'Turn back, O children

77. Ibid.
78. Ibid.
79. Ibid.
80. Ibid.

of men!' For a thousand years in thy sight are but as yesterday when it is past, or as a watch in the night. Thou dost sweep men away; they are like a dream, like grass which is renewed in the morning: in the morning it flourishes and is renewed; in the evening it fades and withers" (Ps. 90:3–6). These verses could be taken to signify that God inscribed human death into the order of creation, since human death is compared to the withering of grass, a natural material phenomenon. The natural rhythm of the life cycle of grass, however, is not the psalm's last word about human death. On the contrary, the very next verse of the psalm draws an explicit connection between human death and divine punishment. The psalmist proclaims, "For we are consumed by thy anger; by thy wrath we are overwhelmed. Thou hast set our iniquities before thee, our secret sins in the light of thy countenance" (Ps. 90:7–8). The next two verses of the psalm underscore human death's status as God's punishment for human sin. The psalmist specifies that "all our days pass away under thy wrath" (Ps. 90:9). We know that we are under God's wrath precisely because our lives are so short. As the psalmist says, "Our years come to an end like a sigh" (Ps. 90:9). Even the longest lives are radically short, since the years go by so quickly and, after much suffering, end in death. The psalmist goes on to muse upon "the power of thy anger" (Ps. 90:11) and to advise humans to fear God. Edwards rightly comments on this psalm, "How plain and full is this testimony, that the general mortality of mankind is an evidence of God's anger for the sin of those who are the subjects of such a dispensation!"[81]

Not only does Scripture show repeatedly and explicitly that human death is the punishment of sin, but also Edwards finds passages that indicate that God would not inflict death upon the innocent—and thus death must be a punishment for sin. In this vein he quotes Abimelech's question, "Lord, wilt thou slay an innocent people" (Gen. 20:4)? Abimelech asked this question when "God came to Abimelech in a dream by night, and said to him, 'Behold, you are a dead man, because of the woman [Sarah] whom you have taken; for she is a man's wife'" (Gen. 20:3). God threatened deadly punishment for sin, and Abimelech replied that he was innocent. For Edwards's purposes, the key point is that Abimelech's innocence did indeed ward off God's deadly punishment. On this basis, Edwards reasons that God would not subject to death all humans—"consisting of so many nations, repeating the great slaughter in every generation"—unless all humans, including children, were in fact guilty.[82] If God spared Abimelech from the punishment of death because of Abimelech's innocence, so also God would spare all of us if we were truly innocent.

81. Ibid.
82. Ibid., 173–74.

Taylor proposes, however, that we should distinguish punishment, which is negative, from chastisement, which is positive. In Taylor's view, suffering and death serve as chastisements that God intends for our spiritual good, rather than as punishments. Edwards challenges the applicability and value of this distinction. Consider, Edwards says, "such severe chastisements, as to break the child's bones, when at the same time the father does not suppose any guilt, fault, or offence, in any respect, belonging to the child."[83] Even if such chastisements were (supposedly) for the child's spiritual good, they would clearly be unwarranted. A severe chastisement requires, in justice, an equally severe cause. As Edwards points out, the chastisements that Scripture identifies as good are so because they punish the sin of the people being chastised (i.e., because they are *punishments*). He cites examples of this from both the New Testament and the Old. One such example is 1 Corinthians 11:32, where Paul teaches that "when we are judged by the Lord, we are chastened so that we may not be condemned along with the world." Paul here is speaking of being "judged" and "chastened" for our sins, and the sin that he specifically has in view is that of partaking in the Eucharist "in an unworthy manner" (1 Cor. 11:27). God does not chastise us simply for our spiritual benefit, but expressly because we are sinfully disordered.

Edwards adds that to receive God's chastisements is one thing; to endure death is another. The far greater punishment for sin is death. The distinction between chastisements and the greatest punishment, death, appears in Psalm 118:17–18: "I shall not die, but I shall live, and recount the deeds of the Lord. The Lord has chastened me sorely, but he has not given me over to death." As Edwards remarks, "God's people often pray, when under great affliction, that God would not proceed to this [i.e., to death], as to the greatest extremity."[84] Furthermore, as we have already noted, when Edwards thinks of death as a punishment, he often has in view the death of children. He is adamant, on biblical and logical grounds, that their death makes no sense except as a punishment for sin (original sin). If they merited no punishment, then surely God could not permit them to die "with such dreadful circumstances, and extreme pains."[85] Edwards quotes Taylor's attempt to justify the terrible deaths of utterly innocent children: according to Taylor, "The Lord of all being can never want time, and place, and power, to compensate abundantly any sufferings infants now undergo in subserviency to his good providence."[86] Such reasoning is fallacious, because it assumes that God could

83. Ibid., 174.
84. Ibid., 175.
85. Ibid.
86. Ibid.

"compensate" infants for the extraordinarily unjust sufferings that he permits them to endure during their lives. What kind of God, however, would permit an utterly innocent infant to be burned in an oven as an offering to Moloch, with the intention to make it up to the infant later?

Edwards argues that Taylor, as a matter of logic, "might as well go further still, and say, that God may cast guiltless persons into hell fire, to remain there in the most unutterable torments for ages of ages (which bear no greater proportion to eternity than a quarter of an hour)," simply "because he can never want time, place, and power, abundantly to compensate their sufferings afterwards."[87] The point is that if death is not a punishment for sin, then the horrible deaths of innocent infants that God permits would be indicative of a cruel, unjust God. Edwards mentions here the deaths of the infants who lived in Sodom, and the deaths of the infants of the Egyptians, Canaanites, and Amalekites, as well as the infants who perished when Jerusalem was conquered first by the Babylonians, and then finally by the Romans as prophesied by Jesus. In Deuteronomy 28, Moses even foretells that if Israel abandons God, God will permit the covenantal curses to come upon the people, to such a degree that the exigencies of a siege will cause the people to "eat the offspring of [their] own body, the flesh of [their] sons and daughters, whom the LORD your God has given [them]" (Deut. 28:53). Such death is obviously the punishment of sin, but not personal sin, because infants are too young to sin for themselves. Edwards's point is twofold: Scripture repeatedly and explicitly presents human death—inclusive of the death of infants—as a punishment for sin (personal and/or original), and this is fortunate because otherwise the death of infants would be utterly unintelligible and would reveal an unjust and uncaring God.[88]

Edwards considers that the death that constitutes the punishment of sin is both bodily and spiritual. He notes that the reward promised for righteousness

---

87. Ibid. For Edwards on God's inviolable justice (in relation to the damnation of sinners), see Crisp, *Jonathan Edwards and the Metaphysics of Sin*. Crisp notes that for Edwards, "divine justice is displayed in the damnation of the wicked, by the ordination and causation of the existence and persistence of the wicked through time. God is not morally responsible for the sins that they voluntarily choose, but he is the necessary and sufficient cause of their existence and persistence, through his direct action in creation and conservation" (69). Crisp identifies a problem here, especially given Edwards's occasionalist metaphysics: Edwards "is left with the claim that God's permission (but not his positive agency) in sin is a necessary but not causally sufficient condition of sin, which is exactly what he denies with respect to praise and blame" (ibid.). If God is the cause of all actions—and not only the ultimate cause but the proximate cause, as occasionalist metaphysics requires—it would seem that God is culpable for the sins that we commit.

88. For Edwards's paramount concern to defend God's justice in his treatise on original sin, see Jenson, *America's Theologian*, 148; John E. Smith, *Jonathan Edwards*, 92.

is "life," understood as comprising all the goods of life, bodily and spiritu-al.[89] The punishment for unrighteousness, then, is death in its fullest sense: "the death of the body and the death of the soul, and the eternal, sensible, perfect destruction and misery of both."[90] Edwards develops this position largely on the basis of Romans 6:23, "For the wages of sin is death, but the free gift of God is eternal life in Christ Jesus our Lord." The "wages of sin," he explains, is the fullness of death, the opposite of eternal life. Taylor argues that sin's "wages" consist solely in temporal death, which (as noted above) Taylor considers to be a favor insofar as it curtails our pride and directs our attention to eternal goods. For Edwards, the wages of sin necessarily include not only temporal death but also spiritual death—namely, the soul's loss of "innocence and original righteousness, and the favour of God"—that will be everlasting *unless* God intervenes with grace.[91]

The second aspect of Edwards's position on original sin that I wish to highlight here is his insistence upon human freedom in the original decision to turn away from God. He notes that the question is whether "sinful ac-tion infers a nature originally corrupt."[92] When the first humans sinned, did they do so because their human nature was already corrupt, already sinful? According to Taylor, as quoted by Edwards, the doctrine of "original sin" creates a severe quandary: How could Adam, lacking original sin and its consequences, have possessed "appetites and passions" that "were so irregular and strong, that he did not resist them"?[93] It can easily be understood how people who bear the burden of original sin fail to resist their unruly passions. But in Adam's case, it would seem that he could have easily resisted. Taylor solves the quandary by suggesting simply that Adam and all other humans are in exactly the same position. We all freely sin; sin is universal. We do not have any disadvantage vis-à-vis Adam, because he sinned just like we do. On

89. See Edwards, *Great Christian Doctrine of Original Sin Defended*, 200.

90. Ibid. See also Edwards's less successful exegesis of Old Testament texts on the question of whether the covenant curses entailed "eternal death" or damnation (181–82).

91. See ibid.,186.

92. Ibid., 168.

93. Ibid. For further discussion, see Crisp, *Jonathan Edwards and the Metaphysics of Sin*, 33–37. Crisp raises the concern that Adam's possession of the dispositional property of self-deception before the fall means that Adam may well have been corrupt even prior to the fall. McClymond and McDermott argue that "Thomas Schafer may have been right more than a half-century ago when he concluded that 'Edwards's doctrine of the will, required alike by his theology and his metaphysics, breaks on the impossible task of accounting for both original righteousness and the fall.' At the heart of Edwards's view of the will is the conviction that all action springs from the affections, but his depiction of Adam's action in Eden is inconsistent with this" (*Theology of Jonathan Edwards*, 355; citing Schafer, "Concept of Being in the Thought of Jonathan Edwards").

this view, "original sin" is the wrong answer to the question of why humans sin. All humans, like Adam, sin because they choose to sin. None, including Adam, are burdened by an "original sin." In other words, "original sin" fails to do any explanatory work with respect to our sinfulness. Adam, who did not possess "original sin," nonetheless sinned; and in Taylor's view the same is the case with us.

Edwards answers by differentiating between free will that is not habituated toward sin and free will that does possess such a habituation as a "permanent cause" or a "fixed disposition of mind."[94] Adam's sin produced an "internal fixed propensity," a "fixed inclination," a "settled habit or propensity" toward sin.[95] Adam's sin thereby provides an answer to the question of "how it comes to pass that mankind so universally agree in this evil exercise of their free will."[96] The universal sinfulness of humankind requires some kind of explanation. For Taylor, the explanation is that each and every human chooses to sin. For Edwards, universal sinfulness cannot be explained in this way, because he reasons that at least some humans would choose the good if we were all like Adam in his original state (i.e., lacking original sin). Edwards observes, "A steady effect requires a steady cause; but free will, without any previous propensity to influence its determinations, is no *permanent* cause."[97] What Adam's sin does is to produce this propensity to sin in all humans; this propensity is what Edwards means by an inherited or imputed condition of "original sin."[98] Edwards insists that Adam did not originally have this propensity: Adam was truly free.

94. Edwards, *Great Christian Doctrine of Original Sin Defended*, 168–69. For Edwards on dispositions, see Prud'homme and Schelberg, "Disposition, Potentiality, and Beauty in the Theology of Jonathan Edwards," 34: "These continuing structures or dispositions are logically interrelated, coherent rules prescribing action, which dwell within objects. A disposition is an abiding principle, law-like and logical, that influences the occurrence and character of actual events." See also Lee, *Philosophical Theology of Jonathan Edwards*, 63, 173, and elsewhere; Lee, "God's Relation to the World," 59–60.

95. Edwards, *Great Christian Doctrine of Original Sin Defended*, 169.

96. Ibid.

97. Ibid.

98. For discussion of imputation, see especially Crisp, "Jonathan Edwards on the Imputation of Sin"; Crisp, *Jonathan Edwards and the Metaphysics of Sin*. Crisp notes that for Edwards, "Adam and his posterity are one metaphysical unity in the mind of God," and so God "can 'impute' Adam's sin and guilt to the whole of humanity. They form one corporate spacetime entity, such that Adam's guilt is transmitted to his posterity immediately, though consequent to the imputation of his sin" (*Jonathan Edwards and the Metaphysics of Sin*, 121). Cf. Crisp's conclusion in "Jonathan Edwards on the Imputation of Sin" that Edwards combines Augustinian, federalist, and occasionalist elements to produce "a theory of imputation in which Adam and his posterity are united together by God for the purposes of imputation" (68). I find Crisp's account more persuasive than that of Prud'homme and Schelberg, who argue that Edwards holds that we inherit the condition of original sin "because we possess some 'literal oneness' with Adam as

Thomas Aquinas: Original Justice, Original Sin, and the Power of Redemption

In three areas especially, Aquinas's theology of original sin adds something to what we have explored in Edwards: the relationship of original sin to the grace of original justice, human unity in Adam vis-à-vis the transmission of original sin and its culpability, and why we still suffer and die even after Christ has won the victory over sin. Admittedly, there is pertinent material in Edwards's *The Great Christian Doctrine of Original Sin Defended* (such as his account of Adam as "federal head" of the human race) that I have skipped over both for reasons of space and on the grounds that Aquinas's treatment is particularly helpful. I will limit myself here largely to setting forth the main lines of Aquinas's discussion of original sin in *Summa theologiae* I-II, question 81, to which I will add background regarding original justice.[99]

In the first article of question 81, Aquinas argues that "the first sin of the first man is transmitted to his descendants, by way of origin."[100] In favor of this view, he cites Romans 5:12, "Sin came into the world through one man

individuals, as conscious, voluntary co-participants in Adam's transgression" (Prud'homme and Schelberg, "Disposition, Potentiality, and Beauty in the Theology of Jonathan Edwards," 32). Prud'homme and Schelberg helpfully summarize traditional models of imputation and Adamic federalism: see 29. Prud'homme and Schelberg are right to emphasize that Edwards considers Adam's sin to belong properly, rather than merely extrinsically, to the whole human race. See also Randall E. Otto's defense of imputation and Adamic federalism, "Solidarity of Mankind in Jonathan Edwards' Doctrine of Original Sin"; and the contrasting views represented by Benjamin Warfield's *Studies in Theology*, chap. 18, and Charles Hodge's *Systematic Theology*, 2:205–8 and 2:216–21.

99. For Aquinas's treatment of original sin in his *Commentary on the Sentences* (specifically on book 2, distinctions 30–33, Aquinas's lengthiest discussion of original sin), see Mark Johnson, "Augustine and Aquinas on Original Sin," 152–54; for his treatment of original sin in his *Summa contra gentiles*, see Sean A. Otto, "Felix Culpa." See also Kors, *La justice primitive et le péché originel d'après S. Thomas*; Labourdette, *Le péché originel et les origines de l'homme*; Labourdette, "Le péché originel."

100. *Summa theologiae* (hereafter *ST*) I-II, q. 81, a. 1. Mark Johnson draws attention to the fact that Augustine, while featured prominently in the discussions of original sin presented by other medieval theologians (Johnson cites an array of figures, beginning with Peter Lombard) and in Aquinas's theology as a rule, is "almost non-existent" in *ST* I-II, q. 81, a. 1 ("Augustine and Aquinas on Original Sin," 147). For discussion of Augustine's theology of original sin, see Mann, "Augustine on Evil and Original Sin"; J. Patout Burns, *Development of Augustine's Doctrine of Operative Grace*, 96–109; De Simone, "Modern Research on the Sources of Saint Augustine's Doctrine of Original Sin." De Simone's essay is an erudite response to Beatrice, *Tradux peccati*, which De Simone criticizes for (among other things) rejecting the rootedness of the doctrine of original sin in Rom. 5:12–21. Citing numerous texts from the Greek fathers, De Simone also argues, *pace* Beatrice, that the Greek fathers likewise "maintained: a) all men were involved in Adam's rebellious act; b) the Fall affected our moral nature; c) the sin was transmitted" ("Modern Research on the Sources of Saint Augustine's Doctrine of Original Sin," 210).

and death through sin," and Wisdom of Solomon 2:24, "Through the devil's envy death entered the world."[101] The central question that Aquinas grapples with here consists in how this "first sin" is passed down from generation to generation. Why should a sin committed by a father ("Adam") affect his son, let alone all who descend from him? Aquinas points out that it would appear that just such a transmission, based on origin, is ruled out by God in Ezekiel 18:20: "The soul that sins shall die. The son shall not suffer for the iniquity of the father."[102] This biblical text seems to require that Adam's sons (Cain, Abel, Seth) not suffer for their father's sin.

In response, Aquinas explores how theologians have addressed the problem of the transmission of original sin. He focuses upon two ways in particular: the notion that the rational soul is transmitted in procreation (so that a corrupted soul in the father produces a corrupted soul in the child), and the notion that in procreation "a culpable defect of the soul" can be passed on to the child because "the soul's defects redound into the body, and vice versa."[103] Does either of these ways of explaining the transmission of original sin work? Aquinas thinks not. He recognizes, of course, that "some bodily defects are transmitted by way of origin from parent to child," and he also grants that "some defects of the soul are transmitted in consequence, on account of a defect in the bodily habit"—mental disability being one example.[104] But Aquinas points out that even if one supposed (as he himself does not) that the rational soul or defects of the soul are transmitted in procreation, nonetheless "from the very fact that the stain on the child's soul is not in its will, it would cease to be a guilty stain binding its subject to punishment [*rationem culpae*

101. See *ST* I-II, q. 81, a. 1, *sed contra*. For discussion of Aquinas's view of death, see te Velde, "Evil, Sin, and Death," 160–63. As te Velde observes, for Aquinas, the gift of "original justice" "was intended to enable man to realize himself according to the finality of his spiritual nature within the context of his bodily and earthly existence" (162). Since God is good, God did not allow the corruptibility of the human body to undermine the ability of the first humans to attain the enduring spiritual communion for which they were made. By sinning, however, the first humans lost this gift. Thus for Aquinas "death is both 'natural' and 'penal': natural, because of the condition of the matter, and penal (*poenalis*), because death entered into the life of man as a consequence of the guilty loss of the favor preserving man from death" (ibid.).

102. *ST* I-II, q. 81, a. 1, obj. 1. Michael C. Rea puts the problem in philosophical terms: "If one is guilty, then there must be something—presumably, the obtaining of some state of affairs—*for which* one is guilty. But, one might think, whatever states of affairs obtained at or before the time we were born were not states of affairs whose obtaining we had the power to prevent. . . . It would seem to follow that we can be guilty only for things that happen *after* we are born" ("Metaphysics of Original Sin," 320).

103. *ST* I-II, q. 81, a. 1. The second of these approaches, as Mark Johnson shows in "Augustine and Aquinas on Original Sin," is what Aquinas understood Augustine to hold, and also is what Aquinas himself taught in his *Commentary on the Sentences*.

104. *ST* I-II, q. 81, a. 1.

obligantis ad poenam]."[105] Both these two ways, then, are lacking. It seems to follow that the transmission of original sin—which must indeed be "a guilty stain" in the soul, or fault marked by voluntary choice—is impossible.

To understand how Aquinas resolves this problem, we need first to appreciate original sin's relationship to original justice. Aquinas explains that original justice—the "rectitude of the primitive state"—was a gift of grace whereby God upheld Adam and Eve's reason in subjection to God, their passions in subjection to their reason, and their body in subjection to their soul.[106] The loss of the grace of original justice "dissolved the obedience of the flesh to the soul," thereby deeply wounding human nature.[107] Aquinas defines original sin in us, therefore, as "an inordinate disposition, arising from the destruction of the harmony which was essential to original justice," and he compares original sin to a bodily disease that destroys the "equilibrium which is essential to health."[108] Although we cannot know what it was like to be in full harmony, we know that we are disordered and that, in an intergenerational and social cycle of sin, we act freely (despite our own better knowledge) against God, our neighbor, and our own good. The grace of original justice preserved human nature from such disorder, but the rebellion of the first humans dissolved this preservative justice. As Aquinas puts it, "The sin of our first parent is the cause of death and all such like defects in human nature, in so far as by the sin of our first parent original justice was taken away, whereby not only were the lower powers of the soul held together under the control of reason . . . but also the whole body was held together in subjection to the soul."[109]

---

105. Ibid. For discussion, see Mark Johnson, "Augustine and Aquinas on Original Sin," 155–56.

106. *ST* I, q. 95, a. 1. On "original justice," see also te Velde, "Evil, Sin, and Death," 157–59, 162–63.

107. *ST* I, q. 95, a. 1, and I-II, q. 85, a. 3; cf. *ST* I-II, q. 85, a. 5. Note that God's punishment for original sin is not a harsh punishment, in the sense that God himself does not wound or corrupt our nature in response to Adam and Eve's sin.

108. *ST* I-II, q. 82, a. 1. As Liam Walsh points out, for Aquinas "original sin is *formally* the deprivation of the grace of original justice and *materially* it is the disharmony of our human make-up. . . . Thomas prefers to employ the idea of consequence (*effectus*) rather than punishment to express the relationship between the afflictions that human nature is subject to and original sin" ("Thomas Aquinas, the Doctrine of Original Sin, and the Dogma of the Immaculate Conception," 116).

109. *ST* I-II, q. 85, a. 5. Michael C. Rea explains that Aquinas, indebted to Anselm, "characterizes original justice not as a sort of God-given *rectitude of will* possessed by our first ancestors, but rather as a supernatural gift that made it possible for Adam and Eve to appropriately order the various inclinations that (in us) give rise to sin. Insofar as they were, in Eden, capable of ordering their inclinations appropriately, Adam and Eve were able to refrain from sinning. The corruption brought about by the Fall was the disordering of our inclinations as a result of the withdrawal of the supernatural gift" ("Metaphysics of Original Sin," 324). As Rea points out, "This sort of view, according to which original sin consists in the *loss of*

When humans are born in this state of wounded human nature, inclined to sin and subject to death, they are born into a state of punishment for Adam and Eve's sin.[110] But since only Adam and Eve committed their sin, and we did not designate them to rebel on our behalf, how can this situation be just? In reply, Aquinas first observes that "all men born of Adam may be considered as one man, inasmuch as they have one common nature, which they receive from their first parents."[111] Since all of us humans (so Aquinas assumes) receive our nature from Adam, all humans are "members of one body."[112] Aquinas then notes that as the generative source of all other humans, Adam is "the first mover of the members," "man's first moving principle."[113] Therefore, Adam's volition stands for that of the members in a manner analogous to how the soul's volition stands for the members of a human body (e.g., the hand).

With regard to the justice of our reception of Adam's punishment, therefore, Aquinas holds that "the disorder which is in this man born of Adam,

---

a supernatural gift rather than the acquisition of a new kind of corruption in our nature is sometimes characterized, by way of contrast with the Augustinian view, as one according to which human nature is wounded rather than totally corrupted" (ibid.). See also Anselm, *On the Virgin Conception and Original Sin*, 357–89.

110. Note that Aquinas assigns those who possess original sin but who lack "actual" sins to limbo rather than to the hell of damnation; see Beiting, "Idea of Limbo in Thomas Aquinas." Adam's sin merited the hell of damnation for himself (had he not been redeemed by the grace of the Holy Spirit); whereas Adam's sin as we share in it merits alienation from beatific communion with God and neighbor but does not merit eternal damnation, although our condition of original sin leads us, if not healed by the grace of the Holy Spirit, into "actual" sins that do indeed merit eternal damnation. This distinction between what Adam's sin merited in him and what Adam's sin merits in us is, I suspect, similar to the intention of Reformed theologians who advocate "mediate" imputation, which is explained by Oliver Crisp: "Those who defend a mediate view of imputation believe that the whole nature of original sin consists in that corruption which is hereditary to all humanity because of the fall, and that alone. It denies the actual imputation of Adam's sin to all men" ("Jonathan Edwards on the Imputation of Sin," 61).

111. *ST* I-II, q. 81, a. 1. In his "Metaphysics of Original Sin," Michael Rea argues that Aquinas's view of the unity of all humans in Adam is broadly similar to Edwards's, although Edwards relies upon occasionalist metaphysics (and thus divine decree) in constituting the unity. I think that Aquinas's account of our unity in Adam is much more minimal than Edwards's, since Aquinas generally focuses upon Adam as our "first mover." See also Holbrook, "Jonathan Edwards on Self-Identity and Original Sin," 56–60.

112. *ST* I-II, q. 81, a. 1.

113. Ibid. For discussion, see te Velde, "Evil, Sin, and Death," 156, 159, 163. As Liam Walsh comments, "The body cannot be, in itself, the subject of sin, but only of the effects and manifestation of sin. But it can be the instrument of the transmission of a sin inherent in human nature. . . . Thomas will affirm again and again that it is the soul, not the flesh that is the seat (*subiectum*) of original sin. The flesh can be punished for sin, but it carries no guilt. Guilt resides only in the soul" ("Thomas Aquinas, the Doctrine of Original Sin, and the Dogma of the Immaculate Conception," 117, 119). Walsh rightly notes that "in his treatment of original sin Thomas decisively eliminates any suggestion that it is human sexual disorder that transmits original sin" (118).

is voluntary, not by his will, but by the will of his first parent," just as "the action of one member of the body, of the hand for instance, is voluntary not by the will of that hand, but by the will of the soul, the first mover of the members."[114] The sin is Adam's, but we share justly in the disgrace because our nature is cut off neither from Adam's nature nor from his volition (since he is our "first mover"). To clarify the sense in which we are one with our "first mover"—an important clarification given the obvious limitations of the soul/hand analogy—Aquinas gives the further analogy of a man who from birth is "under a family disgrace, on account of a crime committed by one of his forebears."[115] Although Adam was the one who rebelled and lost original justice, the whole human family is quite justly in a state of disgrace due to the action of its "first mover," Adam. Aquinas thereby distinguishes between original sin (and its level of culpability) in Adam and in us, without separating us from Adam: "Original sin is not the sin of this person, except inasmuch as this person receives his nature from his first parent, for which reason it is called the *sin of nature*."[116]

One might ask, however, whether Adam's further sins, or the sins of others from whom we receive human nature, add to the disgraced woundedness of human nature. In the first article of question 81 Aquinas quoted Ezekiel 18:20 against the notion of inherited sin; now in the second article (objection 1) he quotes Exodus 20:5 in favor of the notion of inherited sin: "I the LORD your God am a jealous God, visiting the iniquity of the fathers upon the children to the third and fourth generation of those who hate me."[117] If in transmitting human nature we transmit Adam's first sin, why do we not transmit Adam's other sins or even our own sins, by which we ourselves have harmed the nature that we received?[118]

In answer to this question, Aquinas explains that Adam, had he not sinned, would have passed on human nature in its state of original justice, since he received it in this state. Once original justice was lost by sin, however,

---

114. *ST* I-II, q. 81, a. 1. Mark Johnson notes that Aquinas here moves beyond Lombard's "rather homogeneous unity of the collective. . . . The accounts of human unity deriving from Augustine in Lombard gave one the sense that, in the homogeneous whole that was humanity in Adam, the infection of original sin in any part of the entity was the same, the *culpa* the same. . . . Thomas's *alia via* makes Adam the primary motive power, by will, in the whole human body" ("Augustine and Aquinas on Original Sin," 156).

115. *ST* I-II, q. 81, a. 1, ad 5.

116. *ST* I-II, q. 81, a. 1. This view accords, Aquinas notes, with Paul's estimation of his condition prior to receiving God's merciful grace through Christ Jesus: "We were by nature children of wrath, like the rest of mankind" (Eph. 2:3).

117. *ST* I-II, q. 81, a. 2, obj. 1.

118. Aquinas notes that Augustine, in his *Enchiridion*, raises this question but does not resolve it.

Adam (and Eve) could only pass on human nature in its wounded state. It is in this way that Adam's first sin, and it alone, damaged human "nature as nature."[119] All other sins damage human nature in the person who sins, rather than damaging human nature as such. Therefore, Aquinas concludes, "other sins are not transmitted."[120] As Aquinas points out in his answer to the first objection, Augustine likewise held that "children are never inflicted with spiritual punishment on account of their parents, unless they share in their guilt . . . because every soul is God's immediate property."[121] Aquinas knows, of course, that sometimes "children receive bodily punishment on their parents' account, inasmuch as the child, as to its body, is part of its father."[122]

Another set of problems arises at this juncture and forms the topic of the third article of question 81. First, it seems that if not all humans die, as 1 Thessalonians 4:14 appears to imply, then in fact not all humans receive original sin and its punishment, death. Likewise, when a baptized person is freed by the sacrament of baptism from original sin, how can such a person pass on to his or her offspring a human nature wounded by original sin? And furthermore, Paul is clear that the grace of Jesus Christ is more powerful than the sin of Adam (see Rom. 5:15–21). But the grace possessed by a person is not transmitted to a person's offspring. If grace is actually more powerful than Adam's sin, then neither should Adam's sin be transmitted.

In reply, Aquinas appeals again to the reasoning that he has already established in the first two articles. He compares our union with Adam to the union of one body. In a human body, the soul governs the members, and each of the members that are moved by the soul shares in a sin willed by the soul. Adam

---

119. *ST* I, q. 81, a. 2. Aquinas explains in ad 3, "The first sin infects nature with a human corruption pertaining to nature; whereas other sins infect it with a corruption pertaining only to the person." Rea, however, is not persuaded: "It is hard to see why Adam's first sin, *and that sin alone*, would involve all of human nature in the way required by the analogy. Even if we grant that there is a sense in which your hand, but not your foot, is to blame for sins you commit with your hand, still it is hard to see why Adam's first sin was a sin *committed with his whole nature*, as it were, rather than a sin that simply involved him as an individual" ("Metaphysics of Original Sin," 331). Rea also emphasizes that Aquinas's account of our metaphysical unity with Adam (like Edwards's account) renders it impossible for us to have prevented Adam's sin. Since we lacked the ability to prevent it, we should not be guilty for it in the way that Adam himself was. Aquinas holds that the voluntary element is always present since Adam is the "first mover" of human nature, but this claim does not satisfy Rea with respect to the punishment of Adam's descendants. I think that focusing upon the fall from the state of original justice helps one to appreciate Aquinas's claim.

120. *ST* I-II, q. 81, a. 2.

121. Ibid., ad 1.

122. Ibid. Aquinas recognizes that certain attributes of nature can be transmitted by one man to his children: for example, "fleetness of body, acuteness of intellect, and so forth" (*ST* I-II, q. 81, a. 2).

has the role of the soul in this analogy, since he is the father of the human race and moves all other humans as their "first mover" in the order of generation. Theologically, Aquinas defends this reasoning both on the basis of Romans 5 and on the basis of the view that if some humans lacked original sin, then "all would not need redemption which is through Christ."[123]

Regarding the problem raised by 1 Thessalonians 4:14, Aquinas holds that it is likely that all will die, even those who are alive at the second coming; but even if some people do not die, "the debt of death is none the less in them"—they owe the penalty of death even if God chooses not to exact it.[124] Regarding baptism and original sin, Aquinas notes that even though baptism takes away the guilt of original sin, the disorder caused by original sin continues to affect the person's nature; the removal of the guilt does not mean that the baptized person can now transmit human nature in its unfallen state. This is evident not only by our ongoing tendency toward sin but also by our ongoing subjection to death. Lastly, the power of Christ's grace has to do with the spiritual order rather than with the corporeal order: Adam's sin is transmitted to all those who come forth from him corporeally, whereas Christ's grace—whose power not only heals Adam's sin but also elevates human nature to a share in the divine life—is transmitted to all those who come forth from him spiritually.

The key issues here have to do with the sufficiency of Christ's redemptive power. Why does this power not simply brush away original sin and all its effects? If it seems that some persons may not have to die, why should anyone have to die who is in Christ? If baptism completely removes the guilt of original sin, why does human nature continue to be transmitted with the fullness of original sin? If Christ's grace is so powerful, then why does it transform fewer people than Adam's sin corrupts? Put another way, this set of problems suggests that the way in which original sin is transmitted makes it more powerful than Christ's grace. Even those who are in Christ still die, still transmit a corrupted nature to the next generation, and still are outnumbered by the universal prevalence of Adam's sin. Do not Christ's passion and resurrection overcome Adam's rebellion in a total and complete way?

Indeed, Aquinas argues that baptism, which incorporates us into Christ's passion, most certainly "has the power to take away the penalties of the

123. *ST* I-II, q. 81, a. 3.
124. Ibid., ad 1. Even Mary, in her immaculate conception (a doctrine not taught by Aquinas), is firmly among the redeemed. Since she must be redeemed, we cannot say that human nature completely starts over in Mary. She is redeemed, however, in a unique fashion: in light of the merits of her Son, God spares her from any taint of sin. But she still is subject to suffering and death. For discussion, see Levering, *Mary's Bodily Assumption*.

present life."[125] Why then does baptism not actually take away such penalties, including suffering and death? It is fitting, Aquinas explains, that baptism not remove them prior to the general resurrection of the dead, when "the mortal puts on immortality" (1 Cor. 15:54). This is so because "it is fitting that what takes place in the Head should take place also in the member incorporated."[126] Jesus Christ suffered and died, and so should we. The freedom from death that the gift of "original justice" gave Adam and Eve at the beginning is not to be ours in this life. Our passage to eternal life in Christ requires taking the same path he took. This path constitutes our "spiritual training" through the grace of the Holy Spirit, so that by struggling against sin and by accepting bodily decay with hope in the resurrection of the dead, we "may receive the crown of victory."[127] Here Aquinas quotes Romans 8:17, where Paul proclaims us "heirs of God and fellow heirs with Christ, provided we suffer with him in order that we may also be glorified with him."

Aquinas adds that if God had willed for the sacrament of baptism to remove entirely the punishment of original sin in the present life, then people would have sought baptism for the wrong reasons. It is necessary to follow the path of Christ completely, because otherwise we tend to cleave to this world as if there were no eternal life. As Aquinas observes, had baptism's effect been to restore us to the immortality enjoyed by Adam, "men might seek to be baptized for the sake of impassibility in the present life, and not for the sake of the glory of life eternal."[128] But he emphasizes that baptism does entirely abolish the punishment of alienation from God, which is by far the greater punishment when compared with the temporal punishment of suffering and death. In this discussion, Aquinas provides a particularly felicitous way of describing the transmission of original sin: "Original sin spread in this way, that at first the person infected the nature, and afterwards the nature infected the person."[129] Christ's redemptive act, communicated to us in baptism, leaves us

---

125. *ST* III, q. 69, a. 3.

126. Ibid.

127. Ibid. Rudi te Velde argues that "the aspect of recognition, by which a human individual assumes and freely acknowledges his belonging to the community of humans, is not given its full due in Aquinas' interpretation of original sin. If the whole of mankind, in its historical sequence of generations, is to have a moral status, as constituting the 'we' of the announcement 'we have all sinned in Adam,' then this 'we' should be understood in terms of the performative act by which we declare ourselves to be part of history, being all children of Adam" ("Evil, Sin, and Death," 164). Surely for Aquinas, this performative act is accomplished in baptism and in the other sacraments; but it needs to be emphasized that humankind has a moral status as a whole whether individual humans acknowledge this or not.

128. *ST* III, q. 69, a. 3. On baptism in connection with original sin, see also Sean A. Otto, "*Felix Culpa*," 787–88.

129. *ST* III, q. 69, a. 3, ad 3.

subject during earthly life to fallen human nature's punishments, but removes the spiritual alienation that otherwise would deprive us of beatitude. We do not recover original justice until the final consummation of all things. Even Jesus did not possess the fullness of original justice in this life, despite being without sin. Aquinas states that Jesus "assumed the nature without sin, and he might likewise have assumed the nature without its penalties. But he wished to bear its penalties in order to carry out the work of redemption"—namely, by suffering and dying.[130]

Aquinas argues that since Jesus's body was formed by the Holy Spirit, Jesus did not contract original sin.[131] On this view, Jesus was "in Adam" with regard to his bodily substance, but he was sinless because he did not derive from Adam "through the active power of generation."[132] Aquinas also holds that original sin comes solely from Adam, not from Eve, since "original sin is contracted, not from the mother, but from the father."[133] Biologically speaking, this view is clearly wrong, presuming as it does that the woman's role is strictly passive and involves the provision not of the ovum but of mere matter. Given faulty Aristotelian biology, and influenced by Augustine, Aquinas interprets Paul's statement that "sin came into the world through one man" (Rom. 5:12) to rule out original sin descending from the woman. He reasons that "if the woman would have transmitted original sin to her children, he [Paul] should have said that it entered by two, since both of them sinned, or rather that it entered by a woman, since she sinned first."[134] In this regard, Enns's clarifications regarding Paul's exegetical practice are deeply helpful.[135]

130. *ST* III, q. 14, a. 3, ad 1.

131. The conception of Mary in the womb of her mother occurred through natural generation, and so her lack of original sin would need to be explained in a different way. Aquinas, however, presumes that she was not conceived without original sin, although God restrained the *fomes* in Mary and healed her entirely from the *fomes* at the moment of the conception of Christ's flesh (see *ST* III, q. 27, a. 3; cf. *ST* I-II, q. 81, a. 5, ad 3).

132. *ST* I-II, q. 81, a. 4. Aquinas is here treating not Christ specifically, but rather any possible human whom God miraculously formed from human flesh (as Aquinas supposes to have occurred in the Virgin's womb). In *ST* III, q. 15, a. 1, ad 2, however, Aquinas makes the connection with Christ explicit.

133. *ST* I-II, q. 81, a. 5. Along these lines, Aquinas observes, "The child pre-exists in its father as in its active principle, and in its mother, as in its material and passive principle" (ibid., ad 1).

134. *ST* I-II, q. 81, a. 5, *sed contra*.

135. We might nonetheless hope that Aquinas's view (and Paul's) went some way toward helping Christians to avoid blaming Eve misogynistically for the fallen human condition. Aquinas comments that if "Adam had not sinned, original sin would not have been transmitted to posterity on account of Eve's sin; it is evident that the children would not have been deprived of original justice: and consequently they would not have been liable to suffer and subject to the necessity of dying" (*ST* I-II, q. 81, a. 5, ad 2).

If all humans descend from an original couple—as Kemp suggests science has not ruled out—then the generative unity of Adam and Eve would give them together the role of "first mover," so that they fill the role that Aquinas gives to Adam and that accounts for the voluntary character of original sin in us. It seems to me that we could also be united to Adam and Eve's will as "first mover" in a broader sense, if God chose two first humans as the representative bearers of human nature so that we are one family with them (Rahner). C. John Collins suggests that this kind of view is biblically acceptable so long as one conceives of the representative Adam and Eve as royal priests, since "a king and queen . . . are legitimately the father and mother of their people," even if not all people descend physically from them.[136]

Conclusion

Peter Enns holds that universal death and sin are simply a reality, and that we cannot ask the "why" question. According to Enns, the stories of Adam and Eve in Genesis function in a variety of ways, including as an account of Israel's history, as a depiction of Israel's temple as a microcosm, and as a revision of the origin narratives of other Near Eastern societies. The one thing, however, that the first chapters of Genesis are not is a historical-scientific description of human origins. Had the authors of the first chapters of Genesis intended to address such questions, they would not have left open such obvious questions as why Cain, having killed his brother, would have feared retaliation, and how Cain could have found a wife. On this view, then, we cannot appeal to the stories of Adam and Eve for historical or scientific information about human origins, although these stories can tell us other important things.

As to Paul's interpretation of Scripture (the Old Testament), Enns maintains that Paul is equally unconcerned with making historical-scientific claims about the first humans. According to Enns, Paul employs Old Testament texts in a free manner that shows that he does not read Scripture through the lens of modern concerns for historical veracity, textual accuracy, and reconstruction of the history behind the text. Although he clearly thought Adam to be the first man, we nevertheless cannot attribute to Paul, in Romans 5, the kind of historical-scientific concerns that we now have.

It is for this reason, Enns argues, that the efforts to fill in the gaps of the Genesis narrative by turning Adam into the first rational hominid from among a group of nonrational but cognitively advanced hominids (e.g., Kemp), or

136. C. John Collins, *Did Adam and Eve Really Exist?*, 125.

by making a "representative man" of Adam or of a group of early humans (e.g., Rahner), are not helpful. In his view, such approaches wrongly interpret the Genesis narrative as a historical-scientific account and seek to augment Genesis along historical-scientific lines. For Enns, this is to yet again misunderstand the Genesis narrative and to refuse to read it on its own terms. To read Genesis 2–3 as though it spoke about two first rational hominids from among a group of cognitively advanced but nonrational hominids, rather than about a first man who was created directly by God "of dust from the ground" (Gen. 2:7) and a first woman created from Adam's rib, separates us from the actual Genesis narrative. Genesis says nothing about a group of nonrational hominids, two of which receive from God a rational soul at conception. Nor does Genesis say anything about a first representative man (or representative group) among many original humans. Genesis, in Enns's view, is simply not this kind of story.

And yet, one cannot avoid the question that Henri Blocher eloquently articulates: "The real issue when we try to interpret Genesis 2–3 is not whether we have a historical account of the fall"—it is clear that we do not—"but whether or not we may read it as the account of a historical fall."[137] Blocher's statement is on point: I think that we can and, indeed, *should* read Genesis 2–3 as an account of a historical fall, since the stories of Adam and Eve make clear that the creator God was not the cause of human sin and death. What Genesis 2–3 shows is that God ensured that his rational creatures possessed full freedom, a freedom which the first humans then subsequently used to rebel against God, with consequences (disharmony, exile, alienation, death) for the entire human race that extend right down into the present.[138] Thus, even though Genesis 2–3 does not offer a historical or scientific account of human origins, Genesis 2–3 does reveal something about these origins, namely, that God did not create humans in a corrupt and sinful predicament. It follows, therefore, that with regard to the event of original sin and its consequences, we are being faithful to the realities depicted by Genesis 2–3 when we conceive of two first rational hominids whose descendants bred with each other and

137. Blocher, *Original Sin*, 50.
138. See also Larchet, *Theology of Illness*. From an Orthodox perspective rooted in numerous quotations from the fathers (mainly Greek fathers, but also some Latin ones), Larchet argues: "According to the Fathers, then, we need to seek the source of illness, infirmities, sufferings, corruption, and death, together with all other evils that presently afflict human nature, in the personal will of man, in the bad use to which he has put his free will, that is, in the sin which he committed in Paradise. . . . Because Adam is the 'root' of human nature, its prototype who embodies the very principle of all human existence, he transmits his state to each of his descendants. Death, corruption, illness and suffering thus become the legacy of the entire human race" (26, 34).

with nonrational hominids (Kemp), just as we are when we conceive of royal representatives (whether one, two, or perhaps a larger group) chosen by God from among the first humans (Rahner).[139]

In my view, Enns does not adequately address Scripture's repeated portrayal of human death as a punishment, demonstrated so clearly by Jonathan Edwards.[140] If God built sin and death into the human condition from the beginning, there could not have been a real rebellion, let alone a just punishment by God. In such a world, we could account for the faultiness of human creatures, but there could not have been a truly free rebellion deserving of punishment. Envisioning just such a world, the philosopher Daniel Dennett argues that the presence of "error"—in the sense of genetic mutations that risk "termination of the reproductive line at worst, or a diminution in the capacity to reproduce"—has shaped the evolutionary history of hominids, so that there was no pure first human who was not shaped by his or her genetic prehistory and its corresponding built-in selfishness.[141] If Dennett's terms were accepted, there would be no room for full freedom or for just punishment. Dennett's position, however, requires ruling out both the good creator God and the grace of original justice. His position is shaped not solely by science but also by philosophical presuppositions that presume, without evidence or

139. For an account that would be consistent with either Kemp's or Rahner's proposal, see also van Inwagen, *Problem of Evil*, 84–94; cf. van Inwagen, "Genesis and Evolution." Without committing himself to affirming the truth of this account, in *Problem of Evil* van Inwagen proposes that the first rational hominids could have been given preternatural gifts so that they were fully in communion with God and each other and were also sustained, for the brief period prior to their sin, from disease and death.

140. Citing a variety of commentaries on Genesis, Astley argues that "whether Genesis 3 intends human death to be seen as a punishment for sin is unclear" ("Evolution and Evil," 179n42). For the view that death is probably not a punishment for sin in Gen. 3, see also Houston, "Sex or Violence?," 141; James Barr, *Garden of Eden and Hope of Immortality*. I think that this view is a misinterpretation. Among the curses that God gives Adam is the following: "In the sweat of your face you shall eat bread, till you return to the ground, for out of it you were taken; you are dust, and to dust you shall return" (Gen. 3:19); and earlier God had promised that "of the tree of the knowledge of good and evil you shall not eat, for in the day that you eat of it you shall die" (Gen. 2:17). Surely this is clear enough. Moreover, Christians read Genesis 2–3 in canonical context, including Rom. 6:23, "the wages of sin is death"—and including the cross of Christ, "whom God put forward as an expiation by his blood" (Rom. 3:25).

141. See Dennett, *Darwin's Dangerous Idea*, 203, 513. For a questionable sociobiological expansion of this point, see also Dawkins, *Selfish Gene*; cf. *Climbing Mount Improbable*, 273. Dawkins holds that animals, including humans, come to be in order to propagate their DNA, and thus are inherently selfish. For further aspects of the problem, see such work as Lindenfors and Tullberg, "Evolutionary Aspects of Aggression"; and the response given in Austriaco, "Theological Fittingness Argument for the Historicity of the Fall of *Homo Sapiens*." On the human inheritance of genetic defects (but not a "selfish" gene) in light of Augustine's theory of original sin, see Rist, *Augustine Deformed*, 380–82. In support of positions such as that of Lindenfors and Tullberg, see also Butler, *Adapting Minds*.

serious argument, the nonexistence of both God and God's grace. By contrast, I hold with Ian McFarland that sin "has no proper place in human nature either as made by God or as destined by God for glory."[142]

Like members of a disgraced family, all humans labor under the damaging consequences of the loss of original justice. Although we are not responsible for original sin in the way that the first humans were, their status as our "first mover" means that the voluntariness of their sin perdures in us, with the result that God is just in not establishing our human nature in the original justice forfeited by the first humans. As noted above, that the first humans are our "first mover" holds good even if this term is broadly construed under the rubric of royal representation, according to which they would be the "first mover" of the human family by divine election rather than by physical generation. The unique status of the first humans befits the fact that the human race unfolds historically. Put simply, it makes sense that the rebellion of the first humans vis-à-vis God's grace would affect the state of human nature in the generations of humans who follow them, not by destroying human nature but by removing grace.[143] After original sin, all humans possess a wounded

142. McFarland, *In Adam's Fall*, 212. This very affirmation, however, is why I disagree with McFarland's view, expressed earlier in his book, that "original sin is a feature of humankind in its fundamental unity from creation to eschaton" rather than "an effect transmitted down the generations from a particular historical cause" (157). For McFarland, "There is no reason why Adam's being the *first* in a series should justify his *representing* the rest of the series in God's sight" (153). But in my view, Adam and Eve's being first in the series simply means that they were created in grace, with original justice that established them in full freedom. This claim is fundamentally a claim about the goodness of the creator. McFarland rejects "the question of how human beings come to be afflicted by original sin" on the grounds that such a question "presupposes that we are (first) agents who (then) receive a human nature" (158). I do not see how this is the case: on the contrary, both the first humans and we ourselves receive human nature and (then) exercise human agency, the sole difference being that the creator not only made the first humans' nature good, but also upheld its harmonious integrity by the grace of original justice (without thereby making their human nature ontologically different from ours, since the loss of original justice does not destroy the goods of human nature). For further viewpoints that, generally without McFarland's level of theological sophistication, envision all humans as sinners from the outset, see Domning and Hellwig, *Original Selfishness*; Patricia Williams, *Doing without Adam and Eve*; Peters, "Evolution of Evil"; Rolston, *Genes, Genesis and God*, 301; Ruse, *Can a Darwinian Be a Christian?*, 210.

143. McFarland states, "We can, of course, reason that we received our wills in this damaged state as part of our natures, and thus that we 'inherited' them from our parents and grandparents and great-grandparents and so on, back up the human family tree. But because the will is the faculty in and through which I recognize my own agency, I can never coherently dissociate any defect in my willing from my agency. Consequently, 'Adam' can only be regarded as the first in a series of sinners and not as the unique 'cause' of subsequent human sin" (*In Adam's Fall*, 160). If I understand McFarland correctly, there was never a time when any mere human, including Adam and Eve, was unfallen or without sin; otherwise what McFarland calls "the unity of the system" would be undermined and one would be able to ask, at least in Adam and

and disordered human nature, which God works to heal not by restoring the grace of original justice but by means of the redemptive and deifying grace of Jesus Christ, which far exceeds original justice.

Does my defense of the plausibility and theological necessity of an original sin at the dawn of human history fall into what Hans Madueme has felicitously termed the "Adam-of-the-gaps fallacy"?[144] I think not, because a God-of-the-gaps is fallacious given God's transcendence, whereas it is quite reasonable to suppose the existence of some first humans who commit a first sin and who thereby, by depriving human nature of the grace of original justice, shape the unfolding of human history. On theological grounds, we should embrace Genesis 2–3's teaching that the creator God is not responsible for sinfulness of humans, which can only be the case if humans brought their condition upon themselves by turning away from the grace God had given them in creating them good. Created in a graced state of justice, Adam and Eve committed the first human sin by freely rebelling against God's order, and the gift of original justice was lost both in them and in the whole of human nature, to which Adam and Eve, as befits their unique status in the human family, are related as "first mover." Disorder, alienation, and death as we now experience it are the punishment for this turning away from the Source of life—not an extrinsic punishment by a harsh God, but a punishment rooted in the nature of the sin.

Eve's case, "the question of how human beings come to be afflicted by original sin" (158–59). McFarland's statement "I can never coherently dissociate any defect in my willing from my agency" is correct in the sense that our freedom means that we cannot blame original sin for our sinful free choices. This fact, however, does not mean that original sin is negligible, since our nature is profoundly disrupted. God did not create human nature in this condition, but after the fall and the loss of original justice, human agency became the site of defective willing (due to the immediate consequences of the loss of original justice).

144. Madueme, "Most Vulnerable Part of the Whole Christian Account," 237.

SEVEN

Atonement

"I will put enmity between you and the woman, and between your seed and her seed; he shall bruise your head, and you shall bruise his heel."

Genesis 3:15

Is there a relationship between the doctrine of creation and the doctrine of atonement? I think that there is, and that it is an important one, as we would expect from creation as a "realm of interrelated and interdependent relations" of creatures to God and of creatures to each other.[1] I agree with the perspective of Symeon the New Theologian, who sees Christ the second Adam in light of the first Adam and holds that the mission of the incarnate Son is to restore the human race to its created condition of justice in relation to the creator.[2] I hold that the order of creation, as an order of justice, is personal and relational rather than being an abstractly juridical reality.[3]

1. McFarlane, "Atonement, Creation and Trinity," 192. With regard to human existence, he spells out this relational dimension further: "*Human* being is determined not in terms of its biological existence alone but much more so by a relational identity. Our true identity is discovered and established only to the degree that the matrix of relations established at creation informs each" (195). See also Webster, "It Was the Will of the Lord to Bruise Him." McFarlane draws upon Welker, *Creation and Reality*, 13.

2. See Symeon the New Theologian, *First-Created Man*, 115; cf. 63.

3. A different approach to creation and cross is advocated in Balthasar, *Theo-Drama*, 4:328–32. Balthasar views creation in terms of infinite freedom risking itself to open up space for finite freedom, and Balthasar advocates a version of substitution theory rooted "in the profound depths of the relations between the divine Hypostases—which are inaccessible to any creature" (336). The approach that Balthasar briefly sketches here, and that he develops further in the remainder of his *Theo-Drama* and in the second volume of his *Theo-Logic*, strikes me as problematic. See also Thomas Joseph White, OP, *Incarnate Lord*, chaps. 6–9.

In making this case, this final chapter first presents Nicholas Wolterstorff's stimulating challenge to doctrines of the atonement such as the one that I advance in this chapter. After presenting and evaluating Wolterstorff's critique, I turn in the chapter's second section to Thomas Aquinas's doctrine of satisfaction, which has a significant place among the various ways that Aquinas interprets the mission of the incarnate Son, filled with the Holy Spirit, for our salvation.[4] Specifically, I argue that the way in which Aquinas grounds his doctrine of satisfaction in the doctrine of creation helps to resolve the central problems raised by Wolterstorff.[5] By perceiving the interpersonal

4. For a summary of Aquinas's view of Christ's satisfaction for sin on the cross, see Bonino, *Il m'a aimé et s'est livré pour moi*, 123; cf. 73, 110–11. Bernard of Clairvaux, in his marvelous response to Peter Abelard and Anselm, emphasizes love, satisfaction, redemption, and sacrifice, all of which are accepted and developed by Aquinas in his presentation of the various ways in which we should understand Christ's saving work on the cross. By focusing upon satisfaction in the present chapter, I do not mean to imply that Aquinas's doctrine of Christ's saving work can be reduced to satisfaction. For the full range of Aquinas's theology of salvation, see Levering, *Christ's Fulfillment of Torah and Temple*. For discussion of Bernard, see Tony Lane, "Bernard of Clairvaux." For the reception of Anselm's satisfaction doctrine by thirteenth-century Franciscans, showing how some of them added a note of penitential punishment to satisfaction, see Rosato, "Interpretation of Anselm's Teaching on Christ's Satisfaction for Sin in the Franciscan Tradition from Alexander of Hales to Duns Scotus." For further background, see also J. Patout Burns, "Concept of Satisfaction in Medieval Redemption Theory"; and Rivière, *Doctrine of the Atonement*.

5. My view of Aquinas's theology of Christ's satisfaction is generally consonant with that of Eleonore Stump in her *Aquinas*, chap. 15. Stump insightfully observes that "the function of satisfaction for Aquinas is not to placate a wrathful God or in some other way remove the constraints which compel God to damn sinners. Instead, the function of satisfaction is to restore a sinner to a state of harmony with God by repairing or restoring in the sinner what sin has damaged" (432). By contrast, I do not agree with the contention of Gerald O'Collins, SJ, that "the way Aquinas adjusted Anselm's theory of satisfaction helped open the door to a sad version of redemption: Christ as a penal substitute who was personally burdened with the sins of humanity, judged, condemned, and deservedly punished in our place" (*Jesus Our Redeemer*, 137). O'Collins contends that the cross lacks any positive relation to retributive justice and punishment, a contention that in my view cannot be upheld exegetically. O'Collins also misreads Aquinas's understanding of satisfaction and sacrifice, not least by suggesting that for Aquinas a sacrifice literally "appeases" an otherwise literally angry God (see 136–37; *Summa theologiae* [hereafter *ST*] III, q. 48, a. 3). However, O'Collins rightly notes Aquinas's emphasis on love. See also Torrell, *Pour nous les hommes et pour notre salut*, 106–24, which emphasizes the centrality of Christ's supreme love in Aquinas's doctrine of satisfaction and warns against making "satisfaction the explicative category *par excellence* of the whole theology of the redemption" (123). For Torrell, the "explicative category *par excellence*" is merit, because merit clearly foregrounds Christ's love. In my view, Torrell downplays satisfaction more than he should (see 146; cf. 112 for concerns regarding Anselmian language). Torrell mistakenly holds that Aquinas "completely abandons in the *Summa theologiae* the idea of restoring the divine order [*l'idée de l'ordre divin à rétablir*]" and that Aquinas, in a crucial text, also abandons "the idea of the payment of a debt" (118–19), especially as regards Christ's bodily life. Certainly these latter themes are neither the only nor the most eminent themes of Aquinas's soteriology—because these themes must be seen in light of God's merciful love—but they remain important, due to the significance of the order of creation for Christ's saving work.

web of justice that characterizes creation, we can fully appreciate Christian salvation's emphasis on "relational love for God, self, others, and the world," since true justice "is *altogether and unabashedly relational.*"[6]

To be clear from the outset, I should emphasize that Christ's satisfactory suffering on the cross is not required or needed by God, nor is it God punishing Jesus, nor is it an individualistic transaction (since it is the action of the head of the human race).[7] The reality of atonement is far from the crude caricatures that one sometimes encounters, such as in Kharalambos Anstall's contention that Anselm and Aquinas reasoned from a "simplistic concept of feudal/legalistic justice" to the conclusion that God "would require, in obedient satisfaction, the agony and death of His only-begotten Son, Jesus Christ, as a blood money (*wergild*) to redeem collective humanity before a reconciliation with God and all the rest of creation could be considered."[8] On the contrary, the incarnate Son's free act of satisfaction is the Triune God's free gift to the entire human race, healing and elevating humans (by the grace of the Holy Spirit) into a just relationship with God, self, neighbor, and world in the body of the Spirit-filled incarnate Son. By his merciful cross, which is "the judgment of this world" (John 12:31), Christ our head freely bears our penalty out of supreme love, much as Isaiah 53 prophesied.[9]

My focus on satisfaction's relationship to creation means that I will not be able to show here how satisfaction relates to the entirety of Jesus's life or to his resurrection and ascension, to the covenantal history of Israel, and to the other ways in which the cross accomplishes our salvation. Neil Ormerod rightly observes that Aquinas "places the work of the incarnation in a much richer context than the single explanatory concept of 'satisfaction.' While it is part of his armory, it is not the whole thing."[10] By focusing upon how

6. McKnight, *Community Called Atonement*, 126, 133. McKnight insightfully underscores the ecclesial dimension of atonement.

7. Thus, in his *Atonement, Law, and Justice*, Adonis Vidu retains the language of punishment but with crucial clarifications: "While the death Jesus died has the quality of punishment, we have no reason to think of this punishment as being directly inflicted by God on Christ" (261).

8. Anstall, "Juridical Justification Theology and a Statement of the Orthodox Teaching," 487–88; the charge of "blasphemy against Christian teaching" is on 488. Purporting to represent the Orthodox position, Anstall's work is colored by a wild array of anti-Western claims. His own position regarding the cross is a version of exemplarism (see 491–92). Aquinas, too, recognizes that the cross is a profound example: "Man knows thereby how much God loves him, and is thereby stirred to love Him in return, and herein lies the perfection of human salvation. . . . He set us an example of obedience, humility, constancy, justice, and the other virtues displayed in the Passion, which are requisite for man's salvation. . . . [Christ] merited justifying grace for him [humankind] and the glory of bliss" (*ST* III, q. 46, a. 3).

9. See also Terry, *Justifying Judgement of God*; Webster, *Holiness*.

10. Ormerod, *Creation, Grace, and Redemption*, 101. Ormerod mistakenly supposes that Aquinas's theology of the cross "makes little direct contact with the historical narrative of Jesus'

satisfaction relates specifically to creation, I hope to show that we can only understand the cross when we recognize that the redeemer is none other than the creator, who from eternity knows and wills the whole of creation in relation to his own goodness, "according to his purpose which he set forth in Christ as a plan for the fulness of time, to unite all things in him, things in heaven and things on earth" (Eph. 1:9–10).[11]

This final chapter should obviously be paired with the previous chapter on original sin, but it should also take us back to our first chapter, on the divine ideas. Charles Journet rightly points out that "the redemptive sacrificial act of Christ on the cross, where the world is given to God and God to the world, is known by God from all eternity in its presentiality."[12] This chapter should lead us back to everything we have discussed about the wisdom and goodness of the simple Triune God's creation, including his creation of humans in his image. God manifests his infinite goodness in creation and redemption for the purpose of drawing his *imago* (and all creation) into eternal communion with him. I agree with Stephen Holmes: "God is not damaged, lessened or hurt at all by our failures, nor is God restored, repaired or set right in his own gracious act of salvation. Instead, and positively, God's act of salvation is a gracious re-ordering of . . . the created order."[13] To exhibit how the cross of the incarnate Son restores and reorders his creation is the task of this chapter.

---

mission as the precursor to his death" (102). On this point, see Levering, *Christ's Fulfillment of Torah and Temple*. For a helpful insistence that soteriology be grounded in "the dogmatics of the immanent Trinity," even if it is possible "to begin at some other point," see Webster, "It Was the Will of the Lord to Bruise Him," 24. As Webster observes, Aquinas's soteriology is deeply biblical and theocentric. Webster cautions against soteriology that orders "its material around some theme (such as 'facing' or 'hospitality')" or that seeks primarily to respond "to a perceived problem (such as violence). Thematic or problem-oriented presentations are commonly nominalist and moralistic, since their centre of gravity lies not in the irreducible person and work of God but rather in some human experience or action of which theological talk of salvation is symbolic" (17). For an attempt to ground soteriology in "the processions and missions of the persons of the Holy Trinity" (25), see Levering, *Engaging the Doctrine of the Holy Spirit*. See also Adam Johnson, *God's Being in Reconciliation*, 1.

11. Here the reminder of Ivor J. Davidson is apropos: "Christian salvation is expounded best when it is seen not in terms of single constituent themes—forgiveness, justification, deliverance, liberation, and so on—but primarily as the good news about God, and all things else in the light of God" ("Introduction," in *God of Salvation*, 7–8).

12. Journet, *The Mass*, 60.

13. Holmes, "Simple Salvation?," 43. Holmes is indebted here to McIntyre, *Shape of Soteriology*, 41. Where I have placed an ellipsis in this quotation, Holmes states: "(at least some parts of)." I have left this out because I think that the whole of the created order is reordered, even if some rational creatures can freely and permanently reject the reordering. I agree with Holmes that "what is changed in soteriology, properly understood, is a *relationship*. The end result of God's saving act is that we stand in a different relation to him: adopted daughters and sons, where once we were alienated rebels. . . . It is a commonplace of classical theology

Nicholas Wolterstorff's *Justice in Love*: A Critique of Satisfaction Theories

The eminent Christian philosopher Nicholas Wolterstorff argues that while it is a mistake to read Jesus's Sermon on the Mount as advocating pacifism, nonetheless Jesus made a crucial ethical advance by rejecting the "reciprocity code" as a standard for justice.[14] What is the reciprocity code? Jesus finds it in God's commandments in the Torah. For example, God gave the following command through Moses regarding permanent injuries caused to innocent parties during a conflict: "If any harm follows, then you shall give life for life, eye for eye, tooth for tooth, hand for hand, foot for foot, burn for burn, wound for wound, stripe for stripe" (Exod. 21:23–25). A similar divine commandment is found in Leviticus 24:19–21: "When a man causes a disfigurement in his neighbor, as he has done it shall be done to him, fracture for fracture, eye for eye, tooth for tooth; as he has disfigured a man, he shall be disfigured. He who kills a beast shall make it good; and he who kills a man shall be put to death." Such laws conceive of justice in terms of reciprocity: when someone has caused permanent harm to an innocent party, the guilty perpetrator shall receive as punishment the same permanent harm. Justice here is conceived to involve retribution so as to restore, as much as possible, the balance of the scales: if I have harmed someone, retributive justice mandates that I suffer the same harm in order to restore a just balance between me and the person whom I have harmed (and in order to avoid an escalating cycle of violence). This understanding of retributive justice prevails throughout the Torah.[15] Thus

---

that there may be a change in a creature, and with it a change in the relationship of God to the creature, without any change in God" ("Simple Salvation?," 44). I also agree with Holmes that "every act of God is simultaneously absolutely just and perfectly merciful" (45).

14. For a persuasive argument, complementing Wolterstorff's, against reading the Sermon on the Mount as advocating pacifism, see Verhey, "Neither Devils nor Angels." Adonis Vidu challenges Wolterstorff's view of the distinctiveness of Jesus's contribution. Drawing upon Homer, Aeschylus, Plato, Aristotle, and Roman law, Vidu argues that "pagan antiquity did not exclusively favor retribution, as Wolterstorff argues, but . . . alongside retribution there was precisely the idea of a (divine) gratuitous forgiveness, precisely in the name of peace and order (and thus justice). . . . The undeniable fact is that the idea of divine forgiveness that is both unconditional and just (Rom. 3:26) was not at all foreign to ancient culture" (*Atonement, Law, and Justice*, 3).

15. Hans S. Reinders argues that an Old Testament exception is the book of Job. According to Reinders's reading of the book of Job, the notion of divine retribution for sin must be rejected because it "implies a scheme of retributive justice that enables God's creatures to lay a claim on how they ought to be dealt with, which elevates them into the position of God's equals" (*Disability, Providence, and Ethics*, 122). As we will see, Aquinas affirms that God need not follow retributive justice—God could forgive all sins without any retribution and yet maintain perfect justice, because all sins are primarily against God—but that out of sheer generosity God does perfectly satisfy retributive justice. As the book of Job shows, however, God does not directly repay sinners in this life, not least because Jesus Christ dies for the forgiveness of all sins and so any further retributive justice requires permanently and everlastingly rejecting Jesus's love.

in Deuteronomy, Moses teaches that if a person has borne false witness in a court of law, "then you shall do to him as he had meant to do to his brother" (Deut. 19:19). Moses goes on to underscore the gravity of this commandment: "Your eye shall not pity; it shall be life for life, eye for eye, tooth for tooth, hand for hand, foot for foot" (Deut. 19:21).[16]

As Wolterstorff points out, Jesus rejected this reciprocity. The key passage is Jesus's teaching in Matthew 5:38–40, part of his Sermon on the Mount: "You have heard that it was said, 'An eye for an eye and a tooth for a tooth.' But I say to you, Do not resist one who is evil. But if any one strikes you on the right cheek, turn to him the other also; and if any one would sue you and take your coat, let him have your cloak as well." Far from retributive justice, rooted in reciprocity, Jesus here teaches us to respond to evil with good. When someone harms us or threatens us with harm, we are to seek no retribution, no reciprocal harm to that person. We are certainly not to seek vengeance. Instead, we are to do good to the one who has harmed us, and not harm the evildoer in any way.

Wolterstorff emphasizes that Jesus's teaching is more radical than many commentators realize. According to Wolterstorff, Jesus's logic means that "when you discern that underlying the prohibition of blind vengeance is the command to love, then you will realize that not only should you refrain from blind vengeance; you should also refrain from paying back evil with proportionate evil. You should return good for evil. You should reject not only blind vengeance but reciprocity as well."[17] Jesus is thereby rejecting, rather than merely adjusting or deepening, the Torah's understanding of the justice that members of God's people should pursue. Even more, Jesus is rejecting *positive* reciprocity. As Jesus goes on to say, "Love your enemies and pray for those who persecute you. . . . For if you love those who love you, what reward have you? Do not even the tax collectors do the same? And if you salute only your brethren, what more are you doing than others? Do not even the Gentiles do the same?" (Matt. 5:44, 46–47). For Jesus, we may not favor our friends, and we may not demand retributive justice with respect to our enemies.

In arguing that Jesus utterly rejects the reciprocity code, Wolterstorff explains further: "The reciprocity code had two aspects. If someone does you

---

I should emphasize that even though Jesus does fulfill retributive justice, he does not thereby make all things that happen (for example, the Holocaust) understandable and acceptable. Rather, in Jesus we encounter the sovereign power of God's love against human sin, but we encounter this power as the scandal of weakness. I think that Reinders is mistaken to claim that the book of Job teaches that "the Creator of the universe cannot be held accountable by the Creator's creatures" (123). The book of Job simply makes clear that the way in which the creator will be accountable cannot be known a priori by humans.

16. For a theological critique of retributive justice—a critique that does not pay sufficient attention to the significance of the created order—see Gorringe, *God's Just Vengeance*.

17. Wolterstorff, *Justice in Love*, 122.

a favor, you owe them an equal favor in return. If someone does you an evil, an equal evil is due them."[18] To show Jesus's critique of this twofold code, Wolterstorff cites Luke 14:12, where Jesus tells the Pharisee who has invited him to dinner: "When you give a dinner or a banquet, do not invite your friends or your brothers or your kinsmen or rich neighbors, lest they also invite you in return, and you be repaid." Commenting on Jesus's command, Wolterstorff remarks, "This is a barbed rejection of that aspect of the reciprocity code which says that favors must be answered with favors."[19] Followers of Jesus must go to some lengths to avoid reciprocity, since love is tested and made meritorious by going beyond reciprocity. We must become like our "Father who is in heaven; for he makes his sun rise on the evil and on the good, and sends rain on the just and on the unjust" (Matt. 5:45).

It seems right to say, as Wolterstorff does, that Jesus rejects "the reciprocity code in favor of the ethic of love," despite the presence of the reciprocity code in the Torah.[20] But I would add that Jesus has not thereby rejected the reciprocity code tout court. The reciprocity code still functions with respect to God's repayment of our acts of love. Thus Jesus adds to his commandment regarding dinner invitations: "You will be repaid at the resurrection of the just" (Luke 14:13–14). Rather than seeking reciprocal justice from humans, in other words, we should now seek it from God; the good that we hope to obtain is something that can only come from God.[21]

Indeed, although Wolterstorff does not mention it, the reciprocity code is on full display in Jesus's depiction of the final judgment in his parable about the sheep and the goats. The "sheep" or righteous will receive the reward of "the kingdom prepared for [them] from the foundation of the world" (Matt. 25:34). This reward will take them by surprise, because they cared for others without realizing that they were thereby caring for Jesus. In response to Jesus's praise for the good deeds that they did to those who could not repay them, the righteous say, "'Lord, when did we see thee hungry and feed thee, or thirsty and give thee drink? . . .' And the King will answer them, 'Truly, I say to you, as you did it to one of the least of these my brethren, you did it to me'" (Matt. 25:37–40). God will reward those who in this life show love for others who cannot repay them; and God will repay, with retributive justice, those who in this life fail to love others in this way (see Matt. 25:41–43). Admittedly, the

18. Ibid., 123.
19. Ibid., 126.
20. Ibid.
21. See Miroslav Volf's description of the Christian vocation in the world: "Assured of God's justice and undergirded by God's presence, they are to break the cycle of violence by refusing to be caught in the automatism of revenge" (*Exclusion and Embrace*, 306).

reward goes beyond pure reciprocity, but it is clearly retributive justice that we see on display in this parable. To underscore the point that there will be both a reciprocal reward and a retributive punishment, Jesus concludes his parable by stating, "And they will go away into eternal punishment, but the righteous into eternal life" (Matt. 25:46).

For his part, Wolterstorff focuses solely on Jesus's rejection of the reciprocity code for his followers with respect to seeking to punish or be recompensed by *other humans*. As Wolterstorff rightly observes, this form of the rejection of the reciprocity code is found not only in the Gospels but also in the Epistles. He cites one representative passage from Peter, and two from Paul. In 1 Peter, in the midst of a discussion of how Christians should live together, we find a statement reminiscent of Jesus's words in the Sermon on the Mount: "Do not return evil for evil or reviling for reviling; but on the contrary bless, for to this you have been called, that you may obtain a blessing" (1 Pet. 3:9). But I would add that the blessing that we are to seek (a *reciprocal* reward) will come from God. To obtain this blessing, we must imitate Jesus, who died for the sins of those who rejected and reviled him. Since we have been healed by Jesus, we must love others as he loved us, and he loved us when we deserved retributive punishment and when we could repay him in no manner. Earlier in 1 Peter, this is made explicit: "Christ also suffered for you, leaving you an example, that you should follow in his steps. . . . When he was reviled, he did not revile in return; when he suffered, he did not threaten; but he trusted to him who judges justly. He himself bore our sins in his body on the tree, that we might die to sin and live to righteousness" (1 Pet. 2:21, 23–24).[22]

The two Pauline passages that Wolterstorff quotes come from 1 Thessalonians 5 and Romans 12. Like 1 Peter 3:9, 1 Thessalonians 5 has to do with the behavior of members of the Christian community toward each other, and we find the same rejection of reciprocity: "See that none of you repays evil for evil, but always seek to do good to one another and to all" (1 Thess. 5:15). Yet Wolterstorff neglects the fact that 1 Thessalonians 5 also envisions a future "wrath" (1 Thess. 5:9) or divine judgment. First Thessalonians contains a clear notion

22. Here might be the place to note René Girard's influential theory of Jesus's cross as the end of scapegoating, as found for example in his *I See Satan Fall like Lightning*. I agree with the criticisms lodged against Girard's theory in Balthasar, *Theo-Drama*, 4:309. For an instructive recent response to Girard, arguing that "the cross makes possible right covenantal relations by removing the covenant sanction and by rendering the eschatological gift of the Holy Spirit" (402) and in this way affirming John Milbank's (and Jean-Luc Marion's) emphasis on the "excess" of the divine gift of love, see Vanhoozer, "Atonement in Postmodernity." Vanhoozer defends "penal substitution" language, on the grounds that God's wrath against sin demands retribution in justice (not abstractly legal, but interpersonally covenantal justice). In this regard, he is responding to Paul Ricoeur, among others; see Ricoeur, "Interpretation of the Myth of Punishment."

of retributive punishment, since it warns against immorality and pleads "that no man transgress, and wrong his brother in this matter, because the Lord is an avenger in all these things, as we solemnly forewarned you" (1 Thess. 4:6).

In the passage from Romans 12 that Wolterstorff quotes, Paul states, "Repay no one evil for evil, but take thought for what is noble in the sight of all. . . . Beloved, never avenge yourselves, but leave it to the wrath of God; for it is written, 'Vengeance is mine, I will repay, says the Lord'" (Rom. 12:17, 19). Wolterstorff concentrates here upon the rejection of reciprocity. It is also clear from this passage, however, that God retains reciprocal or retributive justice, since the "wrath of God" will "repay" at the final judgment. In the present, Christians are to bear witness to Christ's absolute mercy toward us, not least because by so doing we may be able to convert some of our enemies before the final judgment.[23] The latter point—the power of mercy for turning enemies into friends—accords well with Old Testament teaching. Thus, in Romans 12:20, Paul quotes Proverbs 25:21–22: "If your enemy is hungry, give him bread to eat; and if he is thirsty, give him water to drink; for you will heap coals of fire on his head, and the Lord will reward you." Paul understands this proverb to indicate that our good deeds may result in the conversion of our enemy. As Paul emphasizes, much like Jesus, "Do not be overcome by evil, but overcome evil with good" (Rom. 12:21). Earlier in the same chapter, Paul offers a version of Jesus's admonition to love our enemies: "Bless those who persecute you; bless and do not curse them" (Rom. 12:14).

Although Wolterstorff rightly underscores the ways in which Jesus rejects the reciprocity code, therefore, he exaggerates when he argues that Jesus's "rejection of the negative side of the reciprocity code implies opposition to retributive punishment in general."[24] On the contrary, Jesus consistently looks forward to a retributive punishment that God will apply at the final judgment to those who reject God's offer of mercy in Jesus. Wolterstorff is, of course, aware of this, but he does not give it sufficient attention. He states simply, "If redressing injury (harm, evil) has any place at all in the moral order, God will do it. Leave it to God."[25] But if the Gospels and Epistles are any evidence, there is no "if" about whether "redressing injury" has a place in God's moral order. Even so, Wolterstorff is right that with regard to how Christians should behave in this life, "Jesus forbids retribution. Injury imposed on the wrongdoer must be justified by some greater good that it brings about, not by the fact that the wrongdoer imposed an injury."[26]

23. See Jones, *Embodying Forgiveness*; Volf, *Free of Charge*.
24. Wolterstorff, *Justice in Love*, 129.
25. Ibid., 128.
26. Ibid.

Wolterstorff also interprets Romans 13, which presents authorities as "instituted by God" (Rom. 13:1), as not being about retributive punishment.[27] According to Wolterstorff, Paul considers that government authorities "encourage those who do good; and by imposing punishment on wrongdoers, they express anger (*orgē*) against wrongdoing and serve as a terror (*phobos*) to such conduct. Nothing is said about retribution, about getting even, about reciprocating evil with evil, about redress, about vengeance."[28] But it seems to me that retributive justice is indeed envisioned here by Paul, since otherwise he would hardly say that "if you do wrong, be afraid, for he [the government authority] does not bear the sword in vain; he is the servant of God to execute his wrath on the wrongdoer" (Rom. 13:4). Why mention "the sword" and "wrath" if retributive justice is not in play here, especially since it surely would have been in Roman courts?

Clearly, Jesus and Paul require that we forgive those who harm us, rather than seek retribution. Citing Hannah Arendt's remark that "the discoverer of

27. John Howard Yoder, for his part, argues that Rom. 13 does not envision or even allow Christian participation in the state's function of vengeance:

> The function exercised by government is not the function to be exercised by Christians. . . . God can in his own way, in his sovereign permissive providence, "use" an idolatrous Assyria (Isa. 10) or Rome. This takes place, however, without his declaring that such destructive action by pagan powers which he thus uses is morally good or that participation in it is incumbent upon his covenant people. . . . If the statements of 12:19 and 13:4 were not in the same passage, we might not necessarily cross-refer from one to the other. Then we might not have to conclude that the prohibition of vengeance in the one verse excludes the sharing of Christians in the outworking of vengeance as described in the other. (*Politics of Jesus*, 198)

For Yoder, God's instituting of authority in Rom. 13:1 is better translated as God's ordering authority by putting it in its place, using it in his permissive providence, and judging it. For a response to Yoder's pacifism, see Levering, *Betrayal of Charity*, chap. 7. For the ongoing development of Wolterstorff's position, including further discussion of Rom. 13, see Wolterstorff, *Mighty and Almighty*, 110, 113. Wolterstorff develops an important distinction between "performance-authority" (the authority to curb injustice) and "positional authority" (an authority based simply upon occupying a position).

28. Wolterstorff, *Justice in Love*, 128. For a Christian defense of "restorative justice" (including retribution, properly understood) in the political sphere, see Philpott, *Just and Unjust Peace*. Philpott observes critically,

> In country after country, punishment is pitted against reconciliation, just as justice is posed against mercy and retributive justice is positioned against restorative justice. With political reconciliation, however, punishment is restorative—of the political community, of law, of victims, and potentially of perpetrators—and therefore an essential part of reconciliation. . . . Reparations, punishment, and public apologies address past injustices, to be sure, but they do so in an effort to create a better political future. . . . The cardinal virtue running through the practices is mercy. This, too, may sound strange to citizens of the modern West, where mercy most often means forgoing punishment and is understood to be in tension with justice. (6)

Among Philpott's case studies is the response to the Rwandan genocide, particularly the *gacaca* courts (a communal justice system with the goal of healing and rebuilding communities).

the role of forgiveness in the realm of human affairs was Jesus of Nazareth,"[29] Wolterstorff adds that while the Old Testament frequently refers to God's forgiveness of humans, human forgiveness of other humans rarely appears in the Old Testament, and God in the Old Testament never commands humans to forgive those who harm them. So far as I can tell, Wolterstorff is justified in noting the newness of Jesus's teaching to his disciples that "if your brother sins, rebuke him, and if he repents, forgive him; and if he sins against you seven times in the day, and turns to you seven times, and says, 'I repent,' you must forgive him" (Luke 17:3–4).[30] In the Gospel of Matthew, Jesus intensifies this in response to a question from Peter: "'Lord, how often shall my brother sin against me, and I forgive him? As many as seven times?' Jesus said to him, 'I do not say to you seven times, but seventy times seven'" (Matt. 18:21–22).[31] The God who forgives his people expects us to forgive.

On the basis of his arguments that Jesus rejects retributive justice and the reciprocity code, Wolterstorff addresses Anselm's theory that Jesus Christ made "satisfaction" for our sins against God by paying our retributive penalty on the cross. As Wolterstorff emphasizes, this account of how Christ's cross reconciles us to God assumes that forgiveness *requires* retributive justice, and in fact *reverts back* to the reciprocity code as the standard of justice, just as if Jesus had never taught the opposite.[32] Wolterstorff notes that Anselm assumes that forgiveness and justice are in tension; justice cannot be served

29. Arendt, *Human Condition*, 214–15.

30. Wolterstorff affirms that we cannot forgive someone who has wronged us but is unrepentant. We must be willing to forgive this wrongdoer, but the act has been done and full forgiveness requires that both the perpetrator and the victim acknowledge the wrongness of the act. See *Justice in Love*, 172–75.

31. See Wolterstorff, *Justice in Love*, 162–63.

32. See ibid., 163–65. In *Cur Deus homo* 1.12, Anselm teaches that "it is not fitting for God to forgive a sin without punishment," because if a sin "is not punished, it is forgiven without its having been regulated" (*Why God Became Man*, 284). His interlocutor Boso raises an objection similar to Wolterstorff's: "When God teaches us to forgive those who sin against us, he seems to be being contradictory—in teaching us to do something which is not fitting for him to do himself" (1.12, p. 285). Anselm replies to Boso, "There is no contradiction in this, because God is giving us this teaching in order that we should not presume to do something which belongs to God alone. For it belongs to no one to take vengeance, except him who is Lord of all" (ibid.). Boso then raises another crucial objection: "Since God is so free that he is subject to no law and no judgement, and is so benevolent that nothing can be conceived of more benevolent than he, and since there is nothing right or proper except what he wishes, it does seem surprising that we should be saying that he is in no way willing to forgive an injury to himself, or that it is not permissible for him to do so, whereas we are in the habit of seeking forgiveness from him even for things we do to other people" (ibid.). Anselm responds that God can will nothing unjust, because God is justice itself. On this basis, Anselm concludes that "it does not belong to his freedom or benevolence or will to release unpunished a sinner who has not repaid to God what he has taken away from him" (286). Like Aquinas, I disagree with Anselm here, as I discuss further on.

without retribution, that is to say, without the fulfillment of the reciprocity code. Why did Anselm arrive at this position? Wolterstorff observes, "Anselm knew Scripture well and took it as authoritative. He would have known that Jesus enjoined rejection of the reciprocity code. He would have known that Jesus taught that we are not to repay evil with evil but always to seek the good of self and neighbor, even of those who are one's enemies."[33] Yet, despite this knowledge, Anselm still associated justice with retribution in the case of sinners. As Wolterstorff points out, in making this assumption, "Anselm was in line with the majority opinion in the Christian tradition," a majority opinion that leaves Wolterstorff surprised and confounded, given Jesus's clear rejection of the reciprocity code.[34] The result of Anselm's assumption was a theory "of the atonement according to which Christ, in allowing himself to be crucified, suffered on our behalf, thereby satisfying the requirements of retributive justice."[35] On this view, Christ on the cross freely "undergoes the hard treatment that God assigned as our punishment"; he thereby satisfies for our sins by restoring the order of justice between God and us.[36] Justice is

33. Wolterstorff, *Justice in Love*, 192.
34. Ibid.
35. Ibid. Nicholas E. Lombardo, OP, remarks that Anselm "maintains that God wills the heroism of Christ's self-sacrifice, but not his actual suffering and death" (*Father's Will*, 145). Lombardo recognizes that Anselm "rejects the idea that God requires innocent blood or takes pleasure in it, and he affirms that Christ's actual suffering is distasteful and displeasing to God the Father" (148). For Anselm, according to Lombardo, "it cannot be said that the Father commanded or willed his Son's death in any straightforward sense. Instead, the Son, wanting to save the world and knowing that the Father was unwilling to save the world unless he endured crucifixion, went to his death on his own initiative" (153). Lombardo argues that this means that the Son, and indeed the whole Trinity, willed his crucifixion and therefore the Son "committed a kind of suicide" (ibid.). Indeed, in Lombardo's reading of Anselm's account, God "wants the actual crucifying of Christ" (161; cf. 164), and since Christ is innocent, God (wickedly) wills an innocent man to be killed and wills that his crucifiers kill him, thereby willing "to bring about humanity's redemption through morally evil actions" (166). Lombardo also finds that Anselm "describes the Son as choosing to suffer on his own initiative, but he does not adequately locate this independent willing in the Son's humanity" (163); and Lombardo faults Anselm for interpreting "the crucifixion as a transaction" in such a way that "as the recipient of the transaction, the Father inevitably becomes the one who wants the crucifying of Christ" (165). Lombardo is equally dissatisfied with Aquinas's treatment of this theme, although he comments only very briefly on Aquinas; see 145n2. In my view, Aquinas's position (and probably also Anselm's, though I cannot here defend it) is not liable to the charges that Lombardo raises. Christ, in his human will, willed with supreme charity to give his life for our salvation. Insofar as this was an act of love, there is no reason why the divine will could not will this. God does not actively will the sin of anyone, let alone of Christ's killers. God permits, but does not will, the sinful disorder in the world that is the matrix in which just persons, including Christ, suffer out of love for others. The "transaction" is a restoration of justice from the side of the human race, but it involves no change (or "reception" of a sacrifice) on the side of God. See also the background sketched briefly by Vernon White, *Atonement and Incarnation*, 11–12.
36. Wolterstorff, *Justice in Love*, 192.

restored by the greatest injustice (namely, the acts of Jesus's killers, who in fact include all of us) precisely because Jesus's love, in freely offering up his life for us, was by far the greatest act of justice—an act of justice that the Triune God also wills insofar as what God is willing is (Jesus's) love.[37]

Wolterstorff considers Anselm's atonement theory to be a terrible distortion of Christianity.[38] Of course, Wolterstorff affirms that Christ suffered for us, since such a teaching is found clearly in the New Testament. But he argues that "vicarious punishment" not only does not produce forgiveness—since punishment is punishment, not forgiveness—but also goes against Jesus's central teachings. How could Jesus have taught so firmly against retributive justice in Matthew 5 and elsewhere, only to endure God's retributive justice with respect to us? Wolterstorff's point is that if we must not partake in retributive justice, then surely God should not partake in retributive justice either. If we should not "return evil for evil," an eye for an eye, then surely God, too, does not need to punish us—let alone allow Jesus to suffer our penalty for us—in order to establish justice between God and us. Wolterstorff asks with some acerbity, "Why has the declaration that God does not punish the repentant sinner but forgives him, and the injunction that we are to do likewise, not jolted Christian theologians and ethicists into concluding that justice does not require punishment? Why has it instead led them into calling

37. The theological problem arises from such passages as Acts 2:23, "This Jesus, delivered up according to the definite plan and foreknowledge of God . . ."; Mark 14:36 (and parallels), "Abba, Father, all things are possible to thee; remove this cup from me; yet not what I will, but what thou wilt"; Phil. 2:8, "he humbled himself and became obedient unto death, even death on a cross"; and John 10:17, "For this reason the Father loves me, because I lay down my life, that I may take it again." It might seem as though the Father willed to condemn his innocent Son to death. Yet the incarnate Son's freedom in going to the cross is also emphasized throughout the New Testament, in such passages as John 10:18 and 18:37, Luke 13:33, and Gal. 2:20.

38. For a positive view of Anselm's satisfaction theory from an Eastern Orthodox perspective, see Hart, *Beauty of the Infinite*, 360–72. Disagreeing with Vladimir Lossky (and indebted to Hans Urs von Balthasar), Hart considers Anselm's *Cur Deus homo* to be fundamentally in accord with Athanasius's *On the Incarnation*. When Athanasius treats the mode of our salvation, he states, "We will begin . . . with the creation of the world and with God its Maker, for the first fact that you must grasp is this: *the renewal of creation has been wrought by the Self-same Word Who made it in the beginning*" (*On the Incarnation* 1.1, p. 26). Athanasius understands Genesis 2 to mean that if the first humans sinned, "they would come under the natural law of death and live no longer in paradise, but, dying outside of it, continue in death and corruption" (1.3, p. 29). He concludes, therefore, that "there was a debt owing which must needs be paid; for . . . all men were due to die. . . . Death there had to be, and death for all, so that the due of all might be paid" (4.20, p. 49). Because we were created in the rational image of the Word, however, God could hardly leave us to such a dreadful fate. For this reason, says Athanasius, the Word became incarnate and freely "surrendered His body to death in place of all, and offered it to the Father. This He did out of sheer love for us, so that in His death all might die, and the law of death thereby be abolished" (2.8, p. 34).

vicarious punishment of the wrongdoer, *forgiveness* of the wrongdoer?"[39] For Wolterstorff, it is clear both that retributive punishment is not needed for justice and that *vicarious* retributive punishment, whatever it might supposedly accomplish, cannot cause the forgiveness of the persons for whom the vicarious punishment is endured.[40]

Although Wolterstorff rejects retributive punishment (and vicarious retributive punishment), he does not thereby intend to reject all punishment. In his view, punishment has a symbolic significance that is beneficial for both the wrongdoer and society. With regard to the wrongdoer, "the imposition of hard treatment on him counts as condemning *him for his deed*, and it is a way of expressing resentment of *the deed done* and anger at *him* for doing it."[41] Wolterstorff calls his theory of punishment "reprobative" rather than "retributive." He distinguishes *reprobative* punishment from the goals of "rehabilitation, deterrence, or protection," since punishment should look backward to the deed done, not forward to a future good. Reprobative punishment expresses "a judgment of condemnation and an expression of negative feelings toward deed and doer," and shows that "society does not condone what was done."[42]

Must a victim demand reprobative punishment (not retributive punishment) in order for justice to be fulfilled and forgiveness to be possible? Wolterstorff

39. Wolterstorff, *Justice in Love*, 193. Bernard Sesboüé, though not without some appreciation for Aquinas's teaching on satisfaction, expresses a similar concern about "certain dangerous theories, especially that of compensation or of the adequacy of the reparation to the fault" (*Jésus-Christ l'unique médiateur*, 350).

40. In this regard, see also Hans Boersma's contention that "the Paschal mystery of the cross and the resurrection, then, is a recapitulation of Israel's exilic punishment and return from exile. As Israel's representative, Christ thus reconstitutes and restores—at least in principle—both Israel and (through Israel) all of Adamic existence"—or as Boersma puts it in shorthand on the same page, "Christ suffers the corporate curse of Israel and in rising from the dead reconstitutes the people of God" ("Violence, the Cross, and Divine Intentionality," 56). Cf. Boersma, *Violence, Hospitality, and the Cross*. For Boersma, "The Paschal mystery as a reenactment of Israel's exile and restoration implies that divine punishment (and thus divine violence) has a place within the overall scheme of redemption" ("Violence, the Cross, and Divine Intentionality," 56). If by this Boersma means that God punishes the innocent Jesus, I would disagree, but I do think that Jesus freely endured out of supreme love the penalty (death) for our sins. I agree with Boersma that "an entirely nonpenal understanding of justice is not just" (ibid., 61), and I share Boersma's concerns about the fully nonpenal accounts of atonement offered by J. Denny Weaver and (if Boersma's reading is correct) unsystematically by John Milbank. See Weaver, "Narrative *Christus Victor*"; Weaver, *Nonviolent Atonement*; Milbank, *Word Made Strange*; Milbank, *Being Reconciled*.

41. Wolterstorff, *Justice in Love*, 196.

42. Ibid., 196–97. For his understanding of "reprobative punishment," Wolterstorff is indebted to Feinberg, *Doing and Deserving*, 95–118. By contrast, Philpott envisions punishment (which he calls "restorative punishment," and which is closely linked with what I call "retributive punishment") as follows: "Through punishment the community invites the restoration of the perpetrator in the hope that he will repent and accept his punishment as a sincere expression of this repentance" (*Just and Unjust Peace*, 231).

argues that the answer is no. It is possible to offer full and complete forgiveness even without exacting punishment. Here Wolterstorff responds not only to Anselm, but also to Immanuel Kant, who holds that "failure to punish wrongdoers is a double violation of justice."[43] The key question for Wolterstorff is whether forgoing punishment sends a message to the wrongdoer and to society that one condones evil acts. Wolterstorff concludes that it does not; rather, it sends a message of mercy, just as Jesus commanded.

In arguing against retributive justice vis-à-vis the cross (Anselm), Wolterstorff does not address the numerous New Testament passages that seem indebted to retributive justice, insofar as they connect Jesus's work of atonement with his spilling of his blood (e.g., Mark 14:24 and par.; Rom. 3:23–25; 5:9; 1 Cor. 11:25; Eph. 1:7; 2:13; Col. 1:20; Heb. 13:20; 1 Pet. 1:18–19; Rev. 1:5; 5:9). According to such passages, Jesus's spilling of his blood reconciles humans to God, makes peace between humans and God, takes away and expiates sin, pays the ransom owed by sinners, and establishes the new covenant. His death restores us to justice in relation to God: "While we were yet sinners Christ died for us," so that "we are now justified by his blood" (Rom. 5:8–9).[44] Wolterstorff does not address these passages in his account of Jesus's rejection of the reciprocity code or in his critique of theories of atonement centered upon satisfaction for sin (so as to restore justice). Instead, Wolterstorff grants merely that "Paul held that God justifies sinners on account of the fidelity of Jesus; Christ died *for us*."[45] Since his focus is on "the justice of God's love" and on "the fidelity of Jesus," Wolterstorff thinks that he does not need to spell out the significance of Jesus's dying for us, although he recognizes that the fact that Jesus died *for us* "is an extremely important part of Paul's thought."[46] This seems to me to be an understatement, and I think that Wolterstorff makes a serious mistake by not addressing these passages.

In my view, the above biblical texts about Jesus's cross indicate that the justice that Jesus fulfilled on the cross—as part of his mission to accomplish

---

43. Wolterstorff, *Justice in Love*, 201. See Kant, *Metaphysical Elements of Justice*, 102.

44. I agree with Scot McKnight when he writes: "I don't know how to read elements of (especially) Paul without explaining his soteriology as penal" (*Community Called Atonement*, 43; cf. 64–66). McKnight also points out that Jesus's choosing to give up his life during Passover (in light of his Last Supper), and Jesus's statement in Mark 10:45 that "the Son of Man also came . . . to give his life as a ransom for many," indicate Jesus's intention to take upon himself God's judgment against sin and to liberate us from sin. McKnight explains this in a manner reminiscent of the Greek fathers: "He accomplishes that liberation by entering into enemy territory (sin and enslavement), by being captured to the point of death *instead of* and *for the benefit of* others, and by escaping from that captivity through the resurrection" (88).

45. Wolterstorff, *Justice in Love*, 280.

46. Ibid., 280–81.

the restoration of Israel and to inaugurate the kingdom of God—was in fact retributive justice: Jesus paid the retributive penalty of death for us (see also Gen. 2:17; 3:2; 3:19; Rom. 5:12; 6:23; James 1:15).[47] As I noted above, the New Testament also teaches that those who are being configured to Jesus's love by the Holy Spirit will receive an everlasting reward due in reciprocal justice (though the reward will go beyond any merely human reciprocity), while those who freely reject Jesus's love will receive retributive punishment.[48] Jesus tells those who are fasting: "But when you fast, anoint your head and wash your face, that your fasting may not be seen by men but by your Father who is in secret; and your Father who sees in secret will reward you" (Matt. 6:16–18). He promises that good works will be rewarded: "Lay up for yourselves treasures in heaven" (Matt. 6:20; cf. Matt. 10:41–42 and Luke 6:35). Retributive justice will be enacted at the final judgment toward those who freely reject God's love (see Matt. 25:41–46; Rev. 20:14), though we should keep in view that retributive justice has already been fulfilled on the cross and that God's desire is to "have mercy upon all" (Rom. 11:32).

In addition to these texts that seem to retain reciprocal and retributive justice (without displacing mercy), there is another crucial issue that receives insufficient attention from Wolterstorff, namely, from where does the code of reciprocity come? For Wolterstorff, the code of reciprocity seems to be essentially a cultural prejudice. He states that "the reciprocity code, and the idea of punishment as retribution that goes along with it, have had such a tight grip on human thought and imagination that not even Jesus's rejection of the code and his injunction to forgive rather than punish have been sufficient to loosen that grip, not even on those who take his words as authoritative."[49] But why does the code of reciprocity have such a "tight grip on human thought and imagination"? Some might suppose that the reason is a survival-driven sense of equity. Perhaps this is what Wolterstorff has in mind when he comments, "All about us people talk about getting even, giving malefactors what they have coming to them; it's hard to resist

47. As Eleonore Stump notes, some theologians hold that according to "Christian doctrine, the punishment for sin is not just death but hell" (*Aquinas*, 429). In fact, however, while the punishment for sin is death, the punishment for consciously and freely rejecting God's mercy in Christ is hell. The sin of rejecting mercy for sin is distinct from the sin whose punishment is death; and in both cases the punishment is intrinsic to the crime. The distinction between death and hell is found, e.g., in the words of the risen Lord to the church in Smyrna: "Be faithful unto death, and I will give you the crown of life. . . . He who conquers shall not be hurt by the second death" (Rev. 2:10–11).

48. As I. Howard Marshall observes, "I cannot see how deprivation of eternal life can be seen as anything other than a [retributive] penalty or punishment upon the impenitent sinner" ("Theology of the Atonement," 57).

49. Wolterstorff, *Justice in Love*, 193.

thinking the same way."[50] In my view, however, the reason for the reciprocity code is more profound than the urge to even things up with malefactors or the desire to prevent malefactors from getting away with harming us and our loved ones. I think that the reason for the enduring power of the reciprocity code is that it belongs to the relational justice inscribed in the order of creation.

The remainder of this chapter offers an account of reciprocal justice as grounded in the created order, in hopes of exhibiting the manifold links between creation and atonement.[51] I do so by drawing upon the theology of Thomas Aquinas, since he is well known for his Anselmian insistence that given God's will to free us from sin, it was in a certain sense "necessary that God should become incarnate for the restoration of human nature"—a restoration that was accomplished "by Christ satisfying for us" and that restored our just ordering to God.[52] In this sense, Christ died "for our sins *in our place, instead of us*," as Simon Gathercole rightly emphasizes.[53] The perspective that informs Aquinas's

50. Ibid.

51. Colin E. Gunton emphasizes the role of metaphor in theories of Christ's saving work, but this overlooks the fact that the order of (relational) justice inscribed in creation is not a metaphorical order. Gunton states, "All the main ways of spelling out the saving significance of the life, death and resurrection of Jesus contain a considerable metaphorical and imaginative content, drawing, as is often remarked, from a number of human institutions: notably the legal system, the altar of sacrifice, the battlefield and the slavemarket" (*Actuality of Atonement*, 17–18; cf. 27–52). In my view, the use of the legal system and the altar of sacrifice, both of which depend upon the relational order of justice, need not be described primarily in terms of "metaphorical and imaginative content," since law and sacrificial worship belong to the order of creation just as much as does human rationality itself (though I recognize that law, justice, and sacrificial worship, in their human expressions over the centuries, have changed and developed). In soteriology, we are dealing with *analogous* uses of law, justice, and sacrifice, rather than with metaphorical language. I disagree, then, with Gunton's claim that our descriptions of Christ's saving work "are eschatological concepts, giving up their secrets only by anticipation and through the gift of the Spirit" (105), unless by this he simply means that no concept or category can exhaust the meaning and power of Christ's saving work. Gunton's discussion of Schleiermacher's and Hegel's evacuations of the penal elements of the cross explains why he distances himself so strongly from anything that in his view hints of rationalism (cf. 128). I fully agree with Gunton's spirited defense of "the historically particular" (22) and of the necessary connection "to the story that is told of Jesus of Nazareth, narrated as it is in language containing 'pictorial', representational elements" (23). It is worth noting, too, that Gunton provides a sympathetic account of Anselm's doctrine of atonement and recognizes the significance for Anselm of "the conception of God as the upholder of universal justice" (90, 101; cf. 94–113). As he states, "there can be no restoration of relationships unless the nature of the offence against universal justice is laid bare and attacked at its root" (161). For an approach to metaphor indebted to Gunton, see Blocher, "Biblical Metaphors and the Doctrine of the Atonement."

52. Thomas Aquinas, *ST* III, q. 1, a. 2. For the connection between the incarnation (as taught at the Council of Chalcedon) and the proper understanding of Christ's act of satisfaction, see especially Perrier, "L'enjeu christologique de la satisfaction," 105–36 and 203–47.

53. Gathercole, *Defending Substitution*, 14. Gathercole goes on to say: "I am defining *substitutionary* atonement for the present purposes as Christ's death in our place, instead of

theology of the cross has been well articulated, without reference to Aquinas, by Graham McFarlane: "The cross signifies that our human actions carry with them real consequences, that within creation there is an inbuilt penalty clause for relational unfaithfulness, and that this lies at the very heart of the created order."[54]

Creation and Atonement: Thomas Aquinas's Contribution

Is There Justice in God?

The question of whether reciprocal justice is inscribed in the created order depends in part upon whether there is justice in the creator, since the perfections of creatures participate in a finite mode in the infinite perfections of God. In the question that Aquinas devotes in the *Summa theologiae* to the justice of God, an objection observes that "the act of justice is to pay what is due. But God is no man's debtor. Therefore justice does not belong to God."[55] Why is God not a debtor? The key scriptural passage that Aquinas cites is Romans 11:35: "Who has given a gift to him, that he might be repaid?" The next verse adds a doxology: "For from him and through him and to him are all things" (Rom. 11:36). All things are from God; all things, insofar as they have being and goodness, are his gifts. The created order and everything in it is sheer divine gift. Interestingly, in Romans 11:35 Paul is paraphrasing Job 35, where Elihu criticizes Job for claiming something as his "right before God" (Job 35:2). Elihu

---

us. The 'instead of us' clarifies the point that 'in our place' does not, in substitution at least, mean 'in our place *with us*.' (Jesus was, for example, baptized in *our place with us*—that is, the baptism was not a substitution.) In substitutionary theory of the death of Jesus, he did something, underwent something, so that we did not and would never have to do so" (15). In this sense of "substitutionary," Aquinas's "satisfaction" theory is a "substitutionary" theory (since Christ alone could satisfy for our sins; we could not do it ourselves). The key question, however, is what is meant by Christ bearing our sins: Was Christ the object of the Father's just wrath? Gathercole distances his interpretation from the latter view, but traditional substitutionary theories (Protestant and Catholic) of the atonement have often upheld this view. On this point, see Torrell, *Pour nous les hommes et pour notre salut*, 156–81, which treats Martin Luther and John Calvin as well as such figures as Denys the Carthusian, Jacques Bénigne Bossuet, and Louis Bourdaloue. (For the latter three, Torrell relies upon Sabourin, *Rédemption sacrificielle*.) Gathercole offers instructive critiques, with which I agree, of Gese, "The Atonement"; Hooker, "Interchange in Christ"; and Douglas A. Campbell, *Deliverance of God*, 33, 185, 325.

54. McFarlane, "Atonement, Creation and Trinity," 201. As McFarlane points out, "Whilst the creatures have broken the network of relational associations that links them with God, it would appear that it is not a two-way break. Rather, we see [already in Gen. 3] the character of the Creator, whose initial instinct is to save the fallen image-bearers and preserve them from the ultimate consequences of their actions" (202). In his essay, McFarlane uses the language of "substitution," though he warns against "purely penal interpretations of the death of Christ that source the penal dimension and its consequences in the character of God" (204).

55. *ST* I, q. 21, a. 1, obj. 3.

tries to bring Job back to reality so that Job will not cry out against God. Thus Elihu asks Job, "If you are righteous, what do you give to him; or what does he receive from your hand?" (Job 35:7). Elihu's point is that the gift is all on God's side. Elihu is not a spokesman for God, and yet God later affirms something of what Elihu says. Speaking directly to Job, God asks rhetorically, "Who has given to me, that I should repay him? Whatever is under the whole heaven is mine" (Job 41:11). If everything is gift, it seems that claims to justice on the side of the creature make no sense, since no one has a right to a gift. God is sheer giver, and creatures cannot make claims of justice as though God owed creatures something, since everything that creatures have and are is God's gift.

Aquinas, however, argues that God possesses justice vis-à-vis creatures, since as Psalm 10:8 says (in his Vulgate version), "The Lord is just, and has loved justice."[56] In defending this scriptural claim, Aquinas makes use of Aristotle's distinction between commutative justice (equitable exchange of goods and services) and distributive justice (giving to each person what he or she deserves).[57] Commutative justice does not apply to God, because God is the giver of all things, and he receives nothing in return because he is infinitely actual and because creatures are finite participations of his infinite actuality. God is an utterly free giver, not one who gives out of a neediness or a hoped-for return. God gives because of his infinite goodness; he loves finite things into being and sustains them in being by his love. Whatever goodness creatures have, is the gift of his causal love. But once commutative justice is ruled out (as Paul and Job confirm it must be), distributive justice remains. Every good ruler or steward, Aquinas observes, must be just in the sense of distributive justice, in giving to each what each deserves. Distributive justice means that "the order of the universe, which is seen both in effects of nature and in effects of will, shows forth the justice of God."[58]

---

56. *ST* I, q. 21, a. 1, *sed contra*. Ps. 10:8 in the Vulgate corresponds to Ps. 11:7 in the RSV. The Latin is: "Iustus Dominus, et iustitias dilexit." The RSV translates the verse with essentially the same meaning, substituting righteousness for justice: "For the Lord is righteous, he loves righteous deeds." When Aquinas goes on to appeal to Aristotle, it is not a case of (as Adam Johnson says in another context, without having Aquinas in view) stepping "away from Scripture in order to dwell on some abstractly derived doctrine of God" (Johnson, *God's Being in Reconciliation*, 13).

57. Alister McGrath argues, "Far from endorsing prevailing secular accounts of justice, as some less perceptive critics suggested, Anselm aims to disconnect the theological discussion of redemption from preconceived human patterns of distributive or retributive justice" (*Iustitia Dei*, 76). Although I cannot treat Anselm here, McGrath's claim seems too strong, insofar as it suggests that a just human pattern of distributive justice can or should be sharply disconnected from a just divine pattern of distributive justice (which, as a divine attribute and action, must of course be understood analogously).

58. *ST* I, q. 21, a. 1. The opposite view, insisting that God is not bound to any justice vis-à-vis creatures, is articulated by John Duns Scotus. For discussion, see Vidu, *Atonement, Law,*

To explain this point further, Aquinas cites Dionysius's *The Divine Names* on God's justice as exemplified in creation. Dionysius urges that people who do not perceive the justice of the existing order of things need to "see that God is truly just, in seeing how He gives to all existing things what is proper to the condition of each; and preserves the nature of each one in the order and with the powers that properly belong to it."[59] Each thing that God creates has a nature, and God gives it the powers that belong to its nature and that enable its flourishing as the kind of thing that it is. Aquinas adds that God's justice is always founded upon his mercy, because it is an act of mercy, flowing from "the abundance of his goodness," for God to create things from nothing.[60] As a divine attribute, justice is infinite, and like the other divine attributes, justice is the simple divine essence (though our finite mode of understanding requires many names for God, predicated analogously).[61] Thus, the justice of God belongs equally to each person of the Trinity and is exhibited in the divine work of creation, with regard to which Aquinas consistently holds together the twin truths that "all things caused are the common work of the whole Godhead" and that "God the Father made the creature through his Word, which is his Son; and through his Love, which is the Holy Spirit."[62]

---

and Justice, 79–86. Vidu goes on to note that *"Calvin and Luther both resolutely reject any direct rational link between human ends, as apprehended by natural reason, and divine justice.* Divine justice and divine power form a unity, but their unity is not given, à la Aquinas, by God's knowledge of the end proper to human beings, and the end that we may also know through natural reason" (93). For important differences between Luther and Calvin, however, see 93–97. On the order of the universe in the "effects of nature," see, e.g., William P. Brown's observation: "Each of the forty-one orders of magnitude that constitute the physical universe as we know it, from half a billion light years to one hundredth of the diameter of a proton, exhibits structure. Even galaxies are found to be concentrated in great cosmic clusters and 'sheets,' such as the 'Sloan Great Wall'" (*Seven Pillars of Creation*, 51).

59. This is the English translation of Aquinas's Latin version of Pseudo-Dionysius's work; for a contemporary translation, see Pseudo-Dionysius, *Divine Names* 8.7 (896B), p. 113: "What they really should know is that the righteousness of God is truly righteousness in that it gives the appropriate and deserved qualities to everything and that it preserves the nature of each being in its due order and power."

60. *ST* I, q. 21, a. 4.

61. See *ST* I, q. 4, a. 2; I, q. 7, aa. 1–2; I, q. 13, aa. 2, 4, and 5. God would be just even if there were no creatures toward which to exercise justice, since one can have a just will even if one lacks objects for the exercise of justice. Aquinas specifies that "God's justice is from eternity in respect of the eternal will and purpose (and it is chiefly in this that justice consists); although it is not eternal as regards its effect, since nothing is co-eternal with God" (*ST* II-II, q. 58, a. 2, ad 3). For a helpful discussion of the atonement in light of the "uniqueness of divine agency," due to divine simplicity and perfection, see Vidu, *Atonement, Law, and Justice*, 240–72.

62. *ST* I, q. 45, a. 6 (including the *sed contra*). I treat the trinitarian missions in relation to Jesus's saving work in my *Engaging the Doctrine of the Holy Spirit*, chap. 4. Adam Johnson rightly notes the importance of the doctrine of God for the doctrine of the atonement; see

If God exercises distributive justice toward creatures, however, this may seem to imply that God is not free in what he gives to creatures, or that God is bound to "an impersonal set of rules of the game of the universe" so that creatures determine God rather than the other way around.[63] In response to such concerns, Aquinas's analogy between God and a human artist or craftsman is helpful. Citing Deuteronomy 32:4, "The Rock, his work is perfect; for all his ways are justice," Aquinas notes that God's distributive justice is apparent in the human body.[64] He observes that "every artist intends to give to his work the best disposition; not absolutely the best, but the best as regards the proposed end."[65] Humans therefore receive the "best disposition" suitable to their end or goal of knowing and loving God. As rational creatures, humans do not need horns, claws, and fur in order to remain alive; and human hands serve as the instruments of human rationality. The human being has an upright stature and faces forward "in order that by the senses, and chiefly by sight, which is more subtle and penetrates further into the differences of things, he may freely survey the sensible objects around him, both heavenly and earthly, so as to gather intelligible truth from all things."[66] Since God's plan for distributive justice is an infinitely wise plan, it can be rightly termed a "law" of justice without thereby rendering it unfree.[67] As Aquinas says, rather than creating in an arbitrary fashion, what God "does according to his will he does justly: as we do justly what we do according to law."[68]

Even so, it seems that the fundamental difficulty with attributing distributive justice to God still needs to be answered. Can it really be said that God *owes* something to any creature? Does God really owe to humans that, given the end or goal of our rational nature, we not have (for example) cow bodies?

God's Being in Reconciliation, 9. In *Community Called Atonement*, McKnight also offers valuable insight into the rootedness of atonement in the trinitarian *perichoresis* and missions.

63. Green, "Must We Imagine the Atonement in Penal Substitutionary Terms?," 163. For this problem, see also Vernon White, *Atonement and Incarnation*, 27. Graham McFarlane remarks in this regard that "there is a divine and personal justice: we sin against persons, not an impersonal creation," even though our sin makes manifest a "creational justice, a rule of creation to which we must adhere" ("Atonement, Creation and Trinity," 203–4). I think that McFarlane is moving toward Aquinas's doctrine of satisfaction when he proposes that "for the restoration of a relationship and, therefore, atonement to occur, divine love reshapes divine justice and does so by going beyond the boundaries established by normal law" (204). However, divine love, divine justice, and divine law need not be set in tension.

64. See *ST* I, q. 91, a. 1. The portion of Deut. 32:4 that Aquinas cites (in his Latin translation) reads simply "God's works are perfect."

65. *ST* I, q. 91, a. 3. Aquinas grants that through material generation, individuals of the species will possess defects.

66. *ST* I, q. 91, a. 3, ad 3. In this discussion, Aquinas benefits from Aristotle's *De anima*.

67. *ST* I, q. 21, a. 1, ad 2.

68. Ibid.

If God is our debtor in distributive justice, then it seems as though the order has become topsy-turvy. A true giver does not *owe* someone a gift. If the gift is owed, it is not really a gift but rather is a payment, an obligation. God has no such obligations to pay. Recall God's words to Job (41:11), which Paul takes up and affirms: "Who has given to me, that I should repay him? Whatever is under the whole heaven is mine." How then can there be distributive justice in God the creator?

Aquinas answers in a twofold way. He affirms that God does indeed owe creatures what pertains to their flourishing, to their ability to achieve the end of their nature. In this regard, with particular reference to human nature, he states that it is "due to a created thing that it should possess what is ordered to it; thus it is due to man to have hands."[69] But before making this affirmation, he argues that the primary debt God owes is to himself: to his own goodness. It is because God is good that God owes to himself that he distribute to creatures what is justly due to them. Aquinas observes, "It is due to God that there should be fulfilled in creatures what his will and wisdom require, and what manifests his goodness."[70] In giving creatures what he owes them in distributive justice, God is primarily giving what he owes to himself as the good creator.[71] In ordering creatures to his goodness, God owes them in justice what is due to their natures; but it is the ordering of creatures to God, and thus God's debt to his own goodness, that is fundamental.

For Aquinas, therefore, creation or the created order is imbued with justice in two ways: first insofar as all created things are ordered to God's goodness, and second insofar as "one created thing is ordered to another, as the parts to the whole, accident to substance, and all things whatsoever to their end."[72] For our purposes, the key point is that the created order is imbued

---

69. *ST* I, q. 21, a. 1, ad 3.

70. Ibid. Romanus Cessario, OP, observes in this regard that "Aquinas forges an understanding of God's justice which, as it remains identical with the divine nature itself, therefore must also fully manifest the divine goodness. . . . The divine goodness controls Aquinas' theology of salvation from its start in the Incarnation to its completion in the transformation of the Church into Christ's Bride" ("Aquinas on Christian Salvation," 134). As Cessario goes on to say, the "communication of the divine goodness to the human creature governs everything that Aquinas teaches about Christian salvation" (ibid.).

71. Gunton argues that God's justice in this sense must be metaphorical, since "a concept whose apparently primary meaning is to be found in matters of legality is now used chiefly to explicate relationships between persons, and in particular the all determining relationship between the creator and his erring but never abandoned children" (*Actuality of Atonement*, 113). But I think that an analogical understanding of "legality" would enable Gunton to recognize that God's justice vis-à-vis creatures (and vice versa) is not simply a metaphorical extension of the true meaning of justice.

72. *ST* I, q. 21, a. 1, ad 3.

with distributive justice, both in its own interrelationships and in its relation to God. Again, this justice is rooted in God's goodness, by which the Triune God, not only as creator but also as redeemer, enables creatures to share in the trinitarian life.[73]

It follows that a sharp contrast between a logic of gift/love and a logic of justice is mistaken with respect to creation (and so likewise with respect to redemption).[74] Creation is God's sheer gift, and yet creation is profoundly imbued with structures of justice. Indeed, precisely because creation is God's gift, justice and juridical categories are inseparable from the created order. An example that Aquinas offers begins with our possession of hands: "To possess hands is due to man on account of his rational soul; and his rational soul is due to him that he may be man; and his being man is on account of the divine goodness."[75] God's justice in creating humans with what is due to them has its source in God's goodness and love. Indeed, Aquinas finds that God's mercy is always deeper than his distributive justice: "In every work of God, viewed at its primary source, there appears mercy," since the giver always bestows not only what is due, but far more than what is due.[76]

Creaturely Injustice and Retributive Punishment

Since God's relationship to creation involves not only love and gift, but also justice, rational creatures can rebel against God's goodness in such a way as to fall afoul of justice, and to deserve punishment in retributive justice. Recall Wolterstorff's criticism of "theories of the atonement according to which

73. See *ST* III, q. 1, a. 1, including the quotation from John of Damascus in the *sed contra*; see also—in addition to Cessario, "Aquinas on Christian Salvation"—Davidson, "Salvation's Destiny." Drawing upon Brauch, "Perspectives on 'God's Righteousness' in Recent German Discussion," Gunton notes that "although Luther himself conceived justice as creative and redemptive activity, his contemporaries and successors tended to lapse back into a pre-Reformation understanding of justice as merely distributive" (*Actuality of Atonement*, 103). It is a mistake, however, to suppose that God's distributive justice prevents God from acting (creatively and redemptively) to establish justice; in fact the opposite is the case. At the same time, Gunton recognizes, with Brauch (and indebted to the Old Testament), that "an important aspect of the concept's meaning centres on the notion of God's faithfulness to his entire creation"; and Gunton recognizes that this view of God's faithfulness is apparent in Anselm's (and Athanasius's) perspective. Citing Forsyth, *Justification of God*, Gunton states insightfully that "there is a link between matters of justice more narrowly conceived and the created order as a whole" (*Actuality of Atonement*, 107). He urges us to "learn . . . to realise the interrelatedness of redemption and creation" (ibid., 149), but he does not examine creation in terms of the order of justice (beyond the way in which Christ's victory redeems a fallen creation and brings creation to its intended completion and perfection).

74. In *Justice in Love*, Wolterstorff shows that Søren Kierkegaard and Reinhold Niebuhr, among many others, consider love to be in opposition to justice.

75. *ST* I, q. 21, a. 4.

76. Ibid; cf. *ST* I, q. 21, a. 3.

Christ, in allowing himself to be crucified, suffered on our behalf, thereby satisfying the requirements of retributive justice."[77] For Wolterstorff, such theories go against Jesus's teaching that "we are to stop thinking in terms of paying back, getting even, evening things up, redressing injury with injury, harm with harm, evil with evil."[78] As I noted above, Wolterstorff fails to account for a number of New Testament texts that indicate that Christ paid the penalty for sin by his blood, and that make clear that the code of reciprocity continues to hold, although as believers united to Christ we are required to await divine reward and punishment in the life to come. It should now be clear that Wolterstorff's criticism of atonement theories that involve Christ's "satisfying the requirements of retributive justice" begs the question of whether there is a relationship of justice between rational creatures and the creator. If there is such a relationship, then the order of justice is indeed likely to be something that the incarnate Son, filled with the Holy Spirit, willed to satisfy for us, by restoring the justice of the human race vis-à-vis the Triune God.[79]

Aquinas points out that just as the creator owes a debt to creatures (because of the creator's own goodness), so also rational creatures owe a debt of worship and service to the creator, since "he made all things, and has supreme dominion over all."[80] Reflecting upon the virtue of piety, Aquinas comments that "man becomes a debtor to other men in various ways, according to their various excellence and the various benefits received from them. On both counts God holds first place, for he is supremely excellent, and is for us the first principle of being and government."[81] This debt is both a debt of justice

77. Wolterstorff, *Justice in Love*, 192.

78. Ibid., 193.

79. Gunton comments that "to be part of the creation means *to be related to the Father through the Son and in the Spirit*. But the creation, and particularly the human creation, has lived as if this relation were not real, and so has become subject to the slavery to sin and corruption. The fact that the Son takes flesh in the midst of time means that the relationship is reordered and renewed: redirected to its original and eschatological destiny" (*Actuality of Atonement*, 169). This is well put, although it needs to be added that the reordering of the relationship comes about through the cross and not solely through the incarnation (as Gunton well recognizes).

80. *ST* II-II, q. 81, a. 1, ad 3. It is not that the Triune God, to be happy, requires our worship. Rather, as Gunton remarks, "Praise perfects perfection: it is the movement out of self into free and glad relationship with the other. To be truly human, it must be realised, not to be curved in upon ourselves (one of Luther's definitions of sin) but to be liberated from self-preoccupation by and to the praise of God and each other" (*Actuality of Atonement*, 201). See also Hardy and Ford, *Jubilate*.

81. *ST* II-II, q. 101, a. 1. Thus Peter J. Leithart urges us to become persons "whose first instinct in every circumstance is to offer praise and thanks to the Father. We must learn what it means to offer a continuous sacrifice of thanksgiving" (*Gratitude*, 229). Leithart here urges that Christians restore the Eucharist to its central place, and I agree wholeheartedly. Leithart offers a brief, critical treatment of Aquinas on gratitude at 92–94, concluding that "little of Aquinas' account is distinctively Christian. Believing as he does in creation, he recognizes that

and a debt that rightly calls forth love: the Triune God who lovingly creates us has a just claim upon our love. God's infinite goodness, manifested not least in the gift of creation, makes him infinitely lovable. Indeed, if we were able to apprehend how lovable God actually is, we literally could not help but love him.

When we humans turn away from the divine love and refuse our debt of justice, we lack the justice that we were created to have. Aquinas observes that sin "is not a pure privation but an act deprived of its due order."[82] The sinner rebels against the order of justice that exists between rational creatures and God, an interpersonal order that characterizes full human flourishing (virtue). Aquinas describes the resulting disorder as the "debt of punishment [*reatus poenae*]" that sin produces.[83] Human beings were created for a graced union with the Triune God, in God's kingdom, through knowledge and love. Having rejected God's grace and destroyed "the principle of the order whereby man's will is subject to God," humans fall into disorder and slavery to sin.[84] Sin itself, then, is a punishment for sin. As Aquinas says, "Whatever rises up against an order, is put down by that order or by the principle thereof. And because sin is an inordinate act, it is evident that whoever sins, commits an offense against an order: wherefore he is put down, in consequence, by that same order, which repression is punishment."[85] The order of creation is such that when we rebel against this order, we disorder ourselves, losing our interior justice and our just relation to God. Aquinas adds that "so long as the disturbance of the order [*perversitas ordinis*] remains, the debt of punishment

---

all things are gifts of God. He, of course, endorses the Pauline exhortation to 'give thanks in all circumstances.' Yet when he gives direct attention to gratitude, he follows Seneca and Tully to give a slightly Christianized version of ancient reciprocity. In his work the infinite circle of Christian gift and gratitude contracted" (94). It appears to me, however, that this contraction stems in good part from Leithart's reading of the *secunda pars* of the *Summa theologiae* in isolation. Even so, Leithart is right to identify Aquinas as representative of a position on gratitude that Leithart opposes, because for Leithart, Jesus utterly cancels out human reciprocity (see 71). In my view, however, loving one another includes certain social debts, since love and justice are not in opposition, nor is love the only virtue. In love, we owe debts to, e.g., our parents; the inaugurated kingdom of God does not cancel such debts, but rather allows us to fulfill them with a justice ordered by charity. Since we cannot adequately repay many of our debts (including our debts to our parents), Christ pays our debt for us, in accord with the superabundant generosity of the Trinity. In Christ, the Father calls us to a reward that far exceeds anything owed to us, although the indwelling Spirit enables us to merit this reward. On this latter point, see Charles Raith II's ecumenical studies: *Aquinas and Calvin on Romans*; "Calvin's Critique of Merit, and Why Aquinas (Mostly) Agrees"; and "Aquinas and Calvin on Merit, Part II."

82. *ST* I-II, q. 72, a. 1, ad 2.
83. *ST* I-II, q. 87, a. 1.
84. *ST* I-II, q. 87, a. 3.
85. *ST* I-II, q. 87, a. 1.

[*reatus poenae*] must needs remain also."[86] The "disturbance of the order" is that in pride we have turned away from God as our ultimate end and have cut ourselves off from God by the loss of charity. Aquinas notes that this disorder, considered in itself, is "irreparable, although it is possible to repair it by the power of God."[87] Only God can restore our graced charity and draw us into his kingdom.

Is such punishment, wherein God actually does not inflict anything but rather simply permits humans to have their own way in rejecting God, "retributive" punishment?[88] Aquinas explains that "in so far as sin consists in turning away from something, its corresponding punishment is the *pain of loss* [*poena damni*], which also is infinite, because it is the loss of the infinite good, i.e., God."[89] Humans rebel against the order of love, and as punishment God permits humans to live in this disorder. This is a just punishment, and reflects the inability of sinners truly to overthrow the order of justice. God does not *actively* inflict the punishment, but the punishment is retributive because the punishment consists in a harm that the sinner incurs due to the harm that the sinner has inflicted.[90]

86. *ST* I-II, q. 87, a. 3.
87. Ibid.
88. See Koritansky, *Thomas Aquinas and the Philosophy of Punishment*. Koritansky notes that for the influential utilitarian philosopher Jeremy Bentham, "punishment is evil by definition and must therefore be justified by some good consequence sufficient to outweigh the evil suffered by the criminal," and "retribution is a fundamentally irrational motive for punishing because . . . it cannot be connected with any ostensible good or benefit to society" (191). Aquinas disagrees with Bentham in numerous respects, but he agrees, as Koritansky observes, that "punishment may never be imposed simply as an infliction of harm upon a criminal" (192). With regard to the question of retributive justice, Koritansky states, "In responding to Bentham's suggestion that retribution constitutes a useless reveling in the harm of another person, Aquinas would respond by saying that retribution serves the further purpose of justice. Although Aquinas consistently holds that 'the punishments of this life are more of a medicinal character' [*ST* II-II, q. 108, a. 3, ad 2], reestablishing the equality of justice remains an essential good that punishment achieves. . . . On Aquinas's analysis, the equality of justice is reestablished by imposing something against the criminal's will that represses his inordinate criminal act. What matters, then, is not the kind of crime committed, but the *degree* to which the criminal's will encroached upon the common good in the commission of the crime" (193, 195). See also Koritansky, "Christianity, Punishment, and Natural Law." The crucial differences between Aquinas's account of retributive punishment and those found in Bentham and Immanuel Kant can be seen in Shuster, "Kant on the Role of the Retributive Outlook in Moral and Political Life"; Crimmins, "Principles of Utilitarian Penal Law in Beccaria, Bentham, and J. S. Mill."
89. *ST* I-II, q. 87, a. 4.
90. Scot McKnight raises the concern that this approach (a version of which he finds in C. H. Dodd) depersonalizes God's "wrath" and thereby undermines the biblical portrait of God's anger and jealousy against sin. McKnight comments that

"wrath" has found many who argue that it means the impersonal, inevitable consequences of sin. That is, it is not the momentary, personal reaction of a holy God to

Reflecting further upon the fallen human condition, Aquinas shows that when a person commits a sin, the sin incurs guilt or debt (*reatus*) because of the harm that it causes, and the sin also stains the will by causing the will to lose holiness.[91] The sinner needs to be freed from both the debt and the stain (*macula*). For this to happen, the repentant sinner must willingly embrace the order of justice inscribed in creation and must freely choose to endure the just retributive punishment. With regard to the debt, the sinner must "pay some sort of penal compensation, which restores him to the equality of justice."[92] With regard to the stain, the sinner must willingly "accept the order of divine justice" either by "[taking] upon himself the punishment of his past sin, or [bearing] patiently the punishment which God inflicts upon him."[93] Again, punishment will be given to the sinner whether or not the sinner embraces it. Sin carries with it its own punishment, due to the disorder that it brings. Thus removal of the debt of punishment involves the sinner actively embracing and accepting punishment as justly owed to him or her. By embracing the just punishment in love, the sinner turns it into a "satisfactory" punishment, a punishment that heals the disorder rather than simply reflecting the disorder.[94]

---

specific sins, but instead a system God has established: an impersonal cause and effect, an impersonal establishment of the laws of consequences. Dig a hole, and you'll fall into it. There remains one fundamental problem for this so-called impersonal view of wrath: *Who* established the impersonal, inevitable consequence factor? If God is the one who established this so-called impersonal system of consequences, then one cannot either make it *im*personal (for God is personal in all that God does) or somehow separate it from God (for it is, after all, God who made the system of consequences). (*Community Called Atonement*, 67–68)

In a remark approved by McKnight, Paul Fiddes states that God "consents in an *active* and personal way to the structure of justice in the world, and so this consent can truly be called the 'wrath' of God against sin which spoils his work" (*Past Event and Present Salvation*, 93). This insistence upon God's personal consent to "the structure of justice in the world" is another way of emphasizing that the "order of justice" inscribed in creation is never impersonal, precisely because creation is God's creation. See also Joel B. Green's observation that for Paul in Rom. 1, "sinful activity is the result of God's letting us go our own way, and this letting us go our own way constitutes God's wrath," so that "our sinful acts do not invite God's wrath but prove that God's wrath is already active" ("Must We Imagine the Atonement in Penal Substitutionary Terms?," 163).

91. See *ST* I-II, q. 87, a. 6. On this "stain," see Stump, *Aquinas*, 439, 453. Stump suggests that Jesus's agony on the cross comes from acquiring "all the stains on the soul caused by all the sins of all human beings" (453), and I would agree so long as this acquisition consists in a deep knowledge of and sorrow for these stains, rather than Jesus's own soul becoming stained. Stump seems to suggest that Jesus has "stains on the soul in his human nature" (574n116), but this would entail a lack of holiness in Jesus's soul, and thus a lack of salvific charity.

92. *ST* I-II, q. 87, a. 6.

93. Ibid.

94. For discussion, emphasizing the centrality of love for the act of satisfaction, see Cessario, *Godly Image*, 119.

Is Aquinas right to argue that "the equality of justice" is restored "by penal compensation [*per recompensationem poenae*]"?[95] It would seem that "penal compensation" is not needed once the sinner's will has been healed. In this regard, Aquinas recalls the story of David, who has sexual intercourse with Uriah the Hittite's wife and then, in an attempt to conceal the crime, has Uriah the Hittite killed.[96] The prophet Nathan confronts David with his sin, and David repents, saying to Nathan, "I have sinned against the LORD" (2 Sam. 12:13). In his sincere repentance, David embraces the order of justice anew; his will is healed. In response, Nathan tells David that "the LORD also has put away your sin" (2 Sam. 12:14). Should this suffice, or does David still owe a "penal compensation" for his sin? Scripture suggests the latter: David must endure the death of the child he conceived with Bathsheba.[97]

This story would certainly not persuade Wolterstorff, since he is well aware that the Old Testament endorses retributive punishment and "penal compensation," and he argues that Jesus reverses this teaching. But in Aquinas's view, "when the stain of sin has been removed, there may remain a debt of punishment, not indeed of punishment simply, but of satisfactory punishment."[98] Again, why is this so? If the stain has been removed by the will's return to its holy brightness, which happens when the will embraces the order of justice (which is an order of love), why should a "satisfactory punishment" remain to be paid, let alone a "penal compensation" for the guilt? Aquinas states with respect to the guilt: "Now it is evident that in all actual sins, when the act of sin has ceased, the guilt remains; because the act of sin makes man deserving of punishment, in so far as he transgresses the order of divine justice."[99] In justice, the rational creature owes a debt of worship and service—a debt of love—to the creator God. Sin means that the rational creature turns away from God and refuses unjustly to give the worship and service that the rational creature owes. To restore justice in this situation means not only returning the will to its proper "brightness" (love), but also paying the debt due for failing to give to God what should have been given.[100]

95. *ST* I-II, q. 87, a. 6 and ad 3.
96. See *ST* I-II, q. 87, a. 6, *sed contra*.
97. See Cessario, *Godly Image*, 118–19.
98. *ST* I-II, q. 87, a. 6.
99. Ibid.
100. Indeed, the order of justice requires the same of any thief; he or she must repay the stolen property plus pay a penalty for committing the crime. Aquinas's satisfaction theory differs from "penal substitution" as defined by Scot McKnight (keeping in mind that for both Aquinas and McKnight, the doctrine of Jesus's saving work requires other categories as well):

> Penal substitution contends that God is holy and that humans are sinful. God, because he
> is holy, can't simply ignore human sin and be true to his own holiness. So there must be a

Jesus's Death as Satisfaction for Sin

Although sin places us in radical opposition to the perfect love, justice, and innocence of God—and in this sense the biblical depictions of God's "wrath" against sin are crucially important[101]—God could freely forgive sin without any retributive punishment, since such punishment meets no need of God's and our crimes are against him. Aquinas emphasizes that no "satisfactory punishment" was strictly necessary for salvation. He observes that if God "had willed to free man from sin without any satisfaction, he would not have acted against justice."[102] Rather, since sin "has the formality of fault in that it is committed against himself," God can forgive it "just as anyone

---

just punishment (hence, *penal*). Jesus Christ, the God-Man, stood in the sinner's place, absorbing God's just punishment on sin and sinners (hence, *substitution*). Because God demands utter perfection for entry into God's presence, not only are our sins imputed to Christ on the cross but his righteousness was then imputed to us (hence, *double imputation*). In this the mechanics are explained: God remains holy and just by judging sinners and, at the same time, forgives sin and justifies sinners by imputing Christ's obedience to us. (*Community Called Atonement*, 39; cf. 113–14)
For an exposition and defense of the doctrine of penal substitution, see Packer, "What Did the Cross Achieve?" Since both "penal substitution" and "satisfaction" involve justice, the two approaches are sometimes conflated, as perhaps Adam Johnson does when he speaks of "Thomas with his synthesis and development of what was to become the penal substitution of the Reformers and those who followed them" (*God's Being in Reconciliation*, 4).

101. For Paul on God's "wrath," see especially Fee, "Paul and the Metaphors of Salvation." For a differing view, which argues that divine wrath is a divine emotion and that God directly inflicts punishment (rather than permitting it as an intrinsic consequence of sin), see Marshall, "Theology of the Atonement," 53–54. In defending substitution theory, Marshall helpfully emphasizes that "the death of Jesus is not a means of appeasing a Father who is unable or unwilling to forgive" and that "it is not a case of God punishing Christ but of God in Christ taking on himself the sin and its penalty" (62–63). Marshall states, "It is true that the wrath of God is operative against sinners who have not accepted the gospel, but it is not true that God's wrath has to be appeased before he will be merciful" (62).

102. *ST* III, q. 46, a. 2, ad 3; Aquinas is implicitly responding to Anselm's *Cur Deus homo* 1.12–13. In a passage approvingly cited here by Aquinas, Augustine comments that in showing that it was fitting for Jesus to die for our sins, "we must also show, *not indeed that no other possible way was available to God, since all things are equally within his power*, but that there neither was nor should have been a more suitable way of curing our unhappy state" (Augustine, *Trinity* 13.4.13, p. 353, emphasis added). For contrasting interpretations regarding whether Augustine held that God could forgive sin without retributive justice, see Vidu, *Atonement, Law, and Justice*, 38; Crisp, "Divine Retribution," 37. The key point for Aquinas is that God did not need satisfaction in order to preserve justice or to act in accord with divine justice. Crisp notes that most versions of penal substitution theory require that God must "punish sin rather than pass over or forgive it without punishment," and he affirms that God could not "just forgive human beings without punishment" (Crisp, "Logic of Penal Substitution Revisited," 211, 223). I disagree with Crisp, on the grounds that God's justice is primarily toward what he owes himself. Like Crisp, however, I find Anselmian satisfaction theory to be "a robust doctrine of atonement that delivers much of what penal substitution promises without some of the more problematic aspects of penal substitution" (223).

else, overlooking a personal trespass, without satisfaction, acts mercifully and not unjustly."[103]

If so, however, why did God send his Son to restore the human race by enduring, with perfect love, the penalty of death, thereby removing both the stain and the debt of human sin?[104] According to Aquinas, God did so because he thereby showed "more copious mercy than if he had forgiven sins without satisfaction."[105] Not only did God show how much he loves us and inspire us to love him in return, but also God greatly dignified humanity by healing its sinful disorder through the work of the head of the human race, rather than extrinsically by divine fiat. In this regard, Aquinas underscores that only the incarnate Son could have made condign or perfect satisfaction, fully restoring the order of justice between humans and the Triune God. This is so both because "the goodness of any person or persons could not make up adequately for the harm done to the whole of the nature; and also because a sin committed against God has a kind of infinity from the infinity of the divine majesty."[106]

Is it really possible to affirm that Jesus's cross satisfies for the huge number of human sins, including the sin of Jesus's executioners? In response, Aquinas emphasizes that as the head of all humans, Jesus is not separated from other humans in such a way that his suffering and death are utterly extrinsic to them, as Wolterstorff seems to suppose in his critique of the notion of vicarious punishment. As Aquinas states, "The head and members are one mystic person; and therefore Christ's satisfaction belongs to all the faithful as being

---

103. *ST* III, q. 46, a. 2, ad 3.

104. See also *ST* III, q. 1, a. 1, ad 3, where Aquinas explains further why it is that the incarnate Son of God can bear our penalty but cannot be a sinner:

> Every mode of being wherein any creature whatsoever differs from the Creator has been established by God's wisdom, and is ordained to God's goodness. For God, who is uncreated, immutable, and incorporeal, produced mutable and corporeal creatures for his own goodness. And so also the evil of punishment was established by God's justice for God's glory. But evil of fault is committed by withdrawing from the art of the divine wisdom and from the order of the divine goodness. And therefore it could be fitting to God to assume a nature created, mutable, corporeal, and subject to penalty, but it did not become him to assume the evil of fault.

105. *ST* III, q. 46, a. 1, ad 3. See Adam Johnson, "Fuller Account"; Vidu, *Atonement, Law, and Justice*, 75.

106. *ST* III, q. 1, a. 2, ad 2. Responding to Spence, *Promise of Peace*, Webster points out correctly that "the human history of Jesus may not be allowed to become *in and of itself* soteriologically primitive or constitutive. . . . Jesus' human history is not a quantity in itself. There is no human history of Jesus *in se*, in abstraction from its enhypostatic relation to the divine Word; the only history of Jesus which there is, is the history of the God-man. Jesus' history *is* the Son's mission in the world" ("It Was the Will of the Lord to Bruise Him," 33).

His members."[107] Here it is also important to note that God does not punish Jesus as the vicarious victim in the place of all sinners. Rather, Jesus freely chooses to pay the penalty of death with such love and such dignity (since his death is the death of the divine Son) that the order of justice is restored between the whole human race and God.[108] Since Jesus's death was that of the incarnate Son, Aquinas concludes that the "penal compensation" that Jesus paid was far more "than was required to compensate for the offense of the whole human race."[109]

But why did Jesus choose to die on a cross for us, if a lesser suffering on his part would have sufficed for condign satisfaction? Aquinas answers this question by reference to human death as caused by original sin. He is well aware that material corruption and the death of plants and animals did not result from original sin. But the human experience of death does flow from original sin, as we saw in chapter 6. And in the consummation of his covenantal love for his people, the Triune God freely willed to assume in the person of the Son a human nature "subject to penalty," so that the incarnate Son could heal our sinful alienation by undergoing death out of humility, obedience, and love, and transforming death itself into the path of life, the path by which we obtain "the full participation of the divinity, which is the true bliss of man and end of human life."[110]

---

107. *ST* III, q. 48, a. 2, ad 1. Scot McKnight rightly emphasizes "the *ecclesial* shape of the kingdom and the atoning work of Jesus" (*Community Called Atonement*, 14), as does Colin E. Gunton in chap. 7 of his *Actuality of Atonement*.

108. In this regard, see Eleonore Stump's helpful defense of vicarious satisfaction (which must be sharply distinguished from vicarious substitution), although her point that the aim of satisfaction "is not to make debts and payments balance but to restore a sinner to harmony with God" is a bit too oppositional, since the order of justice ("debts and payments") is indeed superabundantly restored by Christ. Stump rightly emphasizes Jesus's humility, obedience, and charity, which heal the "stain" of sin, but she needs to give more attention to Jesus's death itself as the payment of our penalty. See Stump, *Aquinas*, 434–41. With penal substitution theory in view, Oliver Crisp argues that vicarious substitution is not in fact possible: "If a murderer were able to have the culpability for his crime transferred to another, surely, we would think, this would make a mockery of justice. But this is just what is involved in penal substitution. The murderer remains the one who has committed the crime. He remains the one guilty of committing the crime. But the penal consequences of the crime are transferred to a vicar who serves the punishment in his stead. Despite the valiant attempts of theologians past and present to make sense of this claim, I cannot" ("Logic of Penal Substitution Revisited," 223). I agree with Crisp here, but I think that satisfaction theory removes the problem found in substitution theory.

109. *ST* III, q. 48, a. 2; cf. *ST* III, q. 48, a. 4. See Cessario, *Godly Image*, 134–45.

110. *ST* III, q. 1, a. 1, ad 4; *ST* III, q. 1, a. 2. See also *ST* III, q. 14, a. 1. For a contemporary version of this emphasis, focusing on our existential need to give ourselves to God (rather than cleave to lesser things), see Lewis, *Mere Christianity*, 58–60. Lewis sharply distinguishes his position from the theory that "God wanted to punish men for having deserted and joined the Great Rebel, but Christ volunteered to be punished instead, and so God let us off"

Reflecting upon Romans 5:10, "For if while we were enemies we were reconciled to God by the death of his Son . . . ," Aquinas adds an important clarification about this reconciliation. Namely, God's attitude toward us does not change. Aquinas explains, "Christ is not said to have reconciled us with God, as if God had begun anew to love us, since it is written (Jer. 33:3): 'I have loved thee with an everlasting love'; but because the source of hatred was taken away by Christ's Passion, both through sin being washed away and through compensation being made in the shape of a more pleasing offering."[111] God is not our enemy, since God always loves whatever goodness (ontological and moral) we possess, and God loves us even though we turn away from him. It is we who have chosen to be "God's enemies" by committing crimes that God "hates," since our crimes make us lacking in goodness and produce terrible harm in the world.[112] Thus it is we who need healing and changing, not God. Jesus's loving act of satisfaction restores the justice of the human race in relation to the Triune God and, insofar as the Holy Spirit unites us to Jesus (the head of the human race), opens for us "the gate of heaven's kingdom," the kingdom of God that is the kingdom of love.[113]

---

(57). Importantly, however, Lewis accepts the notion of "debt" and of Christ paying our debt or penalty for us:

> If God was prepared to let us off, why on earth did He not do so? And what possible point could there be in punishing an innocent person instead? None at all that I can see, if you are thinking of punishment in the police-court sense. On the other hand, if you think of a debt, there is plenty of point in a person who has some assets paying it on behalf of someone who has not. Or if you take "paying the penalty," not in the sense of being punished, but in the more general sense of "standing the racket" or "footing the bill," then, of course, it is a matter of common experience that, when one person has got himself into a hole, the trouble of getting him out usually falls on a kind friend." (59)

111. *ST* III, q. 49, a. 4, ad 2. Gerald O'Collins emphasizes, "One must insist that the NT never speaks of redemption altering God's attitudes towards human beings and reconciling God to the world" (*Jesus Our Redeemer*, 140). As Aquinas recognizes, it is humans who are reconciled to God. Aquinas's position is much closer to O'Collins than the latter appreciates; see, e.g., the way in which O'Collins articulates his own position in *Jesus Our Redeemer*, 159–60.

112. *ST* III, q. 49, a. 4 and ad 1. For the levels of harmful alienation caused by original sin, see McFarlane, "Atonement, Creation and Trinity," 196–97.

113. *ST* III, q. 49, a. 5. With regard to the glorification of the people of God, Aquinas reflects upon the sharing of Jesus's members in the superabundant grace merited by Jesus; see *ST* III, q. 48, a. 1, where Aquinas notes that Jesus's cross caused "our salvation by way of merit," due to Jesus's supreme love, and that "grace was bestowed upon Christ, not only as an individual, but inasmuch as he is the Head of the Church, so that it might overflow into his members" (an overflow that takes concrete form in the sacraments). Aquinas's full perspective requires drawing together the various modes in which Jesus's cross saves us, along with the sacramental economy by which believers are made participants in the saving power of Jesus's cross. See Stump, *Aquinas*, 442–48. On merit, see Wawrykow, *God's Grace and Human Action*; Raith, *Aquinas and Calvin on Romans*.

Conclusion

I have argued in this chapter that God's act of creation necessarily entails an order of justice between creatures and God and that the mission of the Spirit-filled incarnate Word (the creator made redeemer) needs to be understood in this light. For Wolterstorff, Jesus's rejection of the code of reciprocity and of retributive justice means that God, despite having approved this code in his commandments to Israel, must consider the code of reciprocity and retributive justice to be wrong. I have argued on the contrary that Jesus came to bear our sin out of supreme love (rooted in the infinite wisdom of God) and to restore the just order of human beings to God. It is because Jesus has fulfilled retributive justice, through an act of perfect mercy, that the people formed by faith in Jesus do not need to pursue their own retributive justice but can instead be a people of mercy.[114] Furthermore, if we imitate his wisdom and love through his Spirit dwelling within us, we will come to share in his eternal reward, which brings to completion his saving action as the Messiah who inaugurates the kingdom of God. The code of reciprocity is not negated. Rather, it takes on a higher significance insofar as the eschatological reward for which believers in Jesus strive, and the punishment that believers seek to avoid, belong to the world to come and can be given only by the Triune God. The reward will be the consummated kingdom marked by the everlasting indwelling of the divine persons in the redeemed (John 14:23) and by "face to face" knowledge of God (1 Cor. 13:12). Believers already have a foretaste of this eternal reward, as Jesus makes clear in the Gospel of John (see John 3:36; 4:14).

114. See Pope Francis, *Name of God Is Mercy*. Like Wolterstorff, Gunton emphasizes that "forgiveness is creative of human moral possibilities in the way that the alternative, a doctrine of the absolute requirement of punishment and vengeance, is not. There is, indeed, a kind of 'natural justice' in vengeance, even in the vendetta. But the gospel is that the cycle of offence and retribution is broken only by something different: by the creative re-establishment of human relations on a new basis" (*Actuality of Atonement*, 191; cf. 193). For his part, McKnight emphasizes our participation in Christ's atoning work, a participation rooted in our forgiving others. Drawing upon 2 Cor. 5:18–20, he states, "God reconciles us to himself and he does this 'through Christ.' And then that reconciliation is given to us so we can have a 'ministry' (*ten diakonian*) of 'reconciliation.' And this is done by being an 'ambassador' (*presbuomenon*) of Christ—that is, as his personal agent of representation. 'Ambassadors' are Eikons of Christ in this world. As ambassadors, they are extending the reconciling/atoning work of God to others. That work involves 'not counting their trespasses against them'" (*Community Called Atonement*, 30; cf. 117–41). McKnight concludes that "a missional life is *participation in atonement*" (141). He explains earlier: "I do not believe humans atone for others and I do not believe humans can atone for themselves. Atonement is the work of God—in Christ, through the Spirit—but God has chosen to summon us to participate in *God's* work, even though we are cracked Eikons or, to use Paul's words, 'clay jars' (2 Cor. 4:7)" (118).

Wolterstorff's supposition that God could have nothing to do with reciprocal justice fails to account for the New Testament's statements about Jesus's cross and the life to come. The core of my argument has been that Wolterstorff undervalues retributive justice because he does not attend to its roots in the order of creation. In creation, God bonds rational creatures to himself through a web of justice. Although creation is pure gift, God can rightly be said to owe creatures something, namely, what pertains to the achievement of the end or goal proper to the nature that he wisely and lovingly gives creatures. The logic of gift and the logic of justice, then, are integrally related even on the side of God. Rational creatures, having received the gift of being, must in justice offer love, worship, and service to the creator God. When we turn away from our creator, we receive punishment in this very turning away, due to our violation of the order of justice. This punishment consists in existential disorder, alienation, and death. As John Webster puts it, "Sin is trespass against creatureliness. . . . By sin the creature is brought to ruin, for as fellowship with God is breached, the creature is estranged from the source of its life and condemned to exist in death's shadow."[115]

I consider that God, in perfect wisdom and love, sent his Son to undergo freely the retributive punishment due to us, so as to restore the order of justice (rooted in God's wisdom and love) between humans and God.[116] God did so not out of a thirst for revenge, let alone out of any need on his part or as a way to punish his innocent Son, but rather because the mission of the Son more eminently discloses God's superabundant mercy in healing and elevating humans. Moved by the Spirit, Jesus, in his free act of supreme love, bears our penalty and takes away the guilt and stain of all human sin by his superabundant love, and displays for us how much God loves us and what humility really is. Jesus shows us what a sinless human being looks like, as God in creation intended for all of us to be.[117] As the incarnate Son, Jesus

115. Webster, "It Was the Will of the Lord to Bruise Him," 19.
116. On God's perfection, see Webster, "God's Perfect Life."
117. In his account of the atonement, Scot McKnight emphasizes the status of humans as the "image of God"; but rather than linking this image with rationality, McKnight argues that "to be an Eikon [image of God] is to be a missional being—one designed to love God, self, and others and to represent God by participating in God's rule in this world. . . . To be an Eikon means to be *in relationship*" (*Community Called Atonement*, 21). Arguably, however, human rationality itself is the power to be in relationship, and human rationality is in fact always in relationship with God and neighbor. What McKnight means by being "in relationship" is largely what I have in view when I speak of the order of justice. This order is harmed when we sinfully alienate ourselves from those with whom we are created to be in relationship. McKnight aptly describes the disorder as follows: "Sin is the hyperrelational distortion and corruption of the Eikon's relationship with God and therefore with self, with others, and with the world" (23). In the context of purely judicial definitions of atonement, McKnight is understandably concerned

is united to all persons as their head, and so his act of satisfaction is by no means extrinsic to those for whom he dies. In light of the gift of creation, with its relational web of justice, we can properly appreciate the cruciform pattern of Jesus's love and the way in which it establishes the interpersonal communion (or kingdom) of the new creation.[118] It is in Jesus that "all the fulness of God was pleased to dwell, and through him to reconcile to himself all things, whether on earth or in heaven, making peace by the blood of his cross" (Col. 1:19–20); and it is this same Jesus who "is the image of the invisible God, the firstborn of all creation; for in him all things were created" (Col. 1:15–16). In sum, atonement and creation must be held together. God does not punish his innocent Son, but rather, as head of the human race, Jesus freely and lovingly bears the punishment of all others, thereby showing the creative Word to be eternally "for us" (Rom. 5:8).[119]

---

that sin not be "defined as guilt against the law" (23), but for Aquinas, "guilt" is a relational reality, as is "law." For similar concerns about a purely judicial understanding of atonement, without denying that the atonement has a juridical aspect, see Boersma, *Violence, Hospitality, and the Cross*, 163–64.

118. On the Church, kingdom, and new creation, see McKnight, *Community Called Atonement*, 70–77. Aquinas discusses the kingdom of God in his *Scriptum super Sententiis*, lib. 4, d. 49, q. 1, a. 2, q. 5; and in his *Commentary on the Gospel of St. Matthew*, 88; he implicitly connects the atonement and the kingdom of God in *ST* III, q. 1, a. 2, and *ST* III, q. 49, a. 5. McKnight rightly observes, "Jesus' kingdom vision and atonement are related; separating them is an act of violence. When the many theories of atonement miss this theme, they are missing the telic vision of what atonement is designed to accomplish. Atonement creates the kingdom of God" (*Community Called Atonement*, 13).

119. Thus I agree with Graham McFarlane, who emphasizes that "it is proper to locate the drama of redemption within the stage of creation. We do so because our understanding of creation provides the blueprint for redemption and therefore informs what can and cannot be said about the means by which the pathology may be redressed and redeemed" ("Atonement, Creation and Trinity," 197). McFarlane sums up his perspective on atonement: "The Creator seeks to establish a network of relations capacious enough, via the human image-bearer, to bring glory to the Creator by offering up an embodied reflection of the unity inherent within creation" (198). See also Jonathan R. Wilson's superb description of the purpose of Jesus's restoration of justice: "The telos of justice is not revenge or simply the righting of wrongs. Rather, the telos of justice is the life of creation in the new creation. For the new creation to be the proper end of creation and redemption . . . the things of this world must be rightly aligned with God" (*God's Good World*, 123). He goes on to say: "Only God's justice in Christ can take the evil of this world seriously, deal with it appropriately, and bring the world through the redemption of creation to the new creation. . . . *Reconciliation* is God's act of aligning all things in their proper relationship to God through Christ's cross" (ibid.). Wilson views the Cross as a definitive judgment of evil and also a judgment of self-gift as good.

Conclusion

According to Paul, the whole creation will be healed at the eschatological consummation, because "the creation was subjected to futility" and placed in "bondage to decay" (Rom. 8:20–21) for the sake of "the revealing of the sons of God" (Rom. 8:19), whose revealing—like the unfolding of the whole cosmos—requires time. At the final judgment, cosmic futility and decay will be replaced, not only for humans but for all creation in union with humans, by "the glorious liberty of the children of God" (Rom. 8:21).[1] Until then, we find fallen but redeemed humans and the whole creation "groaning in travail together" (Rom. 8:22), preparing for the birth of the new creation, whose firstfruits is in Christ and his Church as the inaugurated kingdom of love. This is the "mystery of his [God's] will, according to his purpose which he set forth in Christ as a plan for the fulness of time, to unite all things in him, things in heaven and things on earth" (Eph. 1:9–10).

In this book, I have explored the simple God whose ideas express all the ways his goodness can be shared, and whose free creation of a cosmic theophany of beings reflects his infinite wisdom and goodness and finds its ultimate meaning in "the purpose which he set forth in Christ as a plan for the fulness of time." I have rejoiced in the fact that (in Rudi te Velde's words) "to be created means,

---

1. Paul J. Griffiths faults Thomas Aquinas's eschatology for its "anthropocentric principle," but this emphasis seems to me to be justified by Scripture, including Rom. 8. See Griffiths, *Decreation*, 61 and elsewhere; for Griffiths's reflections on temporality, see ibid., 81–87. Nonetheless, Griffiths's insistence that theologians must attend more deeply to the eschatological end of nonhuman creatures is salutary, and his critique of Aquinas's views on the eschatological end of nonhuman creatures is helpful. See also R. R. Reno's observation regarding human eschatology that "we need to see that what matters most about reality is its role in the future ordained by God, rather than its ontological status. Everything that exists is very good. The body is not a prison. Clay, dust, blood, and flesh—the *realia* of embodied life—are not problems to be overcome. But as good as creation is and always will be, nothing created can provide men and women with the future for which they were created" (*Genesis*, 59, 64).

for every creature but particularly for humankind, to exist in response to the gift of being, a gift that is neither of our own making nor of an external and meaningless given."[2] My aim throughout has been to set forth and defend the Christian doctrine of the creator and his theophanic creatures, in the context of human sin (and death) and our redemption through the cross of Jesus Christ. With Reinhard Hütter, I receive "the doctrine of creation as radical comfort, good news, the invitation to understand the world in its contingency and givenness as God's gift, as a gracious act of love."[3]

Even so, after the fall, human existence is fraught with so much difficulty, darkness, and fragility that we can be tempted to conclude with the Preacher that "all is vanity and a striving after wind" (Eccles. 1:14). When the Preacher of Ecclesiastes studies creation, he despondently concludes that "man has no good thing under the sun but to eat and drink and enjoy himself" and that "the days of darkness will be many" (Eccles. 8:15; 11:8). Even with regard to earthly creatures—and certainly also with regard to the creator of the whole cosmos—the Preacher observes that we can have no real knowledge: "However much man may toil in seeking, he will not find it out; even though a wise man claims to know, he cannot find it out" (Eccles. 8:17).

It is no surprise, therefore, that many educated people today affirm that "we were born by mere chance, and hereafter we shall be as though we had never been" (Wis. 2:2). The view that all things came to be "by mere chance," however, is unreasonable.[4] Indeed, nothing could be more unlikely than the story of creation told by Richard Dawkins in defense of atheism, even though Dawkins attempts to tell it in an inspiring way:

> On one planet, and possibly only one planet in the entire universe, molecules that would normally make nothing more complicated than a chunk of rock, gather themselves into chunks of rock-sized matter of such staggering complexity that they are capable of running, jumping, swimming, flying, seeing, hearing, capturing and eating other such animated chunks of complexity; capable in some cases of thinking and feeling, and falling in love with yet other chunks of complex matter.[5]

2. Te Velde, "Metaphysics and the Question of Creation," 99.
3. Hütter, "*Creatio ex Nihilo*," 6. Hütter here attributes this viewpoint, quite rightly, to Martin Luther. As Hütter goes on to say, in a formulation with which I would agree, "*Creation* is both the process and product of God's free, unmerited giving. Creation *ex nihilo* receives thereby a decisively soteriological twist; it is not primarily a metaphysical claim about the contingency of creation, but a theological claim about the nature of the giver of creation and about creation itself: instead of its sheer givenness, we learn about its radical giftness!" (7).
4. For further discussion see Levering, *Proofs of God*.
5. Dawkins, *God Delusion*, 367. He claims that "we now understand essentially how the trick is done, but only since 1859" (ibid.), but in fact we still do not understand how life came to be.

Dawkins sees how wondrous this is—and yet he insists that it is merely a case of molecules being molecules, no further questions needed! Elsewhere he perhaps comes closer to perceiving the mystery of the profusion of finite being: with some emotion, he evokes what it is like to find oneself "under the stars, dazzled by Orion, Cassiopeia and Ursa Major, tearful with the unheard music of the Milky Way, heady with the night scents of frangipani and trumpet flowers in an African garden."[6] But in the end he can perceive nothing more than a self-explanatory (though, at the moment, utterly unexplainable) material realm, and so he has nothing to look forward to other than his own endless annihilation, fittingly joined to the "heat death of the universe" 100 billion years from now.[7]

I wish to conclude this book, therefore, by reflecting briefly upon how our eyes can be opened to the reasonableness of what can be known in faith about creation.[8] The loss of Aquinas's philosophical theology—which I have sought to retrieve in this book alongside Scripture and the fathers—has inflicted a grievous wound upon contemporary thought. For example, the path by which Richard Dawkins arrives at his presentation of the (in his view fictitious) creator God as an oversized computer needs to be subjected to reasonable analysis. We must insist anew upon a balanced account of the divine ideas and of divine simplicity that resists turning God into what amounts to a big, complex creature, a hodgepodge assemblage whose eternal knowing of

6. Ibid., 11.

7. Alex Rosenberg, *Atheist's Guide to Reality*, 309, 314. This broader account of the universe (culminating in its heat death) should paradoxically remind the Christian believer of the truth of Hütter's observation that "even our legitimate and extremely necessary care for the earth can imply the conceitful presumption that we actually could destroy God's creation. In this regard, the doctrine of creation points out our healthy limitations as creatures: we can very well spoil the earth and torture our co-creatures, and finally destroy them and ourselves, but we cannot destroy God's creation, because it is rooted in God's creative act itself. Thereby we are reminded of our own creaturely and thus inherently limited location, which undermines in a very wholesome way all our modern fantasies of omnipotence" (Hütter, "*Creatio ex Nihilo*," 7).

8. As te Velde observes, "the meaning of 'creation' is not restricted to religious belief or to the pre-modern experience of the world," because

its alleged truth and meaning is open to a genuine philosophical articulation. What people may assert in faith is not necessarily without a *fundamentum in re*—that is, not without an intelligible basis in the general structure of human experience of reality. For Aquinas, creation refers to a "higher origin" beyond the sphere of natural causation within this world. Such a higher origin can only be conceived, he says, when the human intellect raises itself, from its habitual "physical" attitude to the world of sensible things, to a metaphysical level of thought (cf. *ST* I, q. 44, a. 2). The notion of creation, together with that of a universal cause of being (*causa universalis totius esse*), occupies a central place in Aquinas's philosophical enquiries. ("Metaphysics and the Question of Creation," 76)

creatures has been whittled down to the level of mere man or machine. It is equally urgent to highlight the congruence of this wise and simple God with the unfathomably vast profusion of creatures across time and space, as also with the radically mysterious and wondrous ability of humans to commune intelligently, freely, and lovingly. Here we must recognize, in the words of the neurosurgeon Paul Kalanithi, that "to make science the arbiter of metaphysics is to banish not only God from the world but also love, hate, meaning—to consider a world that is self-evidently *not* the world we live in."[9]

Similarly, Christians must not shy away from defending the historical plausibility of the biblical portrait (in symbolic language, of course) of first representative humans to whom God graciously gave complete freedom, and whose rebellion deeply wounded human nature. There is nothing that is implausible about this scenario, since the first truly rational hominids—bearers of the free consciousness that humans enjoy—must have emerged at some point and been subject to the care of God. Furthermore, the notion of atonement is not simply the product of more barbarous times, whether medieval or Second Temple, obsessed with placating a bloodthirsty God. Rather, it is a perfectly sensible idea—though a sheer gift—once one has come to understand, in some measure, the interpersonal bonds of justice that relate rational creatures to their creator.

In my view, the theological tendency over the past century to reject what previously were widely shared perspectives on the themes of my book has left Western theology (Catholic and Protestant) in a deeply vulnerable position. When even theologians deplore the Western theological tradition prior to the twentieth century, the refusal of contemporary academics and elites to pay attention to Christian truth claims becomes ever more understandable.

---

9. Kalanithi, *When Breath Becomes Air*, 169. The full passage deserves to be quoted:
During my sojourn in ironclad atheism, the primary arsenal leveled against Christianity had been its failure on empirical grounds. . . . Although I had been raised in a devout Christian family, where prayer and Scripture readings were a nightly ritual, I, like most scientific types, came to believe in the possibility of a material conception of reality, an ultimately scientific worldview that would grant a complete metaphysics, minus outmoded concepts like souls, God, and bearded men in white robes. I spent a good chunk of my twenties trying to build a frame for such an endeavor. The problem, however, eventually became evident: to make science the arbiter of metaphysics is to banish not only God from the world but also love, hate, meaning—to consider a world that is self-evidently *not* the world we live in. That's not to say that if you believe in meaning, you must also believe in God. It is to say, though, that if you believe that science provides no basis for God, then you are almost obligated to conclude that science provides no basis for meaning and, therefore, life itself doesn't have any. In other words, existential claims have no weight; all knowledge is scientific knowledge. (168–69)

For this view (the one that Kalanithi ultimately rejects), see Alex Rosenberg, *Atheist's Guide to Reality*.

When the Western theological tradition appears to have no clothes, then it is hardly the case—despite the hopes of some scholars—that our educated contemporaries are going to turn back to Second Temple Judaism and be persuaded that Jesus came to do the work that only YHWH can do. If the resurrection of Jesus happened, then it truly accomplished something in history. If so, then the Christian theological tradition, without being free of error, will surely testify richly to Christ's kingdom-inaugurating and saint-making power over the centuries. The point is that the erosion of confidence in the Western theological tradition on the part of theologians, over the past century, goes hand in hand with the noninterest in Christianity among many educated persons today.

In rejecting the doctrine of creation, Western societies have also rejected procreation. The post-Christian West finds itself, on the one hand, in a position of receiving (or trying to fence out) immigrants from countries where having children remains a positive good, while, on the other hand, trying to spread contraceptive practices to those countries before it is "too late." The very heart of Christian faith, however, includes the welcoming of children and the wondrous goodness of God's gift of human existence. Without doubt, Christian faith calls us to live virtuously and to take care not to despoil the good things God has made, but Christians cannot sacrifice the generous welcoming of children unless every other way of virtuously responding to the ecological crisis has been tried and has failed. After all, it is the creator who calls people to everlasting trinitarian communion, and who therefore calls on us to be "fruitful and multiply," not just in light of the joys and sorrows and pressing concerns of this present life, but above all in light of the eschatological horizon that encircles the world as a whole and each human life therein. Nothing could be more fundamentally pro-people than the God who creates us so as to call us to this unfathomably high supernatural destiny, communion with himself.

However, given the scope of the mystery of finite realities—and the deeply mysterious reality from which they spring—rational arguments alone cannot suffice for the renewal of our vision of creation. Aquinas himself, like the fathers, frequently appeals to arguments of fittingness, to the spiritual life, and to the enlightenment brought by faith. Rational argumentation alone is not enough. We need to learn how to perceive the created world with a sense of wonder, rooted in the way in which the created world carries within its own beauty many signs of the infinite beauty of its creator.

It is here that I find the seventeenth-century poet Thomas Traherne to be helpful. Rightly arguing for the necessity of a *conversion* of the mind, Traherne cautions that "you never enjoy the world aright, till you see how a

sand exhibiteth the wisdom and power of God; and prize in everything the
service which they do you, by manifesting His glory and goodness to your
soul."[10] Traherne's perspective, then, may be employed to complement the
theological account of creation that I have offered above.

As a young boy growing up in poverty, Traherne questioned whether
God was really much of a giver. In a manner that should bring high-blown
theological sentiments back to earth, he reasoned that a perfect, wise, and
loving God, if such existed, would surely "do most Glorious Things: and
giv us infinit Riches; how comes it to pass therefore that I am so poor? of
so Scanty and Narrow a fortune, enjoying few and Obscure Comforts?"[11]
Indeed, for those who are impoverished or suffering (spiritually or physically), God can seem stingy, arbitrary, and cruel. The young Traherne concluded, "I could not believe Him a GOD to me, unless all His Power were
empowered to Glorify me."[12] Thus the young Traherne fell away from his
Christian faith. Here we have the path of many Enlightenment and post-
Enlightenment persons.

As he grew older, however, Traherne remained captivated by his earliest experiences of the world. As he recalls these earliest perceptions: "All
appeared New, and Strange at the first, inexpressibly rare, and Delightfull,
and Beautifull. . . . The Corn was Orient and Immortal Wheat, which never
should be reaped, nor was ever sown. . . . The Dust and Stones of the Street
were as Precious as GOLD. The Gates were at first the End of the World."[13]
He encourages us to think about what tremendous excitement and awe
each and every thing of this world would inspire in us if we were just now
discovering it. He draws together the beauty of plants with the astounding
beauty of humans: "The Green Trees when I saw them first through one of
the Gates Transported and Ravished me; their Sweetnes and unusual Beauty
made my Heart to leap, and almost mad with Extasie. . . . The Men! O
what Venerable and Reverend Creatures did the Aged seem! . . . And yong

10. Traherne, *Centuries of Meditation* 1:27, in *Selected Poems and Prose*; cited in David
Bentley Hart, *Doors of the Sea*, 56. See also the nature mysticism of Pierre Teilhard de Chardin,
for instance in his *Hymn of the Universe*. At times Teilhard de Chardin's formulations are
exaggerated, as when he praises the Lord's "descent into the universal species" and states,
"You are incarnate in the world," so that "everything around me is the body and blood of the
Word" (27). The fact that the Word is incarnate in the flesh of Jesus Christ does not mean
that the Word is incarnate in all matter, even though the incarnate Word renews all creation.
See also Margaret Barker's observation, on behalf of her rather eccentric way of reclaiming
biblical wisdom, that we must regain "the vision at the heart of creation, and the ability to see
that vision" (*Creation*, 287).

11. Traherne, *Poetry and Prose*, 23.

12. Ibid.

13. Ibid., 17.

Men Glittering and Sparkling Angels and Maids strange Seraphick Pieces of Life and Beauty!"[14]

Traherne then tells us that the specific impetus for his recovery of faith in the creator came when he realized that all things, his soul, body, and the wonders of the cosmos, were "made out of Nothing for me."[15] The key here is that not only did God create such an extraordinary cosmos "out of Nothing," but God did so "for me." God created the cosmos not simply in order to commune with vast oceans of material things or even with a whole throng of trillions of rational creatures, but rather to commune with *each* rational creature with profound intimacy and fullness—a love that is fully "for me" even as it is fully for all of us together. Traherne therefore recognizes that not an abstract love for the general goodness of things, but a specific and personal love "for me" inspired the creation of the universe. In Augustinian terms, the creative divine presencing at the heart of all things is profoundly intimate and personal. God is closer to us than we are to ourselves, and God loves each of us with his infinite love rather than having to parcel out his love among the vast variety of creatures. This is a discovery of the real God, the living God, the God of Abraham, Isaac, and Jacob, as distinct from a deistic demiurge who dwells in realms far removed from everyday human experience.

The implications of Traherne's purification of vision for the present book are the following. First, we must not conceive God's transcendence as an aloof or remote distance from creatures, since God's knowledge of all creatures is ineffably and perfectly intimate in his eternal presencing (chapter 1: divine ideas). Second, the creator God must not be conceived ontologically as though God were a creature, since this would render us unable to perceive either God or creatures accurately, due to a failure to understand how greatly we must

14. Ibid. See also the cognate insights in Foltz, "Traces of Divine Fragrance, Droplets of Divine Love," 324–36. Foltz adds the observation that

> in authentic, patristic Christianity we are cautioned about created beauty not in order to deter us from it, nor even less to cultivate contempt for it, but to exhort us to pursue it more deeply, more radically, more authentically to its very source—and thus to warn us against getting sidetracked in the swift currents and swirling eddies of the material world. . . . And this holds true not just for the beauty of nature but for the beauty of icons and chant and liturgies and vestments as well. All these visible beauties are traces of divine fragrance, "droplets of divine love," to which dissolute and unrighteous souls will tend idolatrously to attach themselves but through which instead the original and originating beauty of the Creator can be seen by those whose hearts have been purified. (335)

15. Traherne, *Poetry and Prose*, 23. David Bentley Hart urges us to recover this "primordial astonishment" if we wish to value creation rightly; we must see "God in all things" as "the truth that shines in and through and beyond the world of ordinary experience" (*Experience of God*, 332).

stammer when face-to-face with the free creator (chapter 2: divine simplicity). Third, when we strive to make sense of the purpose of hundreds of millions of years in which dinosaurs ruled the earth or the incomprehensible vastness of time and space, we must recall that the creator rejoices in the superabundance of finite ways of imitating his infinite being, and so what God speaks to each of us via the created world is not an *impersonal* word but rather expresses his infinitely wise creative Word (chapter 3: creatures).[16] Fourth, God created humans in the image of God and gave humans a royal and priestly mission, but this image does not depend for its existence (as distinct from its fullness) upon how wise and loving we are, since the image is in our rational powers rather than solely in our acts (chapter 4: image of God). Fifth, the terrible failures of human images of God, including ecological devastation, should not lead us to the further failure of seeking to constrict the circle of interpersonal communion for which God created the whole cosmos (chapter 5: be fruitful and multiply). Sixth, in the search for the first rational hominids, and in the difficulties of conceiving of original sin and its transmission, we should be aware that there was a first, fully free sin, because the good creator created the human race good and graciously sustained this goodness until the first humans rebelled (chapter 6: original sin). Seventh, the cross of the incarnate

16. I owe the observation that "what God speaks to us via the created world is not an impersonal word" to a remark by Guy Mansini, OSB, which he made during the question-and-answer period after he lectured on whether it is theologically necessary that humans be able to know something about God by reason. See also the helpful insights of the Catholic philosopher Jason West in his *How to Become a Rational Animal*, 105–6:

> God could indeed have chosen to make a better world than the one he actually did make. Nevertheless, he freely chose to make this one anyway. . . . It is sobering to think that had God really created the best of possible worlds, it would probably be a world without you and me in it. Yet, God did choose to create us, even though he foresaw we would frequently make a mess of things. God's only justification for allowing the imperfections we find in the world is the fact that he loved us enough to create each of us as we are. As St. Thomas Aquinas frequently argued, it is better that all kinds and degrees of goodness exist rather than just the perfect good. Indeed, the logic of those who object that a good God cannot create a world in which evil occurs implies that a good God should not create anything imperfect, but that is to say he should not create at all. What legitimizes the existence of evil and suffering is not some other long-range good that it buys in the course of this world's history. God's creation is not the result of a cost-benefit analysis. From the perspective of faith, we can see that in Christ God has conquered evil. What is most significant is not that God permits evil, but that he has provided the remedy for it. The goodness of God does not entail that suffering never occur in our lives. It does not even ensure that all suffering will, in some mysterious way, always work out for the best. What God does provide are ways for our suffering to become meaningful. A full elaboration of this point is a task for the theologian, not the philosopher. However, one does not need to be a scripture scholar or a theologian to realize that the entire Bible is a response to the problem of evil.

Word testifies to God's surpassing love for creation and for each human being, and makes manifest the significance of the creation's relational justice vis-à-vis the good creator (chapter 7: atonement).

Seeing creation rightly, therefore, ultimately involves an attitude not only of the mind but of the whole person on his or her knees, a point upon which all Christians converge. From an Orthodox perspective, Metropolitan Kallistos Ware observes of our enactment of true creatureliness: "In thanksgiving we *become ourselves*. . . . Only in the attitude of offering and blessing do we attain authentic personhood."[17] From a Catholic perspective, Joseph Ratzinger (Pope Benedict XVI) makes a similar point about the human creature: "Dependence in the form of love precisely constitutes the self as self and sets it free," because the creator loves each of us, rather than being our dominative competitor.[18] And the Reformed theologian John Webster identifies the embrace of creatureliness as being at the heart of our redemption: "Yielding to God means giving up the whole enterprise of being my own maker, giving it up because it is the heart of sin, and giving it up because it is a ruinous affair. . . . Positively, yielding to God means coming to realize who we are, and living in the light of who we are."[19]

Let us close then with personal words of praise and thanksgiving for what the wise and good God, in and through his Son and Holy Spirit, has created, judged, redeemed, and renewed.[20] "O LORD, how manifold are thy works! In wisdom hast thou made them all; the earth is full of thy creatures. . . . When

17. Metropolitan Kallistos Ware, "Through Creation to the Creator," 99. As an act of relational justice, this royal-priestly offering of "the created world back to God the Creator," preeminently in the eucharistic liturgy, cannot be given if the human person is unjust: care for neighbor and for the earth belongs intrinsically to the act of offering, not least since (in Metropolitan Kallistos's words) "as offerers, whether in the Eucharist or in other ways, we do not act alone but in union with our fellow humans" (ibid.). Metropolitan Kallistos adds that "we are offerers rather than rulers or even stewards" (100). He takes this position, which strikes me as a mistaken polarity, because of the misunderstandings that can be associated with the word "rulers": "The language of ruling and also sometimes of stewardship can easily be misinterpreted to signify arbitrary control and exploitation, as if the creation were our exclusive property rather than a gift that we hold in trust for the Creator" (ibid.). Much like Metropolitan Kallistos, Pope Francis teaches, "It is in the Eucharist that all that has been created finds its greatest exaltation. . . . The Eucharist joins heaven and earth; it embraces and penetrates all creation. The world which came forth from God's hands returns to him in blessed and undivided adoration" (*Laudato Si'*, §236).

18. Ratzinger, *In the Beginning* . . ., 98.

19. Webster, *Grace of Truth*, 50–51.

20. Reinhard Hütter pinpoints the significance of doxology: "Doxological praise thus amounts to the practical distinction between God and the effects of God's creative activity. . . . Thus, doxological praise of the Creator means for us occupying and acknowledging our proper place as co-creatures with all the rest of God's creation, as we are neither gods nor animals, neither omnipotent nor powerless. Doxology of the Creator genuinely humanizes us, i.e., teaches us how to accept the *others*, our co-creatures as gift and grace" ("*Creatio ex Nihilo*," 9). Hütter adds

thou sendest forth thy Spirit, they are created; and thou renewest the face of the ground" (Ps. 104:24, 30). "Praise him, sun and moon; praise him, all you shining stars! Praise him, you highest heavens and you waters above the heavens! Let them praise the name of the LORD, for he commanded and they were created" (Ps. 148:3–5).[21]

that "respect of and care for all God's creatures is the primary doxological acknowledgment of God the Creator in creation" (ibid.).

21. See Mays, "Maker of Heaven and Earth."

Bibliography

Alexander, Andrew, CJ. "Human Origins and Genetics." *Clergy Review* 49 (1964): 344–53.

Alexander, Denis. *Creation or Evolution: Do We Have to Choose?* Oxford: Monarch, 2008.

———. *Rebuilding the Matrix: Science and Faith in the 21st Century.* Grand Rapids: Zondervan, 2001.

Allen, Diogenes. "Persons in Philosophical and Biblical Perspective." In Jeeves, *From Cells to Souls—and Beyond*, 165–78.

Alter, Robert. *Genesis.* New York: W. W. Norton, 1996.

Anatolios, Khaled. *Retrieving Nicaea: The Development and Meaning of Trinitarian Doctrine.* Grand Rapids: Baker Academic, 2011.

Anderson, Bernhard W. *Creation versus Chaos: The Reinterpretation of Mythical Symbolism in the Bible.* 2nd ed. Philadelphia: Fortress, 1987.

Anderson, Gary A. "*Necessarium Adae Peccatum*: The Problem of Original Sin." In Braaten and Jenson, *Sin, Death, and the Devil*, 22–44.

Anderson, Kevin. "Going beyond Dangerous Climate Change: Exploring the Void between Rhetoric and Reality in Reducing Carbon Emissions." Public lecture presented at the London School of Economics, October 21, 2011. www.lse.ac.uk/publicEvents/events/2011/20111021t1600vHKT.aspx.

Anizor, Uche. *Kings and Priests: Scripture's Theological Account of Its Readers.* Eugene, OR: Pickwick, 2014.

Anselm. *Monologion and Proslogion.* Translated by Thomas Williams. Indianapolis: Hackett, 1996.

———. *On the Virgin Conception and Original Sin.* Translated by Camilla McNab. In *The Major Works*, edited by Brian Davies and G. R. Evans, 357–89. Oxford: Oxford University Press, 1998.

———. *Why God Became Man.* Translated by Janet Fairweather. In *The Major Works*, edited by Brian Davies and G. R. Evans, 260–356. Oxford: Oxford University Press, 1998.

Anstall, Kharalambos. "Juridical Justification Theology and a Statement of the Orthodox Teaching." In *Stricken by God? Nonviolent Identification and the Victory of Christ*, edited by Brad Jersak and Michael Hardin, 482–502. Grand Rapids: Eerdmans, 2007.

Arendt, Hannah. *The Human Condition.* Garden City, NY: Doubleday, 1959.

Aristotle. *Metaphysics, X–XIV.* Translated by Hugh Tredennick (with the *Oeconomica* and *Magna Moralia*). Loeb Classical Library. Cambridge, MA: Harvard University Press, 1935.

Arnold, Bill T. *Genesis.* Cambridge: Cambridge University Press, 2009.

Ashley, Benedict M., OP, and John Deely. *How Science Enriches Theology.* South Bend, IN: St. Augustine's Press, 2012.

Astley, Jeff. "Evolution and Evil: The Difference Darwinism Makes in Theology and Spirituality." In Barton and Wilkinson, *Reading Genesis after Darwin,* 163–80.

Athanasius. *On the Incarnation.* Translated by a Religious of CSMV. Crestwood, NY: St. Vladimir's Seminary Press, 1993.

Athanasopoulos, C., and C. Schneider, eds. *Divine Essence and Divine Energies: Ecumenical Reflections on the Presence of God in Eastern Orthodoxy.* Cambridge: Clarke, 2013.

Attridge, Harold W. *Hebrews: A Commentary on the Epistle to the Hebrews.* Minneapolis: Fortress, 1989.

Augustine. *Confessions.* Translated by Henry Chadwick. Oxford: Oxford University Press, 1991.

———. *The Literal Meaning of Genesis.* Vol. 1, Books 1–6. Translated by John Hammond Taylor, SJ. New York: Newman Press, 1982.

———. *The Trinity.* Translated by Edmund Hill, OP. Hyde Park, NY: New City Press, 1991.

Austriaco, Nicanor Pier Giorgio, OP. "A Theological Fittingness Argument for the Historicity of the Fall of *Homo Sapiens*." *Nova et Vetera* 13 (2015): 651–67.

Axe, Douglas. *Undeniable: How Biology Confirms Our Intuition That Life Is Designed.* New York: HarperCollins, 2016.

Ayala, Francisco, et al. "Molecular Genetics of Speciation and Human Origins." *Proceedings of the National Academy of Sciences* 91 (1994): 6787–94.

Ayres, Lewis. *Augustine and the Trinity.* Cambridge: Cambridge University Press, 2010.

———. "The Christological Context of *De Trinitate* XIII: Toward Relocating Books VIII–XV." *Augustinian Studies* 29 (1998): 111–39.

———. *Nicaea and Its Legacy: An Approach to Fourth-Century Trinitarian Theology.* Oxford: Oxford University Press, 2004.

Bahnson, Fred, and Norman Wirzba. *Making Peace with the Land: God's Call to Reconcile with Creation.* With a Foreword by Bill McKibben. Downers Grove, IL: InterVarsity, 2012.

Bailleux, Emile. "À l'image du Fils premier-né." *Revue Thomiste* 76 (1976): 181–207.

Baker, Joanne. *50 Universe Ideas You Really Need to Know.* London: Quercus, 2010.

Ball, Philip. *The Elements: A Very Short Introduction.* Oxford: Oxford University Press, 2002.

Balthasar, Hans Urs von. *Theo-Drama: Theological Dramatic Theory.* Vol. 2, *The Dramatis Personae: Man in God.* Translated by Graham Harrison. San Francisco: Ignatius, 1990.

———. *Theo-Drama: Theological Dramatic Theory.* Vol. 4, *The Action.* Translated by Graham Harrison. San Francisco: Ignatius, 1994.

———. *Theo-Drama: Theological Dramatic Theory.* Vol. 5, *The Last Act.* Translated by Graham Harrison. San Francisco: Ignatius, 1998.

———. *Theo-Logic: Theological Logical Theory.* Vol. 1, *Truth of the World.* Translated by Adrian J. Walker. San Francisco: Ignatius, 2000.

Barbour, Ian. *Issues in Science and Religion.* New York: Harper & Row, 1971.

Barker, Margaret. *Creation: A Biblical Vision for the Environment.* London: T&T Clark International, 2010.

Barnes, Michel René. *The Power of God: Δύναμις in Gregory of Nyssa's Trinitarian Theology.* Washington, DC: Catholic University of America Press, 2001.

Barr, James. *The Garden of Eden and the Hope of Immortality.* London: SCM, 1992.

——. "The Image of God in Genesis—A Study in Terminology." *Bulletin of the John Rylands Library* 51 (1968): 11–26.

Barr, Stephen M. *Modern Physics and Ancient Faith.* Notre Dame, IN: University of Notre Dame Press, 2003.

Barrett, Matthew, and Ardel B. Caneday, eds. *Four Views on the Historical Adam.* Grand Rapids: Zondervan, 2013.

Barron, Robert. *Exploring Catholic Theology: Essays on God, Liturgy, and Evangelization.* Grand Rapids: Baker Academic, 2015.

Barth, Karl. *Christ and Adam: Man and Humanity in Romans 5.* Translated by T. A. Smail. New York: Collier, 1962.

——. *Church Dogmatics* II/1, *The Doctrine of God.* Edited by G. W. Bromiley and T. F. Torrance. Translated by T. H. L. Parker, W. B. Johnston, Harold Knight, and J. L. M. Haire. Edinburgh: T&T Clark, 1957.

——. *Church Dogmatics* III/1, *The Doctrine of Creation.* Edited by G. W. Bromiley and T. F. Torrance. Translated by J. W. Edwards, O. Bussey, and H. Knight. Edinburgh: T&T Clark, 1958.

——. *Church Dogmatics* III/2, *The Doctrine of Creation.* Edited by G. W. Bromiley and T. F. Torrance. Translated by H. Knight, G. W. Bromiley, J. K. S. Reid, and R. H. Fuller. Edinburgh: T&T Clark, 1960.

——. *Church Dogmatics* IV/1, *The Doctrine of Reconciliation.* Edited by G. W. Bromiley and T. F. Torrance. Translated by G. W. Bromiley. Edinburgh: T&T Clark, 1956.

——. *The Epistle to the Romans.* Translated by Edwyn C. Hoskyns. Oxford: Oxford University Press, 1933.

Bartlett, Albert. "Reflections on Sustainability and Population Growth." In Cafaro and Crist, *Life on the Brink*, 29–40.

Barton, Stephen C., and David Wilkinson, eds. *Reading Genesis after Darwin.* Oxford: Oxford University Press, 2009.

Basil. *Hexaemeron.* In *Basil: Letters and Select Works.* Vol. 8 of the Nicene and Post-Nicene Fathers, Series 2. Edited by Philip Schaff and Henry Wace. Translated by Blomfield Jackson. Peabody, MA: Hendrickson, 1994 (1895).

Bauckham, Richard. *Living with Other Creatures: Green Exegesis and Theology.* Waco: Baylor University Press, 2011.

Bavinck, Herman. *Reformed Dogmatics.* Vol. 2, *God and Creation.* Edited by John Bolt. Translated by John Vriend. Grand Rapids: Baker Academic, 2004.

Beatrice, Pier Franco. *Tradux peccati: Alle fonti della dottrina agostiniana del peccato originale.* Milan: Vita e pensiero, 1978.

Beiting, Christopher. "The Idea of Limbo in Thomas Aquinas." *The Thomist* 62 (1998): 217–44.

Bellah, Robert N. *Religion in Human Evolution: From the Paleolithic to the Axial Age.* Cambridge, MA: Harvard University Press, 2011.

Bellah, Robert N., and Hans Joas, eds. *The Axial Age and Its Consequences.* Cambridge, MA: Harvard University Press, 2012.

Benton, Michael J. *The History of Life: A Very Short Introduction.* Oxford: Oxford University Press, 2008.

Béresniak, Daniel. *Le mythe du péché origi-nel: Une légende substituée*. Monaco: Éditions du Rocher, 1997.

Bergmann, Michael, and Jeffrey Brower. "A Theistic Argument against Platonism (and in Support of Truthmakers and Divine Simplicity)." In *Oxford Studies in Metaphysics*, vol. 2, edited by Dean W. Zimmerman, 257–86. Oxford: Claren-don, 2006.

Berkouwer, G. C. *Man: The Image of God*. Translated by Dirk W. Jellema. Grand Rapids: Eerdmans, 1962.

Berkowitz, Jacob. *The Stardust Revolution: The New Story of Our Origin in the Stars*. Amherst, NY: Prometheus Books, 2012.

Betts, Richard A., Matthew Collins, Debo-rah L. Hemming, et al. "When Could Global Warming Reach 4° C?" *Philo-sophical Transactions of the Royal Soci-ety* 369 (2011): 67–84.

Betz, John R. "After Barth: A New Introduc-tion to Erich Przywara's *Analogia Entis*." In White, *Analogy of Being*, 35–87.

———. "The Beauty of the Metaphysical Imagination." In Cunningham and Can-dler, *Belief and Metaphysics*, 41–65.

Bieler, Martin. "*Analogia Entis* as an Ex-pression of Love according to Ferdinand Ulrich." In White, *Analogy of Being*, 314–37.

Blanchette, Oliva. "Metaphysics as Preamble to Religious Belief." In Cunningham and Candler, *Belief and Metaphysics*, 141–60.

———. *The Perfection of the Universe ac-cording to Aquinas: A Teleological Cos-mology*. University Park: Pennsylvania State University Press, 1992.

Blenkinsopp, Joseph. *Creation, Un-Cre-ation, Re-Creation: A Discursive Com-mentary on Genesis 1–11*. New York: T&T Clark International, 2011.

Blocher, Henri. "Biblical Metaphors and the Doctrine of the Atonement." *Journal of the Evangelical Theological Society* 47 (2004): 629–45.

———. *Original Sin: Illuminating the Rid-dle*. Grand Rapids: Eerdmans, 1997.

Bloomquist, Karen L., ed. *God, Creation and Climate Change: Spiritual and Ethi-cal Perspectives*. Minneapolis: Lutheran University Press, 2009.

Blowers, Paul M. *Drama of the Divine Economy: Creator and Creation in Early Christian Theology and Piety*. Oxford: Oxford University Press, 2012.

Bockmuehl, Markus. "*Creatio ex Nihilo* in Palestinian Judaism and Early Chris-tianity." *Scottish Journal of Theology* 65 (2012): 253–70.

Boersma, Hans. *Violence, Hospitality, and the Cross: Reappropriating the Atone-ment Tradition*. Grand Rapids: Baker Academic, 2004.

———. "Violence, the Cross, and Divine Intentionality: A Modified Reformed View." In *Atonement and Violence: A Theological Conversation*, edited by John Sanders, 47–69. Nashville: Abing-don, 2006.

Boland, Vivian, OP. *Ideas in God according to Saint Thomas Aquinas: Sources and Synthesis*. Leiden: Brill, 1996.

Bonhoeffer, Dietrich. *Creation and Fall; Temptation: Two Biblical Studies*. Trans-lated by John C. Fletcher and Kathleen Downham. New York: Touchstone, 1997.

Bonino, Serge-Thomas, OP. *Angels and Demons*. Translated by Michael Miller. Washington, DC: Catholic University of America Press, forthcoming.

———. *Il m'a aimé et s'est livré pour moi: Entretiens sur le Rédempteur en sa Pas-sion*. Paris: Parole et Silence, 2013.

———. Review of *Analogia Entis*, by Steven A. Long. *The Thomist* 77 (2013): 629–33.

Bonnette, Dennis. "The Impenetrable Mystery of a Literal Adam and Eve." Forthcoming in *Nova et Vetera*.

———. *Origin of the Human Species*. 2nd ed. Ypsilanti, MI: Sapientia, 2003.

Bostrom, Nick. *Anthropic Bias: Observation Selection Effects in Science and Philosophy*. New York: Routledge, 2002.

Bouma-Prediger, Steven. *For the Beauty of the Earth: A Christian Vision for Creation Care*. Grand Rapids: Baker Academic, 2001.

Bouteneff, Peter C. *Beginnings: Ancient Christian Readings of the Biblical Creation Narratives*. Grand Rapids: Baker Academic, 2008.

Bowman, Donna, and Clayton Crocket, eds. *Cosmology, Ecology, and the Energy of God*. New York: Fordham University Press, 2012.

Braaten, Carl E., and Robert W. Jenson, eds. *Sin, Death, and the Devil*. Grand Rapids: Eerdmans, 2000.

Bradshaw, David. *Aristotle East and West: Metaphysics and the Division of Christendom*. Cambridge: Cambridge University Press, 2004.

———. "The Concept of Divine Energies." *Philosophy and Theology* 18 (2006): 93–120. Reprinted in Athanasopoulos and Schneider, *Divine Essence and Divine Energies*, 27–49.

———. "In Defence of the Essence/Energy Distinction: A Reply to Critics." In Athanasopoulos and Schneider, *Divine Essence and Divine Energies*, 256–73.

———. "The *Logoi* of Beings in Greek Patristic Thought." In Chryssavgis and Foltz, *Toward an Ecology of Transfiguration*, 9–22.

Braine, David. *The Human Person: Animal and Spirit*. Notre Dame, IN: University of Notre Dame Press, 1992.

———. *Language and Human Understanding: The Roots of Creativity in Speech and Thought*. Washington, DC: Catholic University of America Press, 2014.

Brakke, David. *The Gnostics: Myth, Ritual, and Diversity in Early Christianity*. Cambridge, MA: Harvard University Press, 2010.

Brauch, M. T. "Perspectives on 'God's Righteousness' in Recent German Discussion." Appendix to Sanders, *Paul and Palestinian Judaism*, 523–42.

Brennan, William. *John Paul II: Confronting the Language Empowering the Culture of Death*. Naples, FL: Sapientia, 2008.

Briggs, Richard S. "Humans in the Image of God and Other Things Genesis Does Not Make Clear." *Journal of Theological Interpretation* 4 (2010): 111–26.

Brock, Brian, and John Swinton, eds. *Disability in the Christian Tradition: A Reader*. Grand Rapids: Eerdmans, 2012.

Brock, Rita Nakashima, and Rebecca Parker. *Saving Paradise: How Christianity Traded Love of This World for Crucifixion and Empire*. Boston: Beacon, 2008.

Brower, Jeffrey E. "Making Sense of Divine Simplicity." *Faith and Philosophy* 25 (2008): 3–30.

Brown, Edward R. *Our Father's World: Mobilizing the Church to Care for Creation*. 2nd ed. Downers Grove, IL: InterVarsity, 2008.

Brown, Raymond E., SS. *The Gospel according to John (i–xii)*. Garden City, NY: Doubleday, 1966.

Brown, William P. *The Ethos of the Cosmos: The Genesis of Moral Imagination in the Bible*. Grand Rapids: Eerdmans, 1999.

———. *The Seven Pillars of Creation: The Bible, Science, and the Ecology of Wonder*. Oxford: Oxford University Press, 2010.

Brueggemann, Walter. *Genesis*. Atlanta: John Knox, 1982.

Brungs, Robert A., SJ, and Marianne Post-iglione, RSM, eds. *Some Christian and Jewish Perspectives on the Creation: Proceedings of ITEST Workshop, March 15–17, 1991*. St. Louis: ITEST Faith/Science, 1991.

Bryson, Bill. *A Short History of Nearly Everything*. New York: Broadway Books, 2003.

Bulgakov, Sergius. *The Bride of the Lamb*. Translated by Boris Jakim. Grand Rapids: Eerdmans, 2002.

Burns, J. Patout. "The Concept of Satisfaction in Medieval Redemption Theory." *Theological Studies* 36 (1975): 285–304.

———. *The Development of Augustine's Doctrine of Operative Grace*. Paris: Études augustiniennes, 1980.

Burns, Robert M. "The Divine Simplicity in St. Thomas." *Religious Studies* 25 (1989): 271–93.

Burrell, David B., CSC. "Analogy, Creation, and Theological Language." In Van Nieuwenhove and Wawrykow, *Theology of Thomas Aquinas*, 77–98.

———. "Aquinas's Appropriation of *Liber de causis* to Articulate the Creator as Cause-of-Being." In Kerr, *Contemplating Aquinas*, 75–83.

———. "*Creatio ex Nihilo* Recovered." *Modern Theology* 29 (2013): 5–21.

———. "Creation and 'Actualism': The Dialectical Dimension of Philosophical Theology." In *Faith and Freedom: An Interfaith Perspective*, 76–90. Oxford: Blackwell, 2004.

———. *Deconstructing Theodicy: Why Job Has Nothing to Say to the Puzzle of Suffering*. Grand Rapids: Brazos, 2008.

———. *Freedom and Creation in Three Traditions*. Notre Dame, IN: University of Notre Dame Press, 1993.

———. *Knowing the Unknowable God: Ibn-Sina, Maimonides, Aquinas*. Notre

Dame, IN: University of Notre Dame Press, 1986.

Burrell, David B., CSC, Carol Cogliati, Janet M. Soskice, and William R. Stoeger, eds. *Creation and the God of Abraham*. Cambridge: Cambridge University Press, 2010.

Butler, David J. *Adapting Minds: Evolutionary Psychology and the Persistent Quest for Human Nature*. Cambridge, MA: MIT Press, 2005.

Cafaro, Philip, and Eileen Crist, eds. *Life on the Brink: Environmentalists Confront Overpopulation*. Athens: University of Georgia Press, 2012.

Cafaro, Philip, and Winthrop Staples III. "The Environmental Argument for Reducing Immigration into the United States." In Cafaro and Crist, *Life on the Brink*, 172–88.

Cahall, Perry J. *The Mystery of Marriage: A Theology of the Body and the Sacrament*. Chicago: Hillenbrand, 2016.

Caldecott, Stratford. *Not as the World Gives: The Way of Creative Justice*. Kettering, OH: Angelico, 2014.

Campbell, Douglas A. *The Deliverance of God: An Apocalyptic Rereading of Justification in Paul*. Grand Rapids: Eerdmans, 2009.

Campbell, Nancy. *Be Fruitful and Multiply: What the Bible Says about Having Children*. San Antonio, TX: The Vision Forum, 2003.

Carey, James. "Sedimentation of Meaning in the Concepts of Nature and the Environment." In Chryssavgis and Foltz, *Toward an Ecology of Transfiguration*, 175–85.

Carras, Costa. "Environment and Security: Toward a Systemic Crisis of Humanity?" In Chryssavgis and Foltz, *Toward an Ecology of Transfiguration*, 226–34.

Casarella, Peter. "Hans Urs von Balthasar, Erich Przywara's *Analogia Entis*, and the

Problem of a Catholic *Denkform*." In White, *Analogy of Being*, 192–206.

Catechism of the Catholic Church. 2nd ed. Vatican City: Libreria Editrice Vaticana, 1997.

Cessario, Romanus, OP. "Aquinas on Christian Salvation." In Weinandy, Keating, and Yocum, *Aquinas on Doctrine*, 117–37.

———. *The Godly Image: Christ and Salvation in Catholic Thought from Anselm to Aquinas*. Petersham, MA: St. Bede's Publications, 1990.

———. *Introduction to Moral Theology*. Washington, DC: Catholic University of America Press, 2001.

———. "Sonship, Sacrifice, and Satisfaction: The Divine Friendship in Aquinas and the Renewal of Christian Anthropology." In *Theology and Sanctity*, edited by Cajetan Cuddy, OP, 69–98. Ave Maria, FL: Sapientia, 2014.

———. "The Trinitarian Imprint on the Moral Life." In *The Oxford Handbook of the Trinity*, edited by Gilles Emery, OP, and Matthew Levering, 487–92. Oxford: Oxford University Press, 2011.

Chalmers, David J. *The Character of Consciousness*. Oxford: Oxford University Press, 2010.

Charlesworth, Brian, and Deborah Charlesworth. *Evolution: A Very Short Introduction*. Oxford: Oxford University Press, 2003.

Charlesworth, James H. *The Good and Evil Serpent*. New Haven: Yale University Press, 2010.

Chenu, M.-D., OP. *Toward Understanding Saint Thomas*. Translated by A. M. Landry, OP, and D. Hughes, OP. Chicago: Henry Regnery, 1964.

Chesterton, G. K. *Saint Thomas Aquinas*. New York: Doubleday, 1956.

Chilton, David. *Paradise Regained: A Biblical Theology of Dominion*. Tyler, TX: Reconstruction Press, 1985.

Chryssavgis, John. "A New Heaven and a New Earth: Orthodox Christian Insights from Theology, Spirituality, and the Sacraments." In Chryssavgis and Foltz, *Toward an Ecology of Transfiguration*, 152–62.

Chryssavgis, John, and Bruce V. Foltz, eds. *Toward an Ecology of Transfiguration: Orthodox Christian Perspectives on Environment, Nature, and Creation*. New York: Fordham University Press, 2013.

Clarke, W. Norris, SJ. "The Immediate Creation of the Human Soul by God and Some Contemporary Challenges." In *The Creative Retrieval of St. Thomas Aquinas: Essays in Thomistic Philosophy, New and Old*, 179–90. New York: Fordham University Press, 2009.

———. *The One and the Many: A Contemporary Thomistic Metaphysics*. Notre Dame, IN: University of Notre Dame Press, 2001.

———. "The Problem of the Reality and Multiplicity of Divine Ideas in Christian Neoplatonism." In O'Meara, *Neoplatonism and Christian Thought*, 109–27.

Collins, C. John. *Did Adam and Eve Really Exist? Who They Were and Why You Should Care*. Wheaton: Crossway, 2011.

———. "A Historical Adam: Old-Earth Creation View." In Barrett and Caneday, *Four Views on the Historical Adam*, 143–75.

Collins, John J. *Jewish Wisdom in the Hellenistic Age*. Louisville: Westminster John Knox, 1997.

Collins, Robin. "Evolution and Original Sin." In K. B. Miller, *Perspectives on an Evolving Creation*, 469–501.

———. "A Scientific Argument for the Existence of God: The Fine-Tuning

Phenomena." In Murray, *Reason for the Hope Within*, 47–75.

Conly, Sarah. *One Child: Do We Have a Right to More?* Oxford: Oxford University Press, 2016.

Cook, Jill. *Ice Age Art: Arrival of the Modern Mind*. London: British Museum Press, 2013.

Cooper, John W. *Panentheism, the Other God of the Philosophers: From Plato to the Present*. Grand Rapids: Baker Academic, 2006.

Coote, Robert B., and David Robert Ord. *The Bible's First History: From Eden to the Court of David with the Yahwist*. Philadelphia: Fortress, 1989.

Copan, Paul, and William Lane Craig. *Creation out of Nothing: A Biblical, Philosophical, and Scientific Exploration*. Grand Rapids: Baker Academic, 2004.

Cotter, David W., OSB. *Genesis*. Collegeville, MN: Liturgical Press, 2003.

Couenhoven, Jesse. "St. Augustine's Doctrine of Original Sin." *Augustinian Studies* 36 (2005): 359–96.

———. *Stricken by Sin, Cured by Christ: Agency, Necessity, and Culpability in Augustinian Theology*. Oxford: Oxford University Press, 2013.

Craig, William Lane. "The Existence of God and the Beginning of the Universe." *Truth: A Journal of Modern Thought* 3 (1991): 85–96.

———. *God, Time, and Eternity: The Coherence of Theism II; Eternity*. Dordrecht: Kluwer Academic Publishers, 2001.

———. "Timelessness and Omnitemporality." In Ganssle, *God and Time*, 129–60.

Crain, Steven D. "God Embodied in, God Bodying Forth the World: Emergence and Christian Theology." *Zygon* 41 (2006): 665–73.

Creegan, Nicola Hoggard. "The Salvation of Creatures." In Davidson and Rae, *God of Salvation*, 77–87.

Crimmins, James E. "The Principles of Utilitarian Penal Law in Beccaria, Bentham, and J. S. Mill." In Koritansky, *Philosophy of Punishment*, 136–71.

Crisp, Oliver D. "Divine Retribution: A Defense." *Sophia* 42 (2003): 35–52.

———. *Jonathan Edwards and the Metaphysics of Sin*. Aldershot: Ashgate, 2005.

———. "Jonathan Edwards on the Imputation of Sin." In *Retrieving Doctrine*, 47–68.

———. "The Logic of Penal Substitution Revisited." In Tidball, Hilborn, and Thacker, *Atonement Debate*, 208–27.

———. *Retrieving Doctrine: Essays in Reformed Theology*. Downers Grove, IL: IVP Academic, 2010.

Cromartie, Michael, ed. *The Nine Lives of Population Control*. Grand Rapids: Eerdmans, 1995.

Cross, Richard. *Duns Scotus on God*. Aldershot: Ashgate, 2005.

Crysdale, Cynthia, and Neil Ormerod. *Creator God, Evolving World*. Minneapolis: Fortress, 2013.

Cunningham, Conor. "Being Recalled: Life as Anamnesis." In *Divine Transcendence and Immanence in the Work of Thomas Aquinas*, edited by Harm Goris, Herwi Rikhof, and Henk Schoot, 59–80. Leuven: Peeters, 2009.

———. *Darwin's Pious Idea: Why the Ultra-Darwinists and Creationists Both Get It Wrong*. Grand Rapids: Eerdmans, 2010.

Cunningham, Conor, and Peter M. Candler, eds. *Belief and Metaphysics*. London: SCM, 2007.

Cunningham, Mary Kathleen, ed. *God and Evolution: A Reader*. New York: Routledge, 2007.

Curtis, Edward Mason. "Man as the Image of God in Genesis in the Light of Ancient Near Eastern Parallels." PhD diss., University of Pennsylvania, 1984.

Daly, Herman, and John B. Cobb. *For the Common Good: Redirecting the Economy towards Community, the Environment and a Sustainable Future.* London: Green Print, 1990.

Dauphinais, Michael. "Loving the Lord Your God: The *Imago Dei* in Saint Thomas Aquinas." *The Thomist* 63 (1999): 241–67.

Dauphinais, Michael, Barry David, and Matthew Levering, eds. *Aquinas the Augustinian.* Washington, DC: Catholic University of America Press, 2007.

Davidson, Ivor J., and Murray A. Rae. *God of Salvation: Soteriology in Theological Perspective.* Burlington, VT: Ashgate, 2011.

———. "Salvation's Destiny: Heirs of God." In *God of Salvation,* 155–75.

Davies, Paul. *The Goldilocks Enigma: Why Is the Universe Just Right for Life?* New York: Houghton Mifflin Harcourt, 2008.

Davis, Ellen F. *Biblical Prophecy: Perspectives for Christian Theology, Discipleship, and Ministry.* Louisville: Westminster John Knox, 2014.

———. *Scripture, Culture, and Agriculture: An Agrarian Reading of the Bible.* Cambridge: Cambridge University Press, 2009.

Dawkins, Richard. *The Blind Watchmaker: Why the Evidence of Evolution Reveals a Universe without Design.* 2nd ed. New York: Norton, 1996.

———. *Climbing Mount Improbable.* New York: W. W. Norton, 1996.

———. *The God Delusion.* Boston: Houghton Mifflin, 2006.

———. *River out of Eden.* New York: HarperCollins, 1996.

———. *The Selfish Gene.* 2nd ed. Oxford: Oxford University Press, 1989.

Day, John. *From Creation to Babel: Studies in Genesis 1–11.* London: Bloomsbury, 2013.

DeHart, Paul J. "What Is Not, Was Not, and Will Never Be: Creaturely Possibility, Divine Ideas and the Creator's Will in Thomas Aquinas." *Nova et Vetera* 13 (2015): 1009–58.

DeLetter, P., SJ. "If Adam Had Not Sinned . . ." *Irish Theological Quarterly* 28 (1961): 115–25.

de Lubac, Henri, SJ. *Catholicism: Christ and the Common Destiny of Man.* Translated by Lancelot C. Sheppard and Elizabeth Englund, OCD. San Francisco: Ignatius, 1988.

———. *The Mystery of the Supernatural.* Translated by Rosemary Sheed. New York: Herder & Herder, 1967.

Demacopoulos, George E., and Aristotle Papanikolaou. "Augustine and the Orthodox: 'The West' in the East." In Demacopoulos and Papanikolaou, *Orthodox Readings of Augustine,* 11–40.

Demacopoulos, George E., and Aristotle Papanikolaou, eds. *Orthodox Readings of Augustine.* Crestwood, NY: St. Vladimir's Seminary Press, 2008.

Demetracopoulos, John A. "Palamas Transformed: Palamite Interpretations of the Distinction between God's 'Essence' and 'Energies' in Late Byzantium." In *Greeks, Latins, and Intellectual History, 1204–1500,* edited by Chris Schabel and Martin Hinterberger, 263–371. Leuven: Peeters, 2011.

———. "Thomas Aquinas' Impact on Late Byzantine Theology and Philosophy: The Issues of Method or *Modus Sciendi* and *Dignitas Hominis.*" In *Knotenpunkt Byzanz: Wissenformen und kulturelle Wechselbeziehungen,* edited by A. Speer and P. Steinkrüger, 333–410. Berlin: De Gruyter, 2012.

Dennett, Daniel C. *Darwin's Dangerous Idea: Evolution and the Meaning of Life.* New York: Simon & Schuster, 1995.

Derr, Thomas Sieger. "Environmental Ethics and Christian Humanism." In Derr, Nash, and Neuhaus, *Environmental Ethics and Christian Humanism*, 17–103.

Derr, Thomas Sieger, James A. Nash, and Richard John Neuhaus. *Environmental Ethics and Christian Humanism.* Edited by Max L. Stackhouse. Nashville: Abingdon, 1996.

De Simone, Russell J. "Modern Research on the Sources of Saint Augustine's Doctrine of Original Sin." *Augustinian Studies* 11 (1980): 205–27.

De Villalmonte, Alejandro. *El pecado original: Veinticinco años de controversia, 1950–1975.* Salamanca: Naturaleza y Gracia, 1978.

Dewan, Lawrence, OP. "Saint Thomas, Alvin Plantinga, and the Divine Simplicity." *The Modern Schoolman* 66 (1989): 141–51.

———. "St. Thomas, James Ross, and Exemplarism: A Reply." *American Catholic Philosophical Quarterly* 65 (1991): 221–34.

Di Noia, J. Augustine, OP. "Imago Dei— Imago Christi: The Theological Foundations of Christian Humanism." *Nova et Vetera* 2 (2004): 267–78.

Dodds, Michael J., OP. *The Unchanging God of Love: Thomas Aquinas and Contemporary Theology on Divine Immutability.* 2nd ed. Washington, DC: Catholic University of America Press, 2008.

———. *Unlocking Divine Action: Contemporary Science and Thomas Aquinas.* Washington, DC: Catholic University of America Press, 2012.

Dolezal, James E. *God without Parts: Divine Simplicity and the Metaphysics of God's Absoluteness.* Eugene, OR: Pickwick, 2011.

Domning, Daryl, and Monika Hellwig. *Original Selfishness: Original Sin and Evil in the Light of Evolution.* Burlington, VT: Ashgate, 2006.

Donald, Merlin. *A Mind So Rare: The Evolution of Human Consciousness.* New York: Norton, 1999.

———. *Origins of the Modern Mind: Three Stages in the Evolution of Culture and Cognition.* Cambridge, MA: Harvard University Press, 1991.

Doolan, Gregory T. "Aquinas on Creation: Transitive or Immanent Action?" Unpublished.

———. "Aquinas on the Divine Ideas and the Really Real." *Nova et Vetera* 13 (2015): 1059–92.

———. *Aquinas on the Divine Ideas as Exemplar Causes.* Washington, DC: Catholic University of America Press, 2008.

Dubarle, André-Marie, OP. *Le péché originel dans l'Écriture.* 2nd ed. Paris: Cerf, 1967. Reprinted in André-Marie Dubarle, OP, *Le péché originel: Écriture et tradition.* Paris: Cerf, 1999.

Duby, Stephen. *Divine Simplicity: A Dogmatic Account.* London: T&T Clark, forthcoming.

Duffy, Stephen J. "Our Hearts of Darkness: Original Sin Revisited." *Theological Studies* 49 (1988): 597–622.

Durand, Emmanuel, OP. *La périchorèse des personnes divines: Immanence mutuelle, réciprocité et communion.* Paris: Cerf, 2005.

Eddy, G. T. *Dr Taylor of Norwich: Wesley's Arch-Heretic.* Werrington: Epworth, 2003.

Edwards, Denis. *Breath of Life: A Theology of the Creator Spirit.* Maryknoll, NY: Orbis Books, 2004.

Edwards, Jonathan. *The Great Christian Doctrine of Original Sin Defended.* In *The Works of Jonathan Edwards*, 1:146–233.

———. *The Works of Jonathan Edwards.* Vol. 1. Peabody, MA: Hendrickson, 1998 (1834).

Emery, Gilles, OP. "Essentialism or Personalism in the Treatise on God in St. Thomas Aquinas?" In *Trinity in Aquinas*, 165–208.

———. "Le 'monothéisme trinitaire.'" *Nova et Vetera* 90 (2015): 157–76.

———. *The Trinitarian Theology of Saint Thomas Aquinas.* Translated by Francesca Aran Murphy. Oxford: Oxford University Press, 2007.

———. *La Trinité créatrice: Trinité et création dans les commentaires aux "Sentences" de Thomas d'Aquin et de ses précurseurs Albert le Grand et Bonaventure.* Paris: Vrin, 1995.

———. "Trinity and Creation: The Trinitarian Principle of the Creation in the Commentaries of Albert the Great, Bonaventure, and Thomas Aquinas on the *Sentences.*" Translated by Heather Buttery. In *Trinity in Aquinas*, 33–70.

———. *Trinity in Aquinas.* Ypsilanti, MI: Sapientia, 2003.

Engelhardt, H. Tristram, Jr. "Ecology, Morality, and the Challenges of the Twenty-First Century: The Earth in the Hands of the Sons of Noah." In Chryssavgis and Foltz, *Toward an Ecology of Transfiguration*, 276–90.

Enns, Peter. *The Evolution of Adam: What the Bible Does and Doesn't Say about Human Origins.* Grand Rapids: Brazos, 2012.

Eschmann, Ignatius, OP. "The Ethics of the Image of God." In *The Ethics of Saint Thomas Aquinas: Two Courses*, edited by Edward A. Synan, 159–231. Toronto: Pontifical Institute of Mediaeval Studies, 1997.

Estes, Daniel. *Handbook on the Wisdom Books and Psalms.* Grand Rapids: Baker Academic, 2005.

Fabro, Cornelius. *Participation et causalité selon S. Thomas d'Aquin.* Paris: Béatrice-Nauwelaerts, 1961.

Farthing, John L. "The Problem of Divine Exemplarity in St. Thomas." *The Thomist* 49 (1985): 183–222.

Fee, Gordon D. "Paul and the Metaphors of Salvation: Some Reflections on Pauline Soteriology." In *The Redemption*, edited by Stephen T. Davis, Daniel Kendall, SJ, and Gerald O'Collins, SJ, 43–67. Oxford: Oxford University Press, 2004.

Feinberg, Joel. *Doing and Deserving.* Princeton: Princeton University Press, 1970.

Feldmeier, Reinhard, and Hermann Spieckermann. *God of the Living: A Biblical Theology.* Translated by Mark E. Biddle. Waco: Baylor University Press, 2011.

Fergusson, David. *Creation.* Grand Rapids: Eerdmans, 2014.

———. "Interpreting the Story of Creation: A Case Study in the Dialogue between Theology and Science." In MacDonald, Elliott, and Macaskill, *Genesis and Christian Theology*, 155–74.

Ferris, Timothy. *The Whole Shebang: A State-of-the-Universe(s) Report.* New York: Simon & Schuster, 1997.

Feser, Edward. *The Last Superstition: A Refutation of the New Atheism.* South Bend, IN: St. Augustine's Press, 2008.

———. *Philosophy of Mind: A Beginner's Guide.* Oxford: OneWorld, 2006.

Fiddes, Paul. *Past Event and Present Salvation.* Louisville: Westminster John Knox, 1989.

Finn, Daniel K., ed. *The Moral Dynamics of Economic Life: An Extension and Critique of "Caritas in Veritate."* Oxford: Oxford University Press, 2013.

———. "Theology and Sustainable Economics." In R. Miller, *God, Creation, and Climate Change*, 95–111.

Fisher, Simcha. *A Sinner's Guide to Natural Family Planning*. Huntingdon, IN: Our Sunday Visitor, 2014.

Flannery, Austin, OP, ed. *Vatican Council II*. Vol. 1, *The Conciliar and Post Conciliar Documents*. Rev. ed. Northport, NY: Costello, 1996.

Floss, Johannes P. "Schöpfung als Geschehen? Von der Syntax zur Semantik in der priesterschriftlichen Schöpfungsdarstellung Genesis 1,1–2,4a." In *Nachdenken über Israel, Bibel und Theologie: Festschrift für Klaus-Dietrich Schunck zu seinem 65. Geburtstag*, edited by Hermann M. Niemann, Matthias Augustin, and Werner H. Schmidt, 311–18. Frankfurt am Main: Lang, 1994.

Foltz, Bruce V. "Traces of Divine Fragrance, Droplets of Divine Love: On the Beauty of Visible Creation." In Chryssavgis and Foltz, *Toward an Ecology of Transfiguration*, 324–36.

Foreman, Dave. "The Great Backtrack." In Cafaro and Crist, *Life on the Brink*, 56–74.

————. *Man Swarm and the Killing of Wildlife*. Durango, CO: Raven's Eye, 2011.

Forsyth, P. T. *The Justification of God*. London: Duckworth, 1916.

Fortey, Richard. *Life: A Natural History of the First Four Billion Years of Life on Earth*. New York: Knopf, 1998.

Francis, Pope. *Laudato Si'*. Encyclical. Website of the Holy See, May 24, 2015. www.vatican.va.

————. *The Name of God Is Mercy*. Translated by Oonagh Stransky. New York: Random House, 2016.

Francis of Assisi. "Canticle of Brother Sun." In Francis and Clare, *The Complete Works*, translated by Regis J. Armstrong, OFMCap, and Ignatius C. Brady, OFM, 38–39. New York: Paulist Press, 1982.

Friedman, Richard Elliott. *Commentary on the Torah*. New York: HarperCollins, 2001.

Gaine, Simon, OP. *Will There Be Free Will in Heaven? Freedom, Impeccability and Beatitude*. London: T&T Clark, 2003.

Ganssle, Gregory E., ed. *God and Time: Four Views*. Downers Grove, IL: InterVarsity, 2001.

Gathercole, Simon. *Defending Substitution: An Essay on Atonement in Paul*. Grand Rapids: Baker Academic, 2015.

Gaudium et spes. In Flannery, *Conciliar and Post Conciliar Documents*, 903–1001.

Gavrilyuk, Paul. *The Suffering of the Impassible God: The Dialectics of Patristic Thought*. Oxford: Oxford University Press, 2004.

Gese, Hartmut. "The Atonement." In *Essays on Biblical Theology*, 93–116. Minneapolis: Augsburg, 1981.

Gilson, Étienne. *Christian Philosophy: An Introduction*. Translated by Armand Maurer. Toronto: Pontifical Institute of Mediaeval Studies, 1993.

————. *The Christian Philosophy of St. Thomas Aquinas*. Translated by L. K. Shook, CSB. Notre Dame, IN: University of Notre Dame Press, 1956.

————. *Jean Duns Scot: Introduction à ses positions fondamentales*. Paris: Vrin, 1952.

————. *The Spirit of Medieval Philosophy*. Translated by A. H. C. Downes. New York: Scribner's, 1936.

Gioia, Luigi, OSB. *The Theological Epistemology of Augustine's "De Trinitate."* Oxford: Oxford University Press, 2008.

Girard, René. *I See Satan Fall like Lightning*. Translated by James G. Williams. Maryknoll, NY: Orbis Books, 2001.

Glacken, Clarence J. *Traces on the Rhodian Shore: Nature and Culture in Western Thought from Ancient Times to the End* of the Eighteenth Century. Berkeley: University of California Press, 1967.

Goldstein, Jonathan A. *II Maccabees: A New Translation with Introduction and Commentary*. Garden City, NY: Doubleday, 1983.

Goodman, Lenn E. *Creation and Evolution*. London: Routledge, 2010.

Goodwin, Stephanie, and Angela Handley, eds. *The Encyclopedia of Animals: A Complete Visual Guide*. Berkeley: University of California Press, 2004.

Goris, Harm. "Angelic Knowledge in Aquinas and Bonaventure." In *A Companion to Angels in Medieval Philosophy*, edited by Tobias Hoffman, 149–85. Leiden: Brill, 2012.

———. "Divine Foreknowledge, Providence, Predestination, and Human Freedom." In Van Nieuwenhove and Wawrykow, *Theology of Thomas Aquinas*, 99–122.

———. *Free Creatures of an Eternal God: Thomas Aquinas on God's Infallible Foreknowledge and Irresistible Will*. Leuven: Peeters, 1996.

Gorringe, Timothy. *God's Just Vengeance: Crime, Violence and the Rhetoric of Salvation*. Cambridge: Cambridge University Press, 1996.

Gould, Stephen Jay. *Rocks of Ages: Science and Religion in the Fullness of Life*. New York: Ballantine Books, 1999.

Grant, W. Matthews. "Aquinas, Divine Simplicity, and Divine Freedom." *Proceedings of the American Catholic Philosophical Association* 77 (2003): 129–44.

Green, Joel B. *Body, Soul, and Human Life: The Nature of Humanity in the Bible*. Grand Rapids: Baker Academic, 2008.

———. "Must We Imagine the Atonement in Penal Substitutionary Terms? Questions, Caveats and a Plea." In Tidball, Hilborn, and Thacker, *Atonement Debate*, 153–71.

Greenhalgh, Susan, ed. *Situating Fertility: Anthropology and Demographic Inquiry*. Cambridge: Cambridge University Press, 1995.

Gregory of Nyssa. *Contra Eunomium*. In *Gregorii Nysseni Opera*, vol. 2, edited by Werner Jaeger. Leiden: Brill, 1960.

———. *In inscriptiones psalmorum*. In *Patrologia Graeca*, vol. 44, edited by J.-P. Migne. Paris: Migne, 1863.

———. *The Life of Moses*. Translated by Abraham J. Malherbe and Everett Ferguson. Mahwah, NJ: Paulist Press, 1978.

Gregory Palamas. *Topics of Natural and Theological Science and on the Moral and Ascetic Life: One Hundred and Fifty Texts*. In *The Philokalia*, vol. 4, translated and edited by G. E. H. Palmer, Philip Sherrard, and Kallistos Ware, 346–417. London: Faber and Faber, 1995.

Grenz, Stanley. *The Social God and the Relational Self: A Trinitarian Theology of the Imago Dei*. Louisville: Westminster John Knox, 2001.

Griffiths, Paul J. *Decreation: The Last Things of All Creatures*. Waco: Baylor University Press, 2014.

Gschwandtner, Christina M. "'All Creation Rejoices in You': Creation in the Liturgies for the Feasts of the Theotokos." In Chryssavgis and Foltz, *Toward an Ecology of Transfiguration*, 307–23.

Guichardan, Sébastien. *Le problème de la simplicité divine en Orient et en Occident au XIVe et XVe siècles: Grégoire Palamas, Duns Scot, Georges Scholarios*. Lyon: Legendre, 1933.

Gunton, Colin E. *The Actuality of Atonement: A Study of Metaphor, Rationality and the Christian Tradition*. Edinburgh: T&T Clark, 1988.

———. "Between Allegory and Myth: The Legacy of the Spiritualising of Genesis." In Gunton, *Doctrine of Creation*, 47–62.

―――, ed. *The Cambridge Companion to Christian Doctrine*. Cambridge: Cambridge University Press, 1997.

―――. *Christ and Creation*. London: Paternoster, 1992.

―――. "The Doctrine of Creation." In *Cambridge Companion to Christian Doctrine*, 141–57. Cambridge: Cambridge University Press, 1997.

―――, ed. *The Doctrine of Creation: Essays in Dogmatics, History and Philosophy*. London: T&T Clark International, 1997.

―――. "The End of Causality? The Reformers and Their Predecessors." In Gunton, *Doctrine of Creation*, 63–82.

―――. "Introduction." In *Doctrine of Creation*, 1–15.

―――. *The Triune Creator: A Historical and Systematic Study*. Grand Rapids: Eerdmans, 1998.

Haarsma, Deborah B., and Loren D. Haarsma. *Origins: Christian Perspectives on Creation, Evolution, and Intelligent Design*. Rev. ed. Grand Rapids: Faith Alive Christian Resources, 2011.

Hall, Douglas John. *Imaging God: Dominion as Stewardship*. Grand Rapids: Eerdmans, 1986.

Hanby, Michael. *No God, No Science? Theology, Cosmology, Biology*. Oxford: Wiley-Blackwell, 2013.

Hannan, Sarah, Samantha Brennan, and Richard Vernon, eds. *Permissible Progeny? The Morality of Procreation and Parenting*. Oxford: Oxford University Press, 2015.

Hardy, Daniel W., and David F. Ford. *Jubilate: Theology in Praise*. London: Darton, Longman & Todd, 1984.

Harrison, Nonna Verna. *God's Many-Splendored Image: Theological Anthropology for Christian Formation*. Grand Rapids: Baker Academic, 2010.

Hart, David Bentley. *Atheist Delusions: The Christian Revolution and Its Fashionable Enemies*. New Haven: Yale University Press, 2009.

―――. *The Beauty of the Infinite: The Aesthetics of Christian Truth*. Grand Rapids: Eerdmans, 2003.

―――. "The Destiny of Christian Metaphysics: Reflections on the *Analogia Entis*." In White, *Analogy of Being*, 395–410.

―――. *The Doors of the Sea: Where Was God in the Tsunami?* Grand Rapids: Eerdmans, 2005.

―――. *The Experience of God: Being, Consciousness, Bliss*. New Haven: Yale University Press, 2013.

―――. "The Hidden and the Manifest: Metaphysics after Nicaea." In Demacopoulos and Papanikolaou, *Orthodox Readings of Augustine*, 191–226.

Hart, John. *Sacramental Commons: Christian Ecological Ethics*. Lanham, MD: Rowman & Littlefield, 2006.

Hasker, William. *Metaphysics and the Tri-Personal God*. Oxford: Oxford University Press, 2013.

Hauerwas, Stanley. "Seeing Peace: L'Arche as a Peace Movement." In Reinders, *Paradox of Disability*, 113–26.

―――. "Sinsick." In Braaten and Jenson, *Sin, Death, and the Devil*, 7–21.

―――. *Suffering Presence: Theological Reflections on Medicine, the Mentally Handicapped, and the Church*. Notre Dame, IN: University of Notre Dame Press, 1986.

Haught, John F. "Evolution, Tragedy, and Cosmic Purpose." In M. Cunningham, *God and Evolution*, 310–24.

―――. *God after Darwin: A Theology of Evolution*. 2nd ed. Boulder, CO: Westview, 2008.

————. *Science and Religion.* Mahwah, NJ: Paulist Press, 1995.

Hawking, Stephen, and Leonard Mlodinow. *The Grand Design.* New York: Random House, 2010.

Hayes, Zachary, OFM. *The Gift of Being: A Theology of Creation.* Collegeville, MN: Liturgical Press, 2001.

Hector, Kevin. *Theology without Metaphysics: God, Language and the Spirit of Recognition.* Cambridge: Cambridge University Press, 2011.

Helm, Paul. "Eternal Creation: The Doctrine of the Two Standpoints." In Gunton, *Doctrine of Creation,* 29–46.

————. "Response to Nicholas Wolterstorff." In Ganssle, *God and Time,* 214–18.

Henle, Robert J. *Saint Thomas and Platonism: A Study of the "Plato" and "Platonici" Texts in the Writings of Saint Thomas.* The Hague: Martinus Nijhoff, 1956.

Heschel, Abraham Joshua. *The Sabbath: Its Meaning for Modern Man.* New York: Farrar, Straus & Giroux, 1951.

Hess, Rick, and Jan Hess. *A Full Quiver: Family Planning and the Lordship of Christ.* Brentwood, TN: Wolgemuth & Hyatt, 1990.

Hibbs, Thomas. "*Imitatio Christi* and the Foundation of Aquinas's Ethics." *Communio* 18 (1991): 556–73.

Hinze, Bradford E., and D. Lyle Dabney, eds. *Advents of the Spirit: An Introduction to the Current Study of Pneumatology.* Milwaukee: Marquette University Press, 2001.

Hochschild, Joshua P. "Proportionality and Divine Naming: Did St. Thomas Change His Mind about Analogy?" *The Thomist* 77 (2013): 531–58.

Hodge, Charles. *Systematic Theology.* Vol. 2. Grand Rapids: Eerdmans, 1981.

Hoekema, Anthony A. *Created in God's Image.* Grand Rapids: Eerdmans, 1986.

Holbrook, Clyde A. "Jonathan Edwards Addresses Some 'Modern Critics' of Original Sin." *Journal of Religion* 63 (1983): 211–30.

————. "Jonathan Edwards on Self-Identity and Original Sin." *The Eighteenth Century* 25 (1984): 45–63.

Holland, Peter. *The Animal Kingdom: A Very Short Introduction.* Oxford: Oxford University Press, 2011.

Holmes, Stephen R. "A Simple Salvation? Soteriology and the Perfections of God." In Davidson and Rae, *God of Salvation,* 35–46.

Holsinger-Friesen, Thomas. *Irenaeus and Genesis: A Study of Competition in Early Christian Hermeneutics.* Winona Lake, IN: Eisenbrauns, 2009.

Honnefelder, Ludger. *Scientia transcendens: Die formale Bestimmung der Seiendheit und Realität in der Metaphysik des Mittelalters und der Neuzeit (Duns Scotus–Suárez–Wolff–Kant–Peirce).* Hamburg: Felix Meiner Verlag, 1990.

Hooker, Morna D. "Interchange in Christ." In *From Adam to Christ,* 13–25. Cambridge: Cambridge University Press, 1990.

Hore-Lacy, Ian. *Responsible Dominion: A Christian Approach to Sustainable Development.* Vancouver: Regent College Publishing, 2006.

Houghton, Craig. *Family UNplanning: A Guide for Christian Couples Seeking God's Truth on Having Children.* Longwood, FL: Xulon, 2006.

Houston, Walter J. "Sex or Violence? Thinking Again with Genesis about Fall and Original Sin." In MacDonald, Elliott, and Macaskill, *Genesis and Christian Theology,* 140–45.

Howard, Jonathan. *Darwin: A Very Short Introduction.* Oxford: Oxford University Press, 1982.

Hughes, Christopher. *On a Complex Theory of a Simple God: An Investigation into Aquinas' Philosophical Theology.* Ithaca, NY: Cornell University Press, 1989.

Hughes, John. "*Creatio ex Nihilo* and the Divine Ideas in Aquinas." *Modern Theology* 29 (2013): 124–37.

———, ed. *The Unknown God: Sermons Responding to the New Atheists.* Eugene, OR: Cascade Books, 2013.

Hume, David. *Principal Writings on Religion, including "Dialogues concerning Natural Religion" and "The Natural History of Religion,"* edited by J. C. A. Gaskin. Oxford: Oxford University Press, 1993.

Hunsinger, George. *Reading Barth with Charity: A Hermeneutical Proposal.* Grand Rapids: Baker Academic, 2015.

Hurd, James P. "Hominids in the Garden?" In K. B. Miller, *Perspectives on an Evolving Creation,* 208–33.

Hütter, Reinhard. "*Creatio ex Nihilo*: Promise of the Gift; Re-membering the Christian Doctrine of Creation in Troubled Times." In Brungs and Postiglione, *Some Christian and Jewish Perspectives on the Creation,* 1–12.

———. *Dust Bound for Heaven: Explorations in the Theology of Thomas Aquinas.* Grand Rapids: Eerdmans, 2012.

Immink, Frederick Gerrit. *Divine Simplicity.* Kampen: Kok, 1987.

Irenaeus. *Against Heresies.* In *The Apostolic Fathers with Justin Martyr and Irenaeus,* edited by A. Cleveland Coxe. Vol. 1 of *Ante-Nicene Fathers,* edited by Alexander Roberts and James Donaldson. Peabody, MA: Hendrickson, 1995.

———. *On the Apostolic Preaching.* Translated by John Behr. Crestwood, NY: St. Vladimir's Seminary Press, 1997.

Janzen, J. Gerald. *Job.* Atlanta: John Knox, 1985.

Jaspers, Karl. *The Origin and Goal of History.* Translated by Michael Bullock. New York: Routledge, 2010.

———. *Way to Wisdom: An Introduction to Philosophy.* Translated by Ralph Manheim. 2nd ed. New Haven: Yale University Press, 2003.

Jeeves, Malcolm, ed. *From Cells to Souls—and Beyond: Changing Portraits of Human Nature.* Grand Rapids: Eerdmans, 2004.

Jenson, Robert W. *America's Theologian: A Recommendation of Jonathan Edwards.* Oxford: Oxford University Press, 1988.

———. *On Thinking the Human: Resolutions of Difficult Notions.* Grand Rapids: Eerdmans, 2003.

John of Damascus. *The Orthodox Faith.* In *Writings,* translated by Frederic H. Chase Jr., 165–406. Washington, DC: Catholic University of America Press, 1958.

John Paul II, Pope. *Familiaris consortio.* Vatican translation. Boston: Pauline Books & Media, 1981.

———. *Man and Woman He Created Them: A Theology of the Body.* Translated by Michael Waldstein. Boston: Pauline Books & Media, 2006.

Johnson, Adam. "A Fuller Account: The Role of 'Fittingness' in Thomas Aquinas' Doctrine of the Atonement." *International Journal of Systematic Theology* 12 (2010): 302–18.

———. *God's Being in Reconciliation: The Theological Basis of the Unity and Diversity of the Atonement in the Theology of Karl Barth.* London: Bloomsbury, 2012.

Johnson, Elizabeth A., CSJ. *Ask the Beasts: Darwin and the God of Love.* London: Bloomsbury, 2014.

Johnson, Luke Timothy. *Reading Romans: A Literary and Theological Commentary.* New York: Crossroad, 1997.

Johnson, Mark F. "Augustine and Aquinas on Original Sin: Doctrine, Authority, and Pedagogy." In Dauphinais, David, and Levering, *Aquinas the Augustinian*, 145–58.

———. "Did St. Thomas Attribute a Doctrine of Creation to Aristotle?" *The New Scholasticism* 63 (1989): 129–55.

Jones, L. Gregory. *Embodying Forgiveness: A Theological Analysis*. Grand Rapids: Eerdmans, 1995.

Journet, Charles. *The Mass: The Presence of the Sacrifice of the Cross*. Translated by Victor Szczurek, OPraem. South Bend, IN: St. Augustine's Press, 2008.

Joyce, Kathryn. *Quiverfull: Inside the Christian Patriarchy Movement*. Boston: Beacon, 2009.

Kalanithi, Paul. *When Breath Becomes Air*. New York: Random House, 2016.

Kant, Immanuel. *The Metaphysical Elements of Justice*. Translated by John Ladd. Indianapolis: Bobbs-Merrill, 1965.

Kappes, Christiaan W. "The Latin Sources of the Palamite Theology of George-Gennadius Scholarius." *Rivista Nicolaus* 40 (2013): 71–114.

Kappes, Christiaan W., J. Isaac Goff, and T. Alexander Giltner. "Palamas among the Scholastics: A Review Essay Discussing D. Bradshaw, C. Athanasopoulos, C. Schneider et al., *Divine Essence and Divine Energies: Ecumenical Reflections on the Presence of God in Eastern Orthodoxy* (Cambridge: Clarke, 2013)." *Logos: A Journal of Eastern Christian Studies* 55 (2014): 175–220.

Kaufmann, Eric. *Shall the Religious Inherit the Earth? Demography and Politics in the Twenty-First Century*. London: Profile Books, 2010.

Keiner, Marco, ed. *The Future of Sustainability*. Dordrecht: Springer, 2006.

Keller, Catherine. "The Energy We Are: A Meditation in Seven Pulsations." In Bowman and Crocket, *Cosmology, Ecology, and the Energy of God*, 11–25.

———. *Face of the Deep: A Theology of Becoming*. New York: Routledge, 2003.

———. *From a Broken Web: Separation, Sexism, and Self*. Boston: Beacon, 1986.

Kelsey, David H. *Eccentric Existence: A Theological Anthropology*. Vol. 2. Louisville: Westminster John Knox, 2009.

Kemp, Kenneth W. "Science, Theology, and Monogenesis." *American Catholic Philosophical Quarterly* 85 (2011): 217–36.

Kenny, Anthony. *Aquinas: A Collection of Critical Essays*. London: Macmillan, 1970.

———. *Aquinas on Being*. Oxford: Clarendon, 2002.

Kerr, Fergus, OP, ed. *Contemplating Aquinas: On the Varieties of Interpretation*. London: SCM, 2003.

Kerr, Gaven, OP. "Aquinas, Stump, and the Nature of a Simple God." *American Catholic Philosophical Quarterly* 90 (2016): 441–54.

Kidner, Derek. *Genesis*. Downers Grove, IL: InterVarsity, 1967.

Kierkegaard, Søren. *The Concept of Anxiety: A Simple Psychologically Orienting Deliberation on the Dogmatic Issue of Hereditary Sin*. Translated by Reidar Thomte with Albert B. Anderson. Princeton: Princeton University Press, 1980.

Kilner, John F. *Dignity and Destiny: Humanity in the Image of God*. Grand Rapids: Eerdmans, 2015.

Kister, Menahem. "*Tohu wa-Bohu*, Primordial Elements and *Creatio ex Nihilo*." *Jewish Studies Quarterly* 14 (2007): 229–56.

Kitcher, Philip. *Living with Darwin*. Oxford: Oxford University Press, 2007.

Klein, Richard G., and Blake Edgar. *The Dawn of Human Culture: A Bold New*

Theory on What Sparked the "Big Bang" of Human Consciousness. New York: Wiley, 2002.

Klima, Gyula. "On Kenny on Aquinas on Being: A Critical Review of *Aquinas on Being* by Anthony Kenny." *International Philosophical Quarterly* 44 (2004): 567–80.

Knasas, John F. X. "Contra Spinoza: Aquinas on God's Free Will." *American Catholic Philosophical Quarterly* 76 (2002): 417–29.

Kolankiewicz, Leon. "Overpopulation versus Biodiversity: How a Plethora of People Produces a Paucity of Wildlife." In Cafaro and Crist, *Life on the Brink*, 75–90.

Koons, Robert C., and George Bealer, eds. *The Waning of Materialism*. Oxford: Oxford University Press, 2010.

Koritansky, Peter Karl. "Christianity, Punishment, and Natural Law: Thomas Aquinas' Premodern Retributivism." In *Philosophy of Punishment*, 74–95.

———, ed. *The Philosophy of Punishment and the History of Political Thought*. Columbia, MO: University of Missouri Press, 2011.

———. *Thomas Aquinas and the Philosophy of Punishment*. Washington, DC: Catholic University of America Press, 2012.

Kors, J. B., OP. *La justice primitive et le péché originel d'après S. Thomas*. Kain, Belgium: Le Saulchoir, 1922.

Korsmeyer, Jerry D. *Evolution and Eden: Balancing Original Sin and Contemporary Science*. New York: Paulist Press, 1998.

Krause, Elizabeth L. *A Crisis of Births: Population Politics and Family-Making in Italy*. Belmont, CA: Wadsworth / Thomson Learning, 2005.

Krauss, Lawrence M. *A Universe from Nothing: Why There Is Something Rather than Nothing*. New York: Free Press, 2012.

Kretzmann, Norman. "A General Problem of Creation: Why Would God Create Anything at All?" In S. MacDonald, *Being and Goodness*, 208–28.

———. "A Particular Problem of Creation: Why Would God Create This World?" In S. MacDonald, *Being and Goodness*, 229–49.

Kupczak, Jarosław, OP. *Gift and Communion: John Paul II's Theology of the Body*. Translated by Agata Rottkamp, Justyna Pawlak, and Orest Pawlak. Washington, DC: Catholic University of America Press, 2014.

Labourdette, Marie-Michel, OP. "Le péché originel." *Revue Thomiste* 70 (1970): 277–91.

———. *Le péché originel et les origines de l'homme*. Paris: Alsatia, 1953.

LaCocque, André. *The Trial of Innocence: Adam, Eve, and the Yahwist*. Eugene, OR: Cascade Books, 2006.

Lamb, Matthew L. *Eternity, Time, and the Life of Wisdom*. Edited by Matthew Levering and Michael Dauphinais. Naples, FL: Sapientia, 2007.

Lamoureux, Denis O. "No Historical Adam: Evolutionary Creation View." In Barrett and Caneday, *Four Views on the Historical Adam*, 37–65.

Lane, Nick. *Life Ascending: The Ten Great Inventions of Evolution*. London: Profile Books, 2009.

Lane, Tony. "Bernard of Clairvaux: Theologian of the Cross." In Tidball, Hilborn, and Thacker, *Atonement Debate*, 249–66.

Larchet, Jean-Claude. *The Theology of Illness*. Translated by John and Michael Breck. Crestwood, NY: St. Vladimir's Seminary Press, 2002.

Le Pichon, Xavier. "The Sign of Contradiction." In Reinders, *Paradox of Disability*, 94–110.

Lee, Sang Hyun. "God's Relation to the World." In Lee, *Princeton Companion to Jonathan Edwards*, 59–72.

———. *The Philosophical Theology of Jonathan Edwards*. Princeton: Princeton University Press, 1988.

———, ed. *The Princeton Companion to Jonathan Edwards*. Princeton: Princeton University Press, 2005.

Leftow, Brian. "Divine Simplicity." *Faith and Philosophy* 23 (2006): 365–68.

Leithart, Peter J. *Gratitude: An Intellectual History*. Waco: Baylor University Press, 2014.

———. *Traces of the Trinity: Signs of God in Creation and Human Experience*. Grand Rapids: Brazos, 2015.

Lennox, John C. *Seven Days That Divide the World: The Beginning according to Genesis and Science*. Grand Rapids: Zondervan, 2011.

Leslie, John. *Universes*. London: Routledge, 1989.

Levenson, Jon D. *Creation and the Persistence of Evil: The Jewish Drama of Divine Omnipotence*. Princeton: Princeton University Press, 1988.

Levering, Matthew. "Augustine on Creation: An Exercise in the Dialectical Retrieval of the Ancients." In *Wisdom and the Renewal of Catholic Theology: Essays in Honor of Matthew L. Lamb*, edited by Thomas P. Harmon and Roger W. Nutt, 49–65. Eugene, OR: Pickwick, 2016.

———. "'Be Fruitful and Multiply, and Fill the Earth': Was and Is This a Good Idea?" In *On Earth as It Is in Heaven: Cultivating a Contemporary Theology of Creation*, edited by David Vincent Meconi, SJ, 80–122. Grand Rapids: Eerdmans, 2016.

———. *The Betrayal of Charity: The Sins That Sabotage Divine Love*. Waco: Baylor University Press, 2011.

———. "The Book of Job and God's Existence." In *A Man of the Church: Honoring the Theology, Life, and Witness of Ralph Del Colle*, edited by Michel René Barnes, 231–40. Eugene, OR: Wipf and Stock, 2012.

———. "Christ, the Trinity, and Predestination: McCormack and Aquinas." In *Trinity and Election in Contemporary Theology*, edited by Michael T. Dempsey, 244–73. Grand Rapids: Eerdmans, 2011.

———. *Christ's Fulfillment of Torah and Temple: Salvation according to Thomas Aquinas*. Notre Dame, IN: University of Notre Dame Press, 2002.

———. *Engaging the Doctrine of Revelation: The Mediation of the Gospel through Church and Scripture*. Grand Rapids: Baker Academic, 2014.

———. *Engaging the Doctrine of the Holy Spirit: Love and Gift in the Trinity and the Church*. Grand Rapids: Baker Academic, 2016.

———. "Eternity, History, and Divine Providence." *Angelicum* 88 (2011): 403–23.

———. *Jesus and the Demise of Death: Resurrection, Afterlife, and the Fate of the Christian*. Waco: Baylor University Press, 2012.

———. *Jewish-Christian Dialogue and the Life of Wisdom: Engagements with the Theology of David Novak*. London: Continuum, 2010.

———. *Mary's Bodily Assumption*. Notre Dame, IN: University of Notre Dame Press, 2014.

———. "A Note on John Milbank and Thomas Aquinas." *New Blackfriars* 95 (2014): 525–34.

———. *Paul in the "Summa theologiae."* Washington, DC: Catholic University of America Press, 2014.

———. *Proofs of God: Classical Arguments from Tertullian to Karl Barth*. Grand Rapids: Baker Academic, 2016.

———. "Response to Michał Paluch's 'Analogical Synthesis: An Impossible Project?'" *Nova et Vetera* 14 (2016): 609-17.

———. Review of *Bodies and Souls, or Spirited Bodies?*, by Nancey Murphy. *National Catholic Bioethics Quarterly* 7 (2007): 635–38.

———. Review of *Face of the Deep: A Theology of Becoming*, by Catherine Keller. *Theological Studies* 66 (2005): 905–7.

———. *Scripture and Metaphysics: Aquinas and the Renewal of Trinitarian Theology.* Oxford: Blackwell, 2004.

Levin, Christoph. "Genesis 2–3: A Case of Inner-Biblical Interpretation." Translated by Margaret Kohl. In MacDonald, Elliott, and Macaskill, *Genesis and Christian Theology*, 85–100. Grand Rapids: Eerdmans, 2012.

Lévy, Antoine, OP. *Le créé et l'incréé: Maxime le Confesseur et Thomas d'Aquin; Aux sources de la querelle palamienne.* Paris: Vrin, 2006.

———. "An Introduction to Divine Relativity: Beyond David Bradshaw's *Aristotle East and West*." *The Thomist* 72 (2008): 173–231.

———. "Lost in *Translatio*? *Diakrisis Kat'epinoian* as a Main Issue in the Discussions between Fourteenth-Century Palamites and Thomists." *The Thomist* 76 (2012): 431–72.

———. "The Woes of Originality: Discussing David Bradshaw's Aristotelian Journey into Neo-Palamism." In Athanasopoulos and Schneider, *Divine Essence and Divine Energies*, 96–121.

Lewis, C. S. *Mere Christianity.* New York: Macmillan, 1952.

———. *The Problem of Pain: How Human Suffering Raises Almost Intolerable Intellectual Problems.* New York: Macmillan, 1962.

Lidsey, James E. *The Bigger Bang.* Cambridge: Cambridge University Press, 2000.

Ligier, Louis, SJ. *Péché d'Adam et péché du monde: Bible–Kippur–Eucharistie.* 2 vols. Paris: Aubier, 1960–61.

Lindenfors, P., and B. S. Tullberg. "Evolutionary Aspects of Aggression: The Importance of Sexual Selection." *Advances in Genetics* 75 (2011): 7–22.

Lombardo, Nicholas E., OP. *The Father's Will: Christ's Crucifixion and the Goodness of God.* Oxford: Oxford University Press, 2013.

Lomborg, Bjørn. *Cool It: The Skeptical Environmentalist's Guide to Global Warming.* London: Cyan-Marschall Cavendish, 2007.

———. *The Skeptical Environmentalist: Measuring the Real State of the World.* Cambridge: Cambridge University Press, 2001.

Lonergan, Bernard, SJ. *Grace and Freedom: Operative Grace in the Thought of St. Thomas Aquinas.* Edited by Frederick E. Crowe, SJ, and Robert M. Doran, SJ. Toronto: University of Toronto Press, 2000.

Long, D. Stephen. *Saving Karl Barth: Hans Urs von Balthasar's Preoccupation.* Minneapolis: Fortress, 2014.

Long, Steven A. *Analogia Entis: On the Analogy of Being, Metaphysics, and the Act of Faith.* Notre Dame, IN: University of Notre Dame Press, 2011.

López, Antonio. *Gift and the Unity of Being.* Eugene, OR: Cascade Books, 2014.

Lossky, Vladimir. *The Mystical Theology of the Eastern Church.* Translated by members of the Fellowship of St. Alban and St. Sergius. Crestwood, NY: St. Vladimir's Seminary Press, 1976.

Loudovikos, Nicholas. "Striving for Participation: Palamite Analogy as Dialogical Syn-energy and Thomist Analogy as Emanational Similitude." In

Athanasopoulos and Schneider, *Divine Essence and Divine Energies*, 122–48.

Louth, Andrew. "Man and the Cosmos in St. Maximus the Confessor." In Chryssavgis and Foltz, *Toward an Ecology of Transfiguration*, 59–71.

————. "The Six Days of Creation according to the Greek Fathers." In Barton and Wilkinson, *Reading Genesis after Darwin*, 39–55.

Lundin, Roger. *Beginning with the Word: Modern Literature and the Question of Belief*. Grand Rapids: Baker Academic, 2014.

MacDonald, Nathan, Mark W. Elliott, and Grant Macaskill, eds. *Genesis and Christian Theology*. Grand Rapids: Eerdmans, 2012.

MacDonald, Scott, ed. *Being and Goodness: The Concept of the Good in Metaphysics and Philosophical Theology*. Ithaca, NY: Cornell University Press, 1991.

MacIntyre, Alasdair. *After Virtue: A Study in Moral Theory*. 3rd ed. Notre Dame, IN: University of Notre Dame Press, 2007.

————. *Dependent Rational Animals: Why Human Beings Need the Virtues*. Chicago: Open Court, 1999.

Madueme, Hans. "'The Most Vulnerable Part of the Whole Christian Account': Original Sin and Modern Science." In Madueme and Reeves, *Adam, the Fall, and Original Sin*, 225–49.

Madueme, Hans, and Michael Reeves, eds. *Adam, the Fall, and Original Sin: Theological, Biblical, and Scientific Perspectives*. Grand Rapids: Baker Academic, 2014.

Mahoney, Jack, SJ. *Christianity in Evolution: An Exploration*. Washington, DC: Georgetown University Press, 2011.

Malloy, Christopher J. "Participation and Theology: A Response to Schindler's 'What's the Difference?'" *Nova et Vetera* 5 (2007): 619–46.

Mann, William E. "Augustine on Evil and Original Sin." In Stump and Kretzmann, *Cambridge Companion to Augustine*, 40–48.

Mansini, Guy. "Tight Neo-Platonist Henology and Slack Christian Ontology: Christianity as an Imperfect Neo-Platonism." *Nova et Vetera* 8 (2010): 593–611.

Maritain, Jacques. *Existence and the Existent: The Christian Answer*. Translated by Lewis Galantière and Gerald B. Phelan. New York: Pantheon Books, 1948.

Marshall, I. Howard. "The Theology of the Atonement." In Tidball, Hilborn, and Thacker, *Atonement Debate*, 49–68.

Martínez, Florentino García, and Eibert J. C. Tigchelaar, eds. *The Dead Sea Scrolls Study Edition*. 2 vols. Grand Rapids: Eerdmans, 1997–98.

Maurer, Armand, CSB. "James Ross on the Divine Ideas: A Reply." *American Catholic Philosophical Quarterly* 65 (1991): 213–20.

Maximus the Confessor. *Chapters on Knowledge*. In *Maximus the Confessor: Selected Writings*, translated by George C. Berthold, 121–80. Mahwah, NJ: Paulist Press, 1985.

————. *The Church's Mystagogy*. In *Maximus the Confessor: Selected Writings*, translated by George C. Berthold, 183–225. Mahwah, NJ: Paulist Press, 1985.

May, Gerhard. *Creatio ex Nihilo: The Doctrine of 'Creation out of Nothing' in Early Christian Thought*. Translated by A. S. Worrall. Edinburgh: T&T Clark, 1994.

Mayr, Ernst. *This Is Biology: The Science of the Living World*. Cambridge, MA: Harvard University Press, 1997.

Mays, James L. "'Maker of Heaven and Earth': Creation in the Psalms." In *God Who Creates*, edited by William P. Brown and S. Dean McBride, 75–85. Grand Rapids: Eerdmans, 2000.

McCabe, Herbert, OP. "Organism, Language and Grace." In *The Good Life: Ethics and the Pursuit of Happiness*, 58–78. London: Continuum, 2005.

McCall, Thomas H. "'But a Heathen Still': The Doctrine of Original Sin in Wesleyan Theology." In Madueme and Reeves, *Adam, the Fall, and Original Sin*, 147–66.

McCann, Hugh J. *Creation and the Sovereignty of God*. Bloomington: Indiana University Press, 2012.

McClymond, Michael J., and Gerald R. McDermott. *The Theology of Jonathan Edwards*. Oxford: Oxford University Press, 2012.

McCormack, Bruce L. *Orthodox and Modern: Studies in the Theology of Karl Barth*. Grand Rapids: Baker Academic, 2008.

———. "Processions and Missions: A Point of Convergence between Thomas Aquinas and Karl Barth." In McCormack and White, *Thomas Aquinas and Karl Barth*, 99–126.

McCormack, Bruce L., and Thomas Joseph White, eds. *Thomas Aquinas and Karl Barth: An Unofficial Catholic-Protestant Dialogue*. Grand Rapids: Eerdmans, 2013.

McDonough, Sean M. *Christ as Creator: Origins of a New Testament Doctrine*. Oxford: Oxford University Press, 2009.

McFadyen, Alistair. *Bound to Sin: Abuse, Holocaust and the Christian Doctrine of Sin*. Cambridge: Cambridge University Press, 2000.

McFarland, Ian A. *Difference and Identity: A Theological Anthropology*. Cleveland, OH: Pilgrim, 2001.

———. *The Divine Image: Envisioning the Invisible God*. Minneapolis: Fortress, 2005.

———. *From Nothing: A Theology of Creation*. Louisville: Westminster John Knox, 2014.

———. *In Adam's Fall: A Meditation on the Christian Doctrine of Original Sin*. Oxford: Wiley-Blackwell, 2010.

McFarlane, Graham. "Atonement, Creation and Trinity." In Tidball, Hilborn, and Thacker, *Atonement Debate*, 192–207.

McGrath, Alister E. *A Fine-Tuned Universe: The Quest for God in Science and Theology*. Louisville: Westminster John Knox, 2009.

———. *Iustitia Dei: A History of the Christian Doctrine of Justification*. 3rd ed. Cambridge: Cambridge University Press, 2005.

———. *The Reenchantment of Nature: The Denial of Religion and the Ecological Crisis*. New York: Doubleday, 2002.

McGuckin, John Anthony. "The Beauty of the World and Its Significance in St. Gregory the Theologian." In Chryssavgis and Foltz, *Toward an Ecology of Transfiguration*, 34–45.

McHugh, James T. "A Catholic Perspective on Population." In Ryan and Whitmore, *Challenge of Global Stewardship*, 85–101.

McIntyre, John. *The Shape of Soteriology: Studies in the Doctrine of the Death of Christ*. Edinburgh: T&T Clark, 1992.

McKee, Jeffrey. "The Human Population Footprint on Global Biodiversity." In Cafaro and Crist, *Life on the Brink*, 91–97.

McKibben, Bill. *Deep Economy: The Wealth of Communities and the Durable Future*. New York: Holt, 2007.

———. *The End of Nature*. New York: Random House, 1989.

———. *Maybe One: A Case for Smaller Families*. New York: Penguin, 1998.

McKnight, Scot. *A Community Called Atonement*. Nashville: Abingdon, 2007.

McMullin, Ernan. "Natural Science and Belief in a Creator." In Russell, Stoeger, and Coyne, *Physics, Philosophy, and Theology*, 49–79.

Merriell, D. Juvenal, CO. *To the Image of the Trinity: A Study in the Development of Aquinas's Teaching*. Toronto: Pontifical Institute of Mediaeval Studies, 1990.

———. "Trinitarian Anthropology." In Van Nieuwenhove and Wawrykow, *Theology of Thomas Aquinas*, 123–42.

Mescher, Marcus. "Neighbor to Nature." In Winright, *Green Discipleship*, 200–216.

Mettinger, Tryggve N. D. *No Graven Image? Israelite Aniconism in Its Ancient Near Eastern Context*. Stockholm: Almqvist & Wiksell International, 1995.

Middleton, J. Richard. *The Liberating Image: The* Imago Dei *in Genesis 1*. Grand Rapids: Brazos, 2005.

Milbank, John. *Being Reconciled: Ontology and Pardon*. London: Routledge, 2003.

———. "Christianity and Platonism in East and West." In Athanasopoulos and Schneider, *Divine Essence and Divine Energies*, 158–209.

———. "Ecumenical Orthodoxy—A Response to Nicholas Loudovikos." In Papst and Schneider, *Encounter between Eastern Orthodoxy and Radical Orthodoxy*, 156–64.

———. *The Word Made Strange: Theology, Language, Culture*. Oxford: Blackwell, 1997.

Miller, Barry. *A Most Unlikely God: A Philosophical Inquiry into the Nature of God*. Notre Dame, IN: University of Notre Dame Press, 1996.

Miller, Keith B., ed. *Perspectives on an Evolving Creation*. Grand Rapids: Eerdmans, 2003.

Miller, Kenneth R. *Finding Darwin's God: A Scientist's Search for Common Ground between God and Evolution*. New York: HarperCollins, 1999.

Miller, Richard W. "Global Climate Disruption and Social Justice: The State of the Problem." In Miller, *God, Creation, and Climate Change*, 1–34.

———, ed. *God, Creation, and Climate Change: A Catholic Response to the Environmental Crisis*. Maryknoll, NY: Orbis, 2010.

Mithen, Steven. *After the Ice: A Global Human History, 20,000–5,000 BC*. Cambridge, MA: Harvard University Press, 2003.

Moloney, Francis J., SDB. *The Gospel of John*. Collegeville, MN: Liturgical Press, 1998.

Montagnes, Bernard, OP. *La doctrine de l'analogie de l'être d'après Saint Thomas d'Aquinas*. Paris: Béatrice-Nauwelaerts, 1963.

———. *The Doctrine of the Analogy of Being according to Thomas Aquinas*. Translated by E. M. Macierowski. Milwaukee: Marquette University Press, 2004.

Moreland, J. P., and William Lane Craig. *Philosophical Foundations for a Christian Worldview*. Downers Grove, IL: InterVarsity, 2003.

Morris, Thomas V. *Our Idea of God: An Introduction to Philosophical Theology*. Notre Dame, IN: University of Notre Dame Press, 1991.

Muers, Rachel. "Creatures." In Northcott and Scott, *Systematic Theology and Climate Change*, 90–107.

Muller, Richard A. *Post-Reformation Reformed Dogmatics: The Rise and Development of Reformed Orthodoxy, ca. 1520 to ca. 1725*. Vol. 3, *The Divine Essence and Attributes*. 2nd ed. Grand Rapids: Baker Academic, 2003.

Mullins, Ryan T. "Doing Hard Time: Is God the Prisoner of the Oldest Dimension?" *Journal of Analytic Theology* 2 (2014): 160–85.

———. "Simply Impossible: A Case against Divine Simplicity." *Journal of Reformed Theology* 7 (2013): 181–203.

Murphy, Francesca Aran. *God Is Not a Story: Realism Revisited*. Oxford: Oxford University Press, 2007.

Murphy, George L. "Roads to Paradise and Perdition: Christ, Evolution, and Original Sin." *Perspectives on Science and Christian Faith* 58 (2006): 109–18.

Murphy, Nancey. *Bodies and Souls, or Spirited Bodies?* Cambridge: Cambridge University Press, 2006.

Murray, Michael J. *Nature Red in Tooth and Claw: Theism and the Problem of Animal Suffering*. Oxford: Oxford University Press, 2008.

———, ed. *Reason for the Hope Within*. Grand Rapids: Eerdmans, 1999.

Neuhaus, Richard John. "Christ and Creation's Longing." In Derr, Nash, and Neuhaus, *Environmental Ethics and Christian Humanism*, 125–37.

———. *In Defense of People: Ecology and the Seduction of Radicalism*. New York: Macmillan, 1971.

Newman, John Henry. *Apologia pro Vita Sua*. New York: Doubleday, 1956.

———. *An Essay in Aid of a Grammar of Assent*. Westminster, MD: Christian Classics, 1973.

Nicolas, Jean-Hervé, OP. *Synthèse dogmatique: De la Trinité à la Trinité*. Paris: Beauchesne, 1985.

Noll, Mark A. *America's God: From Jonathan Edwards to Abraham Lincoln*. Oxford: Oxford University Press, 2002.

Noonan, John T. *Contraception: A History of Its Treatment by the Catholic Theologians and Canonists*. 2nd ed. Cambridge, MA: Harvard University Press, 1986.

Norman, David. *Dinosaurs: A Very Short Introduction*. Oxford: Oxford University Press, 2005.

Northcott, Michael S. *The Environment and Christian Ethics*. Cambridge: Cambridge University Press, 1996.

———. "Holy Spirit." In Northcott and Scott, *Systematic Theology and Climate Change*, 51–68.

———. *A Political Theology of Climate Change*. Grand Rapids: Eerdmans, 2013.

Northcott, Michael S., and Peter M. Scott, eds. *Systematic Theology and Climate Change: Ecumenical Perspectives*. London: Routledge, 2014.

Novak, David. *The Election of Israel: The Idea of the Chosen People*. Cambridge: Cambridge University Press, 1995.

Nuland, Sherwin B. *How We Die: Reflections on Life's Final Chapter*. New York: Random House, 1993.

Oakes, Kenneth. "The Cross and the *Analogia Entis* in Erich Przywara." In White, *Analogy of Being*, 147–71.

O'Callaghan, John P. "*Imago Dei*: A Test Case for St. Thomas's Augustinianism." In Dauphinais, David, and Levering, *Aquinas the Augustinian*, 100–144.

O'Collins, Gerald, SJ. *Jesus Our Redeemer: A Christian Approach to Salvation*. Oxford: Oxford University Press, 2007.

Oderberg, David S. *Real Essentialism*. London: Routledge, 2007.

Oliver, Simon. "Trinity, Motion and Creation *ex Nihilo*." In Burrell, Cogliati, Soskice, and Stoeger, *Creation and the God of Abraham*, 133–51.

O'Meara, Dominic J., ed. *Neoplatonism and Christian Thought*. Albany: State University of New York Press, 1982.

O'Neill, J. C. "How Early Is the Doctrine of *Creatio ex Nihilo*?" *Journal of Theological Studies* 53 (2002): 449–65.

Oord, Thomas Jay, ed. *Theologies of Creation: Creatio ex Nihilo and Its New Rivals*. New York: Routledge, 2015.

Oppy, Graham Robert. "The Devilish Complexities of Divine Simplicity." *Philo* 6 (Spring-Summer 2003): 10–22.

Ormerod, Neil. *Creation, Grace, and Redemption.* Maryknoll, NY: Orbis Books, 2007.

Osborn, Ronald E. *Death before the Fall: Biblical Literalism and the Problem of Animal Suffering.* Downers Grove, IL: InterVarsity, 2014.

Otto, Randall E. "The Solidarity of Mankind in Jonathan Edwards' Doctrine of Original Sin." *Evangelical Quarterly* 62 (1990): 205–21.

Otto, Sean A. "*Felix Culpa*: The Doctrine of Original Sin as Doctrine of Hope in Aquinas's *Summa contra gentiles*." *Heythrop Journal* 50 (2009): 781–92.

Ovitt, George, Jr. *The Restoration of Perfection: Labor and Technology in Medieval Culture.* New Brunswick, NJ: Rutgers University Press, 1987.

Packer, J. I. "What Did the Cross Achieve? The Logic of Penal Substitution." In *The J. I. Packer Collection*, edited by Alister McGrath, 94–136. Downers Grove, IL: InterVarsity, 1999.

Paffhausen, Metropolitan Jonah. "Natural Contemplation in St. Maximus the Confessor and St. Isaac the Syrian." In Chryssavgis and Foltz, *Toward an Ecology of Transfiguration*, 45–58.

Paluch, Michał, OP. "Analogical Synthesis: An Impossible Project?" *Nova et Vetera* 14 (2016): 591–608.

Pannenberg, Wolfhart. *Systematic Theology.* Vol. 2. Translated by Geoffrey W. Bromiley. Grand Rapids: Eerdmans, 1994.

Papanikolaou, Aristotle. "Creation as Communion in Contemporary Orthodox Theology." In Chryssavgis and Foltz, *Toward an Ecology of Transfiguration*, 106–20.

Papst, Adrian, and Christoph Schneider, eds. *Encounter between Eastern Orthodoxy and Radical Orthodoxy: Transfiguring the World through the Word.* Burlington, VT: Ashgate, 2009.

Parker, Andrew. *The Genesis Enigma.* London: Doubleday, 2009.

Parmisano, Stan, OP. *The Craft of Love: Love and Intimacy in Christian Marriage.* Antioch, CA: Solas, 2009.

Pasewark, Kyle A. *A Theology of Power: Being beyond Domination.* Minneapolis: Fortress, 1993.

Paul VI, Pope. *Populorum Progressio.* Boston: Pauline Books & Media, 1967.

Peacocke, Arthur. *Theology for a Scientific Age: Being and Becoming—Natural, Divine and Human.* 2nd ed. Minneapolis: Fortress, 1993.

Perdue, Leo G. *Wisdom and Creation.* Nashville: Abingdon, 1994.

Perl, Eric D. "Hierarchy and Love in St. Dionysius the Areopagite." In Chryssavgis and Foltz, *Toward an Ecology of Transfiguration*, 23–33.

———. "St. Gregory Palamas and the Metaphysics of Creation." *Dionysius* 14 (1990): 105–30.

Perrier, Emmanuel, OP. "L'enjeu christologique de la satisfaction." *Revue thomiste* 103 (2003): 105–36.

Persson, Per Erik. *Sacra Doctrina: Reason and Revelation in Aquinas.* Translated by Ross Mackenzie. Oxford: Blackwell, 1970.

Peters, Ted. "The Evolution of Evil." In Gaymon Bennett et al., *The Evolution of Evil*, 19–52. Göttingen: Vandenhoeck & Ruprecht, 2008.

Philo of Alexandria. *On the Creation* [*De opificio mundi*]. In *The Works of Philo*, rev. ed., translated by C. D. Yonge, 3–24. Peabody, MA: Hendrickson, 1993.

Philpott, Daniel. *Just and Unjust Peace: An Ethic of Political Reconciliation.* Oxford: Oxford University Press, 2012.

Pieper, Josef. "Immortality—a Non-Christian Idea? Philosophical Comments on a Controversial Theological Theme." In *Tradition as Challenge: Essays and Speeches*, translated by Dan Farrelly, 62–85. South Bend, IN: St. Augustine's Press, 2015.

———. *The Silence of St. Thomas: Three Essays*. Translated by John Murray, SJ, and Daniel O'Connor. South Bend, IN: St. Augustine's Press, 1999.

Pius XII, Pope. *Humani generis*. www.vatican.va.

Plantinga, Alvin. *Does God Have a Nature?* Milwaukee: Marquette University Press, 1980.

Plato. *Timaeus*. Translated by Benjamin Jowett. In *The Collected Dialogues*, edited by Edith Hamilton and Huntington Cairns, 1151–1211. Princeton: Princeton University Press, 1961.

Plested, Marcus. *Orthodox Readings of Aquinas*. Oxford: Oxford University Press, 2012.

Plotinus. *Enneads*. Translated by Stephen MacKenna. Abridged ed. New York: Penguin Books, 1991.

Polkinghorne, John. *Exploring Reality: The Intertwining of Science and Religion*. New Haven: Yale University Press, 2005.

———. *Quantum Theory: A Very Short Introduction*. Oxford: Oxford University Press, 2002.

Pontifical Council for Justice and Peace. *Compendium of the Social Doctrine of the Church*. Vatican City: Libreria Editrice Vaticana, 2004.

Provan, Charles. *The Bible and Birth Control*. Monongahela, PA: Zimmer Printing, 1989.

Prud'homme, Joseph, and James Schelberg. "Disposition, Potentiality, and Beauty in the Theology of Jonathan Edwards: A Defense of His *Great Christian Doctrine of Original Sin*." *American Theological Quarterly* 5 (2012): 25–53.

Pruss, Alexander R. *Actuality, Possibility, and Worlds*. London: Continuum, 2011.

———. "On Two Problems of Divine Simplicity." In *Oxford Studies in Philosophy of Religion*, edited by Jonathan L. Kvanvig, 1:150–67. Oxford: Oxford University Press, 2008.

———. *One Body: An Essay in Christian Sexual Ethics*. Notre Dame, IN: University of Notre Dame Press, 2013.

Przywara, Erich. *Analogia Entis: Metaphysics; Original Structure and Universal Rhythm*. Translated by John R. Betz and David Bentley Hart. Grand Rapids: Eerdmans, 2014.

Pseudo-Dionysius. *The Divine Names*. In *The Complete Works*, translated by Colm Luibheid with Paul Rorem, 49–131. New York: Paulist Press, 1987.

Purcell, Brendan. *From Big Bang to Big Mystery: Human Origins in the Light of Creation and Evolution*. Hyde Park, NY: New City Press, 2012.

Quinn, Philip L. "Disputing the Augustinian Legacy: John Locke and Jonathan Edwards on Romans 5:12–19." In *The Augustinian Tradition*, edited by Gareth B. Matthews, 233–50. Berkeley: University of California Press, 1999.

Rad, Gerhard von. *Wisdom in Israel*. Nashville: Abingdon, 1972.

Radde-Gallwitz, Andrew. *Basil of Caesarea, Gregory of Nyssa, and the Transformation of Divine Simplicity*. Oxford: Oxford University Press, 2009.

Rahner, Karl. *Foundations of Christian Faith: An Introduction to the Idea of Christianity*. Translated by William V. Dych. New York: Crossroad, 1993.

———. *Hominisation: The Evolutionary Origin of Man as a Theological Problem*. Translated by W. T. O'Hara. New York: Herder & Herder, 1965.

———. "The Sin of Adam." In *Theological Investigations*, vol. 11, *Confrontations*, translated by David Bourke, 247–62. London: Darton, Longman & Todd, 1974.

———. "Theological Reflexions on Monogenism." In *Theological Investigations*, vol. 1, *God, Christ, Mary and Grace*, translated by Cornelius Ernst, OP, 229–96. London: Darton, Longman & Todd, 1961.

Raith, Charles, II. "Aquinas and Calvin on Merit, Part II: Condignity and Participation." *Pro Ecclesia* 21 (2012): 195–210.

———. *Aquinas and Calvin on Romans: God's Justification and Our Participation*. Oxford: Oxford University Press, 2014.

———. "Calvin's Critique of Merit, and Why Aquinas (Mostly) Agrees." *Pro Ecclesia* 20 (2011): 135–53.

Ratzinger, Joseph. *'In the Beginning . . .' A Catholic Understanding of the Story of Creation and Fall*. Translated by Boniface Ramsey, OP. Grand Rapids: Eerdmans, 1995.

Rea, Michael C. "The Metaphysics of Original Sin." In *Persons: Human and Divine*, edited by Peter van Inwagen and Dean Zimmerman, 319–56. Oxford: Clarendon, 2007.

Redfern, Martin. *The Earth: A Very Short Introduction*. Oxford: Oxford University Press, 2003.

Rees, Martin J. *Just Six Numbers: The Deep Forces That Shape the Universe*. London: Phoenix, 2000.

Reinders, Hans S., ed. *Disability, Providence, and Ethics: Bridging Gaps, Transforming Lives*. Waco: Baylor University Press, 2014.

———, ed. *The Paradox of Disability: Responses to Jean Vanier and L'Arche Communities from Theology and the Sciences*. Grand Rapids: Eerdmans, 2010.

———. *Receiving the Gift of Friendship: Profound Disability, Theological Anthropology, and Ethics*. Grand Rapids: Eerdmans, 2008.

Reno, R. R. *Genesis*. Grand Rapids: Brazos, 2010.

Richards, Jay Wesley. *The Untamed God: A Philosophical Exploration of Divine Perfection, Simplicity, and Immutability*. Downers Grove, IL: InterVarsity, 2003.

Ricoeur, Paul. *Histoire et vérité*. 2nd ed. Paris: Seuil, 1964.

———. "Interpretation of the Myth of Punishment." Translated by Robert Sweeney. In Ricoeur, *The Conflict of Interpretations: Essays in Hermeneutics*, edited by Don Ihde, 354–77. Evanston, IL: Northwestern University Press, 2007.

———. "'Original Sin': A Study in Meaning." Translated by Peter McCormick. In Ricoeur, *The Conflict of Interpretations: Essays in Hermeneutics*, edited by Don Ihde, 269–86. Evanston, IL: Northwestern University Press, 2007.

Riordan, William. *Divine Light: The Theology of Denys the Areopagite*. San Francisco: Ignatius, 2008.

Rist, John M. *Augustine Deformed: Love, Sin and Freedom in the Western Moral Tradition*. Cambridge: Cambridge University Press, 2014.

Rivière, Jean. *The Doctrine of the Atonement: A Historical Essay*. 2 vols. Translated by Luigi Cappadelta. London: Kegan Paul, Trench, Trübner & Co., 1909.

Robinson, Tara Rodden. *Genetics for Dummies*. 2nd ed. Hoboken, NJ: Wiley, 2010.

Robson, Mark Ian Thomas. *Ontology and Providence in Creation: Taking* ex Nihilo *Seriously*. London: Continuum, 2008.

Rocca, Gregory. "'Creatio ex Nihilo' and the Being of Creatures: God's Creative Act and the Transcendence-Immanence Distinction in Aquinas." In *Divine*

Transcendence and Immanence in the Work of Thomas Aquinas, edited by Harm Goris, Herwi Rikhof, and Henk Schoot, 1–17. Leuven: Peeters, 2009.

Rolston, Holmes. *Genes, Genesis and God*. Cambridge: Cambridge University Press, 1999.

Romero, Miguel J. "Aquinas on the *Corporis Infirmitas*: Broken Flesh and the Grammar of Grace." In *Disability in the Christian Tradition: A Reader*, edited by Brian Brock and John Swinton, 101–25. Grand Rapids: Eerdmans, 2012.

Rosato, Andrew. "The Interpretation of Anselm's Teaching on Christ's Satisfaction for Sin in the Franciscan Tradition from Alexander of Hales to Duns Scotus." *Franciscan Studies* 71 (2013): 411–44.

Rose, Steven. *The Making of Memory: From Molecules to Mind*. Rev. ed. London: Random House, 2003.

Rosenberg, Alex. *The Atheist's Guide to Reality: Enjoying Life without Illusions*. New York: W. W. Norton, 2011.

Rosenberg, Randall S. "Being-toward-a-Death-Transformed: Aquinas on the Naturalness and Unnaturalness of Human Death." *Angelicum* 83 (2006): 747–66.

Rosenzweig, Franz. *The Star of Redemption*. Translated by Barbara E. Galli. Madison: University of Wisconsin Press, 2005.

Ross, James F. "Aquinas' Exemplarism; Aquinas' Voluntarism." *American Catholic Philosophical Quarterly* 64 (1990): 171–98.

———. "God, Creator of Kinds and Possibilities: *Requiescant universalia ante res*." In *Rationality, Religious Belief, and Moral Commitment*, edited by Robert Audi and William Wainwright, 315–34. Ithaca, NY: Cornell University Press, 1986.

———. "Response to Maurer and Dewan." *American Catholic Philosophical Quarterly* 65 (1991): 235–43.

———. *Thought and World: The Hidden Necessities*. Notre Dame, IN: University of Notre Dame Press, 2008.

Rowe, C. Kavin. *World Upside Down: Reading Acts in the Graeco-Roman Age*. Oxford: Oxford University Press, 2009.

Ruse, Michael. *Can a Darwinian Be a Christian?* Cambridge: Cambridge University Press, 2001.

Russell, Andrew C. "Polemical Solidarity: John Wesley and Jonathan Edwards Confront John Taylor on Original Sin." *Wesleyan Theological Journal* 47 (2012): 72–88.

Russell, Robert J., William R. Stoeger, and George V. Coyne, eds. *Physics, Philosophy, and Theology*. Rome: Vatican Observatory, 1988.

Ryan, Maura A., and Todd David Whitmore. *The Challenge of Global Stewardship: Roman Catholic Responses*. Notre Dame, IN: University of Notre Dame Press, 1997.

Ryken, Philip G. "We Cannot Understand the World or Our Faith without a Real, Historical Adam." In Barrett and Caneday, *Four Views on the Historical Adam*, 267–79.

Rziha, John. *Perfecting Human Actions: St. Thomas Aquinas on Human Participation in Eternal Law*. Washington, DC: Catholic University of America Press, 2009.

Sabourin, Léopold. *Rédemption sacrificielle: Une enquête exégétique*. Paris: Desclée, 1961.

Sanders, E. P. *Paul and Palestinian Judaism*. London: SCM, 1977.

Savage, Minot Judson. *The Religion of Evolution*. Boston: Lockwood, Brooks, & Co., 1881.

Schafer, Thomas. "The Concept of Being in the Thought of Jonathan Edwards." PhD diss., Duke University, 1951.

Scheffczyk, Leo. *Creation and Providence.* Translated by Richard Strachan. New York: Herder & Herder, 1970.

Schenk, Richard, OP. "Analogy as the *Discrimen Naturae et Gratiae*: Thomism and Ecumenical Learning." In White, *Analogy of Being*, 172–91.

Schilder, Klaas. *Heidelbergsche Catechismus.* Vol. 1. Goes, The Netherlands: Ooesterbaan & Le Cointre, 1947.

Schindler, D. C. "What's the Difference? On the Metaphysics of Participation in Plato, Plotinus, and Aquinas." *Nova et Vetera* 5 (2007): 583–618.

Schnackenburg, Rudolph. *The Johannine Epistles: Introduction and Commentary.* Translated by Reginald and Ilse Fuller. New York: Crossroad, 1992.

Schönborn, Christoph, OP. *Chance or Purpose? Creation, Evolution, and a Rational Faith.* Edited by Hubert Philip Weber. Translated by Henry Taylor. San Francisco: Ignatius, 2007.

———. "Die kirchliche Erbsündenlehre im Umriss." In *Zur kirchlichen Erbsündenlehre: Stellungnahmen zu einer brennenden Frage*, 69–102. Einsiedeln: Johannes Verlag, 1991.

Schoonenberg, Piet, SJ. *Man and Sin: A Theological View.* Translated by J. Donceel, SJ. Notre Dame, IN: University of Notre Dame Press, 1965.

Schoot, Henk J. M. "Divine Transcendence and the Mystery of Salvation according to Thomas Aquinas." In *Divine Transcendence and Immanence in the Work of Thomas Aquinas*, edited by Harm Goris, Herwi Rikhof, and Henk Schoot, 255–81. Leuven: Peeters, 2009.

Schroeder, Gerald L. *Genesis and the Big Bang: The Discovery of Harmony between Modern Science and the Bible.* New York: Bantam Books, 1990.

Schwager, Raymund, SJ. *Banished from Eden: Original Sin and Evolutionary Theory in the Drama of Salvation.* Translated by James Williams. Leominster, UK: Gracewing, 2006.

Schwarz, Hans. *Creation.* Grand Rapids: Eerdmans, 2002.

Schwarz, John C. *Global Population from a Catholic Perspective.* Mystic, CT: Twenty-Third Publications, 1998.

Scola, Angelo. *The Nuptial Mystery.* Translated by Michelle K. Borras. Grand Rapids: Eerdmans, 2005.

Scruton, Roger. *Green Philosophy: How to Think Seriously about the Planet.* London: Atlantic Books, 2012.

Seitz, Christopher R. *Colossians.* Grand Rapids: Brazos, 2014.

Sell, Alan P. F. *Philosophy, Dissent and Nonconformity.* Cambridge: Clarke, 2004.

Selner-Wright, Susan. "Aquinas on Acts of Creation and Procreation." *National Catholic Bioethics Quarterly* 3 (2003): 707–16.

Sen, Amartya. "Population: Delusion and Reality." In Cromartie, *Nine Lives of Population Control*, 101–27.

Sesboüé, Bernard, SJ. *Jésus-Christ l'unique médiateur. Essai sur la redemption et le salut.* Paris: Desclée, 1988.

Shadle, Matthew A. "No Peace on Earth: War and the Environment." In Winright, *Green Discipleship*, 407–24.

Shanley, Brian J., OP. "Eternal Knowledge of the Temporal in Aquinas." *American Catholic Philosophical Quarterly* 70 (1997): 197–224.

Sherman, Robert. *Covenant, Community, and the Spirit: A Trinitarian Theology of Church.* Grand Rapids: Baker Academic, 2015.

Sherrard, Philip. *The Greek East and the Latin West.* 2nd ed. Limni, Greece: Denise Harvey, 1995.

Shochet, Elijah. *Animal Life in Jewish Tradition: Attitudes and Relationships.* New York: KTAV, 1984.

Shuster, Arthur. "Kant on the Role of the Retributive Outlook in Moral and Political Life." In Koritansky, *Philosophy of Punishment*, 114–35.

Smith, John E. *Jonathan Edwards: Puritan, Preacher, Philosopher*. Notre Dame, IN: University of Notre Dame Press, 1992.

Smith, Mark S. *The Early History of God: Yahweh and the Other Deities in Ancient Israel*. 2nd ed. Grand Rapids: Eerdmans, 2002.

Smith, Randall. "Creation and the Environment in the Hebrew Scriptures: A Transvaluation of Values." In Winright, *Green Discipleship*, 74–90.

Sokolowski, Robert. *The God of Faith and Reason: Foundations of Christian Theology*. Washington, DC: Catholic University of America Press, 1995.

Sommer, Benjamin D. *The Bodies of God and the World of Ancient Israel*. Cambridge: Cambridge University Press, 2009.

Sonderegger, Katherine. *Systematic Theology*. Vol. 1, *The Doctrine of God*. Minneapolis: Fortress, 2015.

Soskice, Janet Martin. "Creation and the Glory of Creatures." *Modern Theology* 29 (2013): 172–85.

———, ed. *Creation 'ex Nihilo' and Modern Theology*. Oxford: Wiley-Blackwell, 2013.

Spence, Alan. *The Promise of Peace: A Unified Theory of Atonement*. London: T&T Clark, 2006.

Staniloae, Dumitru. *The Experience of God: Orthodox Dogmatic Theology*. Vol. 2, *The World: Creation and Deification*. Translated and edited by Ioan Ionita and Robert Barringer. Brookline, MA: Holy Cross Orthodox Press, 2000.

Staples, Winthrop, III, and Philip Cafaro. "For a Species Right to Exist." In Cafaro and Crist, *Life on the Brink*, 283–300.

Sterling, Gregory E. "*Creatio Temporalis, Aeterna, vel Continua*? An Analysis of the Thought of Philo of Alexandria." *Studia Philonica Annual* 4 (1992): 15–41.

Stringer, Chris. *African Exodus: The Origins of Modern Humanity*. New York: Henry Holt, 1996.

———. *Lone Survivors: How We Came to Be the Only Humans on Earth*. New York: St. Martin's Press, 2012.

Stringer, Chris, and Peter Andrews. *The Complete World of Human Evolution*. 2nd ed. London: Thames & Hudson, 2012.

Stueckelberger, Christoph. "Who Dies First? Who Is Sacrificed First? Ethical Aspects of Climate Justice." In Bloomquist, *God, Creation and Climate Change*, 47–62.

Stump, Eleonore. *Aquinas*. London: Routledge, 2003.

Stump, Eleonore, and Norman Kretzmann. "Absolute Simplicity." *Faith and Philosophy* 2 (1985): 353–81.

———. *The Cambridge Companion to Augustine*. Cambridge: Cambridge University Press, 2001.

———. "Eternity." *Journal of Philosophy* 78 (1981): 429–58.

Swinburne, Richard. *The Christian God*. Oxford: Oxford University Press, 1994.

Symeon the New Theologian. *Divine Eros: Hymns of St Symeon the New Theologian*. Translated by Daniel K. Griggs. Crestwood, NY: St. Vladimir's Seminary Press, 2010.

———. *The First-Created Man*. Translated by Seraphim Rose from the Russian edition of St. Theophan the Recluse. 3rd ed. Platina, CA: St. Herman of Alaska Brotherhood, 2001.

Tallis, Raymond. *Aping Mankind: Neuromania, Darwinitis and the Misrepresentation of Humanity*. Durham, UK: Acumen, 2011.

Tanner, Kathryn. *Christ the Key*. Cambridge: Cambridge University Press, 2010.

———. "Creation and Salvation in the Image of an Incomprehensible God." In Davidson and Rae, *God of Salvation*, 61–75.

———. *God and Creation in Christian Theology: Tyranny or Empowerment?* Minneapolis: Fortress, 2005.

Tanner, Norman P., SJ, ed. *Decrees of the Ecumenical Councils*. Vol. 2, *Trent to Vatican II*. Washington, DC: Georgetown University Press, 1990.

Tattersall, Ian. *The Fossil Trail: How We Know What We Think We Know about Human Evolution*. Oxford: Oxford University Press, 1995.

Taubes, Jacob. *Occidental Eschatology*. Translated by David Ratmoko. Stanford, CA: Stanford University Press, 2009.

Taylor, John. *The Scripture-Doctrine of Original Sin Proposed to Free and Candid Examination*. London: J. Waugh, 1740.

Te Velde, Rudi. *Aquinas on God: The 'Divine Science' of the "Summa Theologiae."* Aldershot: Ashgate, 2006.

———. "Evil, Sin, and Death: Thomas Aquinas on Original Sin." In Van Nieuwenhove and Wawrykow, *Theology of Thomas Aquinas*, 143–46.

———. "Metaphysics and the Question of Creation: Thomas Aquinas, Duns Scotus and Us." In Cunningham and Candler, *Belief and Metaphysics*, 73–99.

———. *Participation and Substantiality in Thomas Aquinas*. Leiden: Brill, 1995.

———. "Thomas Aquinas's Understanding of Prayer in the Light of the Doctrine of Creatio ex Nihilo." *Modern Theology* 29 (2013): 49–61.

Teilhard de Chardin, Pierre. *Hymn of the Universe*. Translated by Gerald Vann, OP. New York: Harper & Row, 1965.

Tennant, F. R. *The Origin and Propagation of Sin*. 2nd ed. Cambridge: Cambridge University Press, 1906.

Terry, Justyn. *The Justifying Judgement of God: A Reassessment of the Place of Judgement in the Saving Work of Christ*. Milton Keynes: Paternoster, 2007.

Thomas Aquinas. *Commentary on the Gospel of St. Matthew*. Camillus, NY: Dolorosa, 2012.

———. *Commentary on the Letters of Saint Paul to the Corinthians*. Edited by J. Mortensen and E. Alarcón. Translated by F. R. Larcher, OP, B. Mortensen, and D. Keating. Lander, WY: The Aquinas Institute for the Study of Sacred Doctrine, 2012.

———. *On Evil*. Translated by John A. Oesterle and Jean T. Oesterle. Notre Dame, IN: University of Notre Dame Press, 1995.

———. *On the Power of God* [*De Potentia*]. Translated by English Dominican Fathers. Eugene, OR: Wipf and Stock, 2004.

———. *Scriptum super Sententiis*. Paris: Vivès, 1871–80.

———. *Somme théologique*. Vol. 2. Translated into French by A. D. Sertillanges, OP. Paris: Éditions de la Revue des Jeunes, 1926.

———. *Summa contra gentiles: Book Two, Creation*. Translated by James F. Anderson. Notre Dame, IN: University of Notre Dame Press, 1975.

———. *Summa theologiae*. Translated by the Fathers of the English Dominican Province. Westminster, MD: Christian Classics, 1981.

Thompson, Marianne Meye. *Colossians and Philemon*. Grand Rapids: Eerdmans, 2005.

Thomson, Russell, et al. "Recent Common Ancestry of Human Y Chromosomes: Evidence from DNA Sequence Data."

Proceedings of the National Academy of Sciences U.S.A. 97 (2000): 7360–65.

Tidball, Derek, David Hilborn, and Justin Thacker, eds. *The Atonement Debate: Papers from the London Symposium on the Theology of Atonement*. Grand Rapids: Zondervan, 2008.

Tirosh-Samuelson, Hava. "Judaism and the Care for God's Creation." In Winright, *Green Discipleship*, 286–318.

Torrance, Thomas F. *Divine and Contingent Order*. 2nd ed. Edinburgh: T&T Clark, 1998.

Torrell, Jean-Pierre, OP. *Pour nous les hommes et pour notre salut: Jésus notre rédemption*. Paris: Cerf, 2014.

———. *Saint Thomas Aquinas*. Vol. 2, *Spiritual Master*. Translated by Robert Royal. Washington, DC: Catholic University of America Press, 2003.

Traherne, Thomas. *Poetry and Prose*. Edited by Denise Inge. London: SPCK, 2002.

———. *Selected Poems and Prose*. New York: Penguin, 1991.

Tranzillo, Jeffrey. *John Paul II on the Vulnerable*. Washington, DC: Catholic University of America Press, 2013.

Trigo, Pegro. *Creation and History*. Translated by Robert R. Barr. Maryknoll, NY: Orbis Books, 1991.

Trooster, S. G. M., SJ. *Evolution and the Doctrine of Original Sin*. Translated by John A. Ter Haar. Glen Rock, NJ: Newman, 1968.

Trueman, Carl R. "Original Sin and Modern Theology." In Madueme and Reeves, *Adam, the Fall, and Original Sin*, 167–86.

Turner, Denys. *Thomas Aquinas: A Portrait*. New Haven: Yale University Press, 2013.

Turner, J. Scott. *The Tinkerer's Accomplice: How Design Emerges from Life Itself*. Cambridge, MA: Harvard University Press, 2007.

Ulrich, Ferdinand. *Homo Abyssus: Das Wagnis der Seinsfrage*. 2nd ed. Einsiedeln: Johannes Verlag, 1998.

Underhill, Peter A., et al. "Y Chromosome Sequence Variation and the History of Human Populations." *Nature Genetics* 26 (2000): 358–61.

Van Inwagen, Peter. "Genesis and Evolution." In *God, Knowledge, and Mystery*, 128–62. Ithaca, NY: Cornell University Press, 1995.

———. *The Problem of Evil*. Oxford: Oxford University Press, 2006.

Van Nieuwenhove, Rik, and Joseph Wawrykow, eds. *The Theology of Thomas Aquinas*. Notre Dame, IN: University of Notre Dame Press, 2005.

Vanhoozer, Kevin J. "The Atonement in Postmodernity: Guilt, Goats and Gifts." In *The Glory of the Atonement: Biblical, Historical and Practical Perspectives: Essays in Honor of Roger Nicole*, edited by Charles E. Hill and Frank A. James III, 367–404. Downers Grove, IL: InterVarsity, 2004.

Vannier, Marie-Anne. *"Creatio," "conversio," "formatio" chez S. Augustin*. Fribourg: Éditions universitaires, 1991.

Veldman, Meredith. *Fantasy, the Bomb, and the Greening of Britain: Romantic Protest, 1945–1980*. Cambridge: Cambridge University Press, 1994.

Venema, Dennis. "Genesis and the Genome: Genomics Evidence for Human-Ape Common Ancestry and Ancestral Hominid Population Sizes." *Perspectives on Science and Christian Faith* 62 (2010): 166–78.

Verhey, Allen. *Nature and Altering It*. Grand Rapids: Eerdmans, 2010.

———. "Neither Devils nor Angels: Peace, Justice, and Defending the Innocent; A Response to Richard Hays." In *The Word Leaps the Gap: Essays on Scripture and Theology in Honor of Richard B. Hays*, edited by J. Ross Wagner, C. Kavin Rowe, and A. Katherine Grieb, 599–625. Grand Rapids: Eerdmans, 2008.

Vidu, Adonis. *Atonement, Law, and Justice: The Cross in Historical and Cultural Contexts*. Grand Rapids: Baker Academic, 2014.

Vilenkin, Alex. *Many Worlds in One: The Search for Other Universes*. New York: Hill & Wang, 2006.

Vogt, Christopher P. "Catholic Social Teaching and Creation." In Winright, *Green Discipleship*, 220–40.

Volf, Miroslav. *Exclusion and Embrace: A Theological Exploration of Identity, Otherness, and Reconciliation*. Nashville: Abingdon, 1996.

———. *Free of Charge: Giving and Forgiving in a Culture Stripped of Grace*. Grand Rapids: Zondervan, 2005.

Vollert, Cyril, SJ. "The Two Senses of Original Justice in Medieval Theology." *Theological Studies* 5 (1944): 3–23.

Wallace, Mark I. "The Green Face of God: Recovering the Spirit in an Ecocidal Era." In Hinze and Dabney, *Advents of the Spirit*, 442–62.

Walsh, Liam G., OP. "Thomas Aquinas, the Doctrine of Original Sin, and the Dogma of the Immaculate Conception." In *Studying Mary: Reflections on the Virgin Mary in Anglican and Roman Catholic Theology and Devotion*, edited by Adelbert Denaux and Nicholas Sagovsky, 110–30. London: T&T Clark, 2007.

Walton, John H. "A Historical Adam: Archetypal Creation View." In Barrett and Caneday, *Four Views on the Historical Adam*, 89–118.

———. *The Lost World of Genesis One: Ancient Cosmology and the Origins Debate*. Downers Grove, IL: IVP Academic, 2009.

Ward, Keith. *Defending the Soul*. London: Hodder & Stoughton, 1992.

Ware, Kallistos. *The Orthodox Way*. 2nd ed. Crestwood, NY: St. Vladimir's Seminary Press, 1995.

———. "Through Creation to the Creator." In Chryssavgis and Foltz, *Toward an Ecology of Transfiguration*, 86–105.

Warfield, Benjamin. *Studies in Theology*. New York: Oxford University Press, 1932.

Watson, Francis. "Genesis before Darwin: Why Scripture Needed Liberating from Science." In Barton and Wilkinson, *Reading Genesis after Darwin*, 23–37.

Wattenberg, Ben. *Fewer: How the New Demography of Depopulation Will Shape Our Future*. Chicago: Ivan R. Dee, 2004.

Wawrykow, Joseph P. *God's Grace and Human Action: 'Merit' in the Theology of Thomas Aquinas*. Notre Dame, IN: University of Notre Dame Press, 1995.

Weaver, J. Denny. "Narrative *Christus Victor*: The Answer to Anselmian Atonement Violence." In *Atonement and Violence: A Theological Conversation*, edited by John Sanders, 1–29. Nashville: Abingdon, 2006.

———. *The Nonviolent Atonement*. 2nd ed. Grand Rapids: Eerdmans, 2011.

Webb, Stephen H. "*Creatio a Materia ex Christi*." In Oord, *Theologies of Creation*, 69–78.

———. *Jesus Christ, Eternal God: Heavenly Flesh and the Metaphysics of Matter*. Oxford: Oxford University Press, 2012.

Weber, Otto. *Foundations of Dogmatics*. Vol. 1. Translated by Darrell L. Guder. Grand Rapids: Eerdmans, 1981.

Webster, John. "God's Perfect Life." In *God's Life in Trinity*, edited by Miroslav Volf and Michael Welker, 143–52. Minneapolis: Fortress, 2006.

———. *The Grace of Truth*. Edited by Daniel Bush and Brannon Ellis. Farmington Hills, MI: Oil Lamp Books, 2011.

———. *Holiness*. Grand Rapids: Eerdmans, 2003.

———. "'It Was the Will of the Lord to Bruise Him': Soteriology and the Doctrine of God." In Davidson and Rae, *God of Salvation*, 15–34.

———. "'Love Is Also a Lover of Life': *Creatio ex Nihilo* and Creaturely Goodness." *Modern Theology* 29 (2013): 156–71.

———. "Theologies of Retrieval." In Webster, Tanner, and Torrance, *Oxford Handbook of Systematic Theology*, 583–99.

———. "Trinity and Creation." *International Journal of Systematic Theology* 12 (2010): 4–19.

Webster, John, Kathryn Tanner, and Iain Torrance, eds. *The Oxford Handbook of Systematic Theology*. Oxford: Oxford University Press, 2007.

Weigel, Peter. *Aquinas on Simplicity: An Investigation into the Foundations of His Philosophical Theology*. Oxford: Lang, 2008.

Weinandy, Thomas G., OFMCap. *Does God Change? The Word's Becoming in the Incarnation*. Still River, MA: St. Bede's Publications, 1985.

———. *Does God Suffer?* Notre Dame, IN: University of Notre Dame Press, 2000.

———. "Of Men and Angels." *Nova et Vetera* 3 (2005): 295–306.

Weinandy, Thomas G., OFMCap, Daniel A. Keating, and John P. Yocum, eds. *Aquinas on Doctrine: A Critical Introduction*. London: T&T Clark International, 2004.

Weinberg, Rivka. *The Risk of a Lifetime: How, When, and Why Procreation May Be Permissible*. Oxford: Oxford University Press, 2016.

Weir, D. A. *The Origins of the Federal Theology in Sixteenth-Century Reformation Thought*. Oxford: Clarendon, 1990.

Weisman, Alan. *Countdown: Our Last, Best Hope for a Future on Earth?* New York: Little, Brown, 2013.

Welker, Michael. *Creation and Reality*. Translated by John F. Hoffmeyer. Minneapolis: Fortress, 1999.

Wenham, Gordon J. *Genesis 1–15*. Nashville: Nelson, 1987.

Wesley, John. *The Doctrine of Original Sin: According to Scripture, Reason, and Experience*. Bristol: E. Farley, 1757.

West, Jason. *How to Become a Rational Animal: Six Questions Everyone Should Ask*. Ottawa, ON: Justin, 2014.

Westermann, Claus. *Blessing in the Bible and the Life of the Church*. Philadelphia: Fortress, 1978.

———. *Genesis 1–11: A Commentary*. Translated by John J. Scullion, SJ. Minneapolis: Augsburg, 1984.

White, Kevin. "Act and Fact: On a Disputed Question in Recent Thomistic Metaphysics." *Review of Metaphysics* 68 (2014): 287–312.

White, Thomas Joseph, OP, ed. *The Analogy of Being: Invention of the Antichrist or the Wisdom of God?* Grand Rapids: Eerdmans, 2011.

———. "Classical Christology after Schleiermacher and Barth: A Thomistic Perspective." *Pro Ecclesia* 20 (2011): 229–63.

———. "Imperfect Happiness and the Final End of Man: Thomas Aquinas and the Paradigm of Nature-Grace Orthodoxy." *The Thomist* 78 (2014): 247–89.

———. *The Incarnate Lord: A Thomistic Study in Christology*. Washington, DC: Catholic University of America Press, 2015.

———. "Introduction: The *Analogia Entis* Controversy and Its Contemporary Significance." In White, *Analogy of Being*, 1–31.

———. "The 'Pure Nature' of Christology: Human Nature and *Gaudium et Spes* 22." *Nova et Vetera* 8 (2010): 283–322.

————. "'Through Him All Things Were Made' (John 1:3): The Analogy of the Word Incarnate according to St. Thomas Aquinas and Its Ontological Presuppositions." In White, *Analogy of Being*, 246–79.

————. *Wisdom in the Face of Modernity: A Study in Thomistic Natural Theology*. Ave Maria, FL: Sapientia, 2009.

White, Vernon. *Atonement and Incarnation: An Essay in Universalism and Particularity*. Cambridge: Cambridge University Press, 1991.

Whitney, Elspeth. *Paradise Restored: The Mechanical Arts from Antiquity through the Thirteenth Century*. Philadelphia: Temple University Press, 1989.

Wilcox, David. "Finding Adam: The Genetics of Human Origins." In K. B. Miller, *Perspectives on an Evolving Creation*, 234–53.

Wiley, Tatha. *Original Sin: Origins, Developments, Contemporary Meanings*. New York: Paulist Press, 2002.

Williams, A. N. "Does 'God' Exist?" *Scottish Journal of Theology* 58 (2005): 468–84.

————. *The Ground of Union: Deification in Aquinas and Palamas*. Oxford: Oxford University Press, 1999.

Williams, Charles. *The Image of the City, and Other Essays*. Edited by Anne Ridler. London: Oxford University Press, 1958.

————. *The Region of the Summer Stars*. London: Oxford University Press, 1950.

Williams, Patricia. *Doing without Adam and Eve: Sociobiology and Original Sin*. Minneapolis: Fortress, 2001.

Williams, Rowan. *The Edge of Words: God and the Habits of Language*. London: Bloomsbury, 2014.

————. "The Philosophical Structures of Palamism." *Eastern Churches Review* 9 (1977): 27–44.

Wilson, Edward O. *Consilience*. New York: Knopf, 1998.

————. *The Future of Life*. New York: Knopf, 2002.

————. *The Social Conquest of Earth*. New York: Norton, 2012.

Wilson, Jonathan R. *God's Good World: Reclaiming the Doctrine of Creation*. Grand Rapids: Baker Academic, 2013.

Winright, Tobias, ed. *Green Discipleship: Catholic Theological Ethics and the Environment*. Winona, MN: Anselm Academic, 2011.

Winston, David. "*Creation ex Nihilo* Revisited: A Reply to Jonathan Goldstein." *Journal of Jewish Studies* 37 (1986): 88–91.

Wippel, John F. *The Metaphysical Thought of Thomas Aquinas: From Finite Being to Uncreated Being*. Washington, DC: Catholic University of America Press, 2000.

————. "Norman Kretzmann on Aquinas's Attribution of Will and Freedom to Create to God." *Religious Studies* 39 (2003): 287–98.

————. *Thomas Aquinas on the Divine Ideas*. Toronto: Pontifical Institute of Mediaeval Studies, 1993.

Wirzba, Norman. "The Art of Creaturely Life: A Question of Human Propriety." *Pro Ecclesia* 22 (2013): 7–28.

————. *From Nature to Creation: A Christian Vision for Understanding and Loving Our World*. Grand Rapids: Baker Academic, 2015.

————. *The Paradise of God: Renewing Religion in an Ecological Age*. Oxford: Oxford University Press, 2003.

Wolterstorff, Nicholas. *Justice in Love*. Grand Rapids: Eerdmans, 2011.

————. *The Mighty and the Almighty: An Essay in Political Theology*. Cambridge: Cambridge University Press, 2014.

———. "Unqualified Divine Temporality." In Ganssle, *God and Time*, 187–213.

Wood, Bernard. *Human Evolution: A Very Short Introduction*. Oxford: Oxford University Press, 2005.

Wright, Christopher J. H. *Old Testament Ethics for the People of God*. Downers Grove, IL: InterVarsity, 2004.

Wright, N. T. *After You Believe: Why Christian Character Matters*. New York: HarperCollins, 2010.

———. "The Letter to the Romans." In *The New Interpreter's Bible*, vol. 10, *Acts, Romans, 1 Corinthians*, edited by Leander Keck, 393–770. Nashville: Abingdon, 2002.

———. *Surprised by Scripture: Engaging Contemporary Issues*. New York: HarperCollins, 2014.

Yarnold, Edward, SJ. *The Theology of Original Sin*. Hales Corners, WI: Clergy Book Service, 1971.

Yoder, John Howard. *The Politics of Jesus: Vicit Agnus Noster*. 2nd ed. Grand Rapids: Eerdmans, 1994.

Yong, Amos. *The Bible, Disability, and the Church: A New Vision of the People of God*. Grand Rapids: Eerdmans, 2011.

Young, Frances. *God's Presence: A Contemporary Recapitulation of Early Christianity*. Cambridge: Cambridge University Press, 2013.

Zachariah, George. "Discerning the Times: A Spirituality of Resistance and Alternatives." In Bloomquist, *God, Creation and Climate Change*, 75–91.

Zevit, Ziony. *What Really Happened in the Garden of Eden?* New Haven: Yale University Press, 2013.

Zizioulas, Metropolitan John. "Proprietors or Priests of Creation?" In Chryssavgis and Foltz, *Toward an Ecology of Transfiguration*, 163–71.

Scripture Index

Name Index

Subject Index